BATMAN CHRONICLES

VOLUME FIVE

Dan DiDio SENIOR VP-EXECUTIVE EDITOR ☆ Whitney Ellsworth EDITOR-ORIGINAL SERIES ☆ Bob Joy EDITOR-COLLECTED EDITION
Robbin Brosterman SENIOR ART DIRECTOR ☆ Paul Levitz PRESIDENT & PUBLISHER ☆ Georg Brewer VP-DESIGN & DC DIRECT CREATIVE
Richard Bruning SENIOR VP-CREATIVE DIRECTOR ☆ Patrick Caldon EXECUTIVE VP-FINANCE & OPERATIONS ☆ Chris Caramalis VP-FINANCE
John Cunningham VP-MARKETING ☆ Terri Cunningham VP-MANAGING EDITOR ☆ Alison Gill VP-MANUFACTURING
David Hyde VP-PUBLICITY ☆ Hank Kanalz VP-GENERAL MANAGER, WILDSTORM ☆ Jim Lee EDITORIAL DIRECTOR-WILDSTORM
Paula Lowitt SENIOR VP-BUSINESS & LEGAL AFFAIRS ☆ MaryEllen McLaughlin VP-ADVERTISING & CUSTOM PUBLISHING
John Nee SENIOR VP-BUSINESS DEVELOPMENT ☆ Gregory Noveck SENIOR VP-CREATIVE AFFAIRS ☆ Sue Pohja VP-BOOK TRADE SALES
Steve Rotterdam SENIOR VP-SALES & MARKETING ☆ Cheryl Rubin SENIOR VP-BRAND MANAGEMENT
Jeff Trojan VP-BUSINESS DEVELOPMENT, DC DIRECT ☆ Bob Wayne VP-SALES

Cover art by Jack Burnley.

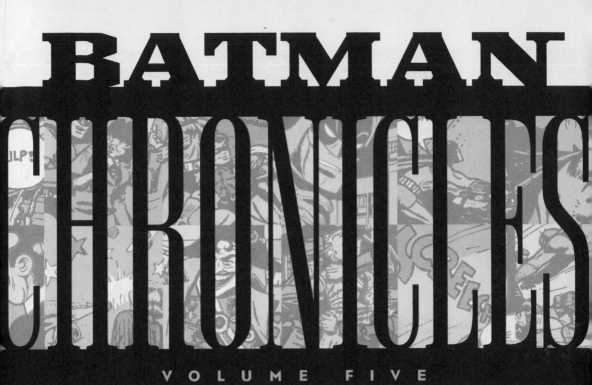

BATMAN CHRONICLES
VOLUME FIVE

BATMAN CREATED BY BOB KANE

*ALL STORIES WRITTEN BY BILL FINGER. ALL COVERS AND STORIES PENCILLED BY BOB KANE
AND INKED BY JERRY ROBINSON UNLESS OTHERWISE NOTED.*

*These stories were originally untitled and are
titled here for reader convenience.

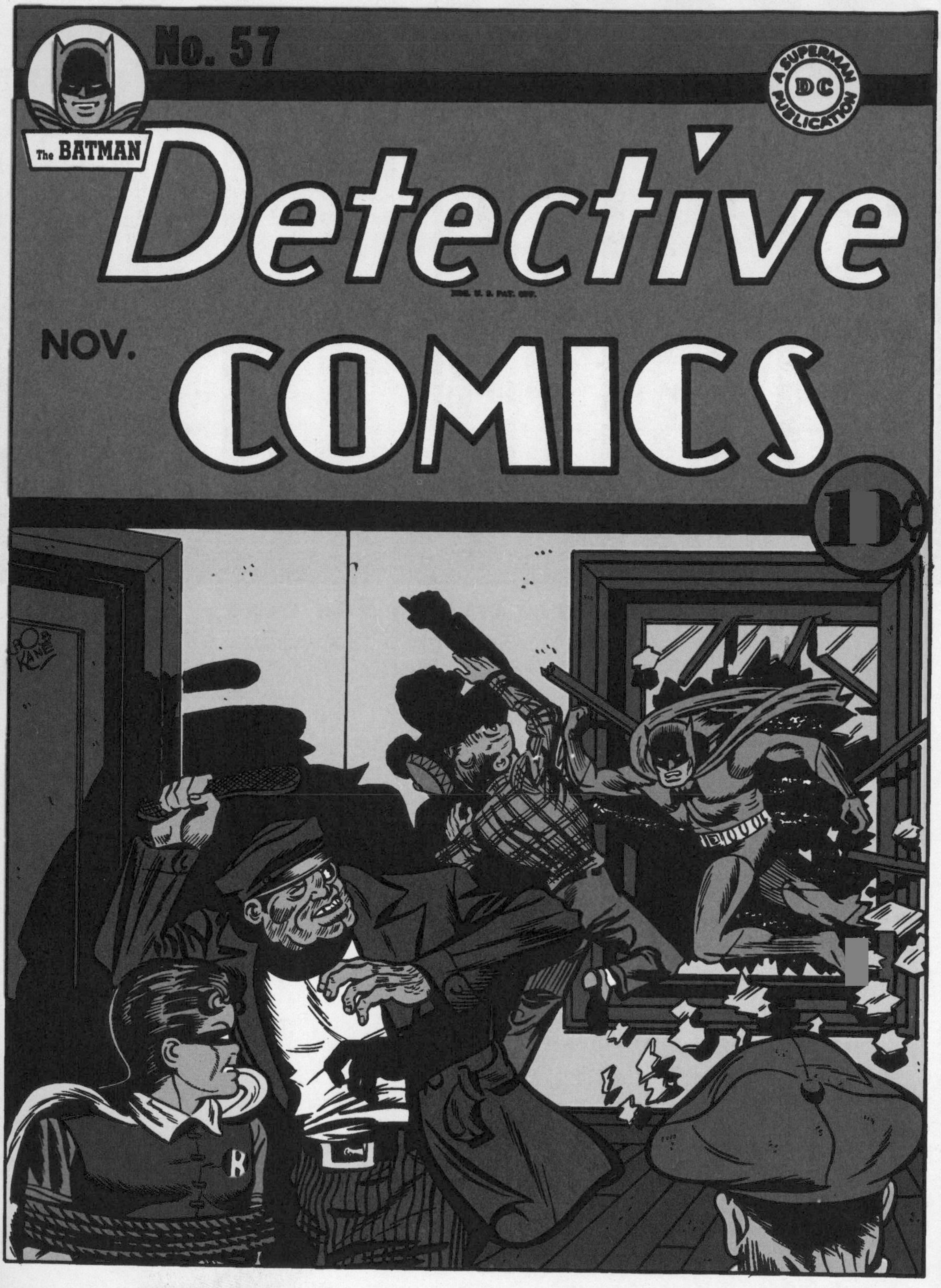
No. 57
The BATMAN
A SUPERMAN DC PUBLICATION
Detective
NOV.
COMICS
10¢
BOB KANE

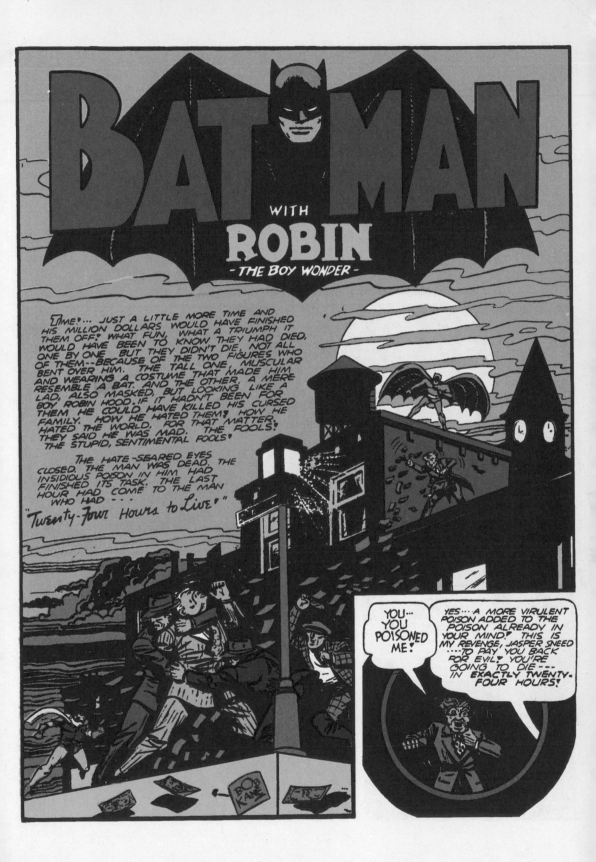

BATMAN

WITH

ROBIN

-THE BOY WONDER-

TIME!.... JUST A LITTLE MORE TIME AND HIS MILLION DOLLARS, WOULD HAVE FINISHED THEM OFF! WHAT FUN, WHAT A TRIUMPH IT WOULD HAVE BEEN TO KNOW THEY HAD DIED, ONE BY ONE. BUT THEY DIDN'T DIE, NOT ALL OF THEM—BECAUSE OF THE TWO FIGURES WHO BENT OVER HIM. THE TALL ONE, MUSCULAR AND WEARING A COSTUME THAT MADE HIM RESEMBLE A BAT. AND THE OTHER, A MERE LAD, ALSO MASKED, BUT LOOKING LIKE A BOY ROBIN HOOD. IF IT HADN'T BEEN FOR THEM HE COULD HAVE KILLED HIS CURSED FAMILY. HOW HE HATED THEM! HOW HE HATED THE WORLD, FOR THAT MATTER. THEY SAID HE WAS MAD. THE FOOLS! THE STUPID, SENTIMENTAL FOOLS!

THE HATE-SEARED EYES CLOSED. THE MAN WAS DEAD. THE INSIDIOUS POISON IN HIM HAD FINISHED ITS TASK. THE LAST HOUR HAD COME TO THE MAN WHO HAD - - -

"Twenty-Four Hours to Live."

YOU... YOU POISONED ME!

YES....A MORE VIRULENT POISON ADDED TO THE POISON ALREADY IN YOUR MIND! THIS IS MY REVENGE, JASPER SNEED ....TO PAY YOU BACK FOR EVIL! YOU'RE GOING TO DIE--- IN EXACTLY TWENTY-FOUR HOURS!

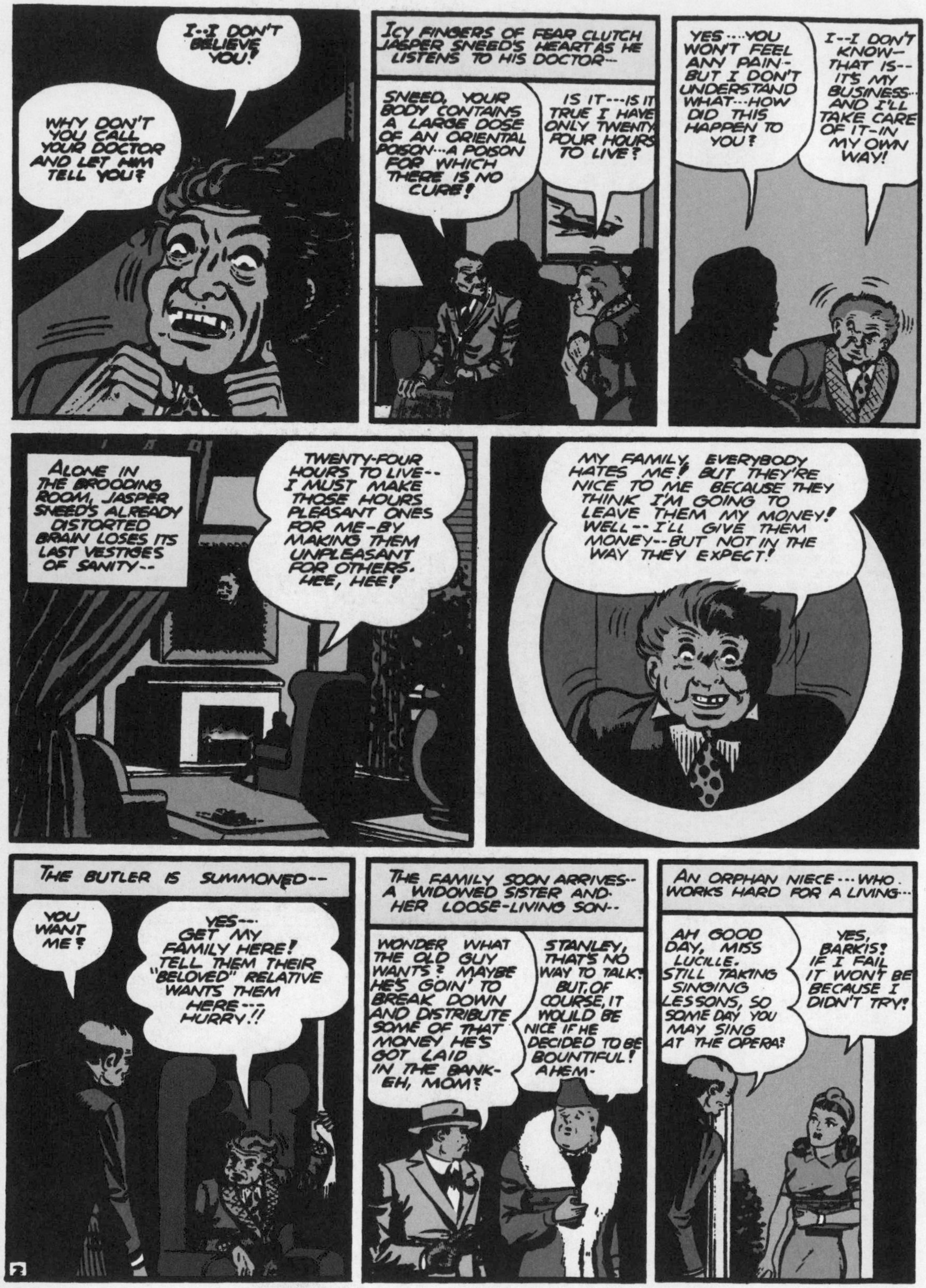
I--I DON'T BELIEVE YOU!
WHY DON'T YOU CALL YOUR DOCTOR AND LET HIM TELL YOU?
ICY FINGERS OF FEAR CLUTCH JASPER SNEED'S HEART AS HE LISTENS TO HIS DOCTOR--
SNEED, YOUR BODY CONTAINS A LARGE DOSE OF AN ORIENTAL POISON...A POISON FOR WHICH THERE IS NO CURE!
IS IT---IS IT TRUE I HAVE ONLY TWENTY FOUR HOURS TO LIVE?
YES....YOU WON'T FEEL ANY PAIN-BUT I DON'T UNDERSTAND WHAT...HOW DID THIS HAPPEN TO YOU?
I--I DON'T KNOW--THAT IS--IT'S MY BUSINESS...AND I'LL TAKE CARE OF IT-IN MY OWN WAY!
ALONE IN THE BROODING ROOM, JASPER SNEED'S ALREADY DISTORTED BRAIN LOSES ITS LAST VESTIGES OF SANITY--
TWENTY-FOUR HOURS TO LIVE--I MUST MAKE THOSE HOURS PLEASANT ONES FOR ME-BY MAKING THEM UNPLEASANT FOR OTHERS. HEE, HEE!
MY FAMILY, EVERYBODY HATES ME! BUT THEY'RE NICE TO ME BECAUSE THEY THINK I'M GOING TO LEAVE THEM MY MONEY! WELL--I'LL GIVE THEM MONEY--BUT NOT IN THE WAY THEY EXPECT!
THE BUTLER IS SUMMONED--
YOU WANT ME?
YES--GET MY FAMILY HERE! TELL THEM THEIR "BELOVED" RELATIVE WANTS THEM HERE---HURRY!!
2
THE FAMILY SOON ARRIVES--A WIDOWED SISTER AND HER LOOSE-LIVING SON--
WONDER WHAT THE OLD GUY WANTS? MAYBE HE'S GOIN' TO BREAK DOWN AND DISTRIBUTE SOME OF THAT MONEY HE'S GOT LAID IN THE BANK-EH, MOM?
STANLEY, THAT'S NO WAY TO TALK! BUT, OF COURSE, IT WOULD BE NICE IF HE DECIDED TO BE BOUNTIFUL! AHEM-
AN ORPHAN NIECE...WHO WORKS HARD FOR A LIVING...
AH GOOD DAY, MISS LUCILLE. STILL TAKING SINGING LESSONS, SO SOME DAY YOU MAY SING AT THE OPERA?
YES, BARKIS! IF I FAIL IT WON'T BE BECAUSE I DIDN'T TRY!

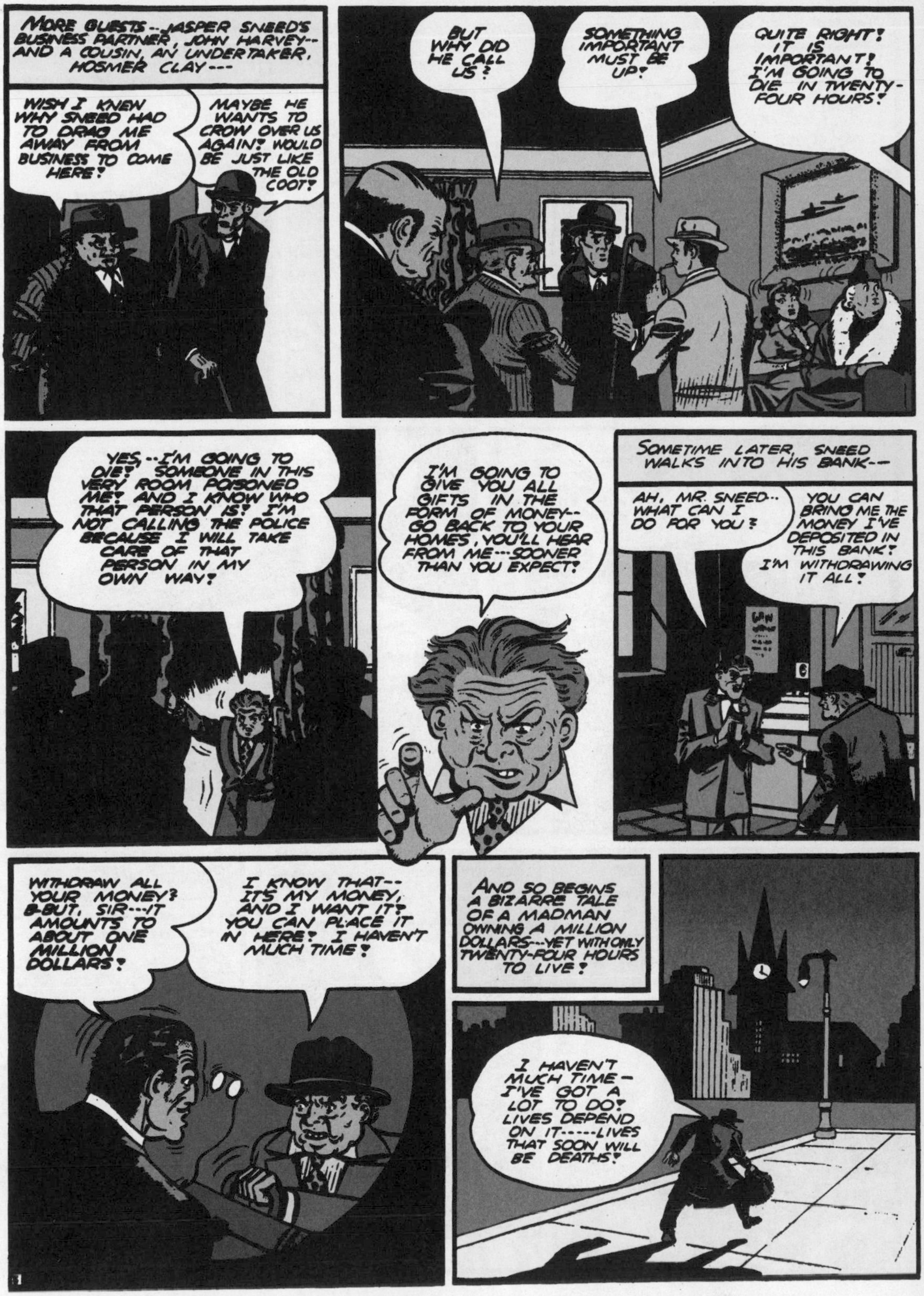
MORE GUESTS--JASPER SNEED'S BUSINESS PARTNER, JOHN HARVEY--AND A COUSIN, AN UNDERTAKER, HOSMER CLAY---
WISH I KNEW WHY SNEED HAD TO DRAG ME AWAY FROM BUSINESS TO COME HERE!
MAYBE HE WANTS TO CROW OVER US AGAIN! WOULD BE JUST LIKE THE OLD COOT!
BUT WHY DID HE CALL US?
SOMETHING IMPORTANT MUST BE UP!
QUITE RIGHT! IT IS IMPORTANT! I'M GOING TO DIE IN TWENTY-FOUR HOURS!
YES,--I'M GOING TO DIE! SOMEONE IN THIS VERY ROOM POISONED ME! AND I KNOW WHO THAT PERSON IS! I'M NOT CALLING THE POLICE BECAUSE I WILL TAKE CARE OF THAT PERSON IN MY OWN WAY!
I'M GOING TO GIVE YOU ALL GIFTS IN THE FORM OF MONEY--GO BACK TO YOUR HOMES, YOU'LL HEAR FROM ME---SOONER THAN YOU EXPECT!
SOMETIME LATER, SNEED WALKS INTO HIS BANK--
AH, MR. SNEED.. WHAT CAN I DO FOR YOU?
YOU CAN BRING ME THE MONEY I'VE DEPOSITED IN THIS BANK! I'M WITHDRAWING IT ALL!
WITHDRAW ALL YOUR MONEY? B-BUT, SIR---IT AMOUNTS TO ABOUT ONE MILLION DOLLARS!
I KNOW THAT--IT'S MY MONEY, AND I WANT IT! YOU CAN PLACE IT IN HERE! I HAVEN'T MUCH TIME!
AND SO BEGINS A BIZARRE TALE OF A MADMAN OWNING A MILLION DOLLARS---YET WITH ONLY TWENTY-FOUR HOURS TO LIVE!
I HAVEN'T MUCH TIME-- I'VE GOT A LOT TO DO! LIVES DEPEND ON IT-----LIVES THAT SOON WILL BE DEATHS!

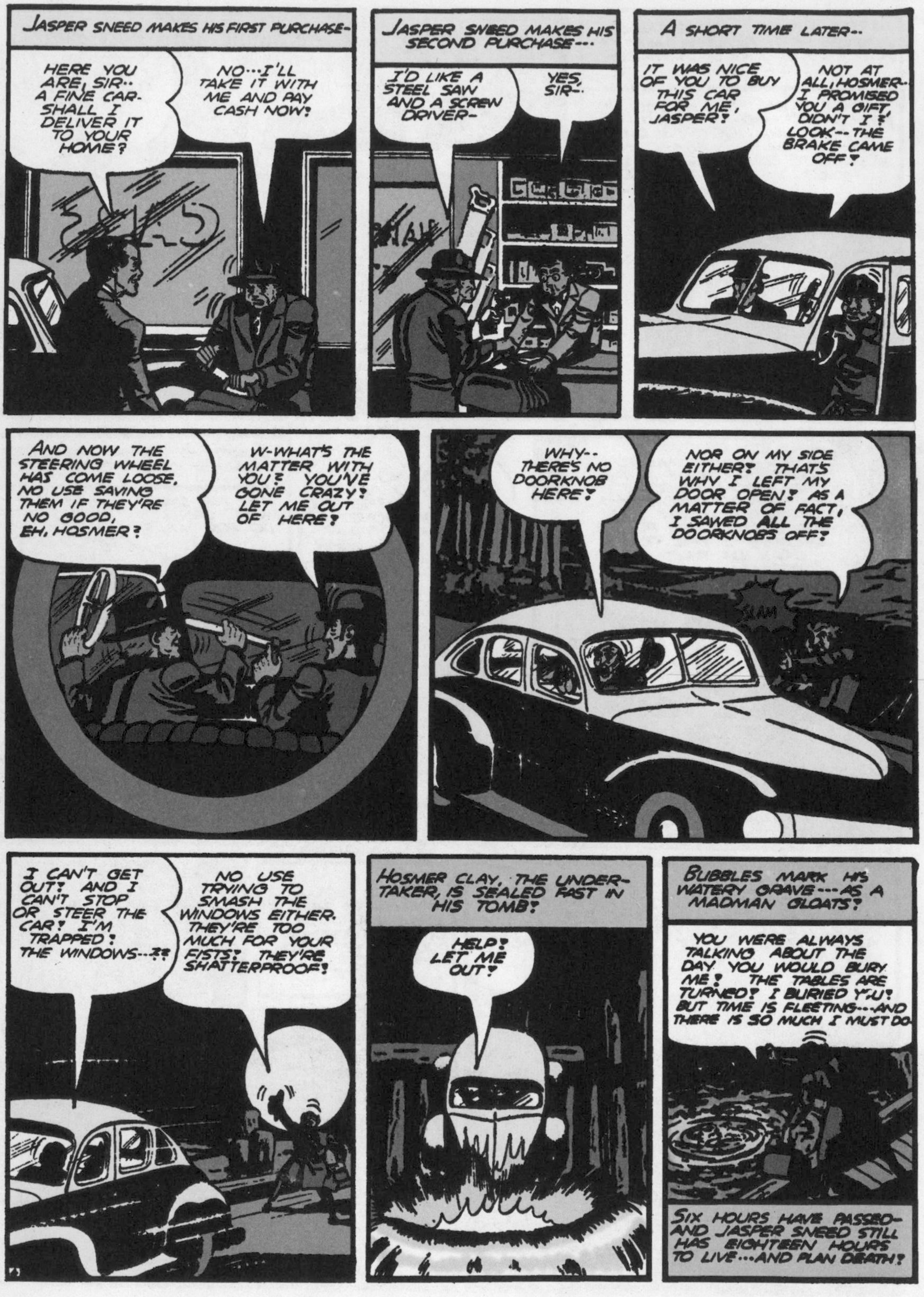
JASPER SNEED MAKES HIS FIRST PURCHASE-
HERE YOU ARE, SIR.. A FINE CAR-SHALL I DELIVER IT TO YOUR HOME?
NO...I'LL TAKE IT WITH ME AND PAY CASH NOW!
JASPER SNEED MAKES HIS SECOND PURCHASE---
I'D LIKE A STEEL SAW AND A SCREW DRIVER-
YES, SIR-.
A SHORT TIME LATER--
IT WAS NICE OF YOU TO BUY THIS CAR FOR ME, JASPER!
NOT AT ALL, HOSMER-- I PROMISED YOU A GIFT, DIDN'T I?! LOOK-- THE BRAKE CAME OFF!
AND NOW THE STEERING WHEEL HAS COME LOOSE. NO USE SAVING THEM IF THEY'RE NO GOOD, EH, HOSMER?
W-WHAT'S THE MATTER WITH YOU? YOU'VE GONE CRAZY! LET ME OUT OF HERE!
WHY-- THERE'S NO DOORKNOB HERE!
NOR ON MY SIDE EITHER! THAT'S WHY I LEFT MY DOOR OPEN! AS A MATTER OF FACT, I SAWED ALL THE DOORKNOBS OFF!
SLAM
I CAN'T GET OUT! AND I CAN'T STOP OR STEER THE CAR! I'M TRAPPED! THE WINDOWS--?!
NO USE TRYING TO SMASH THE WINDOWS EITHER. THEY'RE TOO MUCH FOR YOUR FISTS! THEY'RE SHATTERPROOF!
HOSMER CLAY, THE UNDER-TAKER, IS SEALED FAST IN HIS TOMB!
HELP! LET ME OUT!
BUBBLES MARK HIS WATERY GRAVE---AS A MADMAN GLOATS!
YOU WERE ALWAYS TALKING ABOUT THE DAY YOU WOULD BURY ME! THE TABLES ARE TURNED! I BURIED YOU! BUT TIME IS FLEETING---AND THERE IS SO MUCH I MUST DO
SIX HOURS HAVE PASSED-AND JASPER SNEED STILL HAS EIGHTEEN HOURS TO LIVE...AND PLAN DEATH!

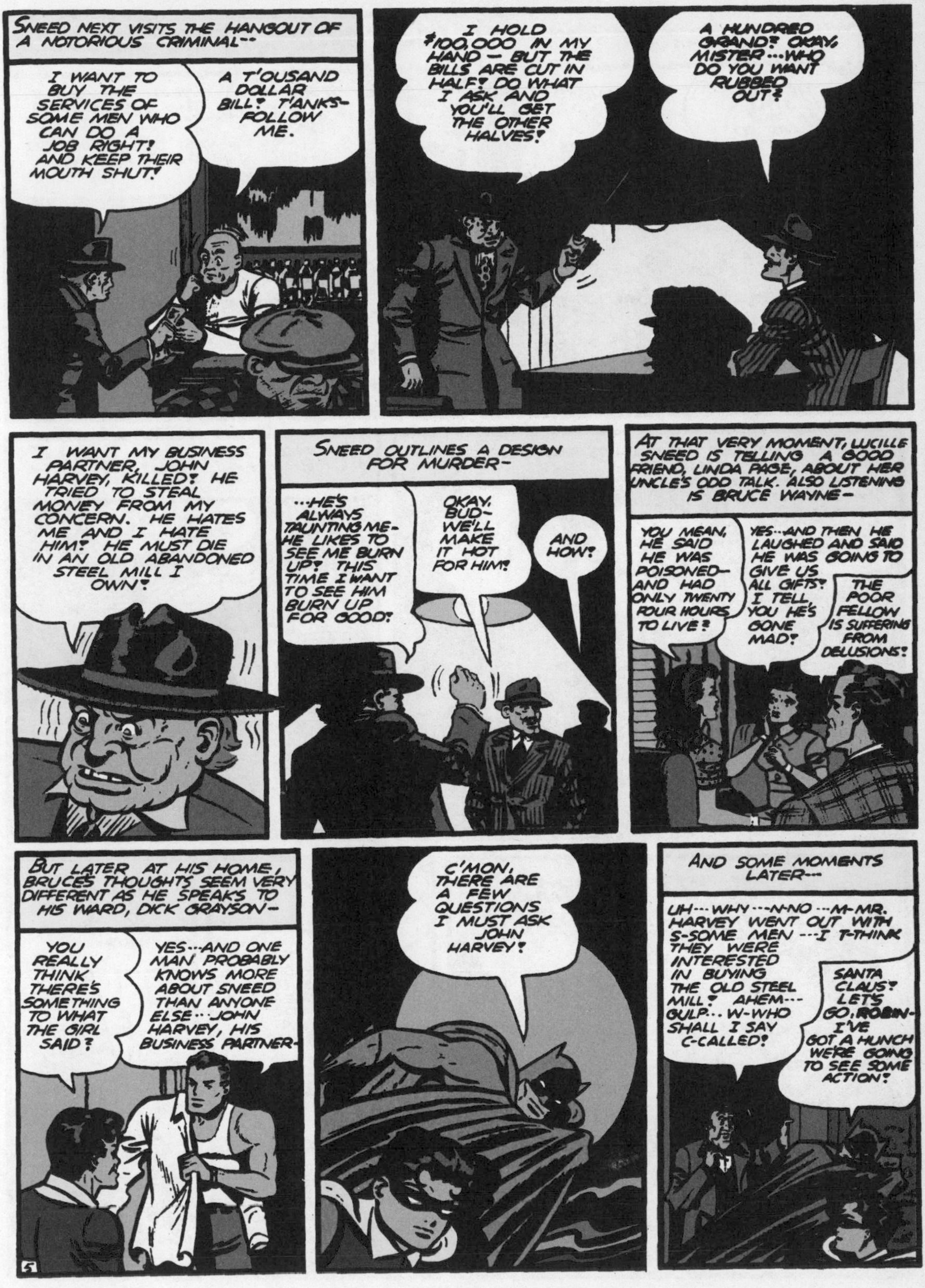
SNEED NEXT VISITS THE HANGOUT OF A NOTORIOUS CRIMINAL--
I WANT TO BUY THE SERVICES OF SOME MEN WHO CAN DO A JOB RIGHT! AND KEEP THEIR MOUTH SHUT!
A T'OUSAND DOLLAR BILL! T'ANKS- FOLLOW ME.
I HOLD $100,000 IN MY HAND -- BUT THE BILLS ARE CUT IN HALF! DO WHAT I ASK AND YOU'LL GET THE OTHER HALVES!
A HUNDRED GRAND! OKAY, MISTER...WHO DO YOU WANT RUBBED OUT?
I WANT MY BUSINESS PARTNER, JOHN HARVEY, KILLED! HE TRIED TO STEAL MONEY FROM MY CONCERN. HE HATES ME AND I HATE HIM! HE MUST DIE IN AN OLD ABANDONED STEEL MILL I OWN!
SNEED OUTLINES A DESIGN FOR MURDER-
...HE'S ALWAYS TAUNTING ME-HE LIKES TO SEE ME BURN UP! THIS TIME I WANT TO SEE HIM BURN UP FOR GOOD!
OKAY, BUD- WE'LL MAKE IT HOT FOR HIM!
AND HOW!
AT THAT VERY MOMENT, LUCILLE SNEED IS TELLING A GOOD FRIEND, LINDA PAGE, ABOUT HER UNCLE'S ODD TALK. ALSO LISTENING IS BRUCE WAYNE-
YOU MEAN, HE SAID HE WAS POISONED- AND HAD ONLY TWENTY FOUR HOURS TO LIVE?
YES...AND THEN HE LAUGHED AND SAID HE WAS GOING TO GIVE US ALL GIFTS! I TELL, YOU HE'S GONE MAD!
THE POOR FELLOW IS SUFFERING FROM DELUSIONS!
BUT LATER AT HIS HOME, BRUCE'S THOUGHTS SEEM VERY DIFFERENT AS HE SPEAKS TO HIS WARD, DICK GRAYSON-
YOU REALLY THINK THERE'S SOMETHING TO WHAT THE GIRL SAID?
YES...AND ONE MAN PROBABLY KNOWS MORE ABOUT SNEED THAN ANYONE ELSE...JOHN HARVEY, HIS BUSINESS PARTNER-
5
C'MON, THERE ARE A FEW QUESTIONS I MUST ASK JOHN HARVEY!
AND SOME MOMENTS LATER---
UH---WHY---N-NO---M-MR. HARVEY WENT OUT WITH S-SOME MEN---I T-THINK THEY WERE INTERESTED IN BUYING THE OLD STEEL MILL! AHEM--- GULP... W-WHO SHALL I SAY C-CALLED?
SANTA CLAUS! LET'S GO, ROBIN- I'VE GOT A HUNCH WE'RE GOING TO SEE SOME ACTION!

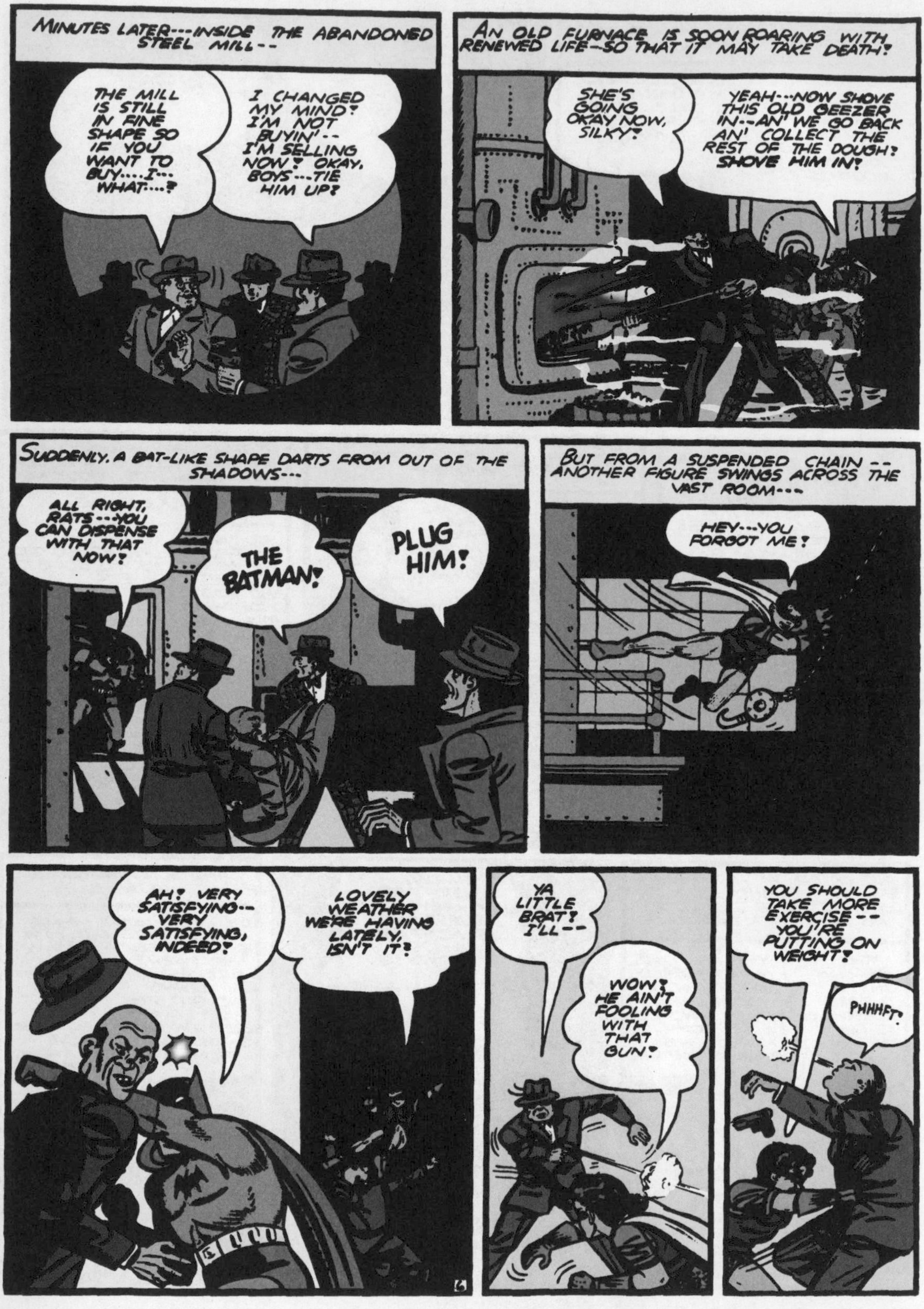

MINUTES LATER---INSIDE THE ABANDONED STEEL MILL--
THE MILL IS STILL IN FINE SHAPE SO IF YOU WANT TO BUY....I-- WHAT--?
I CHANGED MY MIND! I'M NOT BUYIN'-- I'M SELLING NOW! OKAY, BOYS---TIE HIM UP!
AN OLD FURNACE IS SOON ROARING WITH RENEWED LIFE--SO THAT IT MAY TAKE DEATH!
SHE'S GOING OKAY NOW, SILKY!
YEAH---NOW SHOVE THIS OLD GEEZER IN--AN' WE GO BACK AN' COLLECT THE REST OF THE DOUGH! SHOVE HIM IN!
SUDDENLY, A BAT-LIKE SHAPE DARTS FROM OUT OF THE SHADOWS---
ALL RIGHT, RATS---YOU CAN DISPENSE WITH THAT NOW!
THE BATMAN!
PLUG HIM!
BUT FROM A SUSPENDED CHAIN-- ANOTHER FIGURE SWINGS ACROSS THE VAST ROOM---
HEY---YOU FORGOT ME!
AH! VERY SATISFYING-- VERY SATISFYING, INDEED!
LOVELY WEATHER WE'RE HAVING LATELY, ISN'T IT?
YA LITTLE BRAT! I'LL--
WOW! HE AIN'T FOOLING WITH THAT GUN!
YOU SHOULD TAKE MORE EXERCISE-- YOU'RE PUTTING ON WEIGHT!
PHHHFT!

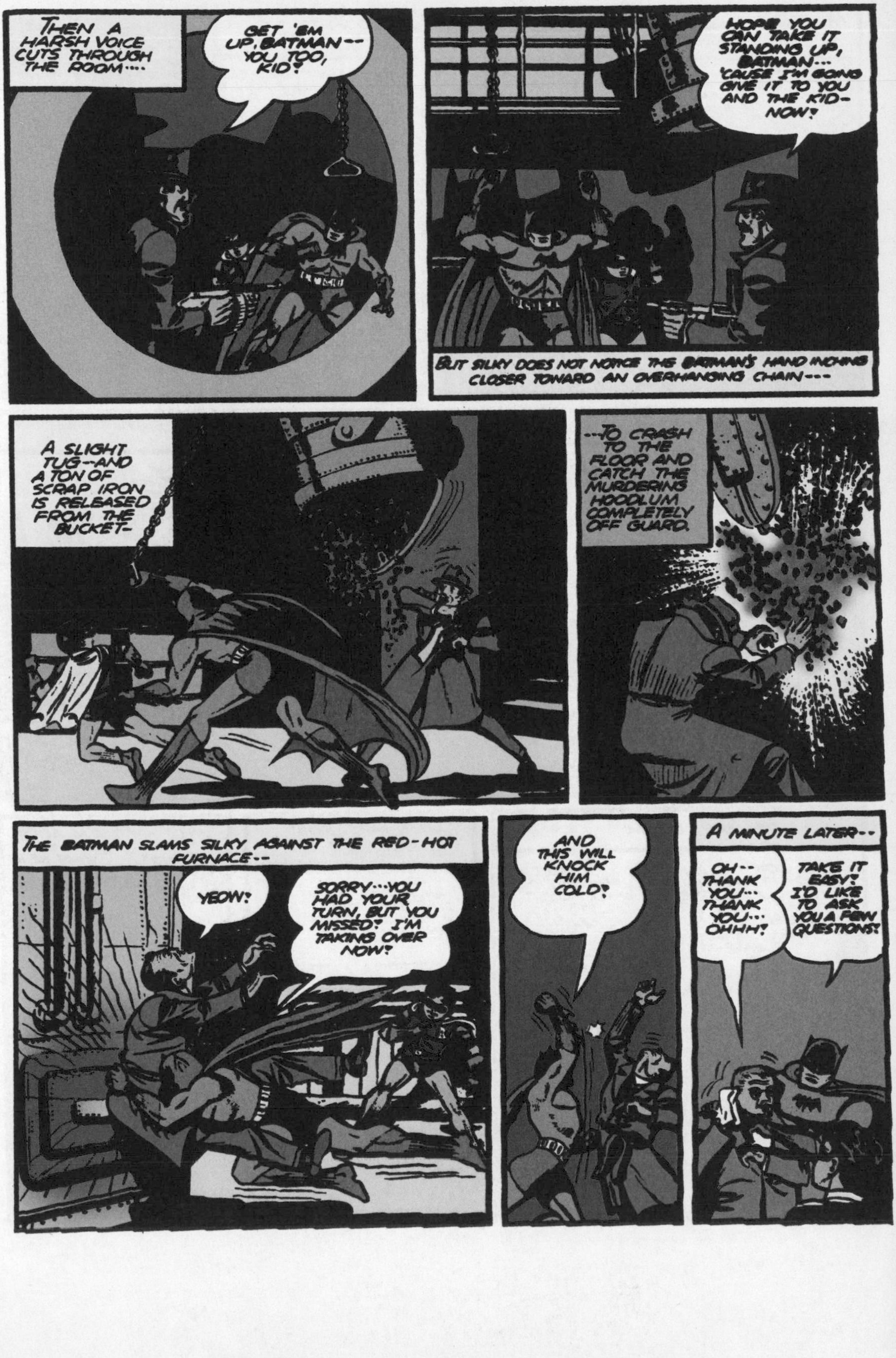
THEN A HARSH VOICE CUTS THROUGH THE ROOM....
GET 'EM UP, BATMAN-- YOU TOO, KID!
HOPE YOU CAN TAKE IT STANDING UP, BATMAN... 'CAUSE I'M GOING GIVE IT TO YOU AND THE KID-- NOW!
BUT SILKY DOES NOT NOTICE THE BATMAN'S HAND INCHING CLOSER TOWARD AN OVERHANGING CHAIN---
A SLIGHT TUG--AND A TON OF SCRAP IRON IS RELEASED FROM THE BUCKET-
--TO CRASH TO THE FLOOR AND CATCH THE MURDERING HOODLUM COMPLETELY OFF GUARD.
THE BATMAN SLAMS SILKY AGAINST THE RED-HOT FURNACE--
YEOW!
SORRY...YOU HAD YOUR TURN, BUT YOU MISSED! I'M TAKING OVER NOW!
AND THIS WILL KNOCK HIM COLD!
A MINUTE LATER--
OH-- THANK YOU... THANK YOU... OHHH!
TAKE IT EASY! I'D LIKE TO ASK YOU A FEW QUESTIONS!

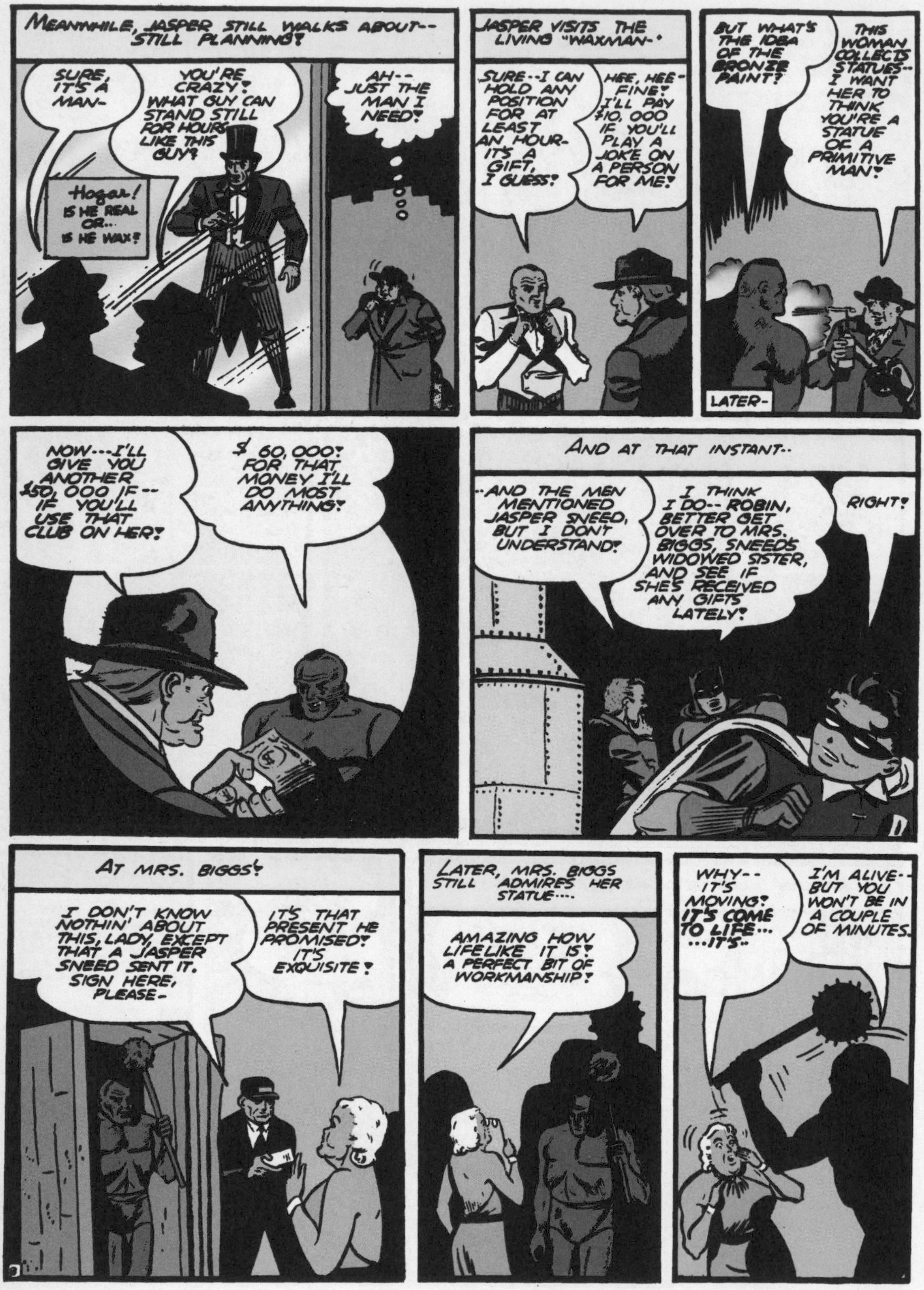

MEANWHILE, JASPER STILL WALKS ABOUT--STILL PLANNING!
SURE, IT'S A MAN-
YOU'RE CRAZY! WHAT GUY CAN STAND STILL FOR HOURS LIKE THIS GUY?
Hogar! IS HE REAL OR... IS HE WAX?
AH--JUST THE MAN I NEED!
JASPER VISITS THE LIVING "WAXMAN-"
SURE--I CAN HOLD ANY POSITION FOR AT LEAST AN HOUR-IT'S A GIFT, I GUESS!
HEE, HEE-FINE! I'LL PAY $10,000 IF YOU'LL PLAY A JOKE ON A PERSON FOR ME!
BUT WHAT'S THE IDEA OF THE BRONZE PAINT?
THIS WOMAN COLLECTS STATUES--I WANT HER TO THINK YOU'RE A STATUE OF A PRIMITIVE MAN!
LATER-
NOW---I'LL GIVE YOU ANOTHER $50,000 IF--IF YOU'LL USE THAT CLUB ON HER!
$60,000! FOR THAT MONEY I'LL DO MOST ANYTHING!
AND AT THAT INSTANT--
--AND THE MEN MENTIONED JASPER SNEED, BUT I DON'T UNDERSTAND!
I THINK I DO-- ROBIN, BETTER GET OVER TO MRS. BIGGS, SNEED'S WIDOWED SISTER, AND SEE IF SHE'S RECEIVED ANY GIFTS LATELY!
RIGHT!
AT MRS. BIGGS'!
I DON'T KNOW NOTHIN' ABOUT THIS, LADY, EXCEPT THAT A JASPER SNEED SENT IT. SIGN HERE, PLEASE-
IT'S THAT PRESENT HE PROMISED! IT'S EXQUISITE!
LATER, MRS. BIGGS STILL ADMIRES HER STATUE....
AMAZING HOW LIFELIKE IT IS! A PERFECT BIT OF WORKMANSHIP!
WHY--IT'S MOVING! IT'S COME TO LIFE... ...IT'S..
I'M ALIVE--BUT YOU WON'T BE IN A COUPLE OF MINUTES.

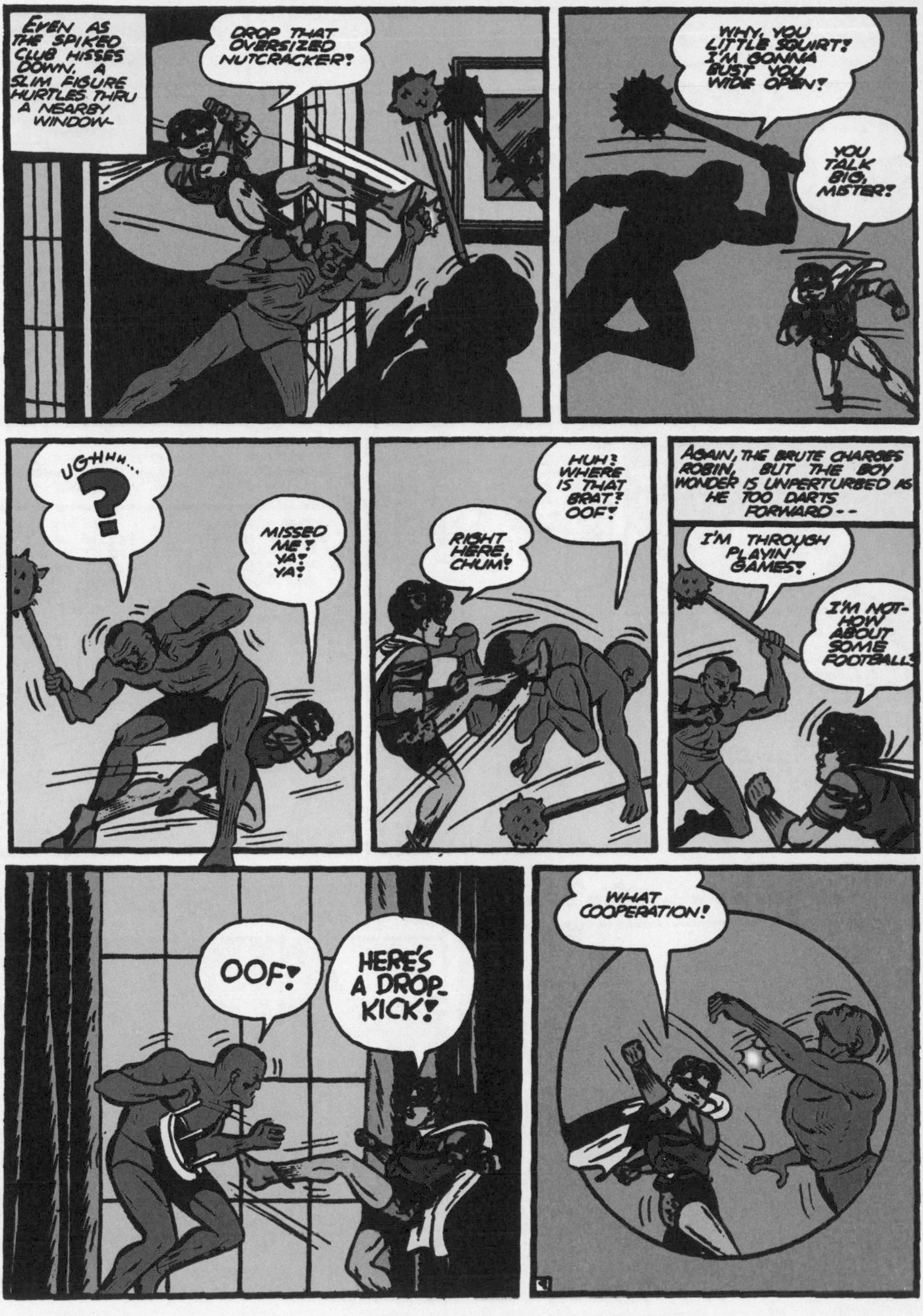
EVEN AS THE SPIKED CLUB HISSES DOWN, A SLIM FIGURE HURTLES THRU A NEARBY WINDOW--
DROP THAT OVERSIZED NUTCRACKER!
WHY, YOU LITTLE SQUIRT! I'M GONNA BUST YOU WIDE OPEN!
YOU TALK BIG, MISTER!
UGHHH...
?
MISSED ME! YA! YA!
HUH? WHERE IS THAT BRAT? OOF!
RIGHT HERE, CHUM!
AGAIN, THE BRUTE CHARGES ROBIN, BUT THE BOY WONDER IS UNPERTURBED AS HE TOO DARTS FORWARD--
I'M THROUGH PLAYIN' GAMES!
I'M NOT-- HOW ABOUT SOME FOOTBALL?
OOF!
HERE'S A DROP-KICK!
WHAT COOPERATION!

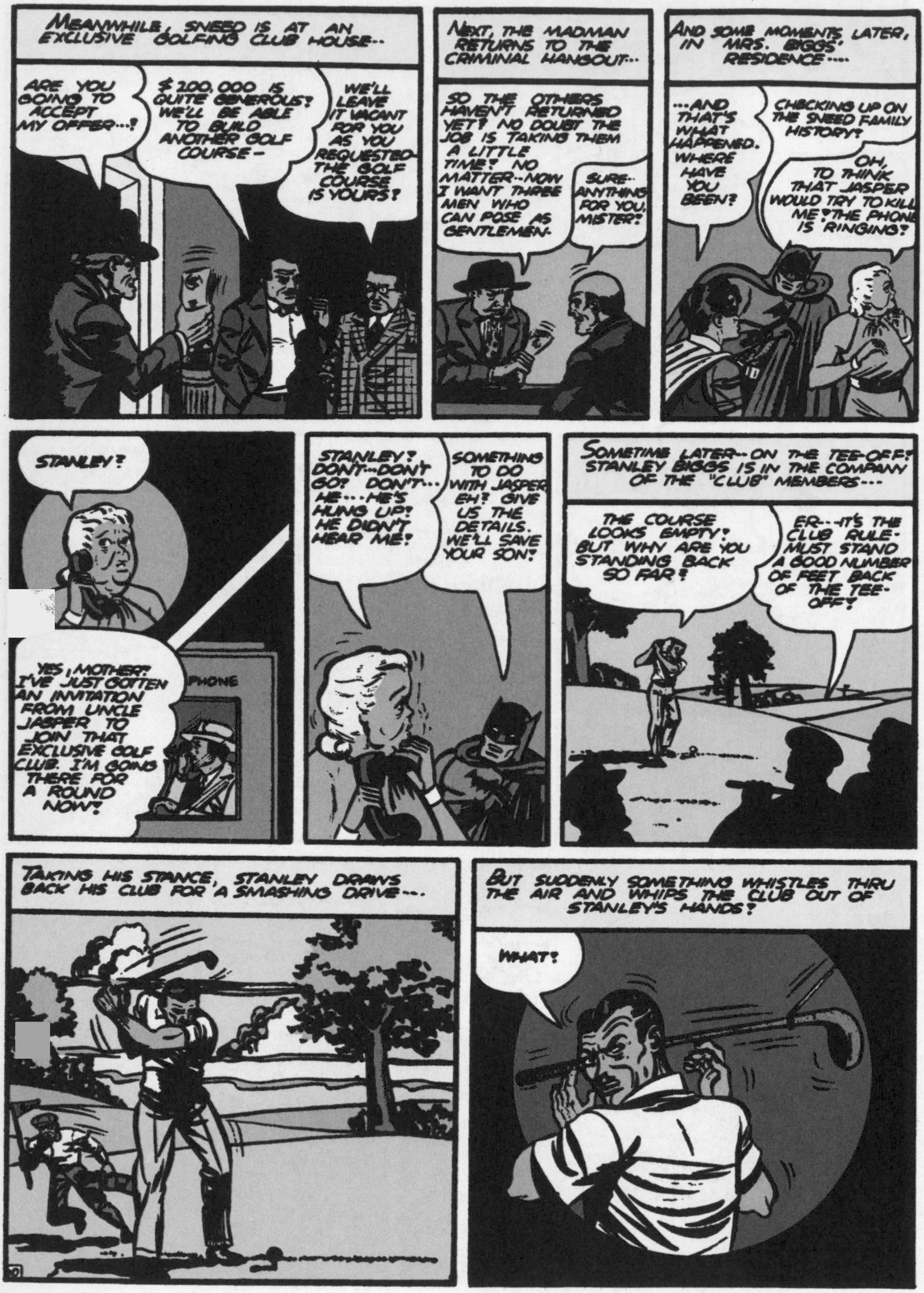
MEANWHILE, SNEED IS AT AN EXCLUSIVE GOLFING CLUB HOUSE--
ARE YOU GOING TO ACCEPT MY OFFER--?
$200,000 IS QUITE GENEROUS! WE'LL BE ABLE TO BUILD ANOTHER GOLF COURSE--
WE'LL LEAVE IT VACANT FOR YOU AS YOU REQUESTED-- THE GOLF COURSE IS YOURS!
NEXT, THE MADMAN RETURNS TO THE CRIMINAL HANGOUT--
SO THE OTHERS HAVEN'T RETURNED YET? NO DOUBT THE JOB IS TAKING THEM A LITTLE TIME! NO MATTER--NOW I WANT THREE MEN WHO CAN POSE AS GENTLEMEN.
SURE--ANYTHING FOR YOU, MISTER!
AND SOME MOMENTS LATER, IN MRS. BIGGS' RESIDENCE----
--AND THAT'S WHAT HAPPENED. WHERE HAVE YOU BEEN?
CHECKING UP ON THE SNEED FAMILY HISTORY!
OH, TO THINK THAT JASPER WOULD TRY TO KILL ME! THE PHONE IS RINGING!
STANLEY!
YES, MOTHER! I'VE JUST GOTTEN AN INVITATION FROM UNCLE JASPER TO JOIN THAT EXCLUSIVE GOLF CLUB. I'M GOING THERE FOR A ROUND NOW!
PHONE
STANLEY! DON'T--DON'T GO! DON'T--- HE---HE'S HUNG UP! HE DIDN'T HEAR ME!
SOMETHING TO DO WITH JASPER EH? GIVE US THE DETAILS. WE'LL SAVE YOUR SON!
SOMETIME LATER--ON THE TEE-OFF! STANLEY BIGGS IS IN THE COMPANY OF THE "CLUB" MEMBERS---
THE COURSE LOOKS EMPTY! BUT WHY ARE YOU STANDING BACK SO FAR?
ER---IT'S THE CLUB RULE-MUST STAND A GOOD NUMBER OF FEET BACK OF THE TEE-OFF!
TAKING HIS STANCE, STANLEY DRAWS BACK HIS CLUB FOR A SMASHING DRIVE---
BUT SUDDENLY SOMETHING WHISTLES THRU THE AIR AND WHIPS THE CLUB OUT OF STANLEY'S HANDS!
WHAT!

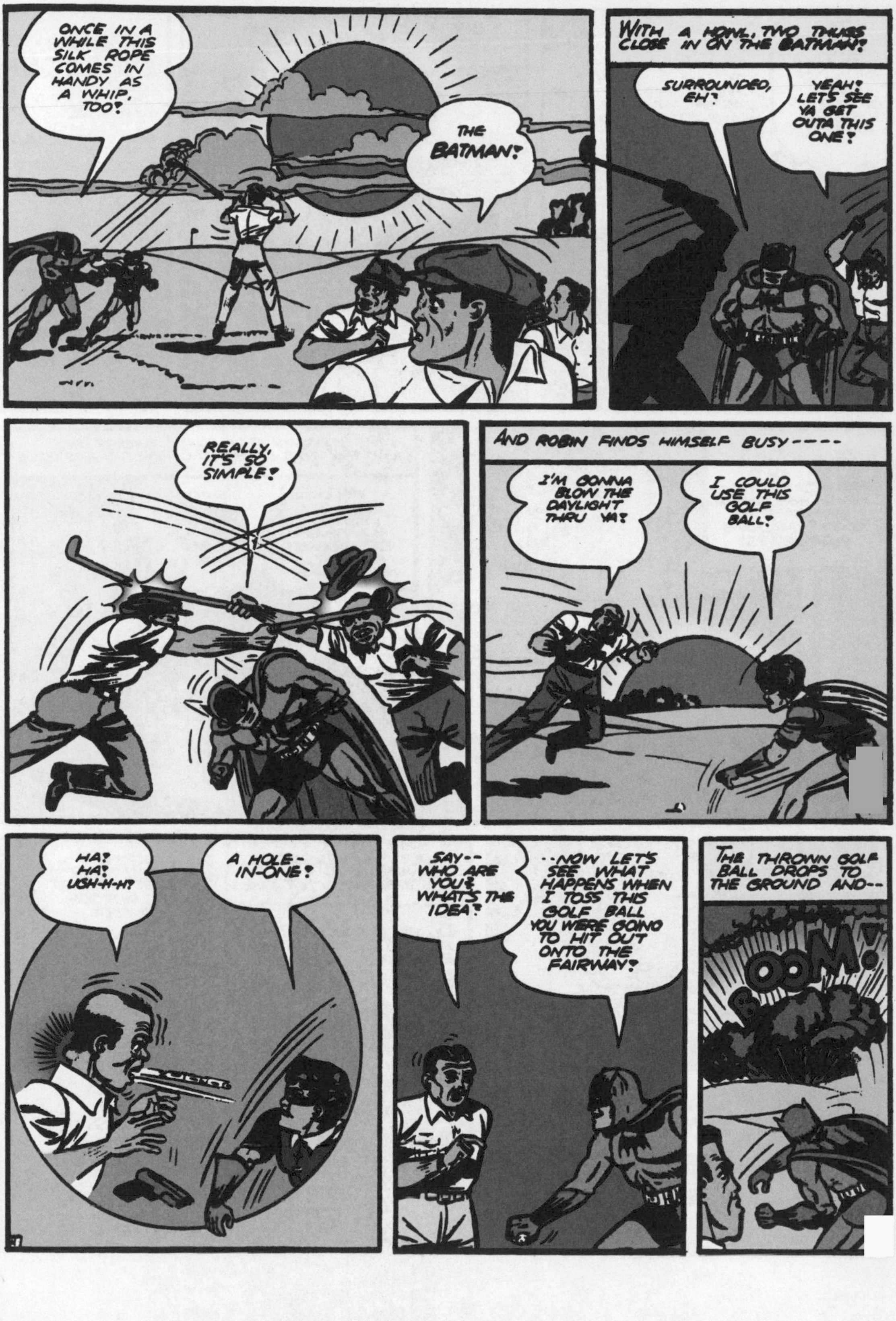
ONCE IN A WHILE THIS SILK ROPE COMES IN HANDY AS A WHIP, TOO!
THE BATMAN!
WITH A HOWL, TWO THUGS CLOSE IN ON THE BATMAN!
SURROUNDED, EH?
YEAH! LET'S SEE YA GET OUTA THIS ONE!
REALLY, IT'S SO SIMPLE!
AND ROBIN FINDS HIMSELF BUSY----
I'M GONNA BLOW THE DAYLIGHT THRU YA!
I COULD USE THIS GOLF BALL!
HA! HA! UGH-H-H!
A HOLE-IN-ONE!
SAY-- WHO ARE YOU? WHAT'S THE IDEA?
--NOW LET'S SEE WHAT HAPPENS WHEN I TOSS THIS GOLF BALL YOU WERE GOING TO HIT OUT ONTO THE FAIRWAY!
THE THROWN GOLF BALL DROPS TO THE GROUND AND--
BOOM!

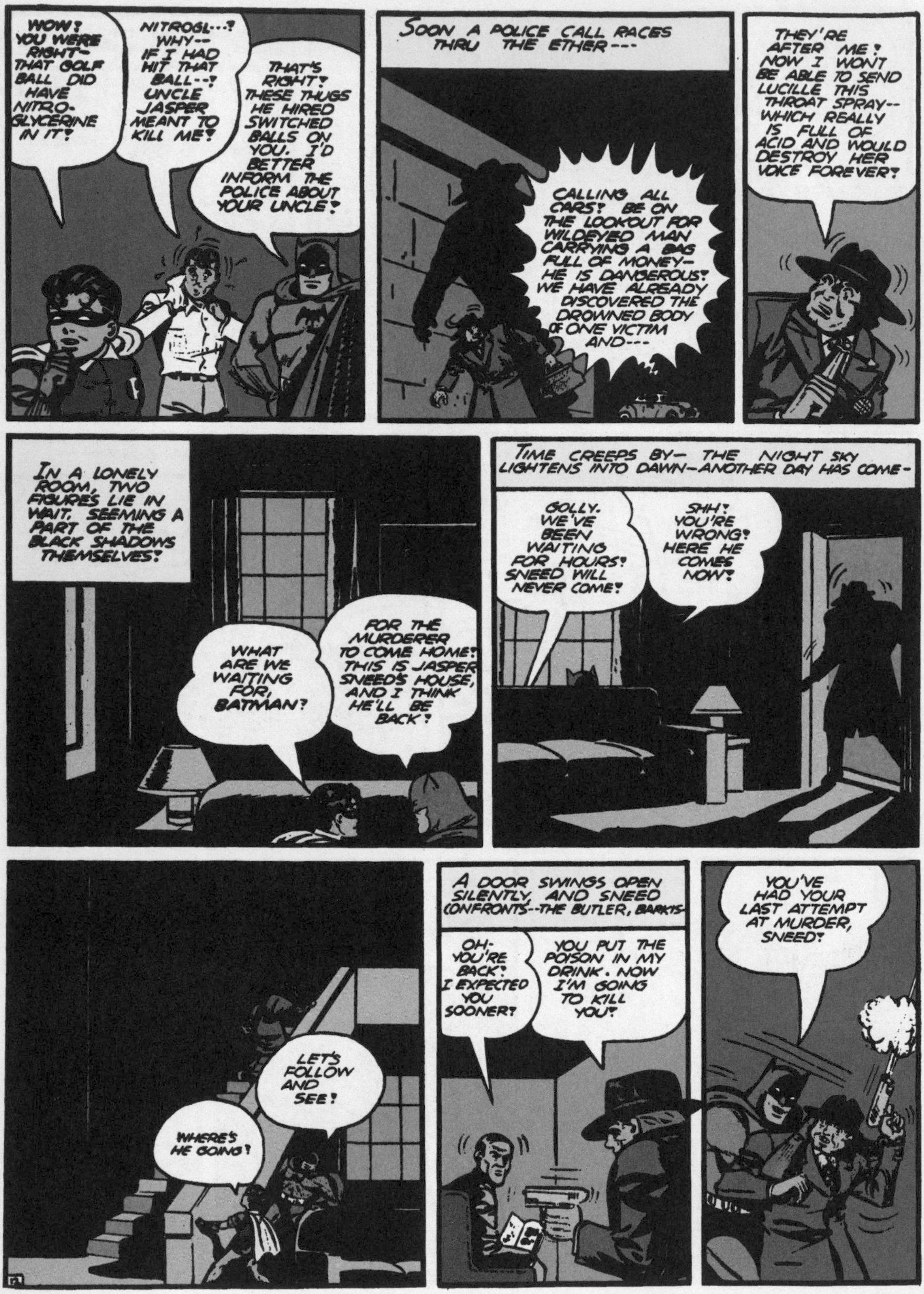
WOW! YOU WERE RIGHT- THAT GOLF BALL DID HAVE NITRO-GLYCERINE IN IT!
NITROGL...? WHY-- IF I HAD HIT THAT BALL--! UNCLE JASPER MEANT TO KILL ME!
THAT'S RIGHT! THESE THUGS HE HIRED SWITCHED BALLS ON YOU. I'D BETTER INFORM THE POLICE ABOUT YOUR UNCLE!
SOON A POLICE CALL RACES THRU THE ETHER---
CALLING ALL CARS! BE ON THE LOOKOUT FOR WILDEYED MAN CARRYING A BAG FULL OF MONEY- HE IS DANGEROUS! WE HAVE ALREADY DISCOVERED THE DROWNED BODY OF ONE VICTIM AND---
THEY'RE AFTER ME! NOW I WON'T BE ABLE TO SEND LUCILLE THIS THROAT SPRAY-- WHICH REALLY IS FULL OF ACID AND WOULD DESTROY HER VOICE FOREVER!
IN A LONELY ROOM, TWO FIGURES LIE IN WAIT, SEEMING A PART OF THE BLACK SHADOWS THEMSELVES!
WHAT ARE WE WAITING FOR, BATMAN?
FOR THE MURDERER TO COME HOME! THIS IS JASPER SNEED'S HOUSE, AND I THINK HE'LL BE BACK!
TIME CREEPS BY- THE NIGHT SKY LIGHTENS INTO DAWN-ANOTHER DAY HAS COME-
GOLLY. WE'VE BEEN WAITING FOR HOURS! SNEED WILL NEVER COME!
SHH! YOU'RE WRONG! HERE HE COMES NOW!
WHERE'S HE GOING?
LET'S FOLLOW AND SEE!
A DOOR SWINGS OPEN SILENTLY, AND SNEED CONFRONTS--THE BUTLER, BARKIS-
OH- YOU'RE BACK! I EXPECTED YOU SOONER!
YOU PUT THE POISON IN MY DRINK. NOW I'M GOING TO KILL YOU!
YOU'VE HAD YOUR LAST ATTEMPT AT MURDER, SNEED!

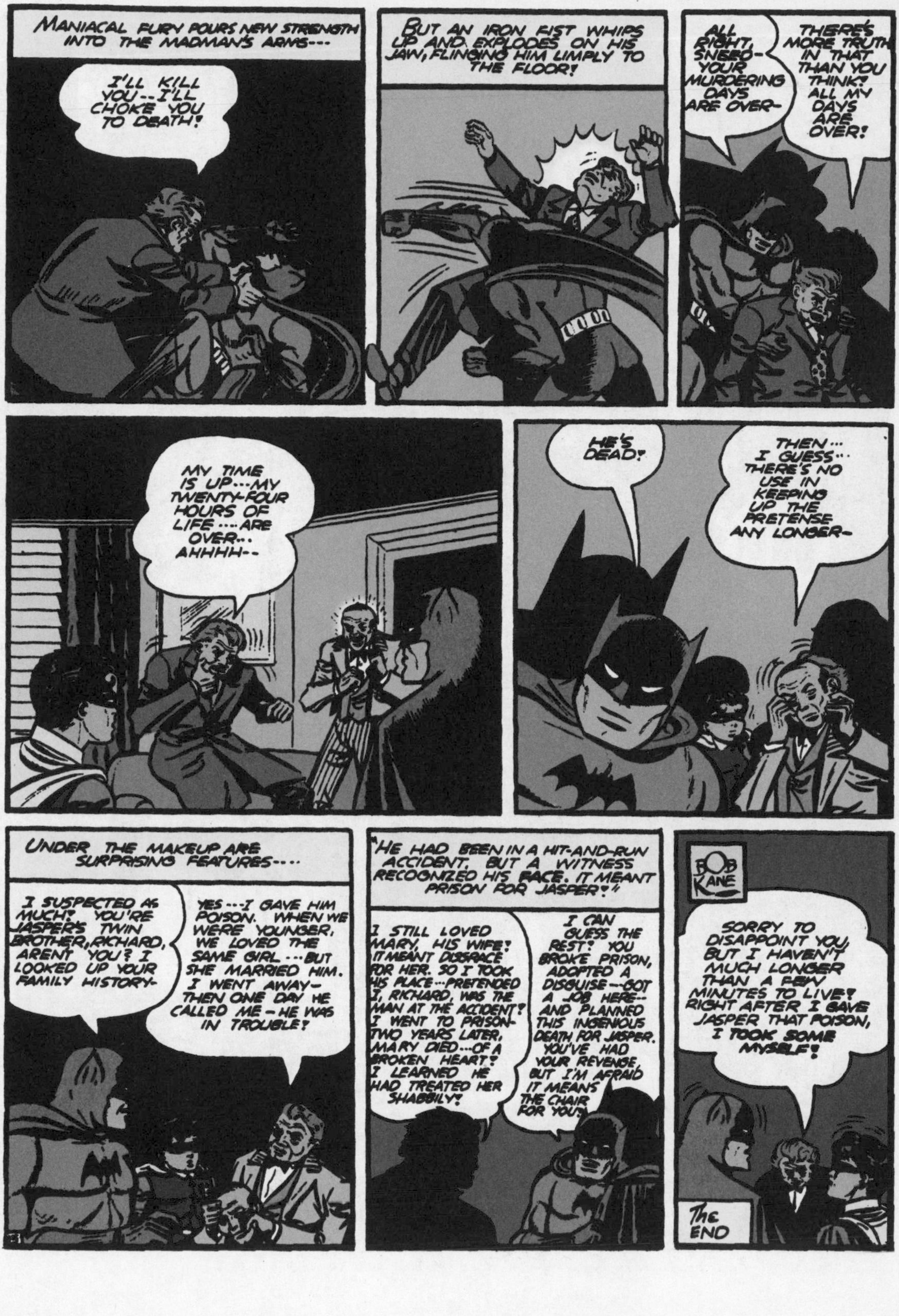
MANIACAL FURY POURS NEW STRENGTH INTO THE MADMAN'S ARMS---
I'LL KILL YOU--I'LL CHOKE YOU TO DEATH!
BUT AN IRON FIST WHIPS UP AND EXPLODES ON HIS JAW, FLINGING HIM LIMPLY TO THE FLOOR!
ALL RIGHT, SNEED-- YOUR MURDERING DAYS ARE OVER-
THERE'S MORE TRUTH IN THAT THAN YOU THINK! ALL MY DAYS ARE OVER!
MY TIME IS UP---MY TWENTY-FOUR HOURS OF LIFE ----ARE OVER... AHHHH--
HE'S DEAD!
THEN... I GUESS... THERE'S NO USE IN KEEPING UP THE PRETENSE ANY LONGER-
UNDER THE MAKEUP ARE SURPRISING FEATURES----
I SUSPECTED AS MUCH! YOU'RE JASPER'S TWIN BROTHER, RICHARD, ARENT YOU? I LOOKED UP YOUR FAMILY HISTORY-
YES---I GAVE HIM POISON. WHEN WE WERE YOUNGER, WE LOVED THE SAME GIRL---BUT SHE MARRIED HIM. I WENT AWAY-- THEN ONE DAY HE CALLED ME - HE WAS IN TROUBLE!
"HE HAD BEEN IN A HIT-AND-RUN ACCIDENT, BUT A WITNESS RECOGNIZED HIS FACE. IT MEANT PRISON FOR JASPER!"
I STILL LOVED MARY, HIS WIFE! IT MEANT DISGRACE FOR HER. SO I TOOK HIS PLACE---PRETENDED I, RICHARD, WAS THE MAN AT THE ACCIDENT! I WENT TO PRISON-TWO YEARS LATER, MARY DIED---OF A BROKEN HEART! I LEARNED HE HAD TREATED HER SHABBILY!
I CAN GUESS THE REST! YOU BROKE PRISON, ADOPTED A DISGUISE--GOT A JOB HERE--AND PLANNED THIS INGENIOUS DEATH FOR JASPER. YOU'VE HAD YOUR REVENGE, BUT I'M AFRAID IT MEANS THE CHAIR FOR YOU!
BOB KANE
SORRY TO DISAPPOINT YOU, BUT I HAVEN'T MUCH LONGER THAN A FEW MINUTES TO LIVE! RIGHT AFTER I GAVE JASPER THAT POISON, I TOOK SOME MYSELF!
THE END

No. 58
The BATMAN
A SUPERMAN DC PUBLICATION
INC
Detective
COMICS
DEC.
10¢

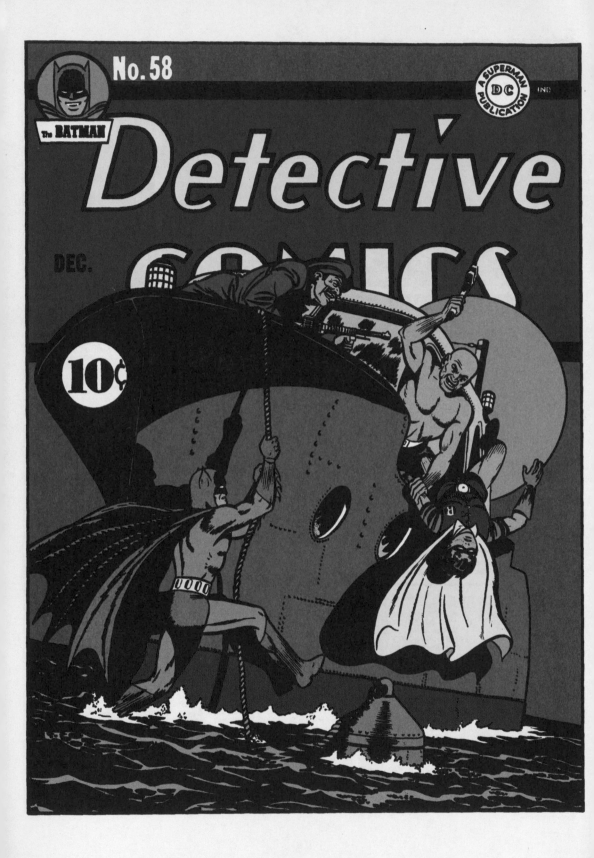

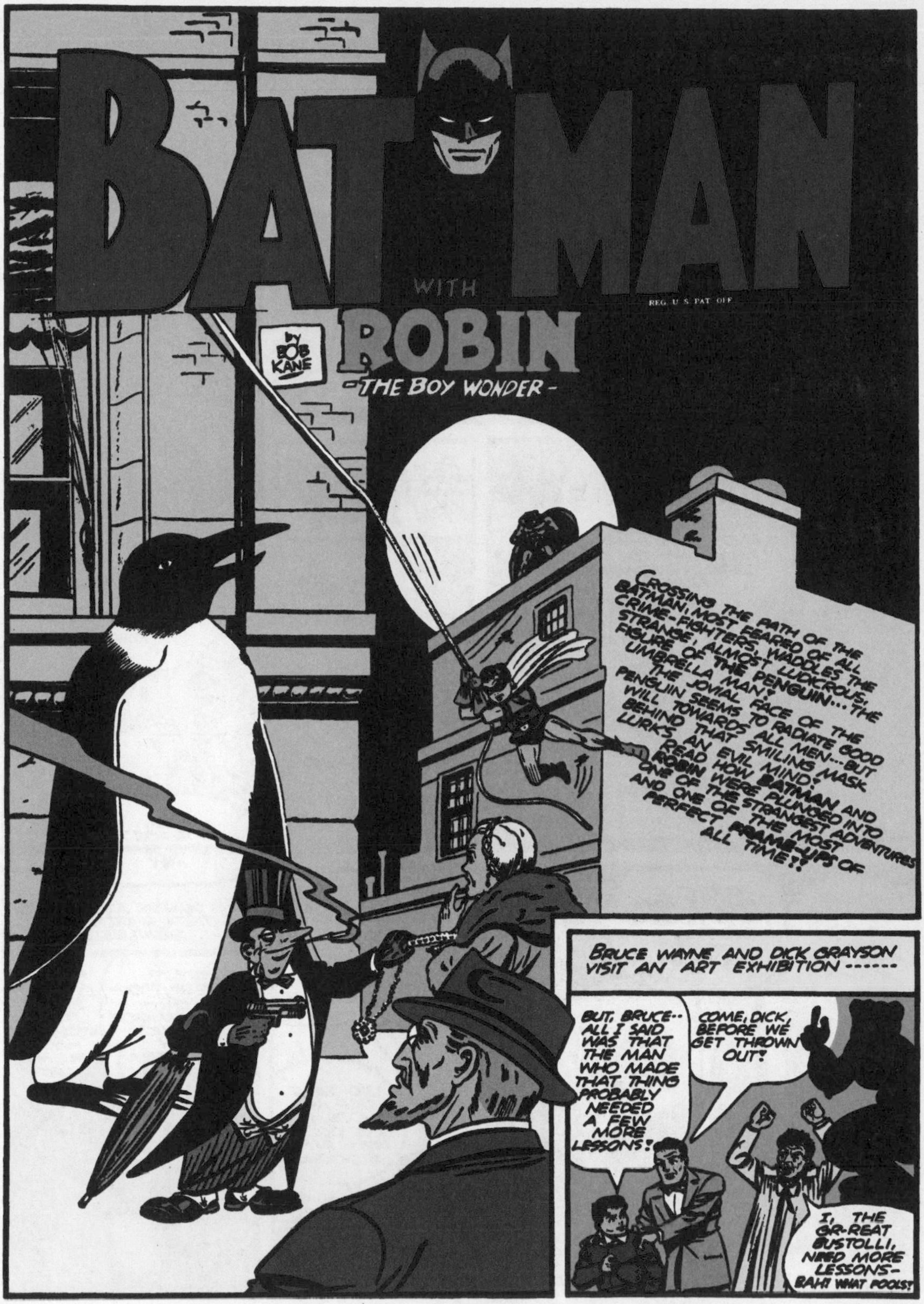
BATMAN
WITH
REG. U.S. PAT. OFF.
by BOB KANE
ROBIN
-THE BOY WONDER-
CROSSING THE PATH OF THE BATMAN, MOST FEARED OF ALL CRIME-FIGHTERS, WADDLES THE STRANGE, ALMOST LUDICROUS, FIGURE OF THE PENGUIN... THE UMBRELLA MAN! THE JOVIAL FACE OF THE PENGUIN SEEMS TO RADIATE GOOD WILL TOWARDS ALL MEN...BUT BEHIND THAT SMILING MASK LURKS AN EVIL MIND! READ HOW BATMAN AND ROBIN WERE PLUNGED INTO ONE OF THE STRANGEST ADVENTURES AND ONE OF THE MOST PERFECT FRAME-UPS OF ALL TIME!!
BRUCE WAYNE AND DICK GRAYSON VISIT AN ART EXHIBITION ------
BUT, BRUCE-- ALL I SAID WAS THAT THE MAN WHO MADE THAT THING PROBABLY NEEDED A FEW MORE LESSONS!
COME, DICK, BEFORE WE GET THROWN OUT!
I, THE GR-REAT BUSTOLLI, NEED MORE LESSONS- BAH! WHAT FOOLS!

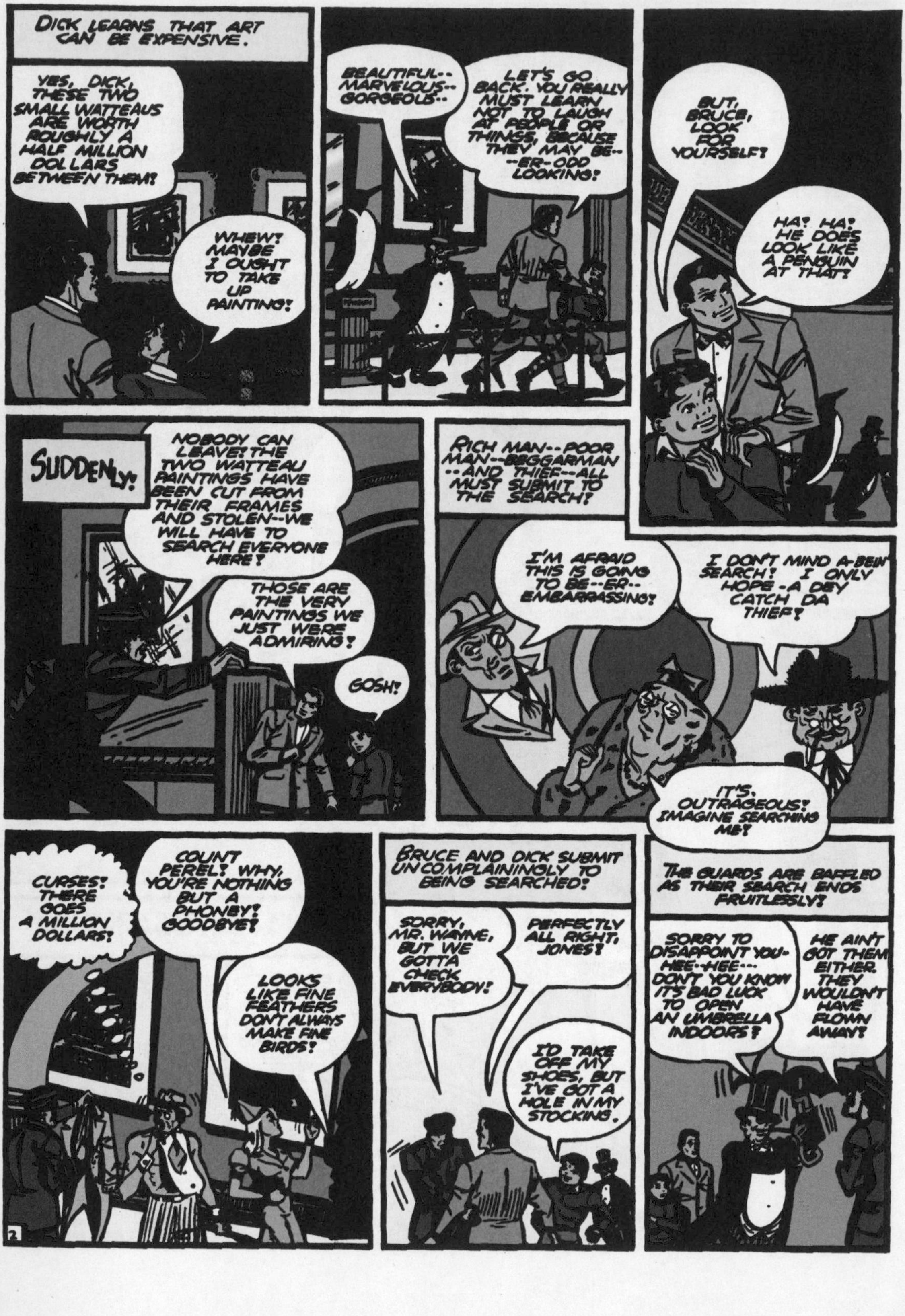
DICK LEARNS THAT ART CAN BE EXPENSIVE.
YES, DICK, THESE TWO SMALL WATTEAUS ARE WORTH ROUGHLY A HALF MILLION DOLLARS BETWEEN THEM!
WHEW! MAYBE I OUGHT TO TAKE UP PAINTING!
BEAUTIFUL--MARVELOUS--GORGEOUS--
LET'S GO BACK. YOU REALLY MUST LEARN NOT TO LAUGH AT PEOPLE OR THINGS, BECAUSE THEY MAY BE--ER-ODD LOOKING!
BUT, BRUCE, LOOK FOR YOURSELF!
HA! HA! HE DOES LOOK LIKE A PENGUIN AT THAT!
SUDDENLY!
NOBODY CAN LEAVE! THE TWO WATTEAU PAINTINGS HAVE BEEN CUT FROM THEIR FRAMES AND STOLEN--WE WILL HAVE TO SEARCH EVERYONE HERE!
THOSE ARE THE VERY PAINTINGS WE JUST WERE ADMIRING!
GOSH!
RICH MAN--POOR MAN--BEGGARMAN--AND THIEF--ALL MUST SUBMIT TO THE SEARCH!
I'M AFRAID THIS IS GOING TO BE--ER--EMBARRASSING!
I DON'T MIND A-BEIN' SEARCH! I ONLY HOPE-A DEY CATCH DA THIEF!
IT'S OUTRAGEOUS! IMAGINE SEARCHING ME!
CURSES! THERE GOES A MILLION DOLLARS!
COUNT PEREL! WHY, YOU'RE NOTHING BUT A PHONEY! GOODBYE!
LOOKS LIKE FINE FEATHERS DON'T ALWAYS MAKE FINE BIRDS!
2
BRUCE AND DICK SUBMIT UNCOMPLAININGLY TO BEING SEARCHED!
SORRY, MR. WAYNE, BUT WE GOTTA CHECK EVERYBODY!
PERFECTLY ALL RIGHT, JONES!
I'D TAKE OFF MY SHOES, BUT I'VE GOT A HOLE IN MY STOCKING.
THE GUARDS ARE BAFFLED AS THEIR SEARCH ENDS FRUITLESSLY!
SORRY TO DISAPPOINT YOU-HEE-HEE--- DON'T YOU KNOW IT'S BAD LUCK TO OPEN AN UMBRELLA INDOORS?
HE AIN'T GOT THEM EITHER. THEY WOULDN'T HAVE FLOWN AWAY!

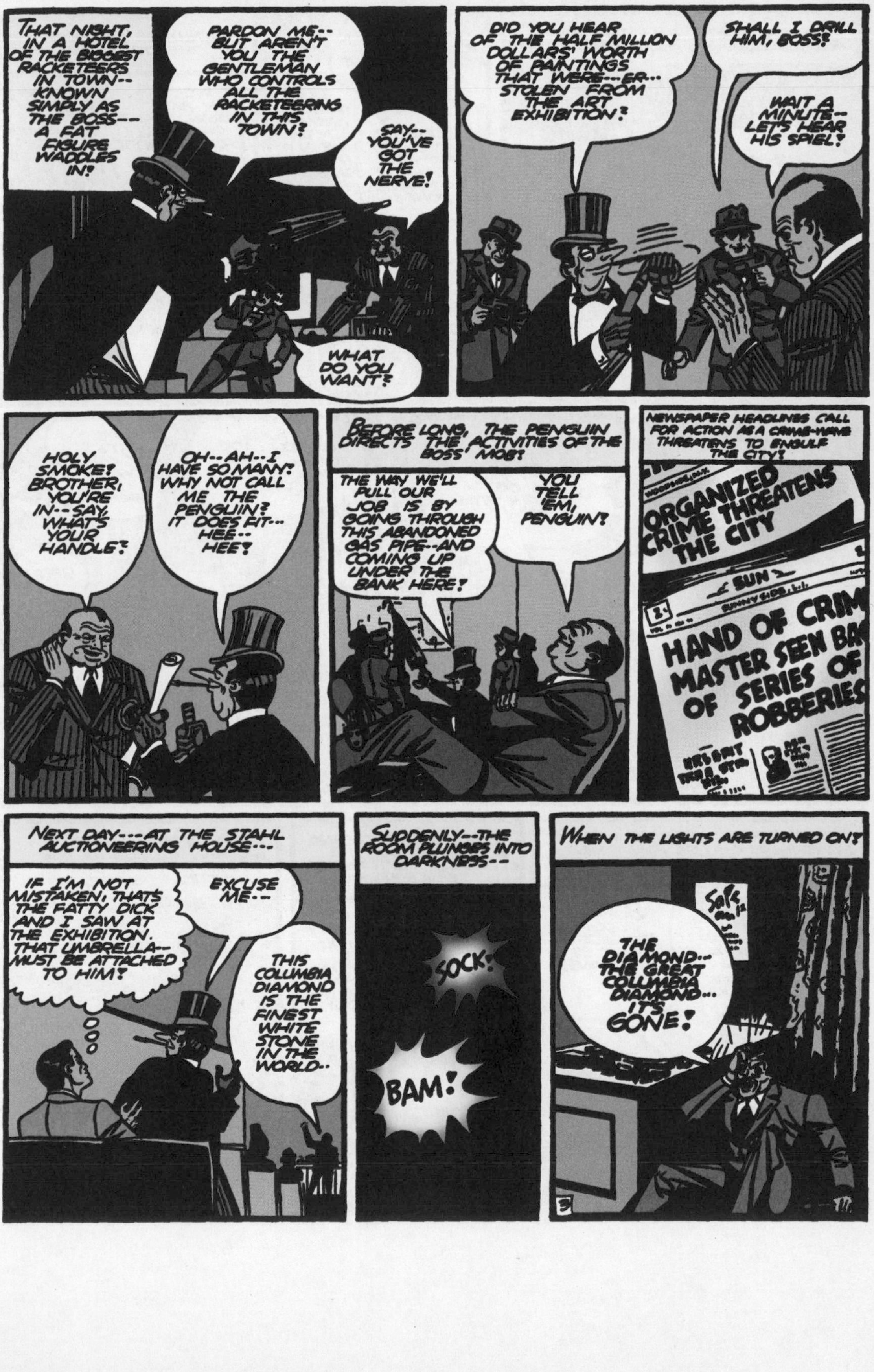
THAT NIGHT, IN A HOTEL OF THE BIGGEST RACKETEERS IN TOWN-- KNOWN SIMPLY AS THE BOSS-- A FAT FIGURE WADDLES IN!
PARDON ME-- BUT AREN'T YOU THE GENTLEMAN WHO CONTROLS ALL THE RACKETEERING IN THIS TOWN?
SAY-- YOU'VE GOT THE NERVE!
WHAT DO YOU WANT?
DID YOU HEAR OF THE HALF MILLION DOLLARS' WORTH OF PAINTINGS THAT WERE--ER-- STOLEN FROM THE ART EXHIBITION?
SHALL I DRILL HIM, BOSS?
WAIT A MINUTE-- LET'S HEAR HIS SPIEL!
HOLY SMOKE! BROTHER, YOU'RE IN--SAY, WHAT'S YOUR HANDLE?
OH--AH--I HAVE SO MANY! WHY NOT CALL ME THE PENGUIN? IT DOES FIT-- HEE-- HEE!
BEFORE LONG, THE PENGUIN DIRECTS THE ACTIVITIES OF THE BOSS' MOB!
THE WAY WE'LL PULL OUR JOB IS BY GOING THROUGH THIS ABANDONED GAS PIPE--AND COMING UP UNDER THE BANK HERE!
YOU TELL 'EM, PENGUIN!
NEWSPAPER HEADLINES CALL FOR ACTION AS A CRIME-WAVE THREATENS TO ENGULF THE CITY!
ORGANIZED CRIME THREATENS THE CITY
SUN
HAND OF CRIM
MASTER SEEN BA
OF SERIES OF
ROBBERIES
NEXT DAY---AT THE STAHL AUCTIONEERING HOUSE---
IF I'M NOT MISTAKEN, THAT'S THE FATTY DICK AND I SAW AT THE EXHIBITION. THAT UMBRELLA-- MUST BE ATTACHED TO HIM!
EXCUSE ME--
THIS COLUMBIA DIAMOND IS THE FINEST WHITE STONE IN THE WORLD--
SUDDENLY--THE ROOM PLUNGES INTO DARKNESS--
SOCK!
BAM!
WHEN THE LIGHTS ARE TURNED ON!
THE DIAMOND-- THE GREAT COLUMBIA DIAMOND-- IT'S GONE!

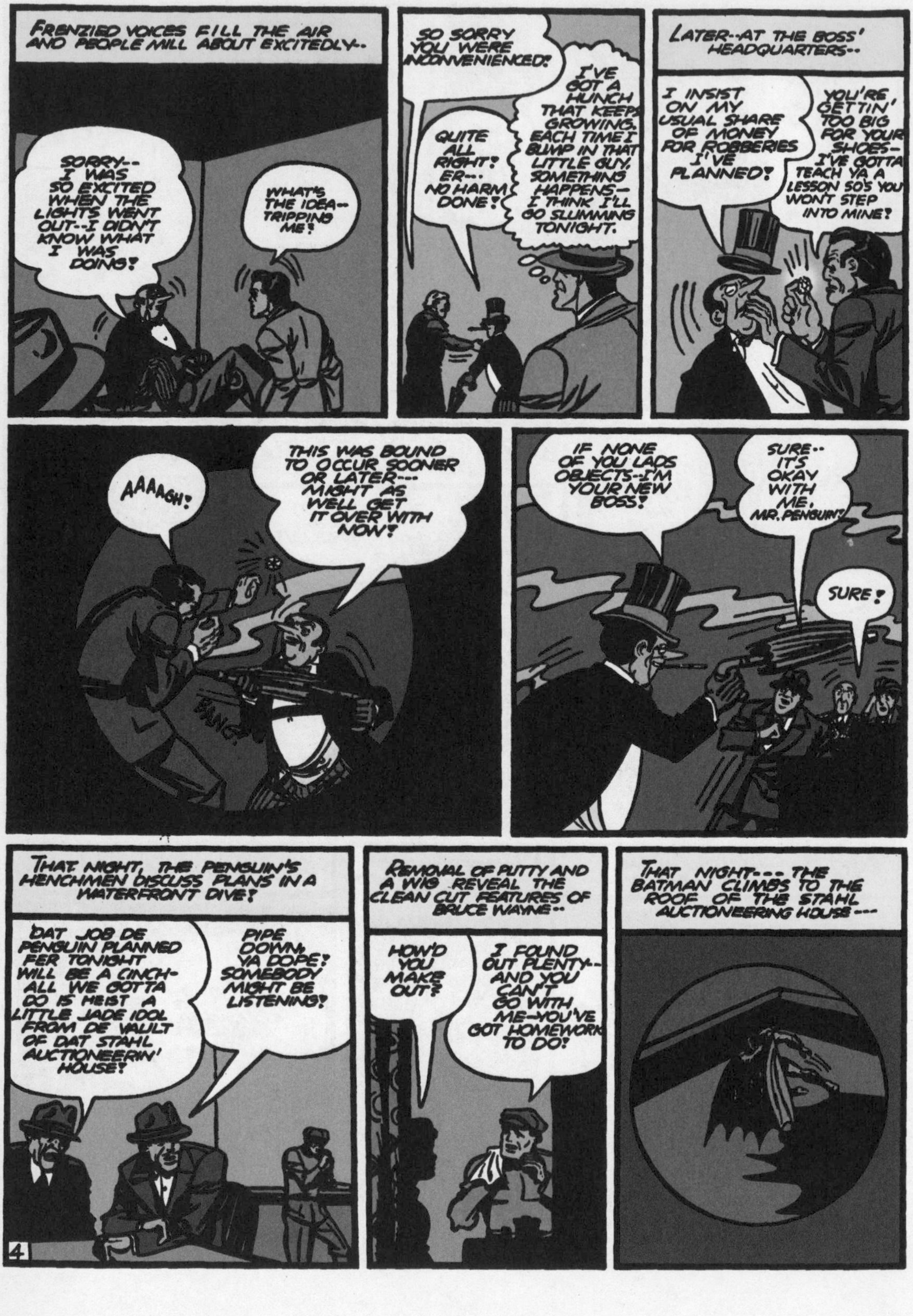

FRENZIED VOICES FILL THE AIR AND PEOPLE MILL ABOUT EXCITEDLY--
SORRY-- I WAS SO EXCITED WHEN THE LIGHTS WENT OUT--I DIDN'T KNOW WHAT I WAS DOING!
WHAT'S THE IDEA-- TRIPPING ME?
SO SORRY YOU WERE INCONVENIENCED!
QUITE ALL RIGHT! ER--- NO HARM DONE!
I'VE GOT A HUNCH THAT KEEPS GROWING. EACH TIME I BUMP IN THAT LITTLE GUY, SOMETHING HAPPENS-- I THINK I'LL GO SLUMMING TONIGHT.
LATER--AT THE BOSS' HEADQUARTERS--
I INSIST ON MY USUAL SHARE OF MONEY FOR ROBBERIES I'VE PLANNED!
YOU'RE GETTIN' TOO BIG FOR YOUR SHOES-- I'VE GOTTA TEACH YA A LESSON SO'S YOU WON'T STEP INTO MINE!
AAAAGH!
THIS WAS BOUND TO OCCUR SOONER OR LATER--- MIGHT AS WELL GET IT OVER WITH NOW!
BANG!
IF NONE OF YOU LADS OBJECTS--I'M YOUR NEW BOSS!
SURE-- IT'S OKAY WITH ME, MR. PENGUIN!
SURE!
THAT NIGHT, THE PENGUIN'S HENCHMEN DISCUSS PLANS IN A WATERFRONT DIVE!
DAT JOB DE PENGUIN PLANNED FER TONIGHT WILL BE A CINCH-- ALL WE GOTTA DO IS HEIST A LITTLE JADE IDOL FROM DE VAULT OF DAT STAHL AUCTIONEERIN' HOUSE!
PIPE DOWN, YA DOPE! SOMEBODY MIGHT BE LISTENING!
4
REMOVAL OF PUTTY AND A WIG REVEAL THE CLEAN CUT FEATURES OF BRUCE WAYNE--
HOW'D YOU MAKE OUT?
I FOUND OUT PLENTY-- AND YOU CAN'T GO WITH ME--YOU'VE GOT HOMEWORK TO DO!
THAT NIGHT--- THE BATMAN CLIMBS TO THE ROOF OF THE STAHL AUCTIONEERING HOUSE---

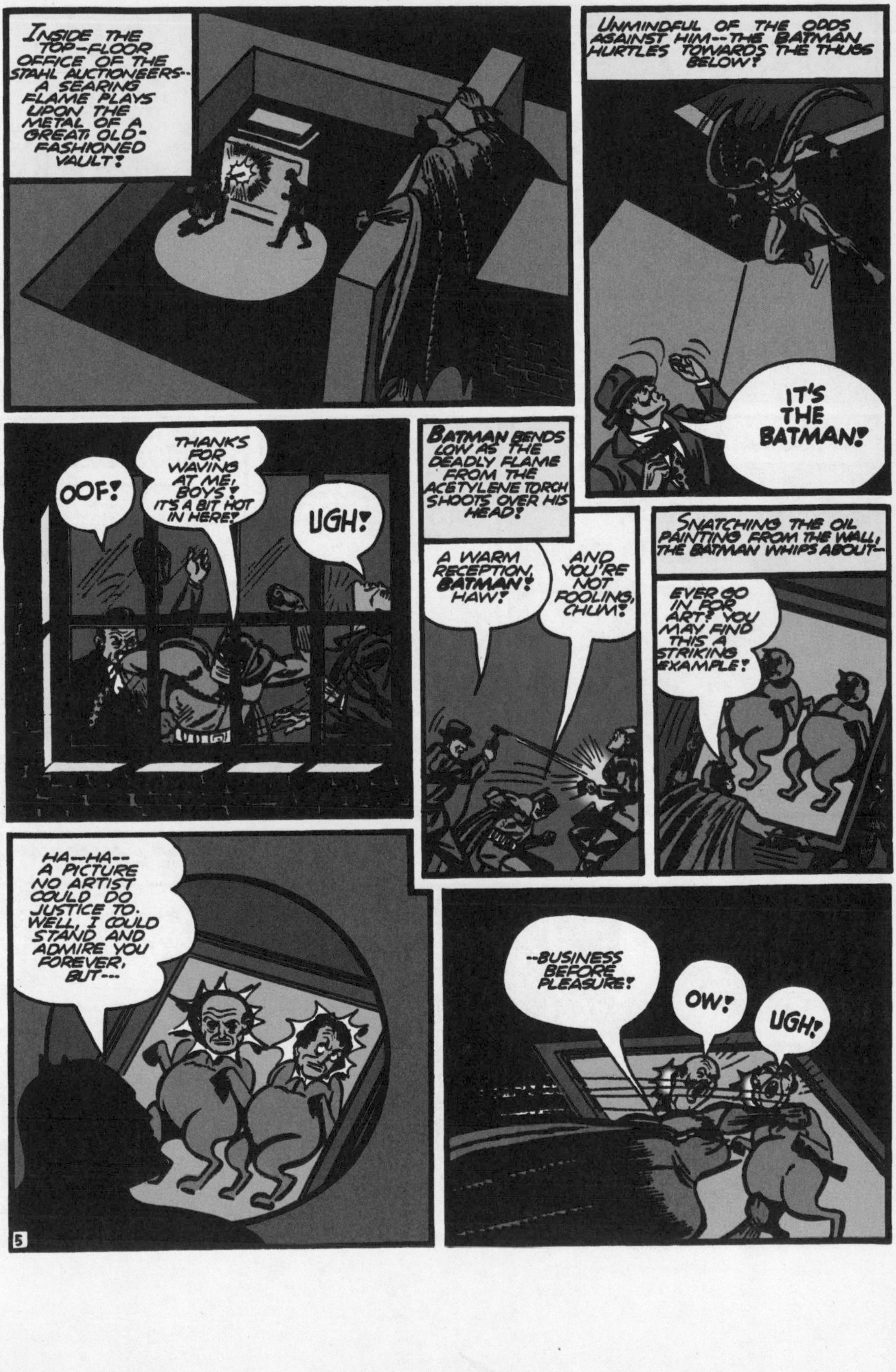
INSIDE THE TOP-FLOOR OFFICE OF THE STAHL AUCTIONEERS-- A SEARING FLAME PLAYS UPON THE METAL OF A GREAT, OLD-FASHIONED VAULT!
UNMINDFUL OF THE ODDS AGAINST HIM--THE BATMAN HURTLES TOWARDS THE THUGS BELOW!
IT'S THE BATMAN!
OOF!
THANKS FOR WAVING AT ME, BOYS! IT'S A BIT HOT IN HERE!
UGH!
BATMAN BENDS LOW AS THE DEADLY FLAME FROM THE ACETYLENE TORCH SHOOTS OVER HIS HEAD!
A WARM RECEPTION, BATMAN! HAW!
AND YOU'RE NOT FOOLING, CHUM!
SNATCHING THE OIL PAINTING FROM THE WALL, THE BATMAN WHIPS ABOUT--
EVER GO IN FOR ART? YOU MAY FIND THIS A STRIKING EXAMPLE!
HA-HA-- A PICTURE NO ARTIST COULD DO JUSTICE TO. WELL, I COULD STAND AND ADMIRE YOU FOREVER, BUT---
5
--BUSINESS BEFORE PLEASURE!
OW!
UGH!

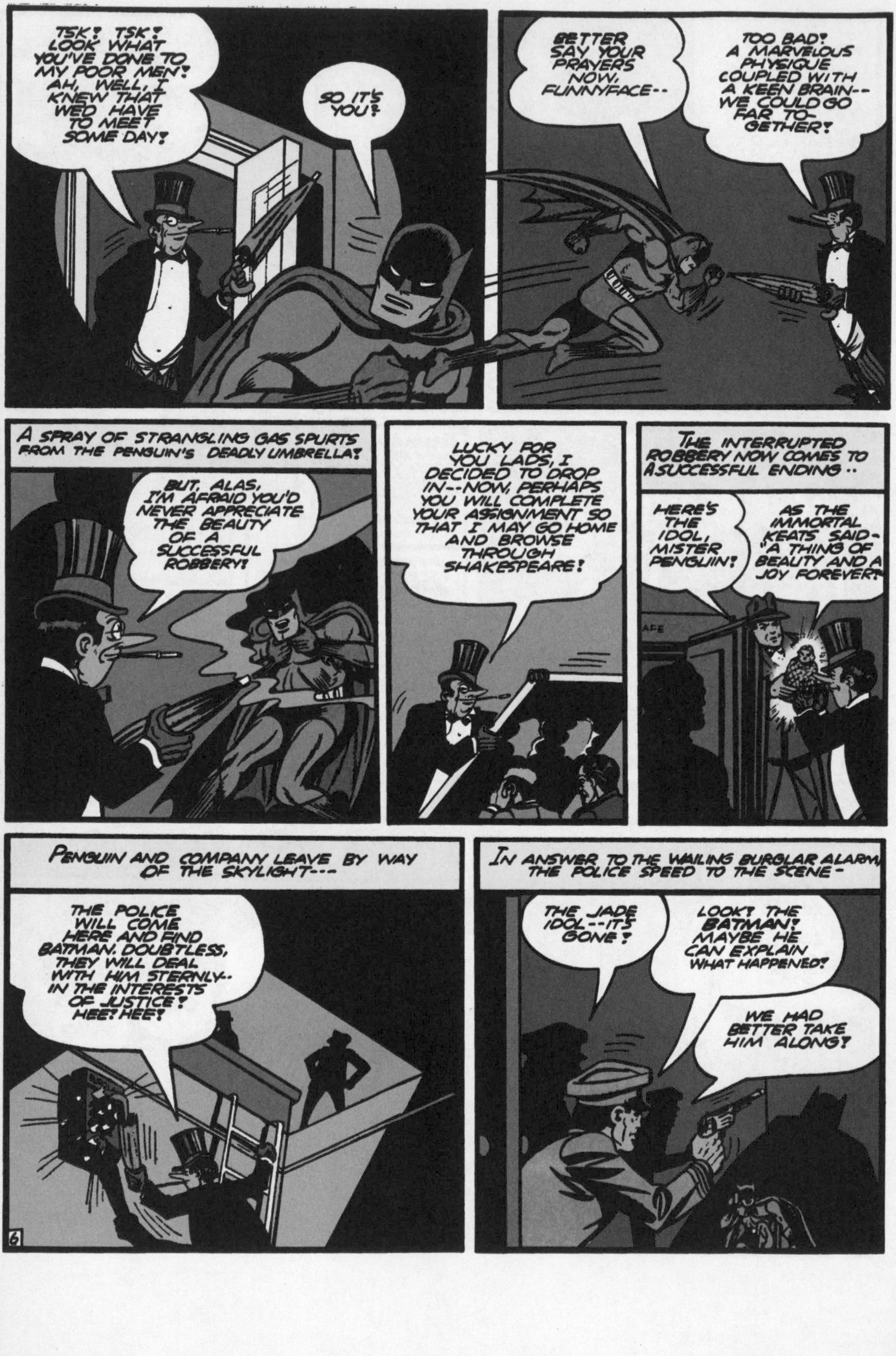
TSK! TSK! LOOK WHAT YOU'VE DONE TO MY POOR MEN! AH, WELL, I KNEW THAT WED HAVE TO MEET SOME DAY!
SO IT'S YOU!
BETTER SAY YOUR PRAYERS NOW, FUNNYFACE--
TOO BAD! A MARVELOUS PHYSIQUE COUPLED WITH A KEEN BRAIN--WE COULD GO FAR TO-GETHER!
A SPRAY OF STRANGLING GAS SPURTS FROM THE PENGUIN'S DEADLY UMBRELLA!
BUT, ALAS, I'M AFRAID YOU'D NEVER APPRECIATE THE BEAUTY OF A SUCCESSFUL ROBBERY!
LUCKY FOR YOU LADS, I DECIDED TO DROP IN--NOW, PERHAPS YOU WILL COMPLETE YOUR ASSIGNMENT SO THAT I MAY GO HOME AND BROWSE THROUGH SHAKESPEARE!
THE INTERRUPTED ROBBERY NOW COMES TO A SUCCESSFUL ENDING..
HERE'S THE IDOL, MISTER PENGUIN!
AS THE IMMORTAL KEATS SAID-"A THING OF BEAUTY AND A JOY FOREVER!"
PENGUIN AND COMPANY LEAVE BY WAY OF THE SKYLIGHT---
THE POLICE WILL COME HERE AND FIND BATMAN. DOUBTLESS, THEY WILL DEAL WITH HIM STERNLY--IN THE INTERESTS OF JUSTICE! HEE! HEE!
6
IN ANSWER TO THE WAILING BURGLAR ALARM, THE POLICE SPEED TO THE SCENE-
THE JADE IDOL--IT'S GONE!
LOOK! THE BATMAN! MAYBE HE CAN EXPLAIN WHAT HAPPENED!
WE HAD BETTER TAKE HIM ALONG!

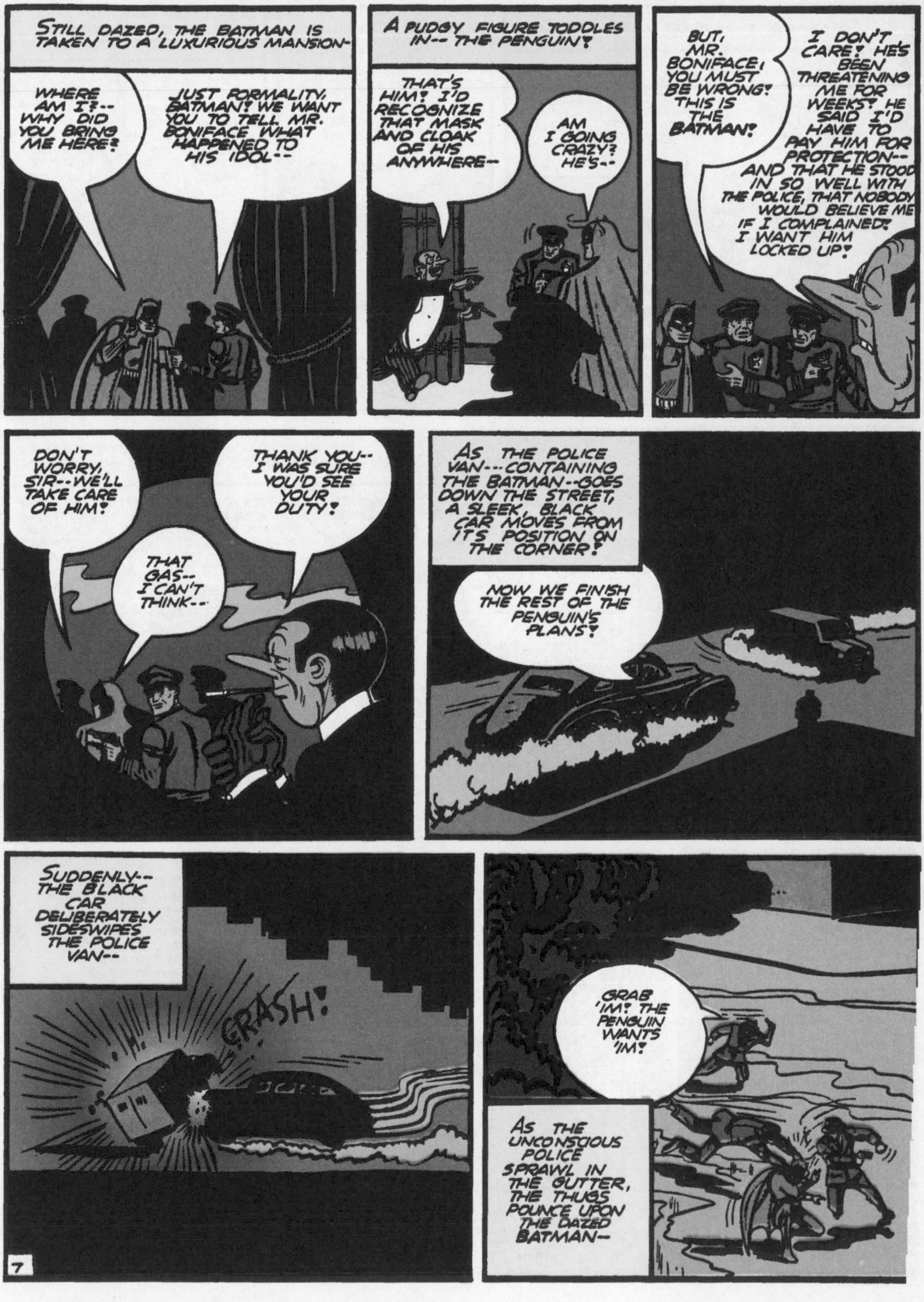
STILL DAZED, THE BATMAN IS TAKEN TO A LUXURIOUS MANSION-
WHERE AM I?-- WHY DID YOU BRING ME HERE?
JUST FORMALITY, BATMAN! WE WANT YOU TO TELL MR. BONIFACE WHAT HAPPENED TO HIS IDOL--
A PUDGY FIGURE TODDLES IN-- THE PENGUIN!
THAT'S HIM! I'D RECOGNIZE THAT MASK AND CLOAK OF HIS ANYWHERE--
AM I GOING CRAZY? HE'S--
BUT, MR. BONIFACE, YOU MUST BE WRONG! THIS IS THE BATMAN!
I DON'T CARE! HE'S BEEN THREATENING ME FOR WEEKS! HE SAID I'D HAVE TO PAY HIM FOR PROTECTION-- AND THAT HE STOOD IN SO WELL WITH THE POLICE, THAT NOBODY WOULD BELIEVE ME IF I COMPLAINED! I WANT HIM LOCKED UP!
DON'T WORRY, SIR--WE'LL TAKE CARE OF HIM!
THANK YOU-- I WAS SURE YOU'D SEE YOUR DUTY!
THAT GAS-- I CAN'T THINK--
AS THE POLICE VAN---CONTAINING THE BATMAN--GOES DOWN THE STREET, A SLEEK, BLACK CAR MOVES FROM IT'S POSITION ON THE CORNER!
NOW WE FINISH THE REST OF THE PENGUIN'S PLANS!
SUDDENLY-- THE BLACK CAR DELIBERATELY SIDESWIPES THE POLICE VAN--
CRASH!
GRAB 'IM! THE PENGUIN WANTS 'IM!
AS THE UNCONSCIOUS POLICE SPRAWL IN THE GUTTER, THE THUGS POUNCE UPON THE DAZED BATMAN--
7

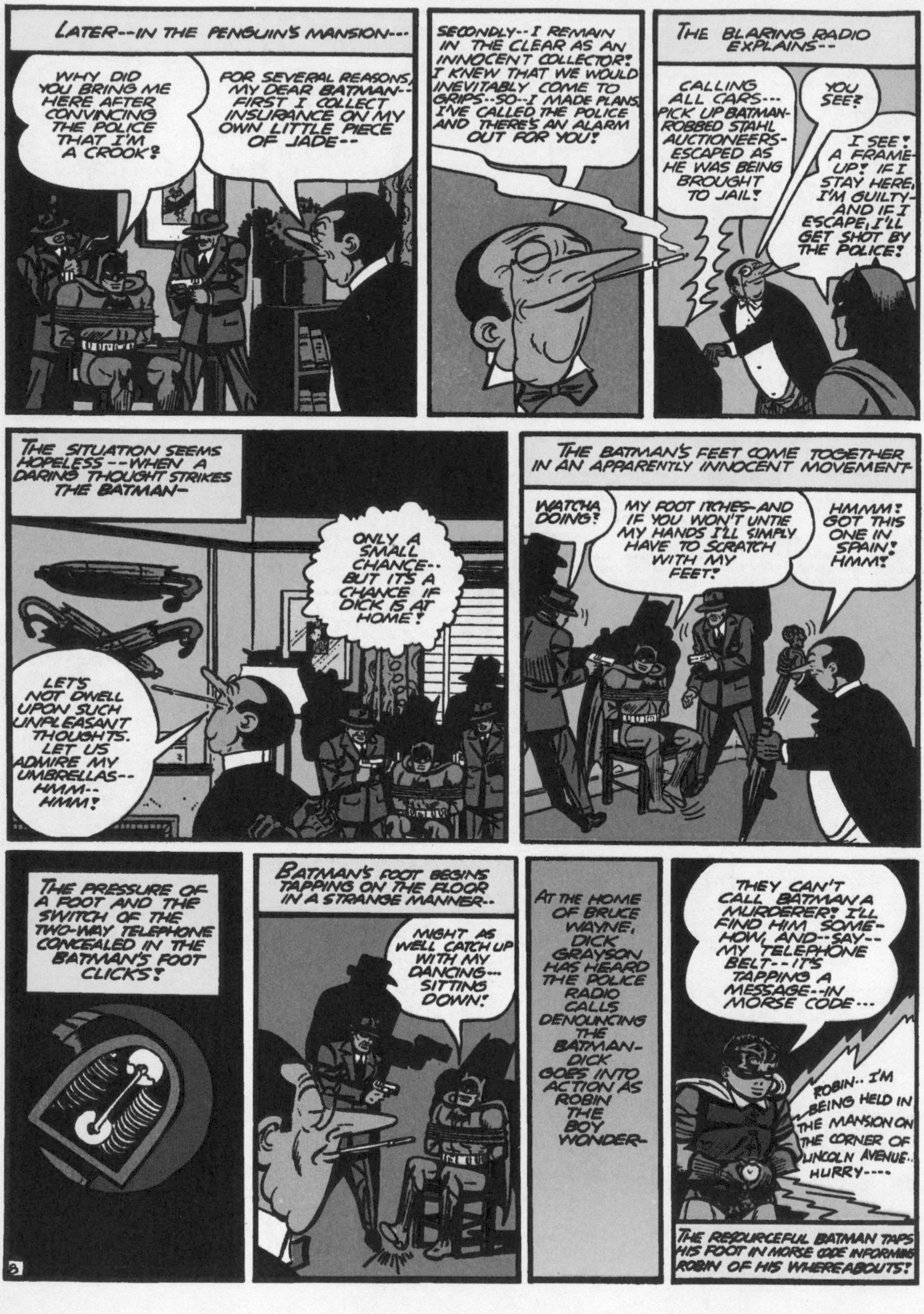
LATER--IN THE PENGUIN'S MANSION---
WHY DID YOU BRING ME HERE AFTER CONVINCING THE POLICE THAT I'M A CROOK?
FOR SEVERAL REASONS, MY DEAR BATMAN--FIRST I COLLECT INSURANCE ON MY OWN LITTLE PIECE OF JADE--
SECONDLY--I REMAIN IN THE CLEAR AS AN INNOCENT COLLECTOR! I KNEW THAT WE WOULD INEVITABLY COME TO GRIPS--SO--I MADE PLANS. I'VE CALLED THE POLICE AND THERE'S AN ALARM OUT FOR YOU!
THE BLARING RADIO EXPLAINS--
CALLING ALL CARS--- PICK UP BATMAN-ROBBED STAHL AUCTIONEERS-ESCAPED AS HE WAS BEING BROUGHT TO JAIL!
YOU SEE?
I SEE! A FRAME-UP! IF I STAY HERE, I'M GUILTY-AND IF I ESCAPE, I'LL GET SHOT BY THE POLICE!
THE SITUATION SEEMS HOPELESS--WHEN A DARING THOUGHT STRIKES THE BATMAN-
ONLY A SMALL CHANCE--BUT IT'S A CHANCE IF DICK IS AT HOME!
LET'S NOT DWELL UPON SUCH UNPLEASANT THOUGHTS. LET US ADMIRE MY UMBRELLAS--HMM--HMM!
THE BATMAN'S FEET COME TOGETHER IN AN APPARENTLY INNOCENT MOVEMENT-
WATCHA DOING?
MY FOOT ITCHES-AND IF YOU WON'T UNTIE MY HANDS I'LL SIMPLY HAVE TO SCRATCH WITH MY FEET!
HMMM! GOT THIS ONE IN SPAIN! HMM!
THE PRESSURE OF A FOOT AND THE SWITCH OF THE TWO-WAY TELEPHONE CONCEALED IN THE BATMAN'S FOOT CLICKS!
BATMAN'S FOOT BEGINS TAPPING ON THE FLOOR IN A STRANGE MANNER--
MIGHT AS WELL CATCH UP WITH MY DANCING--- SITTING DOWN!
AT THE HOME OF BRUCE WAYNE, DICK GRAYSON HAS HEARD THE POLICE RADIO CALLS DENOUNCING THE BATMAN-DICK GOES INTO ACTION AS ROBIN THE BOY WONDER-
THEY CAN'T CALL BATMAN A MURDERER! I'LL FIND HIM SOME-HOW, AND--SAY--MY TELEPHONE BELT--IT'S TAPPING A MESSAGE--IN MORSE CODE---
ROBIN-- I'M BEING HELD IN THE MANSION ON THE CORNER OF LINCOLN AVENUE-- HURRY----
THE RESOURCEFUL BATMAN TAPS HIS FOOT IN MORSE CODE INFORMING ROBIN OF HIS WHEREABOUTS!
8

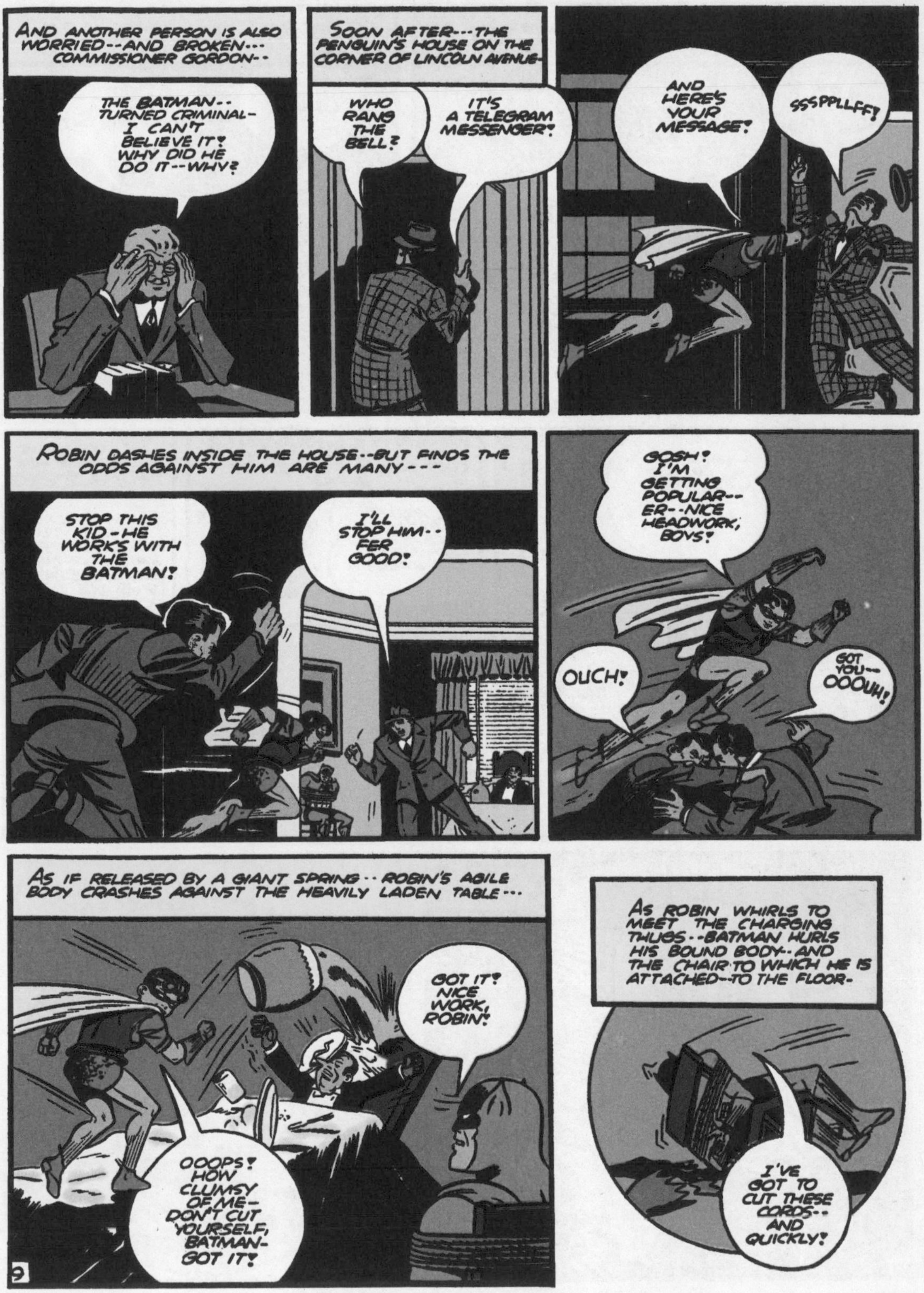
AND ANOTHER PERSON IS ALSO WORRIED--AND BROKEN--- COMMISSIONER GORDON--
THE BATMAN-- TURNED CRIMINAL- I CAN'T BELIEVE IT! WHY DID HE DO IT--WHY?
SOON AFTER---THE PENGUIN'S HOUSE ON THE CORNER OF LINCOLN AVENUE-
WHO RANG THE BELL?
IT'S A TELEGRAM MESSENGER!
AND HERE'S YOUR MESSAGE!
SSSPPLLFF!
ROBIN DASHES INSIDE THE HOUSE--BUT FINDS THE ODDS AGAINST HIM ARE MANY---
STOP THIS KID-HE WORKS WITH THE BATMAN!
I'LL STOP HIM-- FER GOOD!
GOSH! I'M GETTING POPULAR-- ER--NICE HEADWORK, BOYS!
OUCH!
GOT YOU-- OOOUH!
AS IF RELEASED BY A GIANT SPRING--ROBIN'S AGILE BODY CRASHES AGAINST THE HEAVILY LADEN TABLE---
GOT IT! NICE WORK, ROBIN!
OOOPS! HOW CLUMSY OF ME- DON'T CUT YOURSELF, BATMAN- GOT IT!
AS ROBIN WHIRLS TO MEET THE CHARGING THUGS--BATMAN HURLS HIS BOUND BODY--AND THE CHAIR TO WHICH HE IS ATTACHED--TO THE FLOOR-
I'VE GOT TO CUT THESE CORDS-- AND QUICKLY!

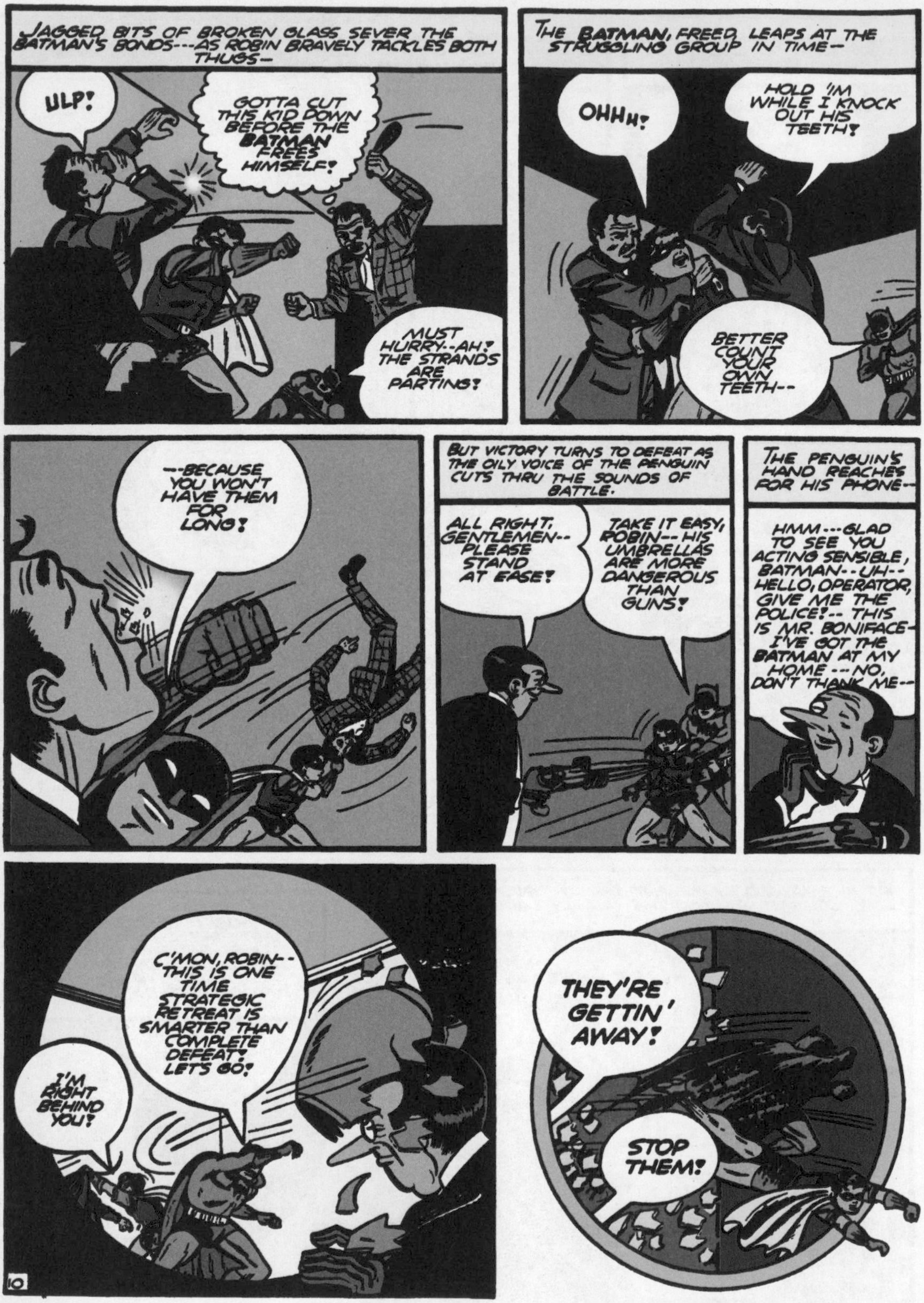
JAGGED BITS OF BROKEN GLASS SEVER THE BATMAN'S BONDS---AS ROBIN BRAVELY TACKLES BOTH THUGS—
ULP!
GOTTA CUT THIS KID DOWN BEFORE THE BATMAN FREES HIMSELF!
MUST HURRY--AH! THE STRANDS ARE PARTING!
THE BATMAN, FREED, LEAPS AT THE STRUGGLING GROUP IN TIME—
OHHH!
HOLD 'IM WHILE I KNOCK OUT HIS TEETH!
BETTER COUNT YOUR OWN TEETH--
--BECAUSE YOU WON'T HAVE THEM FOR LONG!
BUT VICTORY TURNS TO DEFEAT AS THE OILY VOICE OF THE PENGUIN CUTS THRU THE SOUNDS OF BATTLE.
ALL RIGHT, GENTLEMEN-- PLEASE STAND AT EASE!
TAKE IT EASY, ROBIN-- HIS UMBRELLAS ARE MORE DANGEROUS THAN GUNS!
THE PENGUIN'S HAND REACHES FOR HIS PHONE--
HMM---GLAD TO SEE YOU ACTING SENSIBLE, BATMAN--UH-- HELLO, OPERATOR, GIVE ME THE POLICE!-- THIS IS MR. BONIFACE- I'VE GOT THE BATMAN AT MY HOME---NO, DON'T THANK ME--
C'MON, ROBIN-- THIS IS ONE TIME STRATEGIC RETREAT IS SMARTER THAN COMPLETE DEFEAT! LET'S GO!
I'M RIGHT BEHIND YOU!
10
THEY'RE GETTIN' AWAY!
STOP THEM!

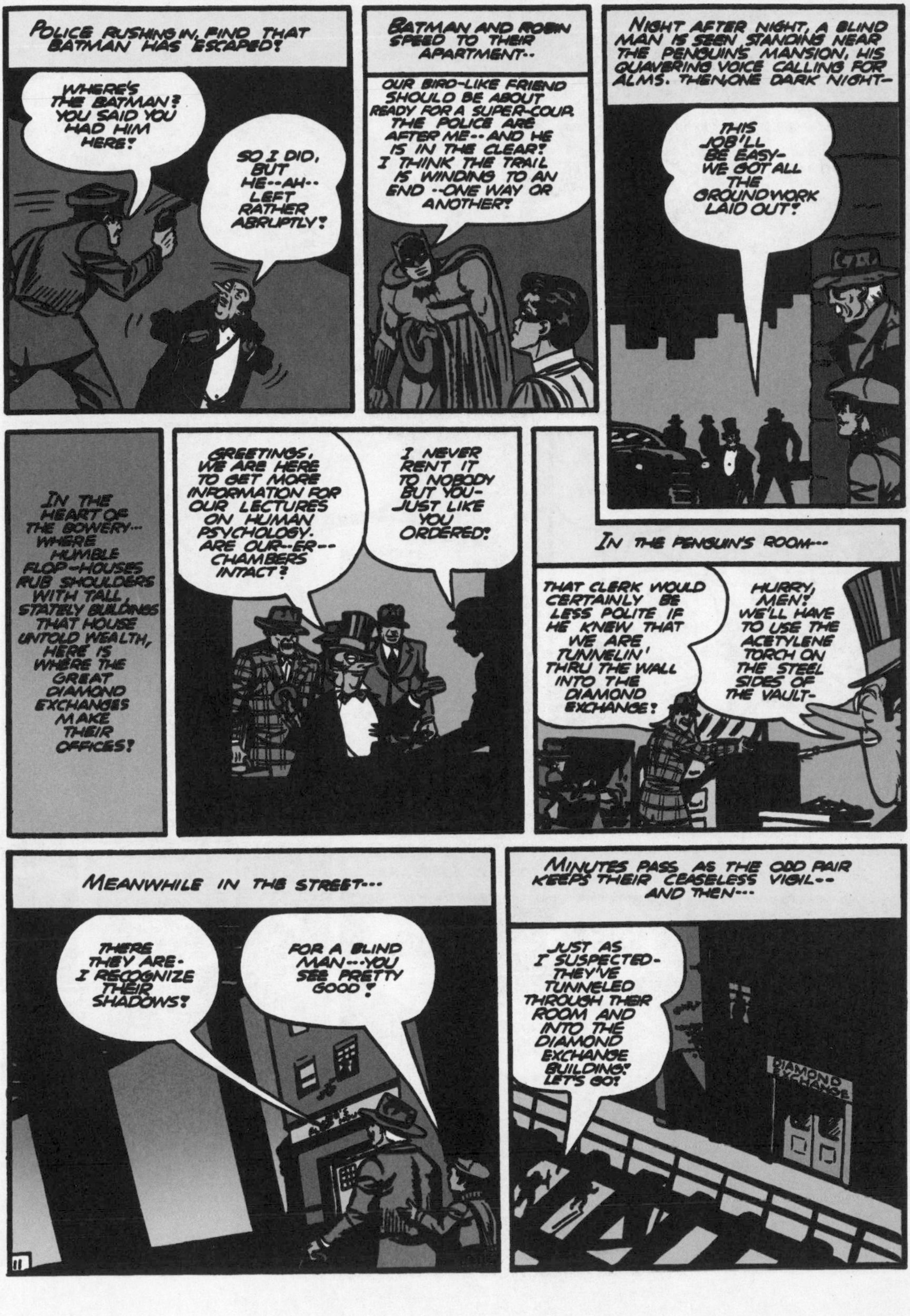
POLICE RUSHING IN, FIND THAT BATMAN HAS ESCAPED!
WHERE'S THE BATMAN? YOU SAID YOU HAD HIM HERE!
SO I DID, BUT HE--AH--LEFT RATHER ABRUPTLY!
BATMAN AND ROBIN SPEED TO THEIR APARTMENT--
OUR BIRD-LIKE FRIEND SHOULD BE ABOUT READY FOR A SUPER-COUP. THE POLICE ARE AFTER ME--AND HE IS IN THE CLEAR! I THINK THE TRAIL IS WINDING TO AN END--ONE WAY OR ANOTHER!
NIGHT AFTER NIGHT, A BLIND MAN IS SEEN STANDING NEAR THE PENGUIN'S MANSION, HIS QUAVERING VOICE CALLING FOR ALMS. THEN,ONE DARK NIGHT-
THIS JOB'LL BE EASY-WE GOT ALL THE GROUNDWORK LAID OUT!
IN THE HEART OF THE BOWERY--WHERE HUMBLE FLOP-HOUSES RUB SHOULDERS WITH TALL, STATELY BUILDINGS THAT HOUSE UNTOLD WEALTH, HERE IS WHERE THE GREAT DIAMOND EXCHANGES MAKE THEIR OFFICES!
GREETINGS, WE ARE HERE TO GET MORE INFORMATION FOR OUR LECTURES ON HUMAN PSYCHOLOGY. ARE OUR--ER--CHAMBERS INTACT?
I NEVER RENT IT TO NOBODY BUT YOU-JUST LIKE YOU ORDERED!
IN THE PENGUIN'S ROOM---
THAT CLERK WOULD CERTAINLY BE LESS POLITE IF HE KNEW THAT WE ARE TUNNELIN' THRU THE WALL INTO THE DIAMOND EXCHANGE!
HURRY, MEN! WE'LL HAVE TO USE THE ACETYLENE TORCH ON THE STEEL SIDES OF THE VAULT-
MEANWHILE IN THE STREET---
THERE THEY ARE-I RECOGNIZE THEIR SHADOWS!
FOR A BLIND MAN---YOU SEE PRETTY GOOD!
11
MINUTES PASS AS THE ODD PAIR KEEPS THEIR CEASELESS VIGIL--AND THEN---
JUST AS I SUSPECTED-THEY'VE TUNNELED THROUGH THEIR ROOM AND INTO THE DIAMOND EXCHANGE BUILDING! LET'S GO!
DIAMOND EXCHANGE

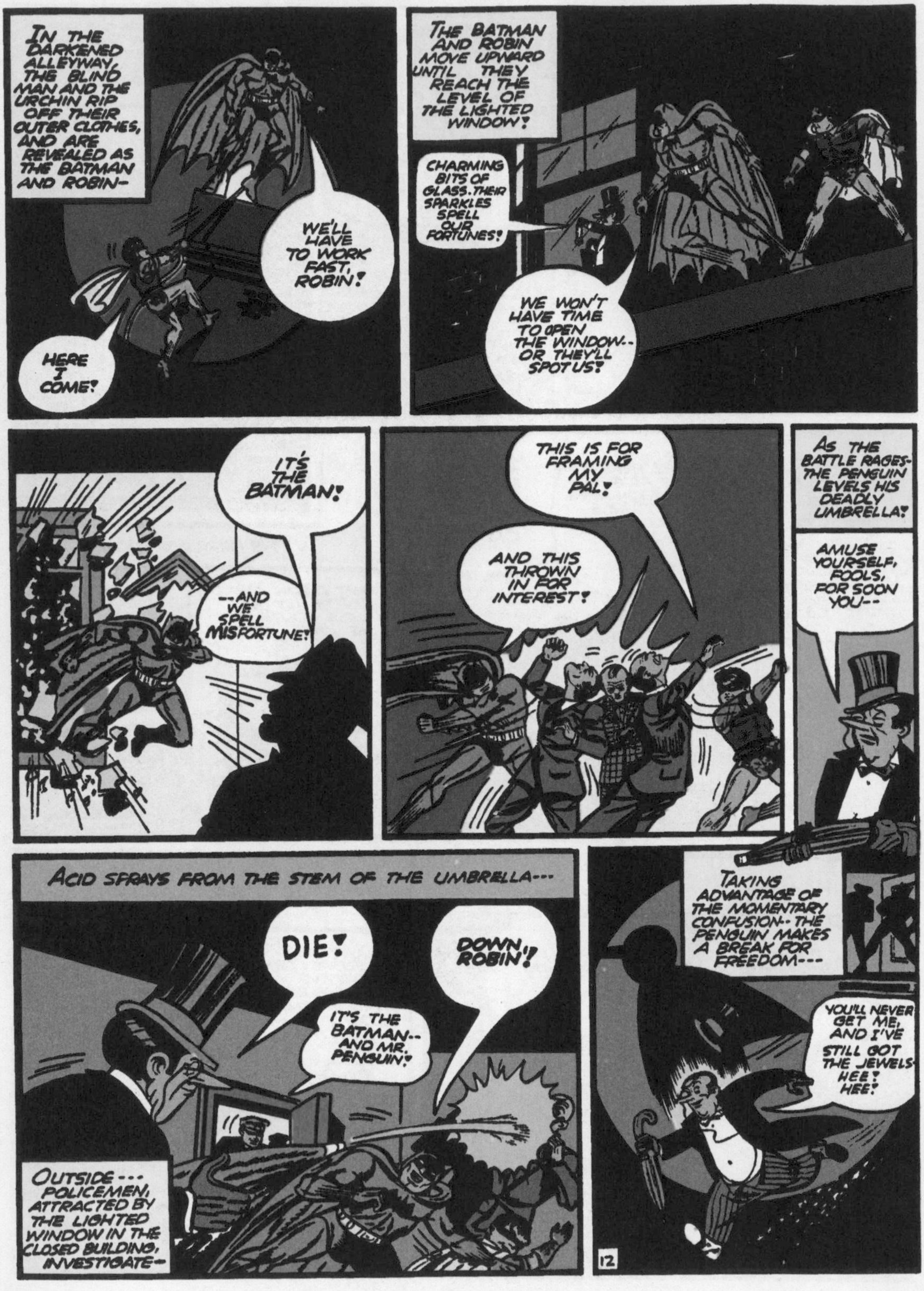
IN THE DARKENED ALLEYWAY, THE BLIND MAN AND THE URCHIN RIP OFF THEIR OUTER CLOTHES, AND ARE REVEALED AS THE BATMAN AND ROBIN-
WE'LL HAVE TO WORK FAST, ROBIN!
HERE I COME!
THE BATMAN AND ROBIN MOVE UPWARD UNTIL THEY REACH THE LEVEL OF THE LIGHTED WINDOW!
CHARMING BITS OF GLASS. THEIR SPARKLES SPELL OUR FORTUNES!
WE WON'T HAVE TIME TO OPEN THE WINDOW-- OR THEY'LL SPOT US!
IT'S THE BATMAN!
--AND WE SPELL MISFORTUNE!
THIS IS FOR FRAMING MY PAL!
AND THIS THROWN IN FOR INTEREST!
AS THE BATTLE RAGES- THE PENGUIN LEVELS HIS DEADLY UMBRELLA!
AMUSE YOURSELF, FOOLS, FOR SOON YOU--
ACID SPRAYS FROM THE STEM OF THE UMBRELLA---
DIE!
DOWN, ROBIN!
IT'S THE BATMAN-- AND MR. PENGUIN!
OUTSIDE--- POLICEMEN, ATTRACTED BY THE LIGHTED WINDOW IN THE CLOSED BUILDING, INVESTIGATE-
TAKING ADVANTAGE OF THE MOMENTARY CONFUSION-- THE PENGUIN MAKES A BREAK FOR FREEDOM---
YOU'LL NEVER GET ME, AND I'VE STILL GOT THE JEWELS- HEE! HEE!
12

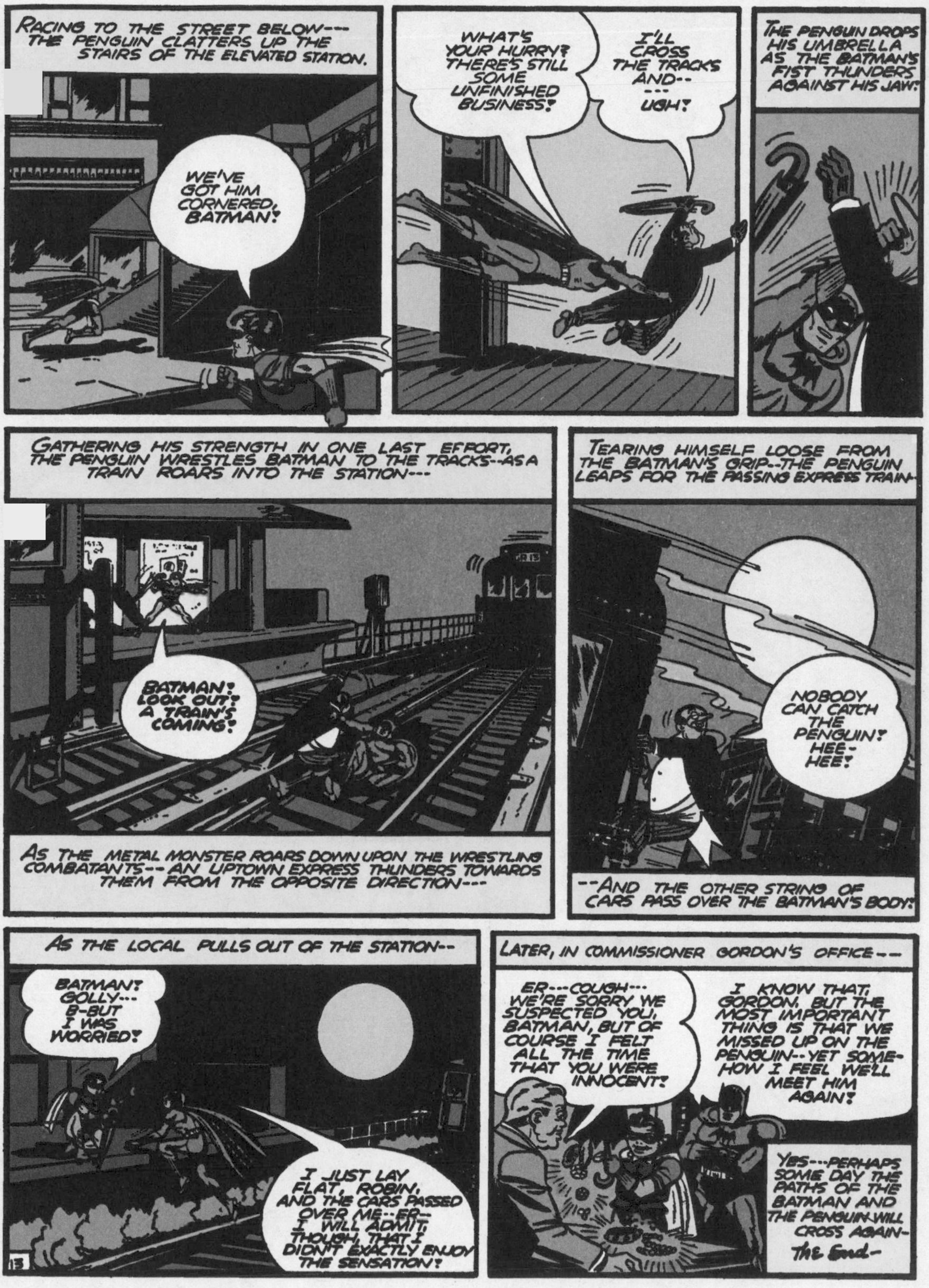

RACING TO THE STREET BELOW--- THE PENGUIN CLATTERS UP THE STAIRS OF THE ELEVATED STATION.
WE'VE GOT HIM CORNERED, BATMAN!
WHAT'S YOUR HURRY? THERE'S STILL SOME UNFINISHED BUSINESS!
I'LL CROSS THE TRACKS AND-- --- UGH!
THE PENGUIN DROPS HIS UMBRELLA AS THE BATMAN'S FIST THUNDERS AGAINST HIS JAW!
GATHERING HIS STRENGTH IN ONE LAST EFFORT, THE PENGUIN WRESTLES BATMAN TO THE TRACKS--AS A TRAIN ROARS INTO THE STATION---
BATMAN! LOOK OUT! A TRAIN'S COMING!
AS THE METAL MONSTER ROARS DOWN UPON THE WRESTLING COMBATANTS-- AN UPTOWN EXPRESS THUNDERS TOWARDS THEM FROM THE OPPOSITE DIRECTION---
TEARING HIMSELF LOOSE FROM THE BATMAN'S GRIP--THE PENGUIN LEAPS FOR THE PASSING EXPRESS TRAIN-
NOBODY CAN CATCH THE PENGUIN! HEE-HEE!
--AND THE OTHER STRING OF CARS PASS OVER THE BATMAN'S BODY!
AS THE LOCAL PULLS OUT OF THE STATION--
BATMAN! GOLLY--- B-BUT I WAS WORRIED!
I JUST LAY FLAT, ROBIN, AND THE CARS PASSED OVER ME--ER-- I WILL ADMIT, THOUGH, THAT I DIDN'T EXACTLY ENJOY THE SENSATION!
13
LATER, IN COMMISSIONER GORDON'S OFFICE---
ER---COUGH--- WE'RE SORRY WE SUSPECTED YOU, BATMAN, BUT OF COURSE I FELT ALL THE TIME THAT YOU WERE INNOCENT!
I KNOW THAT, GORDON, BUT THE MOST IMPORTANT THING IS THAT WE MISSED UP ON THE PENGUIN--YET SOME-HOW I FEEL WE'LL MEET HIM AGAIN!
YES---PERHAPS SOME DAY THE PATHS OF THE BATMAN AND THE PENGUIN WILL CROSS AGAIN-
The End-

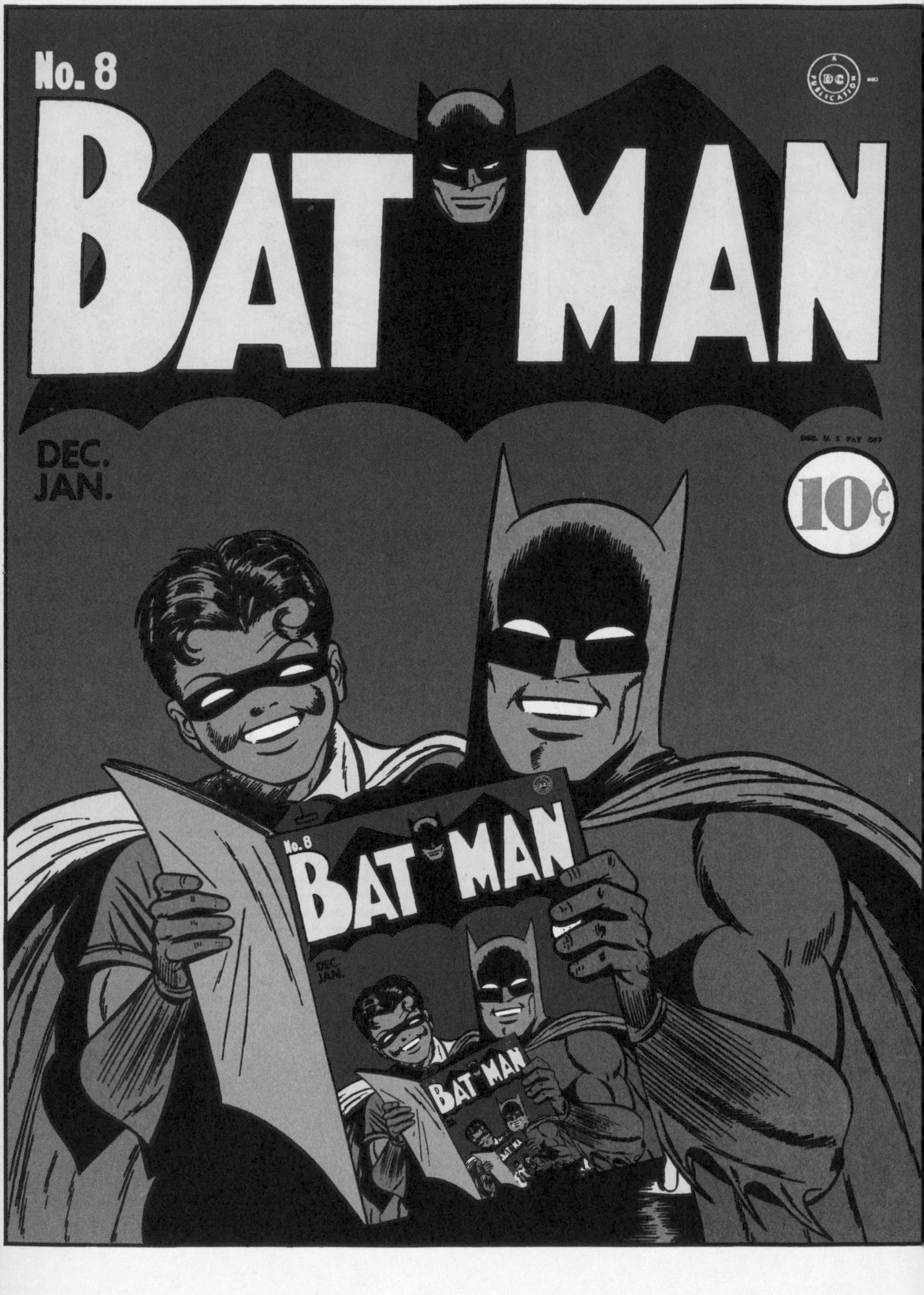
No. 8
BATMAN
A DC PUBLICATION
DEC.
JAN.
10¢

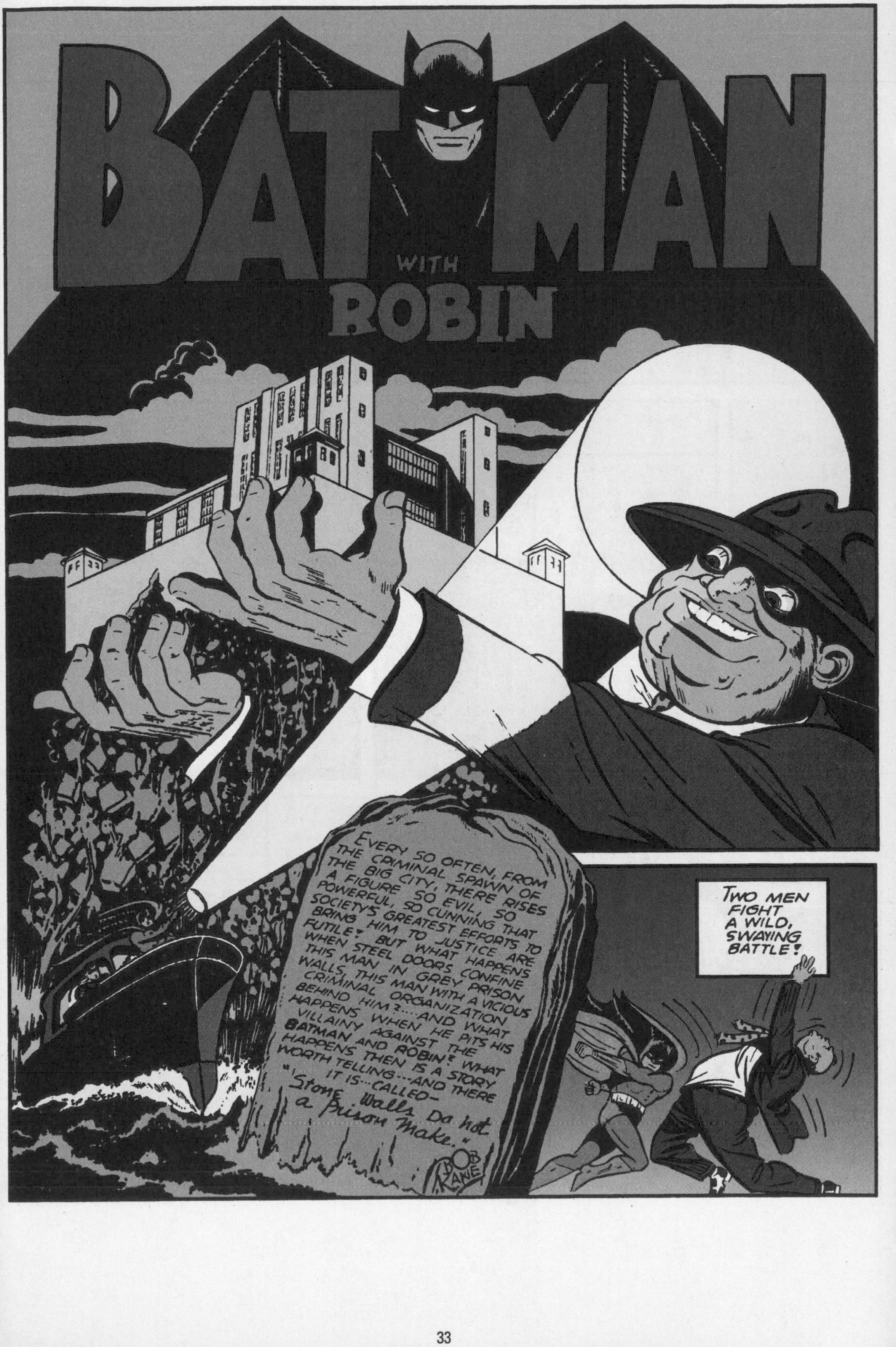
BATMAN
WITH
ROBIN
EVERY SO OFTEN, FROM THE CRIMINAL SPAWN OF THE BIG CITY, THERE RISES A FIGURE SO EVIL, SO POWERFUL, SO CUNNING THAT SOCIETY'S GREATEST EFFORTS TO BRING HIM TO JUSTICE ARE FUTILE! BUT WHAT HAPPENS WHEN STEEL DOORS CONFINE THIS MAN IN GREY PRISON WALLS, THIS MAN WITH A VICIOUS CRIMINAL ORGANIZATION BEHIND HIM?....AND WHAT HAPPENS WHEN HE PITS HIS VILLAINY AGAINST THE BATMAN AND ROBIN! WHAT HAPPENS THEN IS A STORY WORTH TELLING...AND THERE IT IS...CALLED-
"'Stone Walls Do not a Prison Make.'"
BOB KANE
TWO MEN FIGHT A WILD, SWAYING BATTLE!

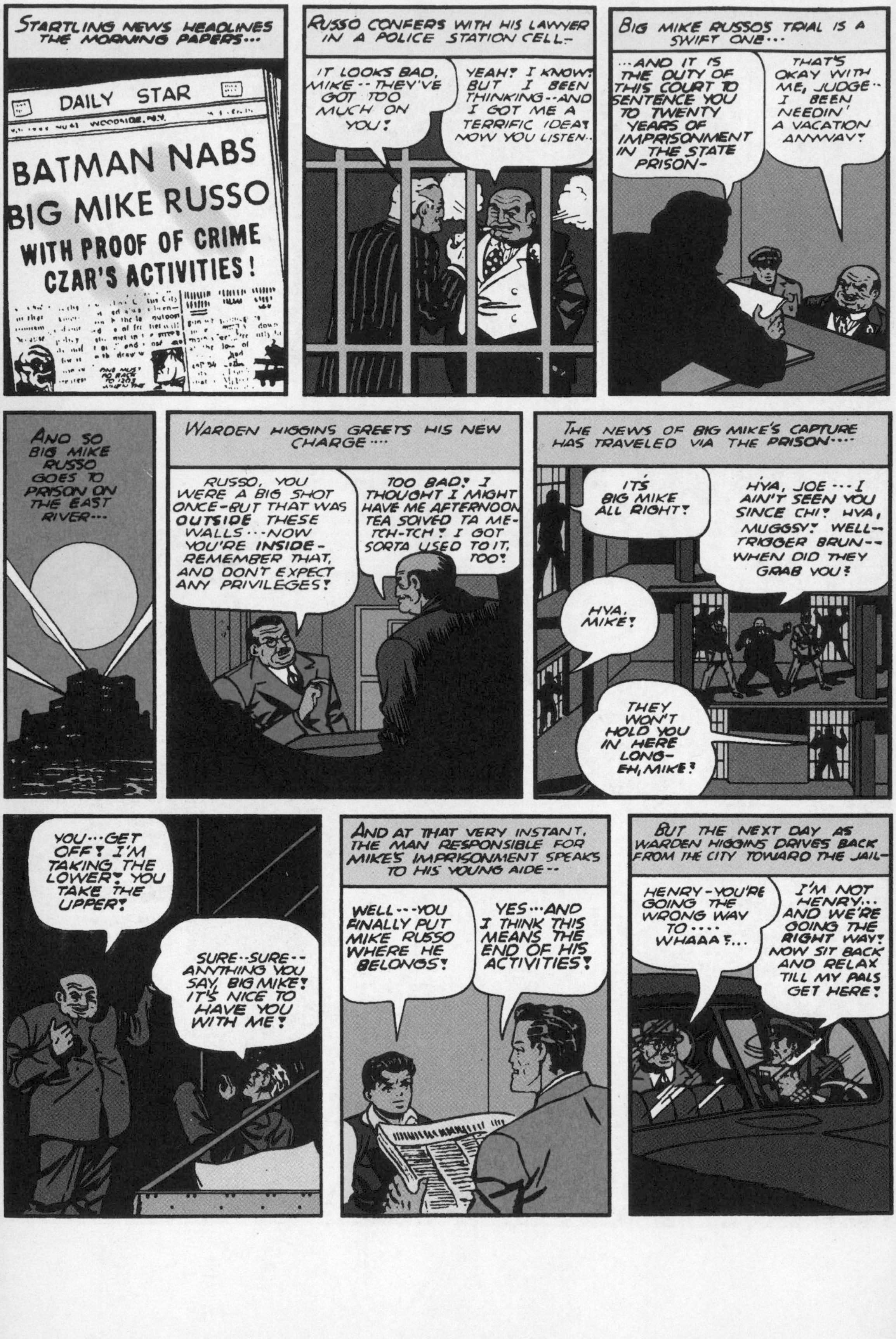
STARTLING NEWS HEADLINES THE MORNING PAPERS...
DAILY STAR
BATMAN NABS BIG MIKE RUSSO WITH PROOF OF CRIME CZAR'S ACTIVITIES!
RUSSO CONFERS WITH HIS LAWYER IN A POLICE STATION CELL.-
IT LOOKS BAD, MIKE--THEY'VE GOT TOO MUCH ON YOU!
YEAH! I KNOW! BUT I BEEN THINKING--AND I GOT ME A TERRIFIC IDEA! NOW YOU LISTEN..
BIG MIKE RUSSO'S TRIAL IS A SWIFT ONE...
...AND IT IS THE DUTY OF THIS COURT TO SENTENCE YOU TO TWENTY YEARS OF IMPRISONMENT IN THE STATE PRISON-
THAT'S OKAY WITH ME, JUDGE.. I BEEN NEEDIN' A VACATION ANYWAY!
AND SO BIG MIKE RUSSO GOES TO PRISON ON THE EAST RIVER...
WARDEN HIGGINS GREETS HIS NEW CHARGE....
RUSSO, YOU WERE A BIG SHOT ONCE-BUT THAT WAS OUTSIDE THESE WALLS...NOW YOU'RE INSIDE-REMEMBER THAT, AND DONT EXPECT ANY PRIVILEGES!
TOO BAD! I THOUGHT I MIGHT HAVE ME AFTERNOON TEA SOIVED TA ME-TCH-TCH! I GOT SORTA USED TO IT, TOO!
THE NEWS OF BIG MIKE'S CAPTURE HAS TRAVELED VIA THE PRISON....
IT'S BIG MIKE ALL RIGHT!
HYA, JOE ---I AIN'T SEEN YOU SINCE CHI! HYA, MUGGSY! WELL-TRIGGER BRUN--WHEN DID THEY GRAB YOU?
HYA, MIKE!
THEY WON'T HOLD YOU IN HERE LONG-EH, MIKE?
YOU...GET OFF! I'M TAKING THE LOWER! YOU TAKE THE UPPER!
SURE--SURE--ANYTHING YOU SAY, BIG MIKE! IT'S NICE TO HAVE YOU WITH ME!
AND AT THAT VERY INSTANT, THE MAN RESPONSIBLE FOR MIKE'S IMPRISONMENT SPEAKS TO HIS YOUNG AIDE--
WELL---YOU FINALLY PUT MIKE RUSSO WHERE HE BELONGS!
YES...AND I THINK THIS MEANS THE END OF HIS ACTIVITIES!
BUT THE NEXT DAY AS WARDEN HIGGINS DRIVES BACK FROM THE CITY TOWARD THE JAIL-
HENRY-YOU'RE GOING THE WRONG WAY TO.... WHAAA?...
I'M NOT HENRY... AND WE'RE GOING THE RIGHT WAY! NOW SIT BACK AND RELAX TILL MY PALS GET HERE!

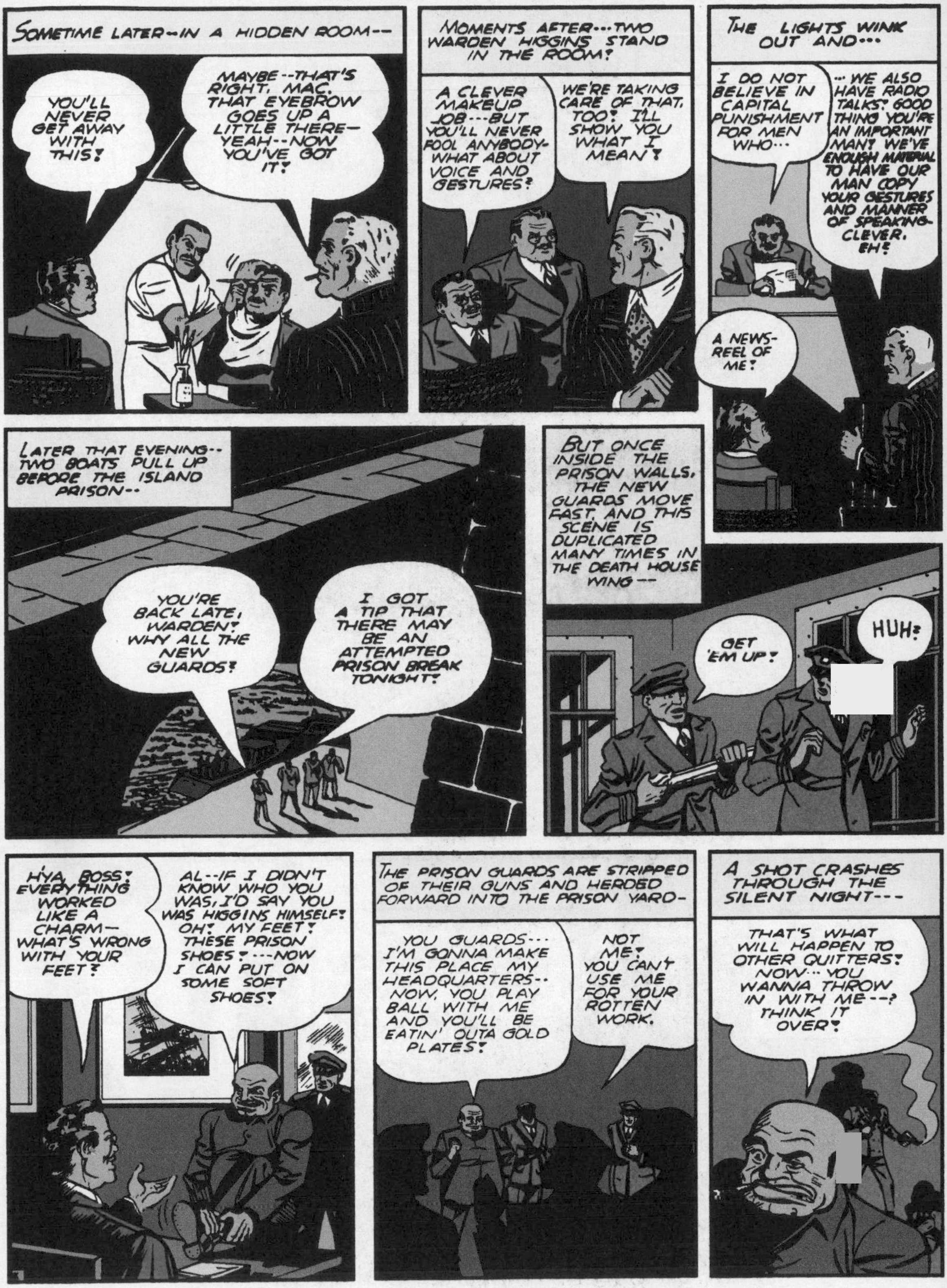
SOMETIME LATER--IN A HIDDEN ROOM--
YOU'LL NEVER GET AWAY WITH THIS!
MAYBE--THAT'S RIGHT, MAC. THAT EYEBROW GOES UP A LITTLE THERE--YEAH--NOW YOU'VE GOT IT!
MOMENTS AFTER---TWO WARDEN HIGGINS STAND IN THE ROOM!
A CLEVER MAKEUP JOB---BUT YOU'LL NEVER FOOL ANYBODY--WHAT ABOUT VOICE AND GESTURES?
WE'RE TAKING CARE OF THAT, TOO! I'LL SHOW YOU WHAT I MEAN!
THE LIGHTS WINK OUT AND...
I DO NOT BELIEVE IN CAPITAL PUNISHMENT FOR MEN WHO...
...WE ALSO HAVE RADIO TALKS! GOOD THING YOU'RE AN IMPORTANT MAN! WE'VE ENOUGH MATERIAL TO HAVE OUR MAN COPY YOUR GESTURES AND MANNER OF SPEAKING-- CLEVER, EH?
A NEWSREEL OF ME!
LATER THAT EVENING--TWO BOATS PULL UP BEFORE THE ISLAND PRISON--
YOU'RE BACK LATE, WARDEN! WHY ALL THE NEW GUARDS?
I GOT A TIP THAT THERE MAY BE AN ATTEMPTED PRISON BREAK TONIGHT!
BUT ONCE INSIDE THE PRISON WALLS, THE NEW GUARDS MOVE FAST, AND THIS SCENE IS DUPLICATED MANY TIMES IN THE DEATH HOUSE WING--
GET 'EM UP!
HUH?
H'YA, BOSS! EVERYTHING WORKED LIKE A CHARM--WHAT'S WRONG WITH YOUR FEET?
AL--IF I DIDN'T KNOW WHO YOU WAS, I'D SAY YOU WAS HIGGINS HIMSELF! OH! MY FEET! THESE PRISON SHOES!---NOW I CAN PUT ON SOME SOFT SHOES!
THE PRISON GUARDS ARE STRIPPED OF THEIR GUNS AND HERDED FORWARD INTO THE PRISON YARD--
YOU GUARDS--- I'M GONNA MAKE THIS PLACE MY HEADQUARTERS--NOW, YOU PLAY BALL WITH ME AND YOU'LL BE EATIN' OUTA GOLD PLATES!
NOT ME! YOU CAN'T USE ME FOR YOUR ROTTEN WORK.
A SHOT CRASHES THROUGH THE SILENT NIGHT---
THAT'S WHAT WILL HAPPEN TO OTHER QUITTERS! NOW... YOU WANNA THROW IN WITH ME--? THINK IT OVER!

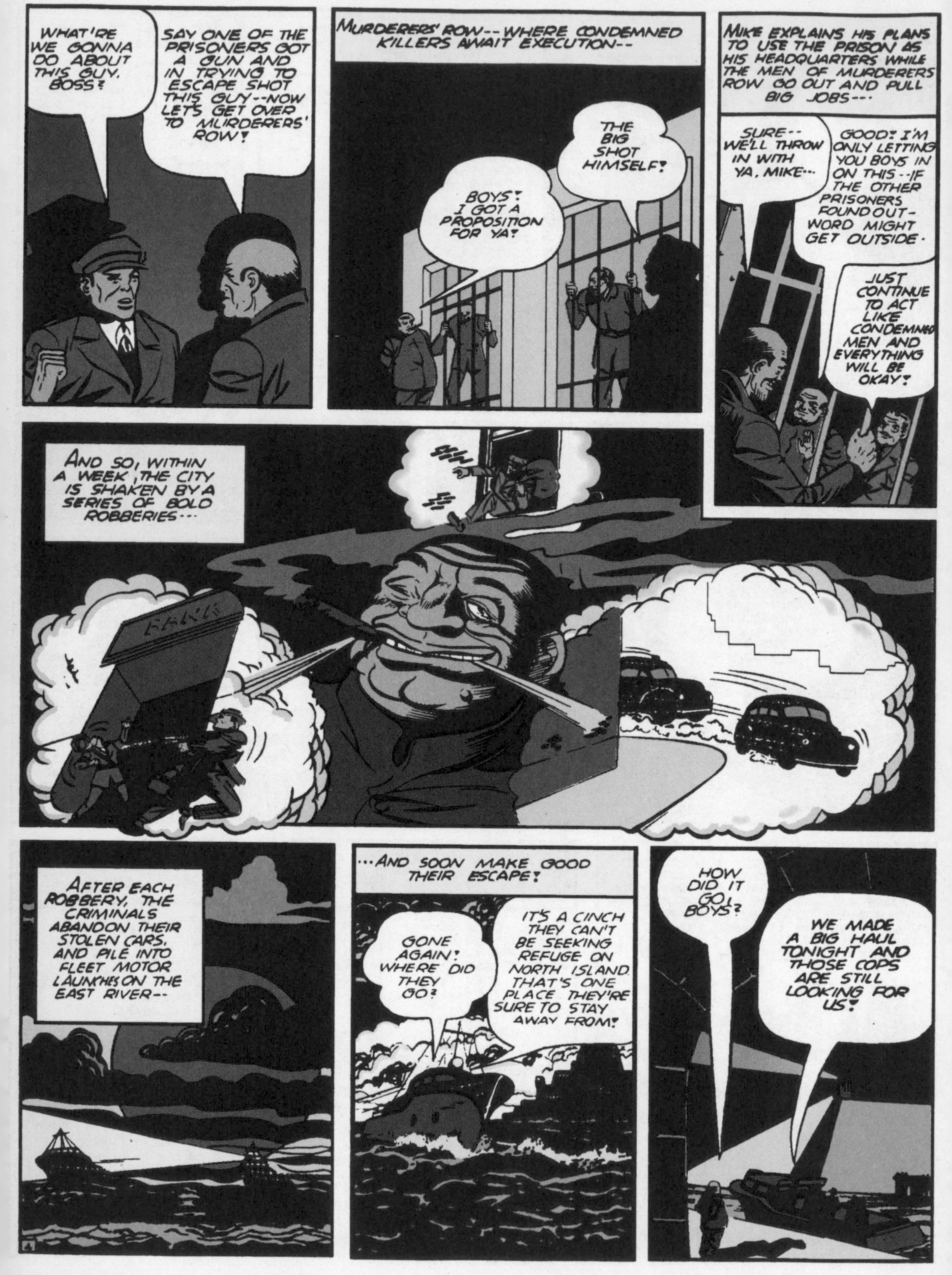
WHAT'RE WE GONNA DO ABOUT THIS GUY, BOSS?
SAY ONE OF THE PRISONERS GOT A GUN AND IN TRYING TO ESCAPE SHOT THIS GUY--NOW LET'S GET OVER TO MURDERERS' ROW!
MURDERERS' ROW--WHERE CONDEMNED KILLERS AWAIT EXECUTION--
THE BIG SHOT HIMSELF!
BOYS! I GOT A PROPOSITION FOR YA!
MIKE EXPLAINS HIS PLANS TO USE THE PRISON AS HIS HEADQUARTERS WHILE THE MEN OF MURDERERS ROW GO OUT AND PULL BIG JOBS---
SURE--WE'LL THROW IN WITH YA, MIKE...
GOOD! I'M ONLY LETTING YOU BOYS IN ON THIS--IF THE OTHER PRISONERS FOUND OUT-WORD MIGHT GET OUTSIDE.
JUST CONTINUE TO ACT LIKE CONDEMNED MEN AND EVERYTHING WILL BE OKAY!
AND SO, WITHIN A WEEK, THE CITY IS SHAKEN BY A SERIES OF BOLD ROBBERIES---
BANK
AFTER EACH ROBBERY, THE CRIMINALS ABANDON THEIR STOLEN CARS, AND PILE INTO FLEET MOTOR LAUNCHES ON THE EAST RIVER--
...AND SOON MAKE GOOD THEIR ESCAPE!
GONE AGAIN! WHERE DID THEY GO?
IT'S A CINCH THEY CAN'T BE SEEKING REFUGE ON NORTH ISLAND. THAT'S ONE PLACE THEY'RE SURE TO STAY AWAY FROM!
HOW DID IT GO, BOYS?
WE MADE A BIG HAUL TONIGHT AND THOSE COPS ARE STILL LOOKING FOR US!

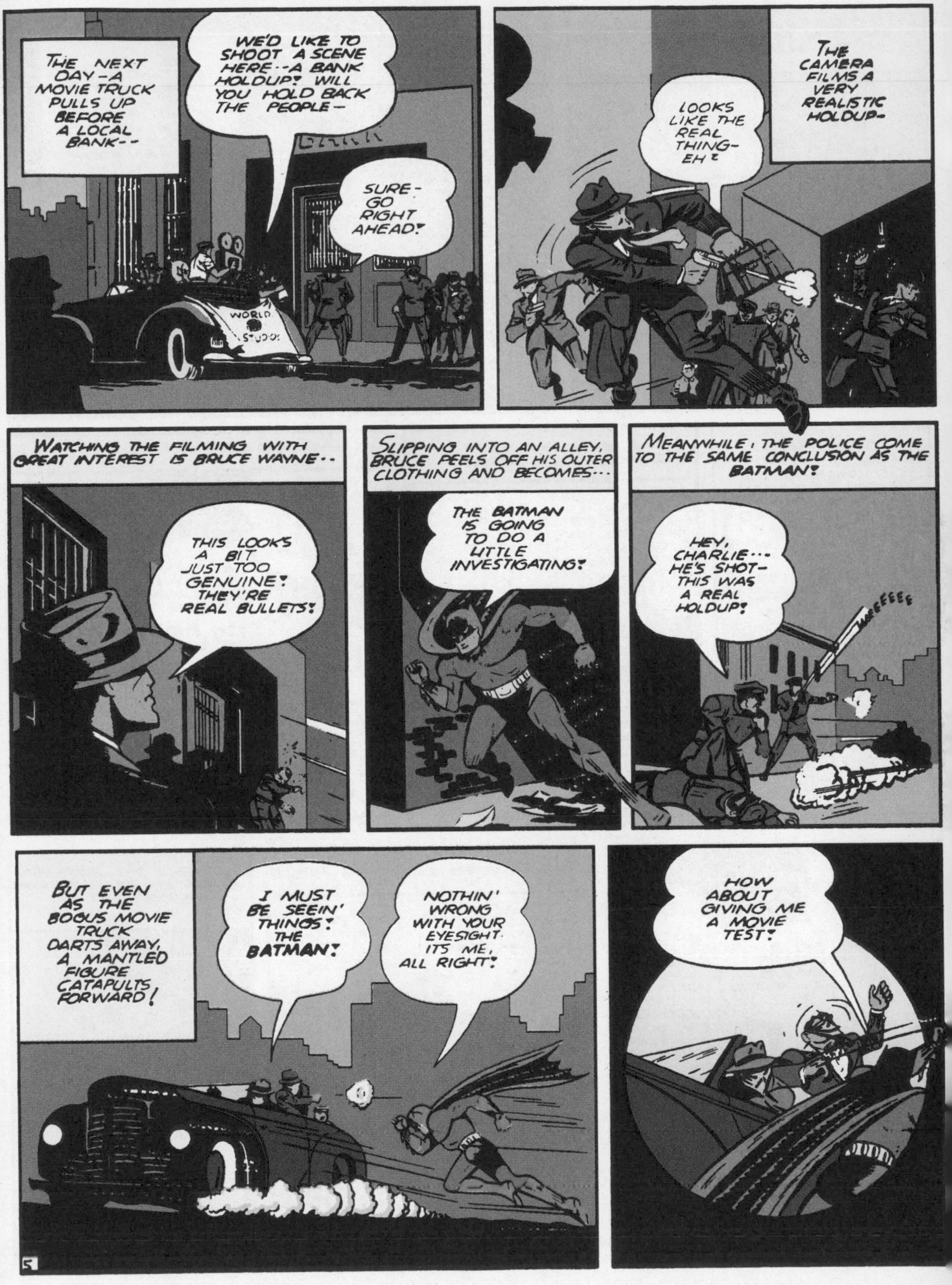
THE NEXT DAY--A MOVIE TRUCK PULLS UP BEFORE A LOCAL BANK--
WE'D LIKE TO SHOOT A SCENE HERE--A BANK HOLDUP! WILL YOU HOLD BACK THE PEOPLE--
SURE-GO RIGHT AHEAD!
WORLD STUDIOS
THE CAMERA FILMS A VERY REALISTIC HOLDUP-
LOOKS LIKE THE REAL THING-EH?
WATCHING THE FILMING WITH GREAT INTEREST IS BRUCE WAYNE..
THIS LOOKS A BIT JUST TOO GENUINE! THEY'RE REAL BULLETS!
SLIPPING INTO AN ALLEY, BRUCE PEELS OFF HIS OUTER CLOTHING AND BECOMES...
THE BATMAN IS GOING TO DO A LITTLE INVESTIGATING!
MEANWHILE, THE POLICE COME TO THE SAME CONCLUSION AS THE BATMAN!
HEY, CHARLIE... HE'S SHOT-THIS WAS A REAL HOLDUP!
BUT EVEN AS THE BOGUS MOVIE TRUCK DARTS AWAY, A MANTLED FIGURE CATAPULTS FORWARD!
I MUST BE SEEIN' THINGS! THE BATMAN!
NOTHIN' WRONG WITH YOUR EYESIGHT. ITS ME, ALL RIGHT!
HOW ABOUT GIVING ME A MOVIE TEST!

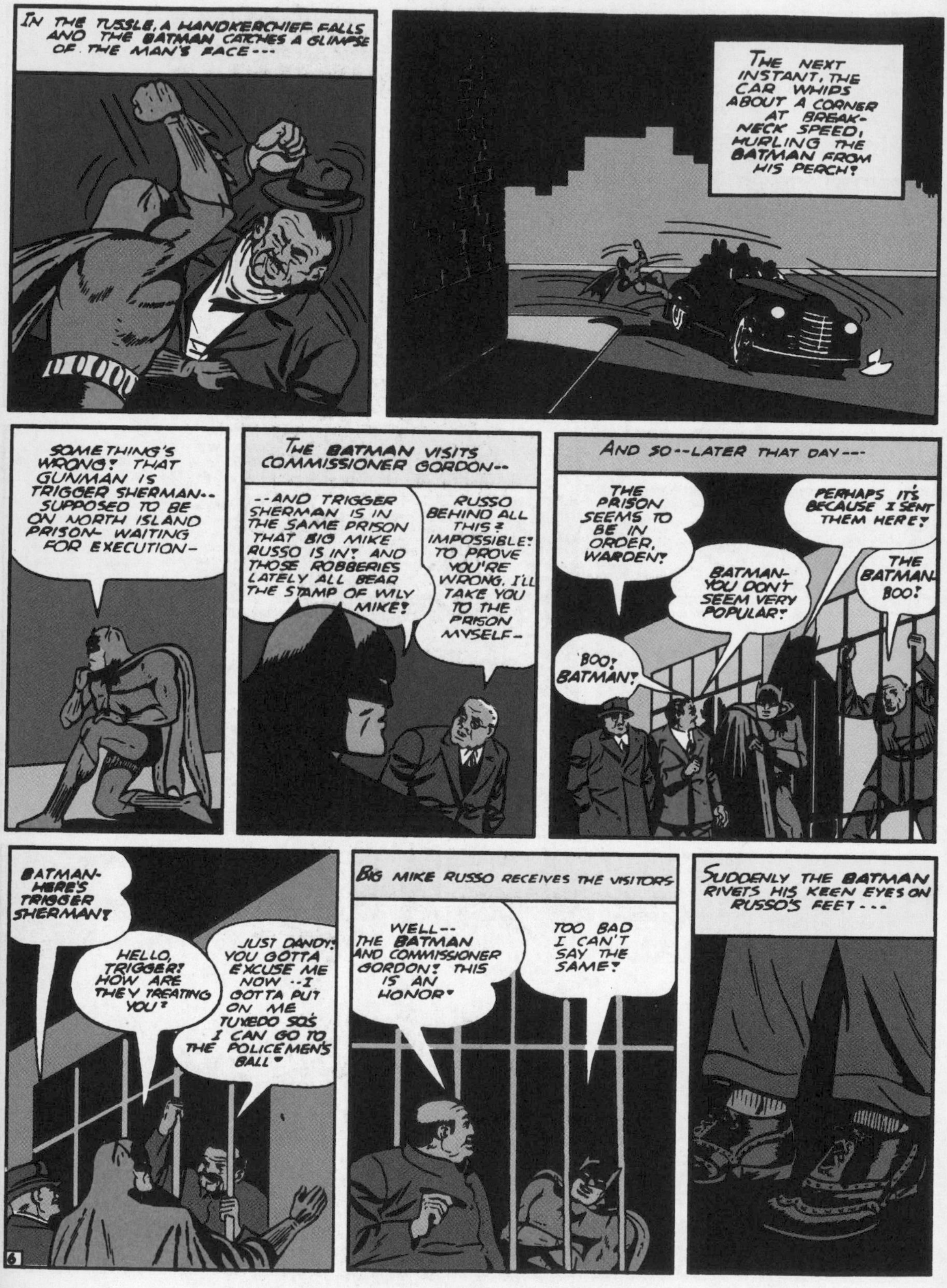
IN THE TUSSLE, A HANDKERCHIEF FALLS AND THE BATMAN CATCHES A GLIMPSE OF THE MAN'S FACE---
THE NEXT INSTANT, THE CAR WHIPS ABOUT A CORNER AT BREAK-NECK SPEED, HURLING THE BATMAN FROM HIS PERCH!
SOMETHING'S WRONG! THAT GUNMAN IS TRIGGER SHERMAN--SUPPOSED TO BE ON NORTH ISLAND PRISON- WAITING FOR EXECUTION-
THE BATMAN VISITS COMMISSIONER GORDON--
--AND TRIGGER SHERMAN IS IN THE SAME PRISON THAT BIG MIKE RUSSO IS IN! AND THOSE ROBBERIES LATELY ALL BEAR THE STAMP OF WILY MIKE!
RUSSO BEHIND ALL THIS? IMPOSSIBLE! TO PROVE YOU'RE WRONG, I'LL TAKE YOU TO THE PRISON MYSELF--
AND SO--LATER THAT DAY---
THE PRISON SEEMS TO BE IN ORDER, WARDEN!
PERHAPS IT'S BECAUSE I SENT THEM HERE!
BATMAN- YOU DON'T SEEM VERY POPULAR!
THE BATMAN- BOO!
BOO! BATMAN!
BATMAN- HERE'S TRIGGER SHERMAN!
HELLO, TRIGGER! HOW ARE THEY TREATING YOU?
JUST DANDY! YOU GOTTA EXCUSE ME NOW--I GOTTA PUT ON ME TUXEDO SO'S I CAN GO TO THE POLICEMEN'S BALL!
6
BIG MIKE RUSSO RECEIVES THE VISITORS
WELL-- THE BATMAN AND COMMISSIONER GORDON! THIS IS AN HONOR!
TOO BAD I CAN'T SAY THE SAME!
SUDDENLY THE BATMAN RIVETS HIS KEEN EYES ON RUSSO'S FEET---

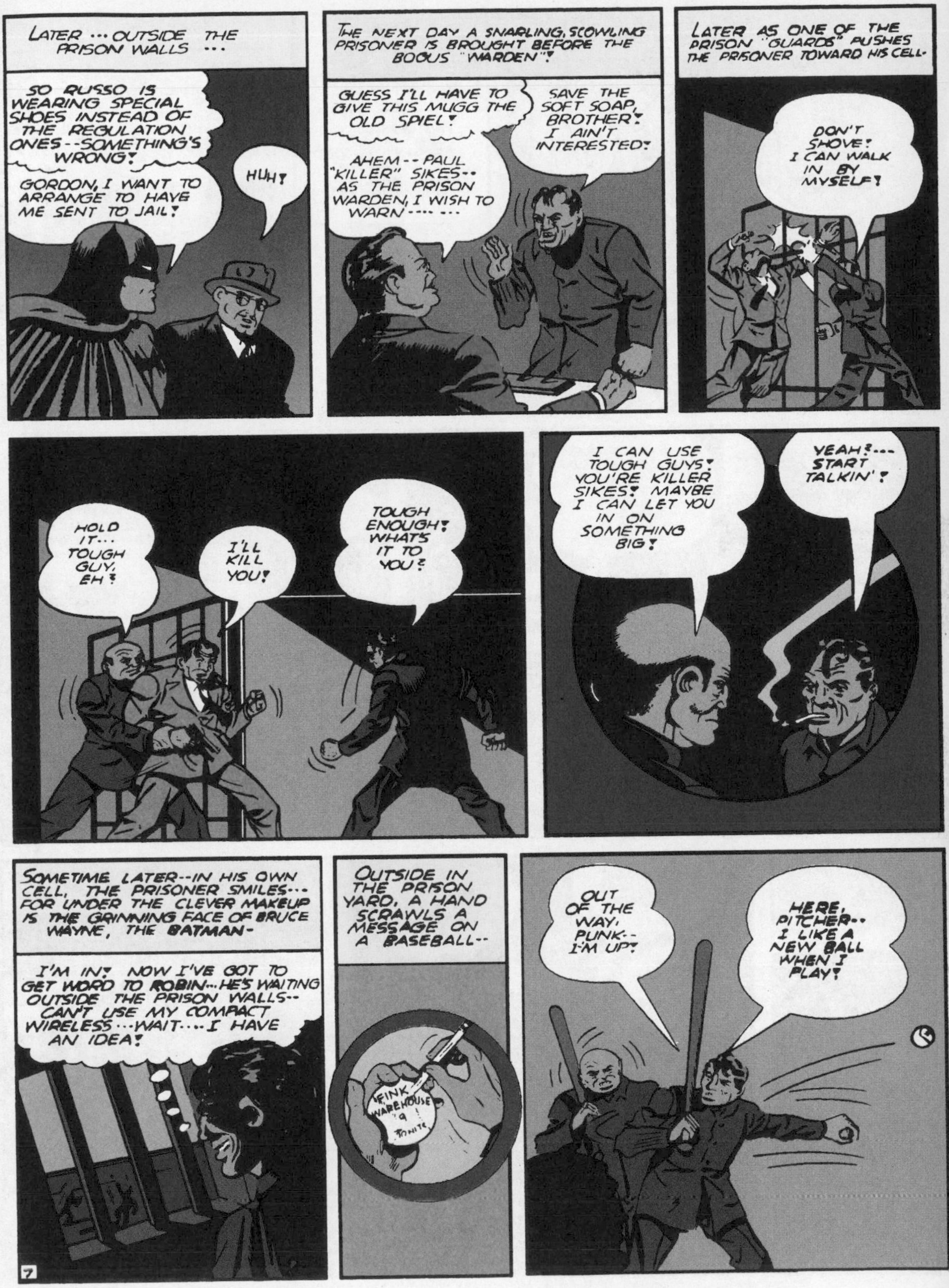
LATER ... OUTSIDE THE PRISON WALLS ...
SO RUSSO IS WEARING SPECIAL SHOES INSTEAD OF THE REGULATION ONES--SOMETHING'S WRONG!
GORDON, I WANT TO ARRANGE TO HAVE ME SENT TO JAIL!
HUH!
THE NEXT DAY A SNARLING, SCOWLING PRISONER IS BROUGHT BEFORE THE BOGUS "WARDEN"!
GUESS I'LL HAVE TO GIVE THIS MUGG THE OLD SPIEL!
AHEM--PAUL "KILLER" SIKES--AS THE PRISON WARDEN, I WISH TO WARN---- ---
SAVE THE SOFT SOAP, BROTHER! I AIN'T INTERESTED!
LATER AS ONE OF THE PRISON "GUARDS" PUSHES THE PRISONER TOWARD HIS CELL-
DON'T SHOVE! I CAN WALK IN BY MYSELF!
HOLD IT... TOUGH GUY, EH?
I'LL KILL YOU!
TOUGH ENOUGH! WHAT'S IT TO YOU?
I CAN USE TOUGH GUYS! YOU'RE KILLER SIKES! MAYBE I CAN LET YOU IN ON SOMETHING BIG!
YEAH?--- START TALKIN'!
SOMETIME LATER--IN HIS OWN CELL, THE PRISONER SMILES---FOR UNDER THE CLEVER MAKEUP IS THE GRINNING FACE OF BRUCE WAYNE, THE BATMAN-
I'M IN! NOW I'VE GOT TO GET WORD TO ROBIN...HE'S WAITING OUTSIDE THE PRISON WALLS--CAN'T USE MY COMPACT WIRELESS---WAIT---I HAVE AN IDEA!
7
OUTSIDE IN THE PRISON YARD, A HAND SCRAWLS A MESSAGE ON A BASEBALL--
FINK WAREHOUSE 9 TONITE
OUT OF THE WAY, PUNK--I'M UP!
HERE, PITCHER--I LIKE A NEW BALL WHEN I PLAY!

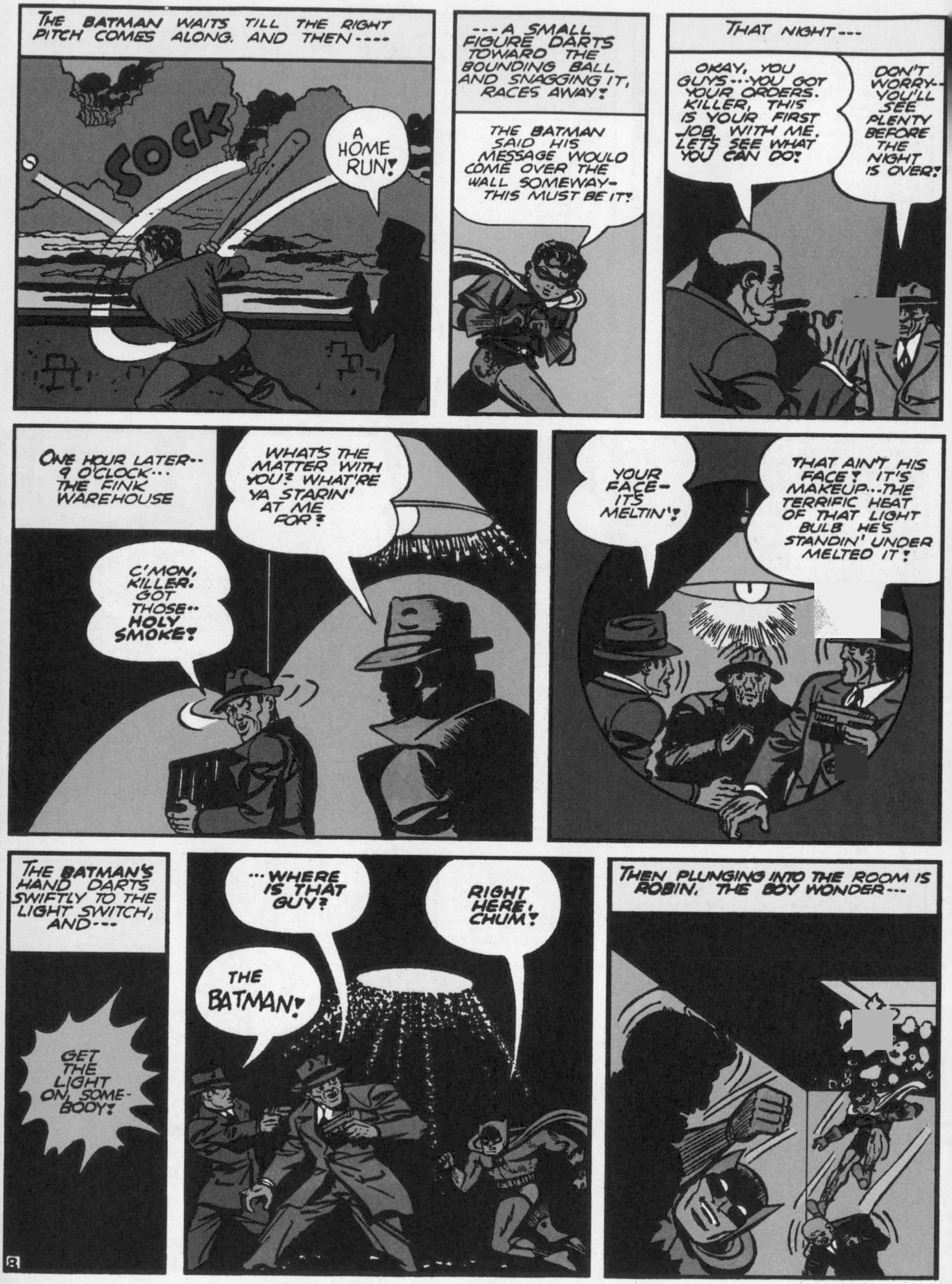
THE BATMAN WAITS TILL THE RIGHT PITCH COMES ALONG, AND THEN----
SOCK
A HOME RUN!
---A SMALL FIGURE DARTS TOWARD THE BOUNDING BALL AND SNAGGING IT, RACES AWAY!
THE BATMAN SAID HIS MESSAGE WOULD COME OVER THE WALL SOMEWAY-THIS MUST BE IT!
THAT NIGHT---
OKAY, YOU GUYS---YOU GOT YOUR ORDERS. KILLER, THIS IS YOUR FIRST JOB WITH ME. LETS SEE WHAT YOU CAN DO!
DON'T WORRY--YOU'LL SEE PLENTY BEFORE THE NIGHT IS OVER!
ONE HOUR LATER-- 9 O'CLOCK--- THE FINK WAREHOUSE
WHAT'S THE MATTER WITH YOU? WHAT'RE YA STARIN' AT ME FOR?
C'MON, KILLER. GOT THOSE-- HOLY SMOKE!
YOUR FACE-ITS MELTIN'!
THAT AIN'T HIS FACE! IT'S MAKEUP...THE TERRIFIC HEAT OF THAT LIGHT BULB HE'S STANDIN' UNDER MELTED IT!
THE BATMAN'S HAND DARTS SWIFTLY TO THE LIGHT SWITCH, AND---
GET THE LIGHT ON, SOME-BODY!
---WHERE IS THAT GUY?
RIGHT HERE, CHUM!
THE BATMAN!
THEN PLUNGING INTO THE ROOM IS ROBIN, THE BOY WONDER---

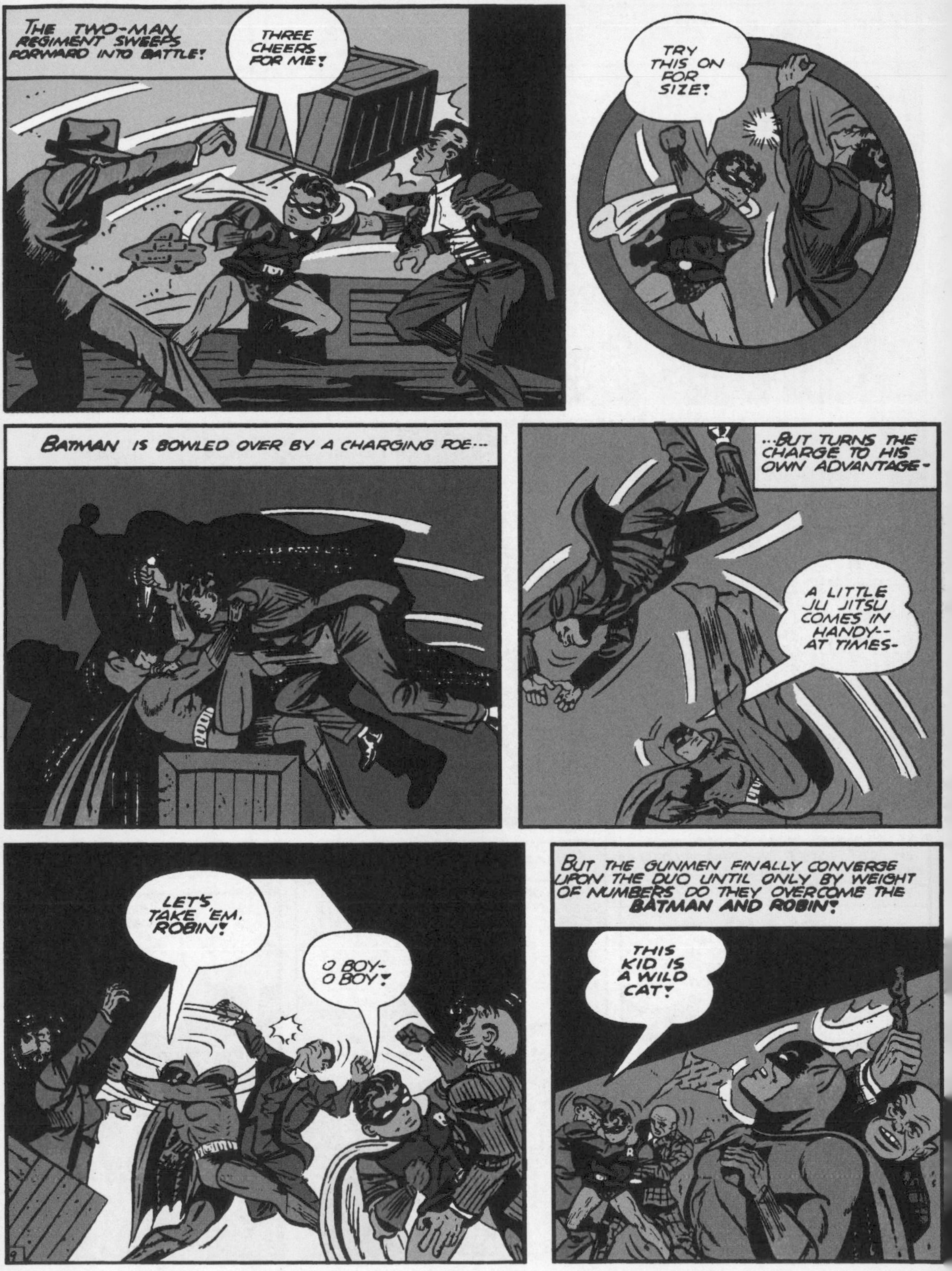
THE TWO-MAN REGIMENT SWEEPS FORWARD INTO BATTLE!
THREE CHEERS FOR ME!
TRY THIS ON FOR SIZE!
BATMAN IS BOWLED OVER BY A CHARGING FOE---
...BUT TURNS THE CHARGE TO HIS OWN ADVANTAGE-
A LITTLE JU JITSU COMES IN HANDY--AT TIMES-
LET'S TAKE 'EM, ROBIN!
O BOY-O BOY!
BUT THE GUNMEN FINALLY CONVERGE UPON THE DUO UNTIL ONLY BY WEIGHT OF NUMBERS DO THEY OVERCOME THE BATMAN AND ROBIN!
THIS KID IS A WILD CAT!

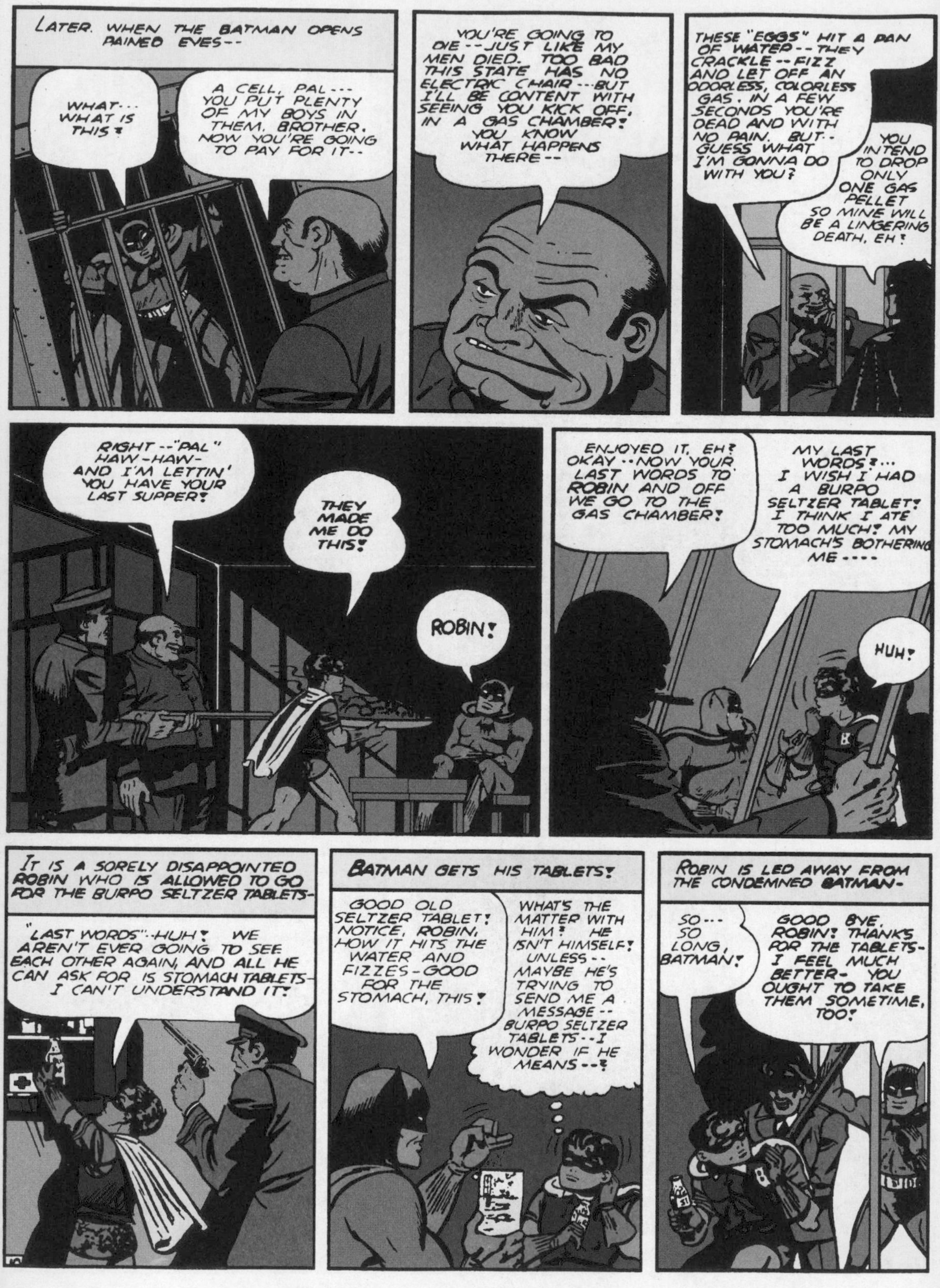
LATER. WHEN THE BATMAN OPENS PAINED EYES--
WHAT... WHAT IS THIS?
A CELL, PAL--- YOU PUT PLENTY OF MY BOYS IN THEM, BROTHER. NOW YOU'RE GOING TO PAY FOR IT--
YOU'RE GOING TO DIE--JUST LIKE MY MEN DIED. TOO BAD THIS STATE HAS NO ELECTRIC CHAIR---BUT I'LL BE CONTENT WITH SEEING YOU KICK OFF, IN A GAS CHAMBER! YOU KNOW WHAT HAPPENS THERE--
THESE "EGGS" HIT A PAN OF WATER--THEY CRACKLE--FIZZ AND LET OFF AN ODORLESS, COLORLESS GAS. IN A FEW SECONDS YOU'RE DEAD AND WITH NO PAIN. BUT-- GUESS WHAT I'M GONNA DO WITH YOU?
YOU INTEND TO DROP ONLY ONE GAS PELLET SO MINE WILL BE A LINGERING DEATH, EH!
RIGHT--"PAL" HAW-HAW- AND I'M LETTIN' YOU HAVE YOUR LAST SUPPER!
THEY MADE ME DO THIS!
ROBIN!
ENJOYED IT, EH? OKAY--NOW YOUR LAST WORDS TO ROBIN AND OFF WE GO TO THE GAS CHAMBER!
MY LAST WORDS?... I WISH I HAD A BURPO SELTZER TABLET! I THINK I ATE TOO MUCH! MY STOMACH'S BOTHERING ME----
HUH!
IT IS A SORELY DISAPPOINTED ROBIN WHO IS ALLOWED TO GO FOR THE BURPO SELTZER TABLETS-
"LAST WORDS"-HUH! WE AREN'T EVER GOING TO SEE EACH OTHER AGAIN, AND ALL HE CAN ASK FOR IS STOMACH TABLETS- I CAN'T UNDERSTAND IT!
BATMAN GETS HIS TABLETS!
GOOD OLD SELTZER TABLET! NOTICE, ROBIN, HOW IT HITS THE WATER AND FIZZES-GOOD FOR THE STOMACH, THIS!
WHAT'S THE MATTER WITH HIM? HE ISN'T HIMSELF! UNLESS-- MAYBE HE'S TRYING TO SEND ME A MESSAGE-- BURPO SELTZER TABLETS--I WONDER IF HE MEANS--?
ROBIN IS LED AWAY FROM THE CONDEMNED BATMAN-
SO--- SO LONG, BATMAN!
GOOD BYE, ROBIN! THANKS FOR THE TABLETS- I FEEL MUCH BETTER- YOU OUGHT TO TAKE THEM SOMETIME, TOO!

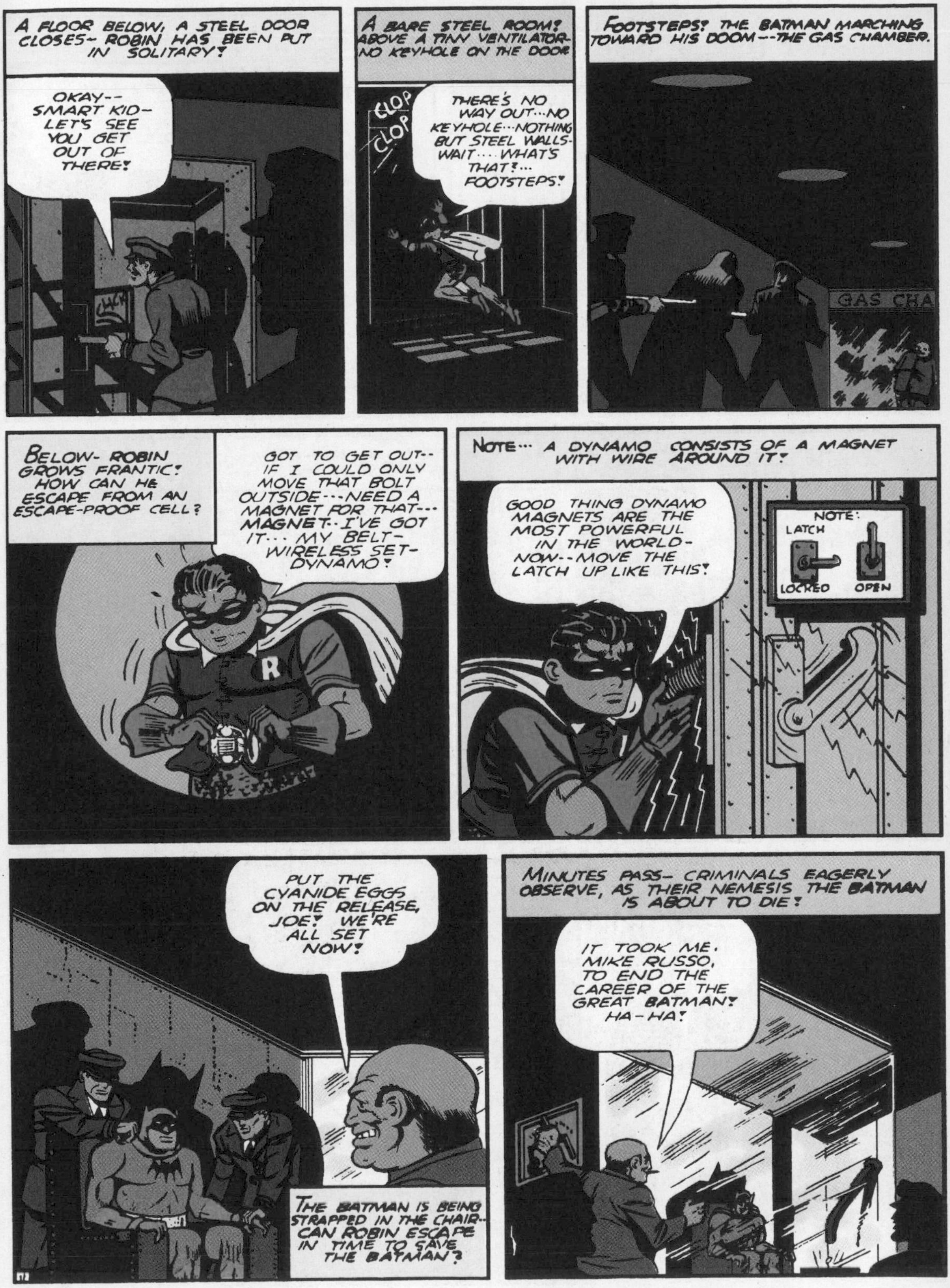
A FLOOR BELOW, A STEEL DOOR CLOSES-- ROBIN HAS BEEN PUT IN SOLITARY!
OKAY-- SMART KID-- LET'S SEE YOU GET OUT OF THERE!
A BARE STEEL ROOM! ABOVE A TINY VENTILATOR-NO KEYHOLE ON THE DOOR
CLOP CLOP
THERE'S NO WAY OUT...NO KEYHOLE...NOTHING BUT STEEL WALLS-WAIT.... WHAT'S THAT?... FOOTSTEPS!
FOOTSTEPS! THE BATMAN MARCHING TOWARD HIS DOOM--THE GAS CHAMBER.
GAS CHA
BELOW- ROBIN GROWS FRANTIC! HOW CAN HE ESCAPE FROM AN ESCAPE-PROOF CELL?
GOT TO GET OUT-- IF I COULD ONLY MOVE THAT BOLT OUTSIDE---NEED A MAGNET FOR THAT--- MAGNET--I'VE GOT IT--- MY BELT-WIRELESS SET-DYNAMO!
NOTE... A DYNAMO CONSISTS OF A MAGNET WITH WIRE AROUND IT!
GOOD THING DYNAMO MAGNETS ARE THE MOST POWERFUL IN THE WORLD-NOW--MOVE THE LATCH UP LIKE THIS!
NOTE:
LATCH
LOCKED
OPEN
PUT THE CYANIDE EGGS ON THE RELEASE, JOE! WE'RE ALL SET NOW!
THE BATMAN IS BEING STRAPPED IN THE CHAIR-- CAN ROBIN ESCAPE IN TIME TO SAVE THE BATMAN?
MINUTES PASS- CRIMINALS EAGERLY OBSERVE, AS THEIR NEMESIS THE BATMAN IS ABOUT TO DIE!
IT TOOK ME, MIKE RUSSO, TO END THE CAREER OF THE GREAT BATMAN! HA-HA!

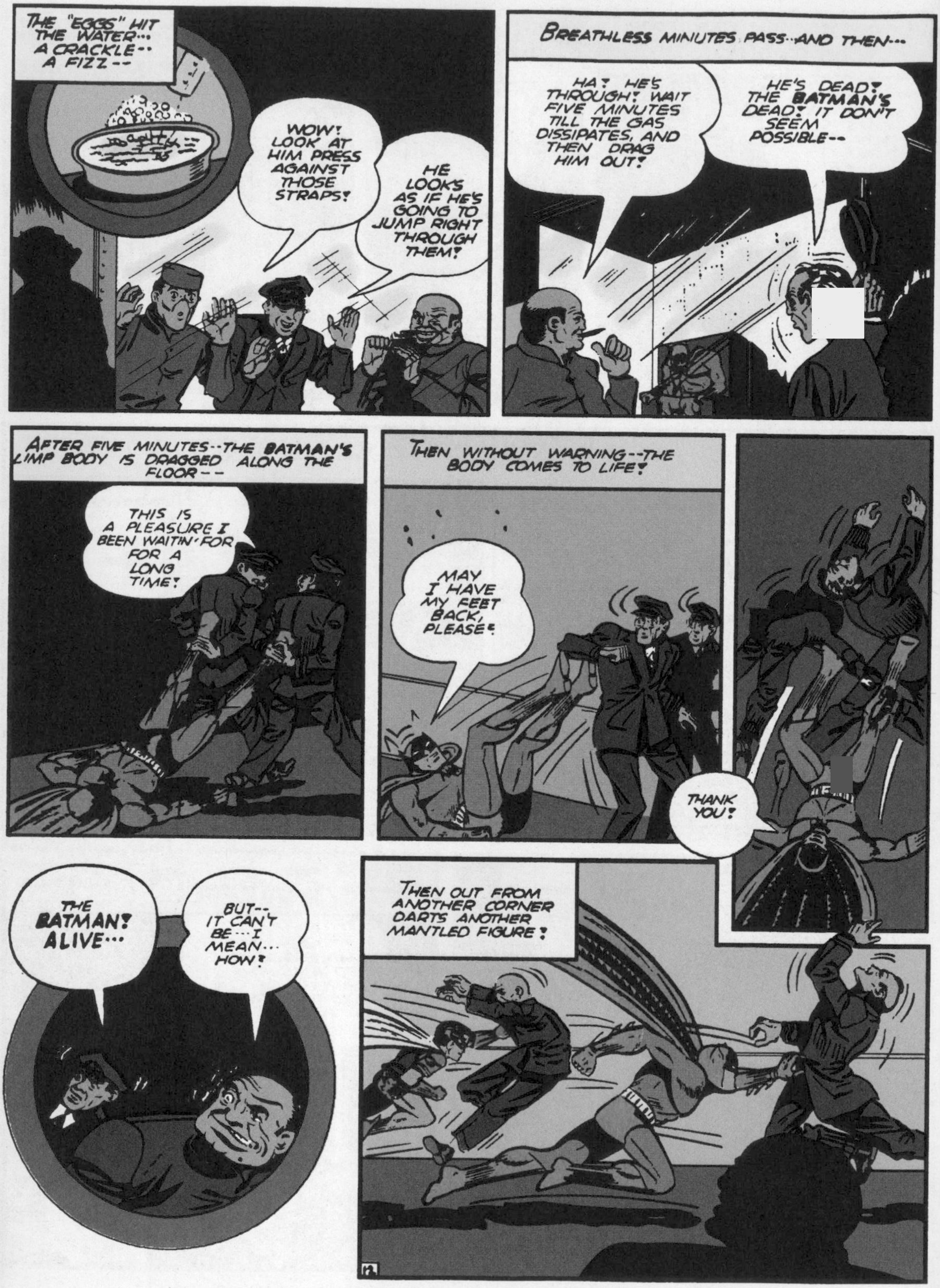
THE "EGGS" HIT THE WATER... A CRACKLE-- A FIZZ--
WOW! LOOK AT HIM PRESS AGAINST THOSE STRAPS!
HE LOOKS AS IF HE'S GOING TO JUMP RIGHT THROUGH THEM!
BREATHLESS MINUTES PASS...AND THEN...
HA! HE'S THROUGH! WAIT FIVE MINUTES TILL THE GAS DISSIPATES, AND THEN DRAG HIM OUT!
HE'S DEAD! THE BATMAN'S DEAD! IT DON'T SEEM POSSIBLE--
AFTER FIVE MINUTES--THE BATMAN'S LIMP BODY IS DRAGGED ALONG THE FLOOR--
THIS IS A PLEASURE I BEEN WAITIN' FOR FOR A LONG TIME!
THEN WITHOUT WARNING--THE BODY COMES TO LIFE!
MAY I HAVE MY FEET BACK, PLEASE!
THANK YOU!
THE BATMAN! ALIVE...
BUT-- IT CAN'T BE... I MEAN... HOW?
THEN OUT FROM ANOTHER CORNER DARTS ANOTHER MANTLED FIGURE!

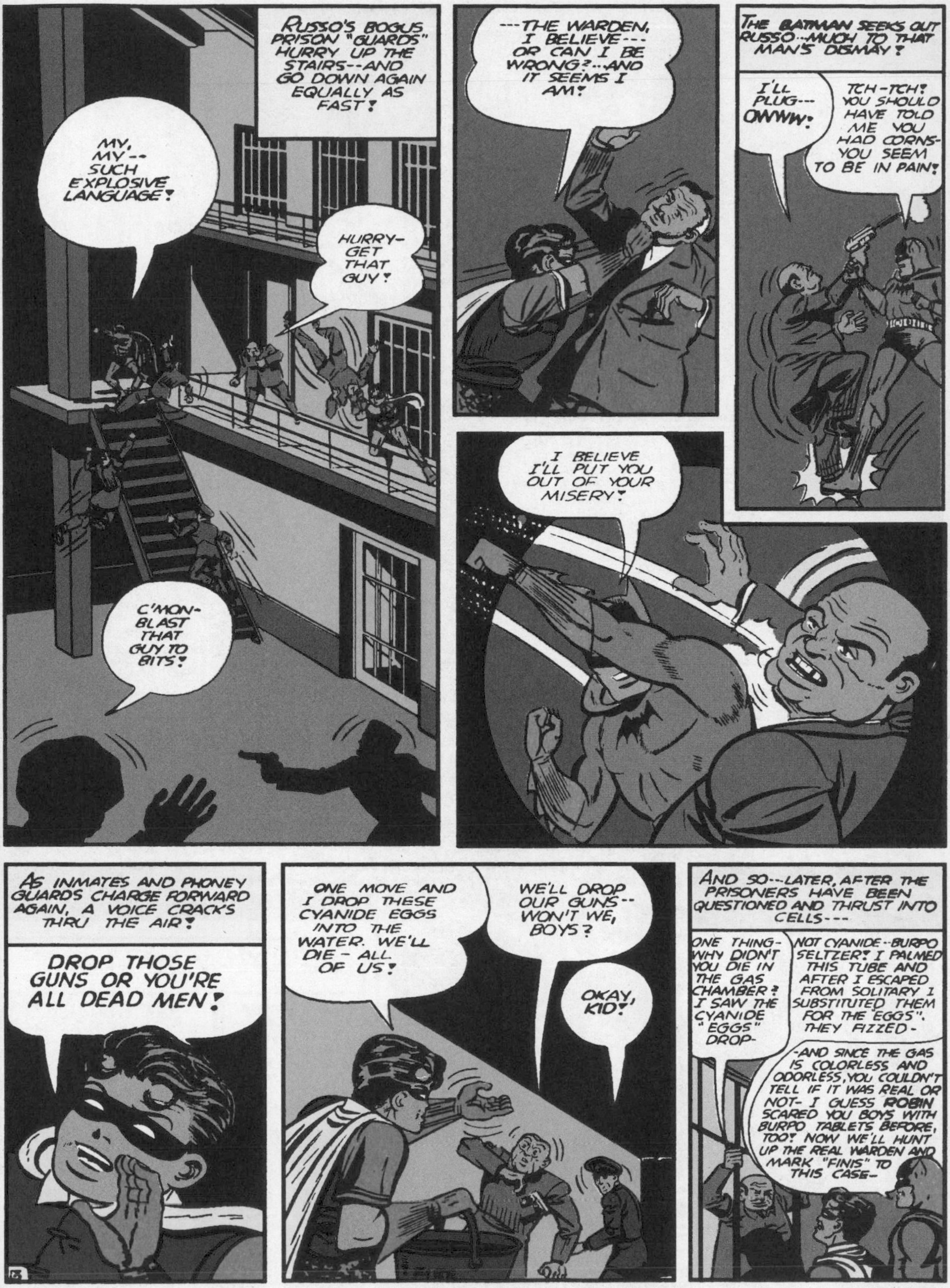
RUSSO'S BOGUS PRISON "GUARDS" HURRY UP THE STAIRS--AND GO DOWN AGAIN EQUALLY AS FAST!
MY, MY-- SUCH EXPLOSIVE LANGUAGE!
HURRY- GET THAT GUY!
C'MON- BLAST THAT GUY TO BITS!
---THE WARDEN, I BELIEVE--- OR CAN I BE WRONG?...AND IT SEEMS I AM!
THE BATMAN SEEKS OUT RUSSO...MUCH TO THAT MAN'S DISMAY!
I'LL PLUG--- OWWW!
TCH-TCH! YOU SHOULD HAVE TOLD ME YOU HAD CORNS- YOU SEEM TO BE IN PAIN!
I BELIEVE I'LL PUT YOU OUT OF YOUR MISERY!
AS INMATES AND PHONEY GUARDS CHARGE FORWARD AGAIN, A VOICE CRACKS THRU THE AIR!
DROP THOSE GUNS OR YOU'RE ALL DEAD MEN!
ONE MOVE AND I DROP THESE CYANIDE EGGS INTO THE WATER. WE'LL DIE - ALL OF US!
WE'LL DROP OUR GUNS-- WON'T WE, BOYS?
OKAY, KID!
AND SO---LATER, AFTER THE PRISONERS HAVE BEEN QUESTIONED AND THRUST INTO CELLS---
ONE THING- WHY DIDN'T YOU DIE IN THE GAS CHAMBER? I SAW THE CYANIDE "EGGS" DROP-
NOT CYANIDE--BURPO SELTZER! I PALMED THIS TUBE AND AFTER I ESCAPED FROM SOLITARY I SUBSTITUTED THEM FOR THE "EGGS". THEY FIZZED-
-AND SINCE THE GAS IS COLORLESS AND ODORLESS, YOU COULDN'T TELL IF IT WAS REAL OR NOT- I GUESS ROBIN SCARED YOU BOYS WITH BURPO TABLETS BEFORE, TOO! NOW WE'LL HUNT UP THE REAL WARDEN AND MARK "FINIS" TO THIS CASE-
13

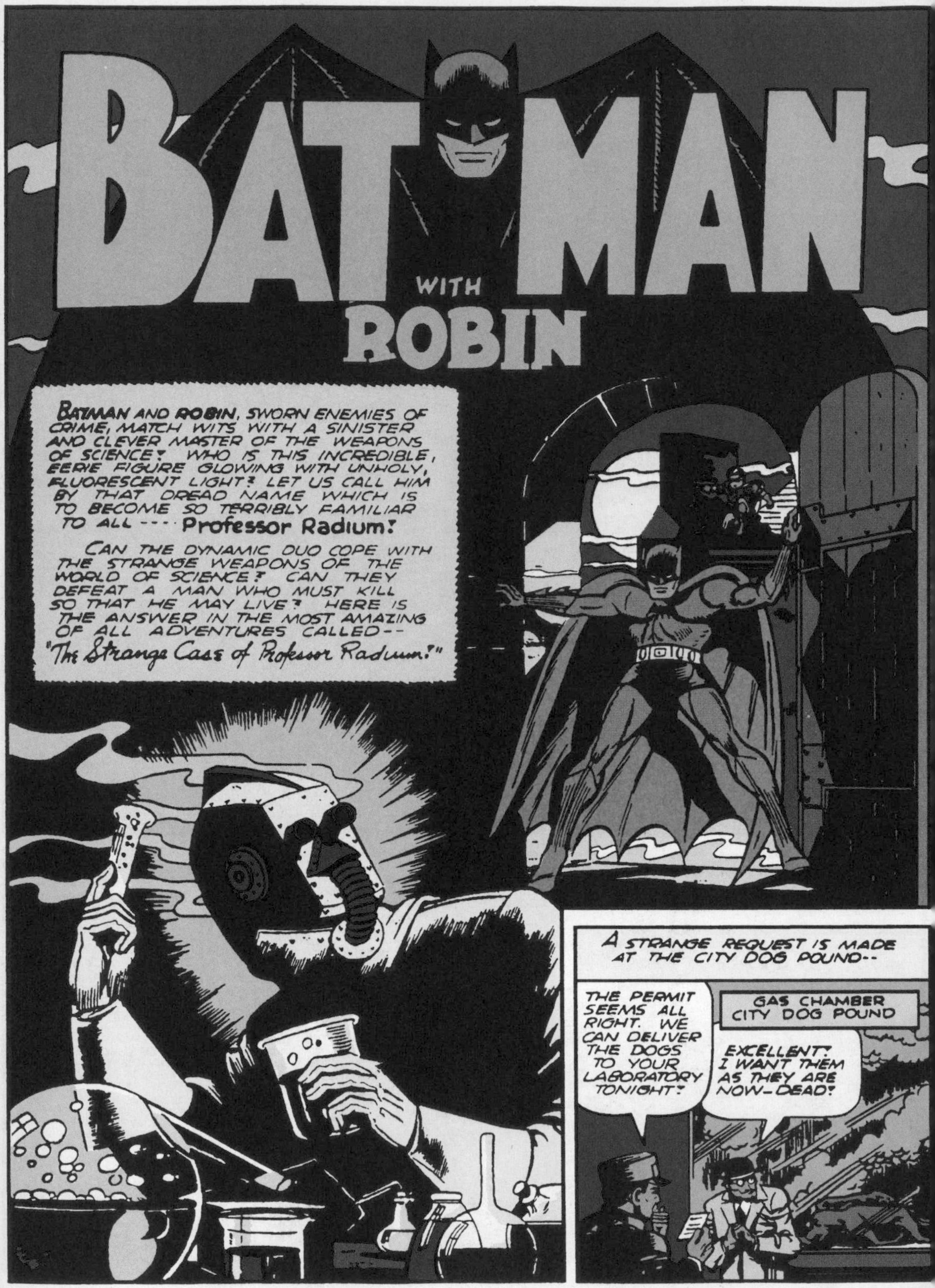
BATMAN
WITH
ROBIN
BATMAN AND ROBIN, SWORN ENEMIES OF CRIME, MATCH WITS WITH A SINISTER AND CLEVER MASTER OF THE WEAPONS OF SCIENCE! WHO IS THIS INCREDIBLE, EERIE FIGURE GLOWING WITH UNHOLY, FLUORESCENT LIGHT? LET US CALL HIM BY THAT DREAD NAME WHICH IS TO BECOME SO TERRIBLY FAMILIAR TO ALL ---- Professor Radium!
CAN THE DYNAMIC DUO COPE WITH THE STRANGE WEAPONS OF THE WORLD OF SCIENCE? CAN THEY DEFEAT A MAN WHO MUST KILL SO THAT HE MAY LIVE? HERE IS THE ANSWER IN THE MOST AMAZING OF ALL ADVENTURES CALLED--
"The Strange Case of Professor Radium!"
A STRANGE REQUEST IS MADE AT THE CITY DOG POUND--
THE PERMIT SEEMS ALL RIGHT. WE CAN DELIVER THE DOGS TO YOUR LABORATORY TONIGHT!
GAS CHAMBER
CITY DOG POUND
EXCELLENT! I WANT THEM AS THEY ARE NOW-DEAD!

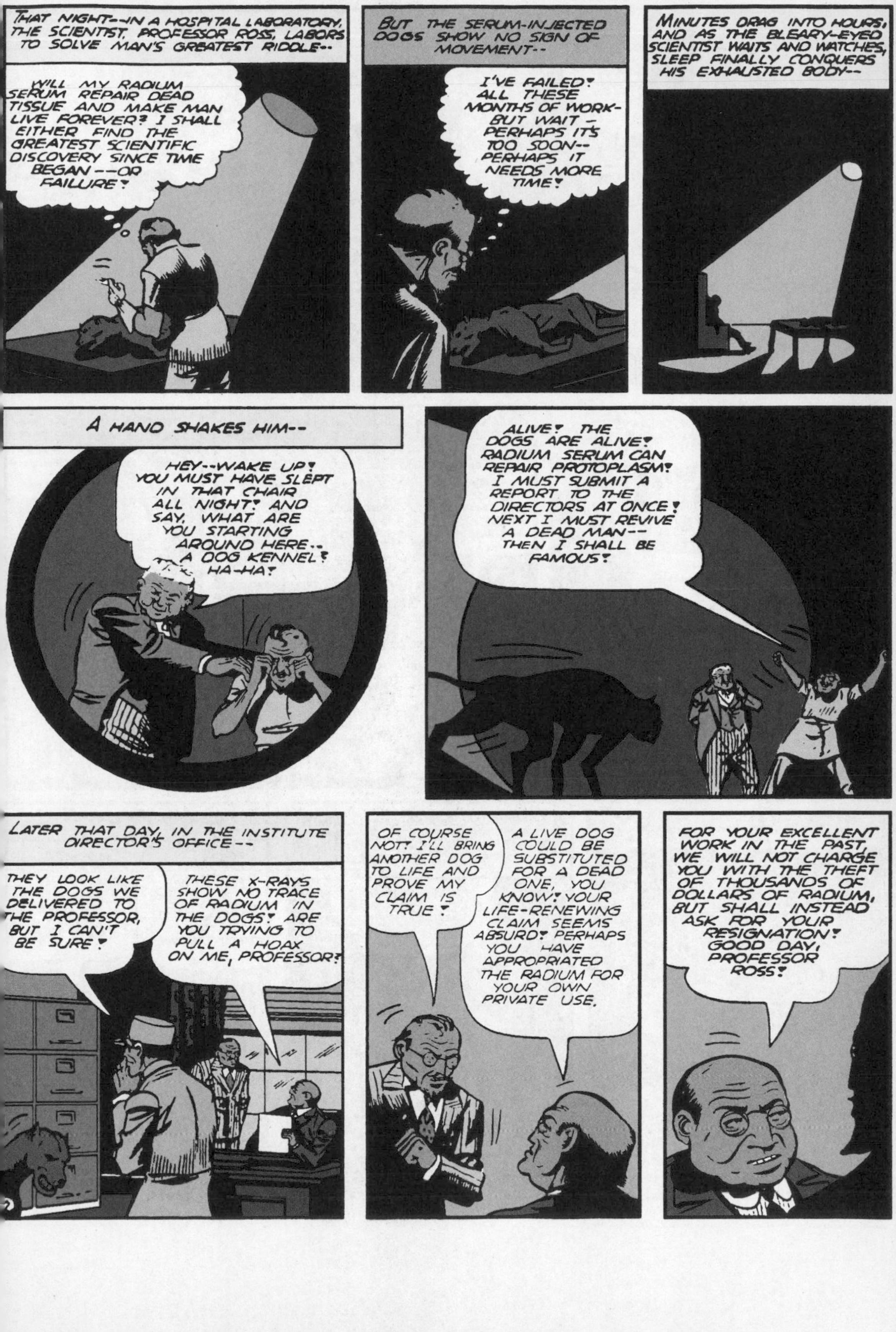

THAT NIGHT--IN A HOSPITAL LABORATORY, THE SCIENTIST, PROFESSOR ROSS, LABORS TO SOLVE MAN'S GREATEST RIDDLE--
WILL MY RADIUM SERUM REPAIR DEAD TISSUE AND MAKE MAN LIVE FOREVER? I SHALL EITHER FIND THE GREATEST SCIENTIFIC DISCOVERY SINCE TIME BEGAN --OR FAILURE!
BUT THE SERUM-INJECTED DOGS SHOW NO SIGN OF MOVEMENT--
I'VE FAILED! ALL THESE MONTHS OF WORK-BUT WAIT -PERHAPS IT'S TOO SOON--PERHAPS IT NEEDS MORE TIME!
MINUTES DRAG INTO HOURS, AND AS THE BLEARY-EYED SCIENTIST WAITS AND WATCHES, SLEEP FINALLY CONQUERS HIS EXHAUSTED BODY--
A HAND SHAKES HIM--
HEY--WAKE UP! YOU MUST HAVE SLEPT IN THAT CHAIR ALL NIGHT! AND SAY, WHAT ARE YOU STARTING AROUND HERE.. A DOG KENNEL? HA-HA!
ALIVE! THE DOGS ARE ALIVE! RADIUM SERUM CAN REPAIR PROTOPLASM! I MUST SUBMIT A REPORT TO THE DIRECTORS AT ONCE! NEXT I MUST REVIVE A DEAD MAN--THEN I SHALL BE FAMOUS!
LATER THAT DAY, IN THE INSTITUTE DIRECTOR'S OFFICE--
THEY LOOK LIKE THE DOGS WE DELIVERED TO THE PROFESSOR, BUT I CAN'T BE SURE!
THESE X-RAYS SHOW NO TRACE OF RADIUM IN THE DOGS! ARE YOU TRYING TO PULL A HOAX ON ME, PROFESSOR?
A LIVE DOG COULD BE SUBSTITUTED FOR A DEAD ONE, YOU KNOW! YOUR LIFE-RENEWING CLAIM SEEMS ABSURD! PERHAPS YOU HAVE APPROPRIATED THE RADIUM FOR YOUR OWN PRIVATE USE.
OF COURSE NOT! I'LL BRING ANOTHER DOG TO LIFE AND PROVE MY CLAIM IS TRUE!
FOR YOUR EXCELLENT WORK IN THE PAST, WE WILL NOT CHARGE YOU WITH THE THEFT OF THOUSANDS OF DOLLARS OF RADIUM, BUT SHALL INSTEAD ASK FOR YOUR RESIGNATION! GOOD DAY, PROFESSOR ROSS!

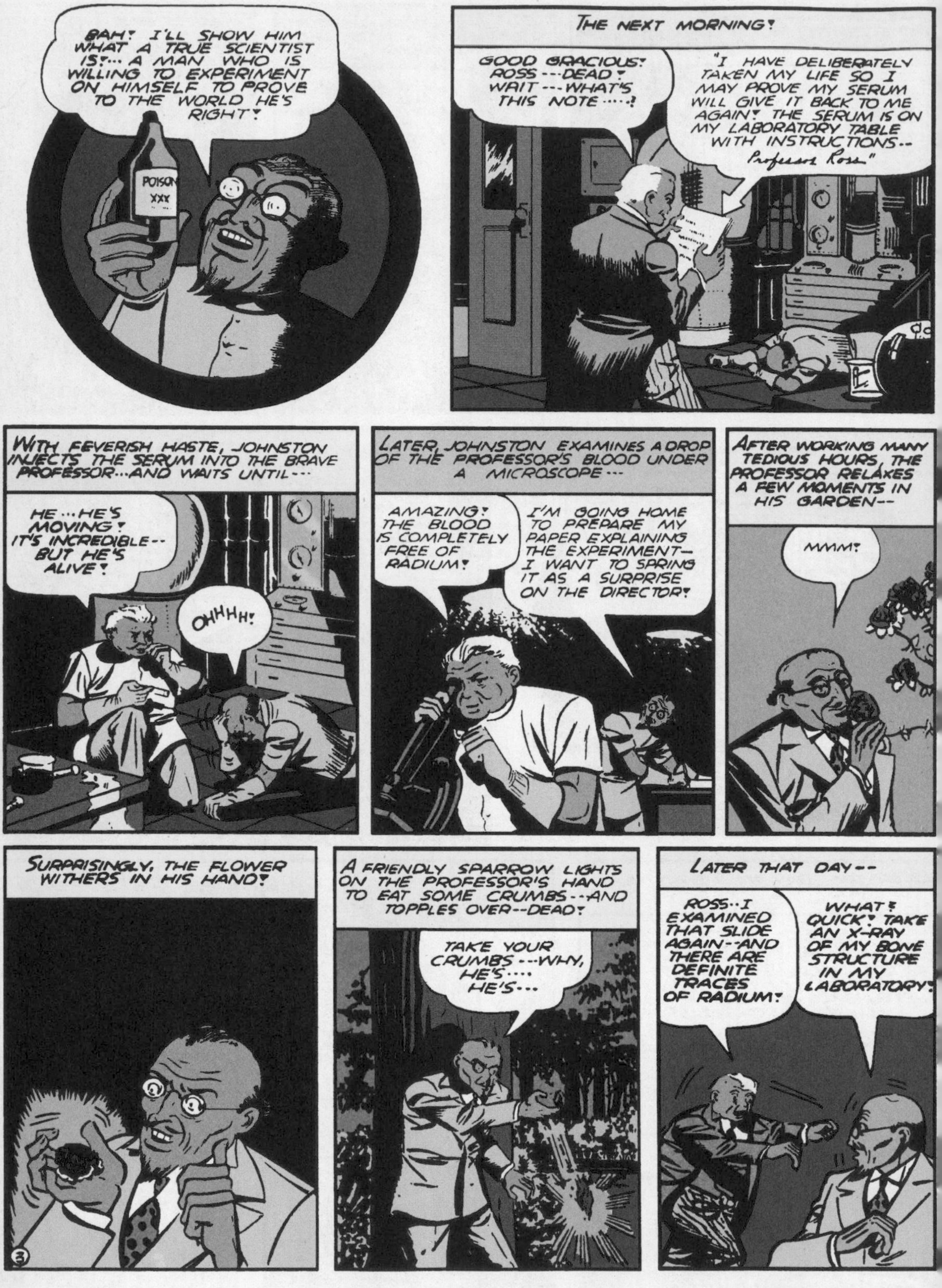
BAH! I'LL SHOW HIM WHAT A TRUE SCIENTIST IS!... A MAN WHO IS WILLING TO EXPERIMENT ON HIMSELF TO PROVE TO THE WORLD HE'S RIGHT!
POISON XXX
THE NEXT MORNING!
GOOD GRACIOUS! ROSS---DEAD! WAIT---WHAT'S THIS NOTE....!
"I HAVE DELIBERATELY TAKEN MY LIFE SO I MAY PROVE MY SERUM WILL GIVE IT BACK TO ME AGAIN! THE SERUM IS ON MY LABORATORY TABLE WITH INSTRUCTIONS-- Professor Ross"
WITH FEVERISH HASTE, JOHNSTON INJECTS THE SERUM INTO THE BRAVE PROFESSOR...AND WAITS UNTIL---
HE...HE'S MOVING! IT'S INCREDIBLE-- BUT HE'S ALIVE!
OHHHH!
LATER, JOHNSTON EXAMINES A DROP OF THE PROFESSOR'S BLOOD UNDER A MICROSCOPE---
AMAZING! THE BLOOD IS COMPLETELY FREE OF RADIUM!
I'M GOING HOME TO PREPARE MY PAPER EXPLAINING THE EXPERIMENT— I WANT TO SPRING IT AS A SURPRISE ON THE DIRECTOR!
AFTER WORKING MANY TEDIOUS HOURS, THE PROFESSOR RELAXES A FEW MOMENTS IN HIS GARDEN--
MMM!
SURPRISINGLY, THE FLOWER WITHERS IN HIS HAND!
3
A FRIENDLY SPARROW LIGHTS ON THE PROFESSOR'S HAND TO EAT SOME CRUMBS--AND TOPPLES OVER--DEAD!
TAKE YOUR CRUMBS---WHY, HE'S.... HE'S---
LATER THAT DAY--
ROSS--I EXAMINED THAT SLIDE AGAIN--AND THERE ARE DEFINITE TRACES OF RADIUM!
WHAT? QUICK! TAKE AN X-RAY OF MY BONE STRUCTURE IN MY LABORATORY!

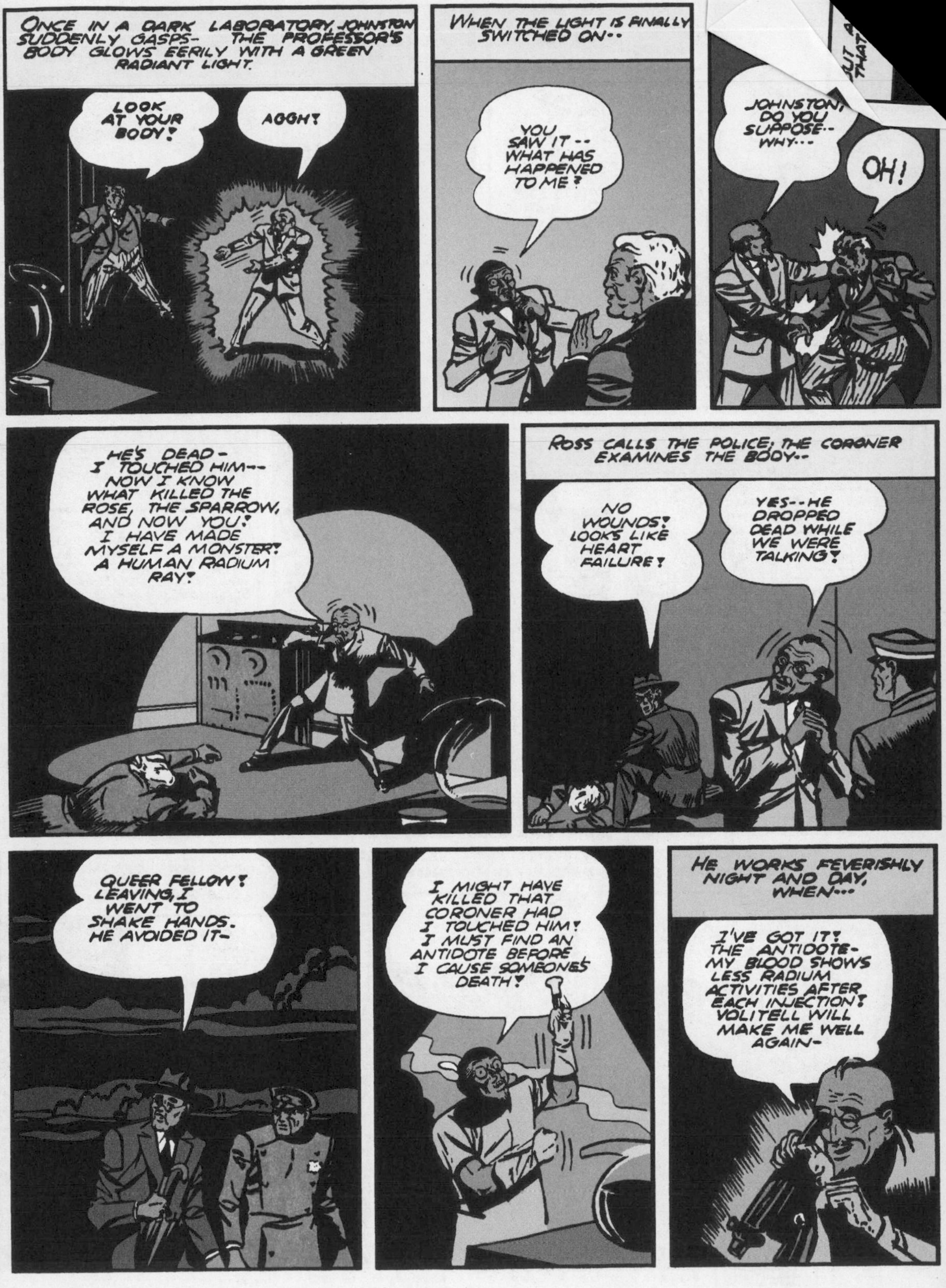
ONCE IN A DARK LABORATORY, JOHNSTON SUDDENLY GASPS- THE PROFESSOR'S BODY GLOWS EERILY WITH A GREEN RADIANT LIGHT.
LOOK AT YOUR BODY!
AGGH!
WHEN THE LIGHT IS FINALLY SWITCHED ON--
YOU SAW IT -- WHAT HAS HAPPENED TO ME?
JOHNSTON! DO YOU SUPPOSE-- WHY---
OH!
HE'S DEAD- I TOUCHED HIM-- NOW I KNOW WHAT KILLED THE ROSE, THE SPARROW, AND NOW YOU! I HAVE MADE MYSELF A MONSTER! A HUMAN RADIUM RAY!
ROSS CALLS THE POLICE; THE CORONER EXAMINES THE BODY--
NO WOUNDS! LOOKS LIKE HEART FAILURE!
YES--HE DROPPED DEAD WHILE WE WERE TALKING!
QUEER FELLOW! LEAVING, I WENT TO SHAKE HANDS. HE AVOIDED IT-
I MIGHT HAVE KILLED THAT CORONER HAD I TOUCHED HIM! I MUST FIND AN ANTIDOTE BEFORE I CAUSE SOMEONE'S DEATH!
HE WORKS FEVERISHLY NIGHT AND DAY, WHEN---
I'VE GOT IT! THE ANTIDOTE- MY BLOOD SHOWS LESS RADIUM ACTIVITIES AFTER EACH INJECTION! VOLITELL WILL MAKE ME WELL AGAIN-

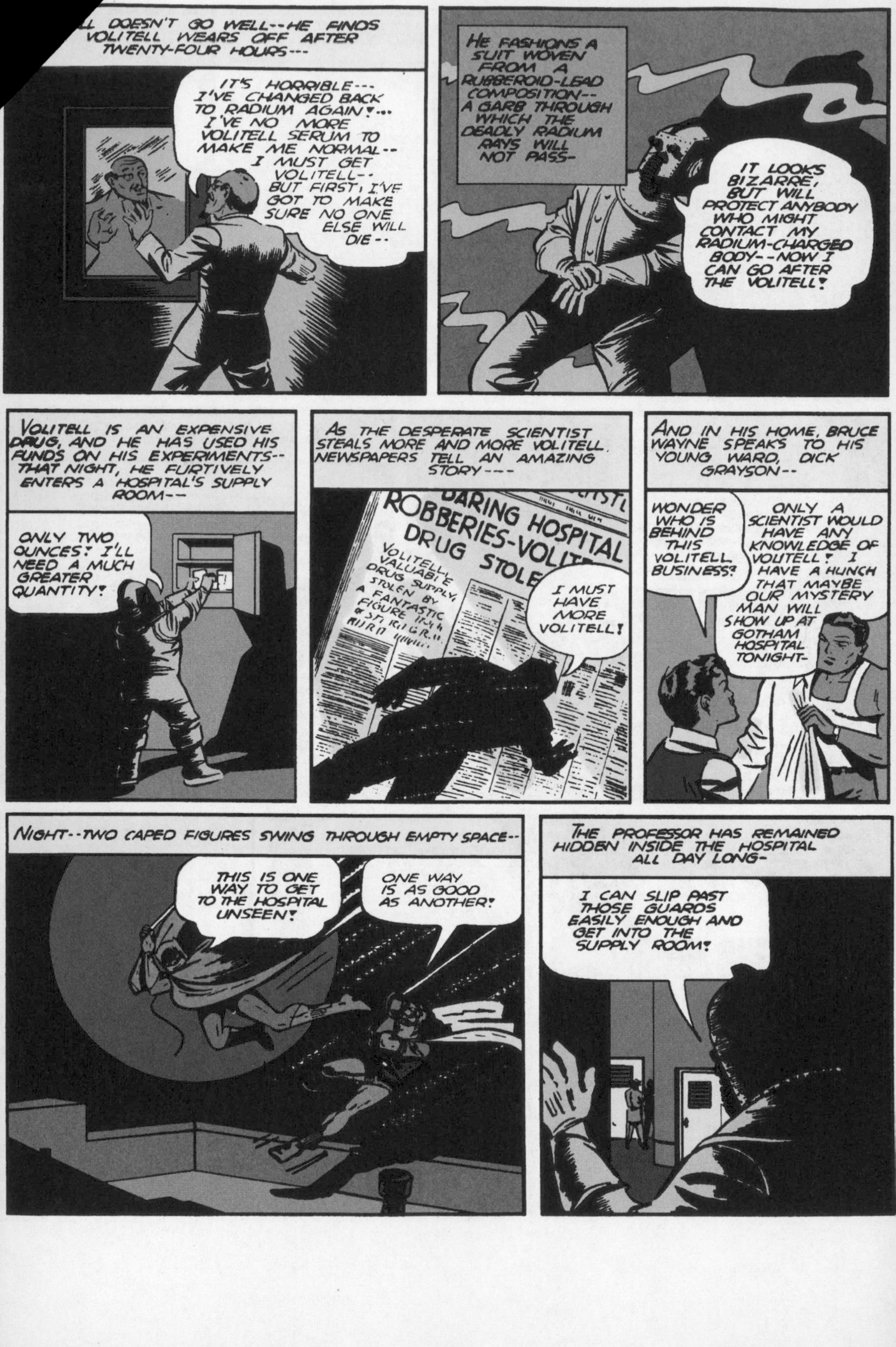
LL DOESN'T GO WELL--HE FINDS VOLITELL WEARS OFF AFTER TWENTY-FOUR HOURS---
IT'S HORRIBLE--- I'VE CHANGED BACK TO RADIUM AGAIN!... I'VE NO MORE VOLITELL SERUM TO MAKE ME NORMAL-- I MUST GET VOLITELL-- BUT FIRST, I'VE GOT TO MAKE SURE NO ONE ELSE WILL DIE--
HE FASHIONS A SUIT WOVEN FROM A RUBBEROID-LEAD COMPOSITION-- A GARB THROUGH WHICH THE DEADLY RADIUM RAYS WILL NOT PASS-
IT LOOKS BIZARRE, BUT WILL PROTECT ANYBODY WHO MIGHT CONTACT MY RADIUM-CHARGED BODY--NOW I CAN GO AFTER THE VOLITELL!
VOLITELL IS AN EXPENSIVE DRUG, AND HE HAS USED HIS FUNDS ON HIS EXPERIMENTS-- THAT NIGHT, HE FURTIVELY ENTERS A HOSPITAL'S SUPPLY ROOM--
ONLY TWO OUNCES! I'LL NEED A MUCH GREATER QUANTITY!
AS THE DESPERATE SCIENTIST STEALS MORE AND MORE VOLITELL, NEWSPAPERS TELL AN AMAZING STORY---
DARING HOSPITAL ROBBERIES-VOLIT DRUG STOLE
VOLITELL, VALUABLE DRUG SUPPLY, STOLEN BY A FANTASTIC FIGURE
I MUST HAVE MORE VOLITELL!
AND IN HIS HOME, BRUCE WAYNE SPEAKS TO HIS YOUNG WARD, DICK GRAYSON--
WONDER WHO IS BEHIND THIS VOLITELL BUSINESS?
ONLY A SCIENTIST WOULD HAVE ANY KNOWLEDGE OF VOLITELL! I HAVE A HUNCH THAT MAYBE OUR MYSTERY MAN WILL SHOW UP AT GOTHAM HOSPITAL TONIGHT-
NIGHT--TWO CAPED FIGURES SWING THROUGH EMPTY SPACE--
THIS IS ONE WAY TO GET TO THE HOSPITAL UNSEEN!
ONE WAY IS AS GOOD AS ANOTHER!
THE PROFESSOR HAS REMAINED HIDDEN INSIDE THE HOSPITAL ALL DAY LONG-
I CAN SLIP PAST THOSE GUARDS EASILY ENOUGH AND GET INTO THE SUPPLY ROOM!

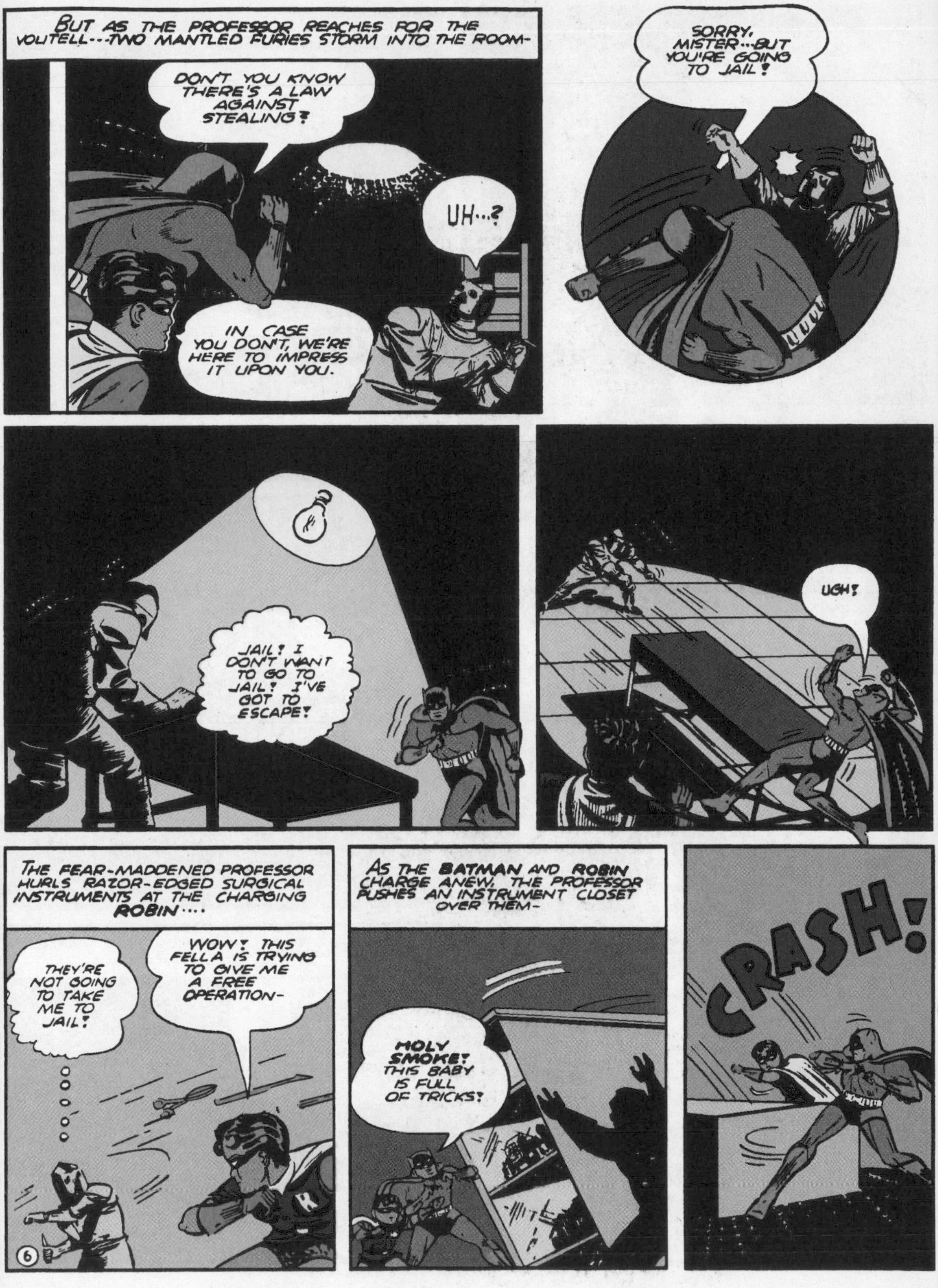
BUT AS THE PROFESSOR REACHES FOR THE VOLTELL---TWO MANTLED FURIES STORM INTO THE ROOM-
DON'T YOU KNOW THERE'S A LAW AGAINST STEALING?
IN CASE YOU DON'T, WE'RE HERE TO IMPRESS IT UPON YOU.
UH...?
SORRY, MISTER...BUT YOU'RE GOING TO JAIL!
JAIL! I DON'T WANT TO GO TO JAIL! I'VE GOT TO ESCAPE!
UGH!
THE FEAR-MADDENED PROFESSOR HURLS RAZOR-EDGED SURGICAL INSTRUMENTS AT THE CHARGING ROBIN....
THEY'RE NOT GOING TO TAKE ME TO JAIL!
WOW! THIS FELLA IS TRYING TO GIVE ME A FREE OPERATION-
6
AS THE BATMAN AND ROBIN CHARGE ANEW, THE PROFESSOR PUSHES AN INSTRUMENT CLOSET OVER THEM-
HOLY SMOKE! THIS BABY IS FULL OF TRICKS!
CRASH!

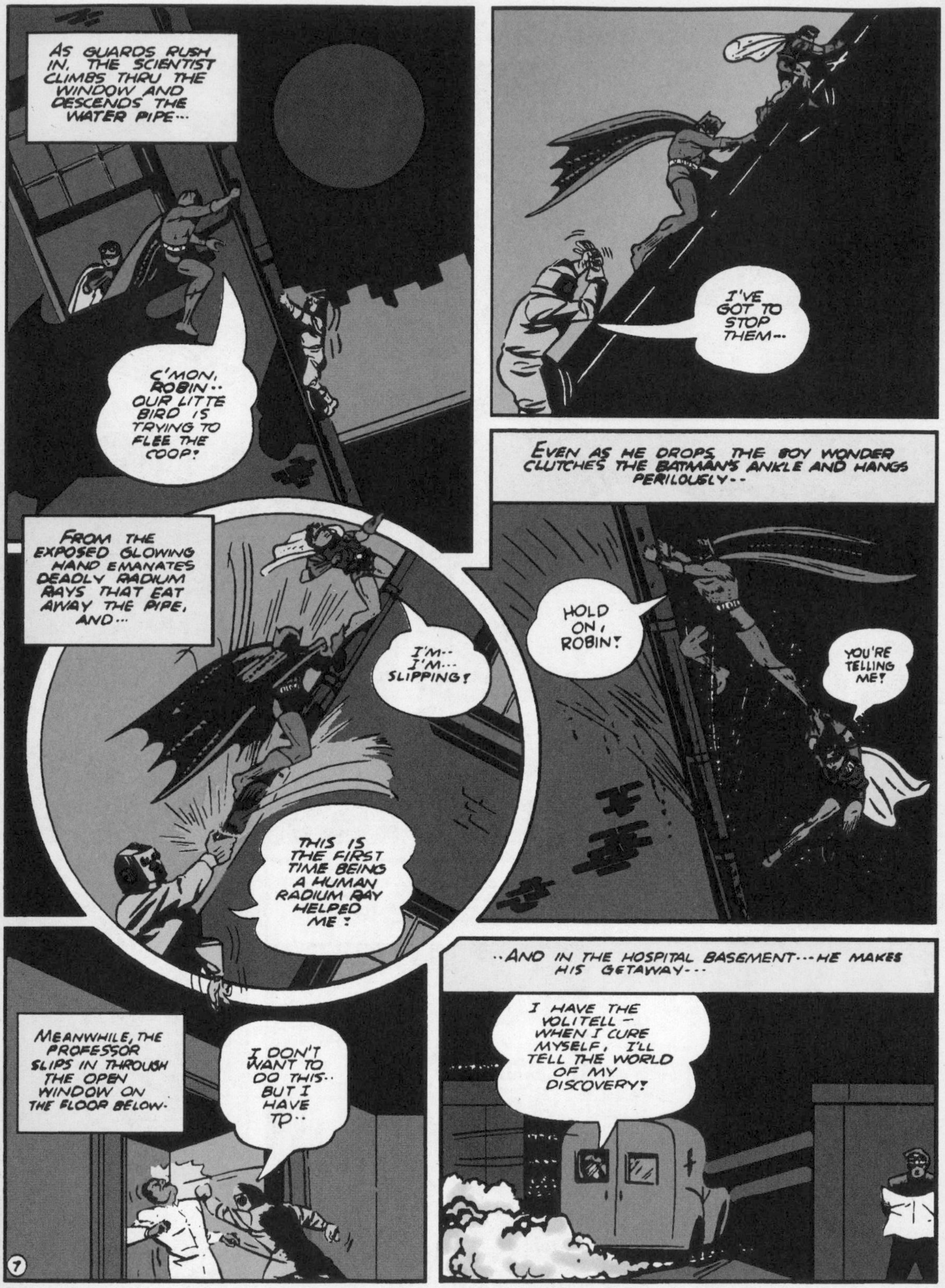

AS GUARDS RUSH IN, THE SCIENTIST CLIMBS THRU THE WINDOW AND DESCENDS THE WATER PIPE...
C'MON, ROBIN.. OUR LITTE BIRD IS TRYING TO FLEE THE COOP!
I'VE GOT TO STOP THEM...
FROM THE EXPOSED GLOWING HAND EMANATES DEADLY RADIUM RAYS THAT EAT AWAY THE PIPE, AND...
I'M.. I'M... SLIPPING!
THIS IS THE FIRST TIME BEING A HUMAN RADIUM RAY HELPED ME!
EVEN AS HE DROPS, THE BOY WONDER CLUTCHES THE BATMAN'S ANKLE AND HANGS PERILOUSLY--
HOLD ON, ROBIN!
YOU'RE TELLING ME!
MEANWHILE, THE PROFESSOR SLIPS IN THROUGH THE OPEN WINDOW ON THE FLOOR BELOW.
I DON'T WANT TO DO THIS.. BUT I HAVE TO..
7
..AND IN THE HOSPITAL BASEMENT---HE MAKES HIS GETAWAY---
I HAVE THE VOLITELL -- WHEN I CURE MYSELF, I'LL TELL THE WORLD OF MY DISCOVERY!

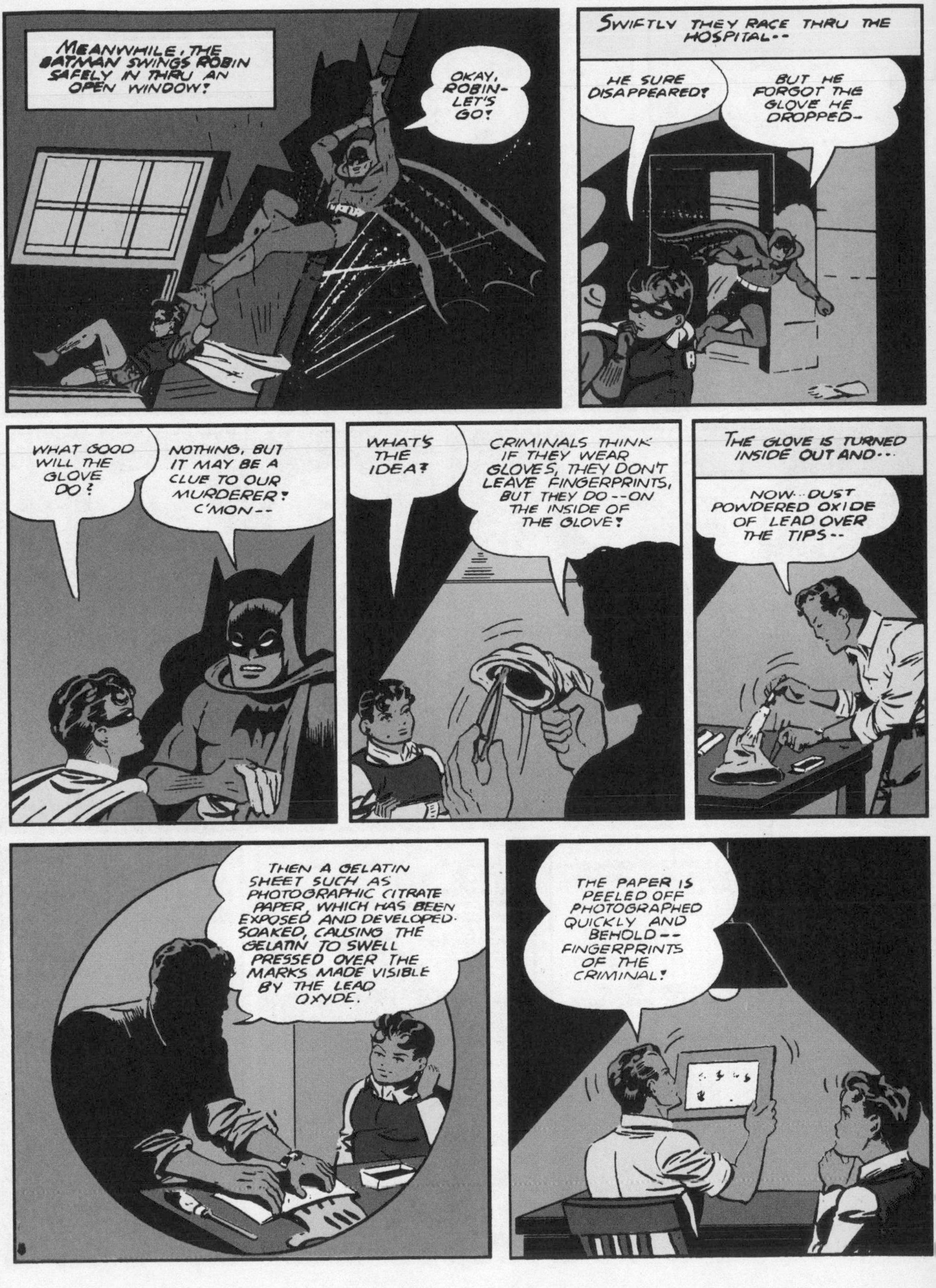
MEANWHILE, THE BATMAN SWINGS ROBIN SAFELY IN THRU AN OPEN WINDOW!
OKAY, ROBIN-LET'S GO!
SWIFTLY THEY RACE THRU THE HOSPITAL--
HE SURE DISAPPEARED!
BUT HE FORGOT THE GLOVE HE DROPPED-
WHAT GOOD WILL THE GLOVE DO?
NOTHING, BUT IT MAY BE A CLUE TO OUR MURDERER! C'MON--
WHAT'S THE IDEA?
CRIMINALS THINK IF THEY WEAR GLOVES, THEY DON'T LEAVE FINGERPRINTS, BUT THEY DO--ON THE INSIDE OF THE GLOVE!
THE GLOVE IS TURNED INSIDE OUT AND---
NOW--DUST POWDERED OXIDE OF LEAD OVER THE TIPS--
THEN A GELATIN SHEET SUCH AS PHOTOGRAPHIC CITRATE PAPER, WHICH HAS BEEN EXPOSED AND DEVELOPED. SOAKED, CAUSING THE GELATIN TO SWELL PRESSED OVER THE MARKS MADE VISIBLE BY THE LEAD OXYDE.
THE PAPER IS PEELED OFF PHOTOGRAPHED QUICKLY AND BEHOLD--FINGERPRINTS OF THE CRIMINAL!

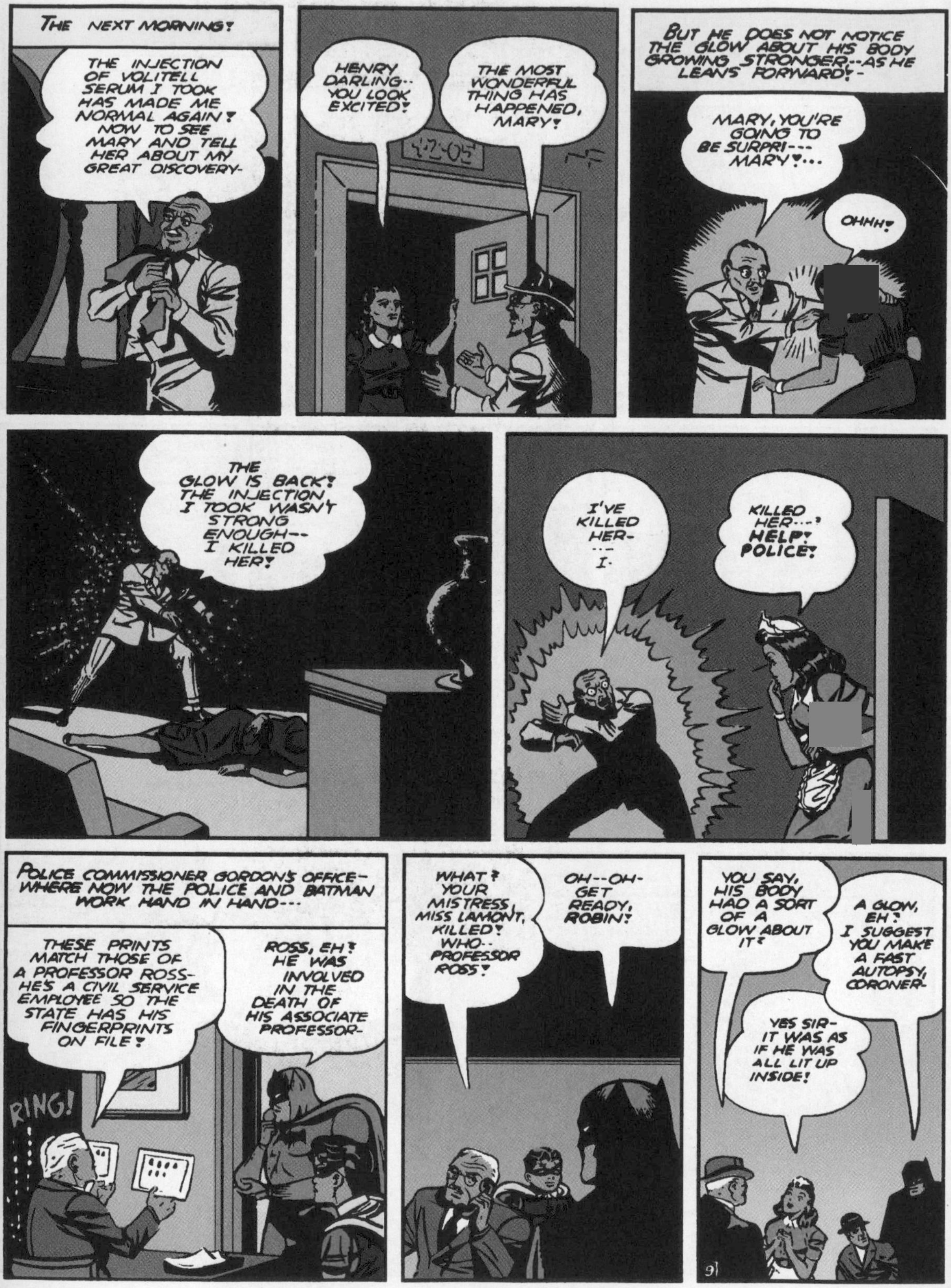
THE NEXT MORNING!
THE INJECTION OF VOLITELL SERUM I TOOK HAS MADE ME NORMAL AGAIN! NOW TO SEE MARY AND TELL HER ABOUT MY GREAT DISCOVERY-
HENRY DARLING-- YOU LOOK EXCITED!
THE MOST WONDERFUL THING HAS HAPPENED, MARY!
BUT HE DOES NOT NOTICE THE GLOW ABOUT HIS BODY GROWING STRONGER--AS HE LEANS FORWARD!-
MARY, YOU'RE GOING TO BE SURPRI--- MARY!...
OHHH!
THE GLOW IS BACK! THE INJECTION I TOOK WASN'T STRONG ENOUGH-- I KILLED HER!
I'VE KILLED HER- --- I-
KILLED HER...? HELP! POLICE!
POLICE COMMISSIONER GORDON'S OFFICE- WHERE NOW THE POLICE AND BATMAN WORK HAND IN HAND---
THESE PRINTS MATCH THOSE OF A PROFESSOR ROSS- HE'S A CIVIL SERVICE EMPLOYEE SO THE STATE HAS HIS FINGERPRINTS ON FILE!
ROSS, EH? HE WAS INVOLVED IN THE DEATH OF HIS ASSOCIATE PROFESSOR-
RING!
WHAT? YOUR MISTRESS, MISS LAMONT, KILLED! WHO-- PROFESSOR ROSS!
OH--OH- GET READY, ROBIN!
YOU SAY, HIS BODY HAD A SORT OF A GLOW ABOUT IT?
A GLOW, EH? I SUGGEST YOU MAKE A FAST AUTOPSY, CORONER-
YES SIR- IT WAS AS IF HE WAS ALL LIT UP INSIDE!

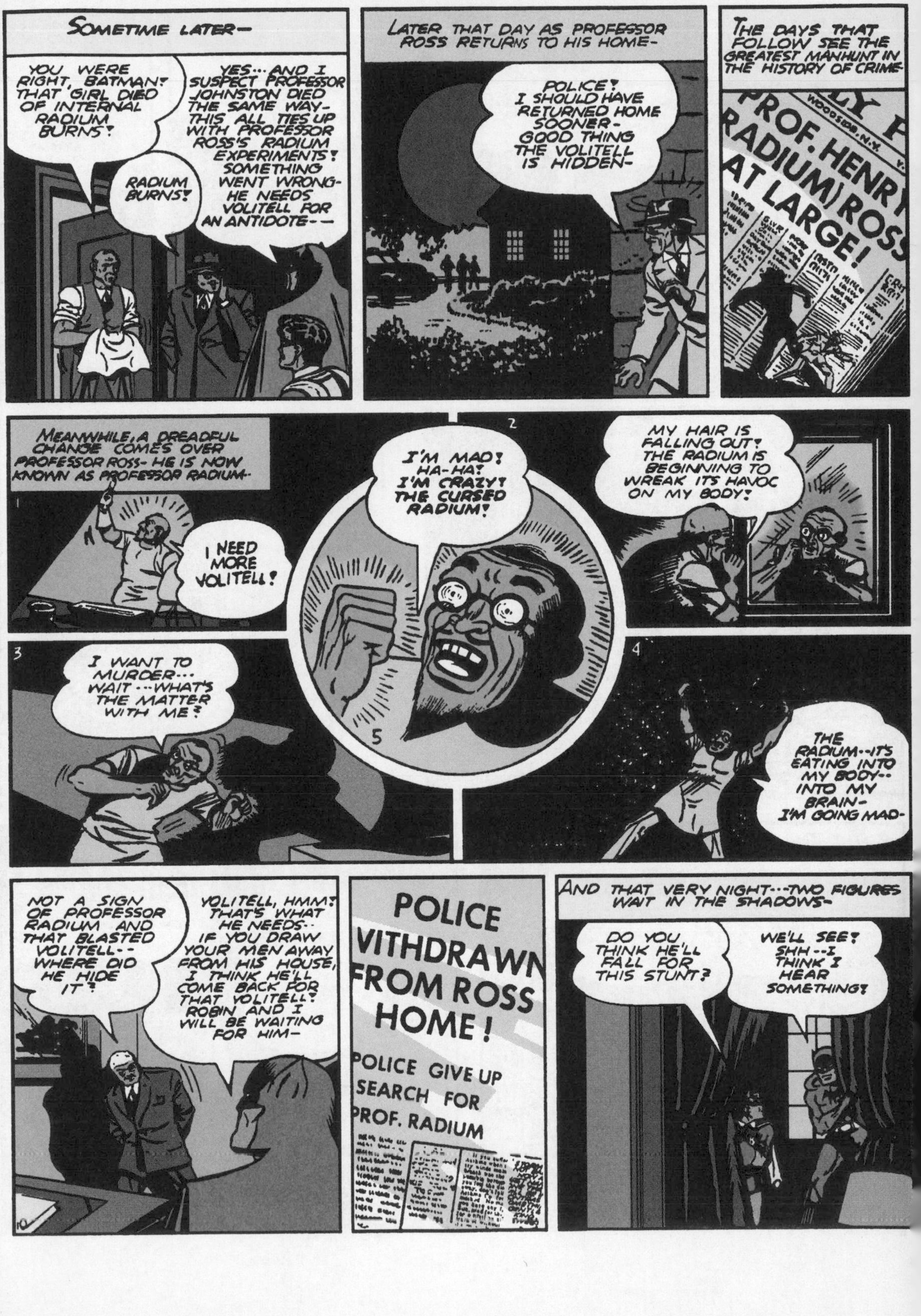
SOMETIME LATER—
YOU WERE RIGHT, BATMAN! THAT GIRL DIED OF INTERNAL RADIUM BURNS!
RADIUM BURNS!
YES...AND I SUSPECT PROFESSOR JOHNSTON DIED THE SAME WAY- THIS ALL TIES UP WITH PROFESSOR ROSS'S RADIUM EXPERIMENTS! SOMETHING WENT WRONG- HE NEEDS VOLITELL FOR AN ANTIDOTE--
LATER THAT DAY AS PROFESSOR ROSS RETURNS TO HIS HOME-
POLICE! I SHOULD HAVE RETURNED HOME SOONER- GOOD THING THE VOLITELL IS HIDDEN-
THE DAYS THAT FOLLOW SEE THE GREATEST MANHUNT IN THE HISTORY OF CRIME-
PROF. HENRY (RADIUM) ROSS AT LARGE!
MEANWHILE, A DREADFUL CHANGE COMES OVER PROFESSOR ROSS- HE IS NOW KNOWN AS PROFESSOR RADIUM-
1
I NEED MORE VOLITELL!
2
MY HAIR IS FALLING OUT! THE RADIUM IS BEGINNING TO WREAK ITS HAVOC ON MY BODY!
3
I WANT TO MURDER--- WAIT---WHAT'S THE MATTER WITH ME?
I'M MAD! HA-HA! I'M CRAZY! THE CURSED RADIUM!
5
4
THE RADIUM--IT'S EATING INTO MY BODY-- INTO MY BRAIN- I'M GOING MAD-
NOT A SIGN OF PROFESSOR RADIUM AND THAT BLASTED VOLITELL-- WHERE DID HE HIDE IT?
VOLITELL, HMM! THAT'S WHAT HE NEEDS-- IF YOU DRAW YOUR MEN AWAY FROM HIS HOUSE, I THINK HE'LL COME BACK FOR THAT VOLITELL! ROBIN AND I WILL BE WAITING FOR HIM-
POLICE WITHDRAWN FROM ROSS HOME!
POLICE GIVE UP SEARCH FOR PROF. RADIUM
AND THAT VERY NIGHT---TWO FIGURES WAIT IN THE SHADOWS-
DO YOU THINK HE'LL FALL FOR THIS STUNT?
WE'LL SEE! SHH--I THINK I HEAR SOMETHING!

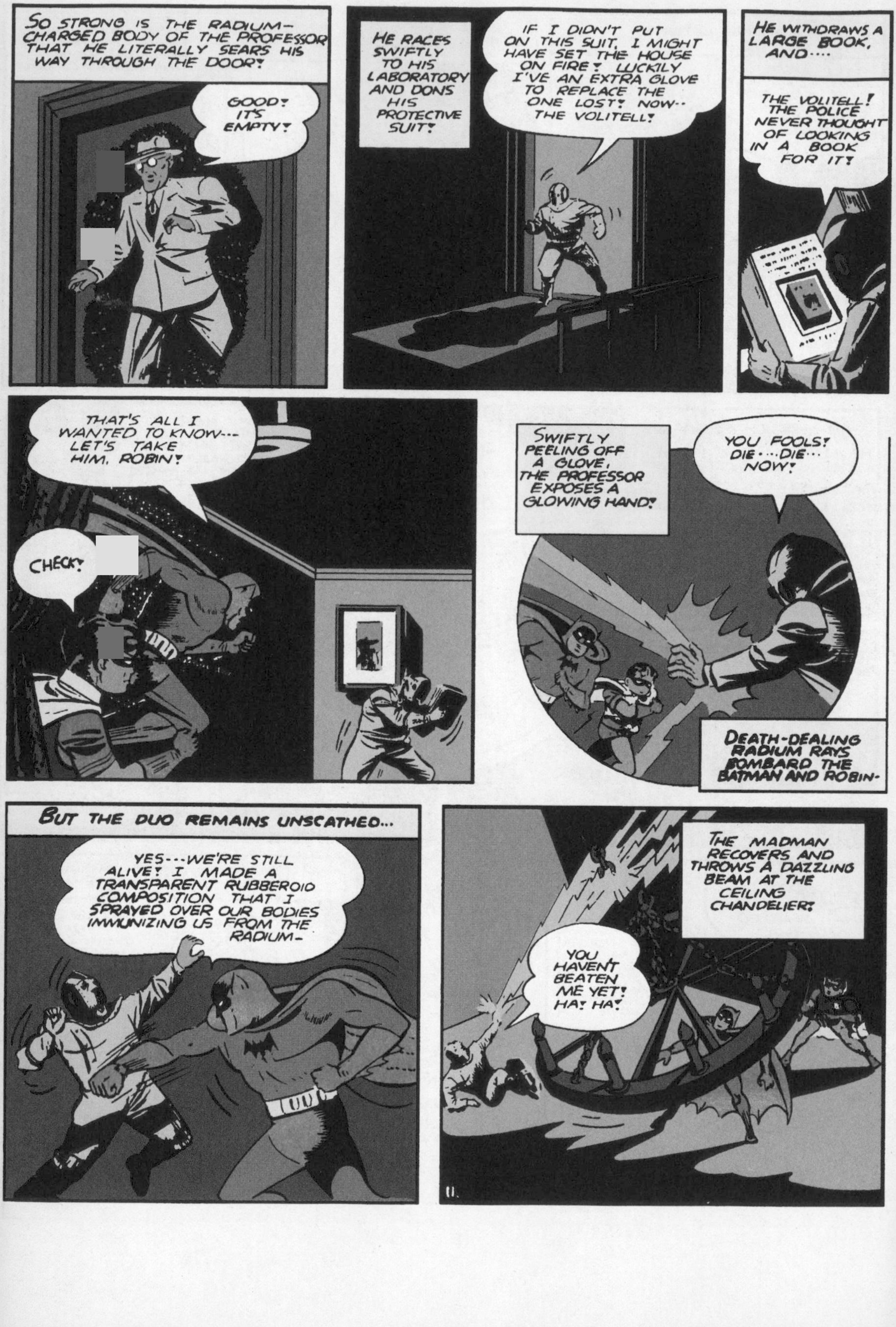
SO STRONG IS THE RADIUM-CHARGED BODY OF THE PROFESSOR THAT HE LITERALLY SEARS HIS WAY THROUGH THE DOOR!
GOOD! IT'S EMPTY!
HE RACES SWIFTLY TO HIS LABORATORY AND DONS HIS PROTECTIVE SUIT!
IF I DIDN'T PUT ON THIS SUIT, I MIGHT HAVE SET THE HOUSE ON FIRE! LUCKILY I'VE AN EXTRA GLOVE TO REPLACE THE ONE LOST! NOW-- THE VOLITELL!
HE WITHDRAWS A LARGE BOOK, AND....
THE VOLITELL! THE POLICE NEVER THOUGHT OF LOOKING IN A BOOK FOR IT!
THAT'S ALL I WANTED TO KNOW--- LET'S TAKE HIM, ROBIN!
CHECK!
SWIFTLY PEELING OFF A GLOVE, THE PROFESSOR EXPOSES A GLOWING HAND!
YOU FOOLS! DIE ...DIE... NOW!
DEATH-DEALING RADIUM RAYS BOMBARD THE BATMAN AND ROBIN-
BUT THE DUO REMAINS UNSCATHED...
YES---WE'RE STILL ALIVE! I MADE A TRANSPARENT RUBBEROID COMPOSITION THAT I SPRAYED OVER OUR BODIES IMMUNIZING US FROM THE RADIUM-
THE MADMAN RECOVERS AND THROWS A DAZZLING BEAM AT THE CEILING CHANDELIER!
YOU HAVEN'T BEATEN ME YET! HA! HA!

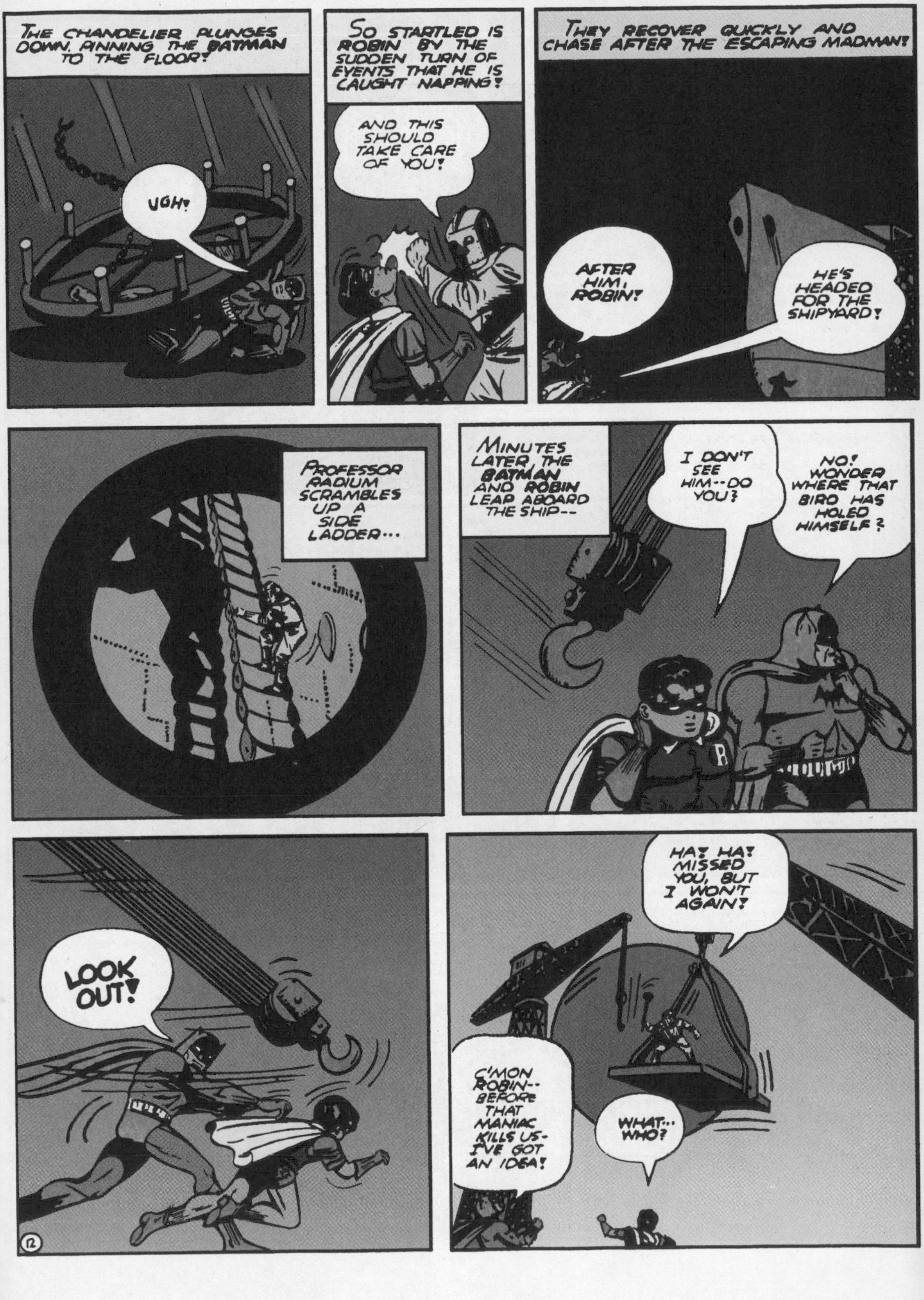
THE CHANDELIER PLUNGES DOWN, PINNING THE BATMAN TO THE FLOOR!
UGH!
SO STARTLED IS ROBIN BY THE SUDDEN TURN OF EVENTS THAT HE IS CAUGHT NAPPING!
AND THIS SHOULD TAKE CARE OF YOU!
THEY RECOVER QUICKLY AND CHASE AFTER THE ESCAPING MADMAN!
AFTER HIM, ROBIN!
HE'S HEADED FOR THE SHIPYARD!
PROFESSOR RADIUM SCRAMBLES UP A SIDE LADDER...
MINUTES LATER THE BATMAN AND ROBIN LEAP ABOARD THE SHIP--
I DON'T SEE HIM--DO YOU?
NO! WONDER WHERE THAT BIRD HAS HOLED HIMSELF?
LOOK OUT!
12
HA! HA! MISSED YOU, BUT I WON'T AGAIN!
C'MON ROBIN-- BEFORE THAT MANIAC KILLS US-- I'VE GOT AN IDEA!
WHAT... WHO?

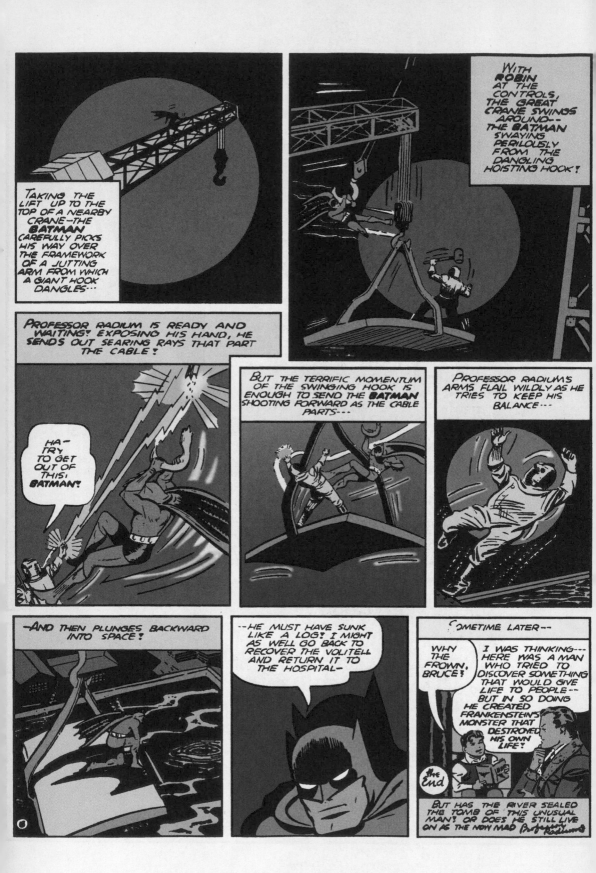

TAKING THE LIFT UP TO THE TOP OF A NEARBY CRANE—THE **BATMAN** CAREFULLY PICKS HIS WAY OVER THE FRAMEWORK OF A JUTTING ARM FROM WHICH A GIANT HOOK DANGLES...

WITH **ROBIN** AT THE CONTROLS, THE GREAT CRANE SWINGS AROUND—THE **BATMAN** SWAYING PERILOUSLY FROM THE DANGLING HOISTING HOOK!

PROFESSOR RADIUM IS READY AND WAITING! EXPOSING HIS HAND, HE SENDS OUT SEARING RAYS THAT PART THE CABLE!

HA—TRY TO GET OUT OF THIS, BATMAN!

BUT THE TERRIFIC MOMENTUM OF THE SWINGING HOOK IS ENOUGH TO SEND THE **BATMAN** SHOOTING FORWARD AS THE CABLE PARTS...

PROFESSOR RADIUM'S ARMS FLAIL WILDLY AS HE TRIES TO KEEP HIS BALANCE...

—AND THEN PLUNGES BACKWARD INTO SPACE!

—HE MUST HAVE SUNK LIKE A LOG! I MIGHT AS WELL GO BACK TO RECOVER THE VOLITELL AND RETURN IT TO THE HOSPITAL—

SOMETIME LATER—

WHY THE FROWN, BRUCE!

I WAS THINKING—HERE WAS A MAN WHO TRIED TO DISCOVER SOMETHING THAT WOULD GIVE LIFE TO PEOPLE—BUT IN SO DOING HE CREATED FRANKENSTEIN'S MONSTER THAT DESTROYED HIS OWN LIFE!

The END

BUT HAS THE RIVER SEALED THE TOMB OF THIS UNUSUAL MAN! OR DOES HE STILL LIVE ON AS THE NOW MAD PROFESSOR RADIUM...

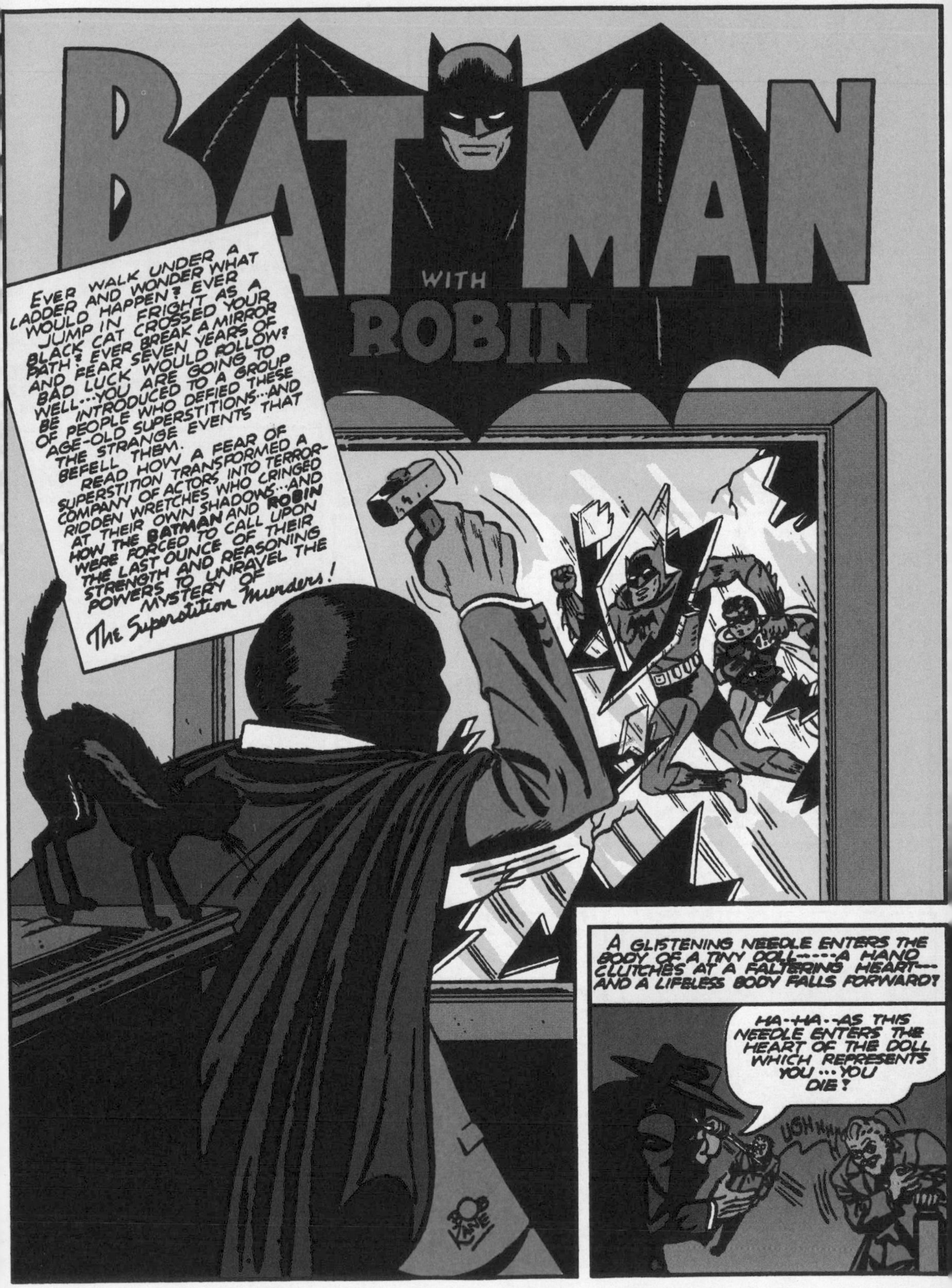
BATMAN
WITH
ROBIN
EVER WALK UNDER A LADDER AND WONDER WHAT WOULD HAPPEN? EVER JUMP IN FRIGHT AS A BLACK CAT CROSSED YOUR PATH? EVER BREAK A MIRROR AND FEAR SEVEN YEARS OF BAD LUCK WOULD FOLLOW? WELL...YOU ARE GOING TO BE INTRODUCED TO A GROUP OF PEOPLE WHO DEFIED THESE AGE-OLD SUPERSTITIONS...AND THE STRANGE EVENTS THAT BEFELL THEM.
READ HOW A FEAR OF SUPERSTITION TRANSFORMED A COMPANY OF ACTORS INTO TERROR-RIDDEN WRETCHES WHO CRINGED AT THEIR OWN SHADOWS...AND HOW THE BATMAN AND ROBIN WERE FORCED TO CALL UPON THE LAST OUNCE OF THEIR STRENGTH AND REASONING POWERS TO UNRAVEL THE MYSTERY OF
The Superstition Murders!
A GLISTENING NEEDLE ENTERS THE BODY OF A TINY DOLL------A HAND CLUTCHES AT A FALTERING HEART---AND A LIFELESS BODY FALLS FORWARD!
HA-HA--AS THIS NEEDLE ENTERS THE HEART OF THE DOLL WHICH REPRESENTS YOU...YOU DIE!
UGHHHH

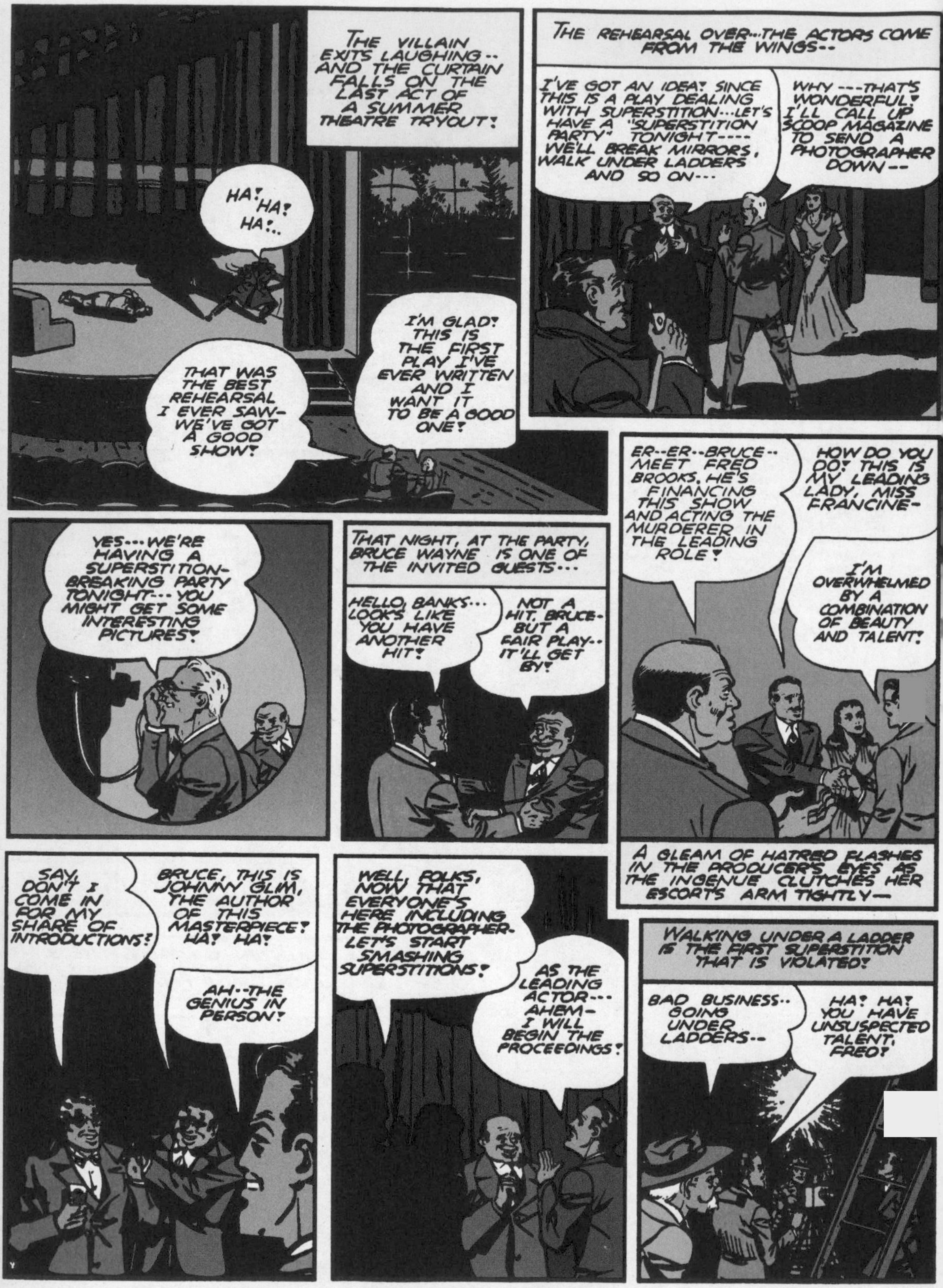
THE VILLAIN EXITS LAUGHING -- AND THE CURTAIN FALLS ON THE LAST ACT OF A SUMMER THEATRE TRYOUT!
HA! HA! HA!..
THAT WAS THE BEST REHEARSAL I EVER SAW- WE'VE GOT A GOOD SHOW!
I'M GLAD! THIS IS THE FIRST PLAY I'VE EVER WRITTEN AND I WANT IT TO BE A GOOD ONE!
THE REHEARSAL OVER--THE ACTORS COME FROM THE WINGS--
I'VE GOT AN IDEA! SINCE THIS IS A PLAY DEALING WITH SUPERSTITION...LET'S HAVE A "SUPERSTITION PARTY" TONIGHT---- WE'LL BREAK MIRRORS, WALK UNDER LADDERS AND SO ON---
WHY ---THAT'S WONDERFUL! I'LL CALL UP SCOOP MAGAZINE TO SEND A PHOTOGRAPHER DOWN --
YES---WE'RE HAVING A SUPERSTITION-BREAKING PARTY TONIGHT--- YOU MIGHT GET SOME INTERESTING PICTURES!
THAT NIGHT, AT THE PARTY, BRUCE WAYNE IS ONE OF THE INVITED GUESTS---
HELLO, BANKS... LOOKS LIKE YOU HAVE ANOTHER HIT!
NOT A HIT, BRUCE- BUT A FAIR PLAY-- IT'LL GET BY!
ER--ER--BRUCE-- MEET FRED BROOKS. HE'S FINANCING THIS SHOW AND ACTING THE MURDERER IN THE LEADING ROLE!
HOW DO YOU DO! THIS IS MY LEADING LADY, MISS FRANCINE-
I'M OVERWHELMED BY A COMBINATION OF BEAUTY AND TALENT!
A GLEAM OF HATRED FLASHES IN THE PRODUCER'S EYES AS THE INGENUE CLUTCHES HER ESCORT'S ARM TIGHTLY—
SAY, DON'T I COME IN FOR MY SHARE OF INTRODUCTIONS?
BRUCE, THIS IS JOHNNY GLIM, THE AUTHOR OF THIS MASTERPIECE! HA! HA!
AH--THE GENIUS IN PERSON!
WELL, FOLKS, NOW THAT EVERYONE'S HERE INCLUDING THE PHOTOGRAPHER- LET'S START SMASHING SUPERSTITIONS!
AS THE LEADING ACTOR--- AHEM- I WILL BEGIN THE PROCEEDINGS!
WALKING UNDER A LADDER IS THE FIRST SUPERSTITION THAT IS VIOLATED!
BAD BUSINESS.. GOING UNDER LADDERS--
HA! HA! YOU HAVE UNSUSPECTED TALENT, FRED!

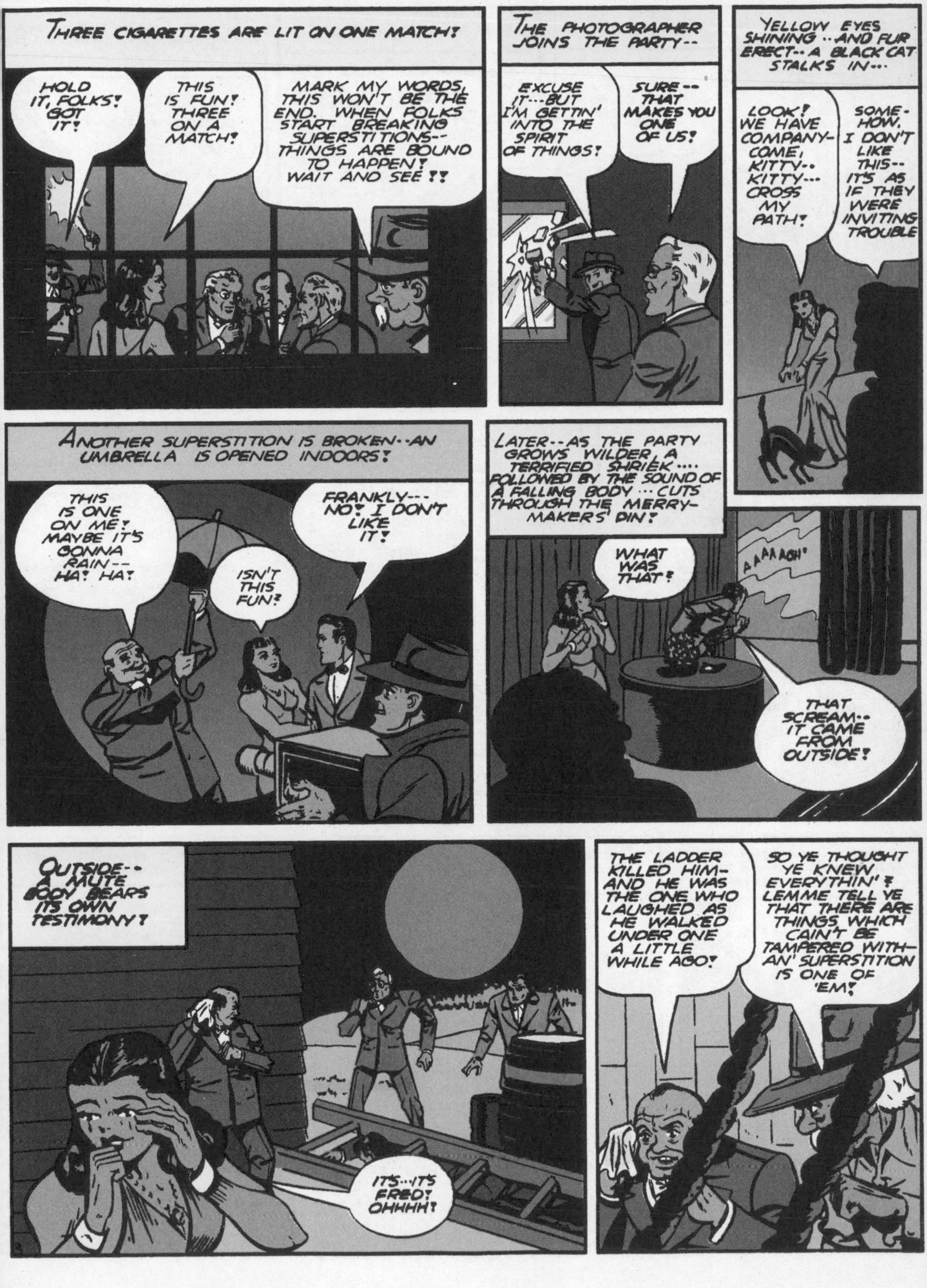
THREE CIGARETTES ARE LIT ON ONE MATCH!
HOLD IT, FOLKS! GOT IT!
THIS IS FUN! THREE ON A MATCH!
MARK MY WORDS, THIS WON'T BE THE END. WHEN FOLKS START BREAKING SUPERSTITIONS-- THINGS ARE BOUND TO HAPPEN! WAIT AND SEE !!
THE PHOTOGRAPHER JOINS THE PARTY--
EXCUSE IT---BUT I'M GETTIN' INTO THE SPIRIT OF THINGS!
SURE-- THAT MAKES YOU ONE OF US!
YELLOW EYES SHINING ..AND FUR ERECT-- A BLACK CAT STALKS IN...
LOOK! WE HAVE COMPANY-COME, KITTY-. KITTY--- CROSS MY PATH!
SOME-HOW, I DON'T LIKE THIS-- IT'S AS IF THEY WERE INVITING TROUBLE
ANOTHER SUPERSTITION IS BROKEN--AN UMBRELLA IS OPENED INDOORS!
THIS IS ONE ON ME! MAYBE IT'S GONNA RAIN-- HA! HA!
ISN'T THIS FUN?
FRANKLY--- NO! I DON'T LIKE IT!
LATER--AS THE PARTY GROWS WILDER, A TERRIFIED SHRIEK.... FOLLOWED BY THE SOUND OF A FALLING BODY ... CUTS THROUGH THE MERRY-MAKERS' DIN!
WHAT WAS THAT?
AAAAAGH!
THAT SCREAM-- IT CAME FROM OUTSIDE!
OUTSIDE-- A MUTE BODY BEARS ITS OWN TESTIMONY!
IT'S...IT'S FRED! OHHHH!
THE LADDER KILLED HIM- AND HE WAS THE ONE WHO LAUGHED AS HE WALKED UNDER ONE A LITTLE WHILE AGO!
SO YE THOUGHT YE KNEW EVERYTHIN'? LEMME TELL YE THAT THERE ARE THINGS WHICH CAIN'T BE TAMPERED WITH- AN' SUPERSTITION IS ONE OF 'EM!

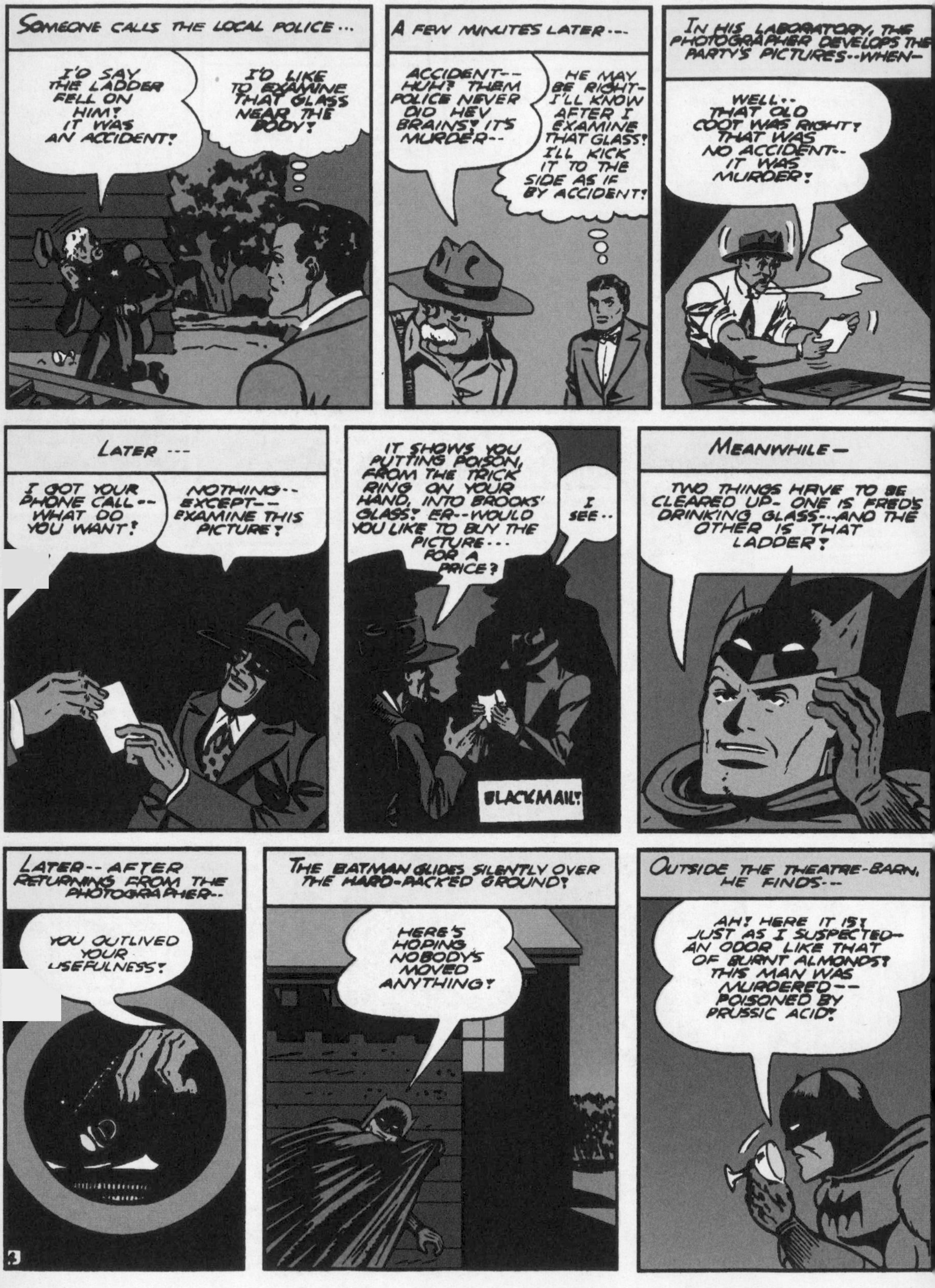
SOMEONE CALLS THE LOCAL POLICE...
I'D SAY THE LADDER FELL ON HIM! IT WAS AN ACCIDENT!
I'D LIKE TO EXAMINE THAT GLASS NEAR THE BODY!
A FEW MINUTES LATER---
ACCIDENT-- HUH? THEM POLICE NEVER DID HEV BRAINS! IT'S MURDER--
HE MAY BE RIGHT- I'LL KNOW AFTER I EXAMINE THAT GLASS! I'LL KICK IT TO THE SIDE AS IF BY ACCIDENT!
IN HIS LABORATORY, THE PHOTOGRAPHER DEVELOPS THE PARTY'S PICTURES--WHEN-
WELL.. THAT OLD COOT WAS RIGHT! THAT WAS NO ACCIDENT-- IT WAS MURDER!
LATER ---
I GOT YOUR PHONE CALL-- WHAT DO YOU WANT!
NOTHING-- EXCEPT-- EXAMINE THIS PICTURE!
IT SHOWS YOU PUTTING POISON, FROM THE TRICK RING ON YOUR HAND, INTO BROOKS' GLASS! ER--WOULD YOU LIKE TO BUY THE PICTURE--- FOR A PRICE?
I SEE--
BLACKMAIL!
MEANWHILE-
TWO THINGS HAVE TO BE CLEARED UP- ONE IS FRED'S DRINKING GLASS--AND THE OTHER IS THAT LADDER!
LATER-- AFTER RETURNING FROM THE PHOTOGRAPHER--
YOU OUTLIVED YOUR USEFULNESS!
THE BATMAN GLIDES SILENTLY OVER THE HARD-PACKED GROUND!
HERE'S HOPING NOBODY'S MOVED ANYTHING!
OUTSIDE THE THEATRE-BARN, HE FINDS--
AH! HERE IT IS! JUST AS I SUSPECTED- AN ODOR LIKE THAT OF BURNT ALMONDS! THIS MAN WAS MURDERED-- POISONED BY PRUSSIC ACID!
4

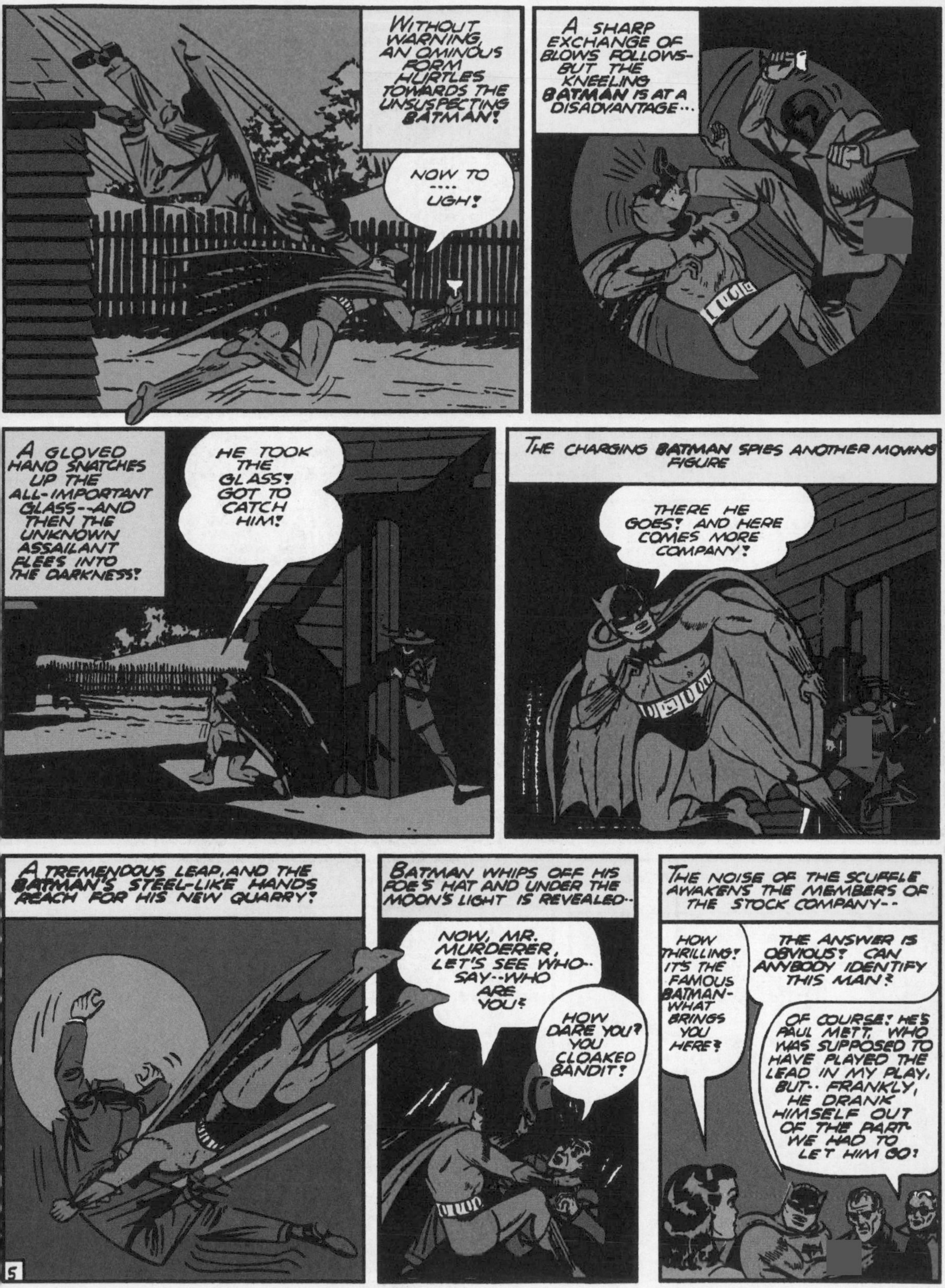
WITHOUT WARNING, AN OMINOUS FORM HURTLES TOWARDS THE UNSUSPECTING BATMAN!
NOW TO .... UGH!
A SHARP EXCHANGE OF BLOWS FOLLOWS-BUT THE KNEELING BATMAN IS AT A DISADVANTAGE...
A GLOVED HAND SNATCHES UP THE ALL-IMPORTANT GLASS--AND THEN THE UNKNOWN ASSAILANT FLEES INTO THE DARKNESS!
HE TOOK THE GLASS! GOT TO CATCH HIM!
THE CHARGING BATMAN SPIES ANOTHER MOVING FIGURE
THERE HE GOES! AND HERE COMES MORE COMPANY!
A TREMENDOUS LEAP, AND THE BATMAN'S STEEL-LIKE HANDS REACH FOR HIS NEW QUARRY!
5
BATMAN WHIPS OFF HIS FOE'S HAT AND UNDER THE MOON'S LIGHT IS REVEALED--
NOW, MR. MURDERER, LET'S SEE WHO-- SAY--WHO ARE YOU?
HOW DARE YOU? YOU CLOAKED BANDIT!
THE NOISE OF THE SCUFFLE AWAKENS THE MEMBERS OF THE STOCK COMPANY--
HOW THRILLING! IT'S THE FAMOUS BATMAN-WHAT BRINGS YOU HERE?
THE ANSWER IS OBVIOUS! CAN ANYBODY IDENTIFY THIS MAN?
OF COURSE! HE'S PAUL METT, WHO WAS SUPPOSED TO HAVE PLAYED THE LEAD IN MY PLAY, BUT-- FRANKLY, HE DRANK HIMSELF OUT OF THE PART- WE HAD TO LET HIM GO!

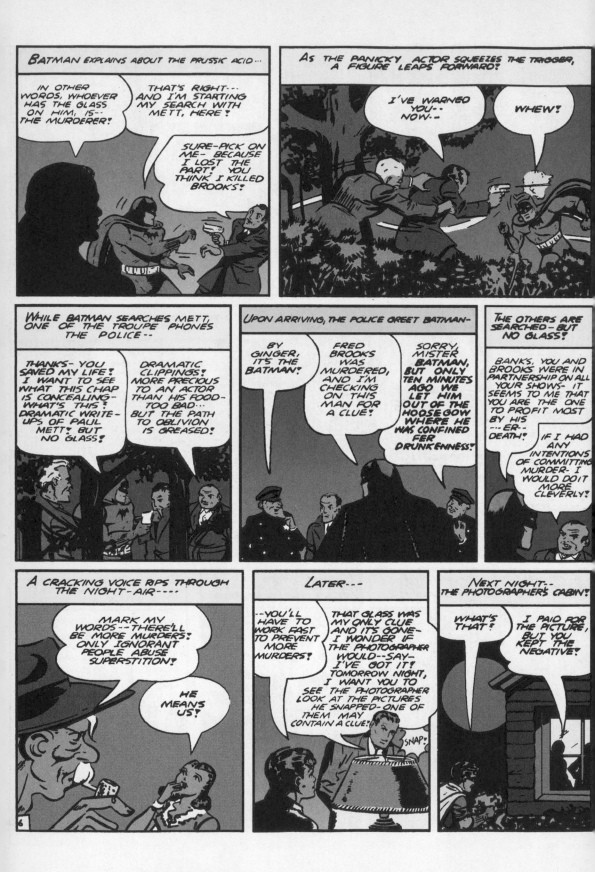

Panel 1 — caption: BATMAN EXPLAINS ABOUT THE PRUSSIC ACID...
- IN OTHER WORDS, WHOEVER HAS THE GLASS ON HIM, IS-- THE MURDERER!
- THAT'S RIGHT-- AND I'M STARTING MY SEARCH WITH METT, HERE!
- SURE-PICK ON ME- BECAUSE I LOST THE PART! YOU THINK I KILLED BROOKS!

Panel 2 — caption: AS THE PANICKY ACTOR SQUEEZES THE TRIGGER, A FIGURE LEAPS FORWARD!
- I'VE WARNED YOU-- NOW--
- WHEW!

Panel 3 — caption: WHILE BATMAN SEARCHES METT, ONE OF THE TROUPE PHONES THE POLICE--
- THANKS- YOU SAVED MY LIFE! I WANT TO SEE WHAT THIS CHAP IS CONCEALING- WHAT'S THIS? DRAMATIC WRITE-UPS OF PAUL METT! BUT NO GLASS!
- DRAMATIC CLIPPINGS! MORE PRECIOUS TO AN ACTOR THAN HIS FOOD-- TOO BAD-- BUT THE PATH TO OBLIVION IS GREASED!

Panel 4 — caption: UPON ARRIVING, THE POLICE GREET BATMAN--
- BY GINGER, IT'S THE BATMAN!
- FRED BROOKS WAS MURDERED, AND I'M CHECKING ON THIS MAN FOR A CLUE!
- SORRY, MISTER BATMAN, BUT ONLY TEN MINUTES AGO WE LET HIM OUT OF THE HOOSEGOW WHERE HE WAS CONFINED FER DRUNKENNESS!

Panel 5 — caption: THE OTHERS ARE SEARCHED- BUT NO GLASS!
- BANKS, YOU AND BROOKS WERE IN PARTNERSHIP ON ALL YOUR SHOWS- IT SEEMS TO ME THAT YOU ARE THE ONE TO PROFIT MOST BY HIS --ER-- DEATH!
- IF I HAD ANY INTENTIONS OF COMMITTING MURDER- I WOULD DO IT MORE CLEVERLY!

Panel 6 — caption: A CRACKING VOICE RIPS THROUGH THE NIGHT-AIR----
- MARK MY WORDS --THERE'LL BE MORE MURDERS! ONLY IGNORANT PEOPLE ABUSE SUPERSTITION!
- HE MEANS US!

Panel 7 — caption: LATER---
- --YOU'LL HAVE TO WORK FAST TO PREVENT MORE MURDERS!
- THAT GLASS WAS MY ONLY CLUE AND IT'S GONE- I WONDER IF THE PHOTOGRAPHER WOULD--SAY- I'VE GOT IT! TOMORROW NIGHT, I WANT YOU TO SEE THE PHOTOGRAPHER LOOK AT THE PICTURES HE SNAPPED- ONE OF THEM MAY CONTAIN A CLUE!
- SNAP!

Panel 8 — caption: NEXT NIGHT-- THE PHOTOGRAPHER'S CABIN!
- WHAT'S THAT?
- I PAID FOR THE PICTURE, BUT YOU KEPT THE NEGATIVE!

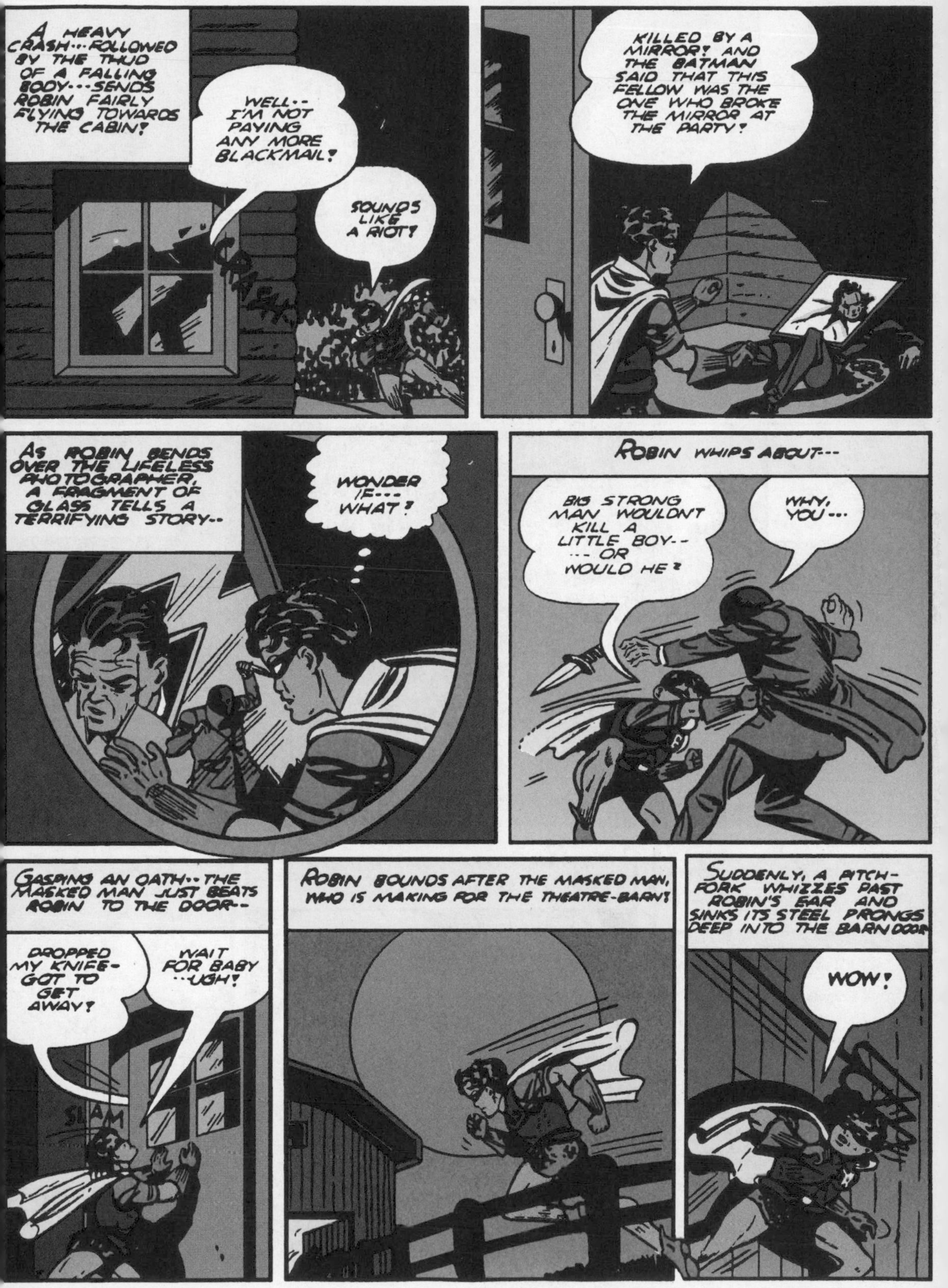
A HEAVY CRASH...FOLLOWED BY THE THUD OF A FALLING BODY---SENDS ROBIN FAIRLY FLYING TOWARDS THE CABIN!
WELL-- I'M NOT PAYING ANY MORE BLACKMAIL!
CRASH
SOUNDS LIKE A RIOT!
KILLED BY A MIRROR! AND THE BATMAN SAID THAT THIS FELLOW WAS THE ONE WHO BROKE THE MIRROR AT THE PARTY!
AS ROBIN BENDS OVER THE LIFELESS PHOTOGRAPHER, A FRAGMENT OF GLASS TELLS A TERRIFYING STORY--
WONDER IF--- WHAT?
ROBIN WHIPS ABOUT---
BIG STRONG MAN WOULDN'T KILL A LITTLE BOY-- --- OR WOULD HE?
WHY, YOU---
GASPING AN OATH--THE MASKED MAN JUST BEATS ROBIN TO THE DOOR--
DROPPED MY KNIFE-GOT TO GET AWAY!
WAIT FOR BABY ---UGH!
SLAM
ROBIN BOUNDS AFTER THE MASKED MAN, WHO IS MAKING FOR THE THEATRE-BARN!
SUDDENLY, A PITCH-FORK WHIZZES PAST ROBIN'S EAR AND SINKS ITS STEEL PRONGS DEEP INTO THE BARN DOOR
WOW!

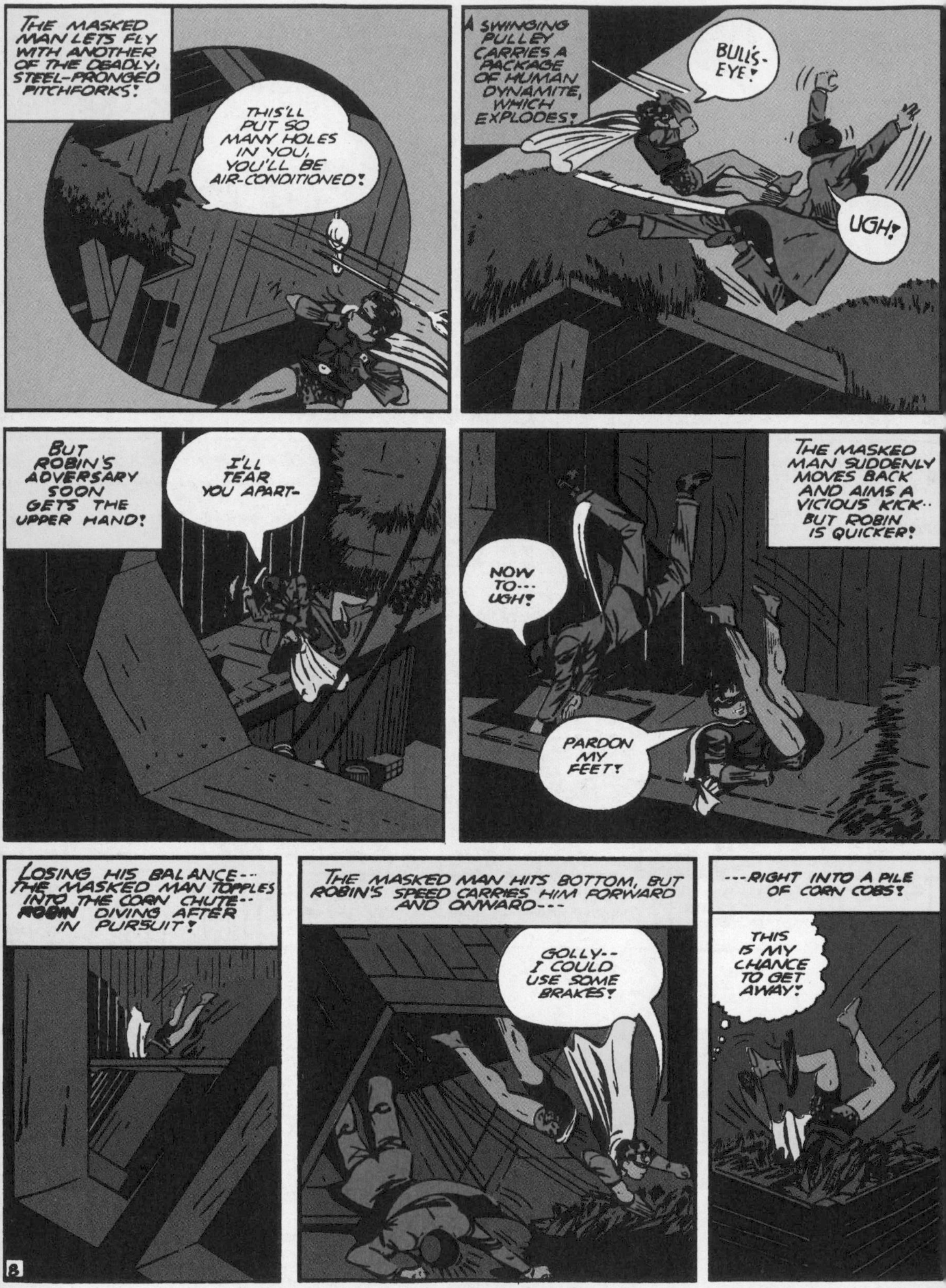
THE MASKED MAN LETS FLY WITH ANOTHER OF THE DEADLY, STEEL-PRONGED PITCHFORKS!
THIS'LL PUT SO MANY HOLES IN YOU, YOU'LL BE AIR-CONDITIONED!
A SWINGING PULLEY CARRIES A PACKAGE OF HUMAN DYNAMITE, WHICH EXPLODES!
BULL'S-EYE!
UGH!
BUT ROBIN'S ADVERSARY SOON GETS THE UPPER HAND!
I'LL TEAR YOU APART-
THE MASKED MAN SUDDENLY MOVES BACK AND AIMS A VICIOUS KICK.. BUT ROBIN IS QUICKER!
NOW TO--- UGH!
PARDON MY FEET!
LOSING HIS BALANCE-- THE MASKED MAN TOPPLES INTO THE CORN CHUTE-- ROBIN DIVING AFTER IN PURSUIT!
8
THE MASKED MAN HITS BOTTOM, BUT ROBIN'S SPEED CARRIES HIM FORWARD AND ONWARD---
GOLLY-- I COULD USE SOME BRAKES!
---RIGHT INTO A PILE OF CORN COBS!
THIS IS MY CHANCE TO GET AWAY!

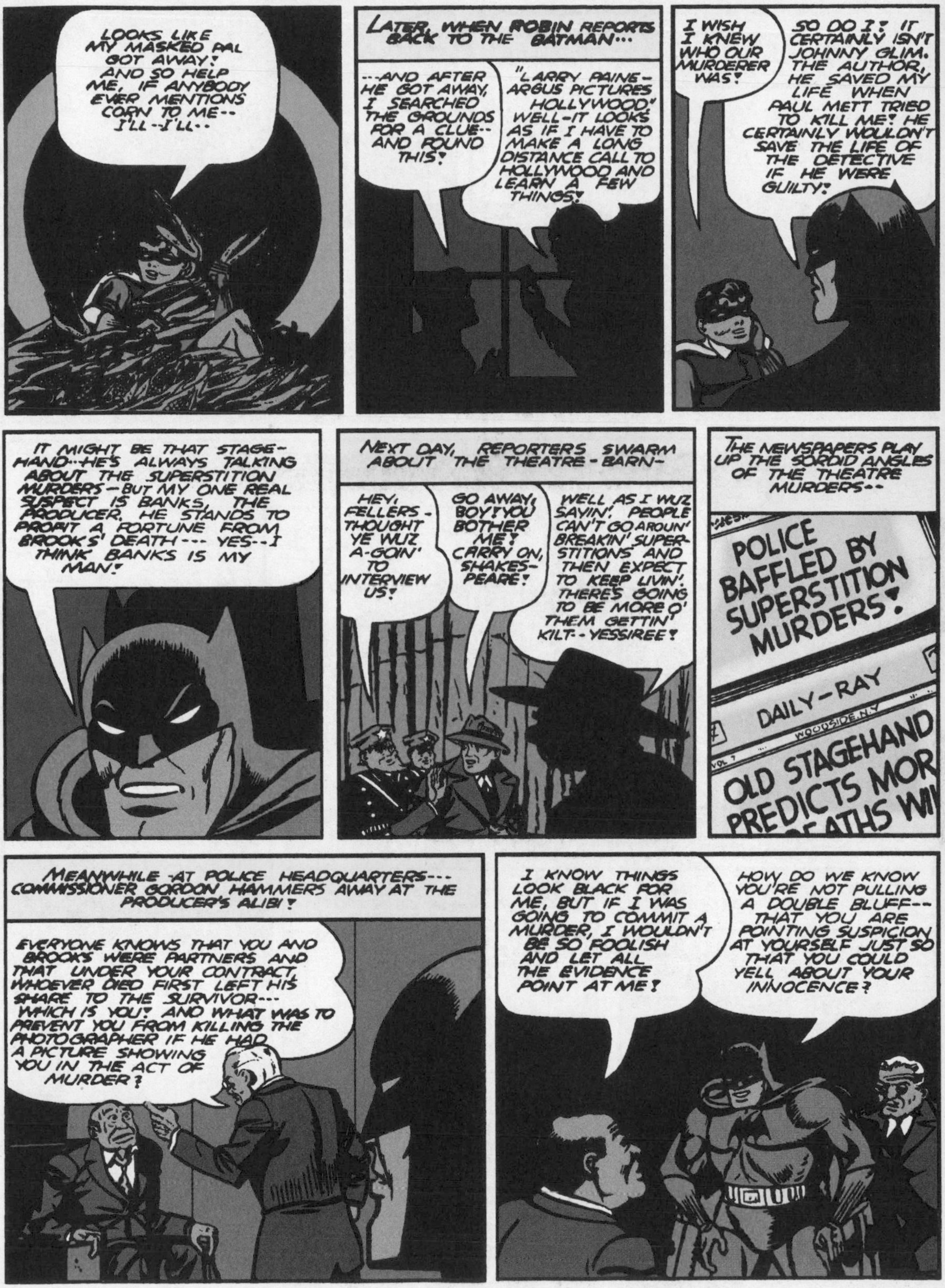
LOOKS LIKE MY MASKED PAL GOT AWAY! AND SO HELP ME, IF ANYBODY EVER MENTIONS CORN TO ME-- I'LL--I'LL--
LATER, WHEN ROBIN REPORTS BACK TO THE BATMAN...
--AND AFTER HE GOT AWAY, I SEARCHED THE GROUNDS FOR A CLUE--AND FOUND THIS!
"LARRY PAINE-ARGUS PICTURES HOLLYWOOD" WELL-IT LOOKS AS IF I HAVE TO MAKE A LONG DISTANCE CALL TO HOLLYWOOD AND LEARN A FEW THINGS!
I WISH I KNEW WHO OUR MURDERER WAS!
SO DO I! IT CERTAINLY ISN'T JOHNNY GLIM, THE AUTHOR. HE SAVED MY LIFE WHEN PAUL METT TRIED TO KILL ME! HE CERTAINLY WOULDN'T SAVE THE LIFE OF THE DETECTIVE IF HE WERE GUILTY!
IT MIGHT BE THAT STAGE-HAND--HE'S ALWAYS TALKING ABOUT THE SUPERSTITION MURDERS--BUT MY ONE REAL SUSPECT IS BANKS, THE PRODUCER. HE STANDS TO PROFIT A FORTUNE FROM BROOK'S' DEATH--- YES--I THINK BANKS IS MY MAN!
NEXT DAY, REPORTERS SWARM ABOUT THE THEATRE-BARN-
HEY, FELLERS-THOUGHT YE WUZ A-GOIN' TO INTERVIEW US!
GO AWAY, BOY! YOU BOTHER ME! CARRY ON, SHAKES-PEARE!
WELL AS I WUZ SAYIN', PEOPLE CAN'T GO AROUN' BREAKIN' SUPER-STITIONS AND THEN EXPECT TO KEEP LIVIN'. THERE'S GOING TO BE MORE O' THEM GETTIN' KILT--YESSIREE!
THE NEWSPAPERS PLAY UP THE SORDID ANGLES OF THE THEATRE MURDERS--
POLICE BAFFLED BY SUPERSTITION MURDERS!
DAILY-RAY
WOODSIDE, N.Y.
OLD STAGEHAND PREDICTS MOR
MEANWHILE-AT POLICE HEADQUARTERS---COMMISSIONER GORDON HAMMERS AWAY AT THE PRODUCER'S ALIBI!
EVERYONE KNOWS THAT YOU AND BROOKS WERE PARTNERS AND THAT UNDER YOUR CONTRACT, WHOEVER DIED FIRST LEFT HIS SHARE TO THE SURVIVOR---WHICH IS YOU! AND WHAT WAS TO PREVENT YOU FROM KILLING THE PHOTOGRAPHER IF HE HAD A PICTURE SHOWING YOU IN THE ACT OF MURDER?
I KNOW THINGS LOOK BLACK FOR ME, BUT IF I WAS GOING TO COMMIT A MURDER, I WOULDN'T BE SO FOOLISH AND LET ALL THE EVIDENCE POINT AT ME!
HOW DO WE KNOW YOU'RE NOT PULLING A DOUBLE BLUFF--THAT YOU ARE POINTING SUSPICION AT YOURSELF JUST SO THAT YOU COULD YELL ABOUT YOUR INNOCENCE?

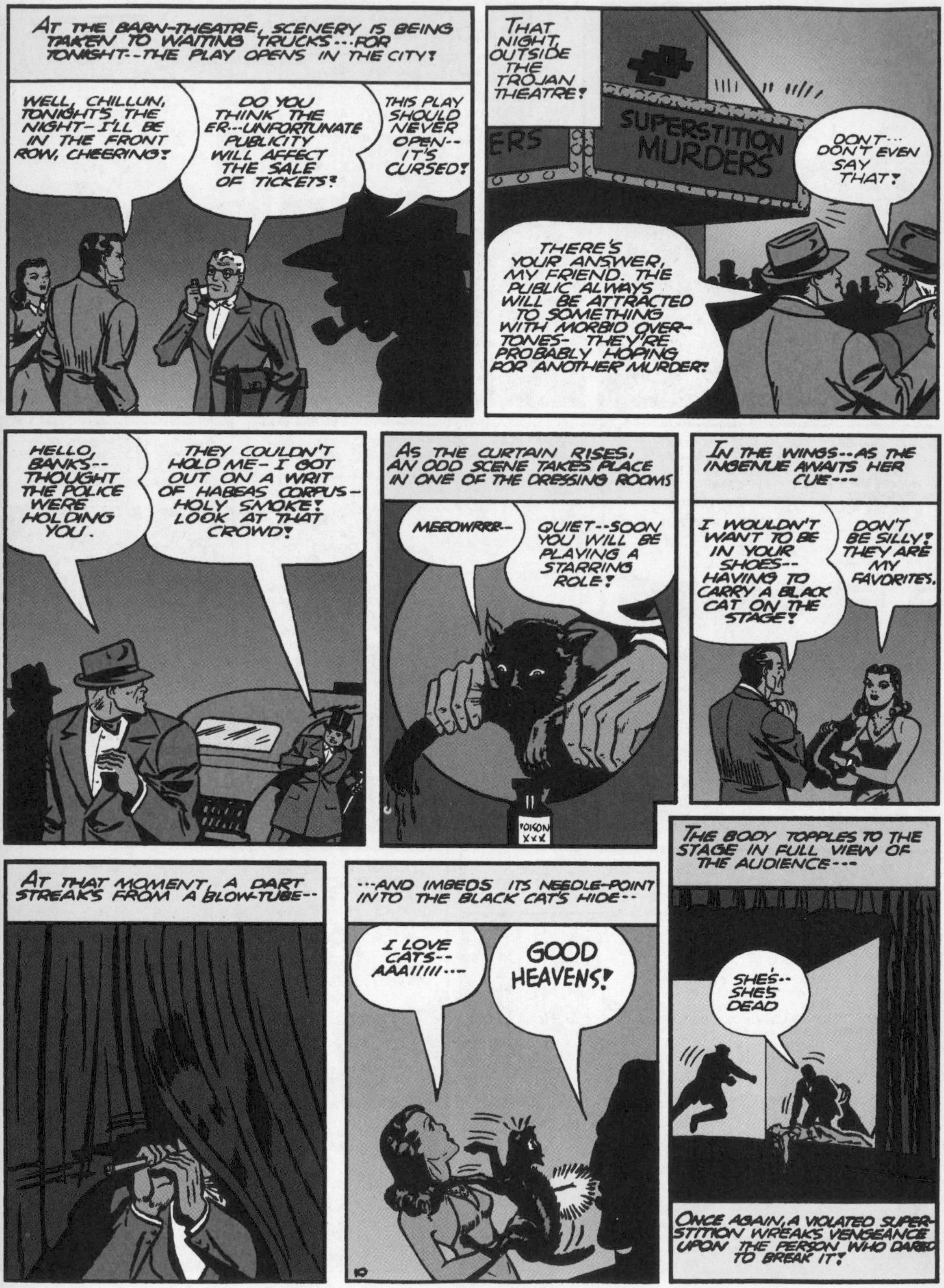
AT THE BARN-THEATRE, SCENERY IS BEING TAKEN TO WAITING TRUCKS---FOR TONIGHT--THE PLAY OPENS IN THE CITY!
WELL, CHILLUN, TONIGHT'S THE NIGHT- I'LL BE IN THE FRONT ROW, CHEERING!
DO YOU THINK THE ER---UNFORTUNATE PUBLICITY WILL AFFECT THE SALE OF TICKETS?
THIS PLAY SHOULD NEVER OPEN-- IT'S CURSED!
THAT NIGHT, OUTSIDE THE TROJAN THEATRE!
SUPERSTITION MURDERS
DON'T--- DON'T EVEN SAY THAT!
THERE'S YOUR ANSWER, MY FRIEND. THE PUBLIC ALWAYS WILL BE ATTRACTED TO SOMETHING WITH MORBID OVERTONES- THEY'RE PROBABLY HOPING FOR ANOTHER MURDER!
HELLO, BANKS-- THOUGHT THE POLICE WERE HOLDING YOU.
THEY COULDN'T HOLD ME- I GOT OUT ON A WRIT OF HABEAS CORPUS- HOLY SMOKE! LOOK AT THAT CROWD!
AS THE CURTAIN RISES, AN ODD SCENE TAKES PLACE IN ONE OF THE DRESSING ROOMS
MEEOWRRR--
QUIET--SOON YOU WILL BE PLAYING A STARRING ROLE!
POISON XXX
IN THE WINGS--AS THE INGENUE AWAITS HER CUE---
I WOULDN'T WANT TO BE IN YOUR SHOES-- HAVING TO CARRY A BLACK CAT ON THE STAGE!
DON'T BE SILLY! THEY ARE MY FAVORITES.
AT THAT MOMENT, A DART STREAKS FROM A BLOW-TUBE--
---AND IMBEDS ITS NEEDLE-POINT INTO THE BLACK CAT'S HIDE--
I LOVE CATS-- AAAIIIII---
GOOD HEAVENS!
THE BODY TOPPLES TO THE STAGE IN FULL VIEW OF THE AUDIENCE---
SHE'S-- SHE'S DEAD
ONCE AGAIN, A VIOLATED SUPERSTITION WREAKS VENGEANCE UPON THE PERSON WHO DARED TO BREAK IT!

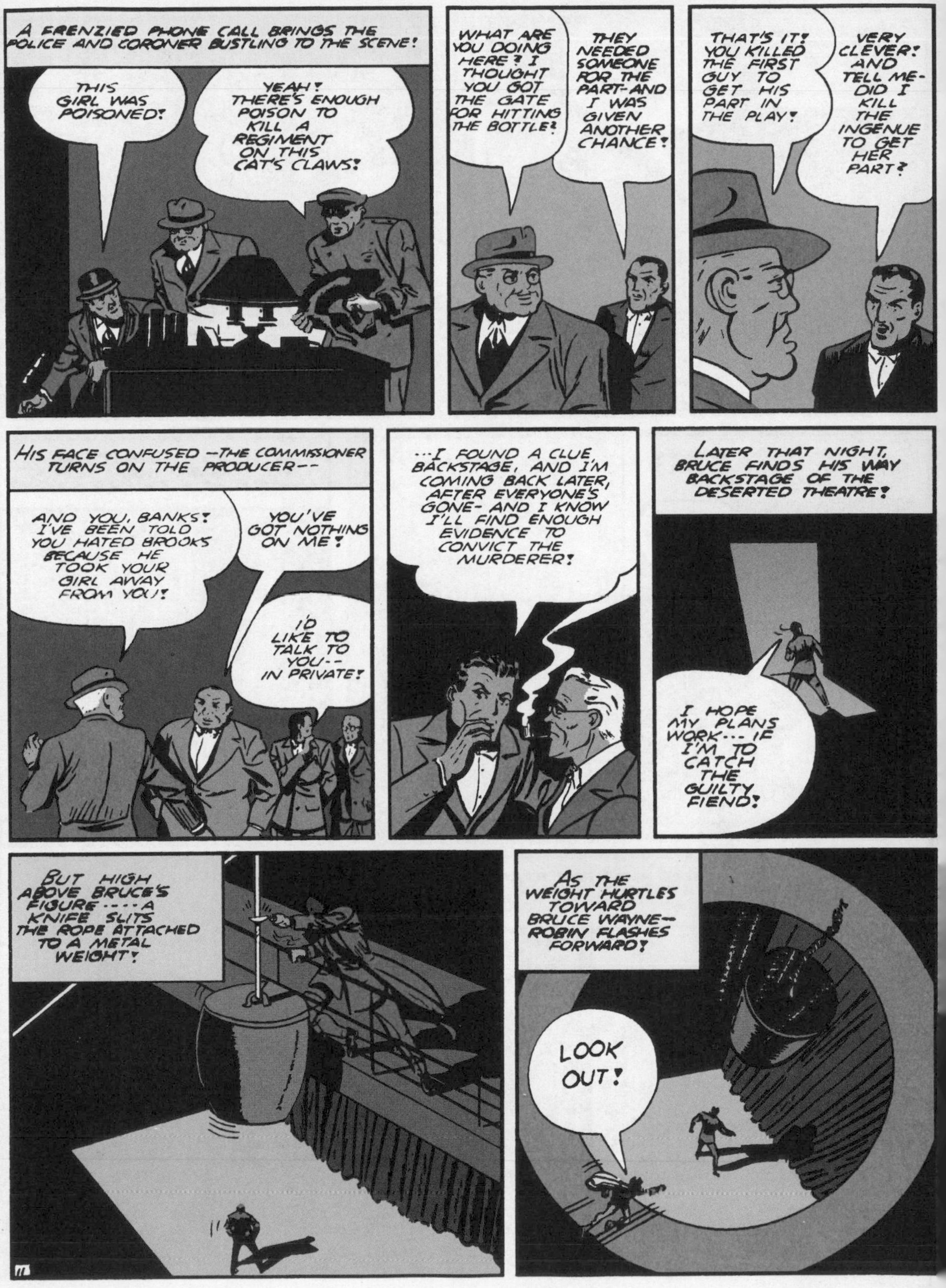
A FRENZIED PHONE CALL BRINGS THE POLICE AND CORONER BUSTLING TO THE SCENE!
THIS GIRL WAS POISONED!
YEAH! THERE'S ENOUGH POISON TO KILL A REGIMENT ON THIS CAT'S CLAWS!
WHAT ARE YOU DOING HERE? I THOUGHT YOU GOT THE GATE FOR HITTING THE BOTTLE?
THEY NEEDED SOMEONE FOR THE PART- AND I WAS GIVEN ANOTHER CHANCE!
THAT'S IT! YOU KILLED THE FIRST GUY TO GET HIS PART IN THE PLAY!
VERY CLEVER! AND TELL ME- DID I KILL THE INGENUE TO GET HER PART?
HIS FACE CONFUSED --THE COMMISSIONER TURNS ON THE PRODUCER--
AND YOU, BANKS! I'VE BEEN TOLD YOU HATED BROOKS BECAUSE HE TOOK YOUR GIRL AWAY FROM YOU!
YOU'VE GOT NOTHING ON ME!
I'D LIKE TO TALK TO YOU-- IN PRIVATE!
...I FOUND A CLUE BACKSTAGE, AND I'M COMING BACK LATER, AFTER EVERYONE'S GONE- AND I KNOW I'LL FIND ENOUGH EVIDENCE TO CONVICT THE MURDERER!
LATER THAT NIGHT, BRUCE FINDS HIS WAY BACKSTAGE OF THE DESERTED THEATRE!
I HOPE MY PLANS WORK--- IF I'M TO CATCH THE GUILTY FIEND!
BUT HIGH ABOVE BRUCE'S FIGURE ---- A KNIFE SLITS THE ROPE ATTACHED TO A METAL WEIGHT!
AS THE WEIGHT HURTLES TOWARD BRUCE WAYNE-- ROBIN FLASHES FORWARD!
LOOK OUT!
11

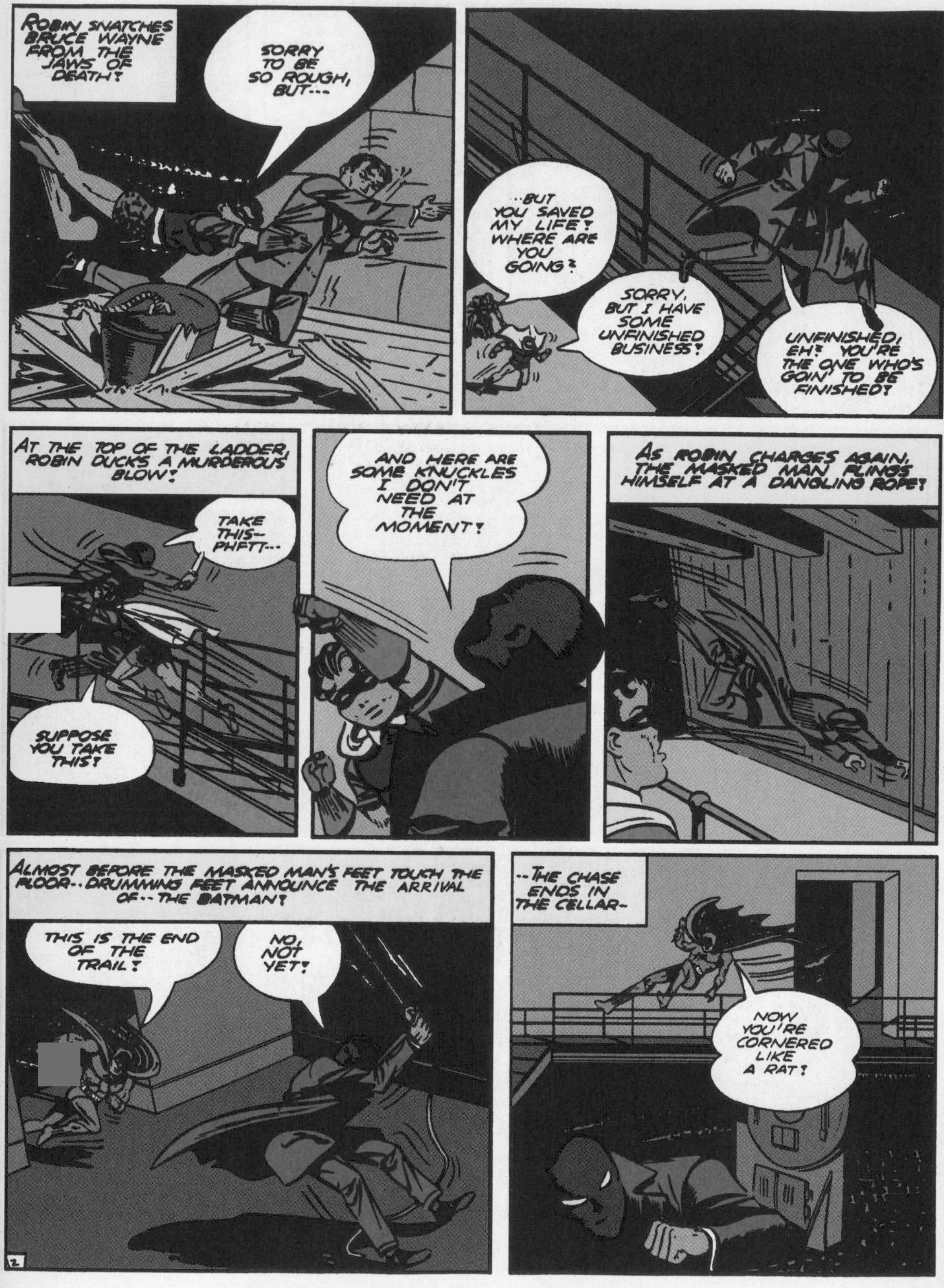
ROBIN SNATCHES BRUCE WAYNE FROM THE JAWS OF DEATH!
SORRY TO BE SO ROUGH, BUT...
...BUT YOU SAVED MY LIFE! WHERE ARE YOU GOING?
SORRY, BUT I HAVE SOME UNFINISHED BUSINESS!
UNFINISHED, EH? YOU'RE THE ONE WHO'S GOIN' TO BE FINISHED!
AT THE TOP OF THE LADDER, ROBIN DUCKS A MURDEROUS BLOW!
TAKE THIS-PHFTT...
SUPPOSE YOU TAKE THIS!
AND HERE ARE SOME KNUCKLES I DON'T NEED AT THE MOMENT!
AS ROBIN CHARGES AGAIN, THE MASKED MAN FLINGS HIMSELF AT A DANGLING ROPE!
ALMOST BEFORE THE MASKED MAN'S FEET TOUCH THE FLOOR.. DRUMMING FEET ANNOUNCE THE ARRIVAL OF..THE BATMAN!
THIS IS THE END OF THE TRAIL!
NO, NOT YET!
2
..THE CHASE ENDS IN THE CELLAR-
NOW YOU'RE CORNERED LIKE A RAT!

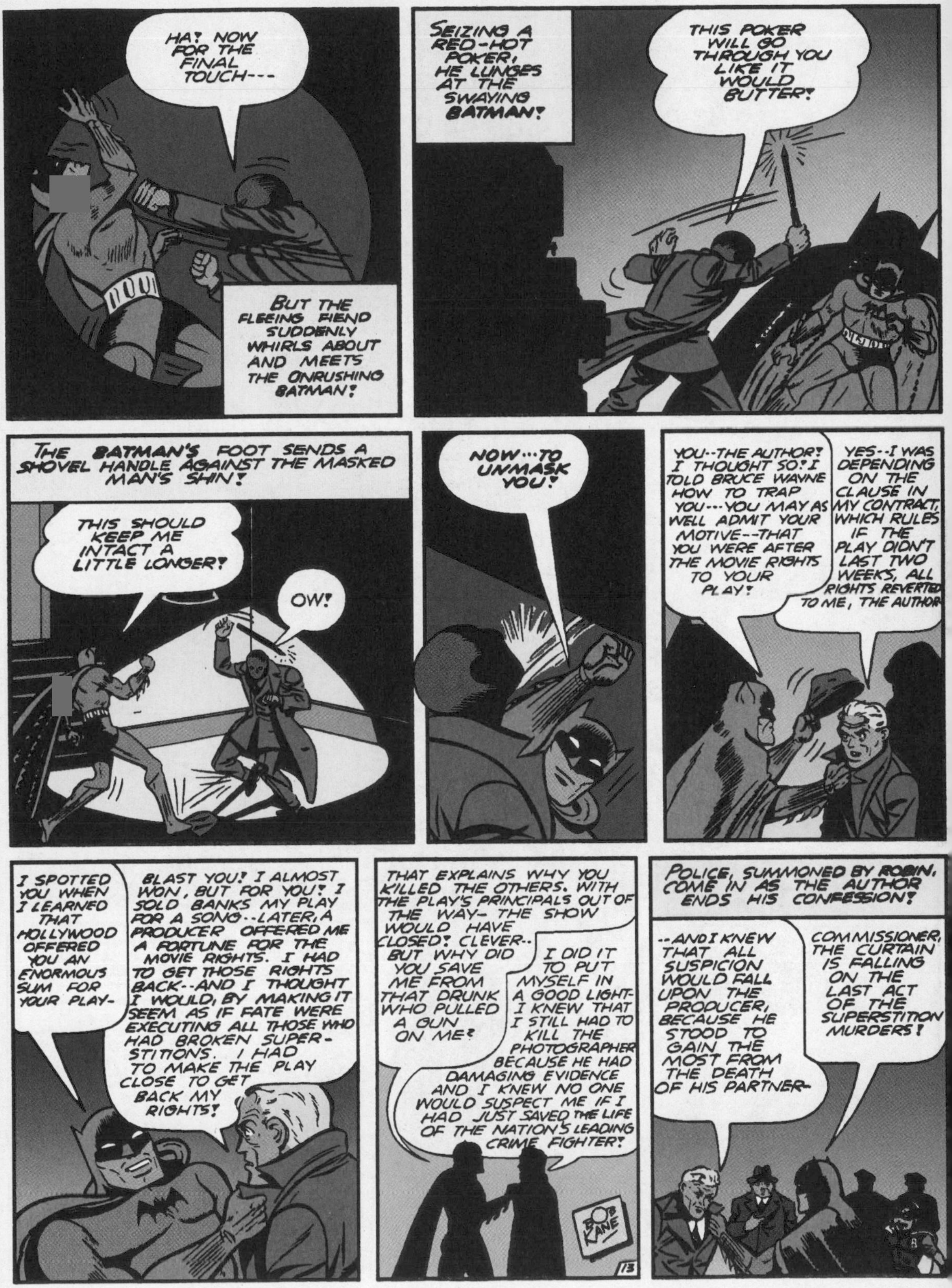
HA! NOW FOR THE FINAL TOUCH---
BUT THE FLEEING FIEND SUDDENLY WHIRLS ABOUT AND MEETS THE ONRUSHING BATMAN!
SEIZING A RED-HOT POKER, HE LUNGES AT THE SWAYING BATMAN!
THIS POKER WILL GO THROUGH YOU LIKE IT WOULD BUTTER!
THE BATMAN'S FOOT SENDS A SHOVEL HANDLE AGAINST THE MASKED MAN'S SHIN!
THIS SHOULD KEEP ME INTACT A LITTLE LONGER!
OW!
NOW...TO UNMASK YOU!
YOU--THE AUTHOR! I THOUGHT SO! I TOLD BRUCE WAYNE HOW TO TRAP YOU---YOU MAY AS WELL ADMIT YOUR MOTIVE--THAT YOU WERE AFTER THE MOVIE RIGHTS TO YOUR PLAY!
YES--I WAS DEPENDING ON THE CLAUSE IN MY CONTRACT, WHICH RULES IF THE PLAY DIDN'T LAST TWO WEEKS, ALL RIGHTS REVERTED TO ME, THE AUTHOR
I SPOTTED YOU WHEN I LEARNED THAT HOLLYWOOD OFFERED YOU AN ENORMOUS SUM FOR YOUR PLAY-
BLAST YOU! I ALMOST WON, BUT FOR YOU! I SOLD BANKS MY PLAY FOR A SONG--LATER, A PRODUCER OFFERED ME A FORTUNE FOR THE MOVIE RIGHTS. I HAD TO GET THOSE RIGHTS BACK--AND I THOUGHT I WOULD, BY MAKING IT SEEM AS IF FATE WERE EXECUTING ALL THOSE WHO HAD BROKEN SUPER-STITIONS. I HAD TO MAKE THE PLAY CLOSE TO GET BACK MY RIGHTS!
THAT EXPLAINS WHY YOU KILLED THE OTHERS. WITH THE PLAY'S PRINCIPALS OUT OF THE WAY- THE SHOW WOULD HAVE CLOSED! CLEVER.. BUT WHY DID YOU SAVE ME FROM THAT DRUNK WHO PULLED A GUN ON ME?
I DID IT TO PUT MYSELF IN A GOOD LIGHT- I KNEW THAT I STILL HAD TO KILL THE PHOTOGRAPHER BECAUSE HE HAD DAMAGING EVIDENCE AND I KNEW NO ONE WOULD SUSPECT ME IF I HAD JUST SAVED THE LIFE OF THE NATION'S LEADING CRIME FIGHTER!
BOB KANE
13
POLICE, SUMMONED BY ROBIN, COME IN AS THE AUTHOR ENDS HIS CONFESSION!
--AND I KNEW THAT ALL SUSPICION WOULD FALL UPON THE PRODUCER, BECAUSE HE STOOD TO GAIN THE MOST FROM THE DEATH OF HIS PARTNER-
COMMISSIONER, THE CURTAIN IS FALLING ON THE LAST ACT OF THE SUPERSTITION MURDERS!

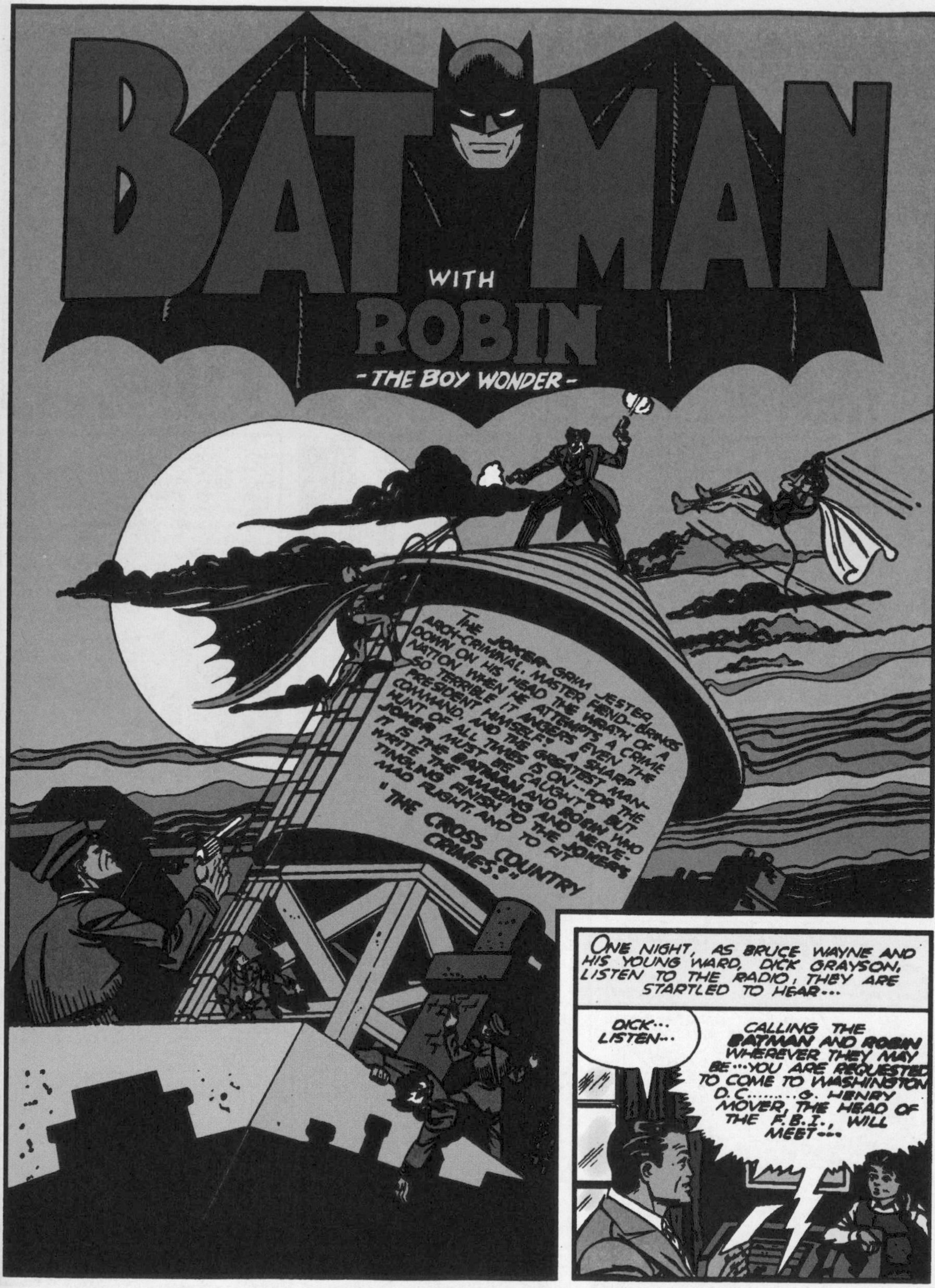
BATMAN
WITH
ROBIN
-THE BOY WONDER-
THE JOKER-GRIM JESTER, ARCH-CRIMINAL, MASTER FIEND--BRINGS DOWN ON HIS HEAD THE WRATH OF A NATION WHEN HE ATTEMPTS A CRIME SO TERRIBLE IT ANGERS EVEN THE PRESIDENT HIMSELF! A SHARP COMMAND, AND THE GREATEST MAN-HUNT OF ALL TIMES IS ON--FOR THE JOKER MUST BE CAUGHT! BUT IT IS THE BATMAN AND ROBIN WHO WRITE THE AMAZING AND NERVE-TINGLING FINISH TO THE JOKER'S MAD FLIGHT, AND TO FIT "THE CROSS COUNTRY CRIMES!"
ONE NIGHT, AS BRUCE WAYNE AND HIS YOUNG WARD, DICK GRAYSON, LISTEN TO THE RADIO, THEY ARE STARTLED TO HEAR...
DICK... LISTEN...
CALLING THE BATMAN AND ROBIN WHEREVER THEY MAY BE...YOU ARE REQUESTED TO COME TO WASHINGTON D.C.......G. HENRY MOVER, THE HEAD OF THE F.B.I., WILL MEET...

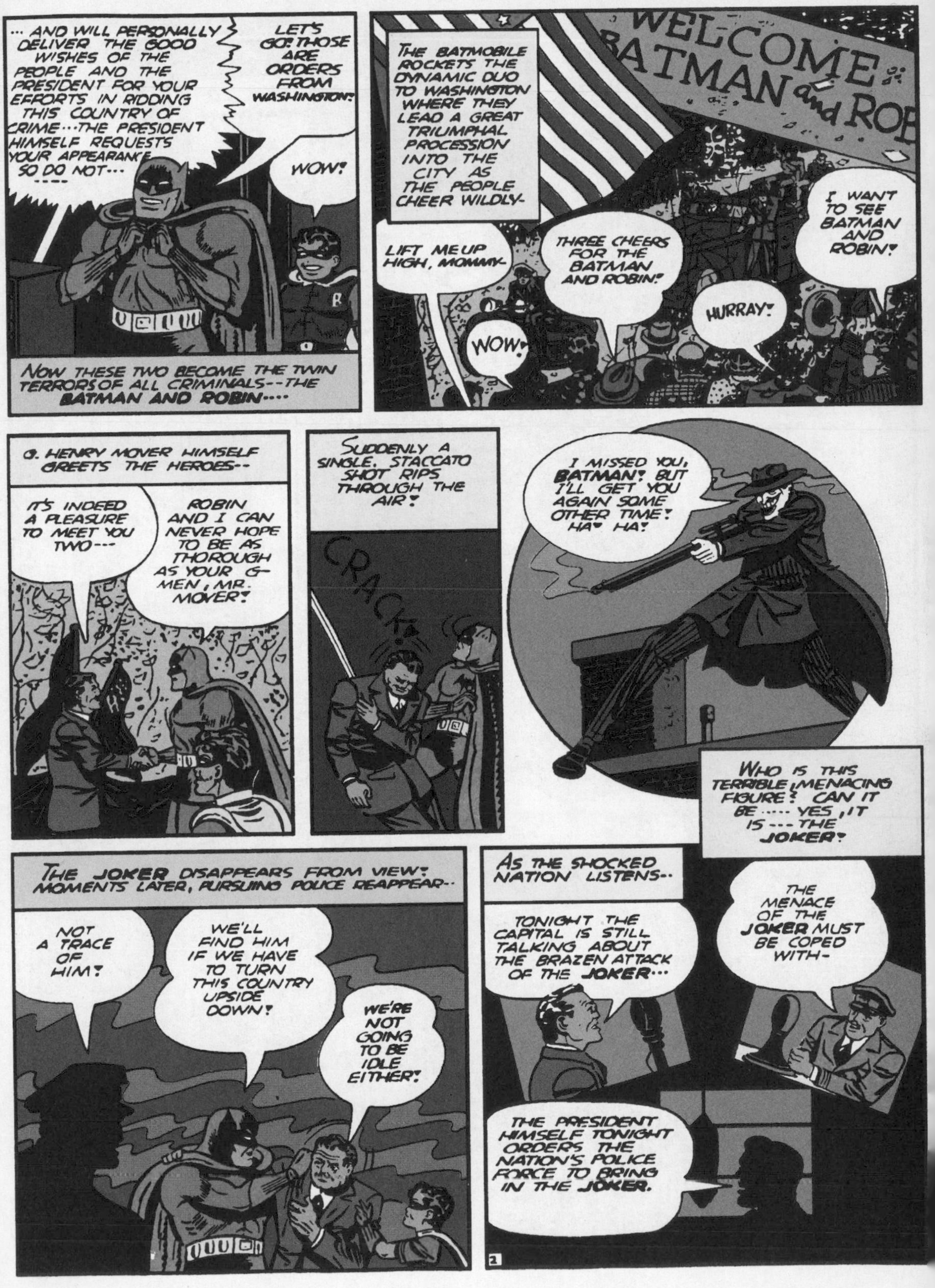

... AND WILL PERSONALLY DELIVER THE GOOD WISHES OF THE PEOPLE AND THE PRESIDENT FOR YOUR EFFORTS IN RIDDING THIS COUNTRY OF CRIME... THE PRESIDENT HIMSELF REQUESTS YOUR APPEARANCE SO DO NOT... ----
LET'S GO! THOSE ARE ORDERS FROM WASHINGTON!
WOW!
NOW THESE TWO BECOME THE TWIN TERRORS OF ALL CRIMINALS--THE BATMAN AND ROBIN....
THE BATMOBILE ROCKETS THE DYNAMIC DUO TO WASHINGTON WHERE THEY LEAD A GREAT TRIUMPHAL PROCESSION INTO THE CITY AS THE PEOPLE CHEER WILDLY-
WELCOME BATMAN and ROB
I WANT TO SEE BATMAN AND ROBIN!
LIFT ME UP HIGH, MOMMY-
THREE CHEERS FOR THE BATMAN AND ROBIN!
HURRAY!
WOW!
G. HENRY MOVER HIMSELF GREETS THE HEROES--
IT'S INDEED A PLEASURE TO MEET YOU TWO---
ROBIN AND I CAN NEVER HOPE TO BE AS THOROUGH AS YOUR G-MEN, MR. MOVER!
SUDDENLY A SINGLE, STACCATO SHOT RIPS THROUGH THE AIR!
CRACK!
I MISSED YOU, BATMAN! BUT I'LL GET YOU AGAIN SOME OTHER TIME! HA! HA!
WHO IS THIS TERRIBLE, MENACING FIGURE? CAN IT BE ..... YES, IT IS --- THE JOKER!
THE JOKER DISAPPEARS FROM VIEW! MOMENTS LATER, PURSUING POLICE REAPPEAR--
NOT A TRACE OF HIM!
WE'LL FIND HIM IF WE HAVE TO TURN THIS COUNTRY UPSIDE DOWN!
WE'RE NOT GOING TO BE IDLE EITHER!
AS THE SHOCKED NATION LISTENS--
TONIGHT THE CAPITAL IS STILL TALKING ABOUT THE BRAZEN ATTACK OF THE JOKER...
THE MENACE OF THE JOKER MUST BE COPED WITH-
THE PRESIDENT HIMSELF TONIGHT ORDERS THE NATION'S POLICE FORCE TO BRING IN THE JOKER.
2

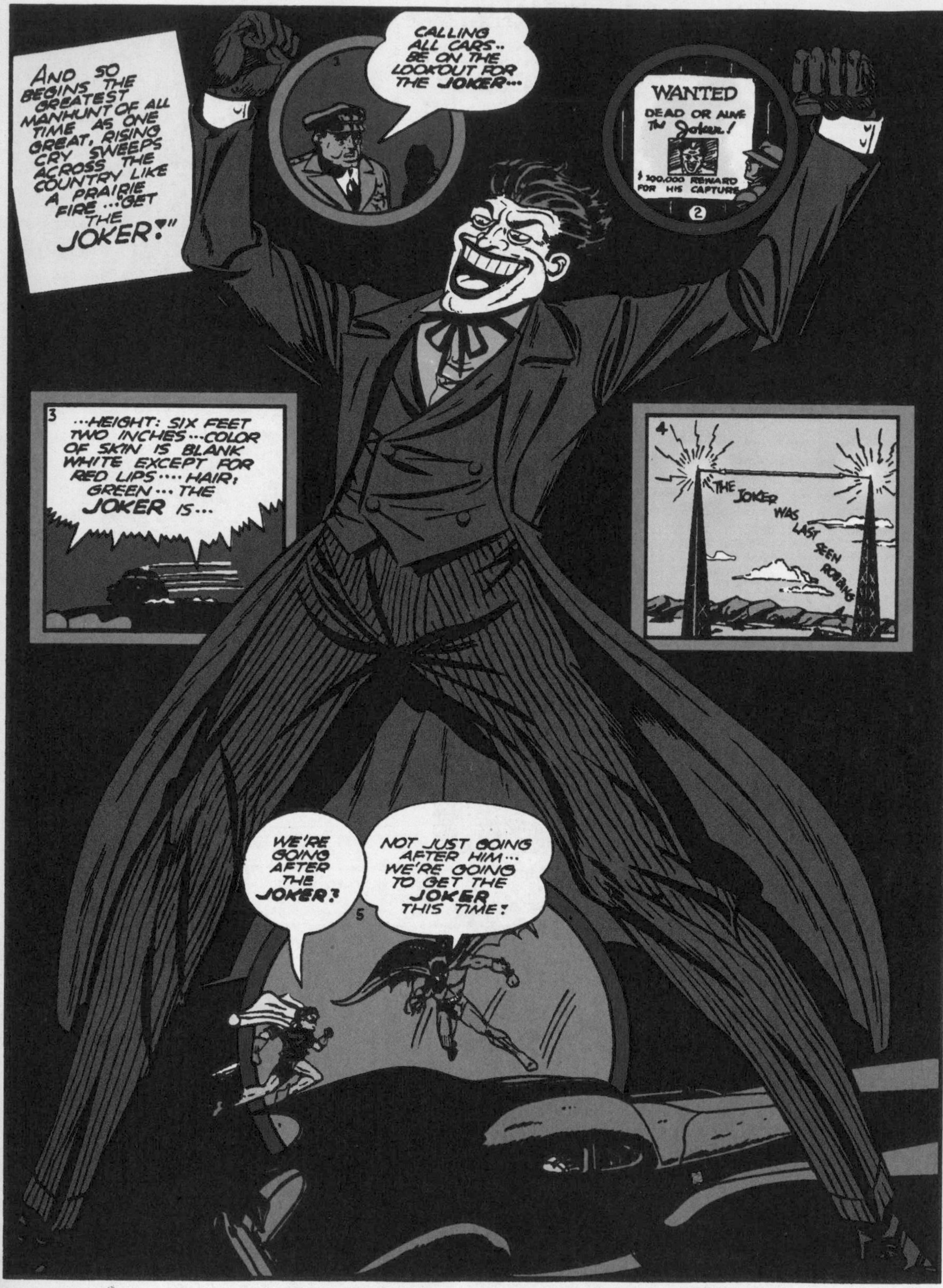
AND SO BEGINS THE GREATEST MANHUNT OF ALL TIME AS ONE GREAT, RISING CRY SWEEPS ACROSS THE COUNTRY LIKE A PRAIRIE FIRE ... "GET THE JOKER!"
CALLING ALL CARS.. BE ON THE LOOKOUT FOR THE JOKER...
WANTED
DEAD OR ALIVE
The Joker!
$100,000 REWARD
FOR HIS CAPTURE
...HEIGHT: SIX FEET TWO INCHES...COLOR OF SKIN IS BLANK WHITE EXCEPT FOR RED LIPS.... HAIR, GREEN... THE JOKER IS...
THE JOKER WAS LAST SEEN ROBBING
WE'RE GOING AFTER THE JOKER?
NOT JUST GOING AFTER HIM... WE'RE GOING TO GET THE JOKER THIS TIME!

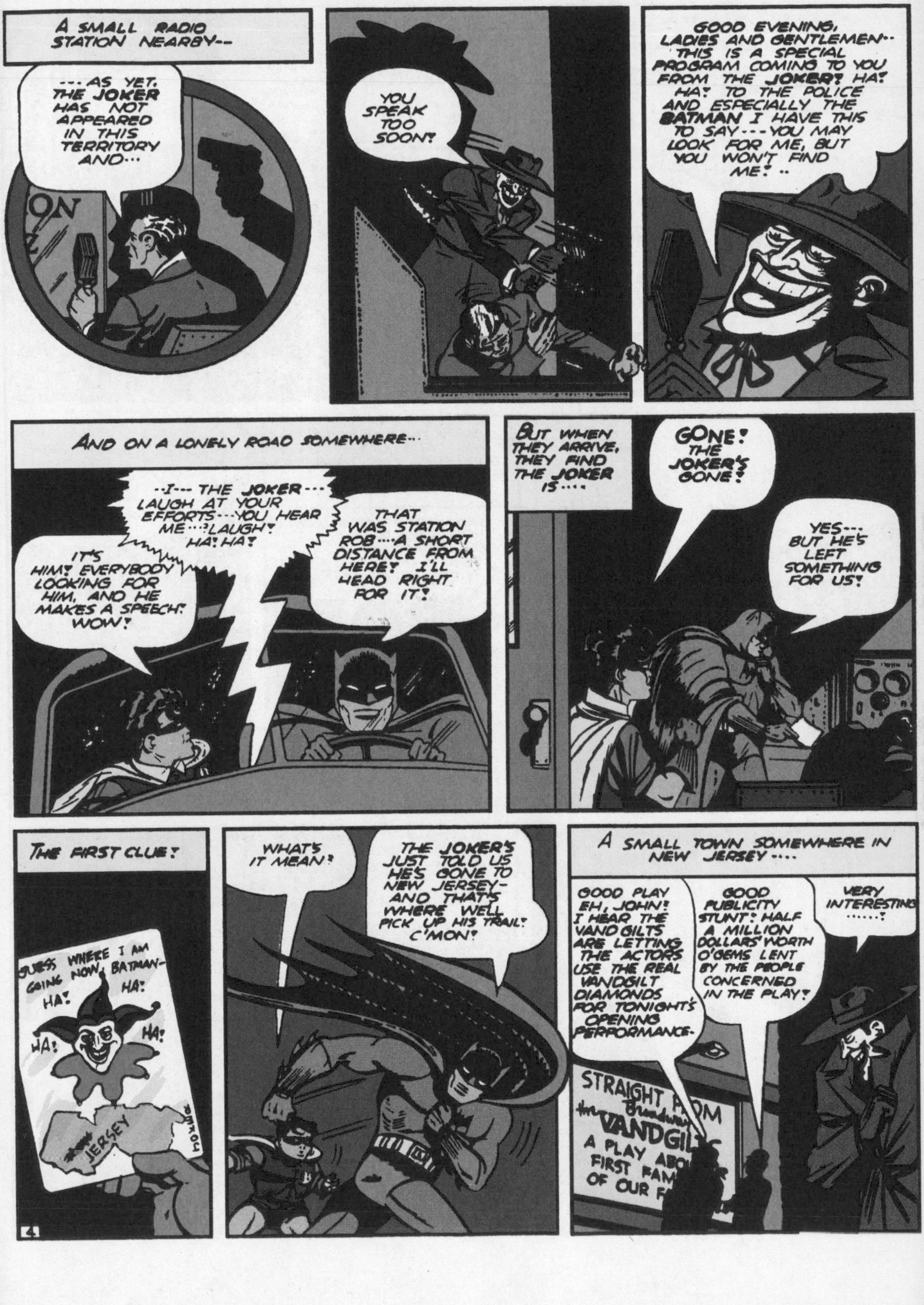
A SMALL RADIO STATION NEARBY--
--- AS YET, THE JOKER HAS NOT APPEARED IN THIS TERRITORY AND---
YOU SPEAK TOO SOON!
GOOD EVENING, LADIES AND GENTLEMEN-- THIS IS A SPECIAL PROGRAM COMING TO YOU FROM THE JOKER! HA! HA! TO THE POLICE AND ESPECIALLY THE BATMAN I HAVE THIS TO SAY---YOU MAY LOOK FOR ME, BUT YOU WON'T FIND ME! --
AND ON A LONELY ROAD SOMEWHERE--
--I--- THE JOKER--- LAUGH AT YOUR EFFORTS---YOU HEAR ME---LAUGH! HA! HA!
IT'S HIM! EVERYBODY LOOKING FOR HIM, AND HE MAKES A SPEECH! WOW!
THAT WAS STATION ROB---A SHORT DISTANCE FROM HERE! I'LL HEAD RIGHT FOR IT!
BUT WHEN THEY ARRIVE, THEY FIND THE JOKER IS----
GONE! THE JOKER'S GONE!
YES--- BUT HE'S LEFT SOMETHING FOR US!
THE FIRST CLUE!
GUESS WHERE I AM GOING NOW, BATMAN- HA! HA!
HA! HA!
JERSEY
WHAT'S IT MEAN?
THE JOKER'S JUST TOLD US HE'S GONE TO NEW JERSEY- AND THAT'S WHERE WE'LL PICK UP HIS TRAIL! C'MON!
A SMALL TOWN SOMEWHERE IN NEW JERSEY----
GOOD PLAY EH, JOHN! I HEAR THE VANDGILTS ARE LETTING THE ACTORS USE THE REAL VANDGILT DIAMONDS FOR TONIGHT'S OPENING PERFORMANCE.
GOOD PUBLICITY STUNT! HALF A MILLION DOLLARS' WORTH O'GEMS LENT BY THE PEOPLE CONCERNED IN THE PLAY!
VERY INTERESTING------!
STRAIGHT FROM
VANDGIL
A PLAY ABO
FIRST FAM
OF OUR F

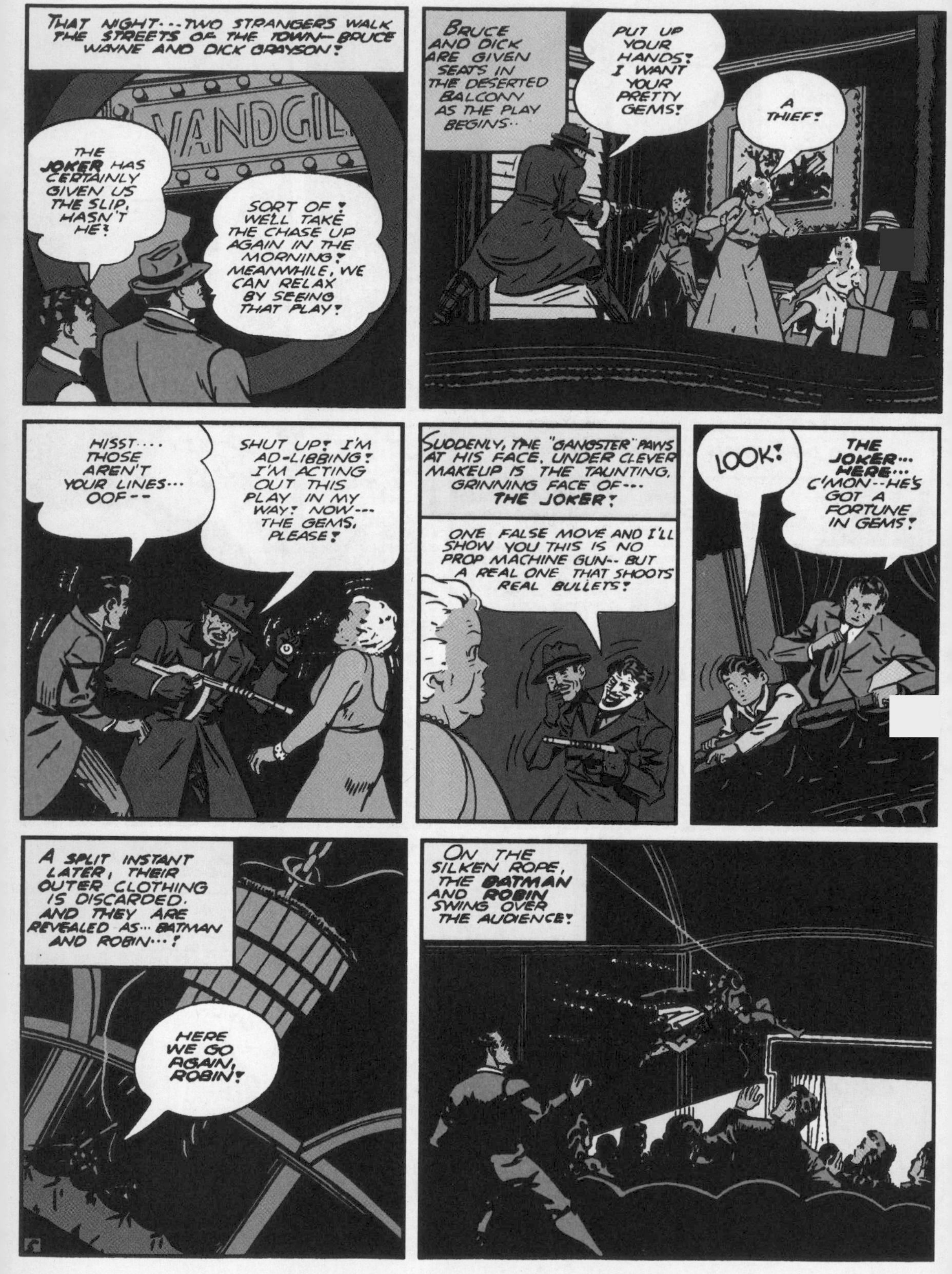
THAT NIGHT---TWO STRANGERS WALK THE STREETS OF THE TOWN--BRUCE WAYNE AND DICK GRAYSON!
VANDGIL
THE JOKER HAS CERTAINLY GIVEN US THE SLIP, HASN'T HE?
SORT OF! WE'LL TAKE THE CHASE UP AGAIN IN THE MORNING! MEANWHILE, WE CAN RELAX BY SEEING THAT PLAY!
BRUCE AND DICK ARE GIVEN SEATS IN THE DESERTED BALCONY AS THE PLAY BEGINS..
PUT UP YOUR HANDS! I WANT YOUR PRETTY GEMS!
A THIEF!
HISST.... THOSE AREN'T YOUR LINES... OOF--
SHUT UP! I'M AD-LIBBING! I'M ACTING OUT THIS PLAY IN MY WAY! NOW--- THE GEMS, PLEASE!
SUDDENLY, THE "GANGSTER" PAWS AT HIS FACE. UNDER CLEVER MAKEUP IS THE TAUNTING, GRINNING FACE OF--- THE JOKER!
ONE FALSE MOVE AND I'LL SHOW YOU THIS IS NO PROP MACHINE GUN-- BUT A REAL ONE THAT SHOOTS REAL BULLETS!
LOOK!
THE JOKER... HERE... C'MON--HE'S GOT A FORTUNE IN GEMS!
A SPLIT INSTANT LATER, THEIR OUTER CLOTHING IS DISCARDED. AND THEY ARE REVEALED AS... BATMAN AND ROBIN...!
HERE WE GO AGAIN, ROBIN!
ON THE SILKEN ROPE, THE BATMAN AND ROBIN SWING OVER THE AUDIENCE!

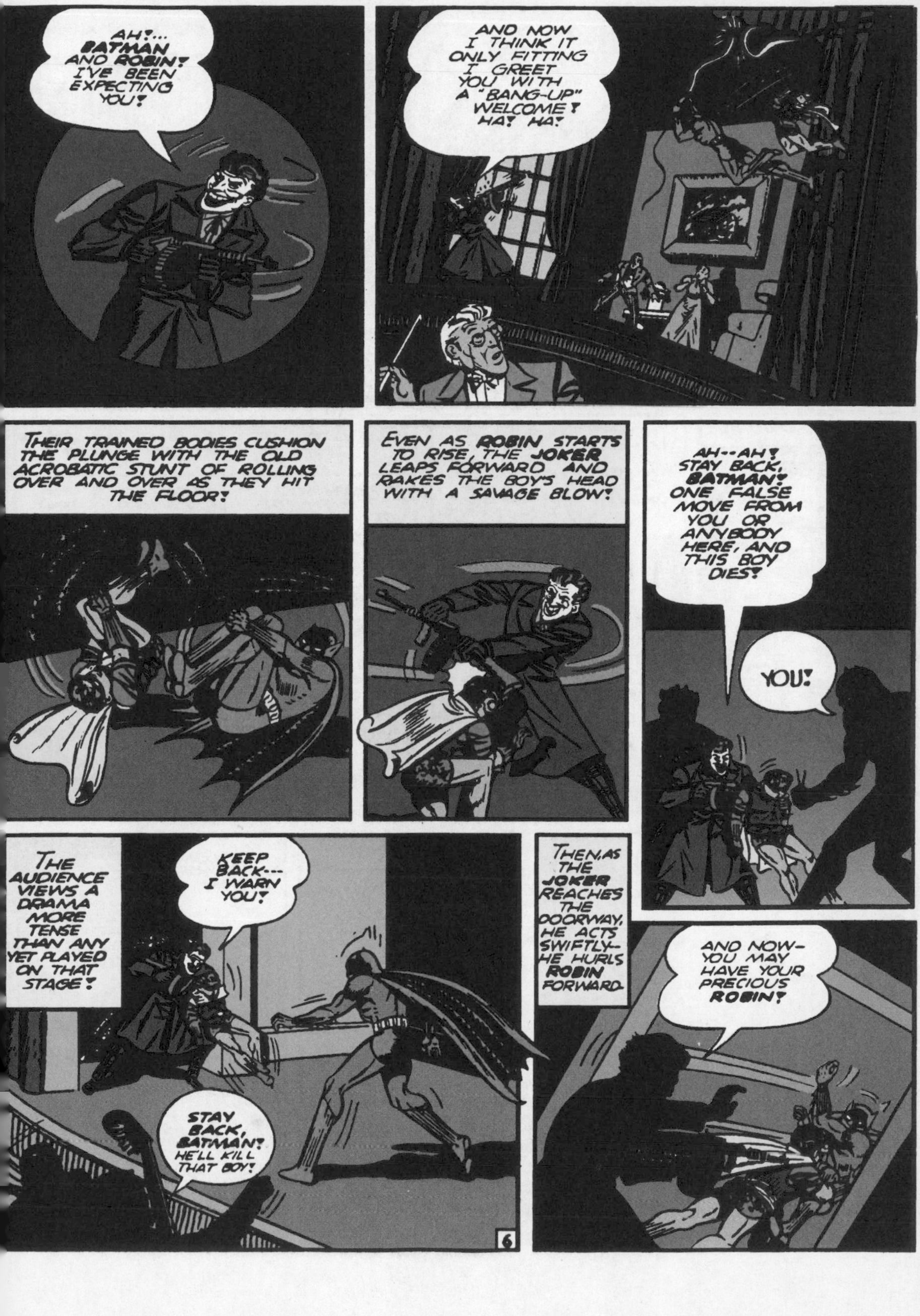
AH?... BATMAN AND ROBIN? I'VE BEEN EXPECTING YOU?
AND NOW I THINK IT ONLY FITTING I GREET YOU WITH A "BANG-UP" WELCOME? HA? HA?
THEIR TRAINED BODIES CUSHION THE PLUNGE WITH THE OLD ACROBATIC STUNT OF ROLLING OVER AND OVER AS THEY HIT THE FLOOR?
EVEN AS ROBIN STARTS TO RISE, THE JOKER LEAPS FORWARD AND RAKES THE BOY'S HEAD WITH A SAVAGE BLOW?
AH--AH? STAY BACK, BATMAN? ONE FALSE MOVE FROM YOU OR ANYBODY HERE, AND THIS BOY DIES?
YOU?
THE AUDIENCE VIEWS A DRAMA MORE TENSE THAN ANY YET PLAYED ON THAT STAGE?
KEEP BACK--- I WARN YOU?
STAY BACK, BATMAN? HE'LL KILL THAT BOY!
6
THEN, AS THE JOKER REACHES THE DOORWAY, HE ACTS SWIFTLY-- HE HURLS ROBIN FORWARD.
AND NOW-- YOU MAY HAVE YOUR PRECIOUS ROBIN?

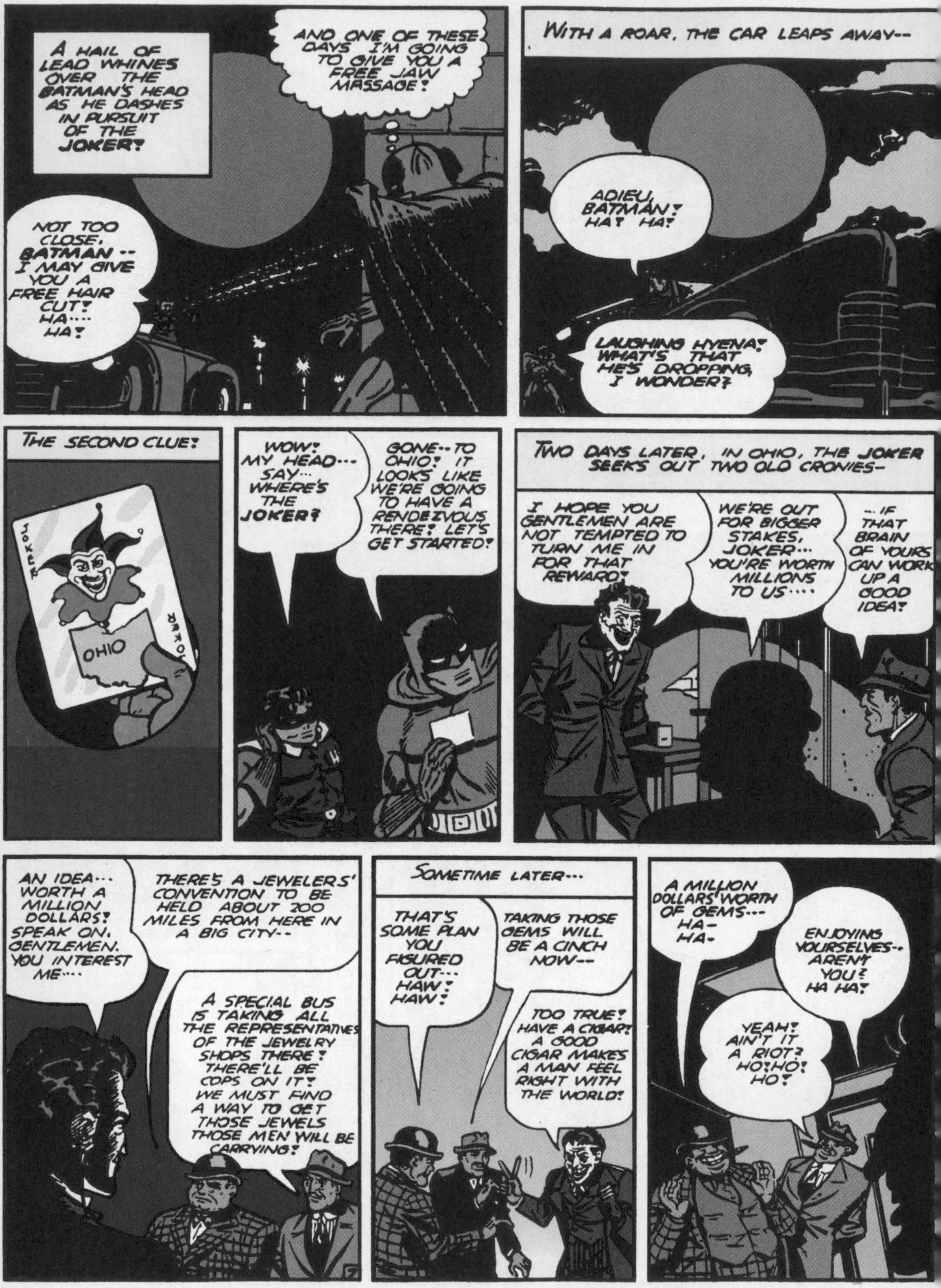
A HAIL OF LEAD WHINES OVER THE BATMAN'S HEAD AS HE DASHES IN PURSUIT OF THE JOKER!
AND ONE OF THESE DAYS I'M GOING TO GIVE YOU A FREE JAW MASSAGE!
NOT TOO CLOSE, BATMAN -- I MAY GIVE YOU A FREE HAIR CUT! HA.... HA!
WITH A ROAR, THE CAR LEAPS AWAY--
ADIEU, BATMAN! HA! HA!
LAUGHING HYENA! WHAT'S THAT HE'S DROPPING, I WONDER?
THE SECOND CLUE!
JOKER
OHIO
WOW! MY HEAD--- SAY... WHERE'S THE JOKER?
GONE--TO OHIO! IT LOOKS LIKE WE'RE GOING TO HAVE A RENDEZVOUS THERE! LET'S GET STARTED!
TWO DAYS LATER, IN OHIO, THE JOKER SEEKS OUT TWO OLD CRONIES-
I HOPE YOU GENTLEMEN ARE NOT TEMPTED TO TURN ME IN FOR THAT REWARD!
WE'RE OUT FOR BIGGER STAKES, JOKER... YOU'RE WORTH MILLIONS TO US....
-- IF THAT BRAIN OF YOURS CAN WORK UP A GOOD IDEA!
AN IDEA... WORTH A MILLION DOLLARS! SPEAK ON, GENTLEMEN. YOU INTEREST ME....
THERE'S A JEWELERS' CONVENTION TO BE HELD ABOUT 200 MILES FROM HERE IN A BIG CITY--
A SPECIAL BUS IS TAKING ALL THE REPRESENTATIVES OF THE JEWELRY SHOPS THERE! THERE'LL BE COPS ON IT! WE MUST FIND A WAY TO GET THOSE JEWELS THOSE MEN WILL BE CARRYING!
SOMETIME LATER...
THAT'S SOME PLAN YOU FIGURED OUT... HAW! HAW!
TAKING THOSE GEMS WILL BE A CINCH NOW--
TOO TRUE! HAVE A CIGAR! A GOOD CIGAR MAKES A MAN FEEL RIGHT WITH THE WORLD!
A MILLION DOLLARS' WORTH OF GEMS--- HA-HA-
ENJOYING YOURSELVES-- AREN'T YOU? HA HA!
YEAH! AIN'T IT A RIOT? HO! HO! HO!

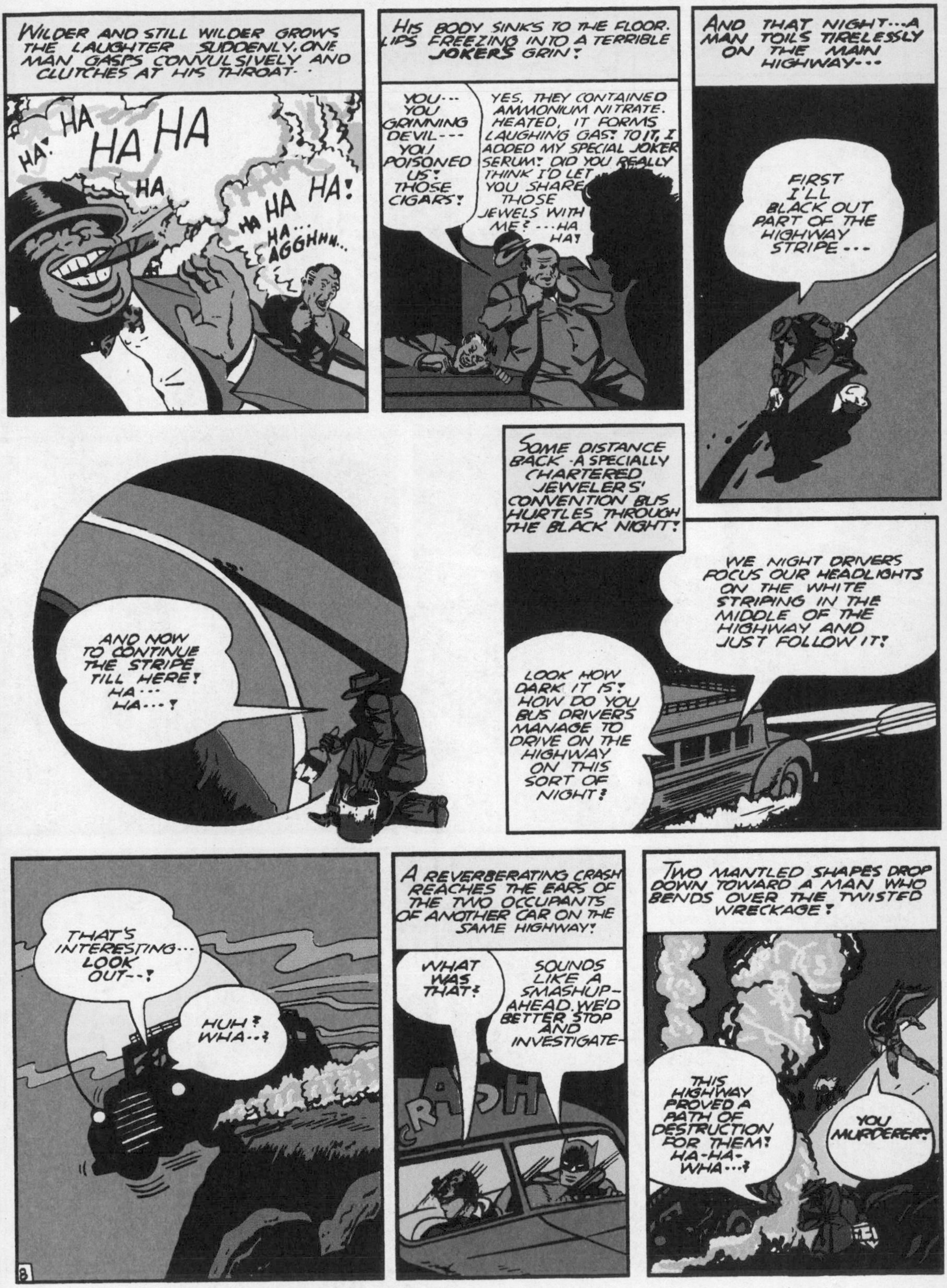
WILDER AND STILL WILDER GROWS THE LAUGHTER SUDDENLY. ONE MAN GASPS CONVULSIVELY AND CLUTCHES AT HIS THROAT--
HA! HA HA HA
HA
HA HA HA!
HA... AGGHHH...
HIS BODY SINKS TO THE FLOOR. LIPS FREEZING INTO A TERRIBLE JOKER'S GRIN!
YOU--YOU GRINNING DEVIL---YOU POISONED US! THOSE CIGARS!
YES, THEY CONTAINED AMMONIUM NITRATE. HEATED, IT FORMS LAUGHING GAS! TO IT, I ADDED MY SPECIAL JOKER SERUM! DID YOU REALLY THINK I'D LET YOU SHARE THOSE JEWELS WITH ME? ---HA HA!
AND THAT NIGHT...A MAN TOILS TIRELESSLY ON THE MAIN HIGHWAY---
FIRST I'LL BLACK OUT PART OF THE HIGHWAY STRIPE---
AND NOW TO CONTINUE THE STRIPE TILL HERE! HA--- HA---!
SOME DISTANCE BACK-A SPECIALLY CHARTERED JEWELERS' CONVENTION BUS HURTLES THROUGH THE BLACK NIGHT!
LOOK HOW DARK IT IS! HOW DO YOU BUS DRIVERS MANAGE TO DRIVE ON THE HIGHWAY ON THIS SORT OF NIGHT?
WE NIGHT DRIVERS FOCUS OUR HEADLIGHTS ON THE WHITE STRIPING IN THE MIDDLE OF THE HIGHWAY AND JUST FOLLOW IT!
THAT'S INTERESTING--- LOOK OUT--!
HUH? WHA--?
8
A REVERBERATING CRASH REACHES THE EARS OF THE TWO OCCUPANTS OF ANOTHER CAR ON THE SAME HIGHWAY!
WHAT WAS THAT?
SOUNDS LIKE A SMASHUP-AHEAD. WE'D BETTER STOP AND INVESTIGATE-
CRASH
TWO MANTLED SHAPES DROP DOWN TOWARD A MAN WHO BENDS OVER THE TWISTED WRECKAGE!
THIS HIGHWAY PROVED A PATH OF DESTRUCTION FOR THEM! HA-HA-WHA---!
YOU MURDERER!

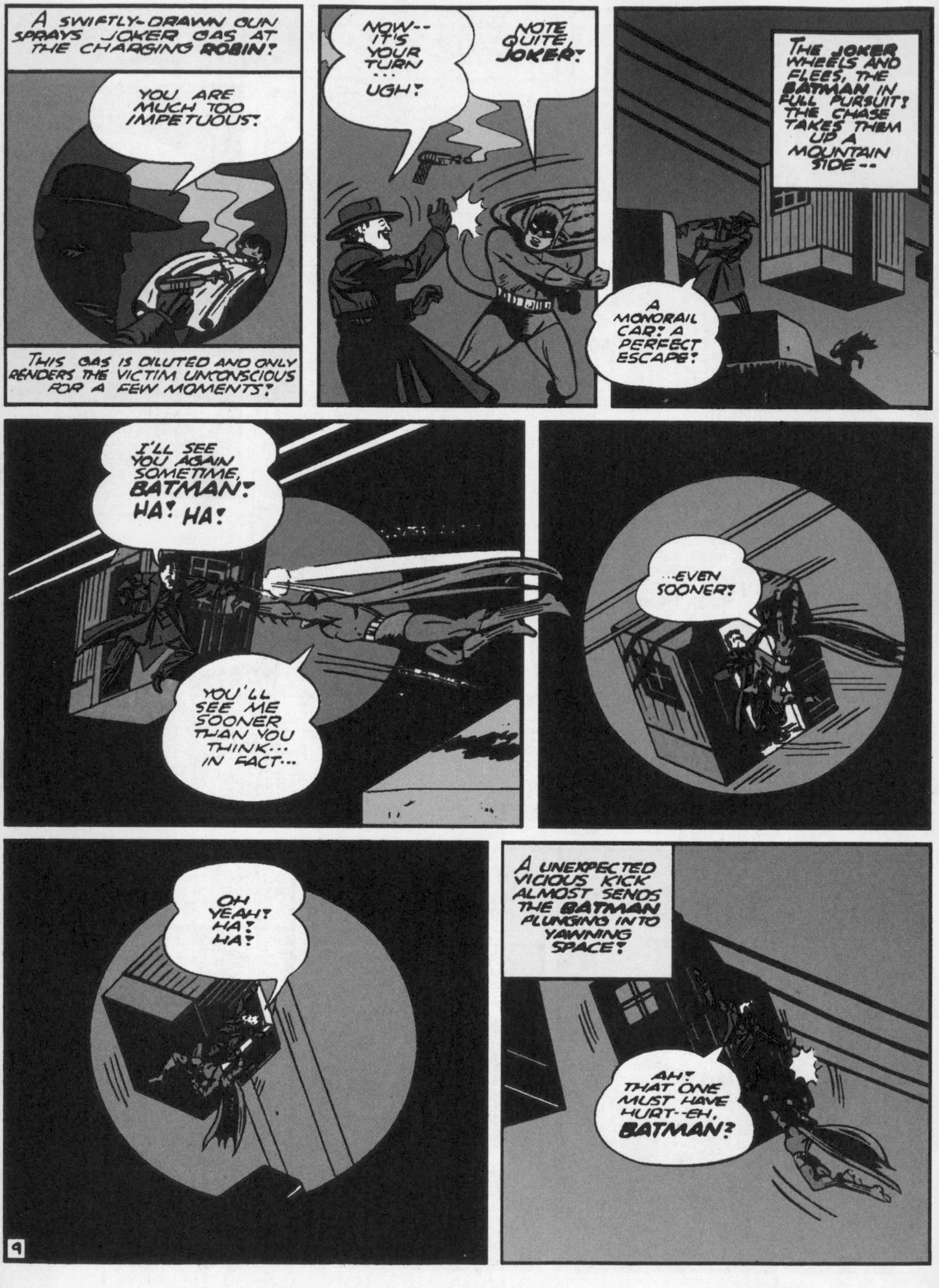
A SWIFTLY-DRAWN GUN SPRAYS JOKER GAS AT THE CHARGING ROBIN!
YOU ARE MUCH TOO IMPETUOUS!
THIS GAS IS DILUTED AND ONLY RENDERS THE VICTIM UNCONSCIOUS FOR A FEW MOMENTS!
NOW-- IT'S YOUR TURN ... UGH!
NOTE QUITE, JOKER!
THE JOKER WHEELS AND FLEES, THE BATMAN IN FULL PURSUIT! THE CHASE TAKES THEM UP A MOUNTAIN SIDE --
A MONORAIL CAR! A PERFECT ESCAPE!
I'LL SEE YOU AGAIN SOMETIME, BATMAN! HA! HA!
YOU'LL SEE ME SOONER THAN YOU THINK... IN FACT...
...EVEN SOONER!
OH YEAH! HA! HA!
9
A UNEXPECTED VICIOUS KICK ALMOST SENDS THE BATMAN PLUNGING INTO YAWNING SPACE!
AH! THAT ONE MUST HAVE HURT--EH, BATMAN?

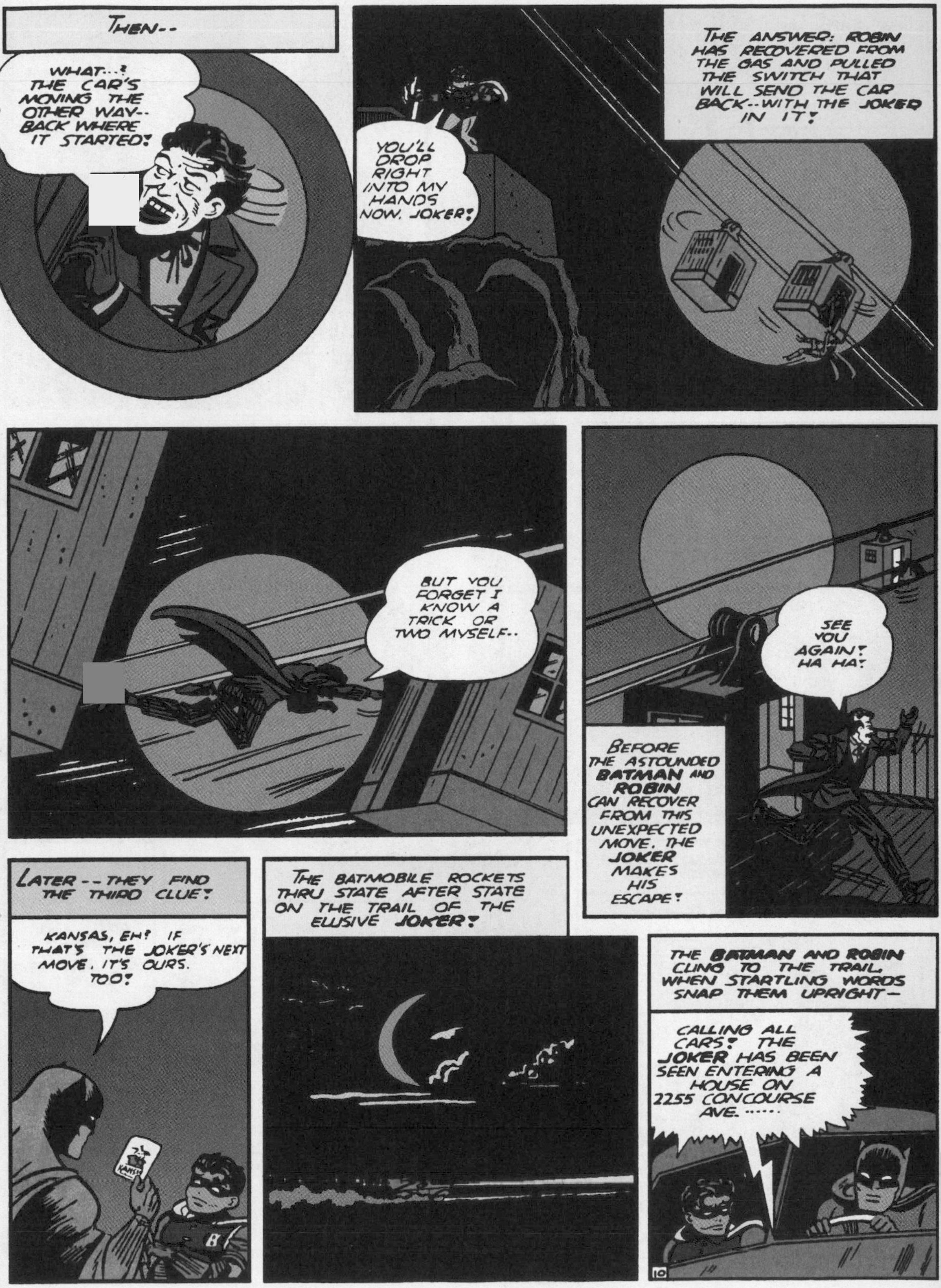
THEN--
WHAT--? THE CAR'S MOVING THE OTHER WAY-- BACK WHERE IT STARTED!
THE ANSWER: ROBIN HAS RECOVERED FROM THE GAS AND PULLED THE SWITCH THAT WILL SEND THE CAR BACK--WITH THE JOKER IN IT!
YOU'LL DROP RIGHT INTO MY HANDS NOW, JOKER!
BUT YOU FORGET I KNOW A TRICK OR TWO MYSELF--
SEE YOU AGAIN! HA HA!
BEFORE THE ASTOUNDED BATMAN AND ROBIN CAN RECOVER FROM THIS UNEXPECTED MOVE, THE JOKER MAKES HIS ESCAPE!
LATER -- THEY FIND THE THIRD CLUE!
KANSAS, EH? IF THAT'S THE JOKER'S NEXT MOVE, IT'S OURS, TOO!
THE BATMOBILE ROCKETS THRU STATE AFTER STATE ON THE TRAIL OF THE ELUSIVE JOKER!
THE BATMAN AND ROBIN CLING TO THE TRAIL, WHEN STARTLING WORDS SNAP THEM UPRIGHT—
CALLING ALL CARS! THE JOKER HAS BEEN SEEN ENTERING A HOUSE ON 2255 CONCOURSE AVE.......
10

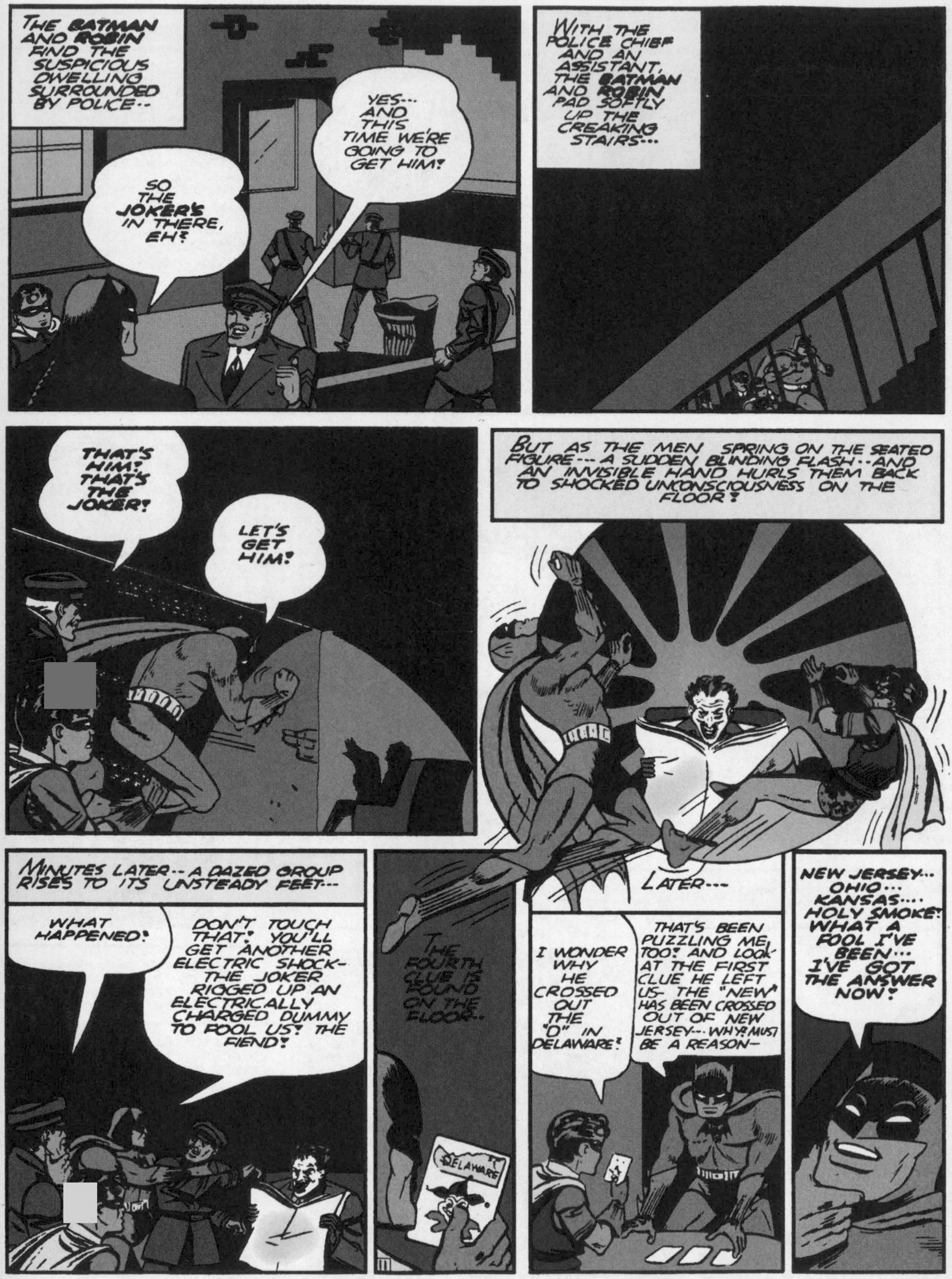
THE BATMAN AND ROBIN FIND THE SUSPICIOUS DWELLING SURROUNDED BY POLICE--
SO THE JOKER'S IN THERE, EH?
YES--- AND THIS TIME WE'RE GOING TO GET HIM!
WITH THE POLICE CHIEF AND AN ASSISTANT, THE BATMAN AND ROBIN PAD SOFTLY UP THE CREAKING STAIRS...
THAT'S HIM! THAT'S THE JOKER!
LET'S GET HIM!
BUT AS THE MEN SPRING ON THE SEATED FIGURE--- A SUDDEN BLINDING FLASH--AND AN INVISIBLE HAND HURLS THEM BACK TO SHOCKED UNCONSCIOUSNESS ON THE FLOOR!
MINUTES LATER-- A DAZED GROUP RISES TO ITS UNSTEADY FEET---
WHAT HAPPENED?
DON'T TOUCH THAT! YOU'LL GET ANOTHER ELECTRIC SHOCK- THE JOKER RIGGED UP AN ELECTRICALLY CHARGED DUMMY TO FOOL US! THE FIEND!
THE FOURTH CLUE IS FOUND ON THE FLOOR--
DELAWARE
LATER---
I WONDER WHY HE CROSSED OUT THE "D" IN DELAWARE?
THAT'S BEEN PUZZLING ME, TOO! AND LOOK AT THE FIRST CLUE HE LEFT US- THE "NEW" HAS BEEN CROSSED OUT OF NEW JERSEY--- WHY? MUST BE A REASON—
NEW JERSEY... OHIO... KANSAS.... HOLY SMOKE! WHAT A FOOL I'VE BEEN... I'VE GOT THE ANSWER NOW!

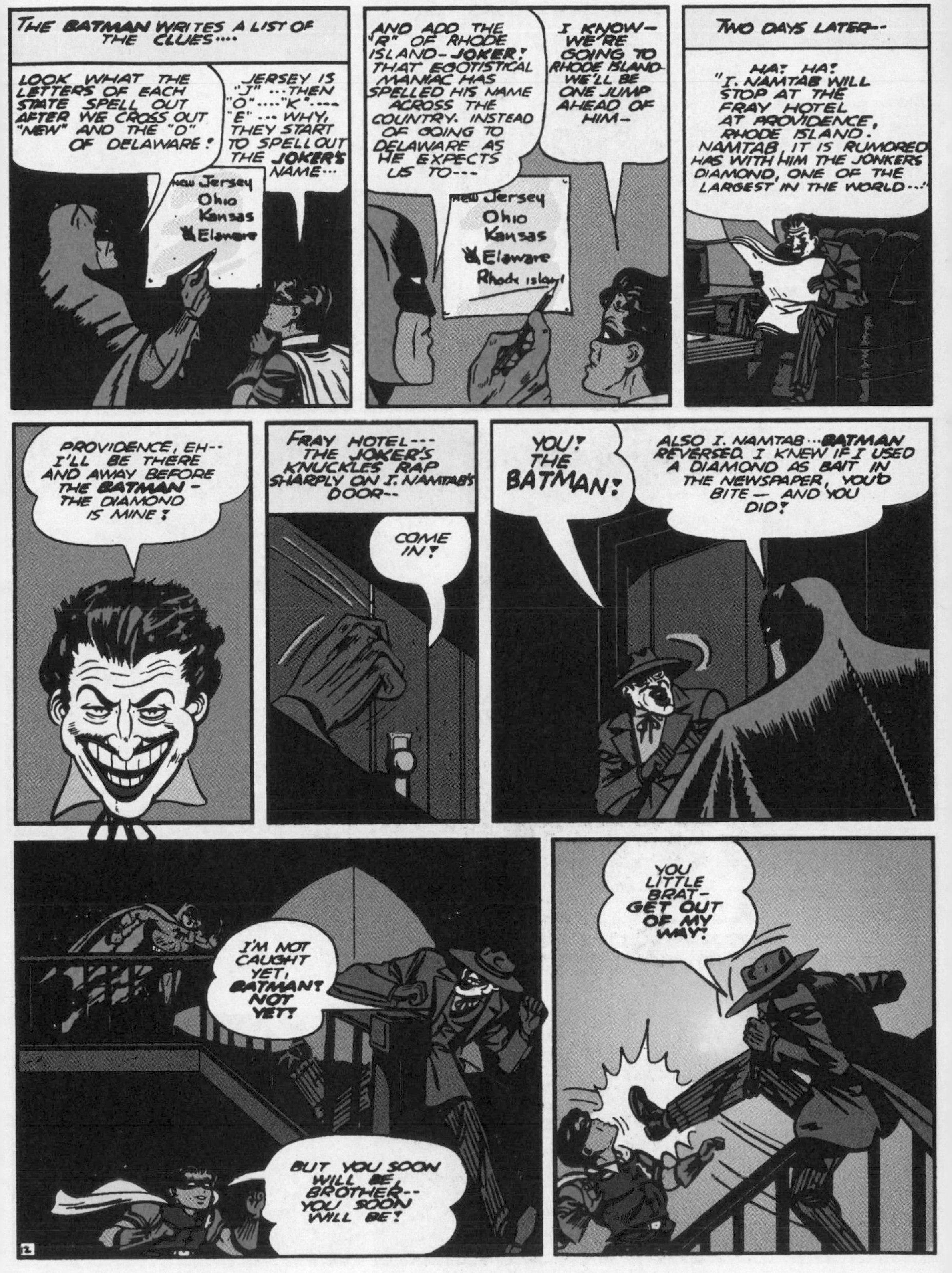
THE BATMAN WRITES A LIST OF THE CLUES....
LOOK WHAT THE LETTERS OF EACH STATE SPELL OUT AFTER WE CROSS OUT "NEW" AND THE "D" OF DELAWARE!
JERSEY IS "J" ... THEN "O"...."K".... "E" ... WHY, THEY START TO SPELL OUT THE JOKER'S NAME...
New Jersey
Ohio
Kansas
Elaware
AND ADD THE "R" OF RHODE ISLAND—JOKER! THAT EGOTISTICAL MANIAC HAS SPELLED HIS NAME ACROSS THE COUNTRY. INSTEAD OF GOING TO DELAWARE AS HE EXPECTS US TO---
I KNOW— WE'RE GOING TO RHODE ISLAND— WE'LL BE ONE JUMP AHEAD OF HIM—
New Jersey
Ohio
Kansas
Elaware
Rhode island
TWO DAYS LATER--
HA! HA! "I. NAMTAB WILL STOP AT THE FRAY HOTEL AT PROVIDENCE, RHODE ISLAND. NAMTAB, IT IS RUMORED HAS WITH HIM THE JONKERS DIAMOND, ONE OF THE LARGEST IN THE WORLD...!"
PROVIDENCE, EH-- I'LL BE THERE AND AWAY BEFORE THE BATMAN - THE DIAMOND IS MINE!
FRAY HOTEL--- THE JOKER'S KNUCKLES RAP SHARPLY ON I. NAMTAB'S DOOR--
COME IN!
YOU! THE BATMAN!
ALSO I. NAMTAB...BATMAN REVERSED. I KNEW IF I USED A DIAMOND AS BAIT IN THE NEWSPAPER, YOU'D BITE— AND YOU DID!
I'M NOT CAUGHT YET, BATMAN! NOT YET!
BUT YOU SOON WILL BE, BROTHER-- YOU SOON WILL BE!
YOU LITTLE BRAT- GET OUT OF MY WAY!

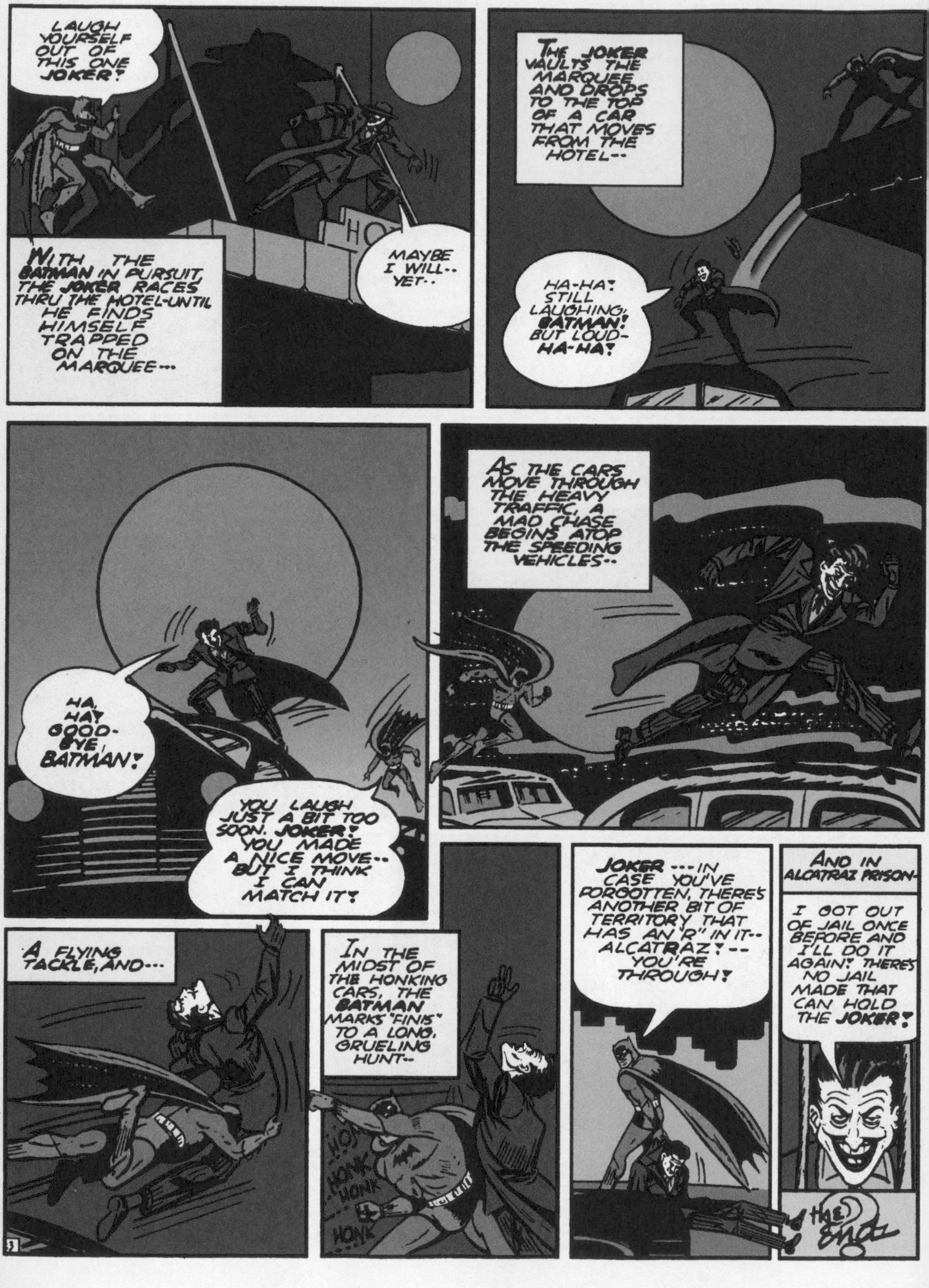
LAUGH YOURSELF OUT OF THIS ONE JOKER!
WITH THE BATMAN IN PURSUIT, THE JOKER RACES THRU THE HOTEL-UNTIL HE FINDS HIMSELF TRAPPED ON THE MARQUEE---
MAYBE I WILL-- YET--
THE JOKER VAULTS THE MARQUEE AND DROPS TO THE TOP OF A CAR THAT MOVES FROM THE HOTEL--
HA-HA! STILL LAUGHING, BATMAN! BUT LOUD-HA-HA!
HA, HA! GOOD-BYE, BATMAN!
YOU LAUGH JUST A BIT TOO SOON, JOKER! YOU MADE A NICE MOVE-- BUT I THINK I CAN MATCH IT!
AS THE CARS MOVE THROUGH THE HEAVY TRAFFIC, A MAD CHASE BEGINS ATOP THE SPEEDING VEHICLES--
A FLYING TACKLE, AND---
IN THE MIDST OF THE HONKING CARS, THE BATMAN MARKS "FINIS" TO A LONG, GRUELING HUNT--
HONK HONK HONK HONK
JOKER ---IN CASE YOU'VE FORGOTTEN, THERE'S ANOTHER BIT OF TERRITORY THAT HAS AN "R" IN IT-- ALCATRAZ! -- YOU'RE THROUGH!
AND IN ALCATRAZ PRISON-
I GOT OUT OF JAIL ONCE BEFORE AND I'LL DO IT AGAIN! THERE'S NO JAIL MADE THAT CAN HOLD THE JOKER!
THE END

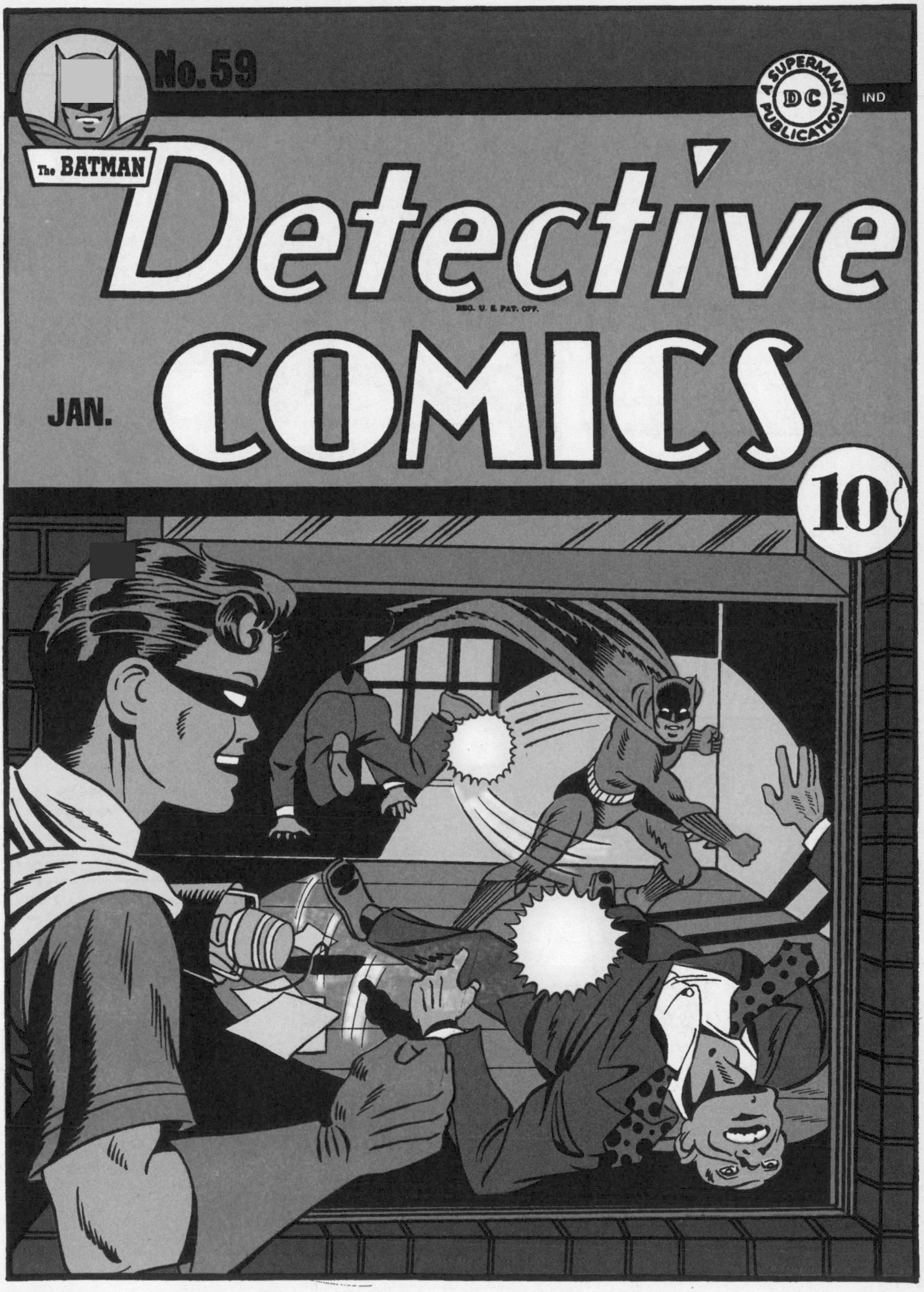

No. 59
The BATMAN
A SUPERMAN DC PUBLICATION
IND
Detective
REG. U.S. PAT. OFF.
JAN.
COMICS
10¢

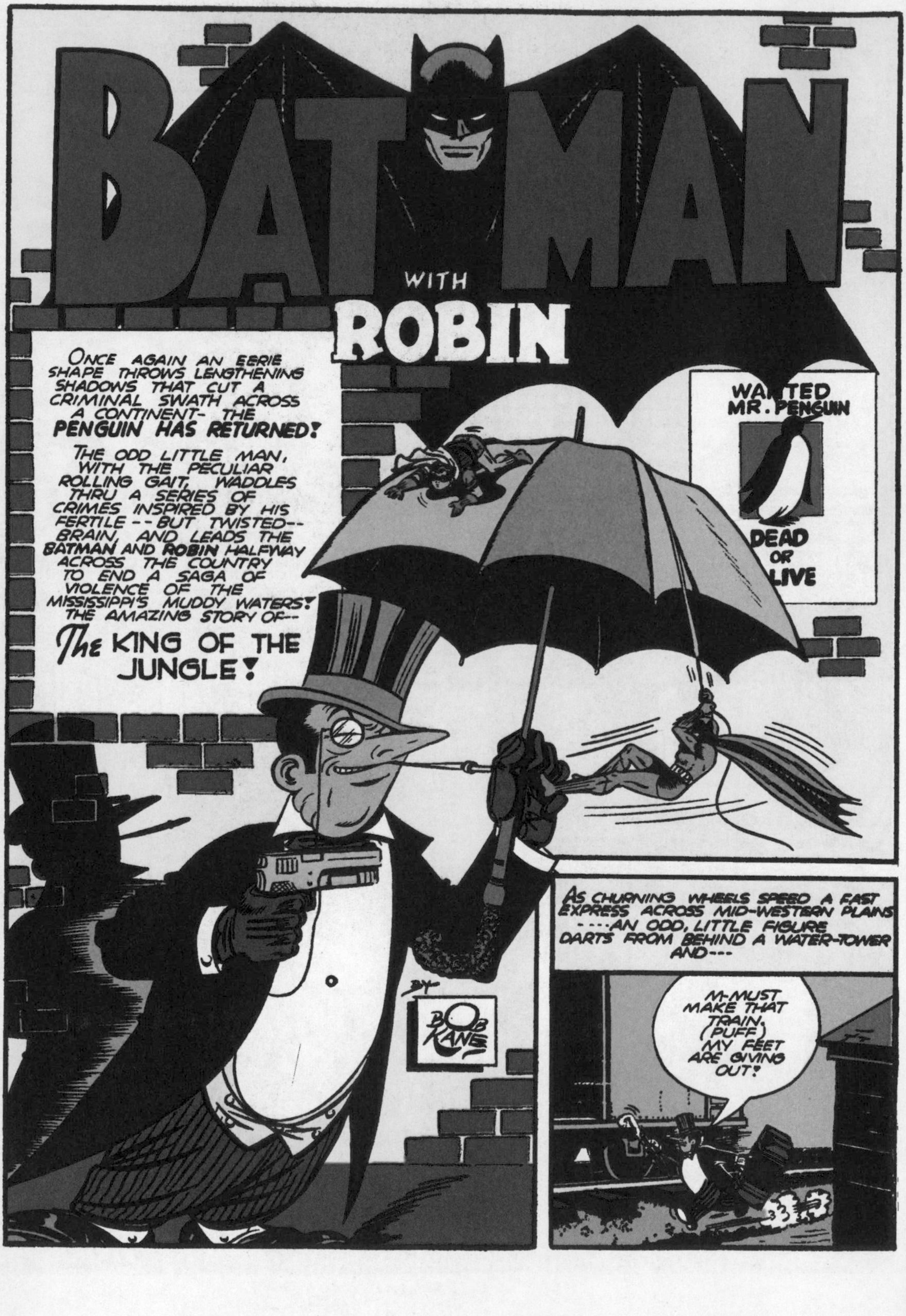

BATMAN
WITH
ROBIN
ONCE AGAIN AN EERIE SHAPE THROWS LENGTHENING SHADOWS THAT CUT A CRIMINAL SWATH ACROSS A CONTINENT- THE PENGUIN HAS RETURNED!
THE ODD LITTLE MAN, WITH THE PECULIAR ROLLING GAIT, WADDLES THRU A SERIES OF CRIMES INSPIRED BY HIS FERTILE -- BUT TWISTED-- BRAIN, AND LEADS THE BATMAN AND ROBIN HALFWAY ACROSS THE COUNTRY TO END A SAGA OF VIOLENCE OF THE MISSISSIPPI'S MUDDY WATERS! THE AMAZING STORY OF--
The KING OF THE JUNGLE!
WANTED MR. PENGUIN
DEAD OR ALIVE
BY BOB KANE
AS CHURNING WHEELS SPEED A FAST EXPRESS ACROSS MID-WESTERN PLAINS ----AN ODD, LITTLE FIGURE DARTS FROM BEHIND A WATER-TOWER AND---
M-MUST MAKE THAT TRAIN, (PUFF) MY FEET ARE GIVING OUT!

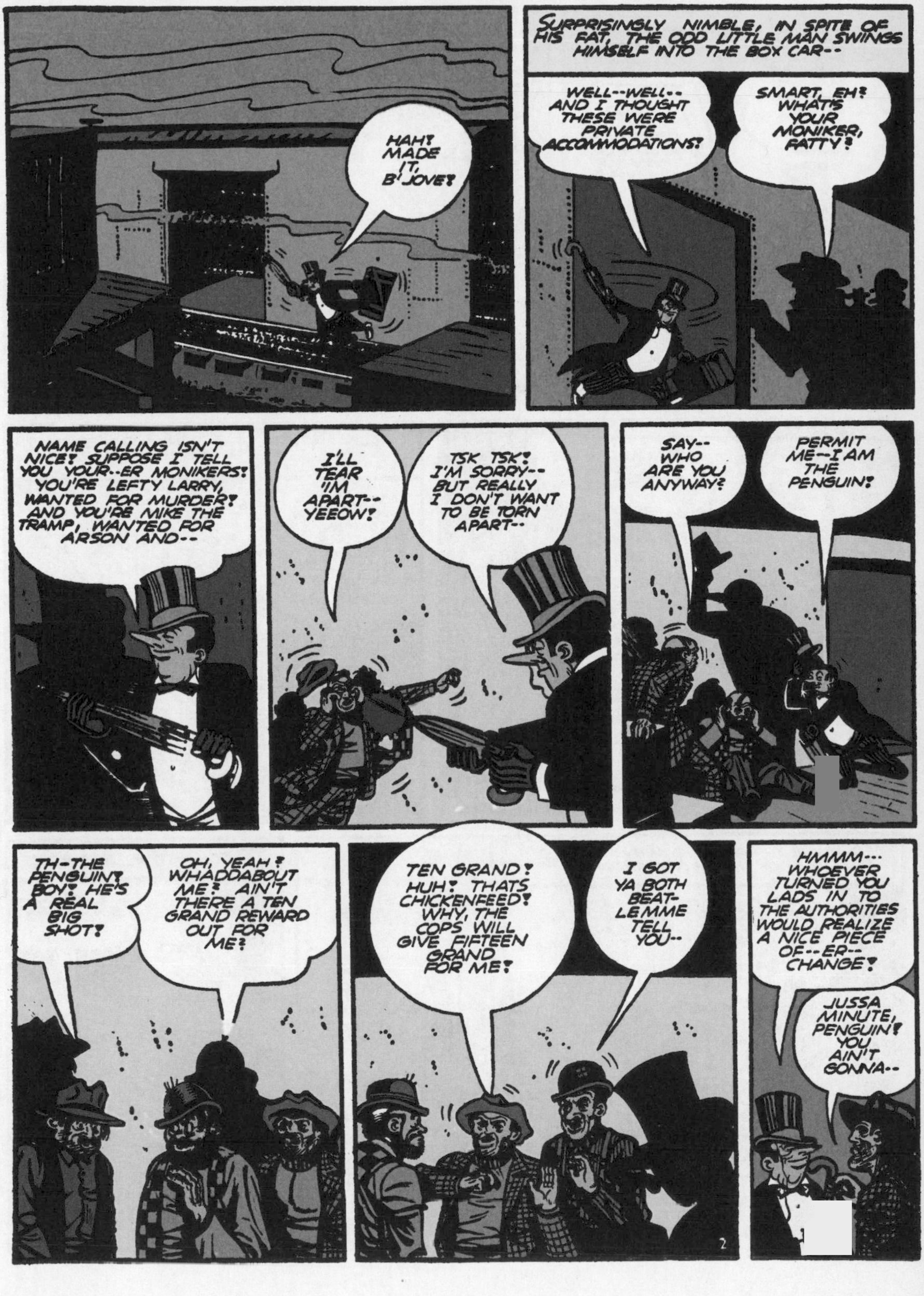

HAH! MADE IT, B'JOVE!
SURPRISINGLY NIMBLE, IN SPITE OF HIS FAT, THE ODD LITTLE MAN SWINGS HIMSELF INTO THE BOX CAR--
WELL--WELL-- AND I THOUGHT THESE WERE PRIVATE ACCOMMODATIONS!
SMART, EH! WHAT'S YOUR MONIKER, FATTY!
NAME CALLING ISN'T NICE! SUPPOSE I TELL YOU YOUR--ER MONIKERS! YOU'RE LEFTY LARRY, WANTED FOR MURDER! AND YOU'RE MIKE THE TRAMP, WANTED FOR ARSON AND--
I'LL TEAR 'IM APART-- YEEOW!
TSK TSK! I'M SORRY-- BUT REALLY I DON'T WANT TO BE TORN APART--
SAY-- WHO ARE YOU ANYWAY!
PERMIT ME--I AM THE PENGUIN!
TH-THE PENGUIN! BOY! HE'S A REAL BIG SHOT!
OH, YEAH! WHADDABOUT ME! AIN'T THERE A TEN GRAND REWARD OUT FOR ME!
TEN GRAND! HUH! THATS CHICKENFEED! WHY, THE COPS WILL GIVE FIFTEEN GRAND FOR ME!
I GOT YA BOTH BEAT- LEMME TELL YOU--
HMMM--- WHOEVER TURNED YOU LADS IN TO THE AUTHORITIES WOULD REALIZE A NICE PIECE OF--ER-- CHANGE!
JUSSA MINUTE, PENGUIN! YOU AIN'T GONNA--
2

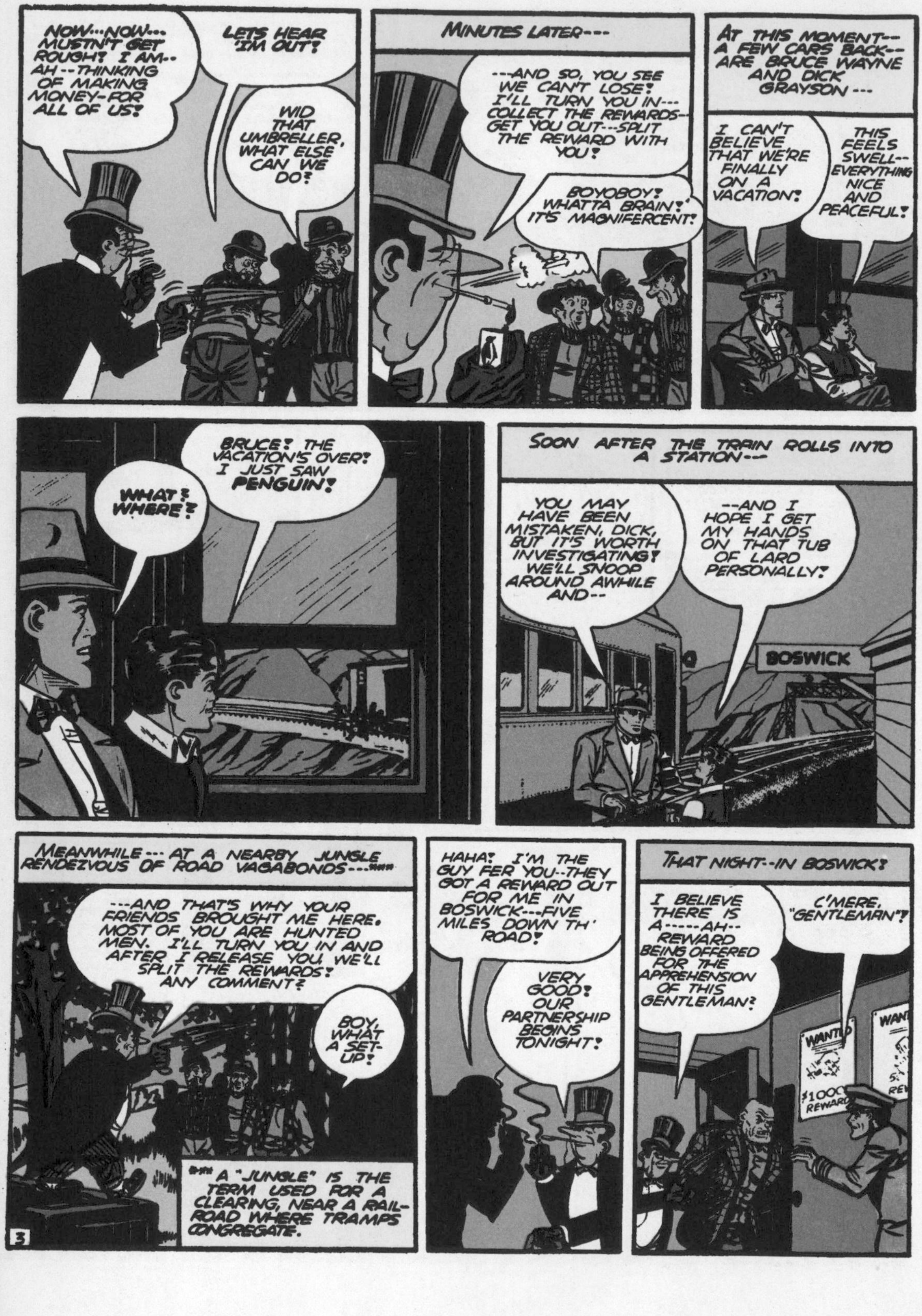
NOW...NOW... MUSTN'T GET ROUGH! I AM-- AH--THINKING OF MAKING MONEY-FOR ALL OF US!
LETS HEAR 'IM OUT!
WID THAT UMBRELLER, WHAT ELSE CAN WE DO?
MINUTES LATER---
--AND SO, YOU SEE WE CAN'T LOSE! I'LL TURN YOU IN--- COLLECT THE REWARDS-- GET YOU OUT---SPLIT THE REWARD WITH YOU!
BOYOBOY! WHATTA BRAIN!' IT'S MAGNIFERCENT!
AT THIS MOMENT-- A FEW CARS BACK-- ARE BRUCE WAYNE AND DICK GRAYSON ---
I CAN'T BELIEVE THAT WE'RE FINALLY ON A VACATION!
THIS FEELS SWELL-- EVERYTHING NICE AND PEACEFUL!
BRUCE! THE VACATION'S OVER! I JUST SAW PENGUIN!
WHAT? WHERE?
SOON AFTER THE TRAIN ROLLS INTO A STATION---
YOU MAY HAVE BEEN MISTAKEN, DICK, BUT IT'S WORTH INVESTIGATING! WE'LL SNOOP AROUND AWHILE AND--
--AND I HOPE I GET MY HANDS ON THAT TUB OF LARD PERSONALLY!
BOSWICK
MEANWHILE--- AT A NEARBY JUNGLE RENDEZVOUS OF ROAD VAGABONDS---***
---AND THAT'S WHY YOUR FRIENDS BROUGHT ME HERE. MOST OF YOU ARE HUNTED MEN. I'LL TURN YOU IN AND AFTER I RELEASE YOU, WE'LL SPLIT THE REWARDS! ANY COMMENT?
BOY, WHAT A SET-UP!
*** A "JUNGLE" IS THE TERM USED FOR A CLEARING, NEAR A RAIL-ROAD WHERE TRAMPS CONGREGATE.
3
HAHA! I'M THE GUY FER YOU--THEY GOT A REWARD OUT FOR ME IN BOSWICK---FIVE MILES DOWN TH' ROAD!
VERY GOOD! OUR PARTNERSHIP BEGINS TONIGHT!
THAT NIGHT--IN BOSWICK!
I BELIEVE THERE IS A-----AH-- REWARD BEING OFFERED FOR THE APPREHENSION OF THIS GENTLEMAN?
C'MERE, "GENTLEMAN"!
WANTED
$1000 REWARD

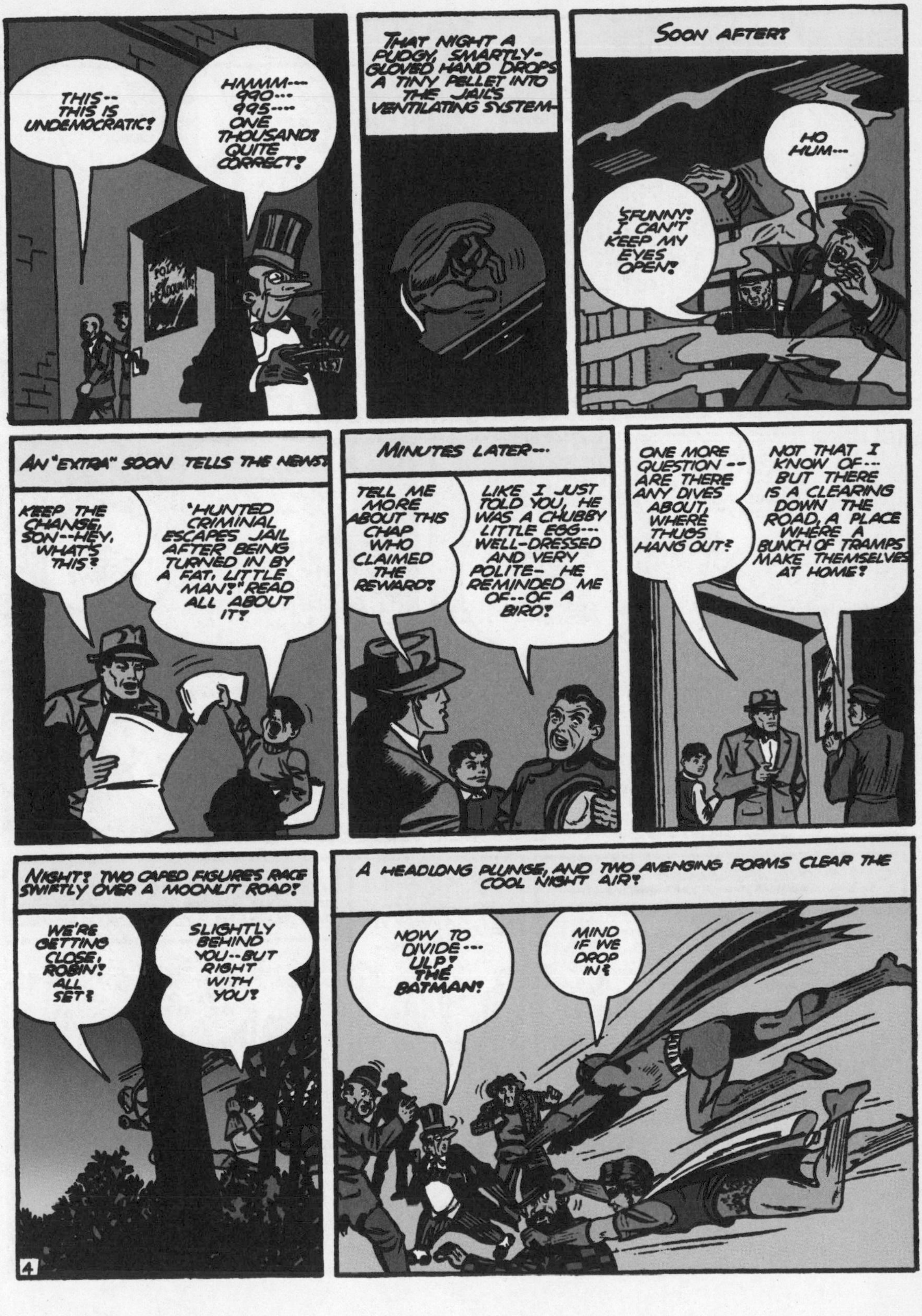
THIS-- THIS IS UNDEMOCRATIC!
HMMM--- 990--- 995---- ONE THOUSAND! QUITE CORRECT!
THAT NIGHT A PUDGY, SMARTLY-GLOVED HAND DROPS A TINY PELLET INTO THE JAIL'S VENTILATING SYSTEM-
SOON AFTER!
HO HUM---
'SFUNNY! I CAN'T KEEP MY EYES OPEN!
AN "EXTRA" SOON TELLS THE NEWS!
KEEP THE CHANGE, SON--HEY, WHAT'S THIS?
"HUNTED CRIMINAL ESCAPES JAIL AFTER BEING TURNED IN BY A FAT, LITTLE MAN!" READ ALL ABOUT IT!
MINUTES LATER---
TELL ME MORE ABOUT THIS CHAP WHO CLAIMED THE REWARD!
LIKE I JUST TOLD YOU, HE WAS A CHUBBY LITTLE EGG--- WELL-DRESSED AND VERY POLITE- HE REMINDED ME OF--OF A BIRD!
ONE MORE QUESTION -- ARE THERE ANY DIVES ABOUT, WHERE THUGS HANG OUT?
NOT THAT I KNOW OF--- BUT THERE IS A CLEARING DOWN THE ROAD, A PLACE WHERE A BUNCH OF TRAMPS MAKE THEMSELVES AT HOME!
NIGHT! TWO CAPED FIGURES RACE SWIFTLY OVER A MOONLIT ROAD!
WE'RE GETTING CLOSE, ROBIN! ALL SET?
SLIGHTLY BEHIND YOU--BUT RIGHT WITH YOU!
A HEADLONG PLUNGE, AND TWO AVENGING FORMS CLEAR THE COOL NIGHT AIR!
NOW TO DIVIDE--- ULP! THE BATMAN!
MIND IF WE DROP IN?
4

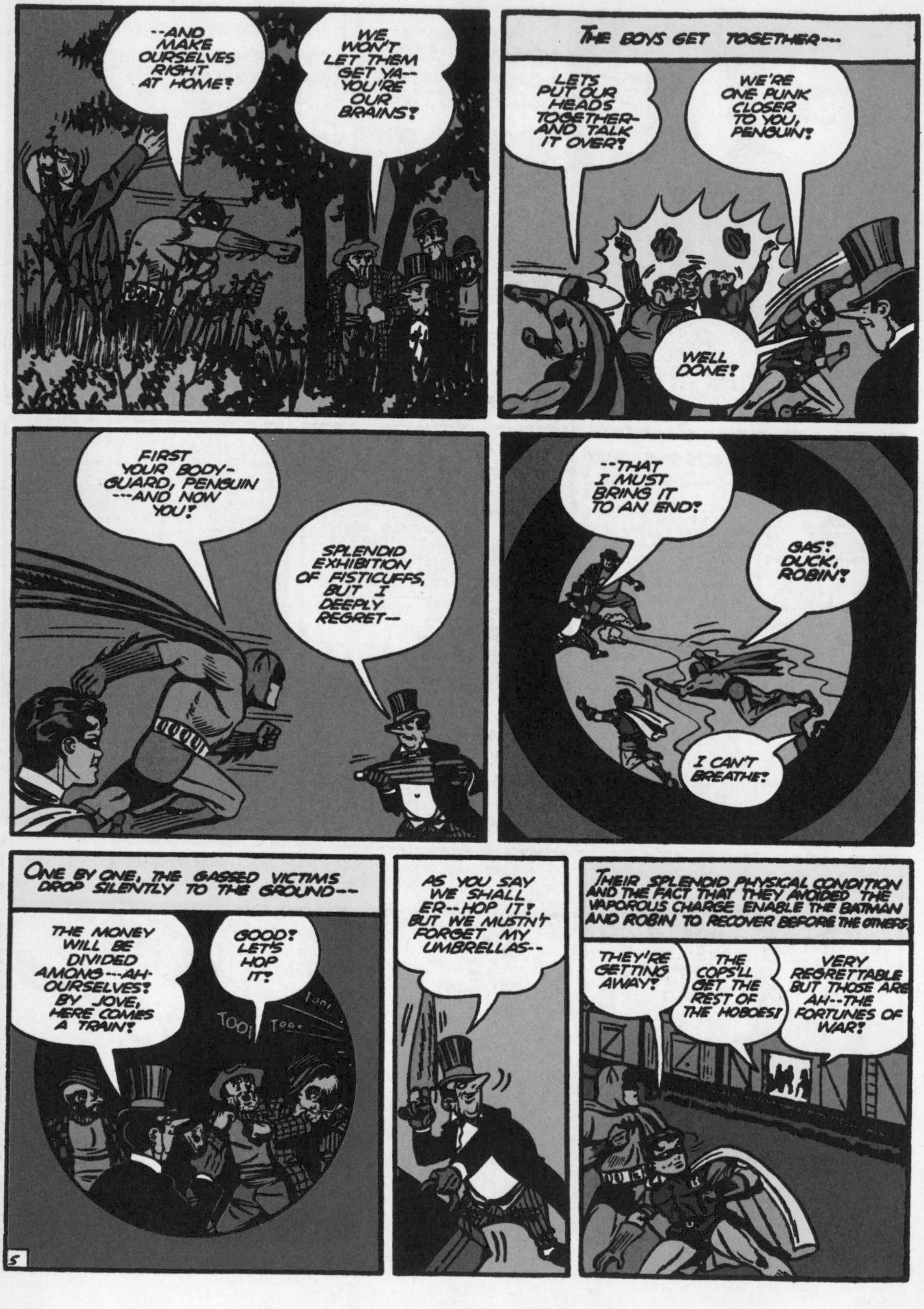
--AND MAKE OURSELVES RIGHT AT HOME!
WE WON'T LET THEM GET YA--YOU'RE OUR BRAINS!
THE BOYS GET TOGETHER---
LETS PUT OUR HEADS TOGETHER- AND TALK IT OVER!
WE'RE ONE PUNK CLOSER TO YOU, PENGUIN!
WELL DONE!
FIRST YOUR BODY-GUARD, PENGUIN ---AND NOW YOU!
SPLENDID EXHIBITION OF FISTICUFFS, BUT I DEEPLY REGRET--
--THAT I MUST BRING IT TO AN END!
GAS! DUCK, ROBIN!
I CAN'T BREATHE!
ONE BY ONE, THE GASSED VICTIMS DROP SILENTLY TO THE GROUND--
THE MONEY WILL BE DIVIDED AMONG---AH-OURSELVES! BY JOVE, HERE COMES A TRAIN!
GOOD! LET'S HOP IT!
TOOT
AS YOU SAY WE SHALL ER--HOP IT! BUT WE MUSTN'T FORGET MY UMBRELLAS--
THEIR SPLENDID PHYSICAL CONDITION AND THE FACT THAT THEY AVOIDED THE VAPOROUS CHARGE ENABLE THE BATMAN AND ROBIN TO RECOVER BEFORE THE OTHERS.
THEY'RE GETTING AWAY!
THE COPS'LL GET THE REST OF THE HOBOES!
VERY REGRETTABLE BUT THOSE ARE AH--THE FORTUNES OF WAR!
5

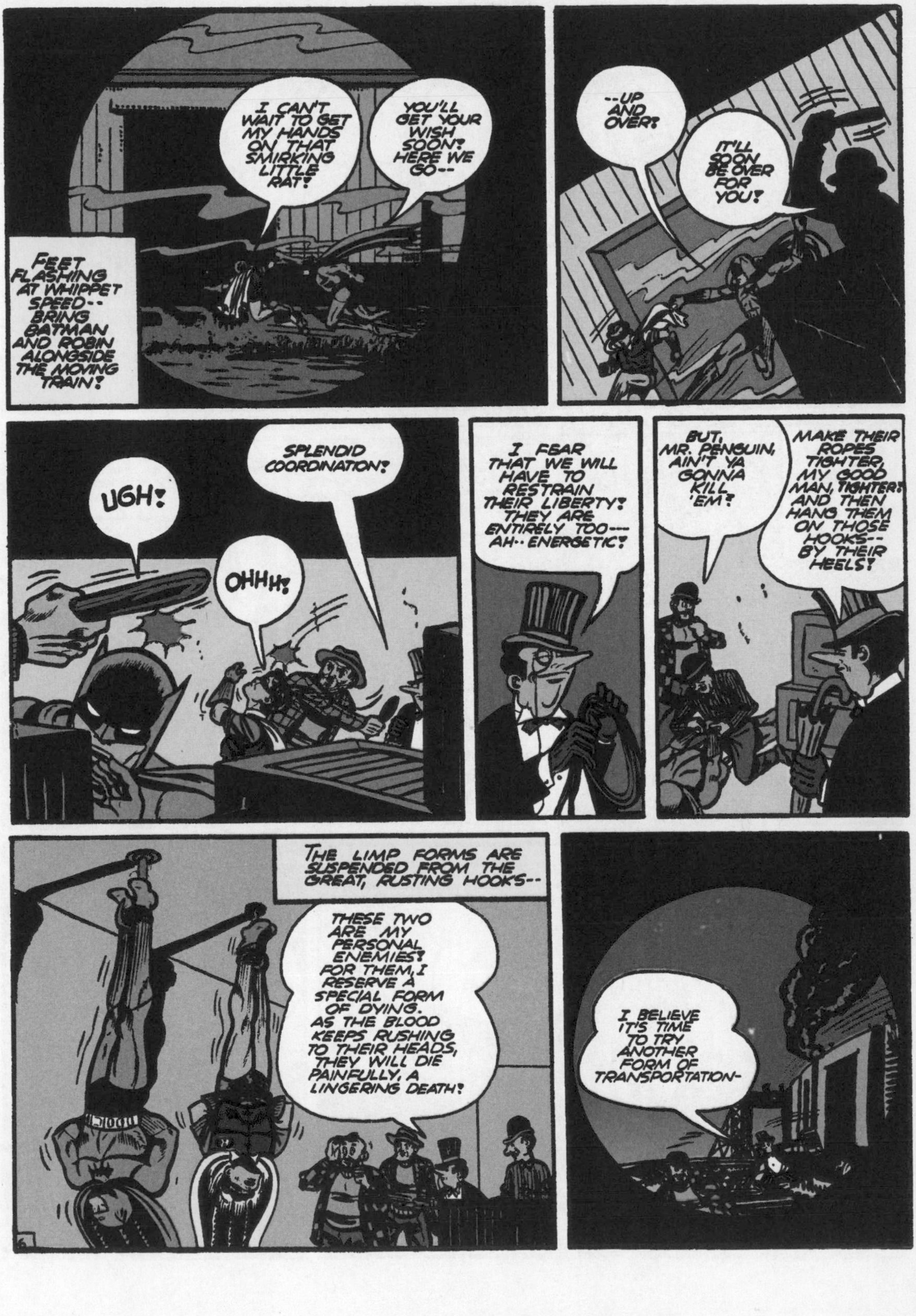
FEET FLASHING AT WHIPPET SPEED-- BRING BATMAN AND ROBIN ALONGSIDE THE MOVING TRAIN!
I CAN'T WAIT TO GET MY HANDS ON THAT SMIRKING LITTLE RAT!
YOU'LL GET YOUR WISH SOON! HERE WE GO--
--UP AND OVER!
IT'LL SOON BE OVER FOR YOU!
UGH!
SPLENDID COORDINATION!
OHHH!
I FEAR THAT WE WILL HAVE TO RESTRAIN THEIR LIBERTY! THEY ARE ENTIRELY TOO--- AH-- ENERGETIC!
BUT, MR. PENGUIN, AIN'T YA GONNA KILL 'EM?
MAKE THEIR ROPES TIGHTER, MY GOOD MAN, TIGHTER! AND THEN HANG THEM ON THOSE HOOKS-- BY THEIR HEELS!
THE LIMP FORMS ARE SUSPENDED FROM THE GREAT, RUSTING HOOKS--
THESE TWO ARE MY PERSONAL ENEMIES! FOR THEM, I RESERVE A SPECIAL FORM OF DYING. AS THE BLOOD KEEPS RUSHING TO THEIR HEADS, THEY WILL DIE PAINFULLY, A LINGERING DEATH!
I BELIEVE IT'S TIME TO TRY ANOTHER FORM OF TRANSPORTATION-

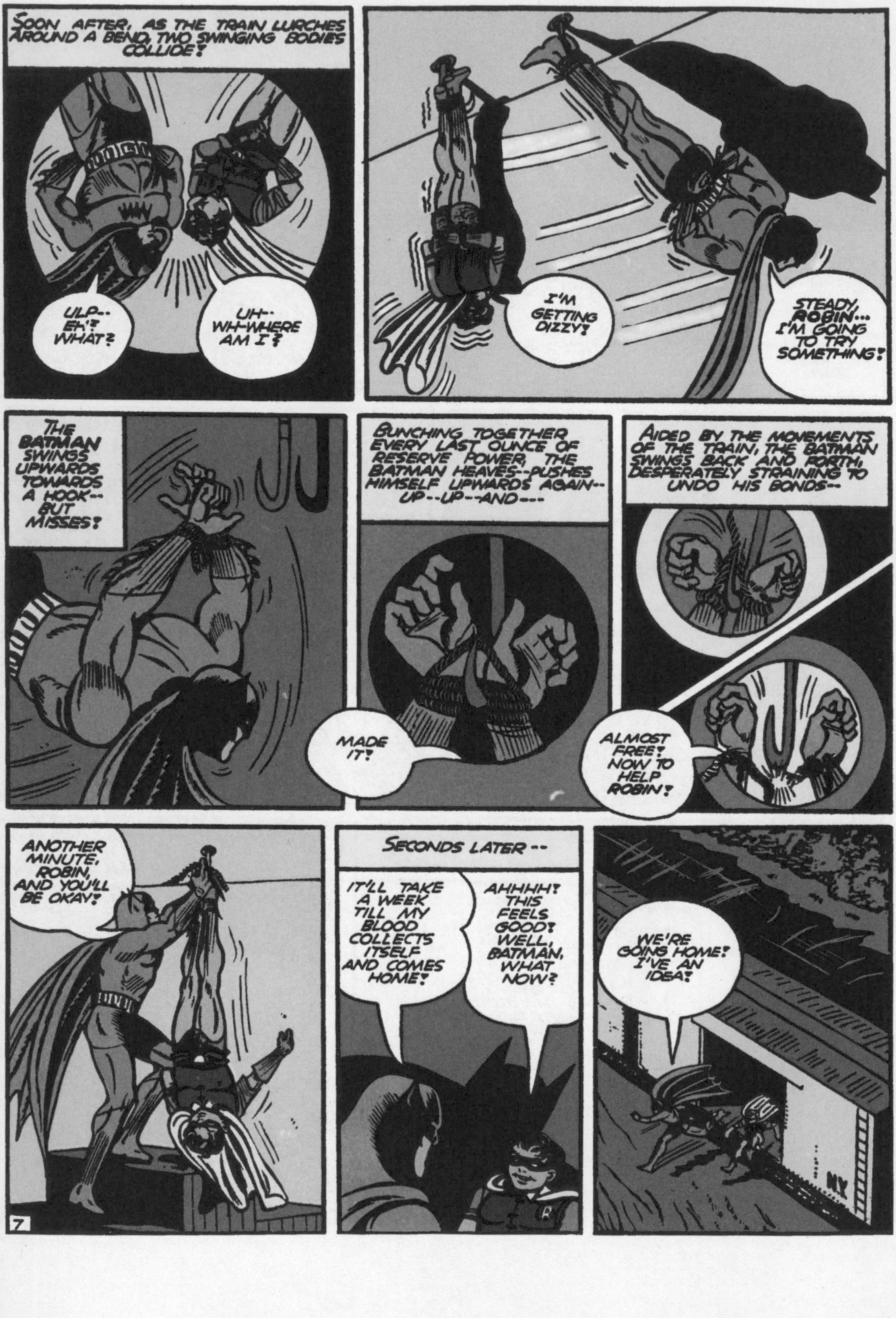
SOON AFTER, AS THE TRAIN LURCHES AROUND A BEND, TWO SWINGING BODIES COLLIDE!
ULP-- EH'? WHAT?
UH-- WH-WHERE AM I?
I'M GETTING DIZZY!
STEADY, ROBIN... I'M GOING TO TRY SOMETHING!
THE BATMAN SWINGS UPWARDS TOWARDS A HOOK-- BUT MISSES!
BUNCHING TOGETHER EVERY LAST OUNCE OF RESERVE POWER, THE BATMAN HEAVES--PUSHES HIMSELF UPWARDS AGAIN-- UP--UP--AND---
MADE IT!
AIDED BY THE MOVEMENTS OF THE TRAIN, THE BATMAN SWINGS BACK AND FORTH, DESPERATELY STRAINING TO UNDO HIS BONDS--
ALMOST FREE! NOW TO HELP ROBIN!
ANOTHER MINUTE, ROBIN, AND YOU'LL BE OKAY!
7
SECONDS LATER --
IT'LL TAKE A WEEK TILL MY BLOOD COLLECTS ITSELF AND COMES HOME!
AHHHH! THIS FEELS GOOD! WELL, BATMAN, WHAT NOW?
WE'RE GOING HOME! I'VE AN IDEA!
N.Y.

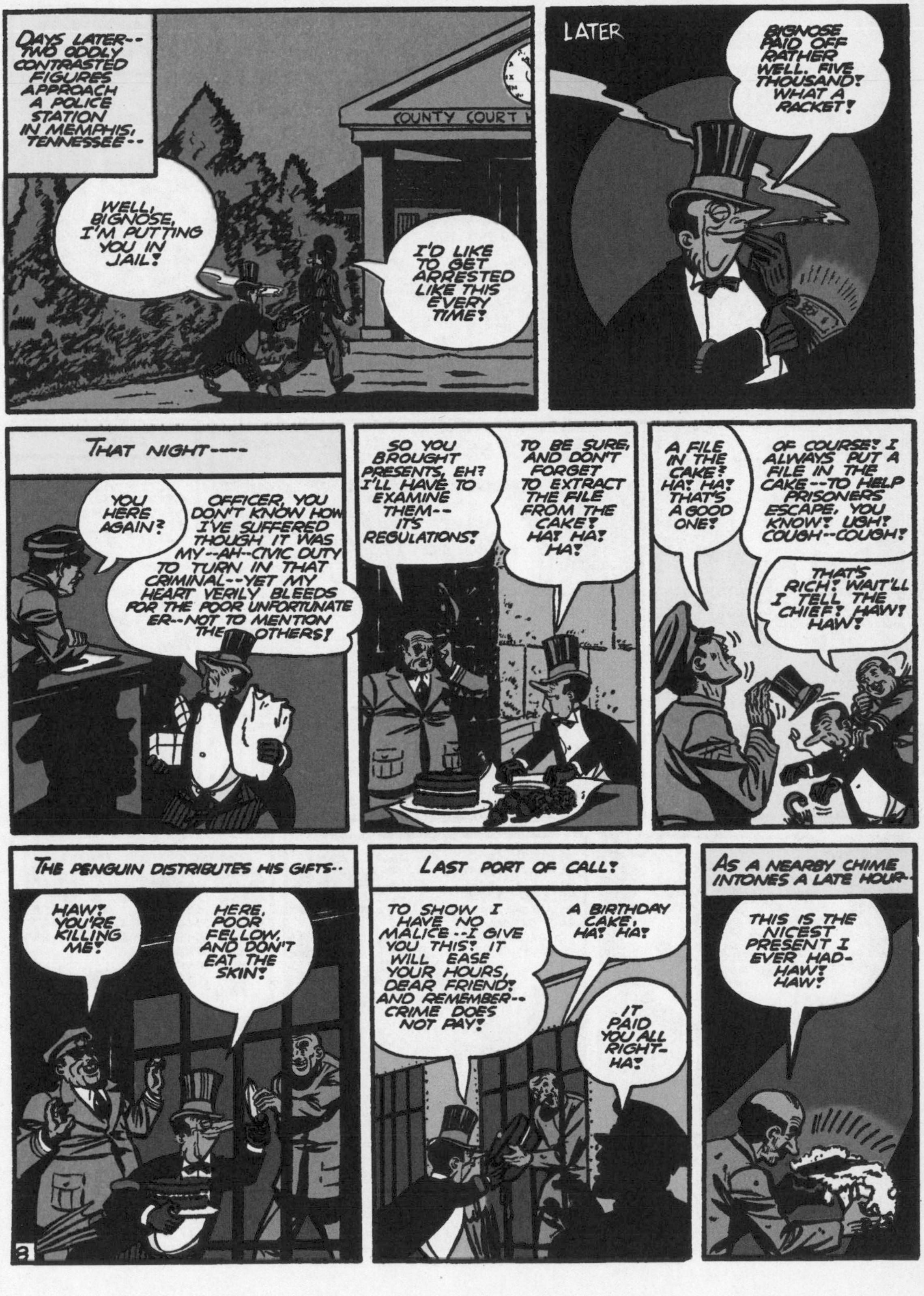
DAYS LATER--TWO ODDLY CONTRASTED FIGURES APPROACH A POLICE STATION IN MEMPHIS, TENNESSEE--
COUNTY COURT
WELL, BIGNOSE, I'M PUTTING YOU IN JAIL!
I'D LIKE TO GET ARRESTED LIKE THIS EVERY TIME!
LATER
BIGNOSE PAID OFF RATHER WELL. FIVE THOUSAND! WHAT A RACKET!
THAT NIGHT----
YOU HERE AGAIN?
OFFICER, YOU DON'T KNOW HOW I'VE SUFFERED THOUGH IT WAS MY--AH--CIVIC DUTY TO TURN IN THAT CRIMINAL--YET MY HEART VERILY BLEEDS FOR THE POOR UNFORTUNATE ER--NOT TO MENTION THE OTHERS!
SO YOU BROUGHT PRESENTS, EH? I'LL HAVE TO EXAMINE THEM--IT'S REGULATIONS!
TO BE SURE, AND DON'T FORGET TO EXTRACT THE FILE FROM THE CAKE! HA! HA! HA!
A FILE IN THE CAKE? HA! HA! THAT'S A GOOD ONE!
OF COURSE! I ALWAYS PUT A FILE IN THE CAKE--TO HELP PRISONERS ESCAPE, YOU KNOW! UGH! COUGH--COUGH!
THAT'S RICH! WAIT'LL I TELL THE CHIEF! HAW! HAW!
THE PENGUIN DISTRIBUTES HIS GIFTS--
HAW! YOU'RE KILLING ME!
HERE, POOR FELLOW, AND DON'T EAT THE SKIN!
8
LAST PORT OF CALL!
TO SHOW I HAVE NO MALICE--I GIVE YOU THIS! IT WILL EASE YOUR HOURS, DEAR FRIEND! AND REMEMBER--CRIME DOES NOT PAY!
A BIRTHDAY CAKE, HA! HA!
IT PAID YOU ALL RIGHT--HA!
AS A NEARBY CHIME INTONES A LATE HOUR--
THIS IS THE NICEST PRESENT I EVER HAD--HAW! HAW!

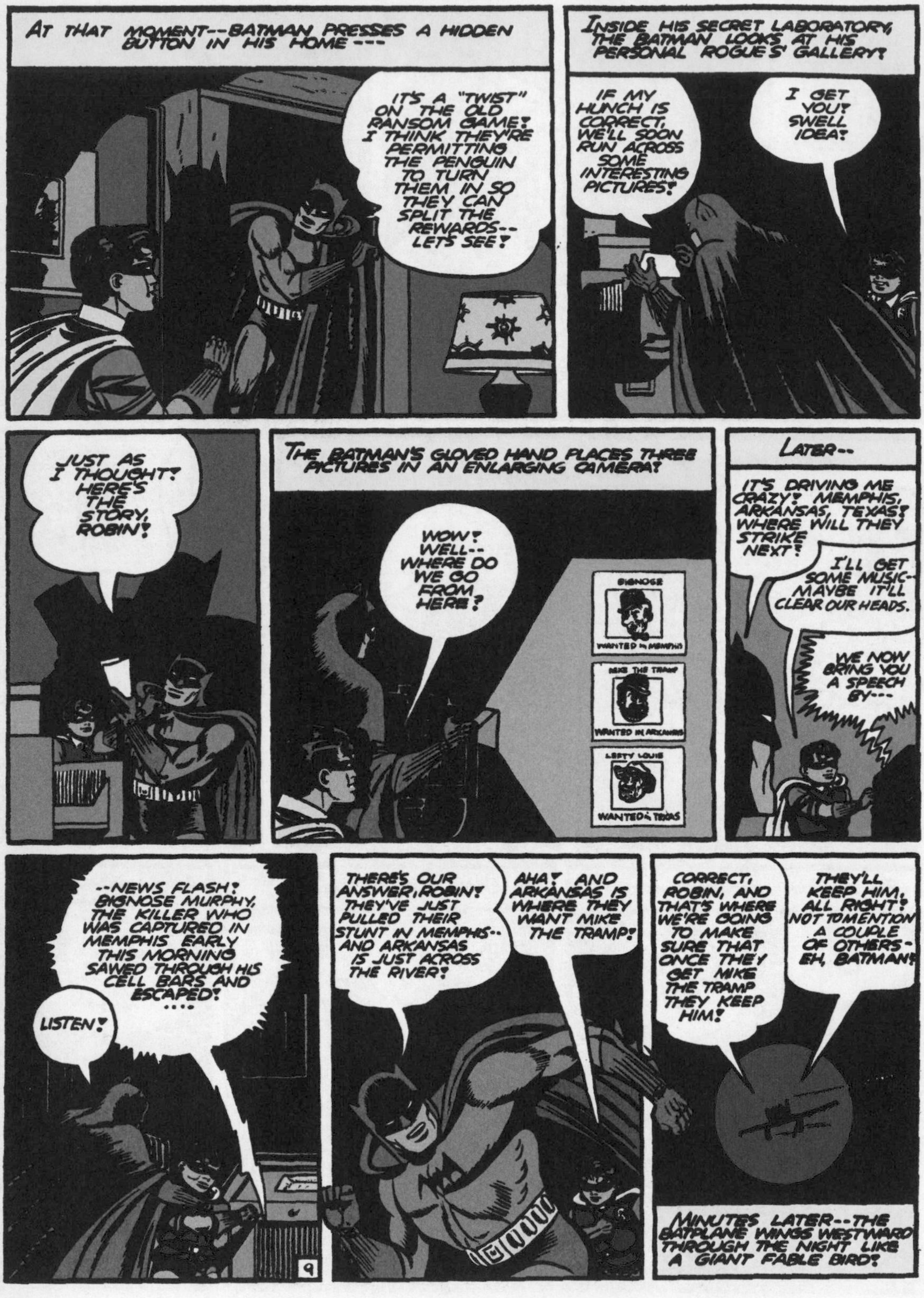
AT THAT MOMENT--BATMAN PRESSES A HIDDEN BUTTON IN HIS HOME---
IT'S A "TWIST" ON THE OLD RANSOM GAME! I THINK THEY'RE PERMITTING THE PENGUIN TO TURN THEM IN SO THEY CAN SPLIT THE REWARDS--LETS SEE!
INSIDE HIS SECRET LABORATORY, THE BATMAN LOOKS AT HIS PERSONAL ROGUE'S' GALLERY!
IF MY HUNCH IS CORRECT, WE'LL SOON RUN ACROSS SOME INTERESTING PICTURES!
I GET YOU! SWELL IDEA!
JUST AS I THOUGHT! HERE'S THE STORY, ROBIN!
THE BATMAN'S GLOVED HAND PLACES THREE PICTURES IN AN ENLARGING CAMERA!
WOW! WELL--WHERE DO WE GO FROM HERE?
BIGNOSE
WANTED IN MEMPHIS
MIKE THE TRAMP
WANTED IN ARKANSAS
LEFTY LOUIE
WANTED IN TEXAS
LATER--
IT'S DRIVING ME CRAZY! MEMPHIS, ARKANSAS, TEXAS! WHERE WILL THEY STRIKE NEXT!
I'LL GET SOME MUSIC--MAYBE IT'LL CLEAR OUR HEADS.
WE NOW BRING YOU A SPEECH BY---
--NEWS FLASH! BIGNOSE MURPHY, THE KILLER WHO WAS CAPTURED IN MEMPHIS EARLY THIS MORNING SAWED THROUGH HIS CELL BARS AND ESCAPED! ....
LISTEN!
9
THERE'S OUR ANSWER, ROBIN! THEY'VE JUST PULLED THEIR STUNT IN MEMPHIS--AND ARKANSAS IS JUST ACROSS THE RIVER!
AHA! AND ARKANSAS IS WHERE THEY WANT MIKE THE TRAMP!
CORRECT, ROBIN, AND THAT'S WHERE WE'RE GOING TO MAKE SURE THAT ONCE THEY GET MIKE THE TRAMP THEY KEEP HIM!
THEY'LL KEEP HIM, ALL RIGHT! NOT TO MENTION A COUPLE OF OTHERS--EH, BATMAN!
MINUTES LATER--THE BATPLANE WINGS WESTWARD THROUGH THE NIGHT LIKE A GIANT FABLE BIRD!

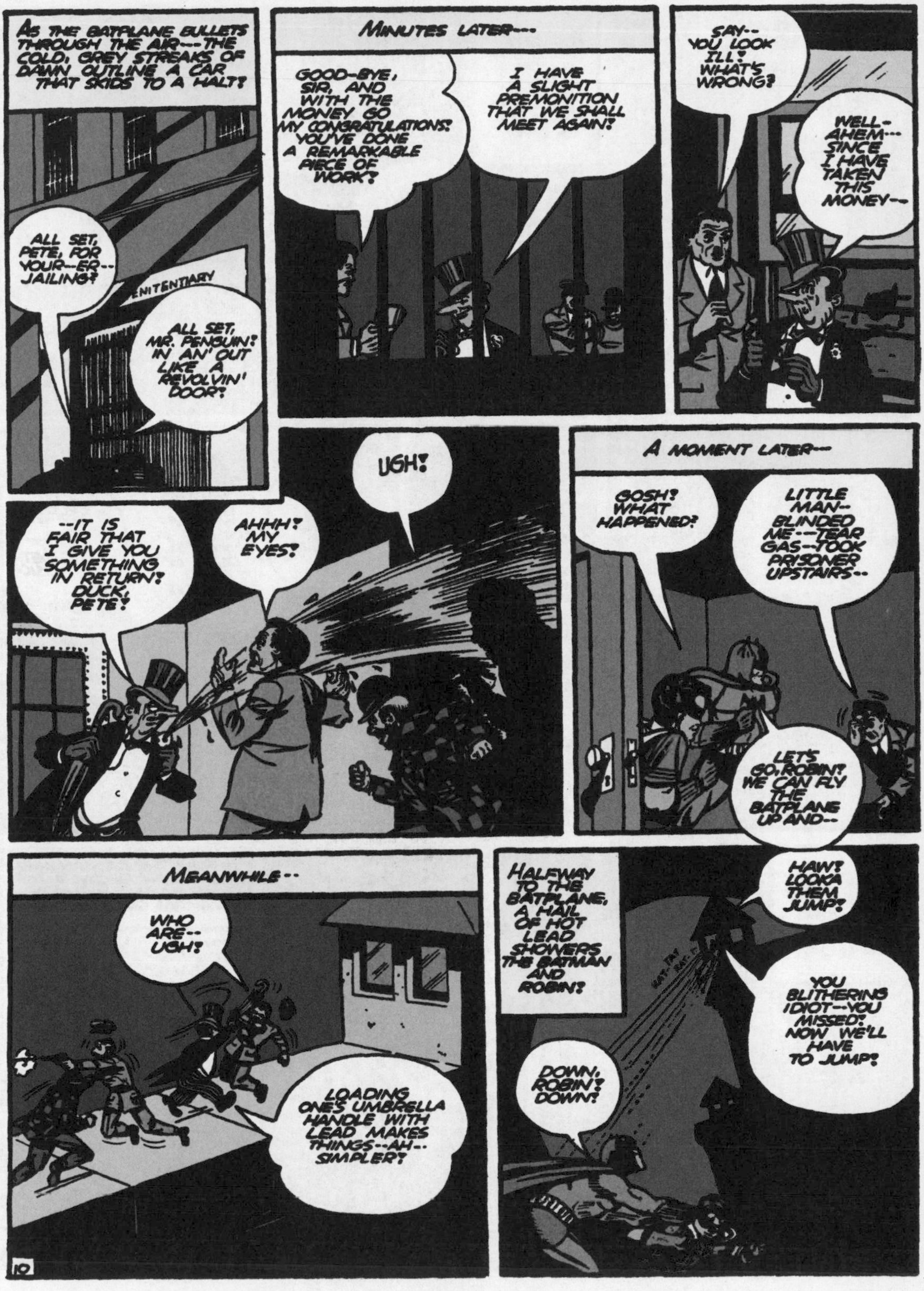
AS THE BATPLANE BULLETS THROUGH THE AIR---THE COLD, GREY STREAKS OF DAWN OUTLINE A CAR THAT SKIDS TO A HALT!
ALL SET, PETE, FOR YOUR--ER--JAILING?
ENITENTIARY
ALL SET, MR. PENGUIN! IN AN' OUT LIKE A REVOLVIN' DOOR!
MINUTES LATER---
GOOD-BYE, SIR, AND WITH THE MONEY GO MY CONGRATULATIONS! YOU'VE DONE A REMARKABLE PIECE OF WORK!
I HAVE A SLIGHT PREMONITION THAT WE SHALL MEET AGAIN!
SAY-- YOU LOOK ILL! WHAT'S WRONG?
WELL-AHEM--- SINCE I HAVE TAKEN THIS MONEY--
--IT IS FAIR THAT I GIVE YOU SOMETHING IN RETURN! DUCK, PETE!
AHHH! MY EYES!
UGH!
A MOMENT LATER---
GOSH! WHAT HAPPENED?
LITTLE MAN-- BLINDED ME--TEAR GAS--TOOK PRISONER UPSTAIRS--
LET'S GO, ROBIN! WE CAN FLY THE BATPLANE UP AND--
MEANWHILE--
WHO ARE-- UGH!
LOADING ONE'S UMBRELLA HANDLE WITH LEAD MAKES THINGS--AH--SIMPLER!
HALFWAY TO THE BATPLANE, A HAIL OF HOT LEAD SHOWERS THE BATMAN AND ROBIN!
HAW! LOOKA THEM JUMP!
YOU BLITHERING IDIOT--YOU MISSED! NOW WE'LL HAVE TO JUMP!
DOWN, ROBIN! DOWN!
10

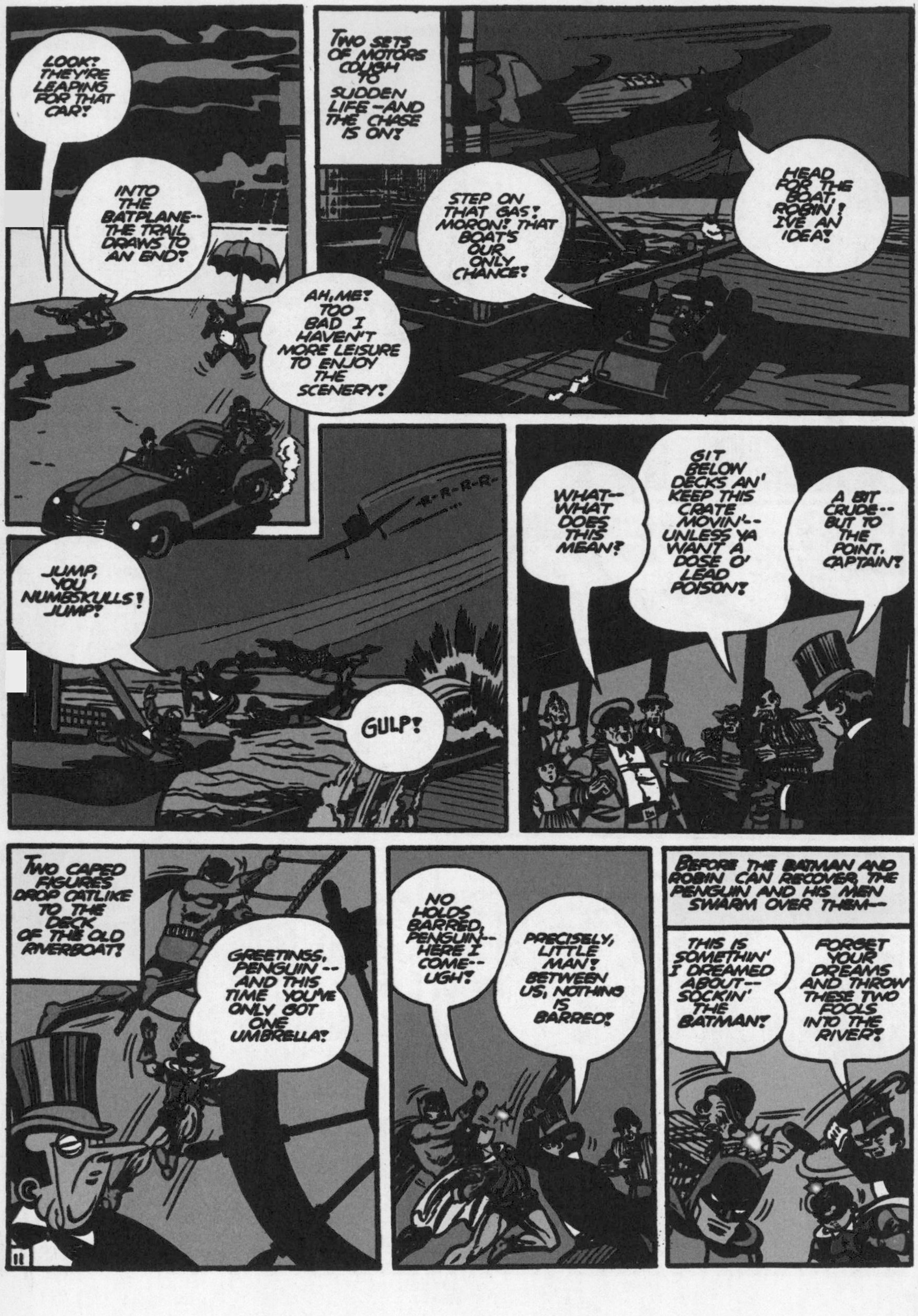
LOOK! THEY'RE LEAPING FOR THAT CAR!
INTO THE BATPLANE--THE TRAIL DRAWS TO AN END!
AH, ME! TOO BAD I HAVEN'T MORE LEISURE TO ENJOY THE SCENERY!
TWO SETS OF MOTORS COUGH TO SUDDEN LIFE--AND THE CHASE IS ON!
STEP ON THAT GAS, MORON! THAT BOAT'S OUR ONLY CHANCE!
HEAD FOR THE BOAT, ROBIN! I'VE AN IDEA!
R-R-R-R-
JUMP, YOU NUMBSKULLS! JUMP!
GULP!
WHAT--WHAT DOES THIS MEAN?
GIT BELOW DECKS AN' KEEP THIS CRATE MOVIN'--UNLESS YA WANT A DOSE O' LEAD POISON!
A BIT CRUDE--BUT TO THE POINT, CAPTAIN!
TWO CAPED FIGURES DROP CATLIKE TO THE DECK OF THE OLD RIVERBOAT!
GREETINGS, PENGUIN--AND THIS TIME YOU'VE ONLY GOT ONE UMBRELLA!
11
NO HOLDS BARRED, PENGUIN--HERE I COME--UGH!
PRECISELY, LITTLE MAN! BETWEEN US, NOTHING IS BARRED!
BEFORE THE BATMAN AND ROBIN CAN RECOVER, THE PENGUIN AND HIS MEN SWARM OVER THEM--
THIS IS SOMETHIN' I DREAMED ABOUT--SOCKIN' THE BATMAN!
FORGET YOUR DREAMS AND THROW THESE TWO FOOLS INTO THE RIVER!

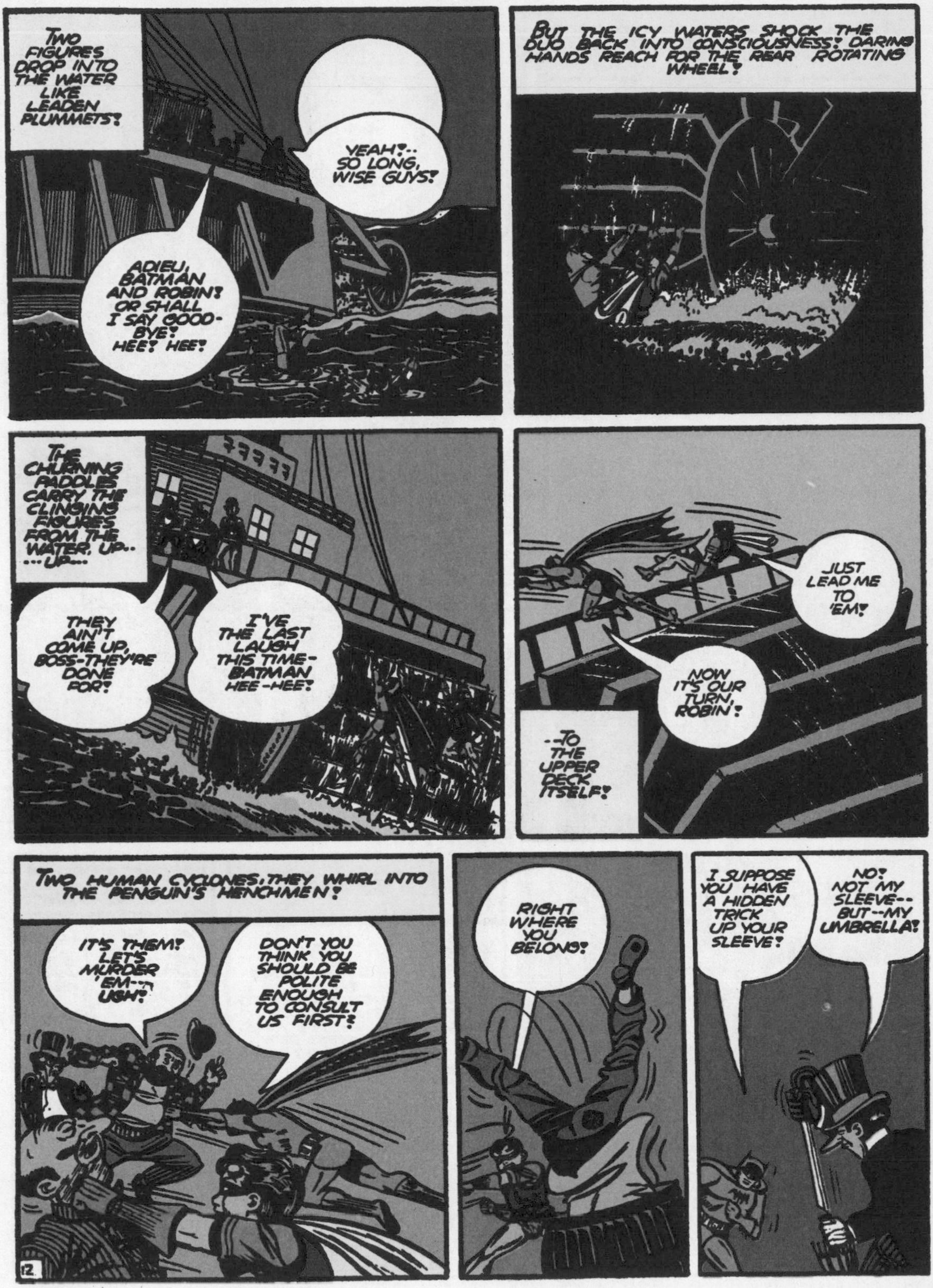
TWO FIGURES DROP INTO THE WATER LIKE LEADEN PLUMMETS!
YEAH!.. SO LONG, WISE GUYS!
ADIEU, BATMAN AND ROBIN! OR SHALL I SAY GOOD-BYE! HEE! HEE!
BUT THE ICY WATERS SHOCK THE DUO BACK INTO CONSCIOUSNESS! DARING HANDS REACH FOR THE REAR ROTATING WHEEL!
THE CHURNING PADDLES CARRY THE CLINGING FIGURES FROM THE WATER, UP.. ...UP...
THEY AIN'T COME UP, BOSS-THEY'RE DONE FOR!
I'VE THE LAST LAUGH THIS TIME-BATMAN HEE-HEE!
JUST LEAD ME TO 'EM!
NOW IT'S OUR TURN, ROBIN!
--TO THE UPPER DECK ITSELF!
TWO HUMAN CYCLONES, THEY WHIRL INTO THE PENGUIN'S HENCHMEN!
IT'S THEM! LET'S MURDER 'EM--UGH!
DON'T YOU THINK YOU SHOULD BE POLITE ENOUGH TO CONSULT US FIRST?
12.
RIGHT WHERE YOU BELONG!
I SUPPOSE YOU HAVE A HIDDEN TRICK UP YOUR SLEEVE?
NO! NOT MY SLEEVE-- BUT--MY UMBRELLA!

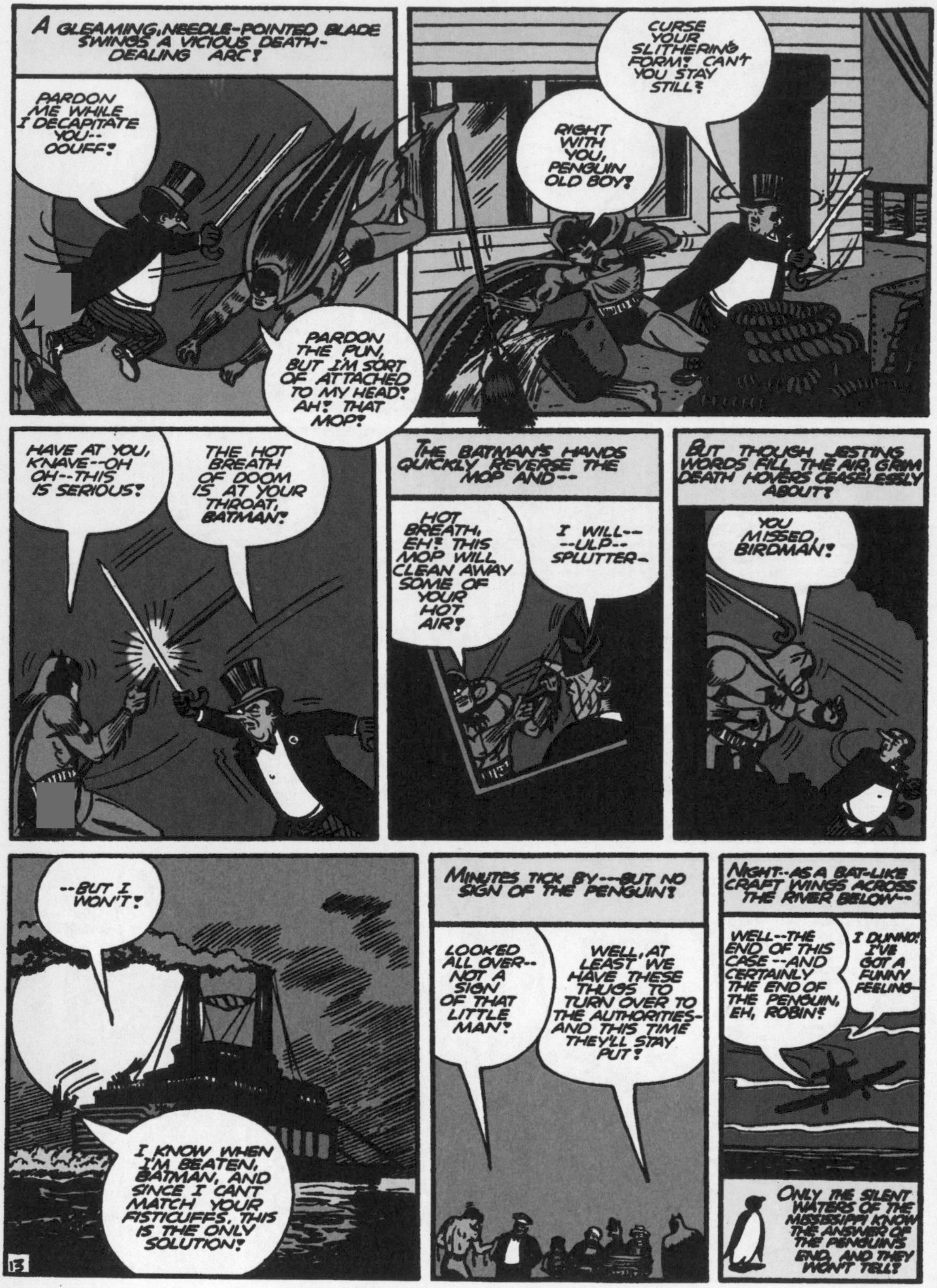
A GLEAMING, NEEDLE-POINTED BLADE SWINGS A VICIOUS DEATH-DEALING ARC!
PARDON ME WHILE I DECAPITATE YOU--OOUFF!
PARDON THE PUN, BUT I'M SORT OF ATTACHED TO MY HEAD! AH! THAT MOP!
CURSE YOUR SLITHERING FORM! CAN'T YOU STAY STILL?
RIGHT WITH YOU, PENGUIN OLD BOY!
HAVE AT YOU, KNAVE--OH OH--THIS IS SERIOUS!
THE HOT BREATH OF DOOM IS AT YOUR THROAT, BATMAN!
THE BATMAN'S HANDS QUICKLY REVERSE THE MOP AND--
HOT BREATH, EH? THIS MOP WILL CLEAN AWAY SOME OF YOUR HOT AIR!
I WILL----ULP--SPLUTTER--
BUT THOUGH JESTING WORDS FILL THE AIR, GRIM DEATH HOVERS CEASELESSLY ABOUT!
YOU MISSED, BIRDMAN!
--BUT I WON'T!
I KNOW WHEN I'M BEATEN, BATMAN, AND SINCE I CAN'T MATCH YOUR FISTICUFFS, THIS IS THE ONLY SOLUTION!
13
MINUTES TICK BY---BUT NO SIGN OF THE PENGUIN!
LOOKED ALL OVER--NOT A SIGN OF THAT LITTLE MAN!
WELL, AT LEAST WE HAVE THESE THUGS TO TURN OVER TO THE AUTHORITIES--AND THIS TIME THEY'LL STAY PUT!
NIGHT--AS A BAT-LIKE CRAFT WINGS ACROSS THE RIVER BELOW--
WELL--THE END OF THIS CASE--AND CERTAINLY THE END OF THE PENGUIN, EH, ROBIN?
I DUNNO! I'VE GOT A FUNNY FEELING--
ONLY THE SILENT WATERS OF THE MISSISSIPPI KNOW THE ANSWER OF THE PENGUIN'S END, AND THEY WON'T TELL!

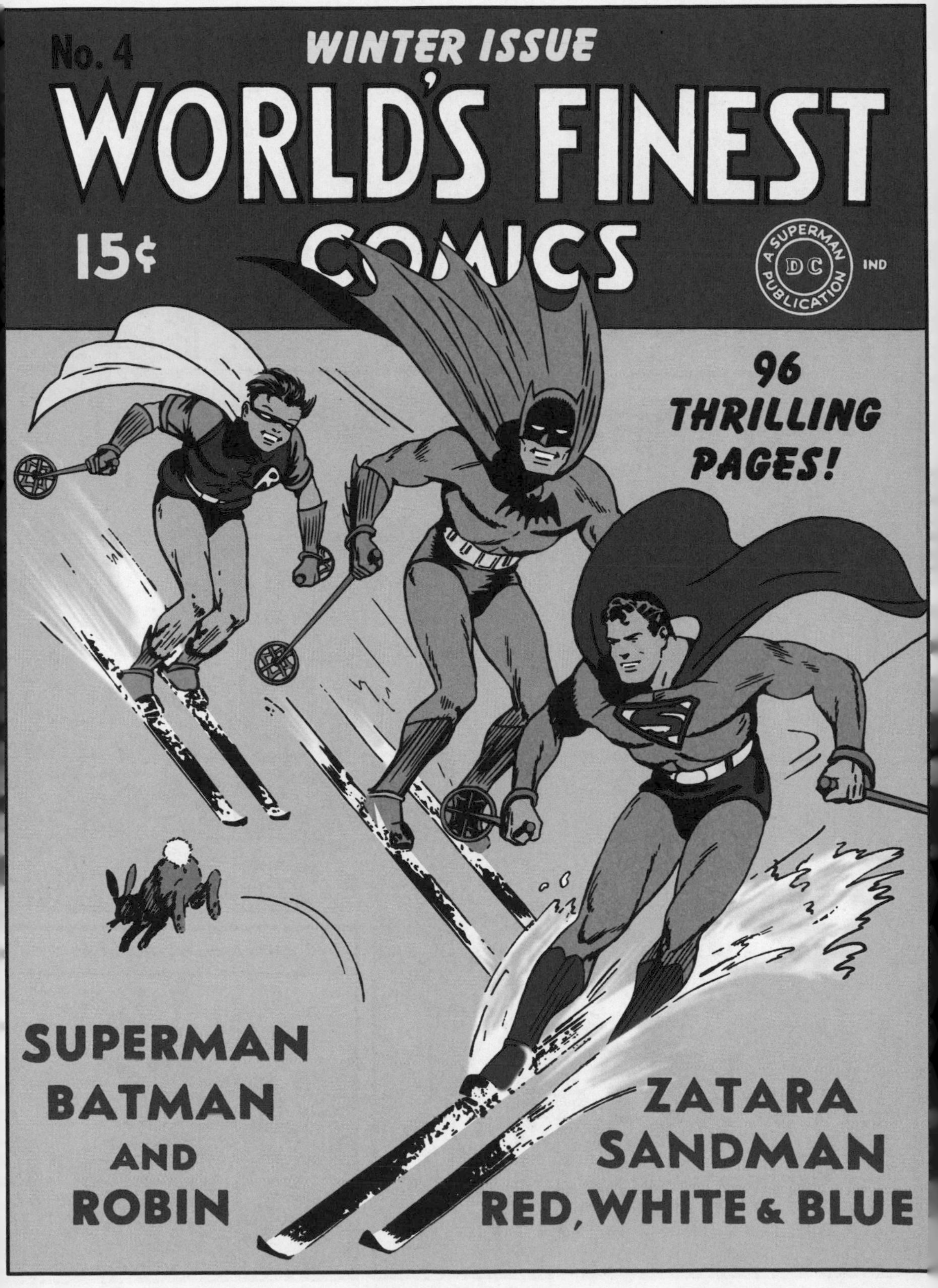
No. 4
WINTER ISSUE
WORLD'S FINEST
COMICS
15¢
A SUPERMAN DC PUBLICATION
IND
96
THRILLING
PAGES!
SUPERMAN
BATMAN
AND
ROBIN
ZATARA
SANDMAN
RED, WHITE & BLUE

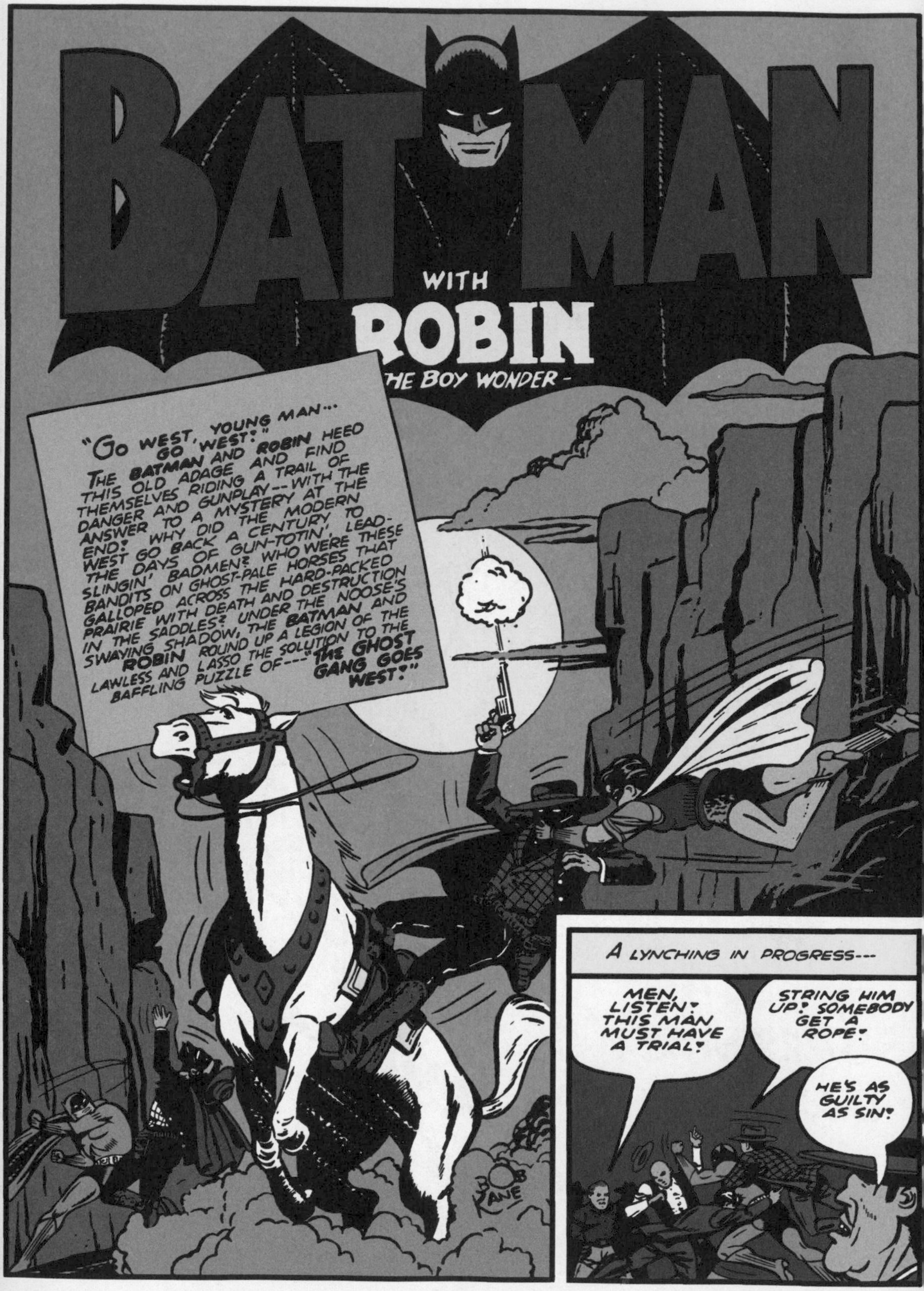
BATMAN
WITH
ROBIN
-THE BOY WONDER-
"GO WEST, YOUNG MAN... GO WEST!" THE BATMAN AND ROBIN HEED THIS OLD ADAGE AND FIND THEMSELVES RIDING A TRAIL OF DANGER AND GUNPLAY--WITH THE ANSWER TO A MYSTERY AT THE END! WHY DID THE MODERN WEST GO BACK A CENTURY TO THE DAYS OF GUN-TOTIN', LEAD-SLINGIN' BADMEN? WHO WERE THESE BANDITS ON GHOST-PALE HORSES THAT GALLOPED ACROSS THE HARD-PACKED PRAIRIE WITH DEATH AND DESTRUCTION IN THE SADDLES? UNDER THE NOOSE'S SWAYING SHADOW, THE BATMAN AND ROBIN ROUND UP A LEGION OF THE LAWLESS AND LASSO THE SOLUTION TO THE BAFFLING PUZZLE OF---"THE GHOST GANG GOES WEST!"
BOB KANE
A LYNCHING IN PROGRESS---
MEN, LISTEN! THIS MAN MUST HAVE A TRIAL!
STRING HIM UP! SOMEBODY GET A ROPE!
HE'S AS GUILTY AS SIN!

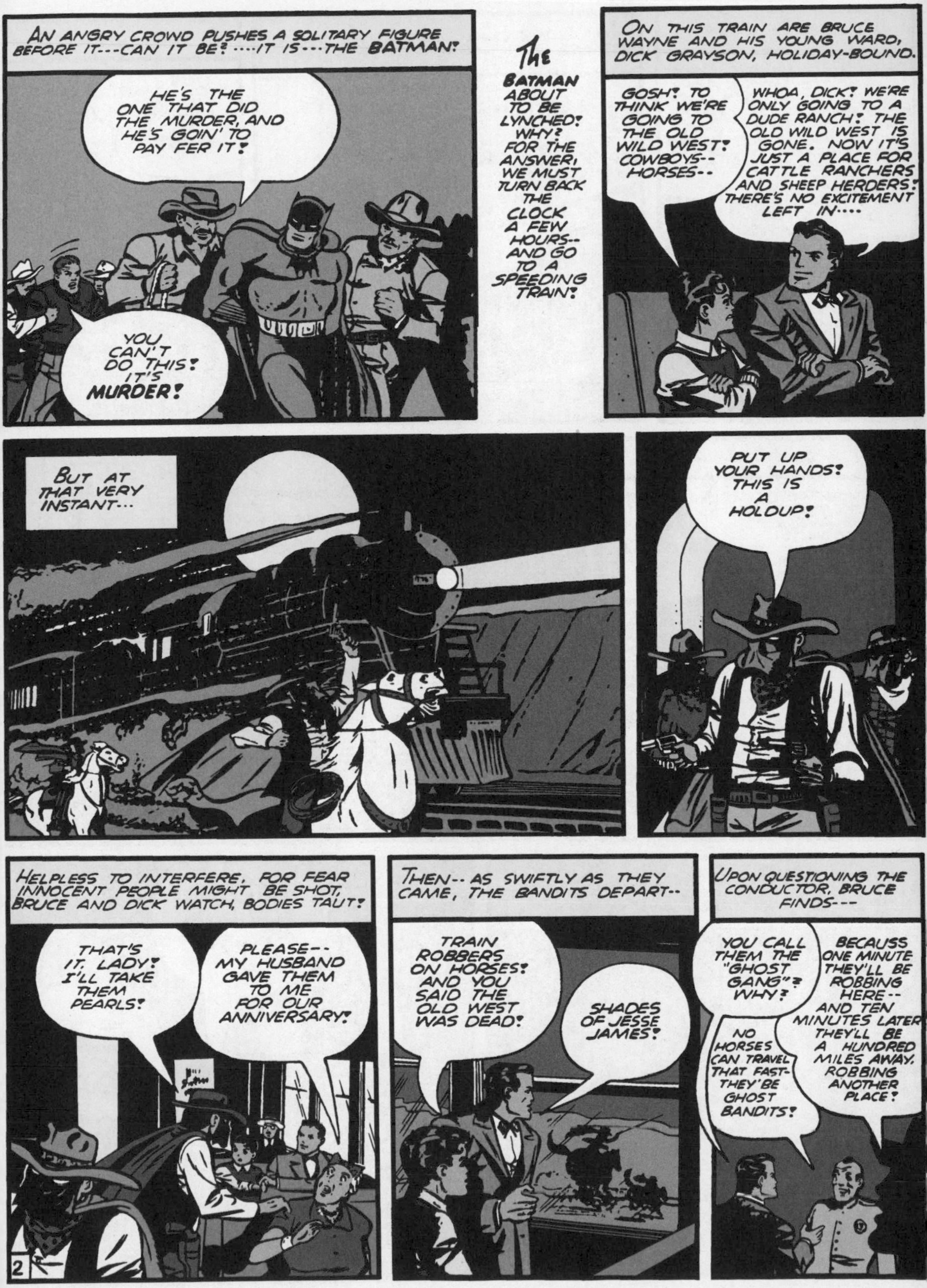

AN ANGRY CROWD PUSHES A SOLITARY FIGURE BEFORE IT---CAN IT BE? ----IT IS---THE BATMAN!
HE'S THE ONE THAT DID THE MURDER, AND HE'S GOIN' TO PAY FER IT!
YOU CAN'T DO THIS! IT'S MURDER!
THE BATMAN ABOUT TO BE LYNCHED! WHY? FOR THE ANSWER, WE MUST TURN BACK THE CLOCK A FEW HOURS-- AND GO TO A SPEEDING TRAIN!
ON THIS TRAIN ARE BRUCE WAYNE AND HIS YOUNG WARD, DICK GRAYSON, HOLIDAY-BOUND.
GOSH! TO THINK WE'RE GOING TO THE OLD WILD WEST! COWBOYS-- HORSES--
WHOA, DICK! WE'RE ONLY GOING TO A DUDE RANCH! THE OLD WILD WEST IS GONE. NOW IT'S JUST A PLACE FOR CATTLE RANCHERS AND SHEEP HERDERS! THERE'S NO EXCITEMENT LEFT IN----
BUT AT THAT VERY INSTANT---
PUT UP YOUR HANDS! THIS IS A HOLDUP!
HELPLESS TO INTERFERE, FOR FEAR INNOCENT PEOPLE MIGHT BE SHOT, BRUCE AND DICK WATCH, BODIES TAUT!
THAT'S IT, LADY! I'LL TAKE THEM PEARLS!
PLEASE-- MY HUSBAND GAVE THEM TO ME FOR OUR ANNIVERSARY!
THEN-- AS SWIFTLY AS THEY CAME, THE BANDITS DEPART--
TRAIN ROBBERS ON HORSES! AND YOU SAID THE OLD WEST WAS DEAD!
SHADES OF JESSE JAMES!
UPON QUESTIONING THE CONDUCTOR, BRUCE FINDS---
YOU CALL THEM THE "GHOST GANG"? WHY?
BECAUSS ONE MINUTE THEY'LL BE ROBBING HERE-- AND TEN MINUTES LATER THEY'LL BE A HUNDRED MILES AWAY, ROBBING ANOTHER PLACE!
NO HORSES CAN TRAVEL THAT FAST-- THEY'BE GHOST BANDITS!

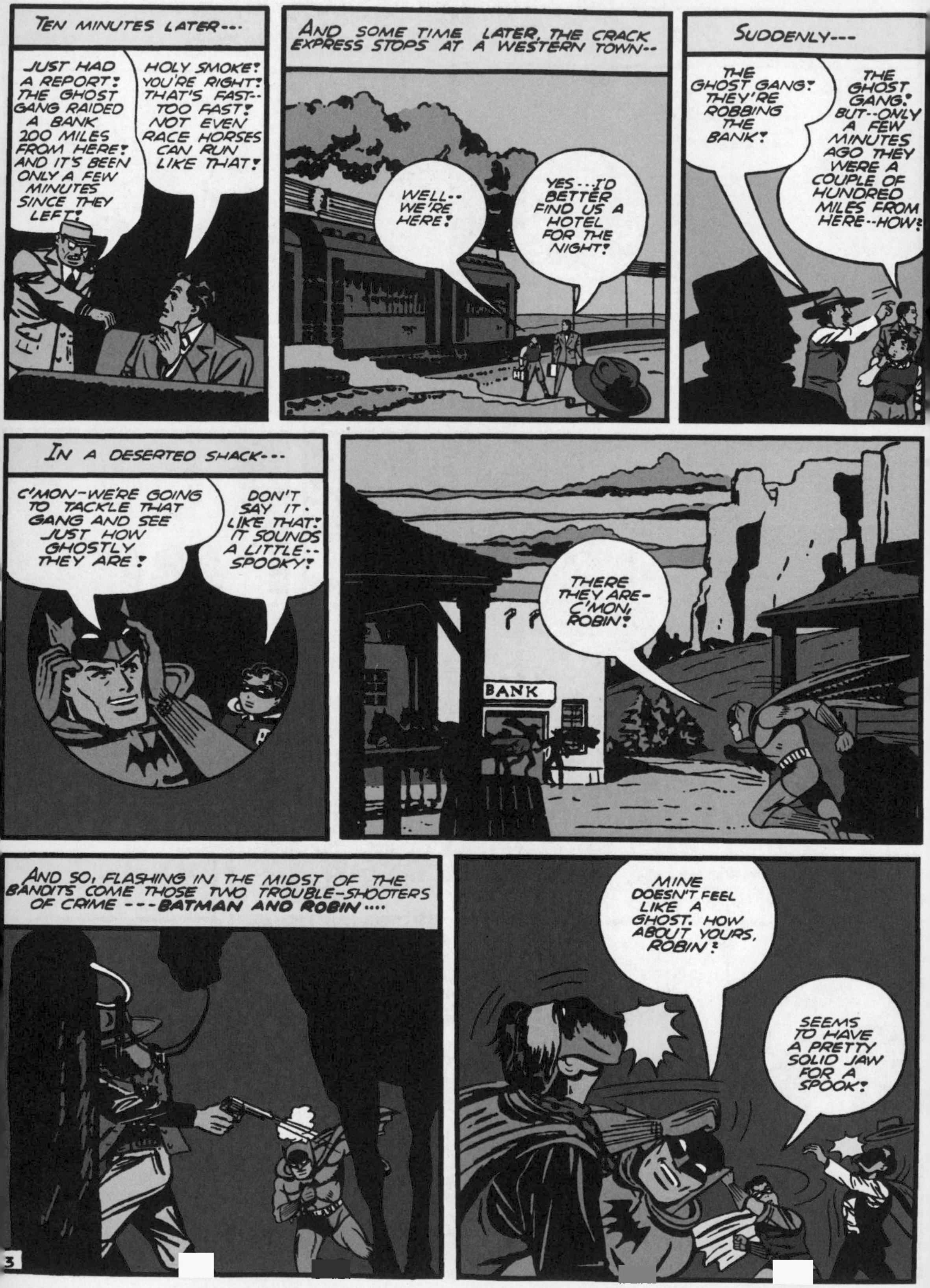
TEN MINUTES LATER---
JUST HAD A REPORT! THE GHOST GANG RAIDED A BANK 200 MILES FROM HERE! AND IT'S BEEN ONLY A FEW MINUTES SINCE THEY LEFT!
HOLY SMOKE! YOU'RE RIGHT! THAT'S FAST--TOO FAST! NOT EVEN RACE HORSES CAN RUN LIKE THAT!
AND SOME TIME LATER, THE CRACK EXPRESS STOPS AT A WESTERN TOWN--
WELL--WE'RE HERE!
YES--I'D BETTER FIND US A HOTEL FOR THE NIGHT!
SUDDENLY---
THE GHOST GANG! THEY'RE ROBBING THE BANK!
THE GHOST GANG! BUT--ONLY A FEW MINUTES AGO THEY WERE A COUPLE OF HUNDRED MILES FROM HERE--HOW?
IN A DESERTED SHACK---
C'MON-WE'RE GOING TO TACKLE THAT GANG AND SEE JUST HOW GHOSTLY THEY ARE!
DON'T SAY IT LIKE THAT! IT SOUNDS A LITTLE--SPOOKY!
THERE THEY ARE-C'MON, ROBIN!
BANK
AND SO, FLASHING IN THE MIDST OF THE BANDITS COME THOSE TWO TROUBLE-SHOOTERS OF CRIME ---BATMAN AND ROBIN....
MINE DOESN'T FEEL LIKE A GHOST. HOW ABOUT YOURS, ROBIN?
SEEMS TO HAVE A PRETTY SOLID JAW FOR A SPOOK!
3

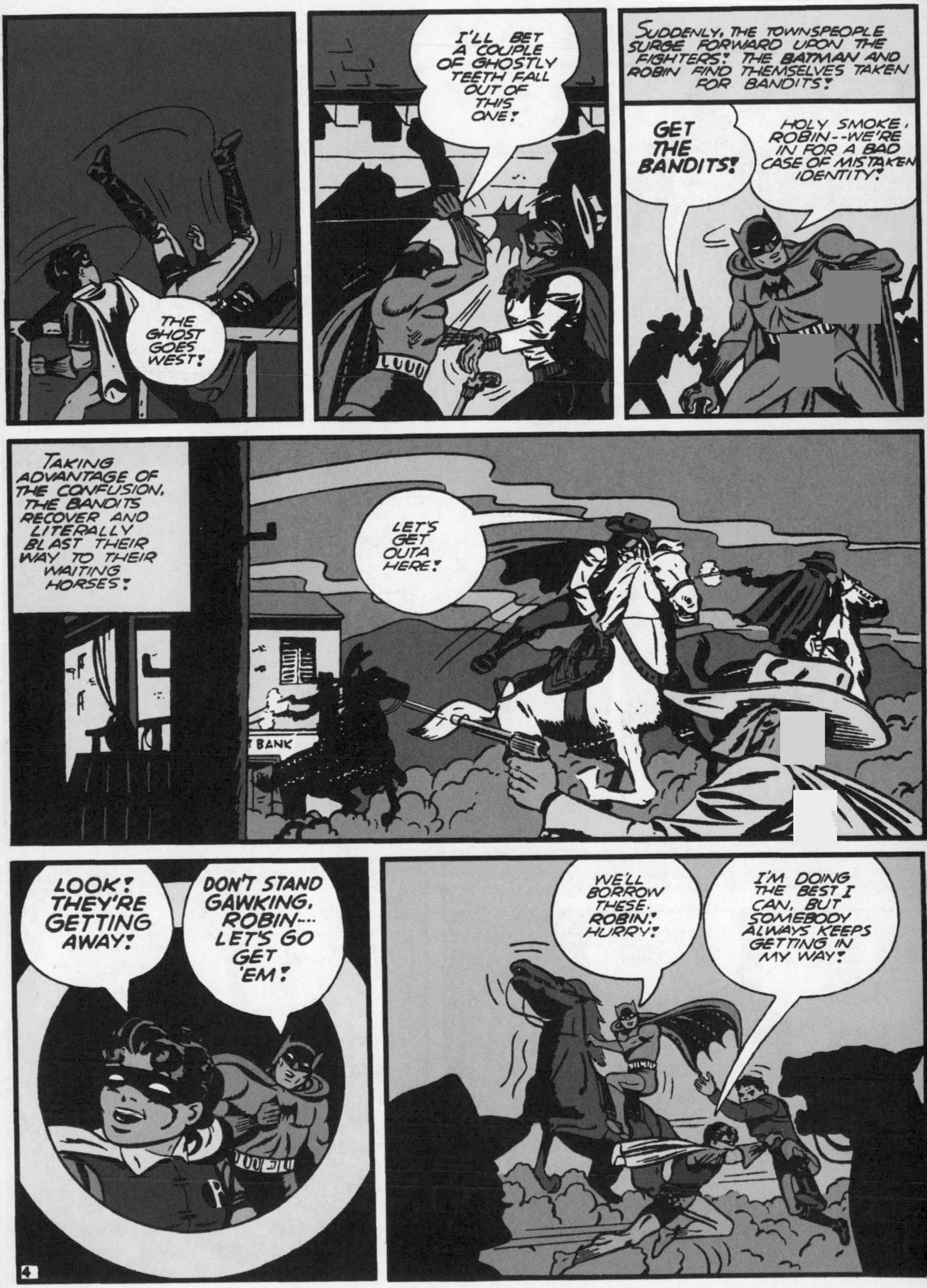
THE GHOST GOES WEST!
I'LL BET A COUPLE OF GHOSTLY TEETH FALL OUT OF THIS ONE!
SUDDENLY, THE TOWNSPEOPLE SURGE FORWARD UPON THE FIGHTERS! THE BATMAN AND ROBIN FIND THEMSELVES TAKEN FOR BANDITS!
GET THE BANDITS!
HOLY SMOKE, ROBIN--WE'RE IN FOR A BAD CASE OF MISTAKEN IDENTITY!
TAKING ADVANTAGE OF THE CONFUSION, THE BANDITS RECOVER AND LITERALLY BLAST THEIR WAY TO THEIR WAITING HORSES!
LET'S GET OUTA HERE!
BANK
LOOK! THEY'RE GETTING AWAY!
DON'T STAND GAWKING, ROBIN.... LET'S GO GET 'EM!
WE'LL BORROW THESE, ROBIN! HURRY!
I'M DOING THE BEST I CAN, BUT SOMEBODY ALWAYS KEEPS GETTING IN MY WAY!
4

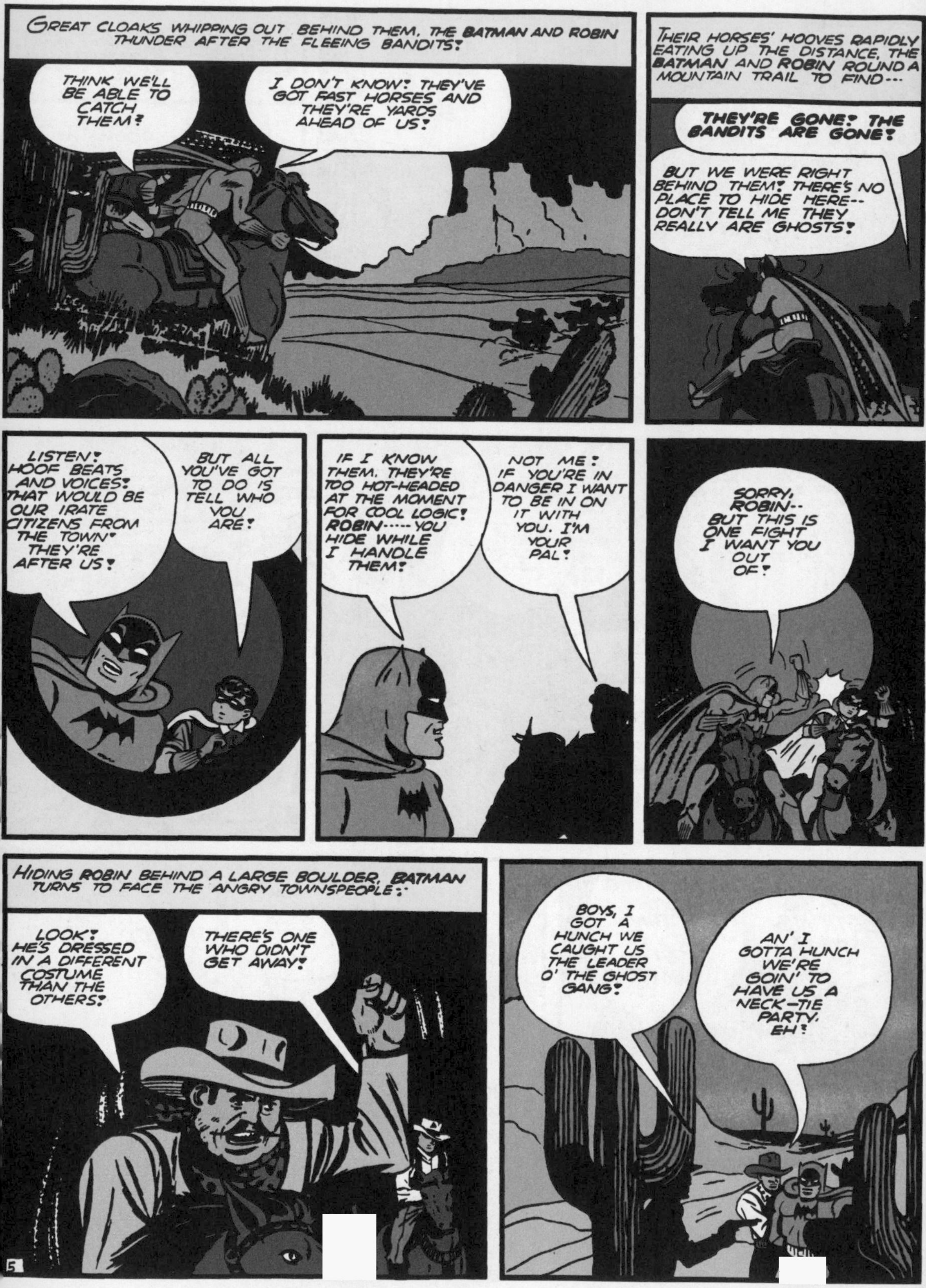
GREAT CLOAKS WHIPPING OUT BEHIND THEM, THE BATMAN AND ROBIN THUNDER AFTER THE FLEEING BANDITS!
THINK WE'LL BE ABLE TO CATCH THEM?
I DON'T KNOW! THEY'VE GOT FAST HORSES AND THEY'RE YARDS AHEAD OF US!
THEIR HORSES' HOOVES RAPIDLY EATING UP THE DISTANCE, THE BATMAN AND ROBIN ROUND A MOUNTAIN TRAIL TO FIND---
THEY'RE GONE! THE BANDITS ARE GONE!
BUT WE WERE RIGHT BEHIND THEM! THERE'S NO PLACE TO HIDE HERE-- DON'T TELL ME THEY REALLY ARE GHOSTS!
LISTEN! HOOF BEATS AND VOICES! THAT WOULD BE OUR IRATE CITIZENS FROM THE TOWN! THEY'RE AFTER US!
BUT ALL YOU'VE GOT TO DO IS TELL WHO YOU ARE!
IF I KNOW THEM, THEY'RE TOO HOT-HEADED AT THE MOMENT FOR COOL LOGIC! ROBIN----- YOU HIDE WHILE I HANDLE THEM!
NOT ME! IF YOU'RE IN DANGER I WANT TO BE IN ON IT WITH YOU. I'M YOUR PAL!
SORRY, ROBIN-- BUT THIS IS ONE FIGHT I WANT YOU OUT OF!
HIDING ROBIN BEHIND A LARGE BOULDER, BATMAN TURNS TO FACE THE ANGRY TOWNSPEOPLE!
LOOK! HE'S DRESSED IN A DIFFERENT COSTUME THAN THE OTHERS!
THERE'S ONE WHO DIDN'T GET AWAY!
5
BOYS, I GOT A HUNCH WE CAUGHT US THE LEADER O' THE GHOST GANG!
AN' I GOTTA HUNCH WE'RE GOIN' TO HAVE US A NECK-TIE PARTY, EH?

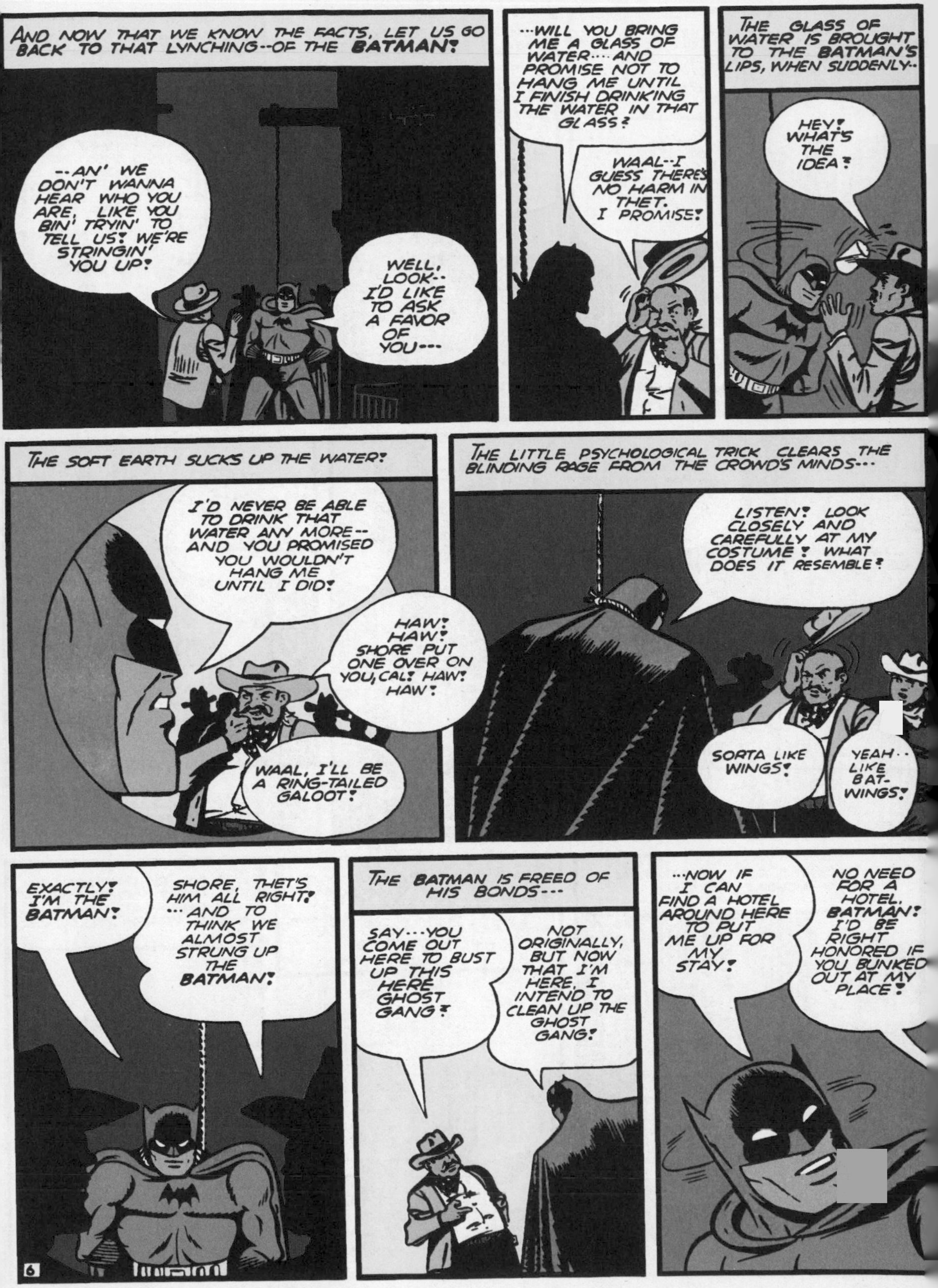
AND NOW THAT WE KNOW THE FACTS, LET US GO BACK TO THAT LYNCHING--OF THE BATMAN!
--AN' WE DON'T WANNA HEAR WHO YOU ARE, LIKE YOU BIN' TRYIN' TO TELL US! WE'RE STRINGIN' YOU UP!
WELL, LOOK-- I'D LIKE TO ASK A FAVOR OF YOU---
...WILL YOU BRING ME A GLASS OF WATER.... AND PROMISE NOT TO HANG ME UNTIL I FINISH DRINKING THE WATER IN THAT GLASS?
WAAL--I GUESS THERE'S NO HARM IN THET. I PROMISE!
THE GLASS OF WATER IS BROUGHT TO THE BATMAN'S LIPS, WHEN SUDDENLY--
HEY! WHAT'S THE IDEA?
THE SOFT EARTH SUCKS UP THE WATER!
I'D NEVER BE ABLE TO DRINK THAT WATER ANY MORE-- AND YOU PROMISED YOU WOULDN'T HANG ME UNTIL I DID!
HAW! HAW! SHORE PUT ONE OVER ON YOU, CAL! HAW! HAW!
WAAL, I'LL BE A RING-TAILED GALOOT!
THE LITTLE PSYCHOLOGICAL TRICK CLEARS THE BLINDING RAGE FROM THE CROWD'S MINDS---
LISTEN! LOOK CLOSELY AND CAREFULLY AT MY COSTUME! WHAT DOES IT RESEMBLE?
SORTA LIKE WINGS!
YEAH-- LIKE BAT-WINGS!
EXACTLY! I'M THE BATMAN!
SHORE, THET'S HIM ALL RIGHT! ...AND TO THINK WE ALMOST STRUNG UP THE BATMAN!
6
THE BATMAN IS FREED OF HIS BONDS---
SAY---YOU COME OUT HERE TO BUST UP THIS HERE GHOST GANG?
NOT ORIGINALLY, BUT NOW THAT I'M HERE, I INTEND TO CLEAN UP THE GHOST GANG!
...NOW IF I CAN FIND A HOTEL AROUND HERE TO PUT ME UP FOR MY STAY!
NO NEED FOR A HOTEL, BATMAN! I'D BE RIGHT HONORED IF YOU BUNKED OUT AT MY PLACE!

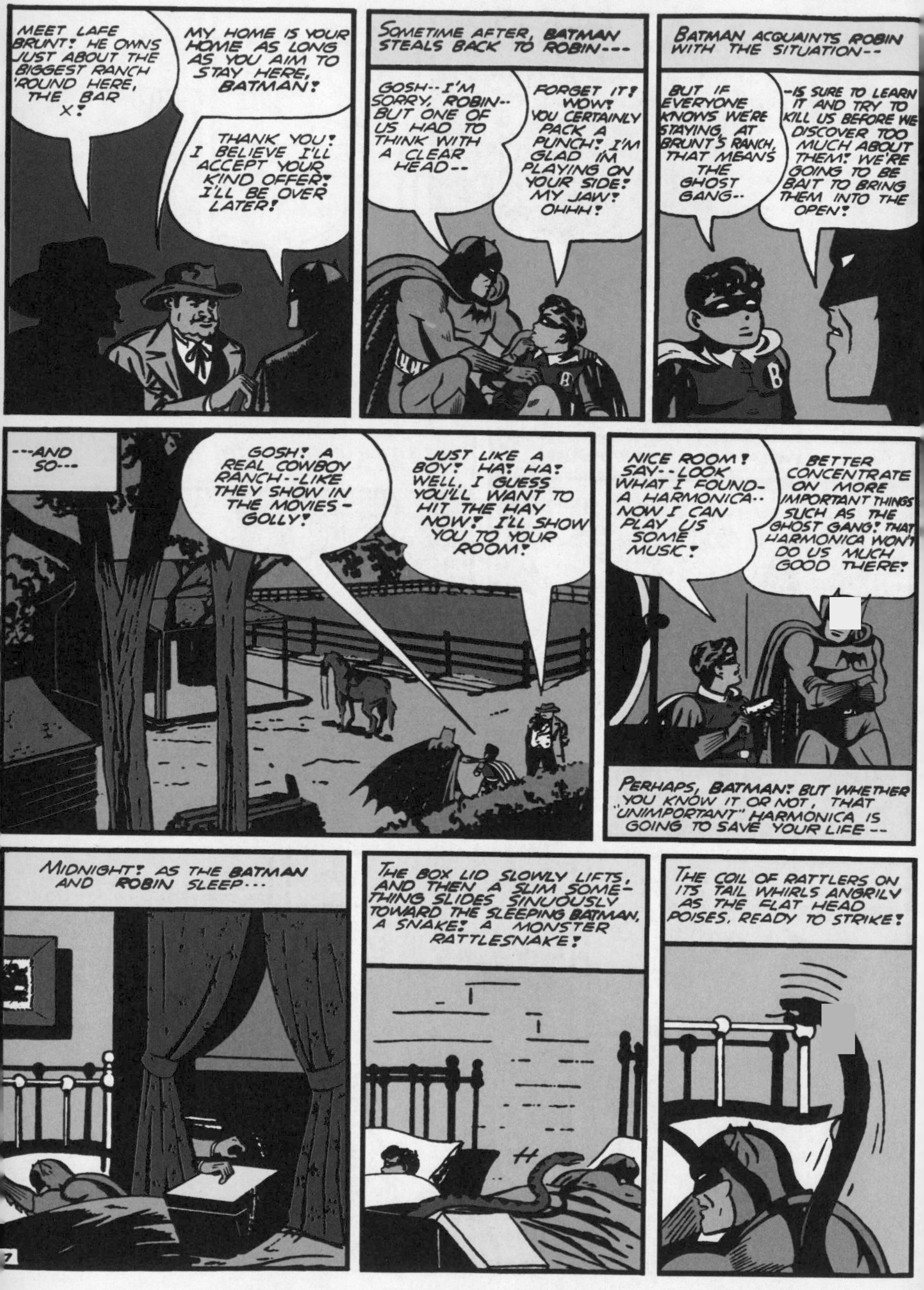
MEET LAFE BRUNT! HE OWNS JUST ABOUT THE BIGGEST RANCH 'ROUND HERE, THE BAR X!
MY HOME IS YOUR HOME AS LONG AS YOU AIM TO STAY HERE, BATMAN!
THANK YOU! I BELIEVE I'LL ACCEPT YOUR KIND OFFER! I'LL BE OVER LATER!
SOMETIME AFTER, BATMAN STEALS BACK TO ROBIN---
GOSH--I'M SORRY, ROBIN-- BUT ONE OF US HAD TO THINK WITH A CLEAR HEAD--
FORGET IT! WOW! YOU CERTAINLY PACK A PUNCH! I'M GLAD I'M PLAYING ON YOUR SIDE! MY JAW! OHHH!
BATMAN ACQUAINTS ROBIN WITH THE SITUATION--
BUT IF EVERYONE KNOWS WE'RE STAYING AT BRUNT'S RANCH, THAT MEANS THE GHOST GANG--
-IS SURE TO LEARN IT AND TRY TO KILL US BEFORE WE DISCOVER TOO MUCH ABOUT THEM! WE'RE GOING TO BE BAIT TO BRING THEM INTO THE OPEN!
---AND SO---
GOSH! A REAL COWBOY RANCH--LIKE THEY SHOW IN THE MOVIES-GOLLY!
JUST LIKE A BOY! HA! HA! WELL, I GUESS YOU'LL WANT TO HIT THE HAY NOW! I'LL SHOW YOU TO YOUR ROOM!
NICE ROOM! SAY--LOOK WHAT I FOUND-A HARMONICA-- NOW I CAN PLAY US SOME MUSIC!
BETTER CONCENTRATE ON MORE IMPORTANT THINGS SUCH AS THE GHOST GANG! THAT HARMONICA WON'T DO US MUCH GOOD THERE!
PERHAPS, BATMAN! BUT WHETHER YOU KNOW IT OR NOT, THAT "UNIMPORTANT" HARMONICA IS GOING TO SAVE YOUR LIFE--
MIDNIGHT! AS THE BATMAN AND ROBIN SLEEP---
THE BOX LID SLOWLY LIFTS, AND THEN A SLIM SOMETHING SLIDES SINUOUSLY TOWARD THE SLEEPING BATMAN. A SNAKE! A MONSTER RATTLESNAKE!
THE COIL OF RATTLERS ON ITS TAIL WHIRLS ANGRILY AS THE FLAT HEAD POISES, READY TO STRIKE!

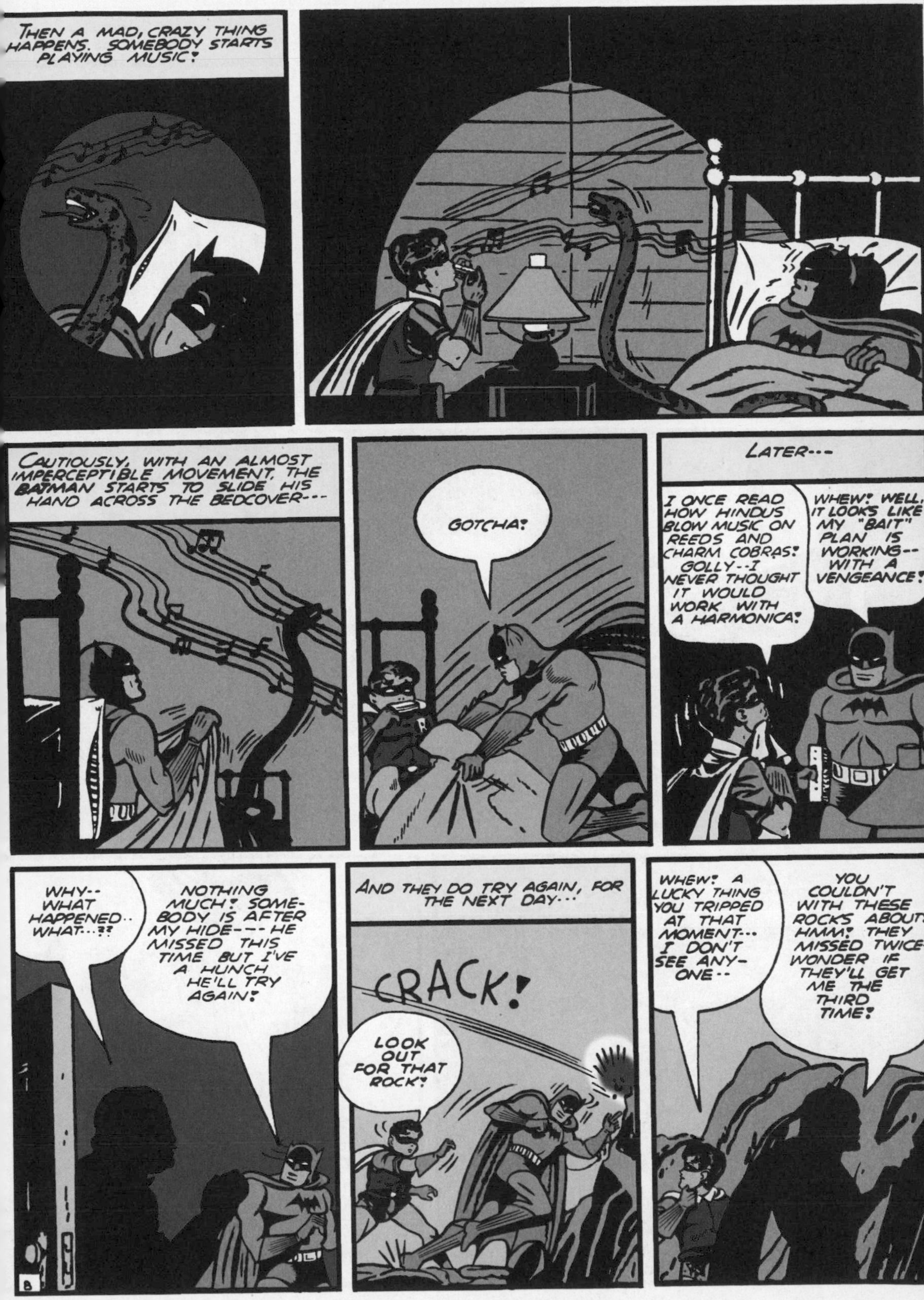
THEN A MAD, CRAZY THING HAPPENS. SOMEBODY STARTS PLAYING MUSIC!
CAUTIOUSLY, WITH AN ALMOST IMPERCEPTIBLE MOVEMENT, THE BATMAN STARTS TO SLIDE HIS HAND ACROSS THE BEDCOVER---
GOTCHA!
LATER---
I ONCE READ HOW HINDUS BLOW MUSIC ON REEDS AND CHARM COBRAS! GOLLY--I NEVER THOUGHT IT WOULD WORK WITH A HARMONICA!
WHEW! WELL, IT LOOKS LIKE MY "BAIT" PLAN IS WORKING--WITH A VENGEANCE!
WHY--WHAT HAPPENED..WHAT...?!
NOTHING MUCH! SOMEBODY IS AFTER MY HIDE--- HE MISSED THIS TIME BUT I'VE A HUNCH HE'LL TRY AGAIN!
AND THEY DO TRY AGAIN, FOR THE NEXT DAY...
CRACK!
LOOK OUT FOR THAT ROCK!
WHEW! A LUCKY THING YOU TRIPPED AT THAT MOMENT... I DON'T SEE ANYONE--
YOU COULDN'T WITH THESE ROCKS ABOUT! HMM! THEY MISSED TWICE--WONDER IF THEY'LL GET ME THE THIRD TIME!

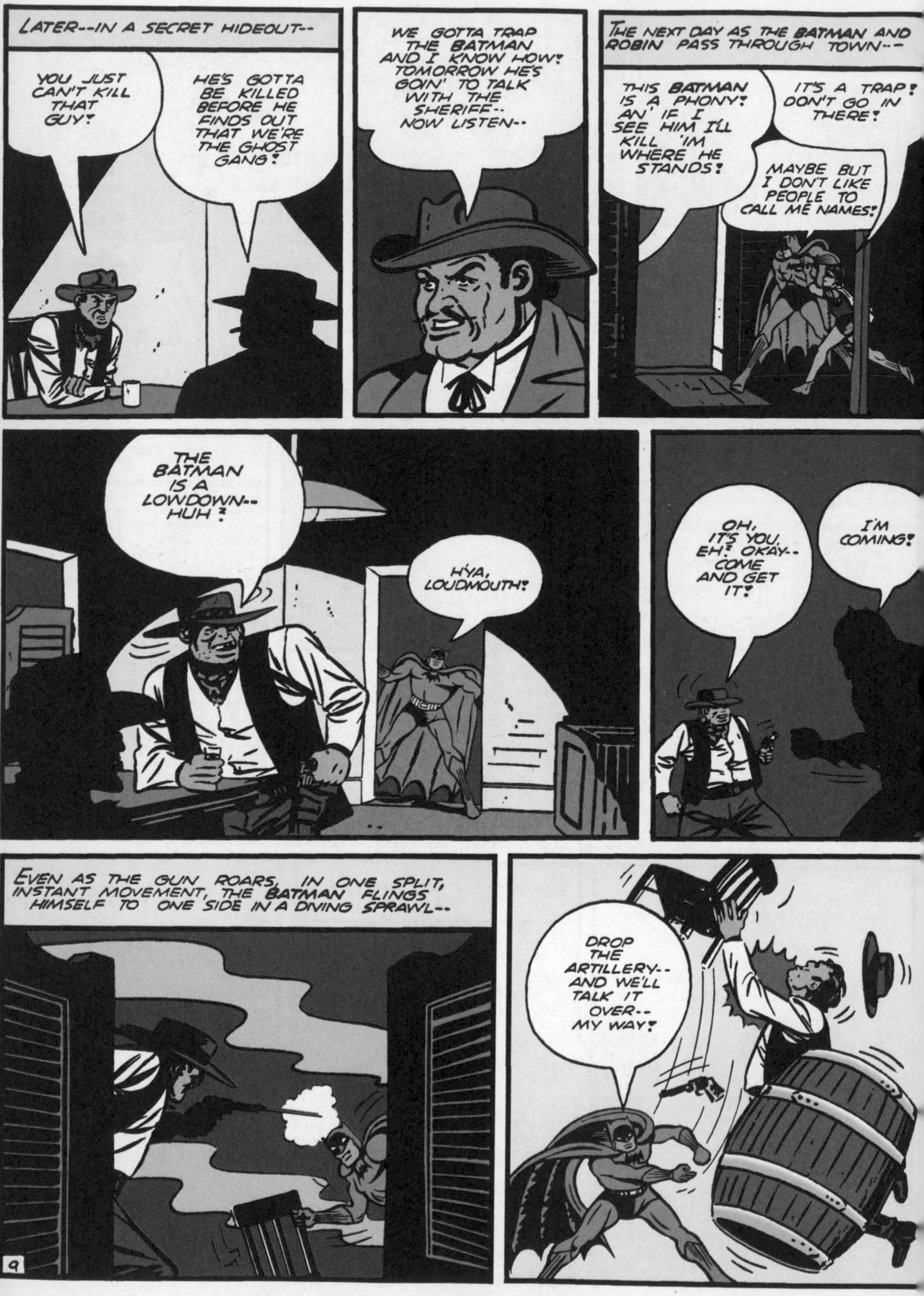

LATER--IN A SECRET HIDEOUT--
YOU JUST CAN'T KILL THAT GUY!
HE'S GOTTA BE KILLED BEFORE HE FINDS OUT THAT WE'RE THE GHOST GANG!
WE GOTTA TRAP THE BATMAN AND I KNOW HOW! TOMORROW HE'S GOIN' TO TALK WITH THE SHERIFF-- NOW LISTEN--
THE NEXT DAY AS THE BATMAN AND ROBIN PASS THROUGH TOWN--
THIS BATMAN IS A PHONY! AN' IF I SEE HIM I'LL KILL 'IM WHERE HE STANDS!
IT'S A TRAP! DON'T GO IN THERE!
MAYBE BUT I DON'T LIKE PEOPLE TO CALL ME NAMES!
THE BATMAN IS A LOWDOWN-- HUH?
H'YA, LOUDMOUTH!
OH, IT'S YOU, EH! OKAY-- COME AND GET IT!
I'M COMING!
EVEN AS THE GUN ROARS, IN ONE SPLIT, INSTANT MOVEMENT, THE BATMAN FLINGS HIMSELF TO ONE SIDE IN A DIVING SPRAWL--
9
DROP THE ARTILLERY-- AND WE'LL TALK IT OVER-- MY WAY!

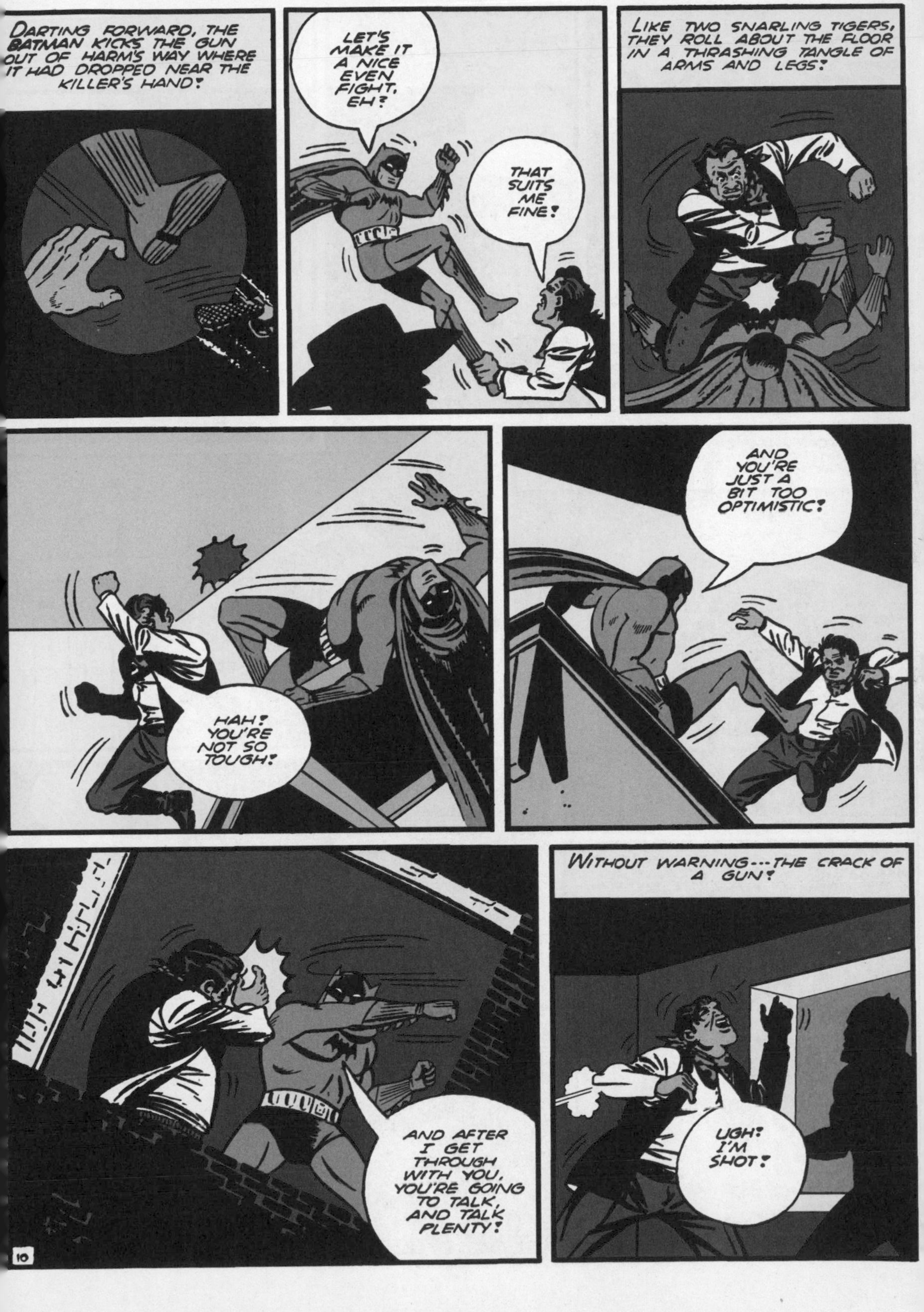

DARTING FORWARD, THE BATMAN KICKS THE GUN OUT OF HARM'S WAY WHERE IT HAD DROPPED NEAR THE KILLER'S HAND!
LET'S MAKE IT A NICE EVEN FIGHT, EH?
THAT SUITS ME FINE!
LIKE TWO SNARLING TIGERS, THEY ROLL ABOUT THE FLOOR IN A THRASHING TANGLE OF ARMS AND LEGS!
HAH! YOU'RE NOT SO TOUGH!
AND YOU'RE JUST A BIT TOO OPTIMISTIC!
AND AFTER I GET THROUGH WITH YOU, YOU'RE GOING TO TALK, AND TALK PLENTY!
10
WITHOUT WARNING... THE CRACK OF A GUN!
UGH! I'M SHOT!

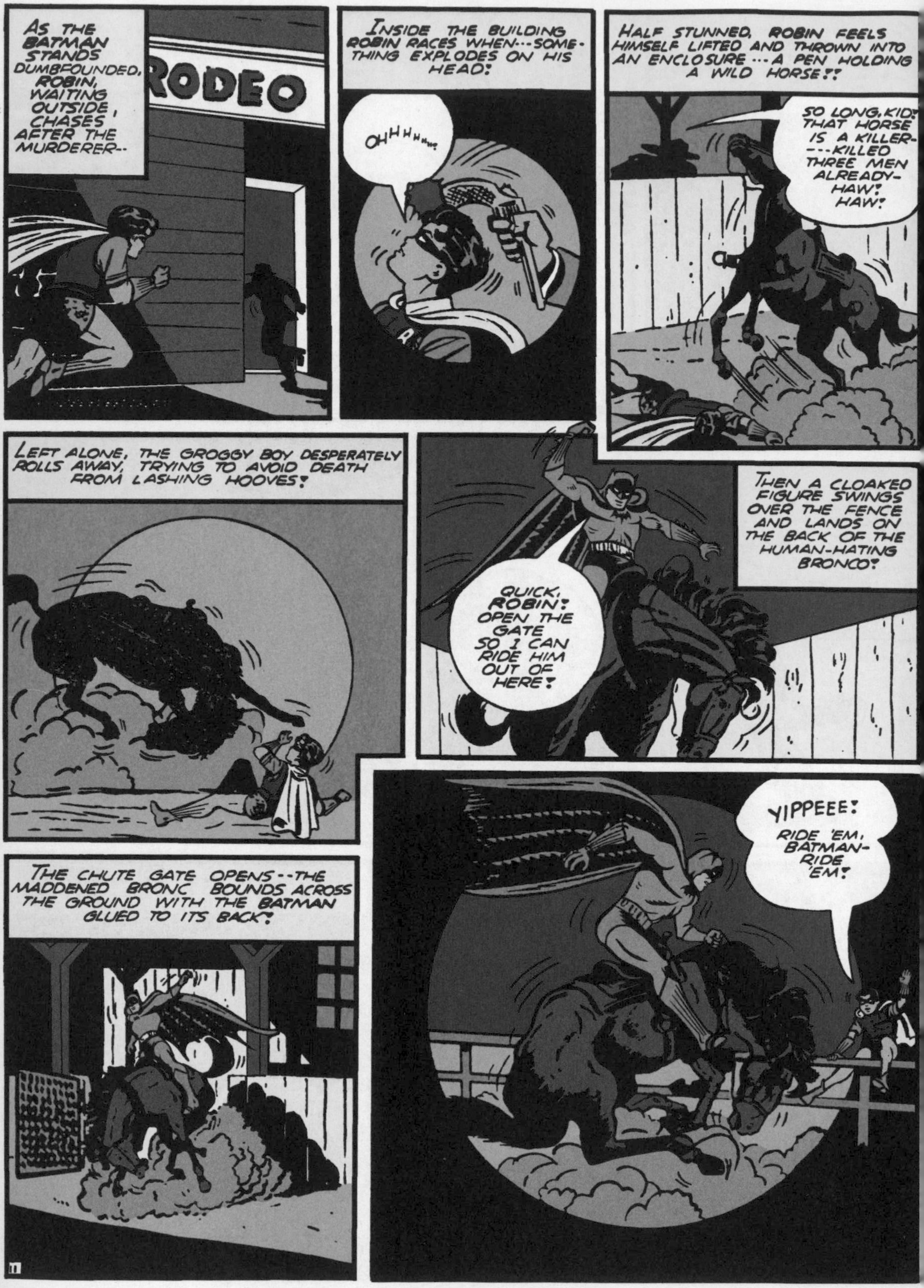
AS THE BATMAN STANDS DUMBFOUNDED, ROBIN, WAITING OUTSIDE, CHASES AFTER THE MURDERER--
RODEO
INSIDE THE BUILDING ROBIN RACES WHEN---SOMETHING EXPLODES ON HIS HEAD!
OHHHHH...
HALF STUNNED, ROBIN FEELS HIMSELF LIFTED AND THROWN INTO AN ENCLOSURE---A PEN HOLDING A WILD HORSE!!
SO LONG, KID! THAT HORSE IS A KILLER---KILLED THREE MEN ALREADY- HAW! HAW!
LEFT ALONE, THE GROGGY BOY DESPERATELY ROLLS AWAY, TRYING TO AVOID DEATH FROM LASHING HOOVES!
THEN A CLOAKED FIGURE SWINGS OVER THE FENCE AND LANDS ON THE BACK OF THE HUMAN-HATING BRONCO!
QUICK, ROBIN! OPEN THE GATE SO I CAN RIDE HIM OUT OF HERE!
THE CHUTE GATE OPENS--THE MADDENED BRONC BOUNDS ACROSS THE GROUND WITH THE BATMAN GLUED TO ITS BACK!
YIPPEEE! RIDE 'EM, BATMAN- RIDE 'EM!

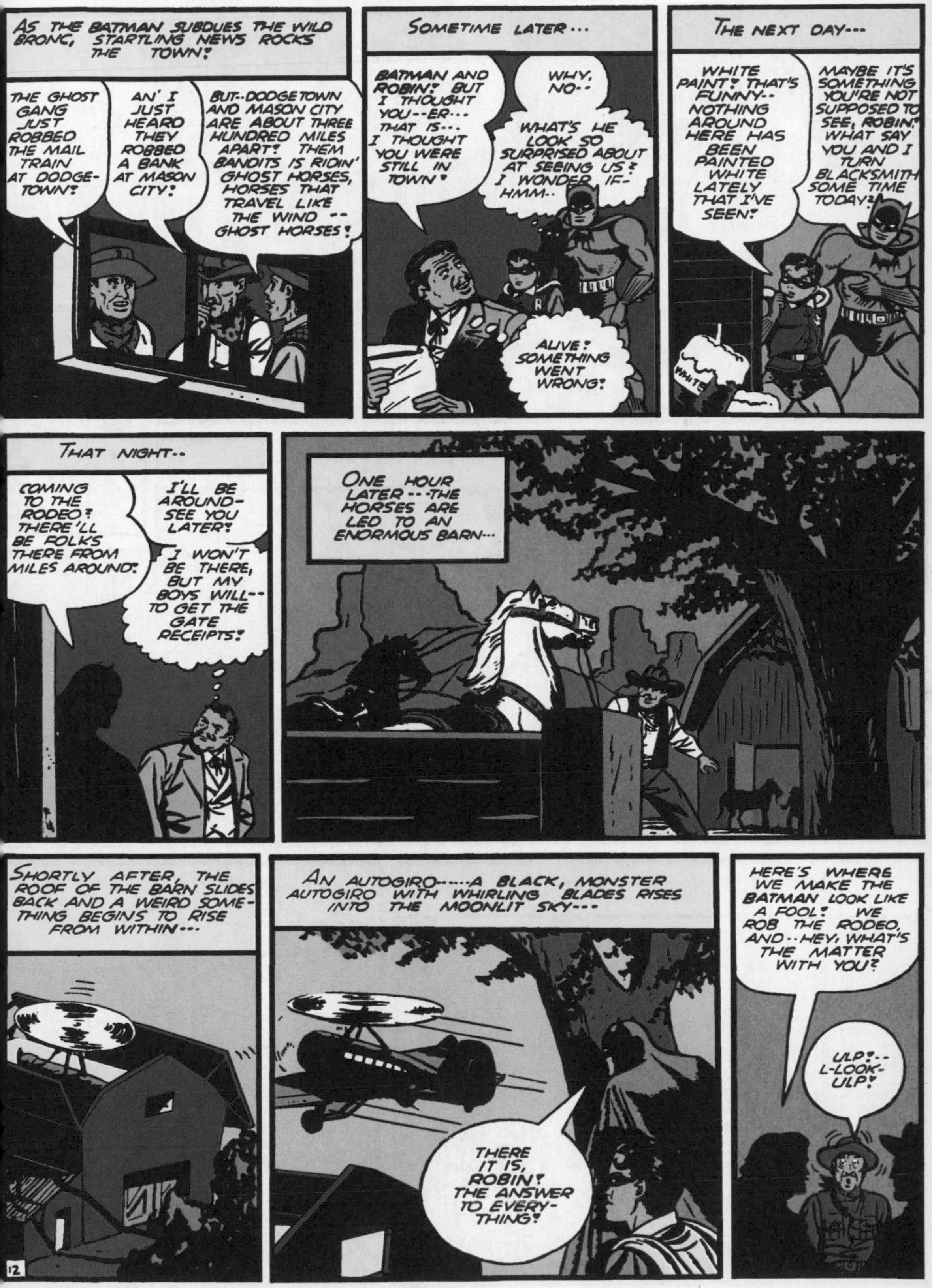

AS THE BATMAN SUBDUES THE WILD BRONC, STARTLING NEWS ROCKS THE TOWN!
THE GHOST GANG JUST ROBBED THE MAIL TRAIN AT DODGETOWN!
AN' I JUST HEARD THEY ROBBED A BANK AT MASON CITY!
BUT--DODGETOWN AND MASON CITY ARE ABOUT THREE HUNDRED MILES APART! THEM BANDITS IS RIDIN' GHOST HORSES, HORSES THAT TRAVEL LIKE THE WIND -- GHOST HORSES!
SOMETIME LATER...
BATMAN AND ROBIN! BUT I THOUGHT YOU--ER... THAT IS... I THOUGHT YOU WERE STILL IN TOWN!
WHY, NO--
WHAT'S HE LOOK SO SURPRISED ABOUT AT SEEING US? I WONDER IF-- HMM..
ALIVE! SOMETHING WENT WRONG!
THE NEXT DAY---
WHITE PAINT! THAT'S FUNNY-- NOTHING AROUND HERE HAS BEEN PAINTED WHITE LATELY THAT I'VE SEEN!
MAYBE IT'S SOMETHING YOU'RE NOT SUPPOSED TO SEE, ROBIN! WHAT SAY YOU AND I TURN BLACKSMITH SOME TIME TODAY?
WHITE
THAT NIGHT--
COMING TO THE RODEO? THERE'LL BE FOLKS THERE FROM MILES AROUND!
I'LL BE AROUND-SEE YOU LATER!
I WON'T BE THERE, BUT MY BOYS WILL-- TO GET THE GATE RECEIPTS!
ONE HOUR LATER---THE HORSES ARE LED TO AN ENORMOUS BARN...
SHORTLY AFTER, THE ROOF OF THE BARN SLIDES BACK AND A WEIRD SOMETHING BEGINS TO RISE FROM WITHIN...
12
AN AUTOGIRO......A BLACK, MONSTER AUTOGIRO WITH WHIRLING BLADES RISES INTO THE MOONLIT SKY---
THERE IT IS, ROBIN! THE ANSWER TO EVERYTHING!
HERE'S WHERE WE MAKE THE BATMAN LOOK LIKE A FOOL! WE ROB THE RODEO, AND--HEY, WHAT'S THE MATTER WITH YOU?
ULP!-- L-LOOK-ULP!

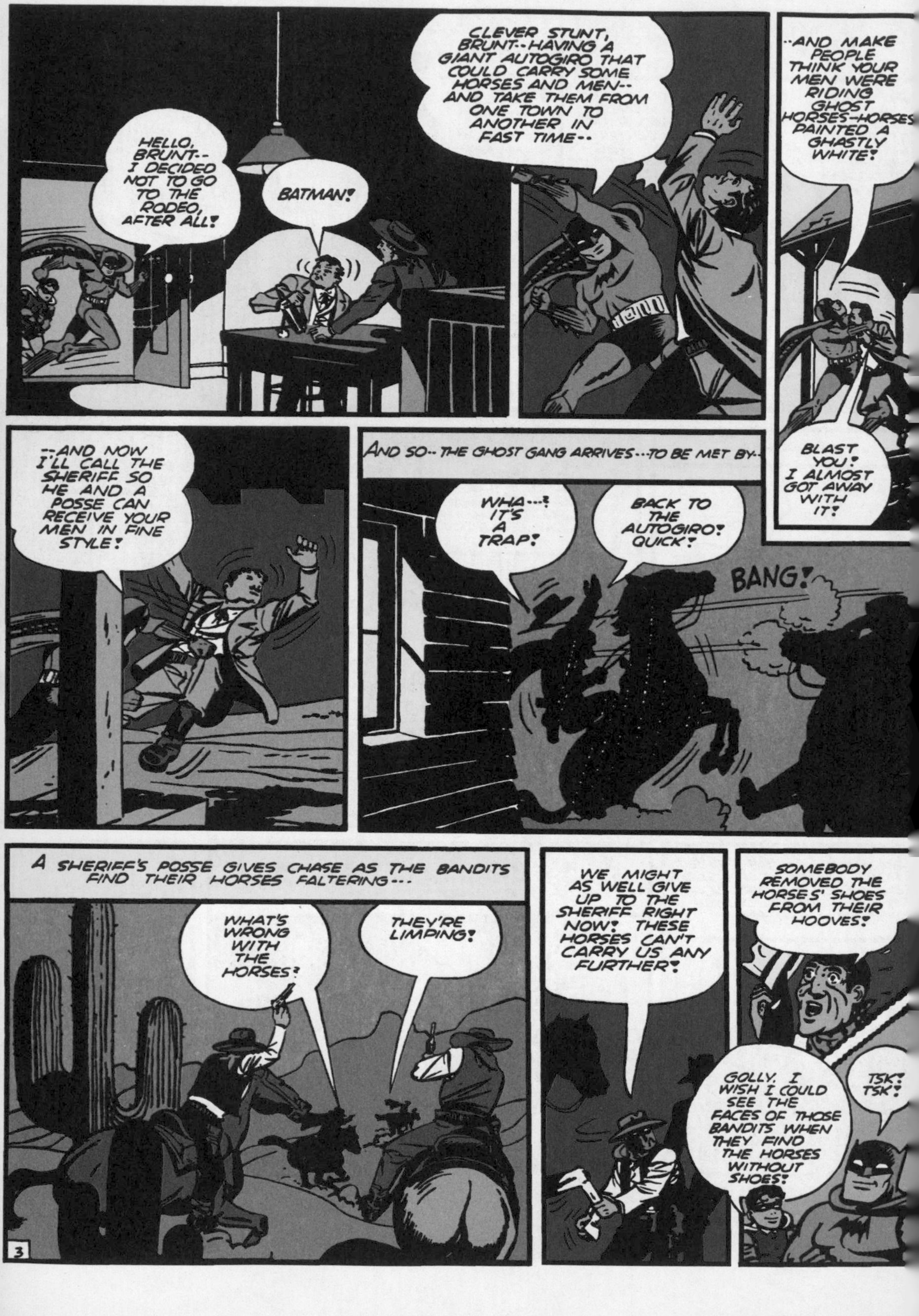
HELLO, BRUNT-- I DECIDED NOT TO GO TO THE RODEO, AFTER ALL!
BATMAN!
CLEVER STUNT, BRUNT--HAVING A GIANT AUTOGIRO THAT COULD CARRY SOME HORSES AND MEN--AND TAKE THEM FROM ONE TOWN TO ANOTHER IN FAST TIME--
--AND MAKE PEOPLE THINK YOUR MEN WERE RIDING GHOST HORSES--HORSES PAINTED A GHASTLY WHITE!
BLAST YOU! I ALMOST GOT AWAY WITH IT!
--AND NOW I'LL CALL THE SHERIFF SO HE AND A POSSE CAN RECEIVE YOUR MEN IN FINE STYLE!
AND SO-- THE GHOST GANG ARRIVES---TO BE MET BY--
WHA---? IT'S A TRAP!
BACK TO THE AUTOGIRO! QUICK!
BANG!
A SHERIFF'S POSSE GIVES CHASE AS THE BANDITS FIND THEIR HORSES FALTERING---
WHAT'S WRONG WITH THE HORSES?
THEY'RE LIMPING!
3
WE MIGHT AS WELL GIVE UP TO THE SHERIFF RIGHT NOW! THESE HORSES CAN'T CARRY US ANY FURTHER!
SOMEBODY REMOVED THE HORSES' SHOES FROM THEIR HOOVES!
GOLLY. I WISH I COULD SEE THE FACES OF THOSE BANDITS WHEN THEY FIND THE HORSES WITHOUT SHOES!
TSK! TSK!

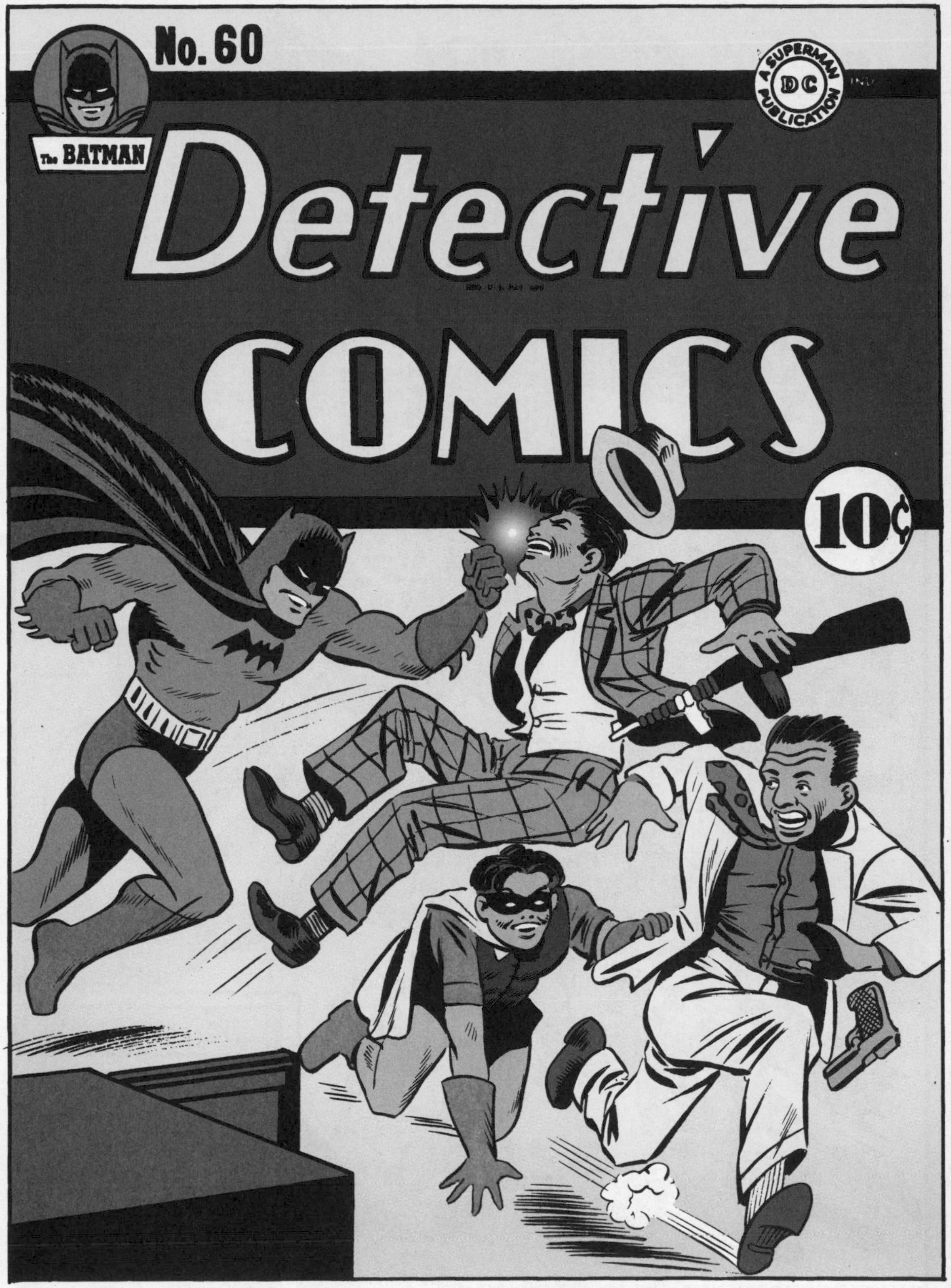
No. 60
The BATMAN
A SUPERMAN DC PUBLICATION
Detective
COMICS
10¢

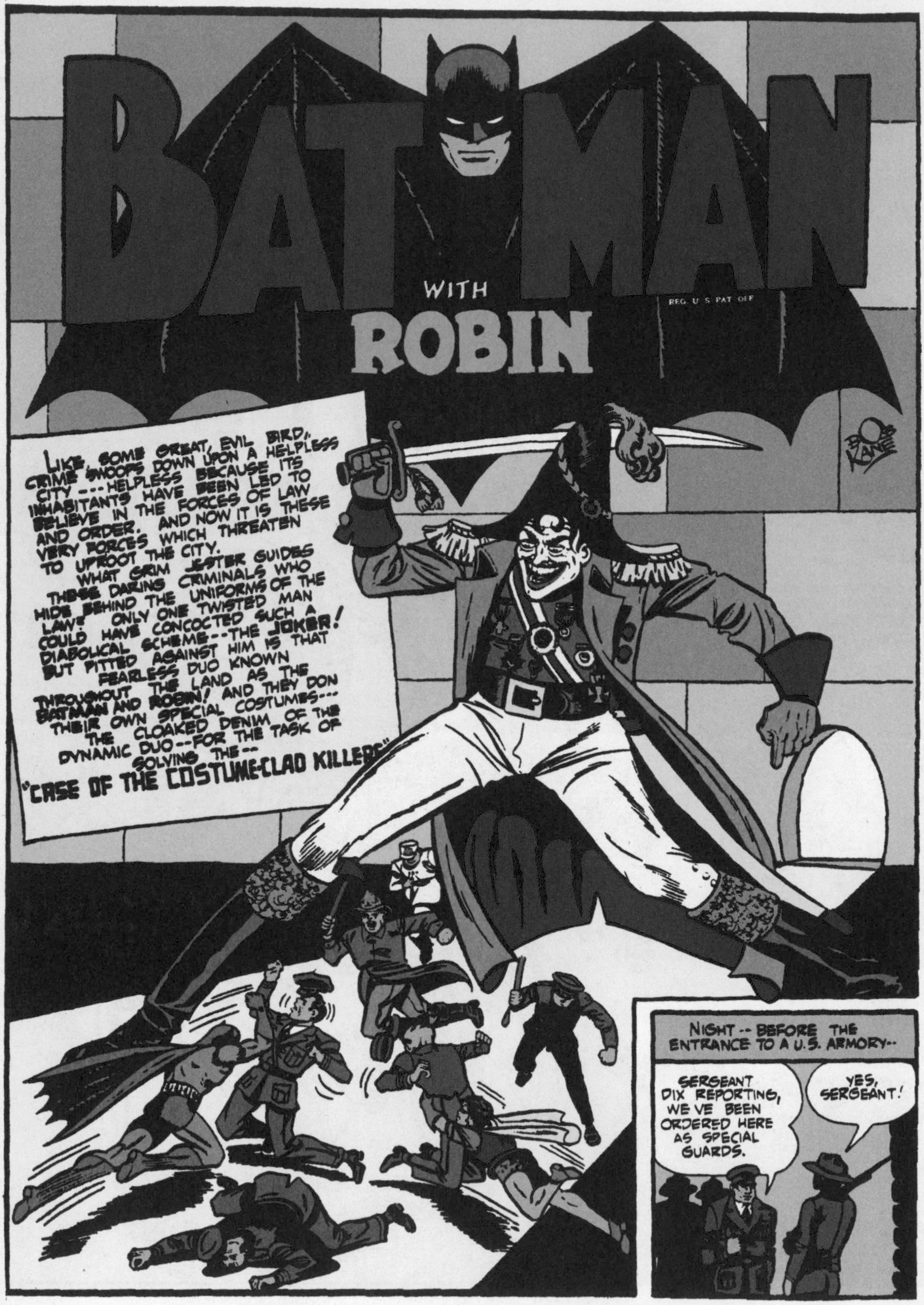
BATMAN
WITH
ROBIN
REG. U.S. PAT. OFF.
BOB KANE
LIKE SOME GREAT, EVIL BIRD, CRIME SWOOPS DOWN UPON A HELPLESS CITY --- HELPLESS BECAUSE ITS INHABITANTS HAVE BEEN LED TO BELIEVE IN THE FORCES OF LAW AND ORDER. AND NOW IT IS THESE VERY FORCES WHICH THREATEN TO UPROOT THE CITY.
WHAT GRIM JESTER GUIDES THESE DARING CRIMINALS WHO HIDE BEHIND THE UNIFORMS OF THE LAW? ONLY ONE TWISTED MAN COULD HAVE CONCOCTED SUCH A DIABOLICAL SCHEME--THE JOKER! BUT PITTED AGAINST HIM IS THAT FEARLESS DUO KNOWN THROUGHOUT THE LAND AS THE BATMAN AND ROBIN! AND THEY DON THEIR OWN SPECIAL COSTUMES--- THE CLOAKED DENIM OF THE DYNAMIC DUO--FOR THE TASK OF SOLVING THE--
"CASE OF THE COSTUME-CLAD KILLERS"
NIGHT -- BEFORE THE ENTRANCE TO A U.S. ARMORY--
SERGEANT DIX REPORTING, WE'VE BEEN ORDERED HERE AS SPECIAL GUARDS.
YES, SERGEANT!

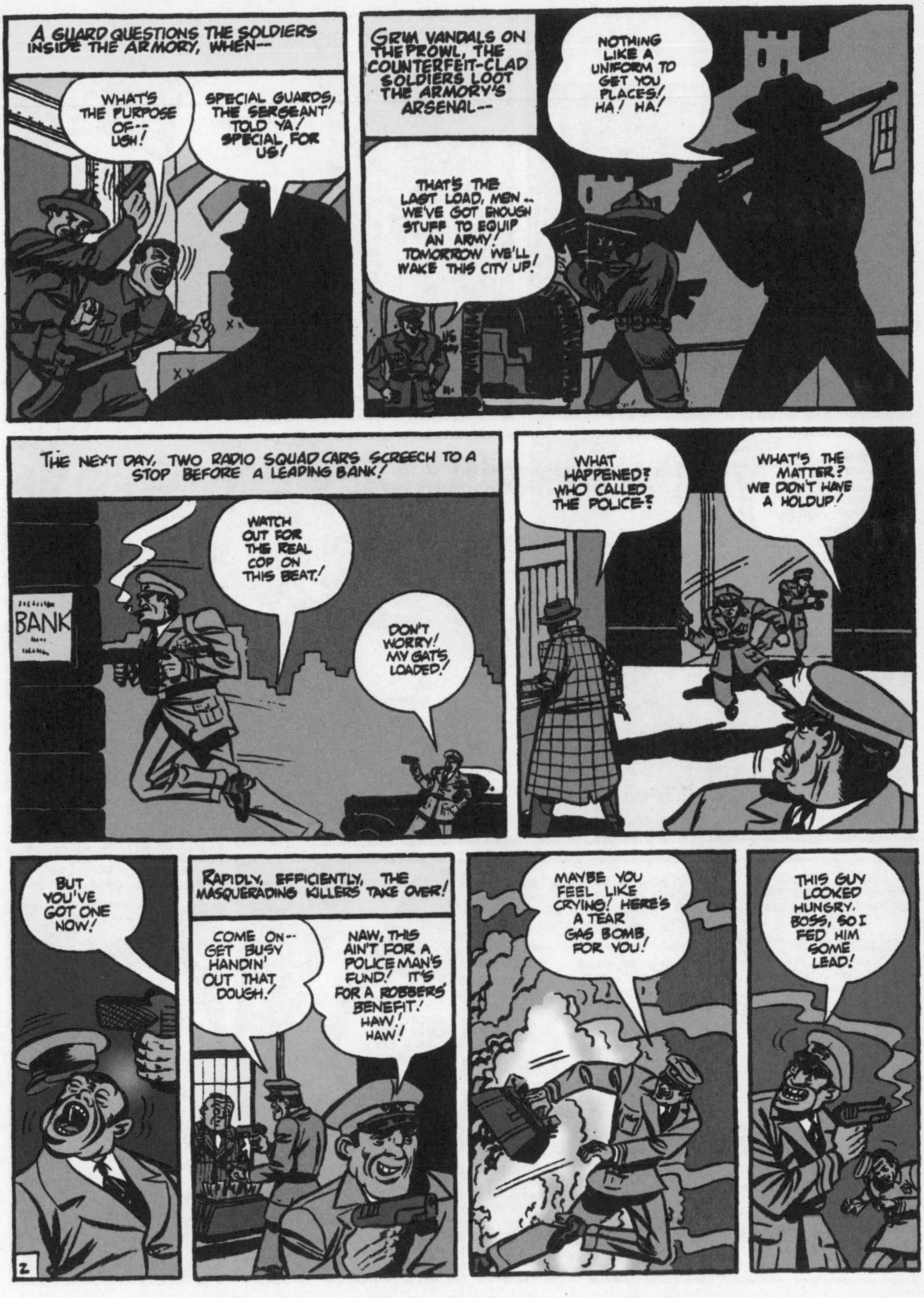
A GUARD QUESTIONS THE SOLDIERS INSIDE THE ARMORY, WHEN--
WHAT'S THE PURPOSE OF-- UGH!
SPECIAL GUARDS, THE SERGEANT TOLD YA! SPECIAL FOR US!
GRIM VANDALS ON THE PROWL, THE COUNTERFEIT-CLAD SOLDIERS LOOT THE ARMORY'S ARSENAL--
NOTHING LIKE A UNIFORM TO GET YOU PLACES! HA! HA!
THAT'S THE LAST LOAD, MEN.. WE'VE GOT ENOUGH STUFF TO EQUIP AN ARMY! TOMORROW WE'LL WAKE THIS CITY UP!
THE NEXT DAY, TWO RADIO SQUAD CARS SCREECH TO A STOP BEFORE A LEADING BANK!
BANK
WATCH OUT FOR THE REAL COP ON THIS BEAT!
DON'T WORRY! MY GAT'S LOADED!
WHAT HAPPENED? WHO CALLED THE POLICE?
WHAT'S THE MATTER? WE DON'T HAVE A HOLDUP!
BUT YOU'VE GOT ONE NOW!
2
RAPIDLY, EFFICIENTLY, THE MASQUERADING KILLERS TAKE OVER!
COME ON-- GET BUSY HANDIN' OUT THAT DOUGH!
NAW, THIS AIN'T FOR A POLICEMAN'S FUND! IT'S FOR A ROBBERS' BENEFIT! HAW! HAW!
MAYBE YOU FEEL LIKE CRYING! HERE'S A TEAR GAS BOMB FOR YOU!
THIS GUY LOOKED HUNGRY, BOSS, SO I FED HIM SOME LEAD!

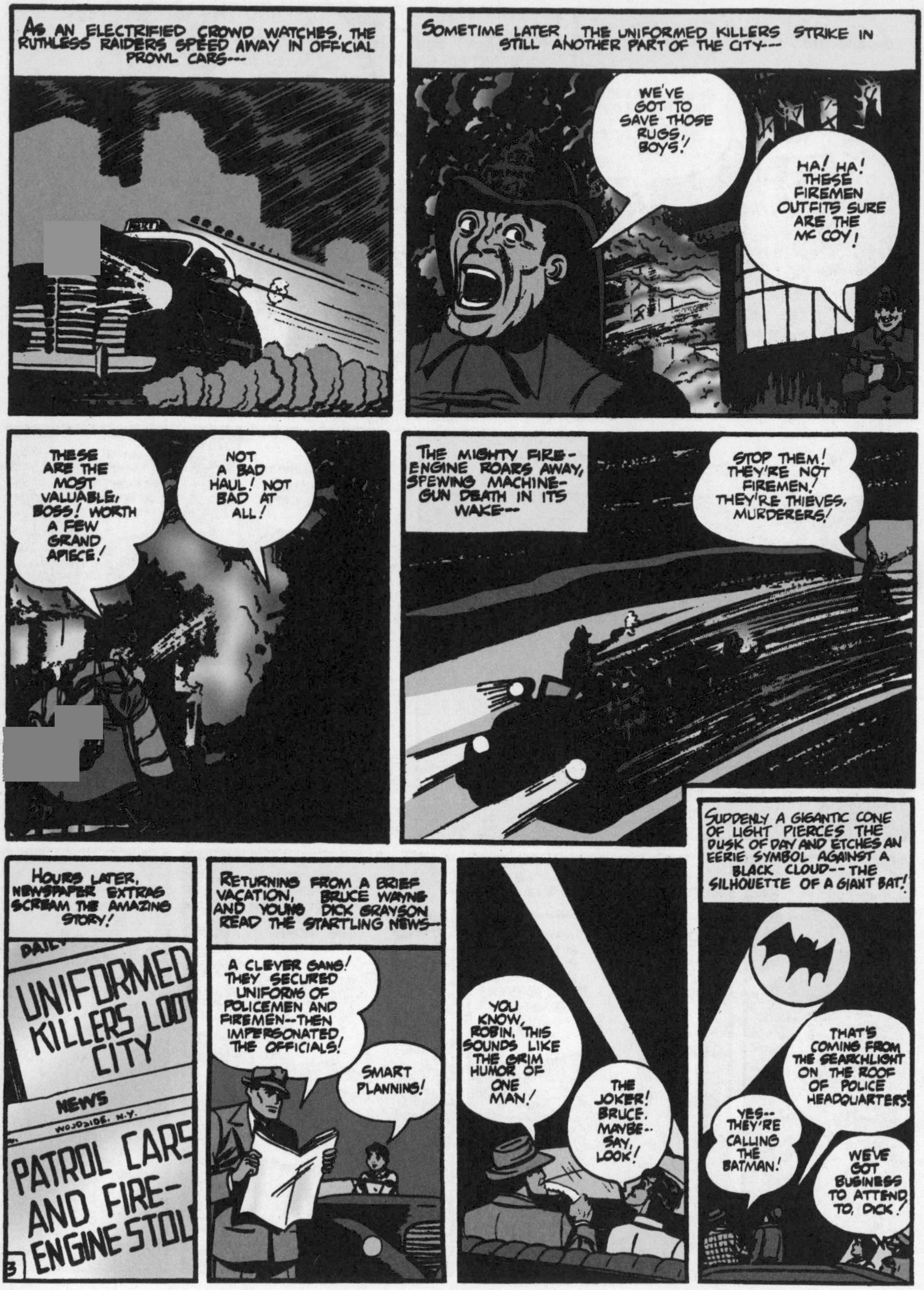
AS AN ELECTRIFIED CROWD WATCHES, THE RUTHLESS RAIDERS SPEED AWAY IN OFFICIAL PROWL CARS---
SOMETIME LATER, THE UNIFORMED KILLERS STRIKE IN STILL ANOTHER PART OF THE CITY---
WE'VE GOT TO SAVE THOSE RUGS, BOYS!
HA! HA! THESE FIREMEN OUTFITS SURE ARE THE MC COY!
THESE ARE THE MOST VALUABLE, BOSS! WORTH A FEW GRAND APIECE!
NOT A BAD HAUL! NOT BAD AT ALL!
THE MIGHTY FIRE-ENGINE ROARS AWAY, SPEWING MACHINE-GUN DEATH IN ITS WAKE---
STOP THEM! THEY'RE NOT FIREMEN! THEY'RE THIEVES, MURDERERS!
HOURS LATER, NEWSPAPER EXTRAS SCREAM THE AMAZING STORY!
UNIFORMED
KILLERS LOO
CITY
NEWS
WOODSIDE, N.Y.
PATROL CARS AND FIRE-ENGINE STOL
3
RETURNING FROM A BRIEF VACATION, BRUCE WAYNE AND YOUNG DICK GRAYSON READ THE STARTLING NEWS--
A CLEVER GANG! THEY SECURED UNIFORMS OF POLICEMEN AND FIREMEN--THEN IMPERSONATED THE OFFICIALS!
SMART PLANNING!
YOU KNOW, ROBIN, THIS SOUNDS LIKE THE GRIM HUMOR OF ONE MAN!
THE JOKER! BRUCE, MAYBE-- SAY, LOOK!
SUDDENLY A GIGANTIC CONE OF LIGHT PIERCES THE DUSK OF DAY AND ETCHES AN EERIE SYMBOL AGAINST A BLACK CLOUD-- THE SILHOUETTE OF A GIANT BAT!
THAT'S COMING FROM THE SEARCHLIGHT ON THE ROOF OF POLICE HEADQUARTERS!
YES-- THEY'RE CALLING THE BATMAN!
WE'VE GOT BUSINESS TO ATTEND TO, DICK!

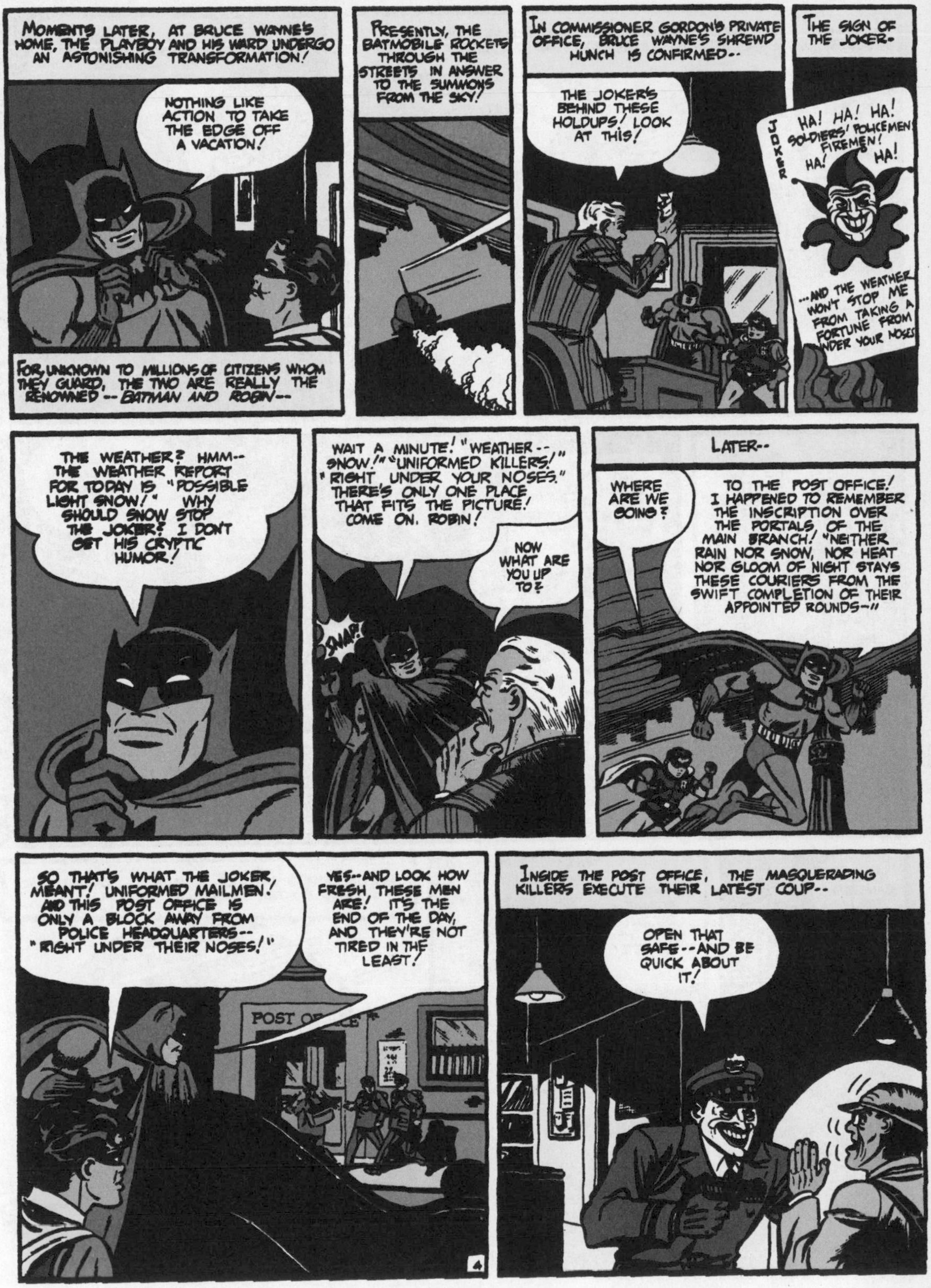
MOMENTS LATER, AT BRUCE WAYNE'S HOME, THE PLAYBOY AND HIS WARD UNDERGO AN ASTONISHING TRANSFORMATION!
NOTHING LIKE ACTION TO TAKE THE EDGE OFF A VACATION!
FOR, UNKNOWN TO MILLIONS OF CITIZENS WHOM THEY GUARD, THE TWO ARE REALLY THE RENOWNED -- BATMAN AND ROBIN --
PRESENTLY, THE BATMOBILE ROCKETS THROUGH THE STREETS IN ANSWER TO THE SUMMONS FROM THE SKY!
IN COMMISSIONER GORDON'S PRIVATE OFFICE, BRUCE WAYNE'S SHREWD HUNCH IS CONFIRMED --
THE JOKER'S BEHIND THESE HOLDUPS! LOOK AT THIS!
THE SIGN OF THE JOKER --
JOKER
HA! HA! HA! SOLDIERS! POLICEMEN! FIREMEN! HA! HA!
...AND THE WEATHER WON'T STOP ME FROM TAKING A FORTUNE FROM UNDER YOUR NOSES
THE WEATHER? HMM-- THE WEATHER REPORT FOR TODAY IS "POSSIBLE LIGHT SNOW!" WHY SHOULD SNOW STOP THE JOKER? I DON'T GET HIS CRYPTIC HUMOR!
WAIT A MINUTE! "WEATHER -- SNOW!" "UNIFORMED KILLERS!" "RIGHT UNDER YOUR NOSES." THERE'S ONLY ONE PLACE THAT FITS THE PICTURE! COME ON, ROBIN!
SNAP!
NOW WHAT ARE YOU UP TO?
LATER --
WHERE ARE WE GOING?
TO THE POST OFFICE! I HAPPENED TO REMEMBER THE INSCRIPTION OVER THE PORTALS OF THE MAIN BRANCH! "NEITHER RAIN NOR SNOW, NOR HEAT NOR GLOOM OF NIGHT STAYS THESE COURIERS FROM THE SWIFT COMPLETION OF THEIR APPOINTED ROUNDS --"
SO THAT'S WHAT THE JOKER MEANT! UNIFORMED MAILMEN! AND THIS POST OFFICE IS ONLY A BLOCK AWAY FROM POLICE HEADQUARTERS -- "RIGHT UNDER THEIR NOSES!"
YES -- AND LOOK HOW FRESH THESE MEN ARE! IT'S THE END OF THE DAY, AND THEY'RE NOT TIRED IN THE LEAST!
POST OF
4
INSIDE THE POST OFFICE, THE MASQUERADING KILLERS EXECUTE THEIR LATEST COUP --
OPEN THAT SAFE -- AND BE QUICK ABOUT IT!

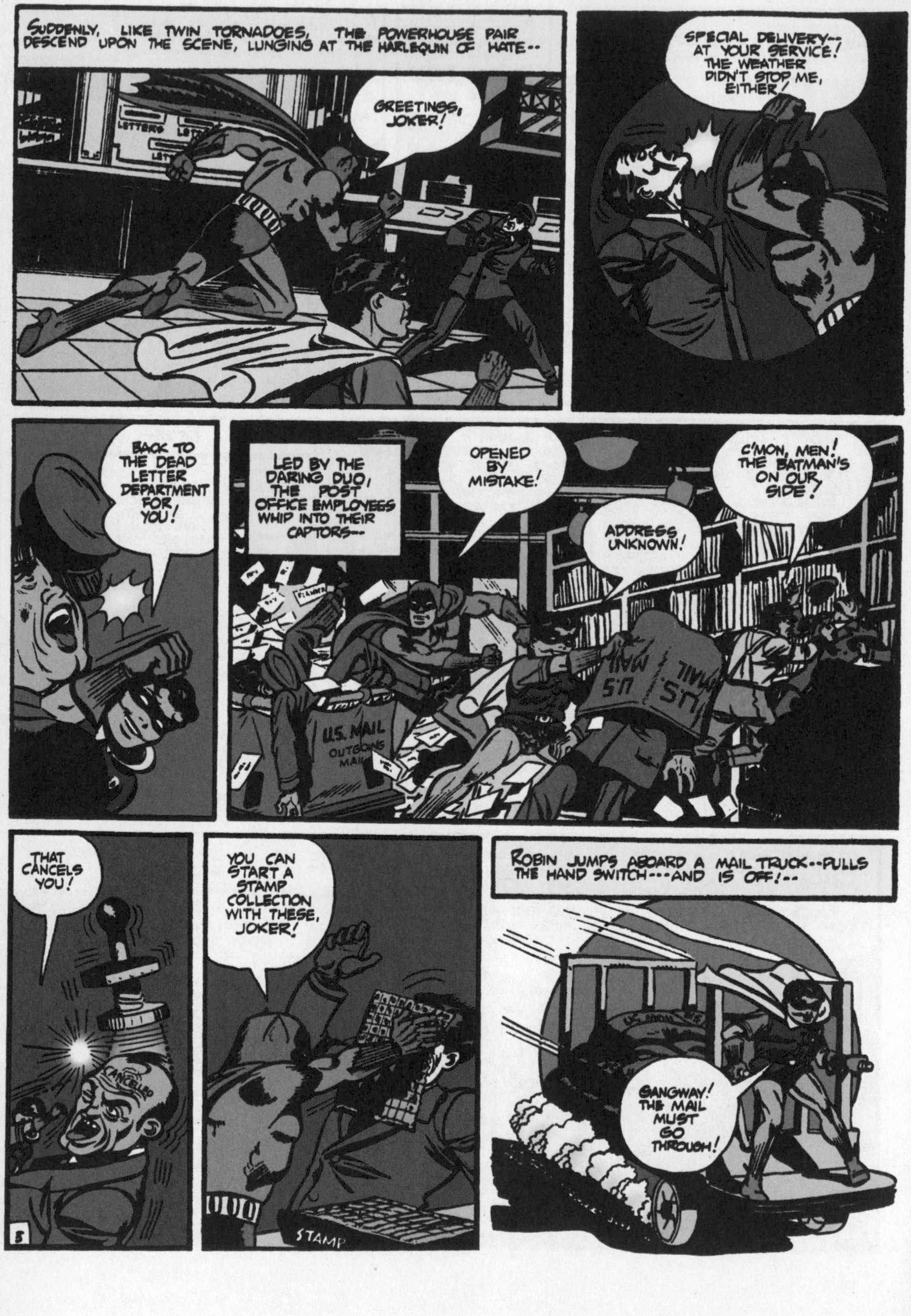
SUDDENLY, LIKE TWIN TORNADOES, THE POWERHOUSE PAIR DESCEND UPON THE SCENE, LUNGING AT THE HARLEQUIN OF HATE--
GREETINGS, JOKER!
SPECIAL DELIVERY-- AT YOUR SERVICE! THE WEATHER DIDN'T STOP ME, EITHER!
BACK TO THE DEAD LETTER DEPARTMENT FOR YOU!
LED BY THE DARING DUO, THE POST OFFICE EMPLOYEES WHIP INTO THEIR CAPTORS--
OPENED BY MISTAKE!
C'MON, MEN! THE BATMAN'S ON OUR SIDE!
ADDRESS UNKNOWN!
U.S. MAIL OUTGOING MAIL
THAT CANCELS YOU!
CANCELLED
YOU CAN START A STAMP COLLECTION WITH THESE, JOKER!
STAMP
ROBIN JUMPS ABOARD A MAIL TRUCK--PULLS THE HAND SWITCH---AND IS OFF!--
GANGWAY! THE MAIL MUST GO THROUGH!

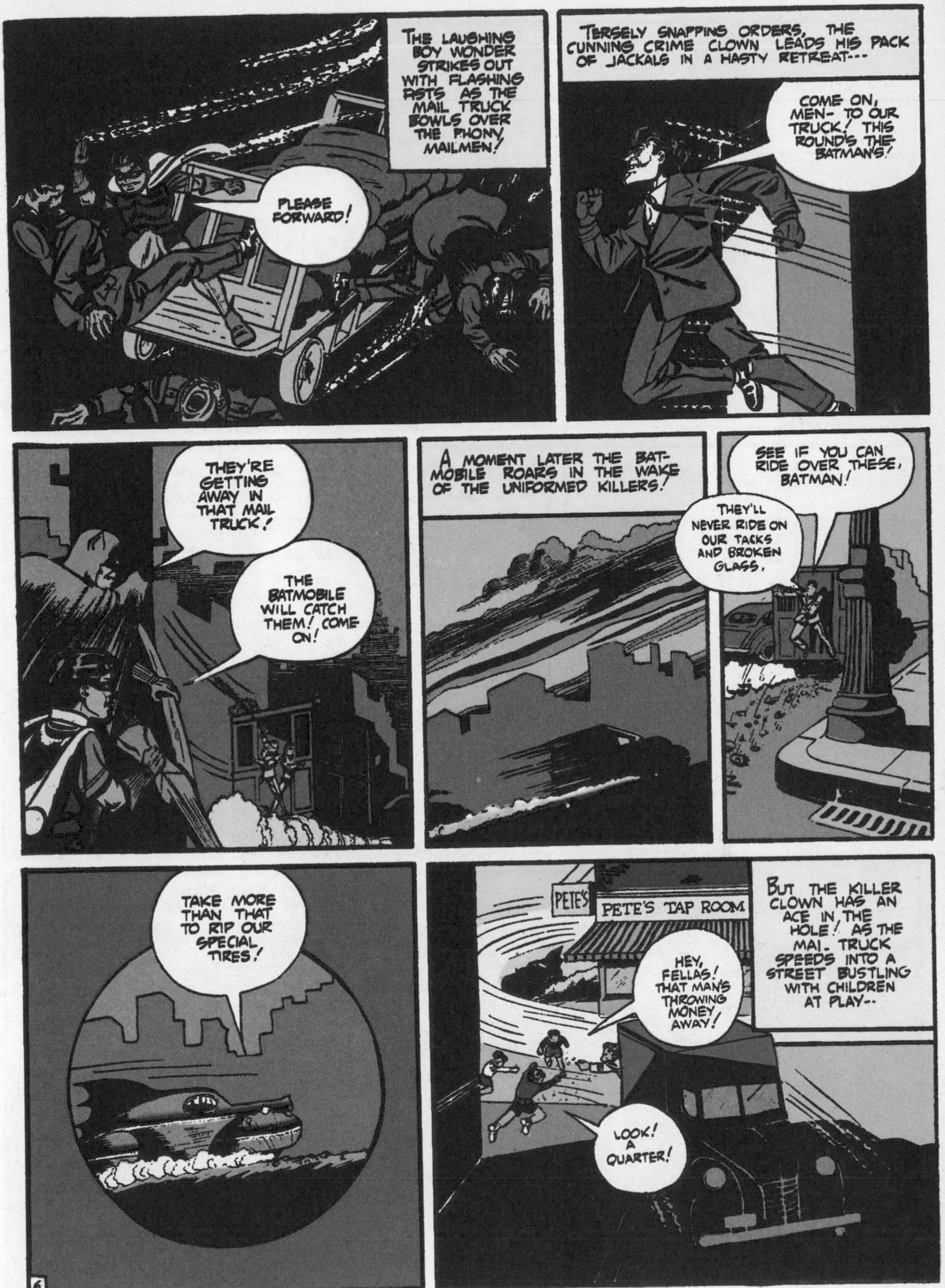
THE LAUGHING BOY WONDER STRIKES OUT WITH FLASHING FISTS AS THE MAIL TRUCK BOWLS OVER THE PHONY MAILMEN!
PLEASE FORWARD!
TERSELY SNAPPING ORDERS, THE CUNNING CRIME CLOWN LEADS HIS PACK OF JACKALS IN A HASTY RETREAT---
COME ON, MEN- TO OUR TRUCK! THIS ROUND'S THE BATMAN'S!
THEY'RE GETTING AWAY IN THAT MAIL TRUCK!
THE BATMOBILE WILL CATCH THEM! COME ON!
A MOMENT LATER THE BATMOBILE ROARS IN THE WAKE OF THE UNIFORMED KILLERS!
SEE IF YOU CAN RIDE OVER THESE, BATMAN!
THEY'LL NEVER RIDE ON OUR TACKS AND BROKEN GLASS.
TAKE MORE THAN THAT TO RIP OUR SPECIAL TIRES!
6
BUT THE KILLER CLOWN HAS AN ACE IN THE HOLE! AS THE MAI_ TRUCK SPEEDS INTO A STREET BUSTLING WITH CHILDREN AT PLAY--
PETE'S
PETE'S TAP ROOM
HEY, FELLAS! THAT MAN'S THROWING MONEY AWAY!
LOOK! A QUARTER!

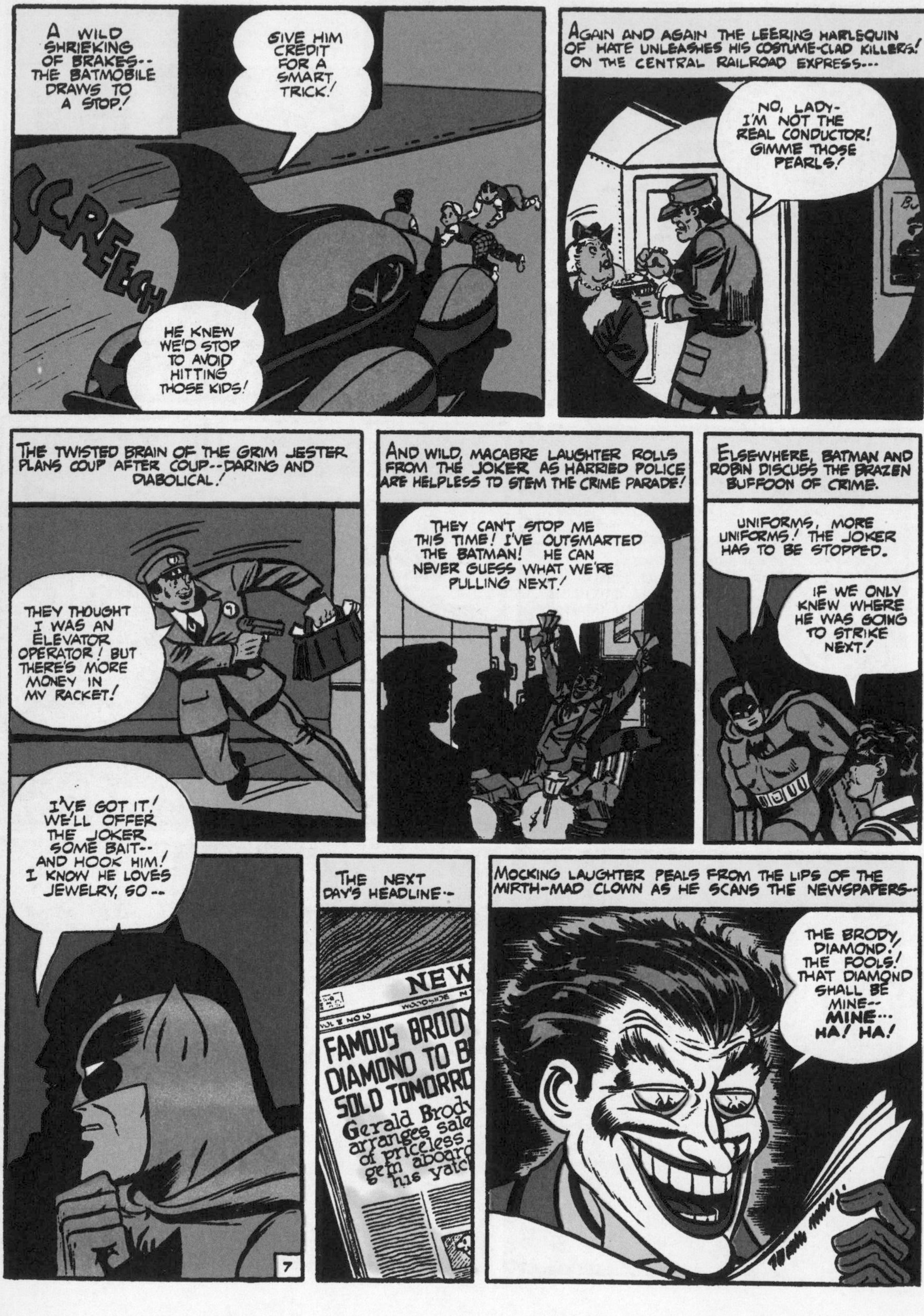

A WILD SHRIEKING OF BRAKES-- THE BATMOBILE DRAWS TO A STOP!
GIVE HIM CREDIT FOR A SMART TRICK!
SCREEECH
HE KNEW WE'D STOP TO AVOID HITTING THOSE KIDS!
AGAIN AND AGAIN THE LEERING HARLEQUIN OF HATE UNLEASHES HIS COSTUME-CLAD KILLERS! ON THE CENTRAL RAILROAD EXPRESS---
NO, LADY- I'M NOT THE REAL CONDUCTOR! GIMME THOSE PEARLS!
THE TWISTED BRAIN OF THE GRIM JESTER PLANS COUP AFTER COUP--DARING AND DIABOLICAL!
THEY THOUGHT I WAS AN ELEVATOR OPERATOR! BUT THERE'S MORE MONEY IN MY RACKET!
AND WILD, MACABRE LAUGHTER ROLLS FROM THE JOKER AS HARRIED POLICE ARE HELPLESS TO STEM THE CRIME PARADE!
THEY CAN'T STOP ME THIS TIME! I'VE OUTSMARTED THE BATMAN! HE CAN NEVER GUESS WHAT WE'RE PULLING NEXT!
ELSEWHERE, BATMAN AND ROBIN DISCUSS THE BRAZEN BUFFOON OF CRIME.
UNIFORMS, MORE UNIFORMS! THE JOKER HAS TO BE STOPPED.
IF WE ONLY KNEW WHERE HE WAS GOING TO STRIKE NEXT!
I'VE GOT IT! WE'LL OFFER THE JOKER SOME BAIT-- AND HOOK HIM! I KNOW HE LOVES JEWELRY, SO --
7
THE NEXT DAY'S HEADLINE--
NEW
FAMOUS BRODY DIAMOND TO B SOLD TOMORRO
Gerald Brody arranges sale of priceless gem aboard his yatc
MOCKING LAUGHTER PEALS FROM THE LIPS OF THE MIRTH-MAD CLOWN AS HE SCANS THE NEWSPAPERS--
THE BRODY DIAMOND! THE FOOLS! THAT DIAMOND SHALL BE MINE-- MINE... HA! HA!

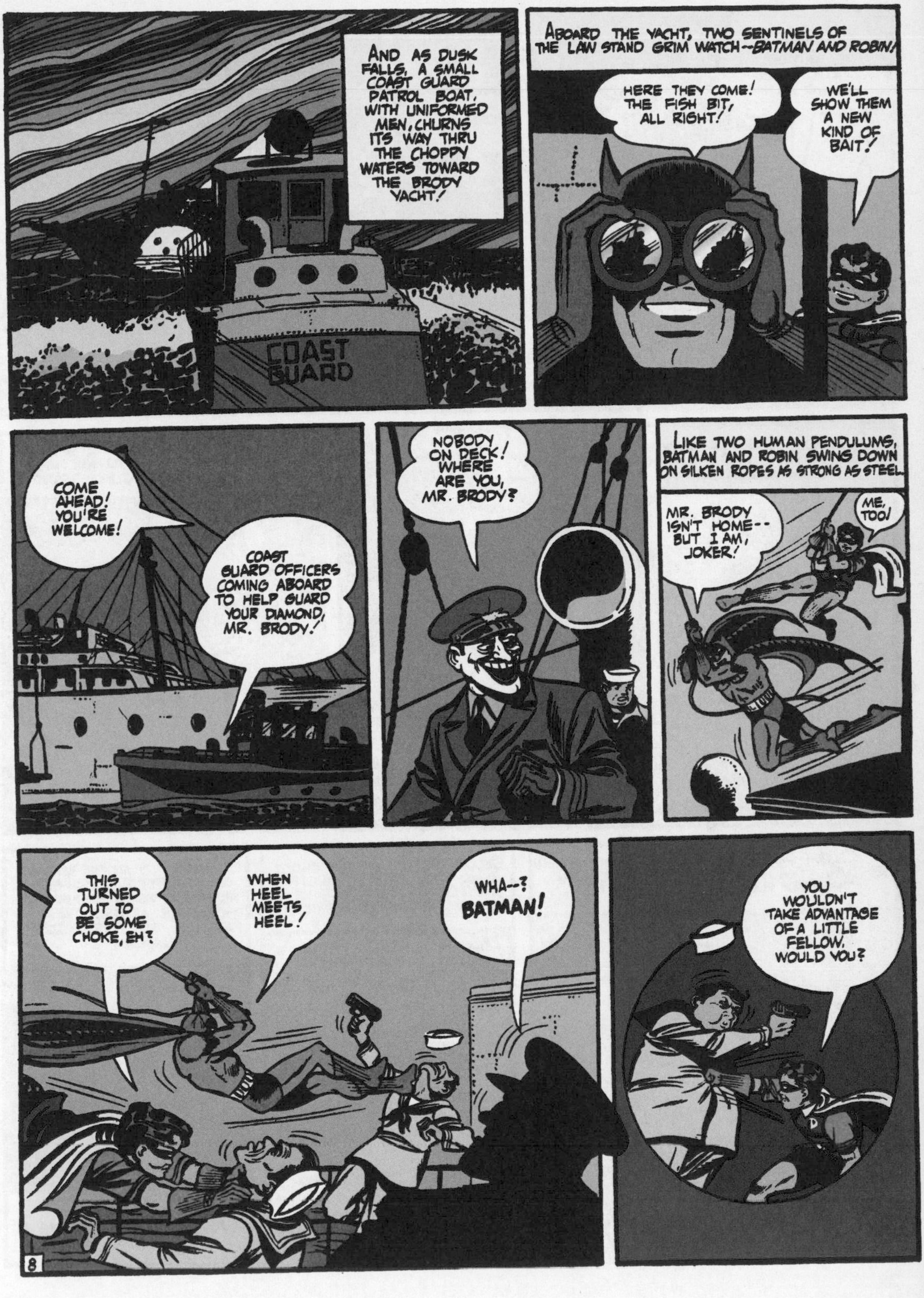
AND AS DUSK FALLS, A SMALL COAST GUARD PATROL BOAT, WITH UNIFORMED MEN, CHURNS ITS WAY THRU THE CHOPPY WATERS TOWARD THE BRODY YACHT!
COAST GUARD
ABOARD THE YACHT, TWO SENTINELS OF THE LAW STAND GRIM WATCH--BATMAN AND ROBIN!
HERE THEY COME! THE FISH BIT, ALL RIGHT!
WE'LL SHOW THEM A NEW KIND OF BAIT!
COME AHEAD! YOU'RE WELCOME!
COAST GUARD OFFICERS COMING ABOARD TO HELP GUARD YOUR DIAMOND, MR. BRODY!
NOBODY ON DECK! WHERE ARE YOU, MR. BRODY?
LIKE TWO HUMAN PENDULUMS, BATMAN AND ROBIN SWING DOWN ON SILKEN ROPES AS STRONG AS STEEL.
MR. BRODY ISN'T HOME-- BUT I AM, JOKER!
ME, TOO!
THIS TURNED OUT TO BE SOME CHOKE, EH?
WHEN HEEL MEETS HEEL!
WHA--? BATMAN!
YOU WOULDN'T TAKE ADVANTAGE OF A LITTLE FELLOW, WOULD YOU?
8

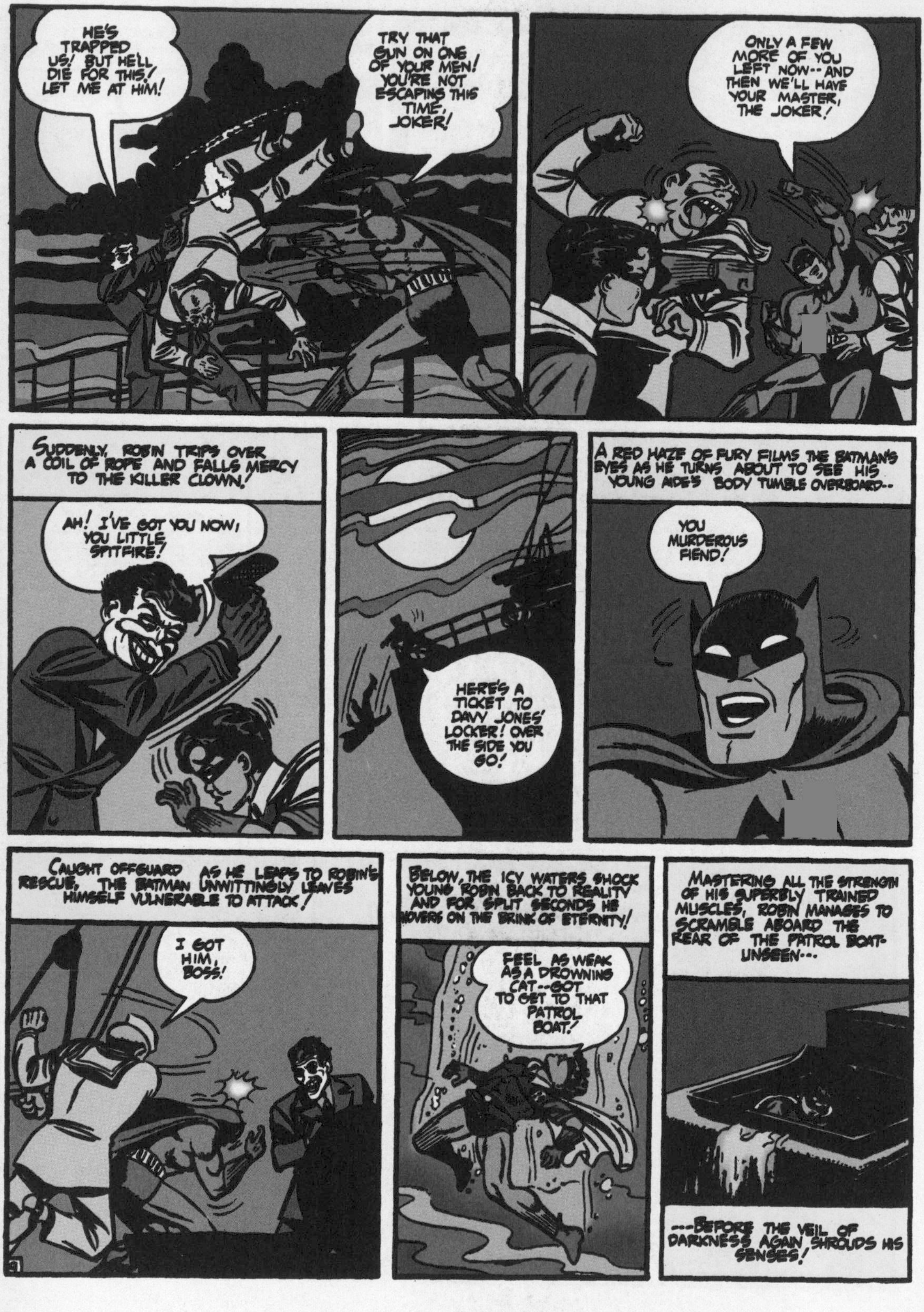

HE'S TRAPPED US! BUT HE'LL DIE FOR THIS! LET ME AT HIM!
TRY THAT GUN ON ONE OF YOUR MEN! YOU'RE NOT ESCAPING THIS TIME, JOKER!
ONLY A FEW MORE OF YOU LEFT NOW--AND THEN WE'LL HAVE YOUR MASTER, THE JOKER!
SUDDENLY, ROBIN TRIPS OVER A COIL OF ROPE AND FALLS MERCY TO THE KILLER CLOWN!
AH! I'VE GOT YOU NOW, YOU LITTLE SPITFIRE!
HERE'S A TICKET TO DAVY JONES' LOCKER! OVER THE SIDE YOU GO!
A RED HAZE OF FURY FILMS THE BATMAN'S EYES AS HE TURNS ABOUT TO SEE HIS YOUNG AIDE'S BODY TUMBLE OVERBOARD--
YOU MURDEROUS FIEND!
CAUGHT OFFGUARD AS HE LEAPS TO ROBIN'S RESCUE, THE BATMAN UNWITTINGLY LEAVES HIMSELF VULNERABLE TO ATTACK!
I GOT HIM, BOSS!
BELOW, THE ICY WATERS SHOCK YOUNG ROBIN BACK TO REALITY AND FOR SPLIT SECONDS HE HOVERS ON THE BRINK OF ETERNITY!
FEEL AS WEAK AS A DROWNING CAT--GOT TO GET TO THAT PATROL BOAT!
MASTERING ALL THE STRENGTH OF HIS SUPERBLY TRAINED MUSCLES, ROBIN MANAGES TO SCRAMBLE ABOARD THE REAR OF THE PATROL BOAT-UNSEEN---
---BEFORE THE VEIL OF DARKNESS AGAIN SHROUDS HIS SENSES!

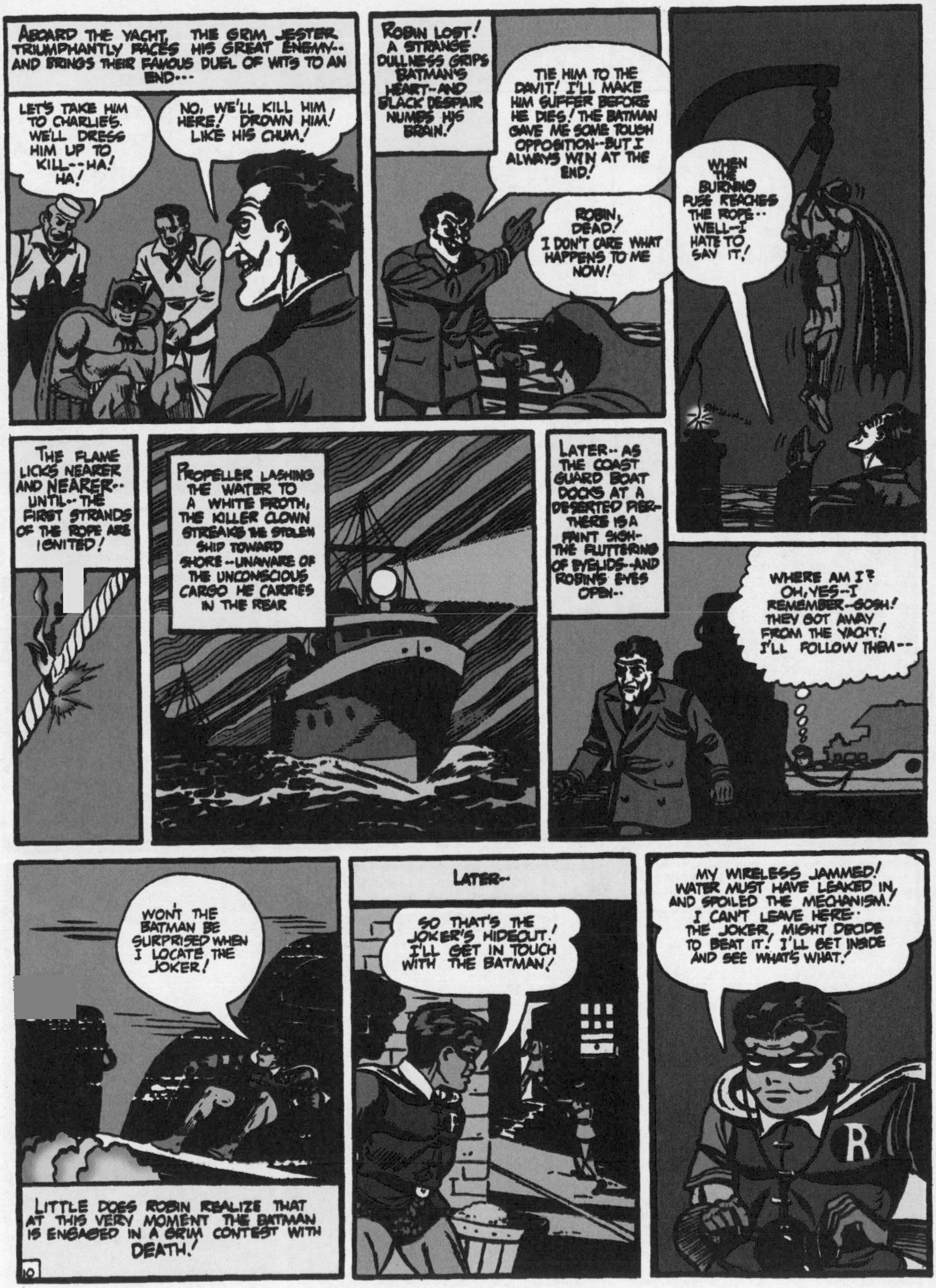
ABOARD THE YACHT, THE GRIM JESTER TRIUMPHANTLY FACES HIS GREAT ENEMY-- AND BRINGS THEIR FAMOUS DUEL OF WITS TO AN END---
LET'S TAKE HIM TO CHARLIE'S. WE'LL DRESS HIM UP TO KILL--HA! HA!
NO, WE'LL KILL HIM HERE! DROWN HIM! LIKE HIS CHUM!
ROBIN LOST! A STRANGE DULLNESS GRIPS BATMAN'S HEART--AND BLACK DESPAIR NUMBS HIS BRAIN!
TIE HIM TO THE DAVIT! I'LL MAKE HIM SUFFER BEFORE HE DIES! THE BATMAN GAVE ME SOME TOUGH OPPOSITION--BUT I ALWAYS WIN AT THE END!
ROBIN, DEAD! I DON'T CARE WHAT HAPPENS TO ME NOW!
WHEN THE BURNING FUSE REACHES THE ROPE-- WELL--I HATE TO SAY IT!
THE FLAME LICKS NEARER AND NEARER-- UNTIL-- THE FIRST STRANDS OF THE ROPE ARE IGNITED!
PROPELLER LASHING THE WATER TO A WHITE FROTH, THE KILLER CLOWN STREAKS THE STOLEN SHIP TOWARD SHORE--UNAWARE OF THE UNCONSCIOUS CARGO HE CARRIES IN THE REAR
LATER-- AS THE COAST GUARD BOAT DOCKS AT A DESERTED PIER-- THERE IS A FAINT SIGH-- THE FLUTTERING OF EYELIDS--AND ROBIN'S EYES OPEN--
WHERE AM I? OH, YES--I REMEMBER--GOSH! THEY GOT AWAY FROM THE YACHT! I'LL FOLLOW THEM--
WON'T THE BATMAN BE SURPRISED WHEN I LOCATE THE JOKER!
LITTLE DOES ROBIN REALIZE THAT AT THIS VERY MOMENT THE BATMAN IS ENGAGED IN A GRIM CONTEST WITH DEATH!
10
LATER--
SO THAT'S THE JOKER'S HIDEOUT! I'LL GET IN TOUCH WITH THE BATMAN!
MY WIRELESS JAMMED! WATER MUST HAVE LEAKED IN, AND SPOILED THE MECHANISM! I CAN'T LEAVE HERE. THE JOKER MIGHT DECIDE TO BEAT IT! I'LL GET INSIDE AND SEE WHAT'S WHAT!

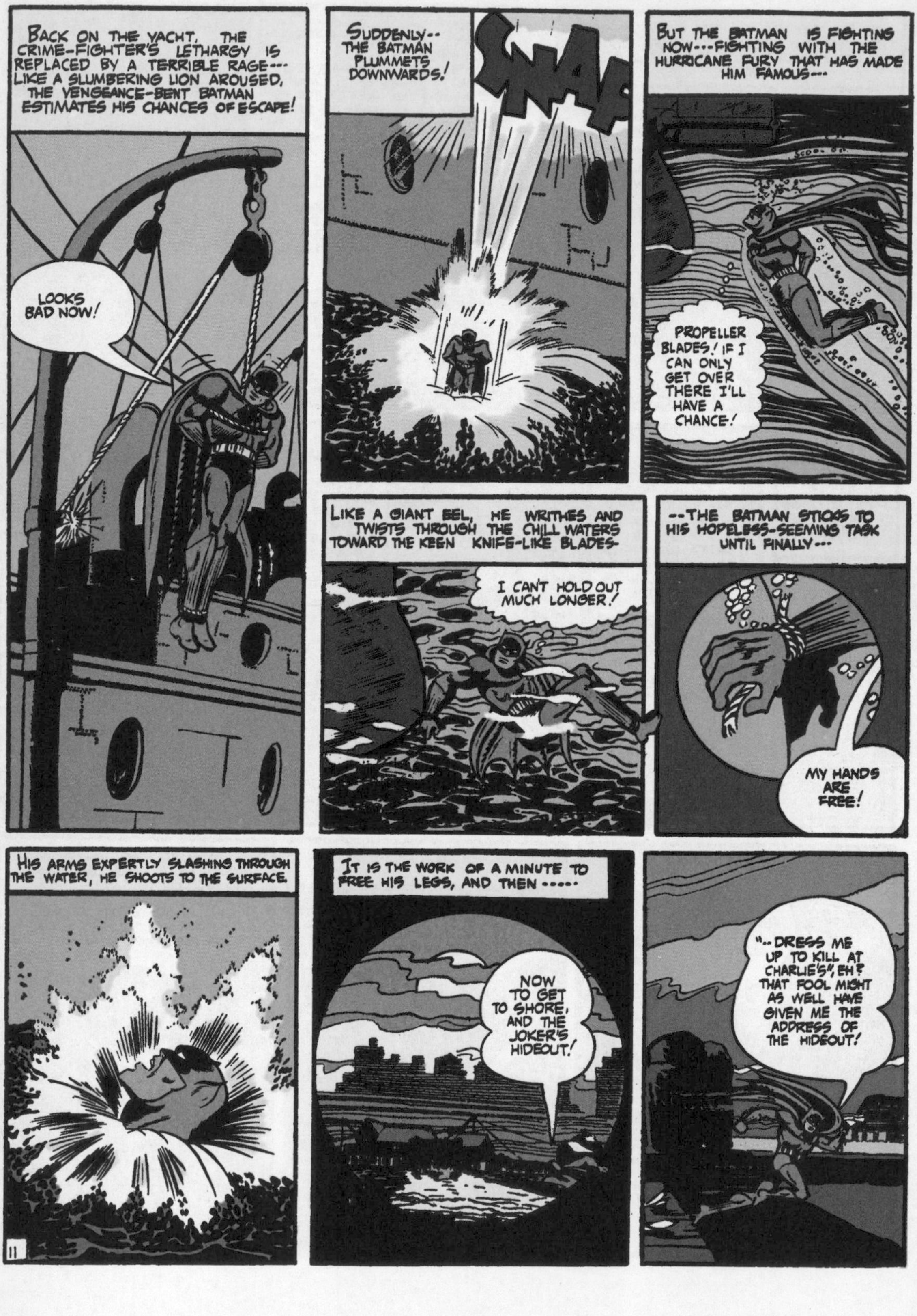
BACK ON THE YACHT, THE CRIME-FIGHTER'S LETHARGY IS REPLACED BY A TERRIBLE RAGE--- LIKE A SLUMBERING LION AROUSED, THE VENGEANCE-BENT BATMAN ESTIMATES HIS CHANCES OF ESCAPE!
LOOKS BAD NOW!
SUDDENLY-- THE BATMAN PLUMMETS DOWNWARDS!
SNAP
BUT THE BATMAN IS FIGHTING NOW---FIGHTING WITH THE HURRICANE FURY THAT HAS MADE HIM FAMOUS---
PROPELLER BLADES! IF I CAN ONLY GET OVER THERE I'LL HAVE A CHANCE!
LIKE A GIANT EEL, HE WRITHES AND TWISTS THROUGH THE CHILL WATERS TOWARD THE KEEN KNIFE-LIKE BLADES-
I CAN'T HOLD OUT MUCH LONGER!
--THE BATMAN STICKS TO HIS HOPELESS-SEEMING TASK UNTIL FINALLY---
MY HANDS ARE FREE!
HIS ARMS EXPERTLY SLASHING THROUGH THE WATER, HE SHOOTS TO THE SURFACE.
11
IT IS THE WORK OF A MINUTE TO FREE HIS LEGS, AND THEN -----
NOW TO GET TO SHORE, AND THE JOKER'S HIDEOUT!
"--DRESS ME UP TO KILL AT CHARLIE'S", EH? THAT FOOL MIGHT AS WELL HAVE GIVEN ME THE ADDRESS OF THE HIDEOUT!

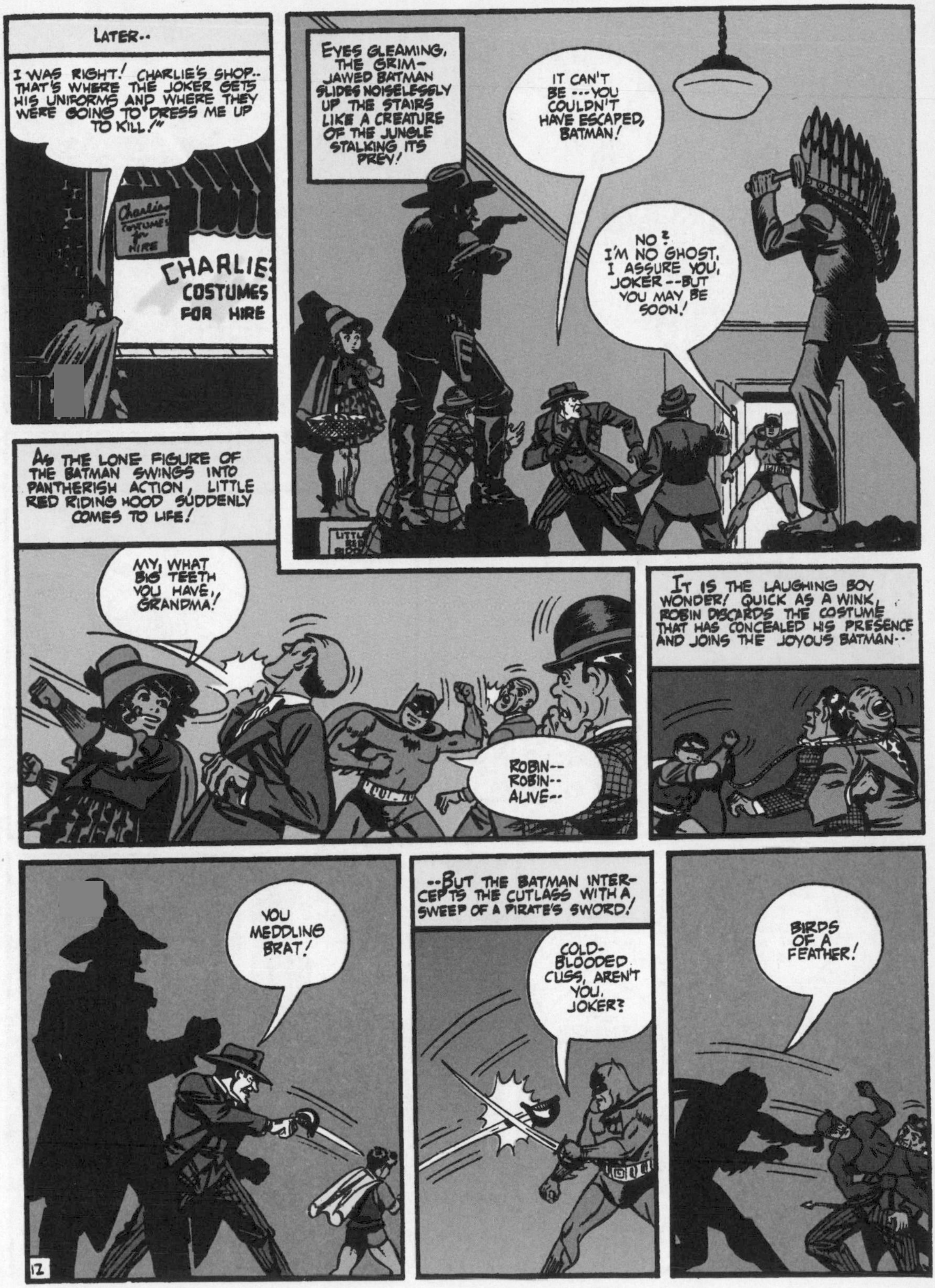
LATER..
I WAS RIGHT! CHARLIE'S SHOP.. THAT'S WHERE THE JOKER GETS HIS UNIFORMS AND WHERE THEY WERE GOING TO DRESS ME UP TO KILL!"
CHARLIE'S COSTUMES FOR HIRE
EYES GLEAMING, THE GRIM-JAWED BATMAN SLIDES NOISELESSLY UP THE STAIRS LIKE A CREATURE OF THE JUNGLE STALKING ITS PREY!
IT CAN'T BE --- YOU COULDN'T HAVE ESCAPED, BATMAN!
NO? I'M NO GHOST, I ASSURE YOU, JOKER -- BUT YOU MAY BE SOON!
AS THE LONE FIGURE OF THE BATMAN SWINGS INTO PANTHERISH ACTION, LITTLE RED RIDING HOOD SUDDENLY COMES TO LIFE!
MY, WHAT BIG TEETH YOU HAVE, GRANDMA!
ROBIN-- ROBIN-- ALIVE--
IT IS THE LAUGHING BOY WONDER! QUICK AS A WINK, ROBIN DISCARDS THE COSTUME THAT HAS CONCEALED HIS PRESENCE AND JOINS THE JOYOUS BATMAN--
YOU MEDDLING BRAT!
12
--BUT THE BATMAN INTERCEPTS THE CUTLASS WITH A SWEEP OF A PIRATE'S SWORD!
COLD-BLOODED CUSS, AREN'T YOU, JOKER?
BIRDS OF A FEATHER!

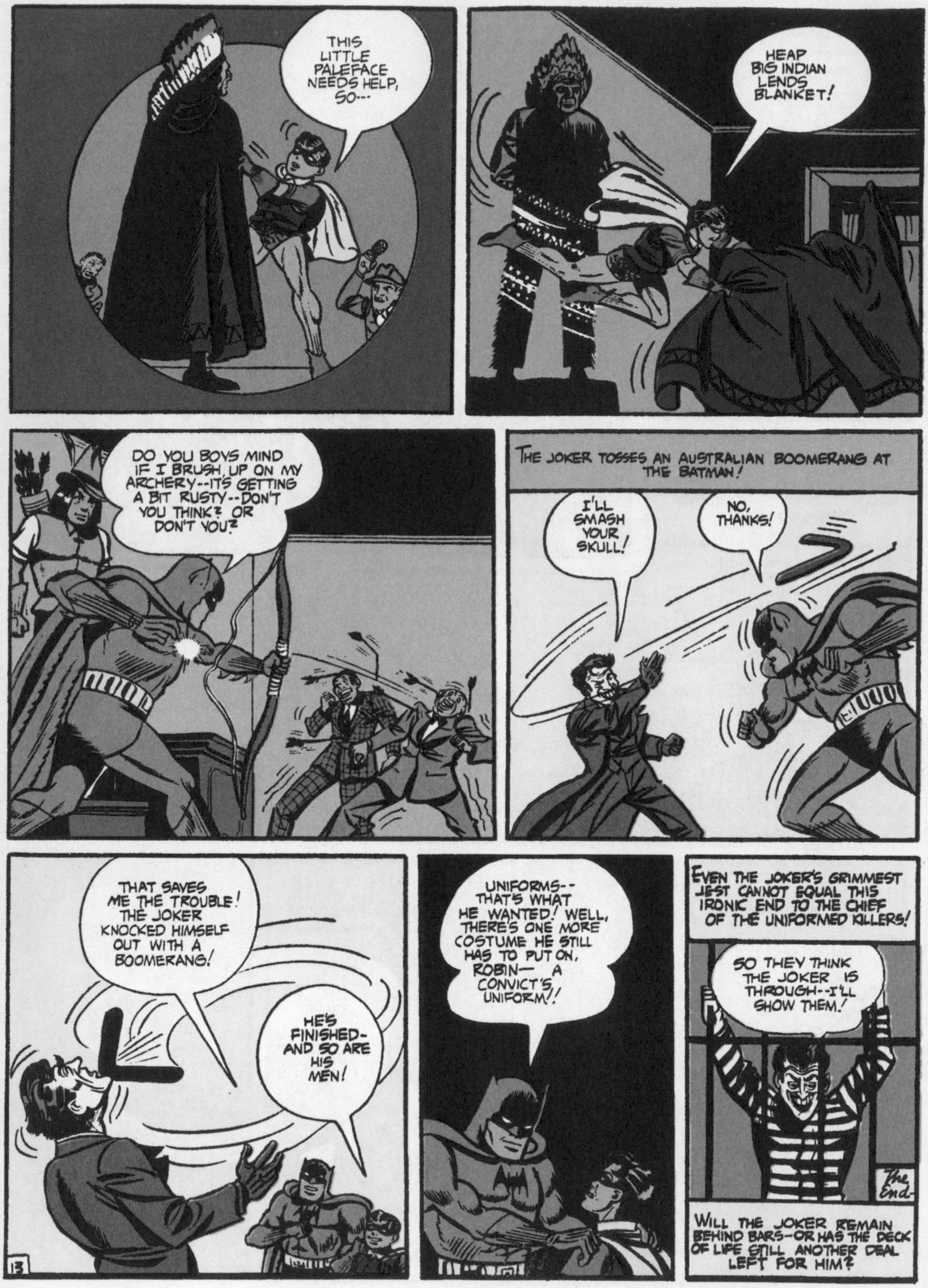
THIS LITTLE PALEFACE NEEDS HELP, SO---
HEAP BIG INDIAN LENDS BLANKET!
DO YOU BOYS MIND IF I BRUSH UP ON MY ARCHERY--IT'S GETTING A BIT RUSTY--DON'T YOU THINK? OR DON'T YOU?
THE JOKER TOSSES AN AUSTRALIAN BOOMERANG AT THE BATMAN!
I'LL SMASH YOUR SKULL!
NO, THANKS!
THAT SAVES ME THE TROUBLE! THE JOKER KNOCKED HIMSELF OUT WITH A BOOMERANG!
HE'S FINISHED- AND SO ARE HIS MEN!
13
UNIFORMS--THAT'S WHAT HE WANTED! WELL, THERE'S ONE MORE COSTUME HE STILL HAS TO PUT ON, ROBIN— A CONVICT'S UNIFORM!!
EVEN THE JOKER'S GRIMMEST JEST CANNOT EQUAL THIS IRONIC END TO THE CHIEF OF THE UNIFORMED KILLERS!
SO THEY THINK THE JOKER IS THROUGH--I'LL SHOW THEM!
The End-
WILL THE JOKER REMAIN BEHIND BARS-OR HAS THE DECK OF LIFE STILL ANOTHER DEAL LEFT FOR HIM?

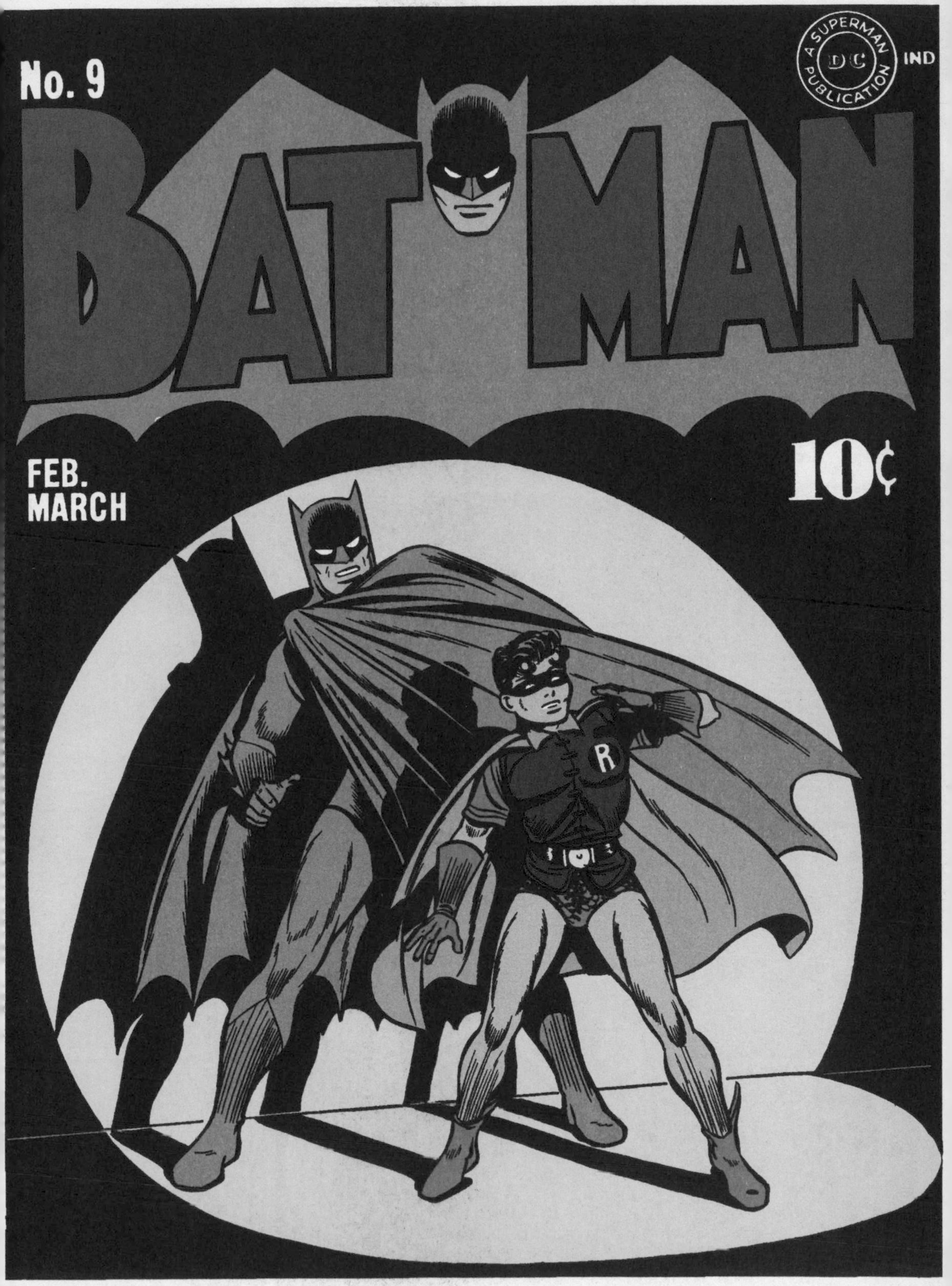
No. 9
A SUPERMAN DC PUBLICATION
IND
BATMAN
FEB.
MARCH
10¢
R

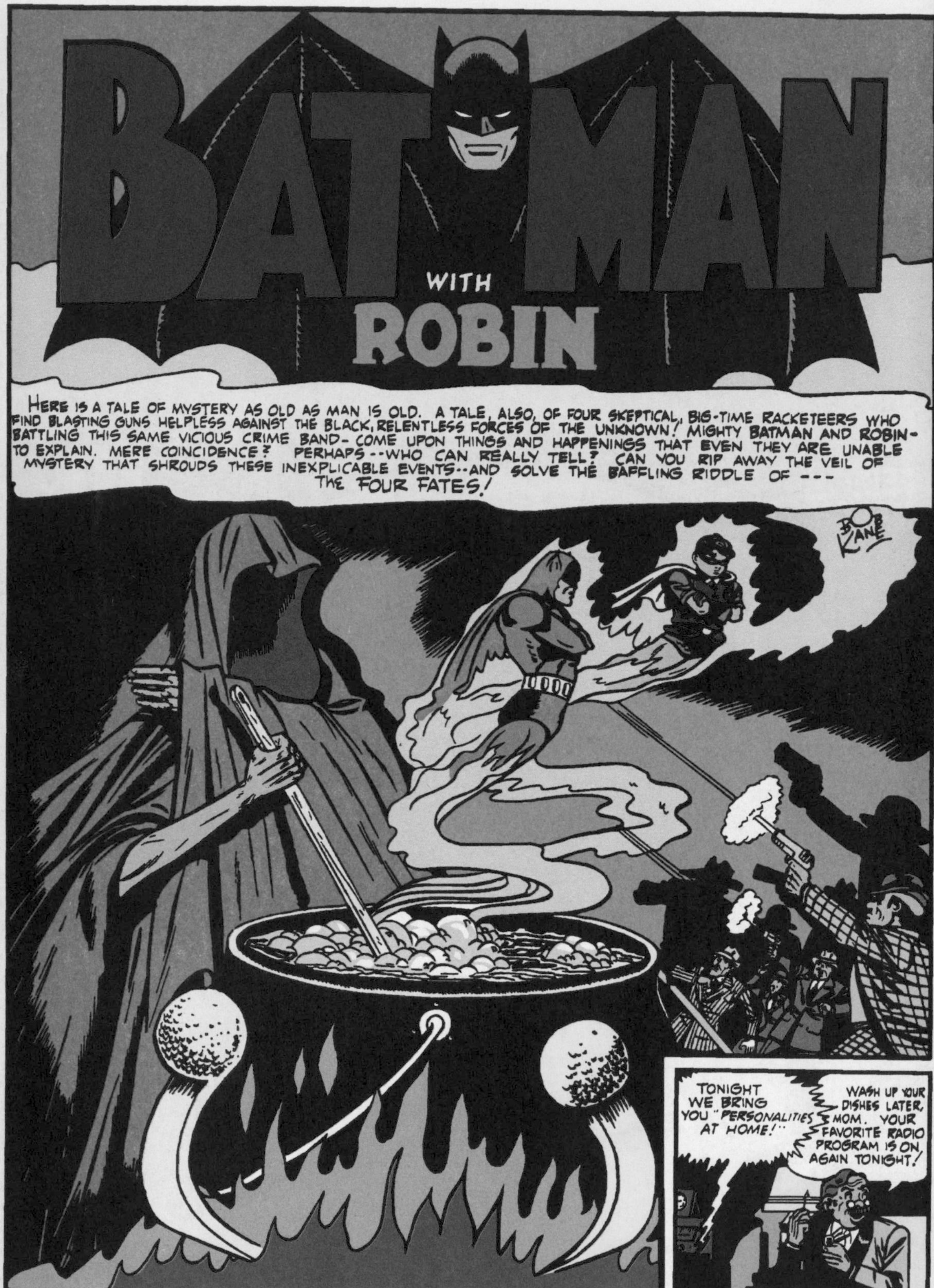
BATMAN
WITH
ROBIN
HERE IS A TALE OF MYSTERY AS OLD AS MAN IS OLD. A TALE, ALSO, OF FOUR SKEPTICAL, BIG-TIME RACKETEERS WHO FIND BLASTING GUNS HELPLESS AGAINST THE BLACK, RELENTLESS FORCES OF THE UNKNOWN! MIGHTY BATMAN AND ROBIN-BATTLING THIS SAME VICIOUS CRIME BAND- COME UPON THINGS AND HAPPENINGS THAT EVEN THEY ARE UNABLE TO EXPLAIN. MERE COINCIDENCE? PERHAPS--WHO CAN REALLY TELL? CAN YOU RIP AWAY THE VEIL OF MYSTERY THAT SHROUDS THESE INEXPLICABLE EVENTS--AND SOLVE THE BAFFLING RIDDLE OF ---
THE FOUR FATES!
BOB KANE
TONIGHT WE BRING YOU "PERSONALITIES AT HOME!"
WASH UP YOUR DISHES LATER, MOM. YOUR FAVORITE RADIO PROGRAM IS ON AGAIN TONIGHT!

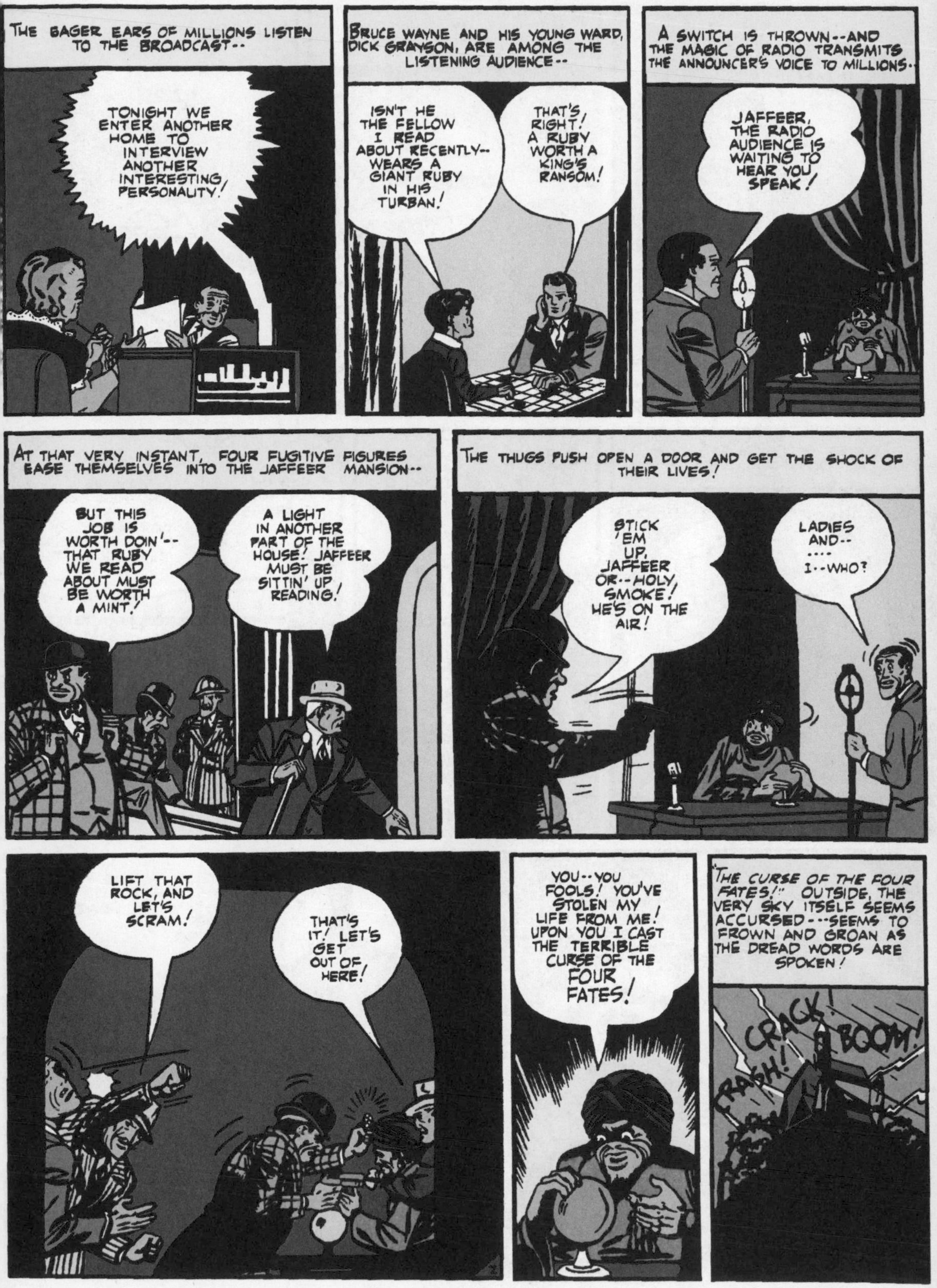
THE EAGER EARS OF MILLIONS LISTEN TO THE BROADCAST--
TONIGHT WE ENTER ANOTHER HOME TO INTERVIEW ANOTHER INTERESTING PERSONALITY!
BRUCE WAYNE AND HIS YOUNG WARD, DICK GRAYSON, ARE AMONG THE LISTENING AUDIENCE--
ISN'T HE THE FELLOW I READ ABOUT RECENTLY--WEARS A GIANT RUBY IN HIS TURBAN!
THAT'S RIGHT! A RUBY WORTH A KING'S RANSOM!
A SWITCH IS THROWN--AND THE MAGIC OF RADIO TRANSMITS THE ANNOUNCER'S VOICE TO MILLIONS..
JAFFEER, THE RADIO AUDIENCE IS WAITING TO HEAR YOU SPEAK!
AT THAT VERY INSTANT, FOUR FUGITIVE FIGURES EASE THEMSELVES INTO THE JAFFEER MANSION--
BUT THIS JOB IS WORTH DOIN'--THAT RUBY WE READ ABOUT MUST BE WORTH A MINT!
A LIGHT IN ANOTHER PART OF THE HOUSE! JAFFEER MUST BE SITTIN' UP READING!
THE THUGS PUSH OPEN A DOOR AND GET THE SHOCK OF THEIR LIVES!
STICK 'EM UP, JAFFEER OR--HOLY SMOKE! HE'S ON THE AIR!
LADIES AND-- .... I--WHO?
LIFT THAT ROCK, AND LET'S SCRAM!
THAT'S IT! LET'S GET OUT OF HERE!
YOU--YOU FOOLS! YOU'VE STOLEN MY LIFE FROM ME! UPON YOU I CAST THE TERRIBLE CURSE OF THE FOUR FATES!
"THE CURSE OF THE FOUR FATES!" OUTSIDE, THE VERY SKY ITSELF SEEMS ACCURSED---SEEMS TO FROWN AND GROAN AS THE DREAD WORDS ARE SPOKEN!
CRASH! CRACK! BOOM!

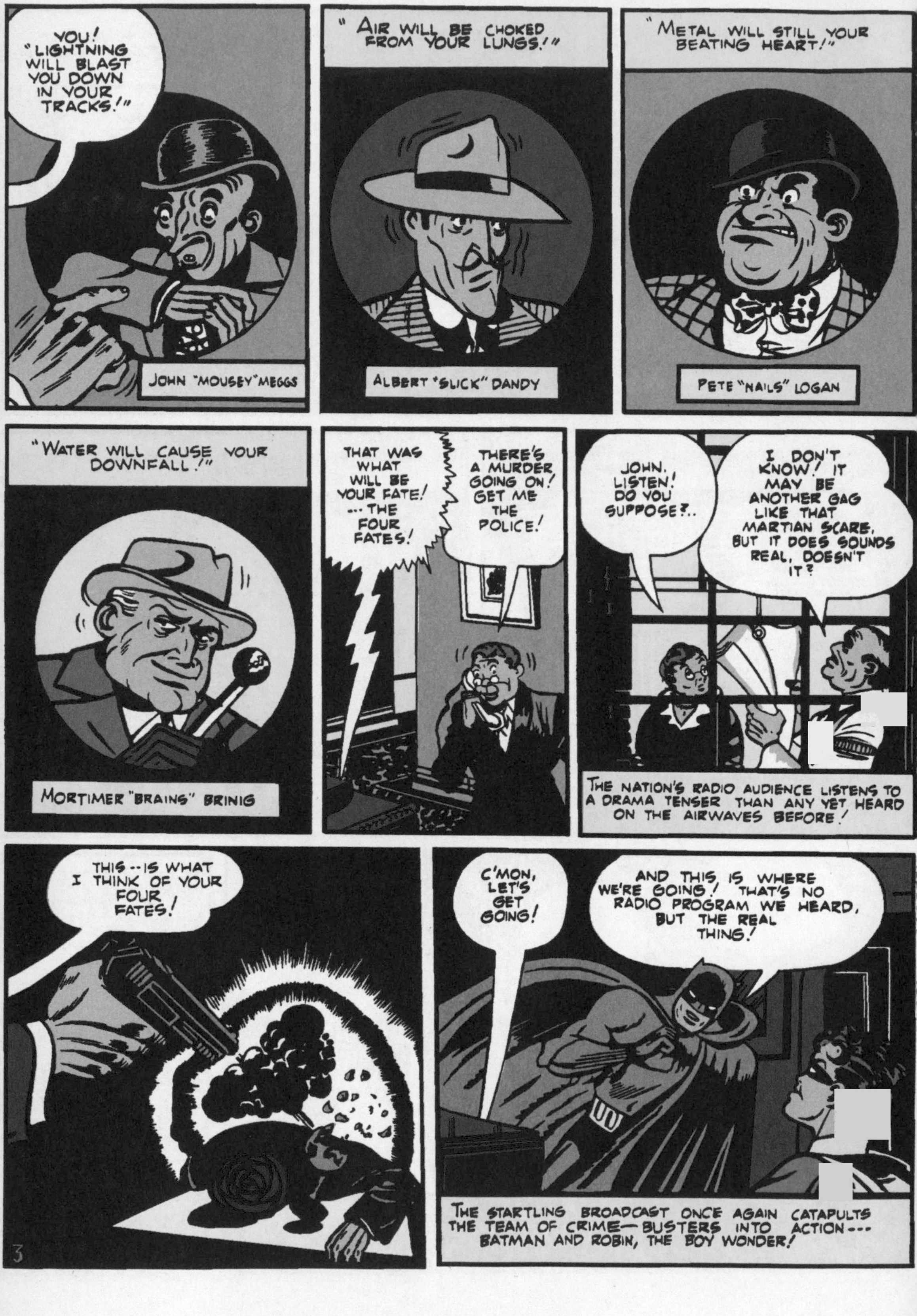
YOU! "LIGHTNING WILL BLAST YOU DOWN IN YOUR TRACKS!"
JOHN "MOUSEY" MEGGS
"AIR WILL BE CHOKED FROM YOUR LUNGS!"
ALBERT "SLICK" DANDY
"METAL WILL STILL YOUR BEATING HEART!"
PETE "NAILS" LOGAN
"WATER WILL CAUSE YOUR DOWNFALL!"
MORTIMER "BRAINS" BRINIG
THAT WAS WHAT WILL BE YOUR FATE! --- THE FOUR FATES!
THERE'S A MURDER GOING ON! GET ME THE POLICE!
JOHN. LISTEN! DO YOU SUPPOSE?..
I DON'T KNOW! IT MAY BE ANOTHER GAG LIKE THAT MARTIAN SCARE, BUT IT DOES SOUNDS REAL, DOESN'T IT?
THE NATION'S RADIO AUDIENCE LISTENS TO A DRAMA TENSER THAN ANY YET HEARD ON THE AIRWAVES BEFORE!
THIS -- IS WHAT I THINK OF YOUR FOUR FATES!
3
C'MON, LET'S GET GOING!
AND THIS IS WHERE WE'RE GOING! THAT'S NO RADIO PROGRAM WE HEARD, BUT THE REAL THING!
THE STARTLING BROADCAST ONCE AGAIN CATAPULTS THE TEAM OF CRIME—BUSTERS INTO ACTION--- BATMAN AND ROBIN, THE BOY WONDER!

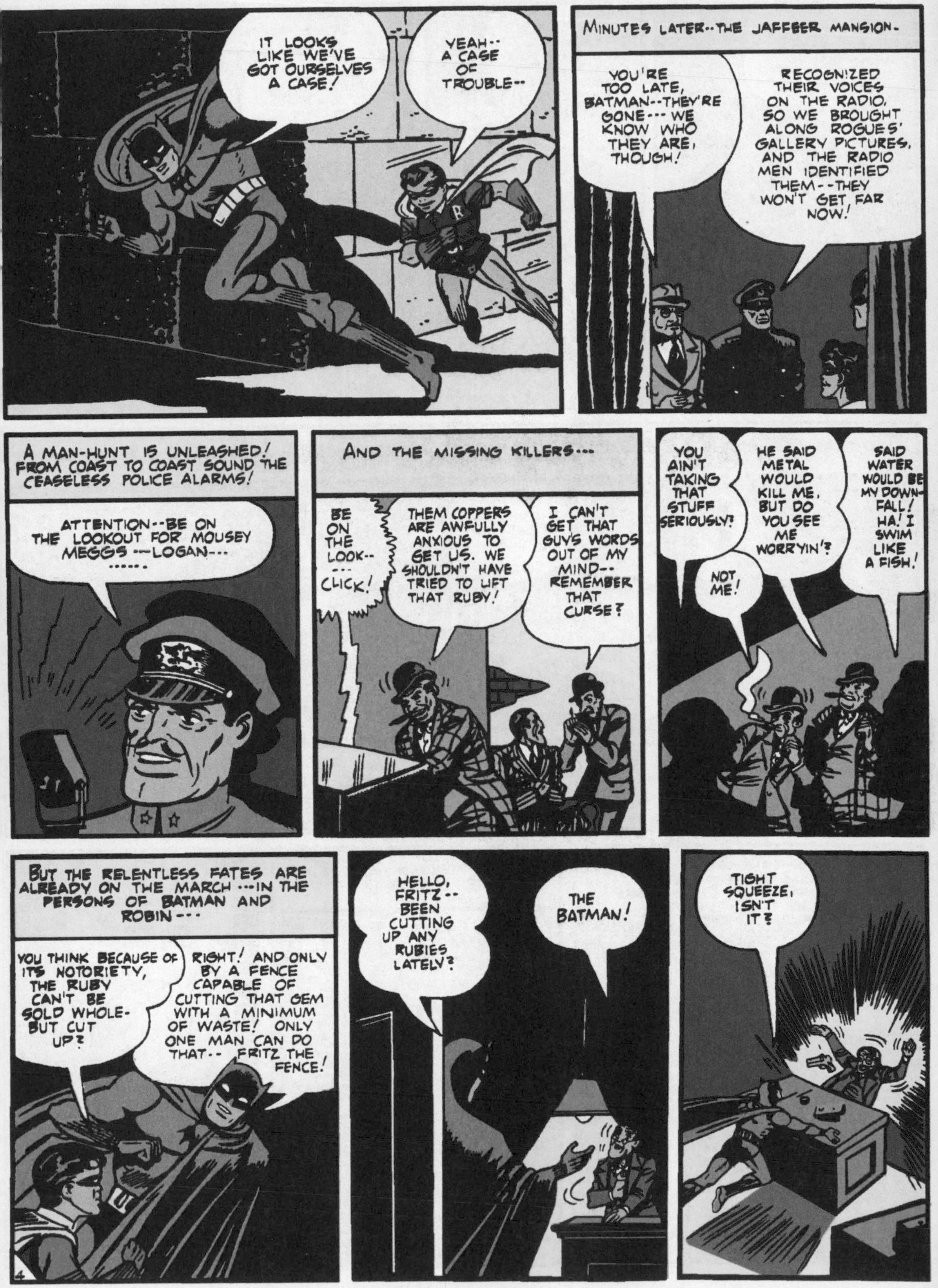
IT LOOKS LIKE WE'VE GOT OURSELVES A CASE!
YEAH-- A CASE OF TROUBLE--
MINUTES LATER--THE JAFFEER MANSION-
YOU'RE TOO LATE, BATMAN--THEY'RE GONE--- WE KNOW WHO THEY ARE, THOUGH!
RECOGNIZED THEIR VOICES ON THE RADIO, SO WE BROUGHT ALONG ROGUES' GALLERY PICTURES, AND THE RADIO MEN IDENTIFIED THEM--THEY WON'T GET FAR NOW!
A MAN-HUNT IS UNLEASHED! FROM COAST TO COAST SOUND THE CEASELESS POLICE ALARMS!
ATTENTION--BE ON THE LOOKOUT FOR MOUSEY MEGGS---LOGAN---......
AND THE MISSING KILLERS---
BE ON THE LOOK-- --- CLICK!
THEM COPPERS ARE AWFULLY ANXIOUS TO GET US. WE SHOULDN'T HAVE TRIED TO LIFT THAT RUBY!
I CAN'T GET THAT GUY'S WORDS OUT OF MY MIND-- REMEMBER THAT CURSE?
YOU AIN'T TAKING THAT STUFF SERIOUSLY?
NOT ME!
HE SAID METAL WOULD KILL ME, BUT DO YOU SEE ME WORRYIN'?
SAID WATER WOULD BE MY DOWN-FALL! HA! I SWIM LIKE A FISH!
BUT THE RELENTLESS FATES ARE ALREADY ON THE MARCH ---IN THE PERSONS OF BATMAN AND ROBIN---
YOU THINK BECAUSE OF ITS NOTORIETY, THE RUBY CAN'T BE SOLD WHOLE- BUT CUT UP?
RIGHT! AND ONLY BY A FENCE CAPABLE OF CUTTING THAT GEM WITH A MINIMUM OF WASTE! ONLY ONE MAN CAN DO THAT-- FRITZ THE FENCE!
4
HELLO, FRITZ-- BEEN CUTTING UP ANY RUBIES LATELY?
THE BATMAN!
TIGHT SQUEEZE, ISN'T IT?

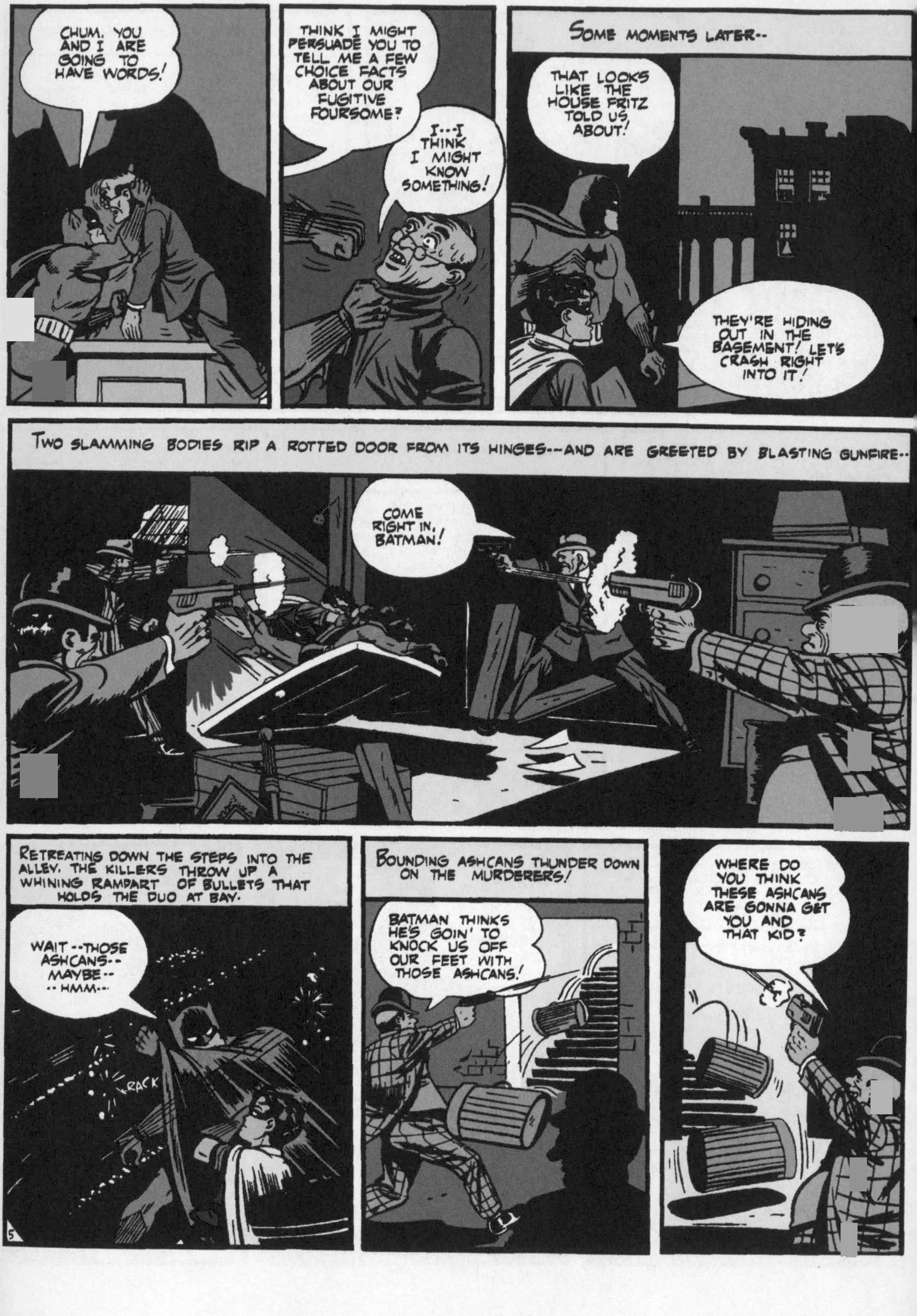
CHUM, YOU AND I ARE GOING TO HAVE WORDS!
THINK I MIGHT PERSUADE YOU TO TELL ME A FEW CHOICE FACTS ABOUT OUR FUGITIVE FOURSOME?
I--I THINK I MIGHT KNOW SOMETHING!
SOME MOMENTS LATER--
THAT LOOKS LIKE THE HOUSE FRITZ TOLD US ABOUT!
THEY'RE HIDING OUT IN THE BASEMENT! LET'S CRASH RIGHT INTO IT!
TWO SLAMMING BODIES RIP A ROTTED DOOR FROM ITS HINGES--AND ARE GREETED BY BLASTING GUNFIRE--
COME RIGHT IN, BATMAN!
RETREATING DOWN THE STEPS INTO THE ALLEY, THE KILLERS THROW UP A WHINING RAMPART OF BULLETS THAT HOLDS THE DUO AT BAY.
WAIT--THOSE ASHCANS--MAYBE-- --HMM--
KRACK
BOUNDING ASHCANS THUNDER DOWN ON THE MURDERERS!
BATMAN THINKS HE'S GOIN' TO KNOCK US OFF OUR FEET WITH THOSE ASHCANS!
WHERE DO YOU THINK THESE ASHCANS ARE GONNA GET YOU AND THAT KID?

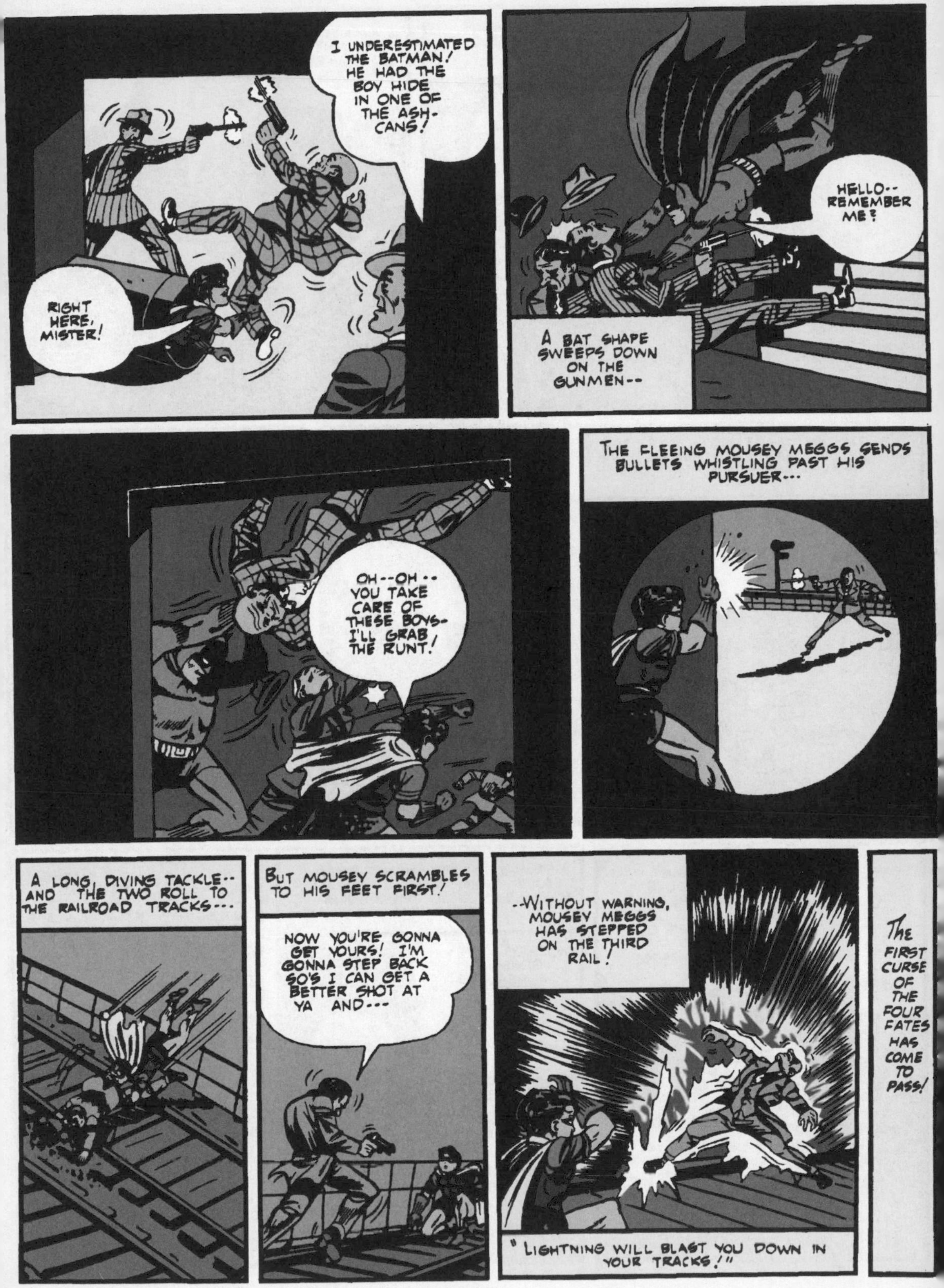
I UNDERESTIMATED THE BATMAN! HE HAD THE BOY HIDE IN ONE OF THE ASH-CANS!
RIGHT HERE, MISTER!
A BAT SHAPE SWEEPS DOWN ON THE GUNMEN--
HELLO--REMEMBER ME?
OH--OH--YOU TAKE CARE OF THESE BOYS--I'LL GRAB THE RUNT!
THE FLEEING MOUSEY MEGGS SENDS BULLETS WHISTLING PAST HIS PURSUER---
A LONG, DIVING TACKLE--AND THE TWO ROLL TO THE RAILROAD TRACKS---
BUT MOUSEY SCRAMBLES TO HIS FEET FIRST!
NOW YOU'RE GONNA GET YOURS! I'M GONNA STEP BACK SO'S I CAN GET A BETTER SHOT AT YA AND---
--WITHOUT WARNING, MOUSEY MEGGS HAS STEPPED ON THE THIRD RAIL!
"LIGHTNING WILL BLAST YOU DOWN IN YOUR TRACKS!"
THE FIRST CURSE OF THE FOUR FATES HAS COME TO PASS!

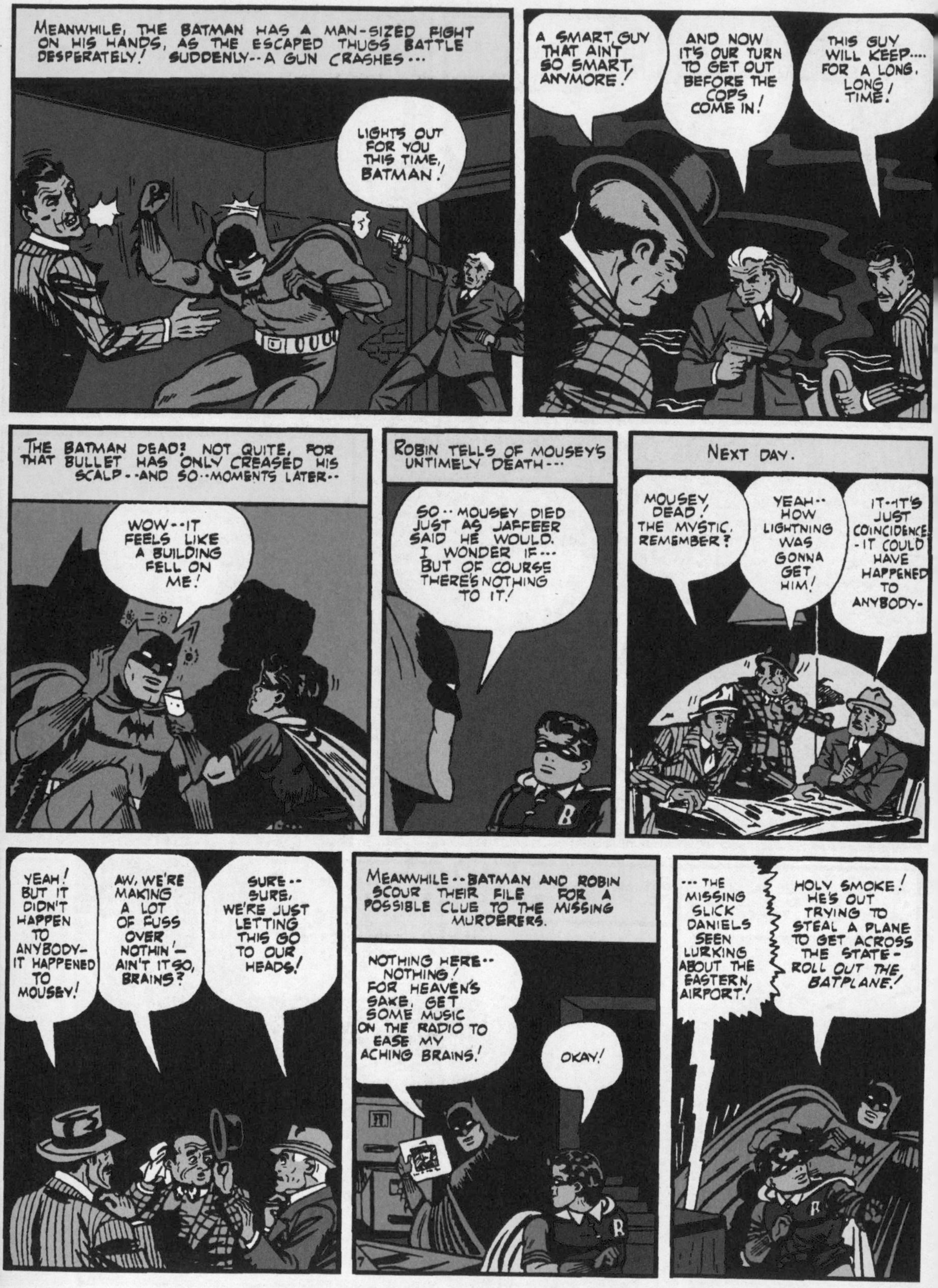
MEANWHILE, THE BATMAN HAS A MAN-SIZED FIGHT ON HIS HANDS, AS THE ESCAPED THUGS BATTLE DESPERATELY! SUDDENLY--A GUN CRASHES...
LIGHTS OUT FOR YOU THIS TIME, BATMAN!
A SMART GUY THAT AINT SO SMART, ANYMORE!
AND NOW IT'S OUR TURN TO GET OUT BEFORE THE COPS COME IN!
THIS GUY WILL KEEP.... FOR A LONG, LONG TIME!
THE BATMAN DEAD? NOT QUITE, FOR THAT BULLET HAS ONLY CREASED HIS SCALP--AND SO--MOMENTS LATER--
WOW--IT FEELS LIKE A BUILDING FELL ON ME!
ROBIN TELLS OF MOUSEY'S UNTIMELY DEATH---
SO-- MOUSEY DIED JUST AS JAFFEER SAID HE WOULD. I WONDER IF--- BUT OF COURSE THERE'S NOTHING TO IT!
NEXT DAY.
MOUSEY DEAD! THE MYSTIC, REMEMBER?
YEAH-- HOW LIGHTNING WAS GONNA GET HIM!
IT--IT'S JUST COINCIDENCE! -IT COULD HAVE HAPPENED TO ANYBODY-
YEAH! BUT IT DIDN'T HAPPEN TO ANYBODY- IT HAPPENED TO MOUSEY!
AW, WE'RE MAKING A LOT OF FUSS OVER NOTHIN'- AIN'T IT SO, BRAINS?
SURE-- SURE, WE'RE JUST LETTING THIS GO TO OUR HEADS!
MEANWHILE--BATMAN AND ROBIN SCOUR THEIR FILE FOR A POSSIBLE CLUE TO THE MISSING MURDERERS.
NOTHING HERE-- NOTHING! FOR HEAVEN'S SAKE, GET SOME MUSIC ON THE RADIO TO EASE MY ACHING BRAINS!
OKAY!
--- THE MISSING SLICK DANIELS SEEN LURKING ABOUT THE EASTERN AIRPORT!
HOLY SMOKE! HE'S OUT TRYING TO STEAL A PLANE TO GET ACROSS THE STATE- ROLL OUT THE BATPLANE!

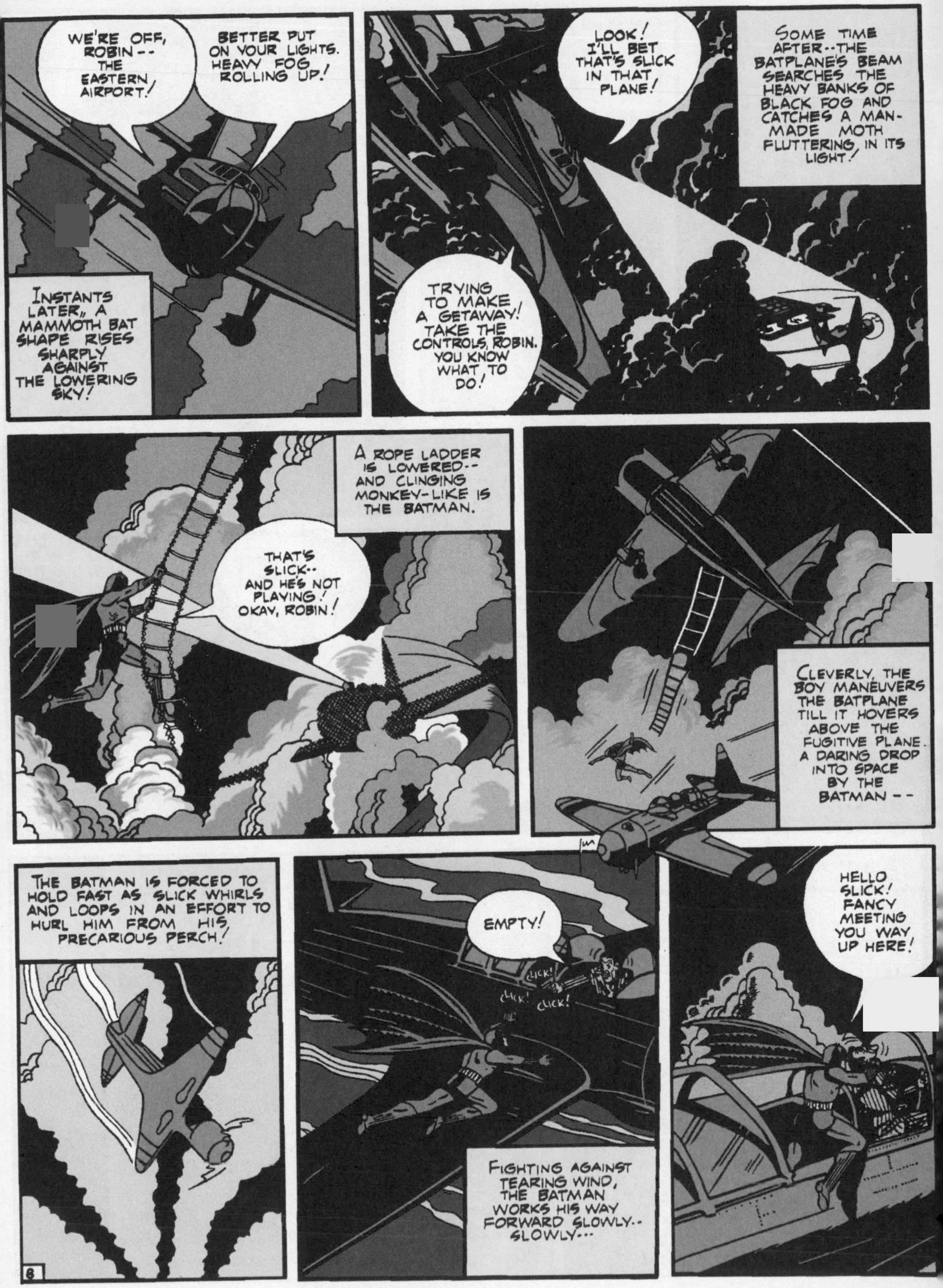
WE'RE OFF, ROBIN -- THE EASTERN AIRPORT!
BETTER PUT ON YOUR LIGHTS. HEAVY FOG ROLLING UP!
INSTANTS LATER,, A MAMMOTH BAT SHAPE RISES SHARPLY AGAINST THE LOWERING SKY!
SOME TIME AFTER--THE BATPLANE'S BEAM SEARCHES THE HEAVY BANKS OF BLACK FOG AND CATCHES A MAN-MADE MOTH FLUTTERING IN ITS LIGHT!
LOOK! I'LL BET THAT'S SLICK IN THAT PLANE!
TRYING TO MAKE A GETAWAY! TAKE THE CONTROLS, ROBIN. YOU KNOW WHAT TO DO!
A ROPE LADDER IS LOWERED-- AND CLINGING MONKEY-LIKE IS THE BATMAN.
THAT'S SLICK-- AND HE'S NOT PLAYING! OKAY, ROBIN!
CLEVERLY, THE BOY MANEUVERS THE BATPLANE TILL IT HOVERS ABOVE THE FUGITIVE PLANE. A DARING DROP INTO SPACE BY THE BATMAN --
THE BATMAN IS FORCED TO HOLD FAST AS SLICK WHIRLS AND LOOPS IN AN EFFORT TO HURL HIM FROM HIS PRECARIOUS PERCH!
EMPTY!
CLICK! CLICK! CLICK!
FIGHTING AGAINST TEARING WIND, THE BATMAN WORKS HIS WAY FORWARD SLOWLY.. SLOWLY...
HELLO SLICK! FANCY MEETING YOU WAY UP HERE!

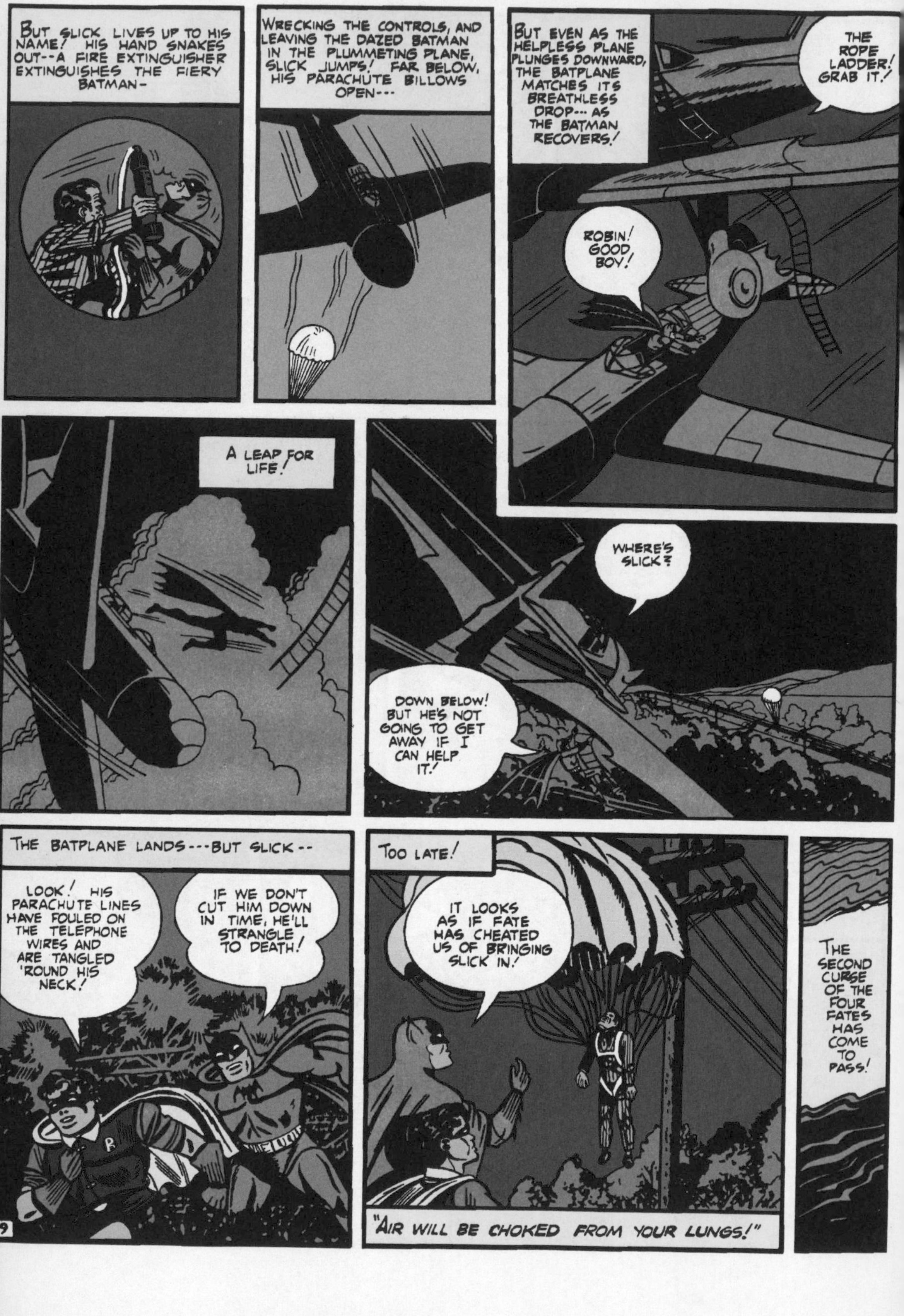

BUT SLICK LIVES UP TO HIS NAME! HIS HAND SNAKES OUT--A FIRE EXTINGUISHER EXTINGUISHES THE FIERY BATMAN-
WRECKING THE CONTROLS, AND LEAVING THE DAZED BATMAN IN THE PLUMMETING PLANE, SLICK JUMPS! FAR BELOW, HIS PARACHUTE BILLOWS OPEN---
BUT EVEN AS THE HELPLESS PLANE PLUNGES DOWNWARD, THE BATPLANE MATCHES ITS BREATHLESS DROP--- AS THE BATMAN RECOVERS!
THE ROPE LADDER! GRAB IT!
ROBIN! GOOD BOY!
A LEAP FOR LIFE!
WHERE'S SLICK?
DOWN BELOW! BUT HE'S NOT GOING TO GET AWAY IF I CAN HELP IT!
THE BATPLANE LANDS---BUT SLICK--
LOOK! HIS PARACHUTE LINES HAVE FOULED ON THE TELEPHONE WIRES AND ARE TANGLED 'ROUND HIS NECK!
IF WE DON'T CUT HIM DOWN IN TIME, HE'LL STRANGLE TO DEATH!
9
TOO LATE!
IT LOOKS AS IF FATE HAS CHEATED US OF BRINGING SLICK IN!
"AIR WILL BE CHOKED FROM YOUR LUNGS!"
THE SECOND CURSE OF THE FOUR FATES HAS COME TO PASS!

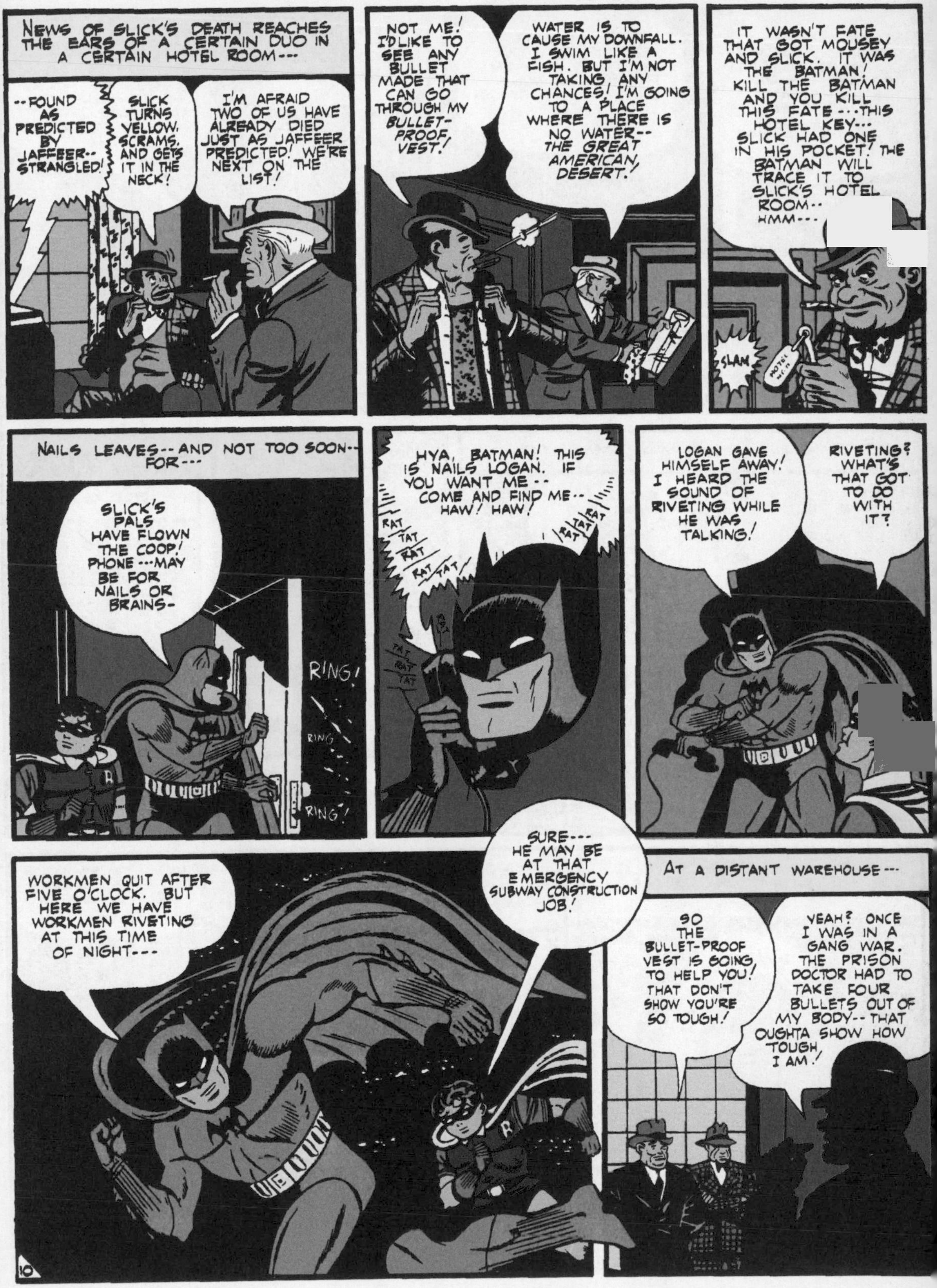
NEWS OF SLICK'S DEATH REACHES THE EARS OF A CERTAIN DUO IN A CERTAIN HOTEL ROOM---
--FOUND AS PREDICTED BY JAFFEER--STRANGLED!
SLICK TURNS YELLOW, SCRAMS, AND GETS IT IN THE NECK!
I'M AFRAID TWO OF US HAVE ALREADY DIED JUST AS JAFFEER PREDICTED! WE'RE NEXT ON THE LIST!
NOT ME! I'D LIKE TO SEE ANY BULLET MADE THAT CAN GO THROUGH MY BULLET-PROOF VEST!
WATER IS TO CAUSE MY DOWNFALL. I SWIM LIKE A FISH. BUT I'M NOT TAKING ANY CHANCES! I'M GOING TO A PLACE WHERE THERE IS NO WATER--THE GREAT AMERICAN DESERT!
IT WASN'T FATE THAT GOT MOUSEY AND SLICK. IT WAS THE BATMAN! KILL THE BATMAN AND YOU KILL THIS FATE---THIS HOTEL KEY--- SLICK HAD ONE IN HIS POCKET! THE BATMAN WILL TRACE IT TO SLICK'S HOTEL ROOM-- HMM---
SLAM
NAILS LEAVES--AND NOT TOO SOON--FOR---
SLICK'S PALS HAVE FLOWN THE COOP! PHONE---MAY BE FOR NAILS OR BRAINS-
RING!
RING
RING!
HYA, BATMAN! THIS IS NAILS LOGAN. IF YOU WANT ME--COME AND FIND ME--HAW! HAW!
RAT TAT RAT RAT TAT
RAT TAT RAT
LOGAN GAVE HIMSELF AWAY! I HEARD THE SOUND OF RIVETING WHILE HE WAS TALKING!
RIVETING? WHAT'S THAT GOT TO DO WITH IT?
WORKMEN QUIT AFTER FIVE O'CLOCK. BUT HERE WE HAVE WORKMEN RIVETING AT THIS TIME OF NIGHT---
SURE---HE MAY BE AT THAT EMERGENCY SUBWAY CONSTRUCTION JOB!
10
AT A DISTANT WAREHOUSE---
SO THE BULLET-PROOF VEST IS GOING TO HELP YOU! THAT DON'T SHOW YOU'RE SO TOUGH!
YEAH? ONCE I WAS IN A GANG WAR. THE PRISON DOCTOR HAD TO TAKE FOUR BULLETS OUT OF MY BODY--THAT OUGHTA SHOW HOW TOUGH I AM!

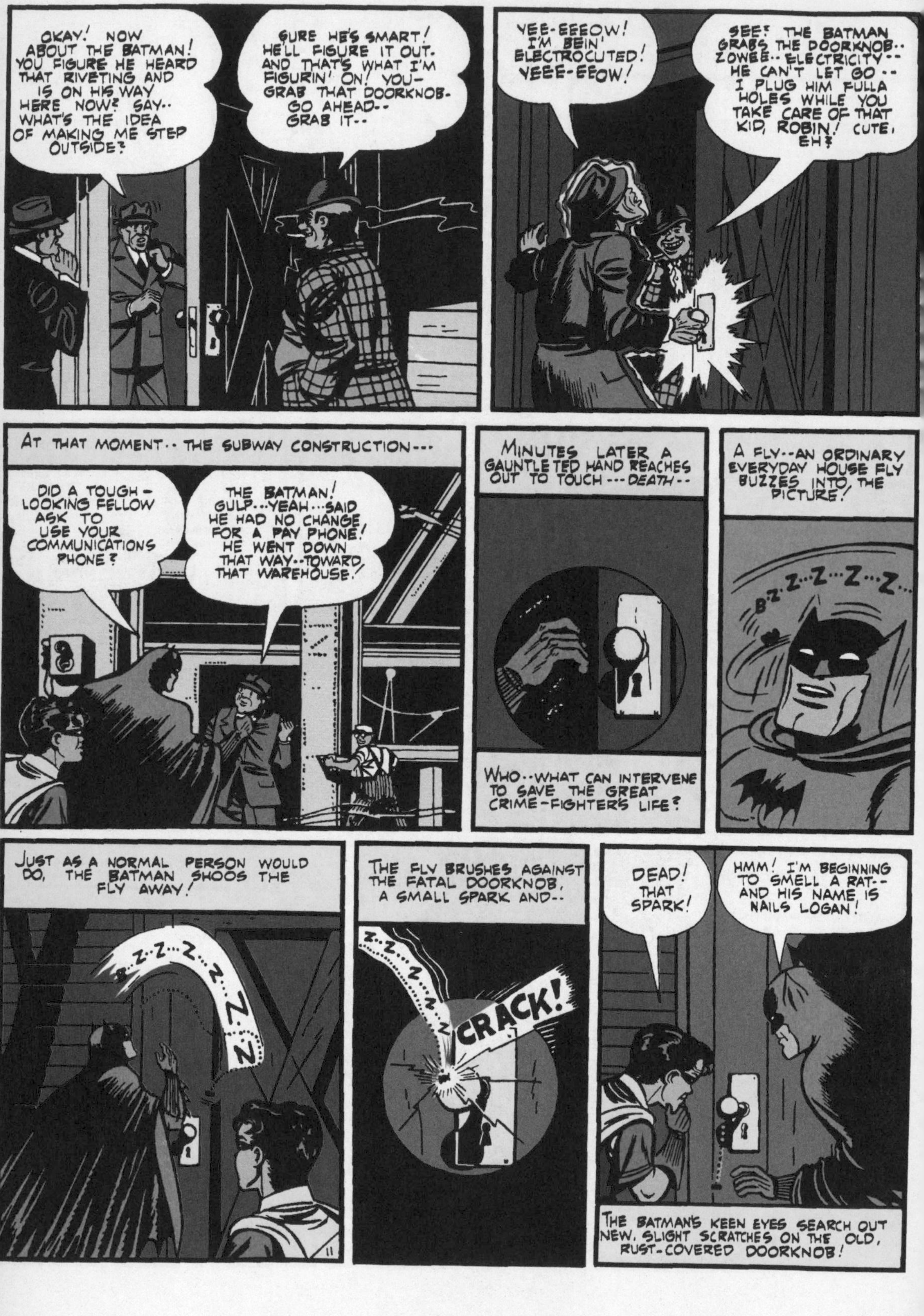
OKAY! NOW ABOUT THE BATMAN! YOU FIGURE HE HEARD THAT RIVETING AND IS ON HIS WAY HERE NOW? SAY.. WHAT'S THE IDEA OF MAKING ME STEP OUTSIDE?
SURE HE'S SMART! HE'LL FIGURE IT OUT. AND THAT'S WHAT I'M FIGURIN' ON! YOU-GRAB THAT DOORKNOB-GO AHEAD--GRAB IT--
YEE-EEEOW! I'M BEIN' ELECTROCUTED! YEEE-EEOW!
SEE? THE BATMAN GRABS THE DOORKNOB.. ZOWEE.. ELECTRICITY-- HE CAN'T LET GO-- I PLUG HIM FULLA HOLES WHILE YOU TAKE CARE OF THAT KID, ROBIN! CUTE, EH?
AT THAT MOMENT.. THE SUBWAY CONSTRUCTION---
DID A TOUGH-LOOKING FELLOW ASK TO USE YOUR COMMUNICATIONS PHONE?
THE BATMAN! GULP...YEAH...SAID HE HAD NO CHANGE FOR A PAY PHONE! HE WENT DOWN THAT WAY--TOWARD THAT WAREHOUSE!
MINUTES LATER A GAUNTLETED HAND REACHES OUT TO TOUCH---DEATH--
WHO..WHAT CAN INTERVENE TO SAVE THE GREAT CRIME-FIGHTER'S LIFE?
A FLY--AN ORDINARY EVERYDAY HOUSE FLY BUZZES INTO THE PICTURE!
B-Z-Z..Z..Z..Z...
JUST AS A NORMAL PERSON WOULD DO, THE BATMAN SHOOS THE FLY AWAY!
B-Z-Z-Z-Z-Z-Z-N
THE FLY BRUSHES AGAINST THE FATAL DOORKNOB, A SMALL SPARK AND--
Z-Z-Z-Z-Z
CRACK!
DEAD! THAT SPARK!
HMM! I'M BEGINNING TO SMELL A RAT--AND HIS NAME IS NAILS LOGAN!
THE BATMAN'S KEEN EYES SEARCH OUT NEW, SLIGHT SCRATCHES ON THE OLD, RUST-COVERED DOORKNOB!

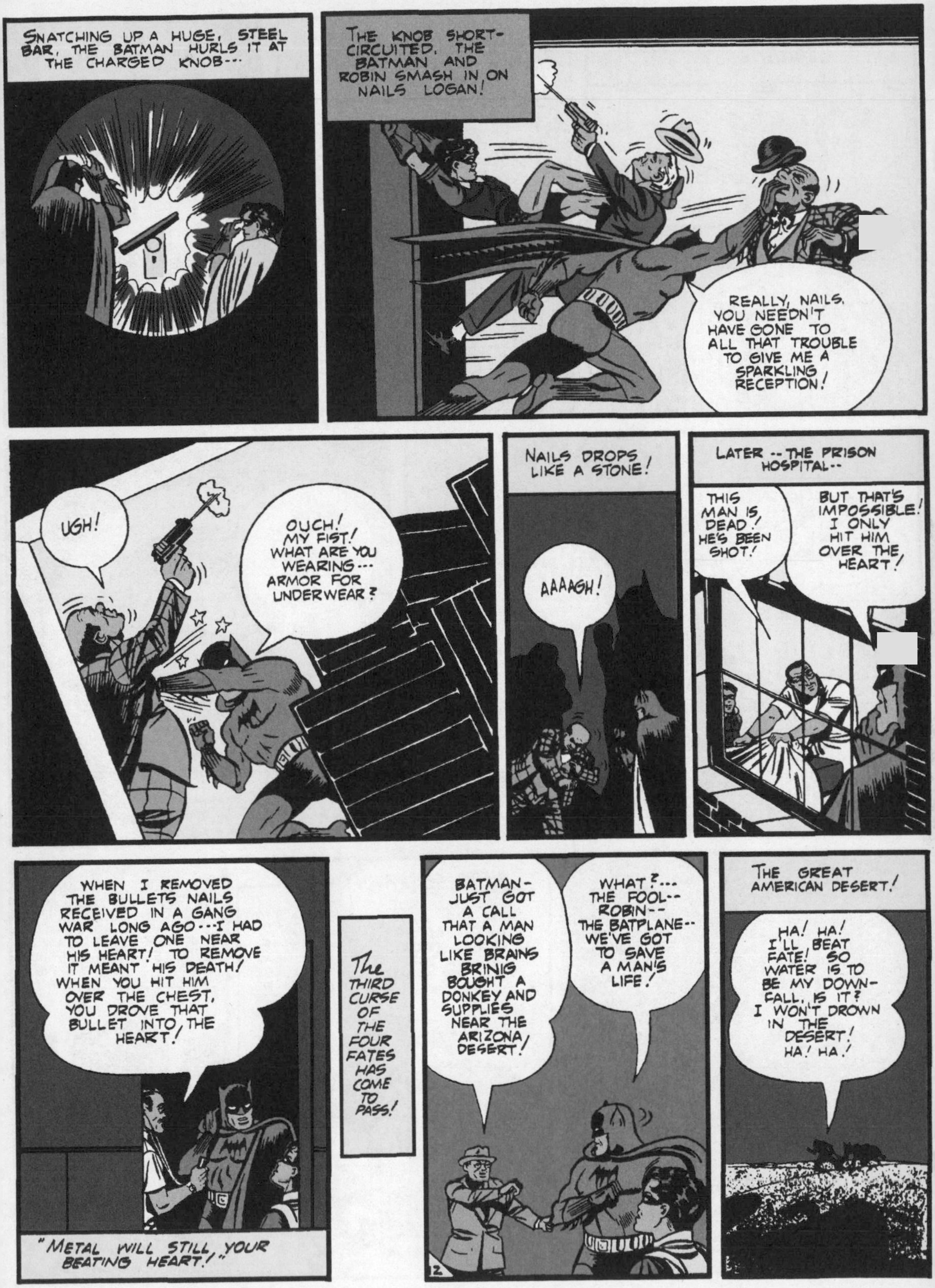
SNATCHING UP A HUGE, STEEL BAR, THE BATMAN HURLS IT AT THE CHARGED KNOB---
THE KNOB SHORT-CIRCUITED, THE BATMAN AND ROBIN SMASH IN ON NAILS LOGAN!
REALLY, NAILS, YOU NEEDN'T HAVE GONE TO ALL THAT TROUBLE TO GIVE ME A SPARKLING RECEPTION!
UGH!
OUCH! MY FIST! WHAT ARE YOU WEARING--- ARMOR FOR UNDERWEAR?
NAILS DROPS LIKE A STONE!
AAAAGH!
LATER -- THE PRISON HOSPITAL --
THIS MAN IS DEAD! HE'S BEEN SHOT!
BUT THAT'S IMPOSSIBLE! I ONLY HIT HIM OVER THE HEART!
WHEN I REMOVED THE BULLETS NAILS RECEIVED IN A GANG WAR LONG AGO---I HAD TO LEAVE ONE NEAR HIS HEART! TO REMOVE IT MEANT HIS DEATH! WHEN YOU HIT HIM OVER THE CHEST, YOU DROVE THAT BULLET INTO THE HEART!
"METAL WILL STILL YOUR BEATING HEART!"
The THIRD CURSE OF THE FOUR FATES HAS COME TO PASS!
BATMAN- JUST GOT A CALL THAT A MAN LOOKING LIKE BRAINS BRINIG BOUGHT A DONKEY AND SUPPLIES NEAR THE ARIZONA DESERT!
WHAT?--- THE FOOL-- ROBIN-- THE BATPLANE-- WE'VE GOT TO SAVE A MAN'S LIFE!
THE GREAT AMERICAN DESERT!
HA! HA! I'LL BEAT FATE! SO WATER IS TO BE MY DOWN-FALL, IS IT? I WON'T DROWN IN THE DESERT! HA! HA!

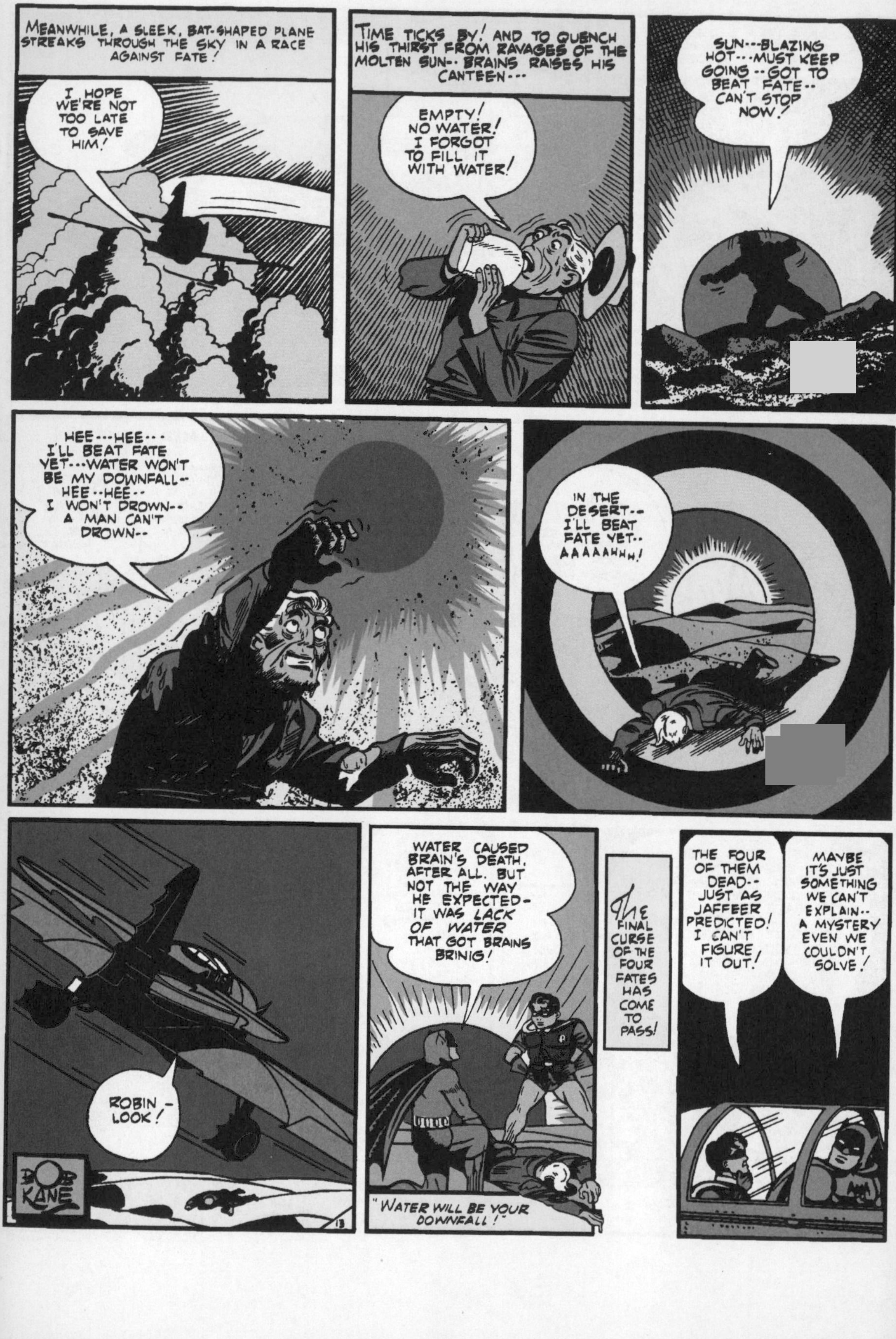
MEANWHILE, A SLEEK, BAT-SHAPED PLANE STREAKS THROUGH THE SKY IN A RACE AGAINST FATE!
I HOPE WE'RE NOT TOO LATE TO SAVE HIM!
TIME TICKS BY! AND TO QUENCH HIS THIRST FROM RAVAGES OF THE MOLTEN SUN-- BRAINS RAISES HIS CANTEEN---
EMPTY! NO WATER! I FORGOT TO FILL IT WITH WATER!
SUN---BLAZING HOT---MUST KEEP GOING--GOT TO BEAT FATE-- CAN'T STOP NOW!
HEE---HEE--- I'LL BEAT FATE YET---WATER WON'T BE MY DOWNFALL-- HEE--HEE-- I WON'T DROWN-- A MAN CAN'T DROWN--
IN THE DESERT-- I'LL BEAT FATE YET-- AAAAAHHHH!
ROBIN - LOOK!
BOB KANE
13
WATER CAUSED BRAIN'S DEATH, AFTER ALL. BUT NOT THE WAY HE EXPECTED- IT WAS LACK OF WATER THAT GOT BRAINS BRINIG!
"WATER WILL BE YOUR DOWNFALL!"
THE FINAL CURSE OF THE FOUR FATES HAS COME TO PASS!
THE FOUR OF THEM DEAD-- JUST AS JAFFEER PREDICTED! I CAN'T FIGURE IT OUT!
MAYBE IT'S JUST SOMETHING WE CAN'T EXPLAIN-- A MYSTERY EVEN WE COULDN'T SOLVE!

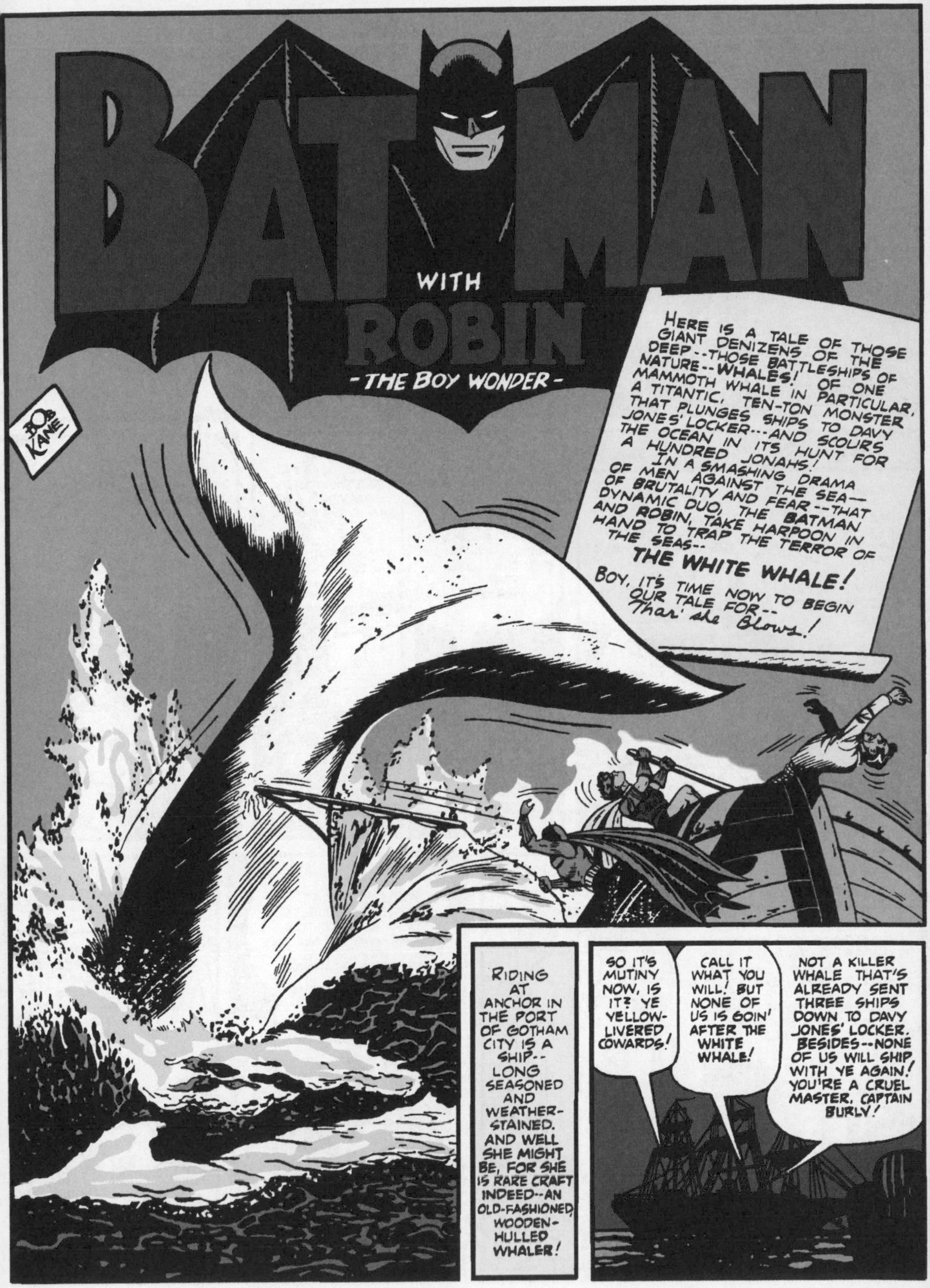
BATMAN
WITH
ROBIN
-THE BOY WONDER-
BOB KANE
HERE IS A TALE OF THOSE GIANT DENIZENS OF THE DEEP--THOSE BATTLESHIPS OF NATURE--WHALES! OF ONE MAMMOTH WHALE IN PARTICULAR, A TITANTIC, TEN-TON MONSTER THAT PLUNGES SHIPS TO DAVY JONES' LOCKER---AND SCOURS THE OCEAN IN ITS HUNT FOR A HUNDRED JONAHS! IN A SMASHING DRAMA OF MEN AGAINST THE SEA— OF BRUTALITY AND FEAR--THAT DYNAMIC DUO, THE BATMAN AND ROBIN, TAKE HARPOON IN HAND TO TRAP THE TERROR OF THE SEAS--
THE WHITE WHALE!
BOY, IT'S TIME NOW TO BEGIN OUR TALE FOR-- Thar' she Blows!
RIDING AT ANCHOR IN THE PORT OF GOTHAM CITY IS A SHIP-- LONG SEASONED AND WEATHER-STAINED. AND WELL SHE MIGHT BE, FOR SHE IS RARE CRAFT INDEED--AN OLD-FASHIONED, WOODEN-HULLED WHALER!
SO IT'S MUTINY NOW, IS IT? YE YELLOW-LIVERED COWARDS!
CALL IT WHAT YOU WILL! BUT NONE OF US IS GOIN' AFTER THE WHITE WHALE!
NOT A KILLER WHALE THAT'S ALREADY SENT THREE SHIPS DOWN TO DAVY JONES' LOCKER. BESIDES--NONE OF US WILL SHIP WITH YE AGAIN! YOU'RE A CRUEL MASTER, CAPTAIN BURLY!

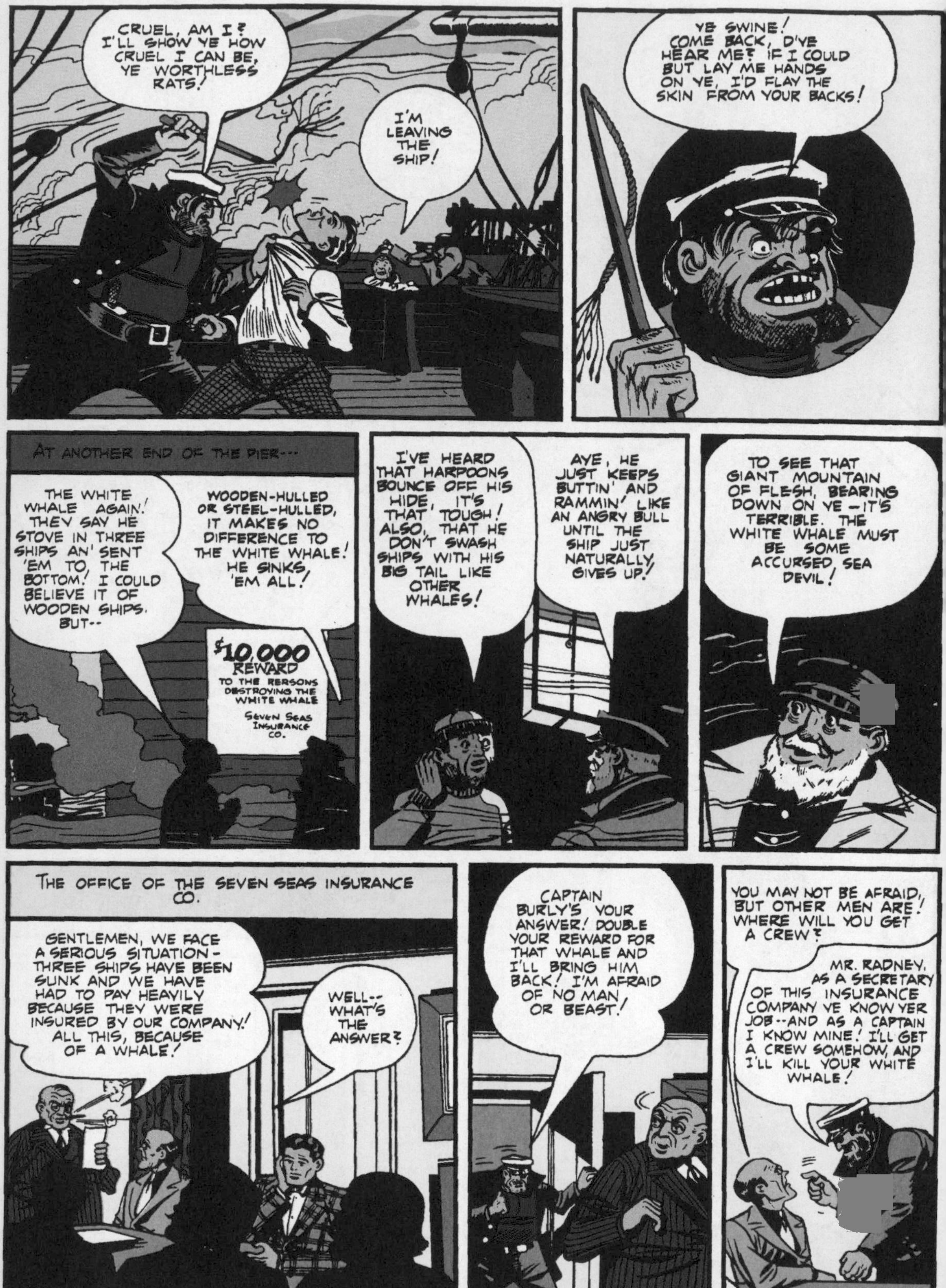
CRUEL, AM I? I'LL SHOW YE HOW CRUEL I CAN BE, YE WORTHLESS RATS!
I'M LEAVING THE SHIP!
YE SWINE! COME BACK, D'YE HEAR ME? IF I COULD BUT LAY ME HANDS ON YE, I'D FLAY THE SKIN FROM YOUR BACKS!
AT ANOTHER END OF THE PIER---
THE WHITE WHALE AGAIN! THEY SAY HE STOVE IN THREE SHIPS AN' SENT 'EM TO THE BOTTOM! I COULD BELIEVE IT OF WOODEN SHIPS. BUT--
WOODEN-HULLED OR STEEL-HULLED, IT MAKES NO DIFFERENCE TO THE WHITE WHALE! HE SINKS 'EM ALL!
$10,000 REWARD
TO THE PERSONS DESTROYING THE WHITE WHALE
SEVEN SEAS INSURANCE CO.
I'VE HEARD THAT HARPOONS BOUNCE OFF HIS HIDE, IT'S THAT TOUGH! ALSO, THAT HE DON'T SWASH SHIPS WITH HIS BIG TAIL LIKE OTHER WHALES!
AYE, HE JUST KEEPS BUTTIN' AND RAMMIN' LIKE AN ANGRY BULL UNTIL THE SHIP JUST NATURALLY GIVES UP!
TO SEE THAT GIANT MOUNTAIN OF FLESH, BEARING DOWN ON YE -- IT'S TERRIBLE. THE WHITE WHALE MUST BE SOME ACCURSED SEA DEVIL!
THE OFFICE OF THE SEVEN SEAS INSURANCE CO.
GENTLEMEN, WE FACE A SERIOUS SITUATION - THREE SHIPS HAVE BEEN SUNK AND WE HAVE HAD TO PAY HEAVILY BECAUSE THEY WERE INSURED BY OUR COMPANY! ALL THIS, BECAUSE OF A WHALE!
WELL-- WHAT'S THE ANSWER?
CAPTAIN BURLY'S YOUR ANSWER! DOUBLE YOUR REWARD FOR THAT WHALE AND I'LL BRING HIM BACK! I'M AFRAID OF NO MAN OR BEAST!
YOU MAY NOT BE AFRAID, BUT OTHER MEN ARE! WHERE WILL YOU GET A CREW?
MR. RADNEY, AS A SECRETARY OF THIS INSURANCE COMPANY YE KNOW YER JOB--AND AS A CAPTAIN I KNOW MINE! I'LL GET A CREW SOMEHOW, AND I'LL KILL YOUR WHITE WHALE!

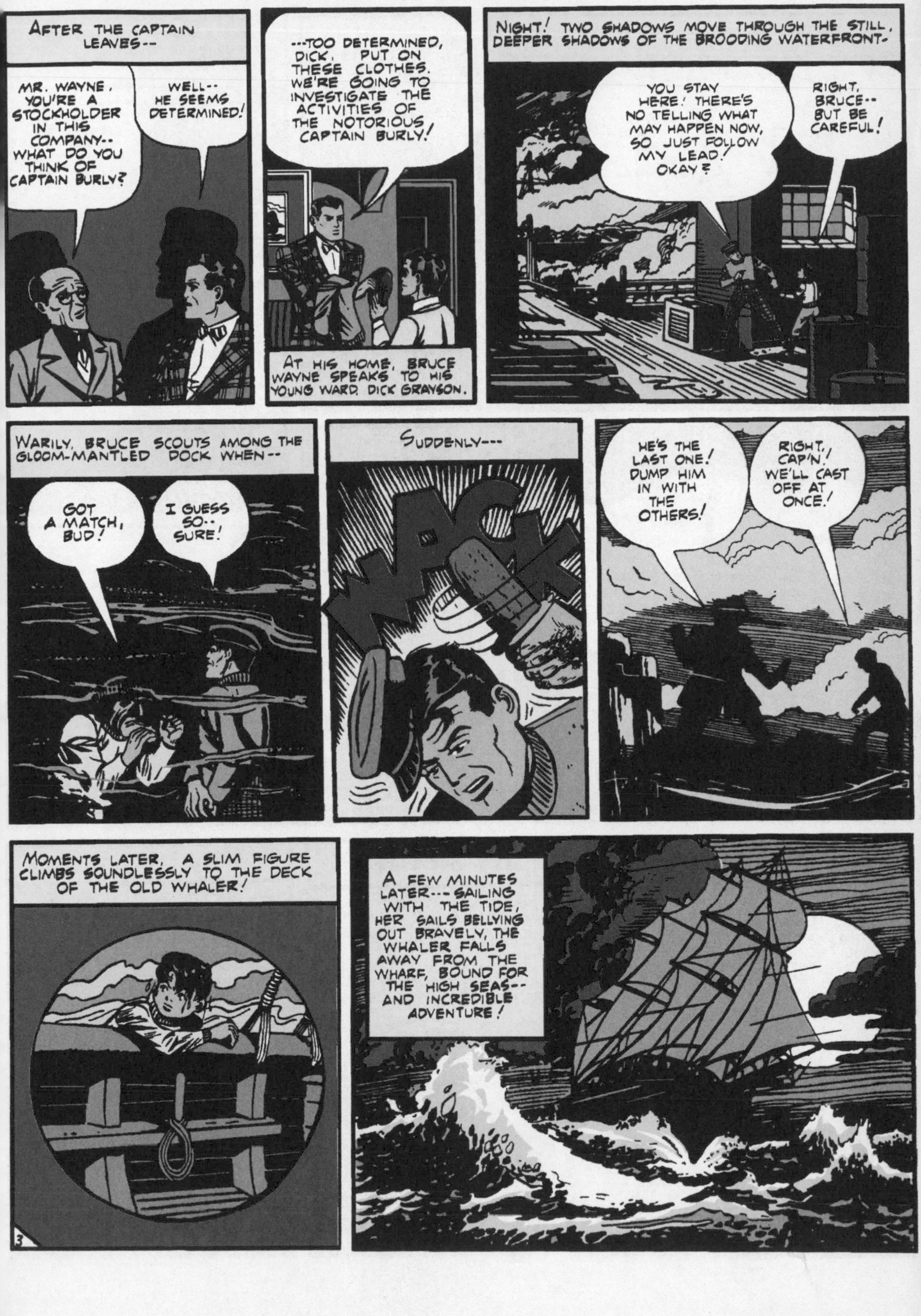
AFTER THE CAPTAIN LEAVES--
MR. WAYNE, YOU'RE A STOCKHOLDER IN THIS COMPANY-- WHAT DO YOU THINK OF CAPTAIN BURLY?
WELL-- HE SEEMS DETERMINED!
---TOO DETERMINED, DICK. PUT ON THESE CLOTHES. WE'RE GOING TO INVESTIGATE THE ACTIVITIES OF THE NOTORIOUS CAPTAIN BURLY!
AT HIS HOME, BRUCE WAYNE SPEAKS TO HIS YOUNG WARD, DICK GRAYSON.
NIGHT! TWO SHADOWS MOVE THROUGH THE STILL, DEEPER SHADOWS OF THE BROODING WATERFRONT-
YOU STAY HERE! THERE'S NO TELLING WHAT MAY HAPPEN NOW, SO JUST FOLLOW MY LEAD! OKAY?
RIGHT, BRUCE-- BUT BE CAREFUL!
WARILY, BRUCE SCOUTS AMONG THE GLOOM-MANTLED DOCK WHEN--
GOT A MATCH, BUD!
I GUESS SO-- SURE!
SUDDENLY---
WACK
HE'S THE LAST ONE! DUMP HIM IN WITH THE OTHERS!
RIGHT, CAP'N! WE'LL CAST OFF AT ONCE!
MOMENTS LATER, A SLIM FIGURE CLIMBS SOUNDLESSLY TO THE DECK OF THE OLD WHALER!
3
A FEW MINUTES LATER--- SAILING WITH THE TIDE, HER SAILS BELLYING OUT BRAVELY, THE WHALER FALLS AWAY FROM THE WHARF, BOUND FOR THE HIGH SEAS-- AND INCREDIBLE ADVENTURE!

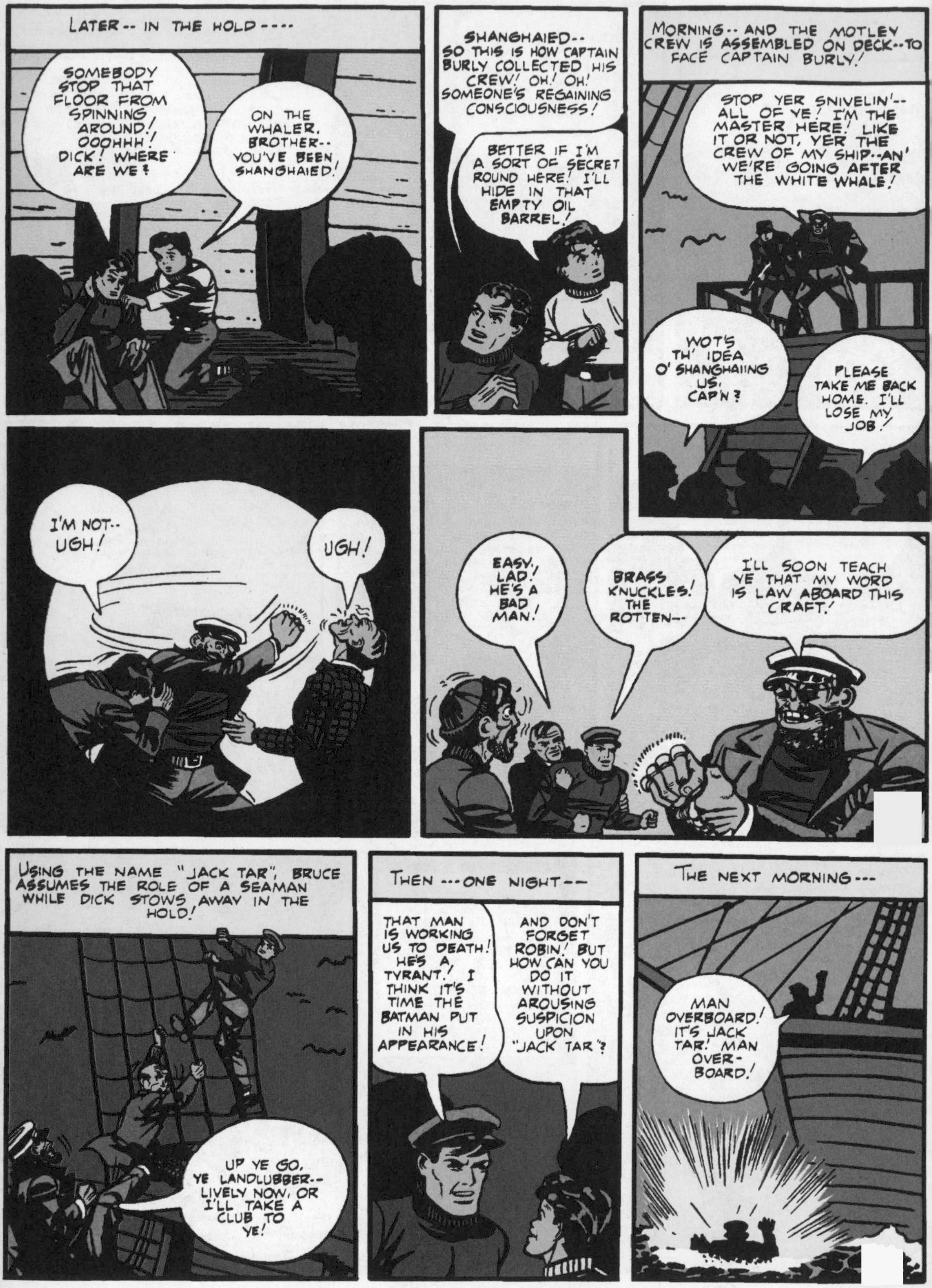
LATER -- IN THE HOLD ----
SOMEBODY STOP THAT FLOOR FROM SPINNING AROUND! OOOHHH! DICK! WHERE ARE WE?
ON THE WHALER, BROTHER-- YOU'VE BEEN SHANGHAIED!
SHANGHAIED-- SO THIS IS HOW CAPTAIN BURLY COLLECTED HIS CREW! OH! OH! SOMEONE'S REGAINING CONSCIOUSNESS!
BETTER IF I'M A SORT OF SECRET ROUND HERE! I'LL HIDE IN THAT EMPTY OIL BARREL!
MORNING -- AND THE MOTLEY CREW IS ASSEMBLED ON DECK -- TO FACE CAPTAIN BURLY!
STOP YER SNIVELIN'-- ALL OF YE! I'M THE MASTER HERE! LIKE IT OR NOT, YER THE CREW OF MY SHIP--AN' WE'RE GOING AFTER THE WHITE WHALE!
WOT'S TH' IDEA O' SHANGHAIING US, CAP'N?
PLEASE TAKE ME BACK HOME. I'LL LOSE MY JOB!
I'M NOT-- UGH!
UGH!
I'LL SOON TEACH YE THAT MY WORD IS LAW ABOARD THIS CRAFT!
BRASS KNUCKLES! THE ROTTEN--
EASY, LAD! HE'S A BAD MAN!
USING THE NAME "JACK TAR", BRUCE ASSUMES THE ROLE OF A SEAMAN WHILE DICK STOWS AWAY IN THE HOLD!
UP YE GO, YE LANDLUBBER-- LIVELY NOW, OR I'LL TAKE A CLUB TO YE!
THEN --- ONE NIGHT --
THAT MAN IS WORKING US TO DEATH! HE'S A TYRANT! I THINK IT'S TIME THE BATMAN PUT IN HIS APPEARANCE!
AND DON'T FORGET ROBIN! BUT HOW CAN YOU DO IT WITHOUT AROUSING SUSPICION UPON "JACK TAR"?
THE NEXT MORNING ---
MAN OVERBOARD! IT'S JACK TAR! MAN OVER-BOARD!

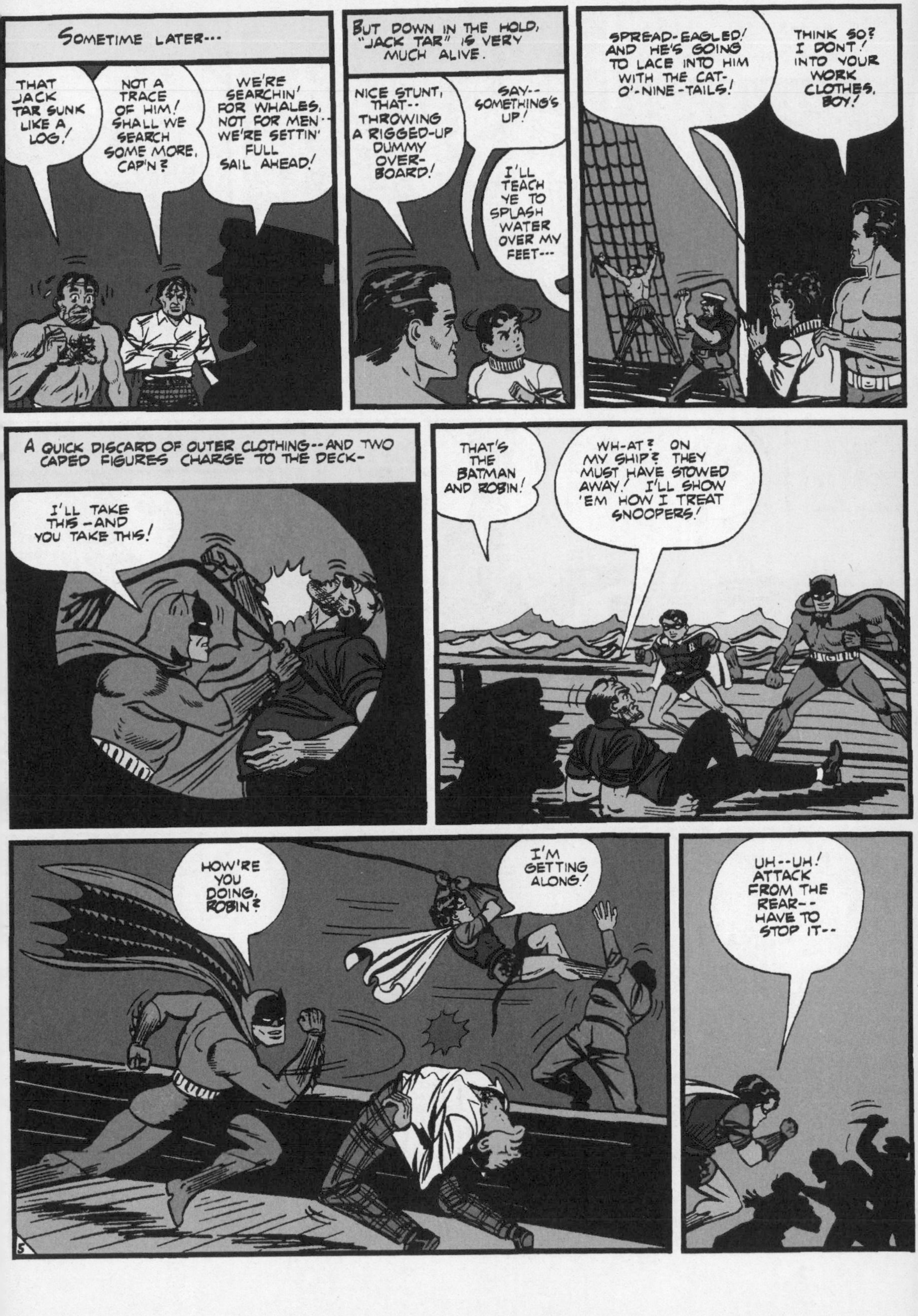
SOMETIME LATER---
THAT JACK TAR SUNK LIKE A LOG!
NOT A TRACE OF HIM! SHALL WE SEARCH SOME MORE, CAP'N?
WE'RE SEARCHIN' FOR WHALES, NOT FOR MEN-- WE'RE SETTIN' FULL SAIL AHEAD!
BUT DOWN IN THE HOLD, "JACK TAR" IS VERY MUCH ALIVE.
NICE STUNT, THAT-- THROWING A RIGGED-UP DUMMY OVER-BOARD!
SAY-- SOMETHING'S UP!
I'LL TEACH YE TO SPLASH WATER OVER MY FEET---
SPREAD-EAGLED! AND HE'S GOING TO LACE INTO HIM WITH THE CAT-O'-NINE-TAILS!
THINK SO? I DONT! INTO YOUR WORK CLOTHES, BOY!
A QUICK DISCARD OF OUTER CLOTHING--AND TWO CAPED FIGURES CHARGE TO THE DECK-
I'LL TAKE THIS -AND YOU TAKE THIS!
THAT'S THE BATMAN AND ROBIN!
WH-AT? ON MY SHIP? THEY MUST HAVE STOWED AWAY! I'LL SHOW 'EM HOW I TREAT SNOOPERS!
HOW'RE YOU DOING, ROBIN?
I'M GETTING ALONG!
UH--UH! ATTACK FROM THE REAR-- HAVE TO STOP IT--
5

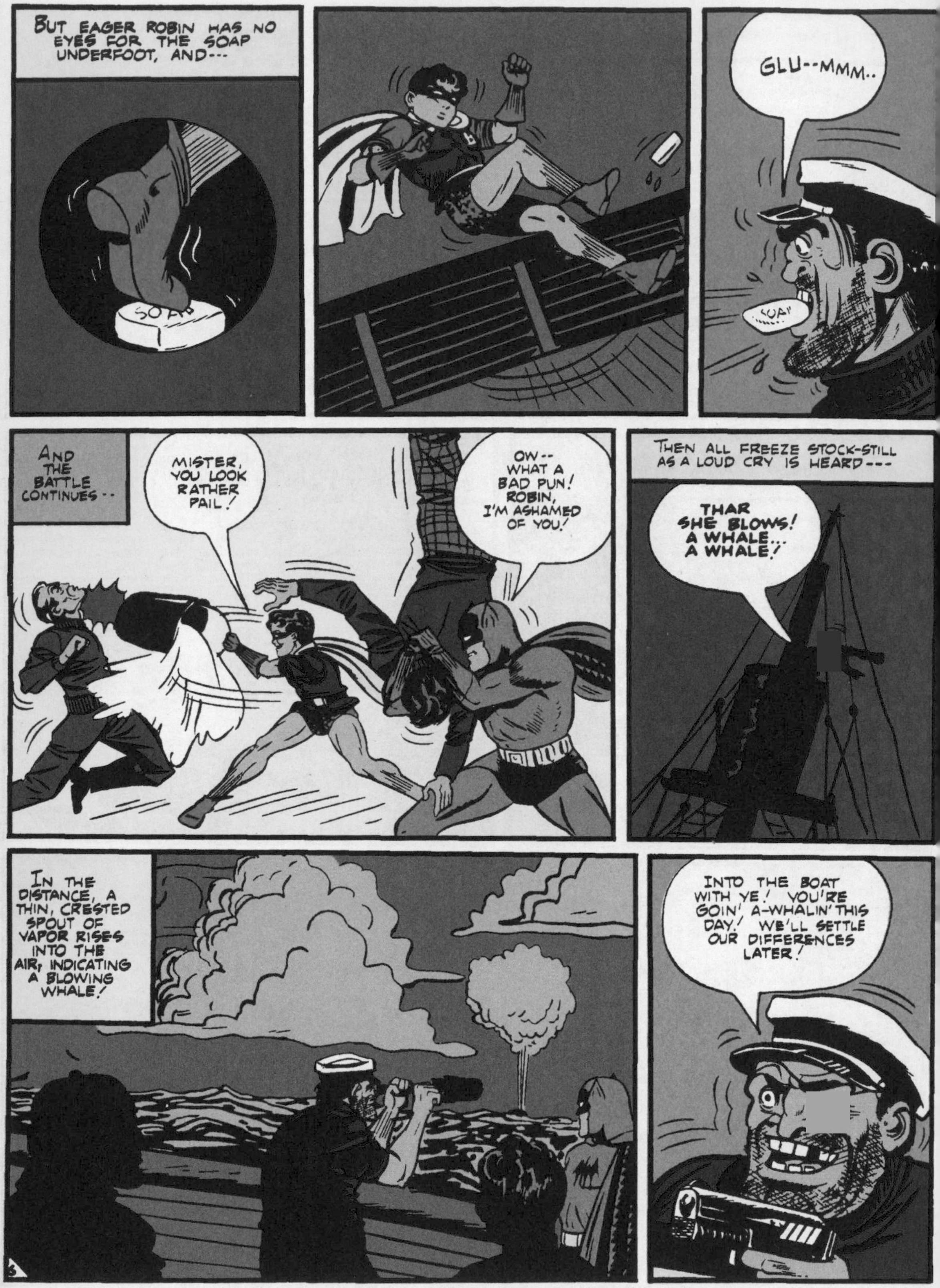
BUT EAGER ROBIN HAS NO EYES FOR THE SOAP UNDERFOOT, AND---
SOAP
GLU--MMM..
AND THE BATTLE CONTINUES--
MISTER, YOU LOOK RATHER PAIL!
OW-- WHAT A BAD PUN! ROBIN, I'M ASHAMED OF YOU!
THEN ALL FREEZE STOCK-STILL AS A LOUD CRY IS HEARD---
THAR SHE BLOWS! A WHALE... A WHALE!
IN THE DISTANCE, A THIN, CRESTED SPOUT OF VAPOR RISES INTO THE AIR, INDICATING A BLOWING WHALE!
INTO THE BOAT WITH YE! YOU'RE GOIN' A-WHALIN' THIS DAY! WE'LL SETTLE OUR DIFFERENCES LATER!

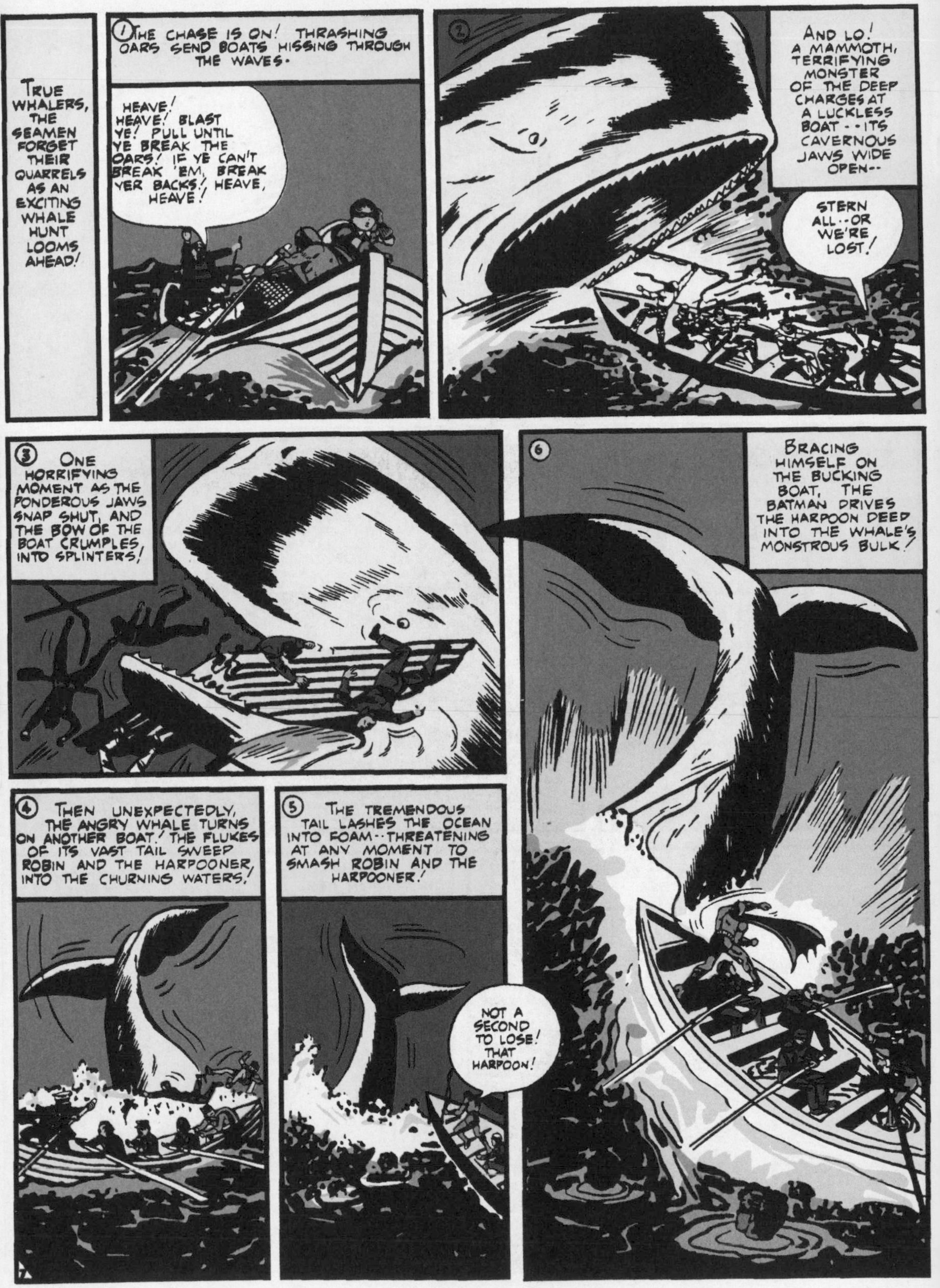
TRUE WHALERS, THE SEAMEN FORGET THEIR QUARRELS AS AN EXCITING WHALE HUNT LOOMS AHEAD!
1
THE CHASE IS ON! THRASHING OARS SEND BOATS HISSING THROUGH THE WAVES.
HEAVE! HEAVE! BLAST YE! PULL UNTIL YE BREAK THE OARS! IF YE CAN'T BREAK 'EM, BREAK YER BACKS! HEAVE, HEAVE!
2
AND LO! A MAMMOTH, TERRIFYING MONSTER OF THE DEEP CHARGES AT A LUCKLESS BOAT--ITS CAVERNOUS JAWS WIDE OPEN--
STERN ALL--OR WE'RE LOST!
3
ONE HORRIFYING MOMENT AS THE PONDEROUS JAWS SNAP SHUT, AND THE BOW OF THE BOAT CRUMPLES INTO SPLINTERS!
4
THEN UNEXPECTEDLY, THE ANGRY WHALE TURNS ON ANOTHER BOAT! THE FLUKES OF ITS VAST TAIL SWEEP ROBIN AND THE HARPOONER INTO THE CHURNING WATERS!
5
THE TREMENDOUS TAIL LASHES THE OCEAN INTO FOAM--THREATENING AT ANY MOMENT TO SMASH ROBIN AND THE HARPOONER!
NOT A SECOND TO LOSE! THAT HARPOON!
6
BRACING HIMSELF ON THE BUCKING BOAT, THE BATMAN DRIVES THE HARPOON DEEP INTO THE WHALE'S MONSTROUS BULK!

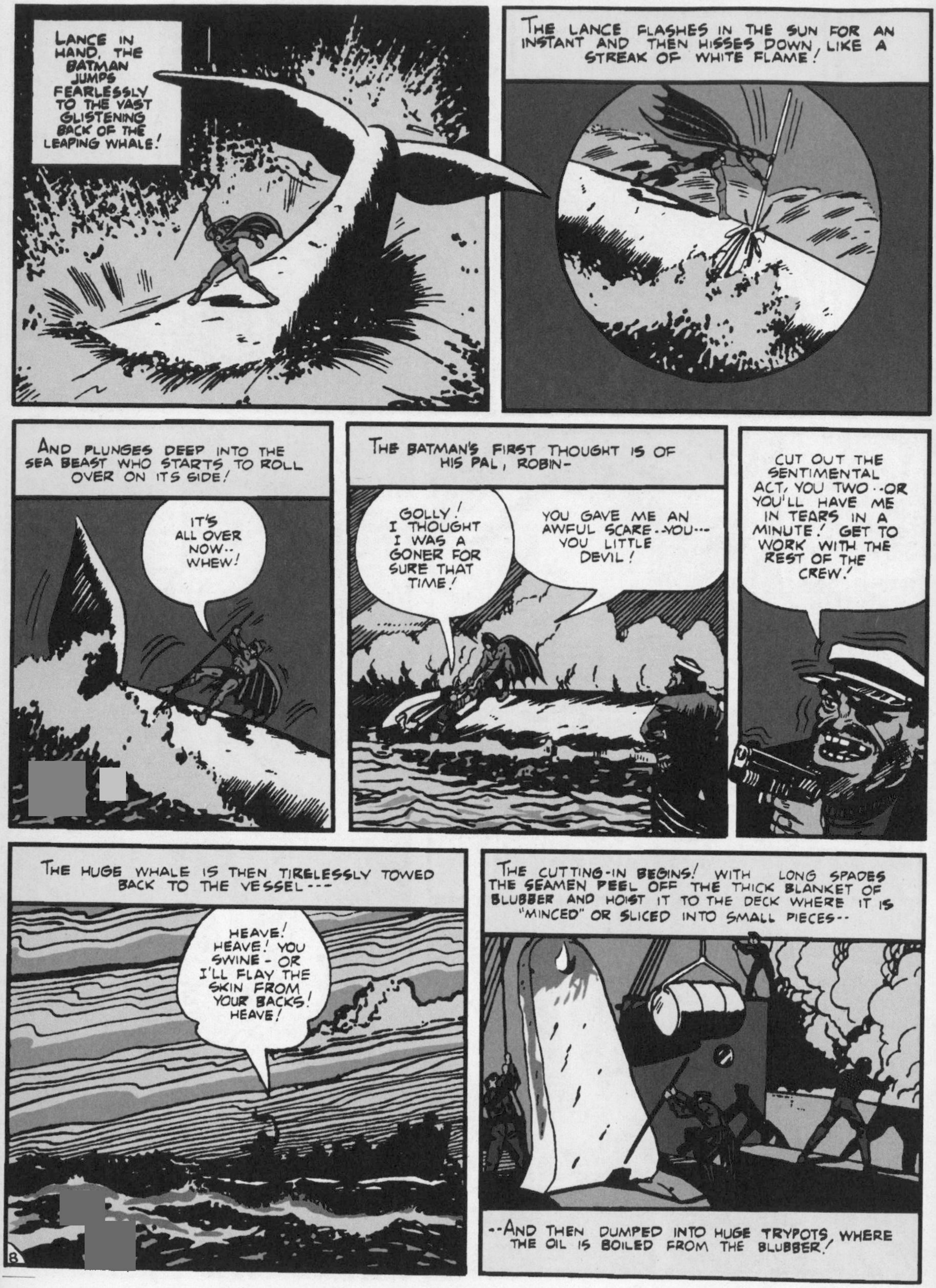
LANCE IN HAND, THE BATMAN JUMPS FEARLESSLY TO THE VAST GLISTENING BACK OF THE LEAPING WHALE!
THE LANCE FLASHES IN THE SUN FOR AN INSTANT AND THEN HISSES DOWN, LIKE A STREAK OF WHITE FLAME!
AND PLUNGES DEEP INTO THE SEA BEAST WHO STARTS TO ROLL OVER ON ITS SIDE!
IT'S ALL OVER NOW.. WHEW!
THE BATMAN'S FIRST THOUGHT IS OF HIS PAL, ROBIN-
GOLLY! I THOUGHT I WAS A GONER FOR SURE THAT TIME!
YOU GAVE ME AN AWFUL SCARE--YOU--- YOU LITTLE DEVIL!
CUT OUT THE SENTIMENTAL ACT, YOU TWO--OR YOU'LL HAVE ME IN TEARS IN A MINUTE! GET TO WORK WITH THE REST OF THE CREW!
THE HUGE WHALE IS THEN TIRELESSLY TOWED BACK TO THE VESSEL---
HEAVE! HEAVE! YOU SWINE - OR I'LL FLAY THE SKIN FROM YOUR BACKS! HEAVE!
8
THE CUTTING-IN BEGINS! WITH LONG SPADES THE SEAMEN PEEL OFF THE THICK BLANKET OF BLUBBER AND HOIST IT TO THE DECK WHERE IT IS "MINCED" OR SLICED INTO SMALL PIECES--
--AND THEN DUMPED INTO HUGE TRYPOTS, WHERE THE OIL IS BOILED FROM THE BLUBBER!

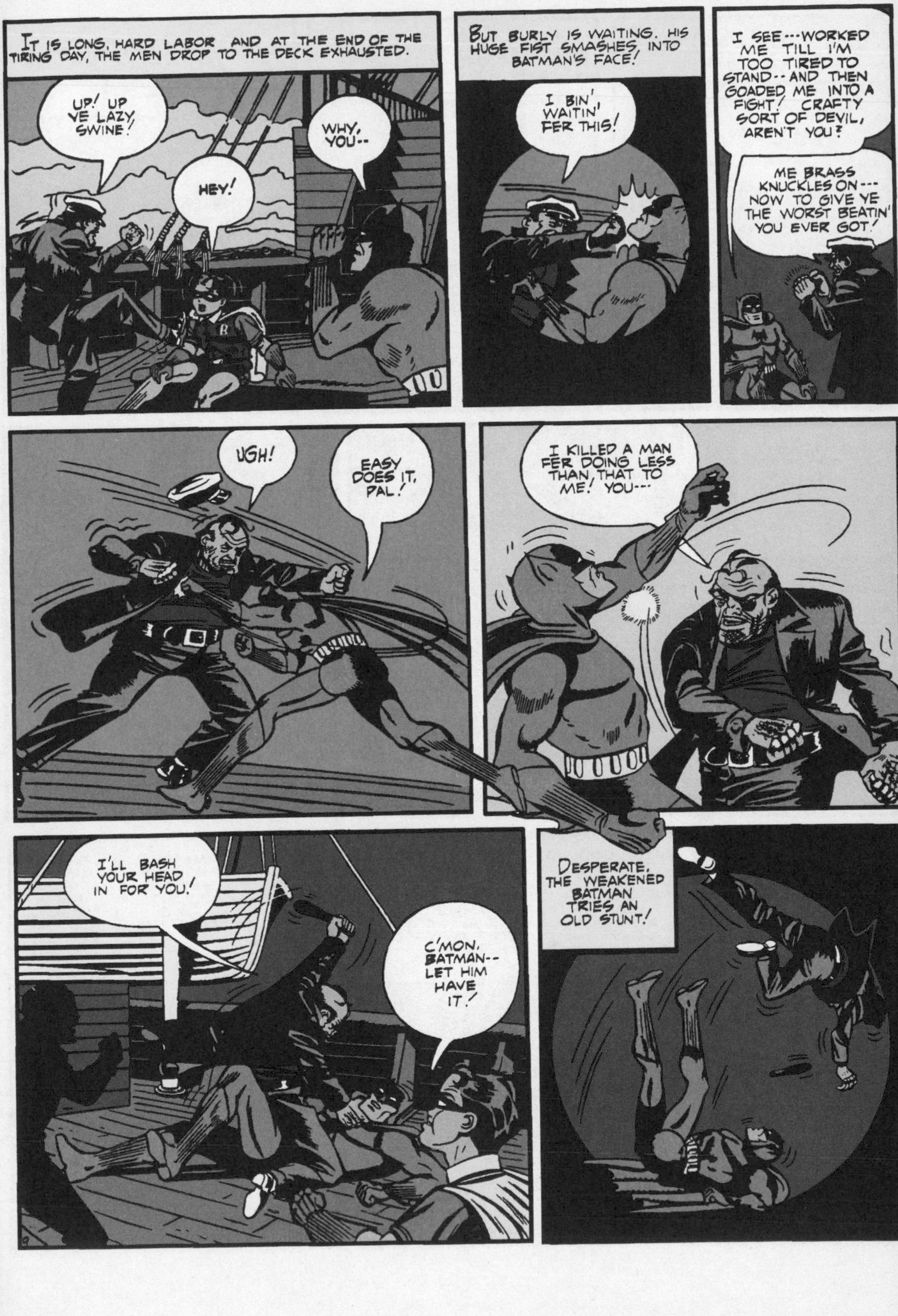
IT IS LONG, HARD LABOR AND AT THE END OF THE TIRING DAY, THE MEN DROP TO THE DECK EXHAUSTED.
UP! UP YE LAZY SWINE!
HEY!
WHY, YOU--
BUT BURLY IS WAITING. HIS HUGE FIST SMASHES, INTO BATMAN'S FACE!
I BIN' WAITIN' FER THIS!
I SEE---WORKED ME TILL I'M TOO TIRED TO STAND--AND THEN GOADED ME INTO A FIGHT! CRAFTY SORT OF DEVIL, AREN'T YOU?
ME BRASS KNUCKLES ON--- NOW TO GIVE YE THE WORST BEATIN' YOU EVER GOT!
UGH!
EASY DOES IT, PAL!
I KILLED A MAN FER DOING LESS THAN THAT TO ME! YOU---
I'LL BASH YOUR HEAD IN FOR YOU!
C'MON, BATMAN-- LET HIM HAVE IT!
DESPERATE, THE WEAKENED BATMAN TRIES AN OLD STUNT!

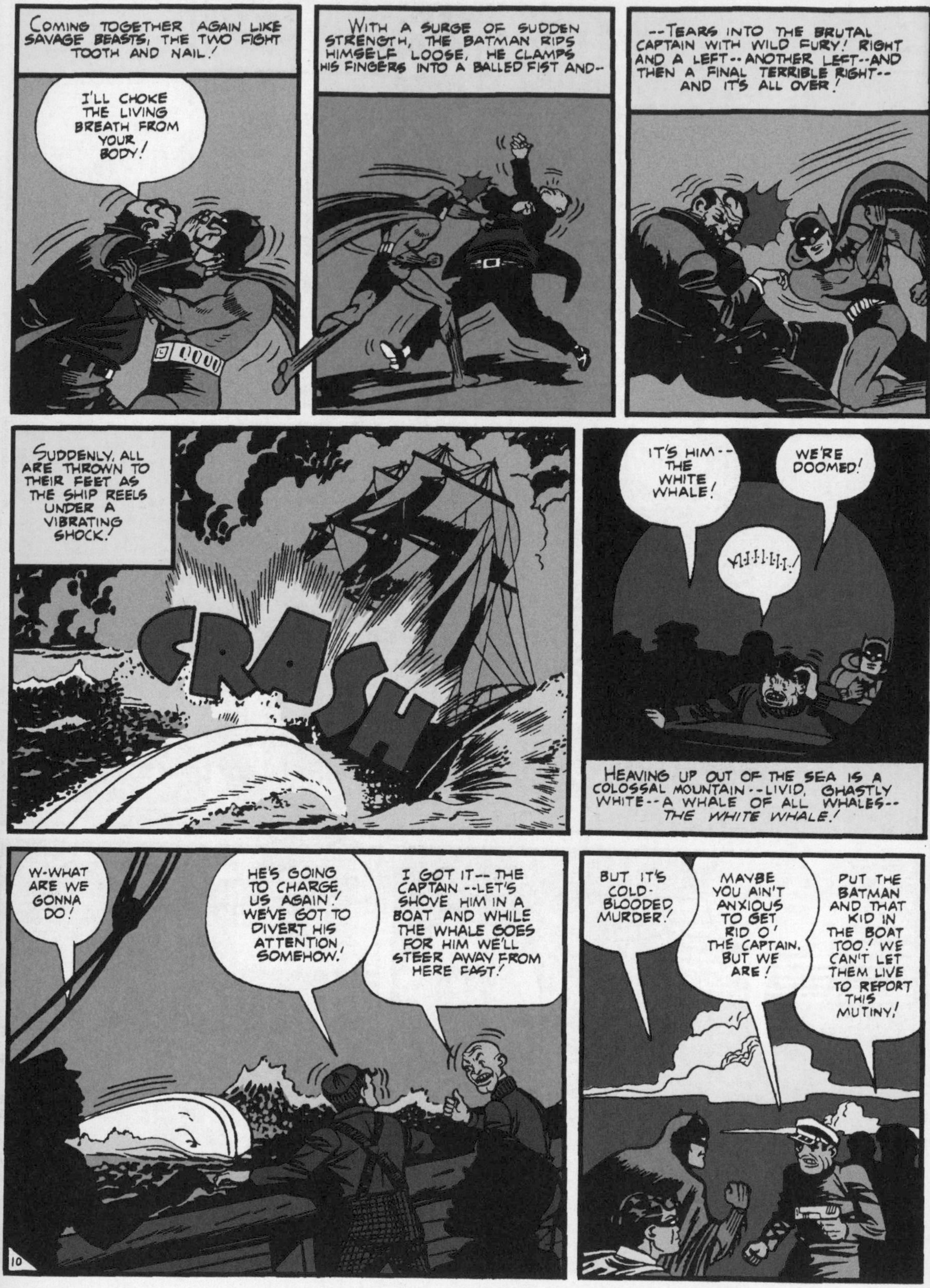
COMING TOGETHER AGAIN LIKE SAVAGE BEASTS, THE TWO FIGHT TOOTH AND NAIL!
I'LL CHOKE THE LIVING BREATH FROM YOUR BODY!
WITH A SURGE OF SUDDEN STRENGTH, THE BATMAN RIPS HIMSELF LOOSE. HE CLAMPS HIS FINGERS INTO A BALLED FIST AND--
--TEARS INTO THE BRUTAL CAPTAIN WITH WILD FURY! RIGHT AND A LEFT--ANOTHER LEFT--AND THEN A FINAL TERRIBLE RIGHT--AND IT'S ALL OVER!
SUDDENLY, ALL ARE THROWN TO THEIR FEET AS THE SHIP REELS UNDER A VIBRATING SHOCK!
CRASH
IT'S HIM--THE WHITE WHALE!
WE'RE DOOMED!
YI-I-I-I-I-I!
HEAVING UP OUT OF THE SEA IS A COLOSSAL MOUNTAIN--LIVID, GHASTLY WHITE--A WHALE OF ALL WHALES--THE WHITE WHALE!
W-WHAT ARE WE GONNA DO!
HE'S GOING TO CHARGE US AGAIN! WE'VE GOT TO DIVERT HIS ATTENTION SOMEHOW!
I GOT IT--THE CAPTAIN--LET'S SHOVE HIM IN A BOAT AND WHILE THE WHALE GOES FOR HIM WE'LL STEER AWAY FROM HERE FAST!
10
BUT IT'S COLD-BLOODED MURDER!
MAYBE YOU AIN'T ANXIOUS TO GET RID O' THE CAPTAIN, BUT WE ARE!
PUT THE BATMAN AND THAT KID IN THE BOAT TOO! WE CAN'T LET THEM LIVE TO REPORT THIS MUTINY!

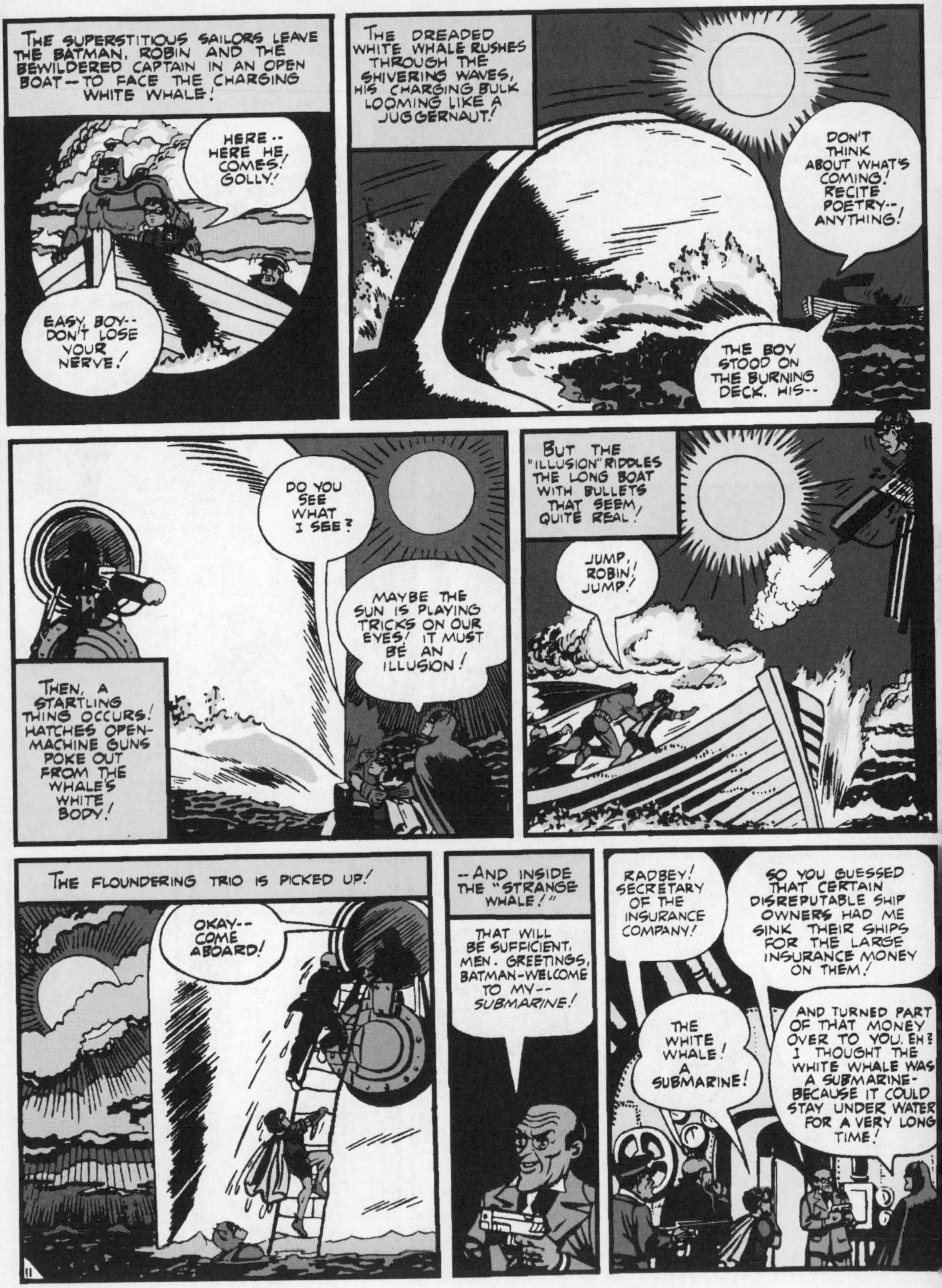
THE SUPERSTITIOUS SAILORS LEAVE THE BATMAN, ROBIN AND THE BEWILDERED CAPTAIN IN AN OPEN BOAT--TO FACE THE CHARGING WHITE WHALE!
HERE-- HERE HE COMES! GOLLY!
EASY, BOY-- DON'T LOSE YOUR NERVE!
THE DREADED WHITE WHALE RUSHES THROUGH THE SHIVERING WAVES, HIS CHARGING BULK LOOMING LIKE A JUGGERNAUT!
DON'T THINK ABOUT WHAT'S COMING! RECITE POETRY-- ANYTHING!
THE BOY STOOD ON THE BURNING DECK. HIS--
DO YOU SEE WHAT I SEE?
MAYBE THE SUN IS PLAYING TRICKS ON OUR EYES! IT MUST BE AN ILLUSION!
THEN, A STARTLING THING OCCURS! HATCHES OPEN-MACHINE GUNS POKE OUT FROM THE WHALE'S WHITE BODY!
BUT THE "ILLUSION" RIDDLES THE LONG BOAT WITH BULLETS THAT SEEM QUITE REAL!
JUMP, ROBIN! JUMP!
THE FLOUNDERING TRIO IS PICKED UP!
OKAY-- COME ABOARD!
--AND INSIDE THE "STRANGE WHALE!"
THAT WILL BE SUFFICIENT, MEN. GREETINGS, BATMAN-WELCOME TO MY-- SUBMARINE!
RADBEY! SECRETARY OF THE INSURANCE COMPANY!
SO YOU GUESSED THAT CERTAIN DISREPUTABLE SHIP OWNERS HAD ME SINK THEIR SHIPS FOR THE LARGE INSURANCE MONEY ON THEM!
THE WHITE WHALE! A SUBMARINE!
AND TURNED PART OF THAT MONEY OVER TO YOU, EH? I THOUGHT THE WHITE WHALE WAS A SUBMARINE-BECAUSE IT COULD STAY UNDER WATER FOR A VERY LONG TIME!
11

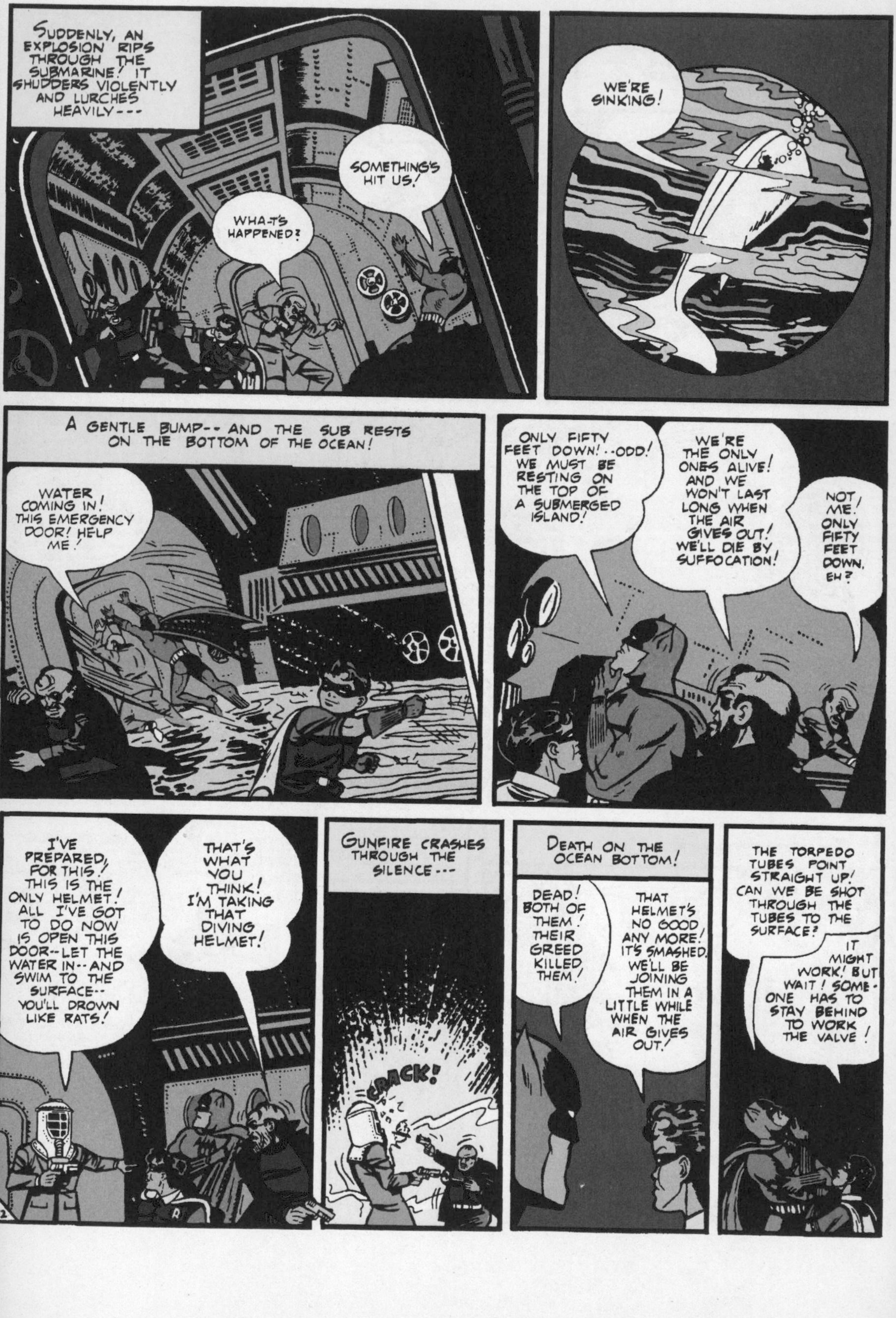
SUDDENLY, AN EXPLOSION RIPS THROUGH THE SUBMARINE! IT SHUDDERS VIOLENTLY AND LURCHES HEAVILY---
SOMETHING'S HIT US!
WHAT'S HAPPENED?
WE'RE SINKING!
A GENTLE BUMP-- AND THE SUB RESTS ON THE BOTTOM OF THE OCEAN!
WATER COMING IN! THIS EMERGENCY DOOR! HELP ME!
ONLY FIFTY FEET DOWN!--ODD! WE MUST BE RESTING ON THE TOP OF A SUBMERGED ISLAND!
WE'RE THE ONLY ONES ALIVE! AND WE WON'T LAST LONG WHEN THE AIR GIVES OUT! WE'LL DIE BY SUFFOCATION!
NOT ME! ONLY FIFTY FEET DOWN, EH?
I'VE PREPARED FOR THIS! THIS IS THE ONLY HELMET! ALL I'VE GOT TO DO NOW IS OPEN THIS DOOR--LET THE WATER IN--AND SWIM TO THE SURFACE-- YOU'LL DROWN LIKE RATS!
THAT'S WHAT YOU THINK! I'M TAKING THAT DIVING HELMET!
GUNFIRE CRASHES THROUGH THE SILENCE---
CRACK!
DEATH ON THE OCEAN BOTTOM!
DEAD! BOTH OF THEM! THEIR GREED KILLED THEM!
THAT HELMET'S NO GOOD ANY MORE! IT'S SMASHED. WE'LL BE JOINING THEM IN A LITTLE WHILE WHEN THE AIR GIVES OUT!
THE TORPEDO TUBES POINT STRAIGHT UP! CAN WE BE SHOT THROUGH THE TUBES TO THE SURFACE?
IT MIGHT WORK! BUT WAIT! SOME-ONE HAS TO STAY BEHIND TO WORK THE VALVE!

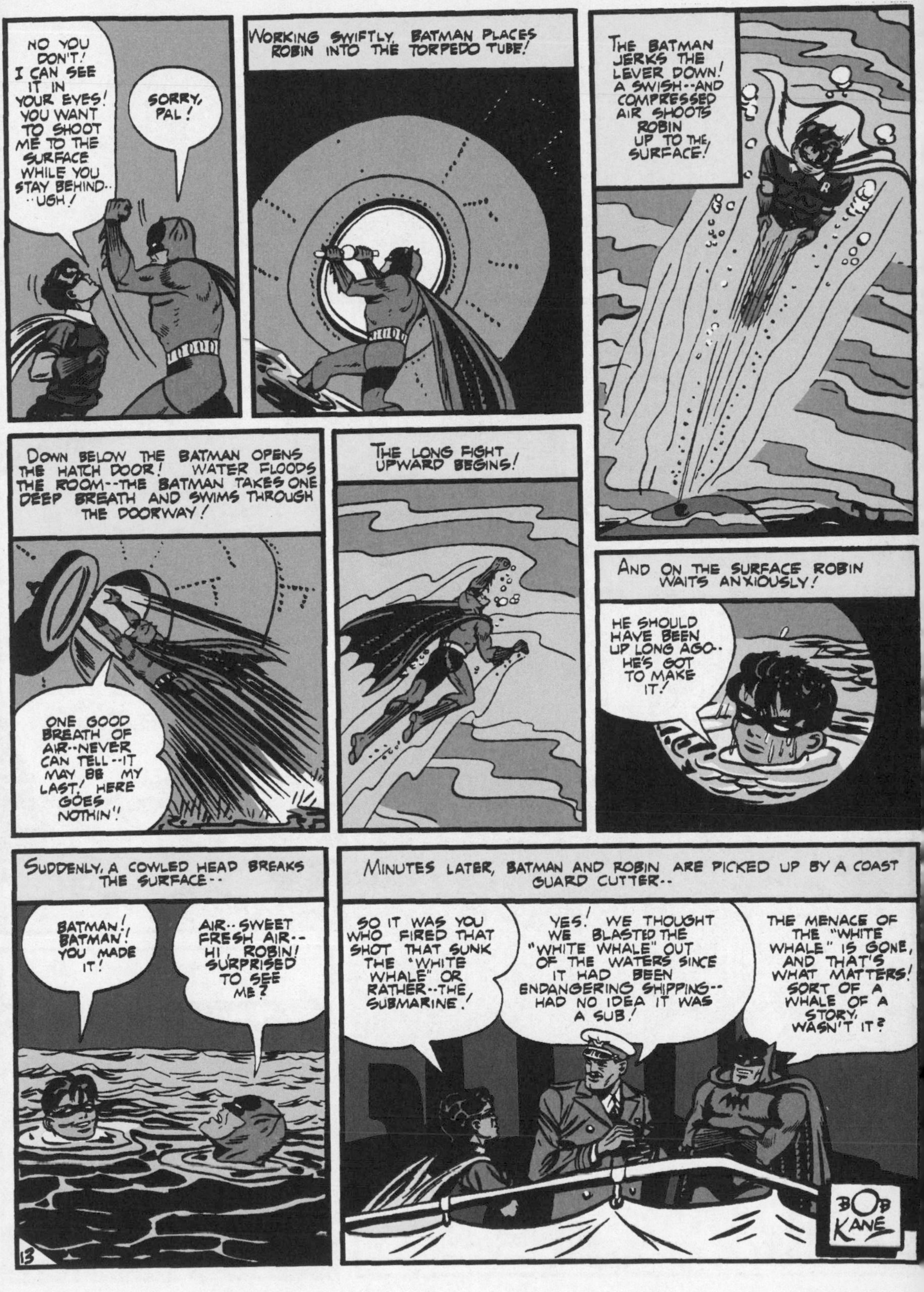
NO YOU DON'T! I CAN SEE IT IN YOUR EYES! YOU WANT TO SHOOT ME TO THE SURFACE WHILE YOU STAY BEHIND.. ..UGH!
SORRY, PAL!
WORKING SWIFTLY, BATMAN PLACES ROBIN INTO THE TORPEDO TUBE!
THE BATMAN JERKS THE LEVER DOWN! A SWISH--AND COMPRESSED AIR SHOOTS ROBIN UP TO THE SURFACE!
DOWN BELOW THE BATMAN OPENS THE HATCH DOOR! WATER FLOODS THE ROOM--THE BATMAN TAKES ONE DEEP BREATH AND SWIMS THROUGH THE DOORWAY!
ONE GOOD BREATH OF AIR--NEVER CAN TELL--IT MAY BE MY LAST! HERE GOES NOTHIN'!
THE LONG FIGHT UPWARD BEGINS!
AND ON THE SURFACE ROBIN WAITS ANXIOUSLY!
HE SHOULD HAVE BEEN UP LONG AGO.. HE'S GOT TO MAKE IT!
SUDDENLY, A COWLED HEAD BREAKS THE SURFACE--
BATMAN! BATMAN! YOU MADE IT!
AIR.. SWEET FRESH AIR-- HI, ROBIN! SURPRISED TO SEE ME?
13
MINUTES LATER, BATMAN AND ROBIN ARE PICKED UP BY A COAST GUARD CUTTER--
SO IT WAS YOU WHO FIRED THAT SHOT THAT SUNK THE "WHITE WHALE" OR RATHER--THE SUBMARINE!
YES! WE THOUGHT WE BLASTED THE "WHITE WHALE" OUT OF THE WATERS SINCE IT HAD BEEN ENDANGERING SHIPPING-- HAD NO IDEA IT WAS A SUB!
THE MENACE OF THE "WHITE WHALE" IS GONE, AND THAT'S WHAT MATTERS! SORT OF A WHALE OF A STORY, WASN'T IT?
BOB KANE

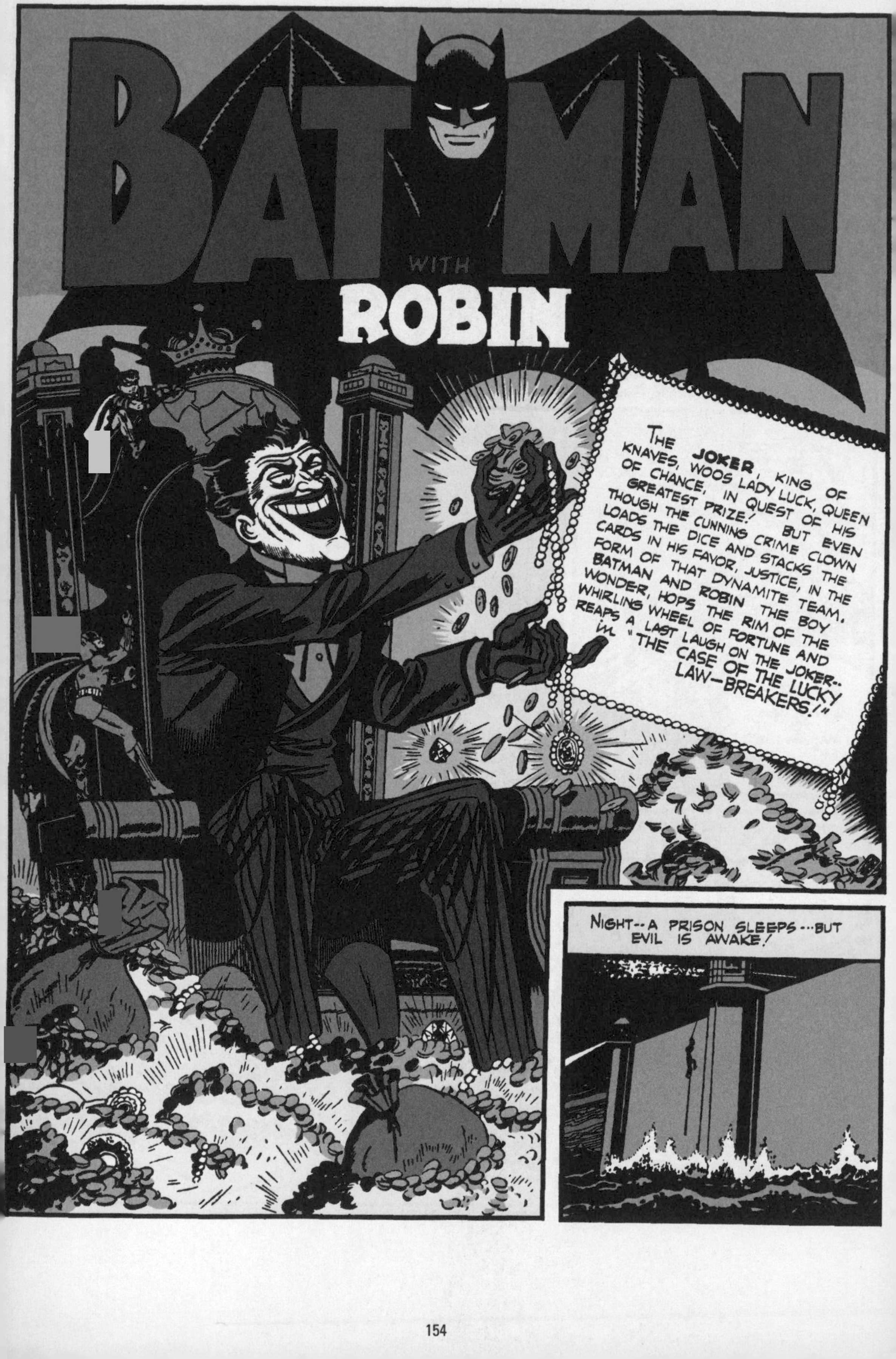
BATMAN
WITH
ROBIN
THE JOKER, KING OF KNAVES, WOOS LADY LUCK, QUEEN OF CHANCE, IN QUEST OF HIS GREATEST PRIZE! BUT EVEN THOUGH THE CUNNING CRIME CLOWN LOADS THE DICE AND STACKS THE CARDS IN HIS FAVOR, JUSTICE, IN THE FORM OF THAT DYNAMITE TEAM, BATMAN AND ROBIN THE BOY WONDER, HOPS THE RIM OF THE WHIRLING WHEEL OF FORTUNE AND REAPS A LAST LAUGH ON THE JOKER-- IN "THE CASE OF THE LUCKY LAW-BREAKERS!"
NIGHT--A PRISON SLEEPS...BUT EVIL IS AWAKE!

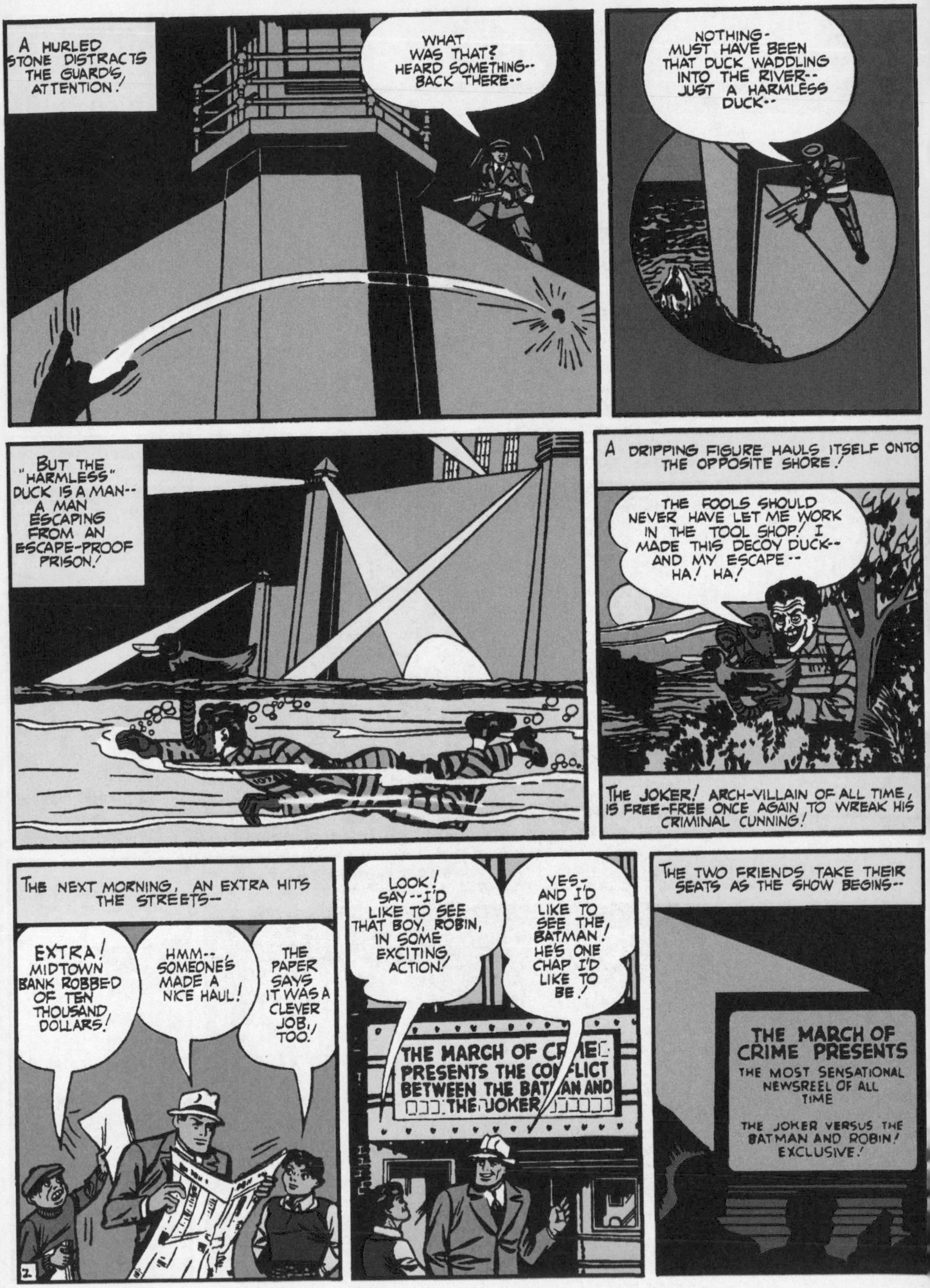
A HURLED STONE DISTRACTS THE GUARD'S ATTENTION!
WHAT WAS THAT? HEARD SOMETHING-- BACK THERE--
NOTHING- MUST HAVE BEEN THAT DUCK WADDLING INTO THE RIVER-- JUST A HARMLESS DUCK--
BUT THE "HARMLESS" DUCK IS A MAN-- A MAN ESCAPING FROM AN ESCAPE-PROOF PRISON!
A DRIPPING FIGURE HAULS ITSELF ONTO THE OPPOSITE SHORE!
THE FOOLS SHOULD NEVER HAVE LET ME WORK IN THE TOOL SHOP! I MADE THIS DECOY DUCK-- AND MY ESCAPE-- HA! HA!
THE JOKER! ARCH-VILLAIN OF ALL TIME, IS FREE-FREE ONCE AGAIN TO WREAK HIS CRIMINAL CUNNING!
THE NEXT MORNING, AN EXTRA HITS THE STREETS--
EXTRA! MIDTOWN BANK ROBBED OF TEN THOUSAND DOLLARS!
HMM-- SOMEONE'S MADE A NICE HAUL!
THE PAPER SAYS IT WAS A CLEVER JOB, TOO!
LOOK! SAY--I'D LIKE TO SEE THAT BOY, ROBIN, IN SOME EXCITING ACTION!
YES- AND I'D LIKE TO SEE THE BATMAN! HE'S ONE CHAP I'D LIKE TO BE!
THE MARCH OF CRIME PRESENTS THE CONFLICT BETWEEN THE BATMAN AND THE JOKER
THE TWO FRIENDS TAKE THEIR SEATS AS THE SHOW BEGINS--
THE MARCH OF CRIME PRESENTS
THE MOST SENSATIONAL NEWSREEL OF ALL TIME
THE JOKER VERSUS THE BATMAN AND ROBIN! EXCLUSIVE!

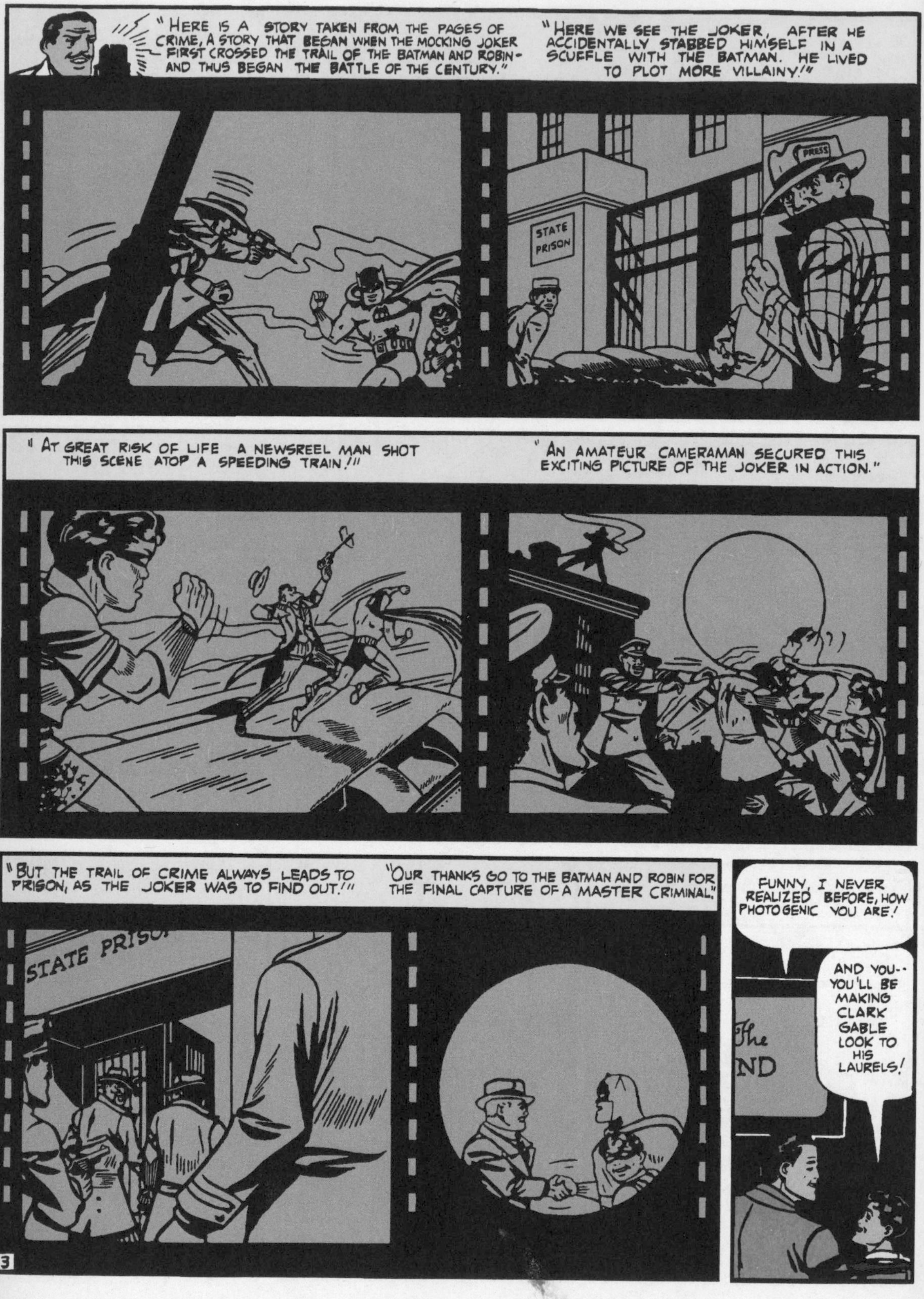
"HERE IS A STORY TAKEN FROM THE PAGES OF CRIME, A STORY THAT BEGAN WHEN THE MOCKING JOKER FIRST CROSSED THE TRAIL OF THE BATMAN AND ROBIN-AND THUS BEGAN THE BATTLE OF THE CENTURY."
"HERE WE SEE THE JOKER, AFTER HE ACCIDENTALLY STABBED HIMSELF IN A SCUFFLE WITH THE BATMAN. HE LIVED TO PLOT MORE VILLAINY!"
STATE PRISON
PRESS
"AT GREAT RISK OF LIFE A NEWSREEL MAN SHOT THIS SCENE ATOP A SPEEDING TRAIN!"
"AN AMATEUR CAMERAMAN SECURED THIS EXCITING PICTURE OF THE JOKER IN ACTION."
"BUT THE TRAIL OF CRIME ALWAYS LEADS TO PRISON, AS THE JOKER WAS TO FIND OUT!"
"OUR THANKS GO TO THE BATMAN AND ROBIN FOR THE FINAL CAPTURE OF A MASTER CRIMINAL."
STATE PRIS
FUNNY, I NEVER REALIZED BEFORE, HOW PHOTOGENIC YOU ARE!
AND YOU--YOU'LL BE MAKING CLARK GABLE LOOK TO HIS LAURELS!
The
ND
3

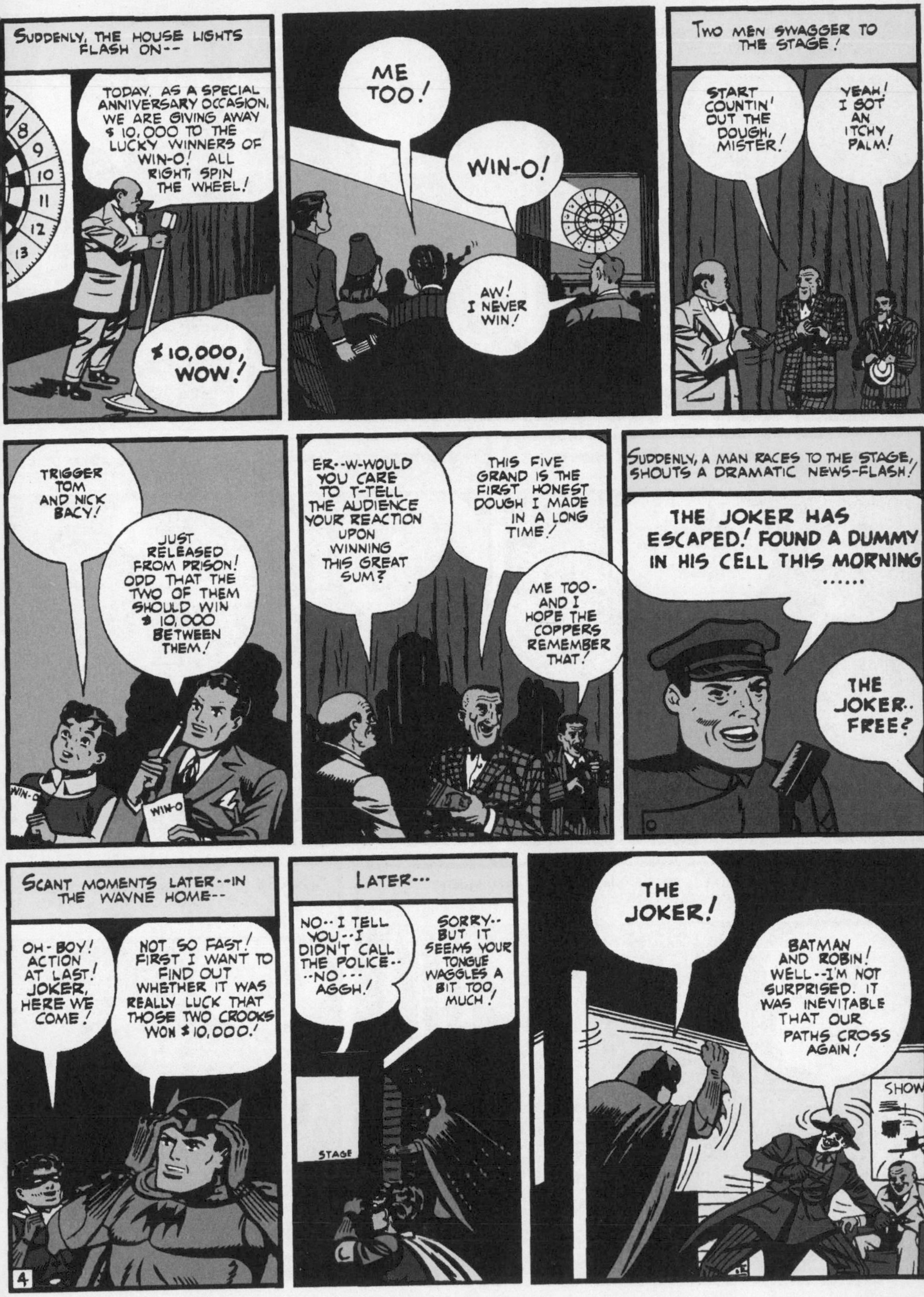
SUDDENLY, THE HOUSE LIGHTS FLASH ON--
TODAY, AS A SPECIAL ANNIVERSARY OCCASION, WE ARE GIVING AWAY $ 10,000 TO THE LUCKY WINNERS OF WIN-O! ALL RIGHT, SPIN THE WHEEL!
$ 10,000, WOW!
ME TOO!
WIN-O!
AW! I NEVER WIN!
TWO MEN SWAGGER TO THE STAGE!
START COUNTIN' OUT THE DOUGH, MISTER!
YEAH! I GOT AN ITCHY PALM!
TRIGGER TOM AND NICK BACY!
JUST RELEASED FROM PRISON! ODD THAT THE TWO OF THEM SHOULD WIN $ 10,000 BETWEEN THEM!
WIN-O
WIN-O
ER--W-WOULD YOU CARE TO T-TELL THE AUDIENCE YOUR REACTION UPON WINNING THIS GREAT SUM?
THIS FIVE GRAND IS THE FIRST HONEST DOUGH I MADE IN A LONG TIME!
ME TOO-AND I HOPE THE COPPERS REMEMBER THAT!
SUDDENLY, A MAN RACES TO THE STAGE, SHOUTS A DRAMATIC NEWS-FLASH!
THE JOKER HAS ESCAPED! FOUND A DUMMY IN HIS CELL THIS MORNING......
THE JOKER.. FREE?
SCANT MOMENTS LATER--IN THE WAYNE HOME--
OH-BOY! ACTION AT LAST! JOKER, HERE WE COME!
NOT SO FAST! FIRST I WANT TO FIND OUT WHETHER IT WAS REALLY LUCK THAT THOSE TWO CROOKS WON $ 10,000!
4
LATER...
NO--I TELL YOU--I DIDN'T CALL THE POLICE-- --NO--- AGGH!
SORRY-- BUT IT SEEMS YOUR TONGUE WAGGLES A BIT TOO MUCH!
STAGE
THE JOKER!
BATMAN AND ROBIN! WELL--I'M NOT SURPRISED. IT WAS INEVITABLE THAT OUR PATHS CROSS AGAIN!
SHOW

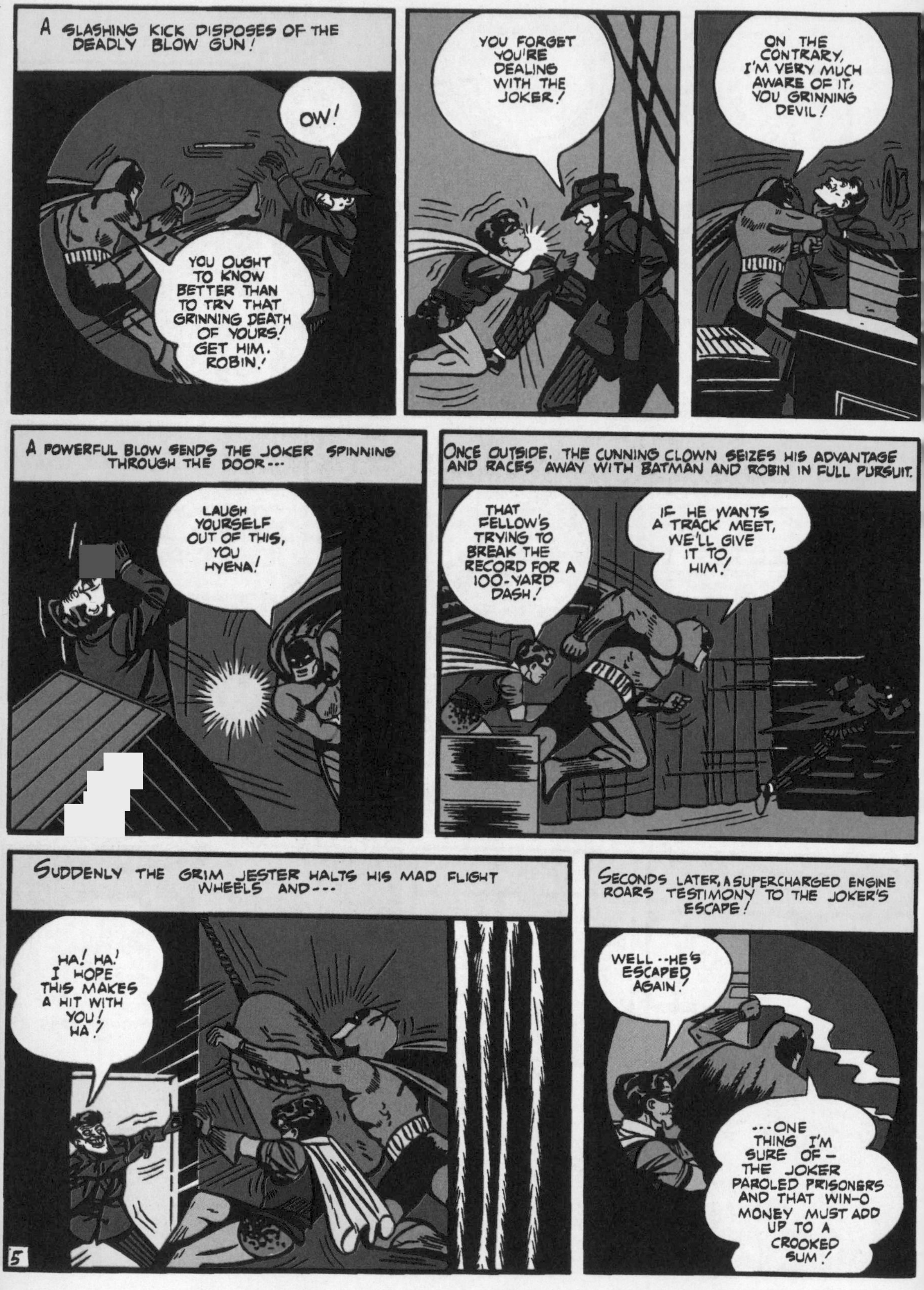
A SLASHING KICK DISPOSES OF THE DEADLY BLOW GUN!
OW!
YOU OUGHT TO KNOW BETTER THAN TO TRY THAT GRINNING DEATH OF YOURS! GET HIM, ROBIN!
YOU FORGET YOU'RE DEALING WITH THE JOKER!
ON THE CONTRARY, I'M VERY MUCH AWARE OF IT, YOU GRINNING DEVIL!
A POWERFUL BLOW SENDS THE JOKER SPINNING THROUGH THE DOOR---
LAUGH YOURSELF OUT OF THIS, YOU HYENA!
ONCE OUTSIDE, THE CUNNING CLOWN SEIZES HIS ADVANTAGE AND RACES AWAY WITH BATMAN AND ROBIN IN FULL PURSUIT.
THAT FELLOW'S TRYING TO BREAK THE RECORD FOR A 100-YARD DASH!
IF HE WANTS A TRACK MEET, WE'LL GIVE IT TO HIM!
SUDDENLY THE GRIM JESTER HALTS HIS MAD FLIGHT WHEELS AND---
HA! HA! I HOPE THIS MAKES A HIT WITH YOU! HA!
5
SECONDS LATER, A SUPERCHARGED ENGINE ROARS TESTIMONY TO THE JOKER'S ESCAPE!
WELL --HE'S ESCAPED AGAIN!
---ONE THING I'M SURE OF -- THE JOKER PAROLED PRISONERS AND THAT WIN-O MONEY MUST ADD UP TO A CROOKED SUM!

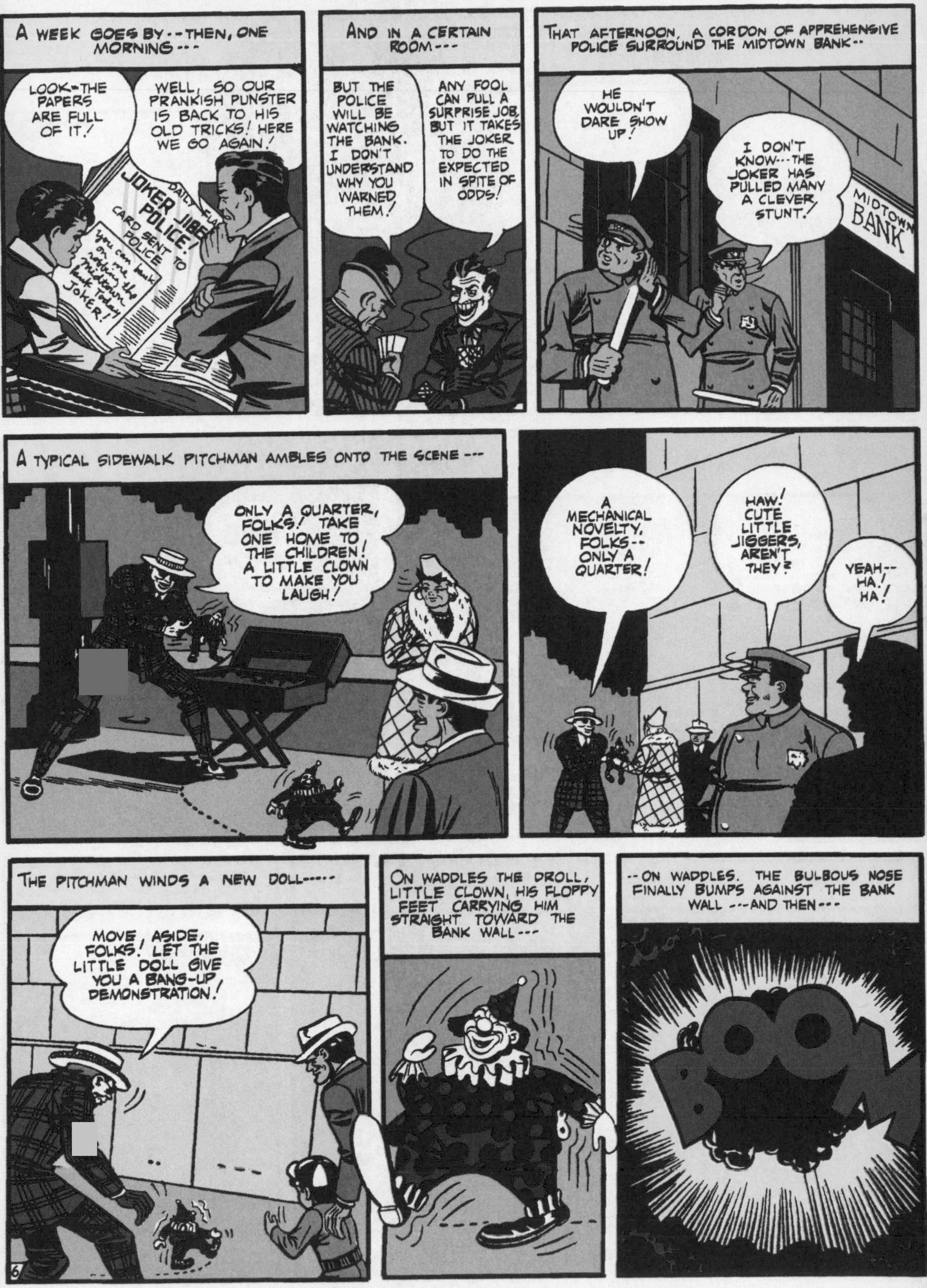
A WEEK GOES BY--THEN, ONE MORNING---
LOOK-THE PAPERS ARE FULL OF IT!
WELL, SO OUR PRANKISH PUNSTER IS BACK TO HIS OLD TRICKS! HERE WE GO AGAIN!
JOKER JIBES POLICE!
CARD SENT TO POLICE
You can bank on me robbing the midtown bank today! JOKER!
AND IN A CERTAIN ROOM---
BUT THE POLICE WILL BE WATCHING THE BANK. I DON'T UNDERSTAND WHY YOU WARNED THEM!
ANY FOOL CAN PULL A SURPRISE JOB, BUT IT TAKES THE JOKER TO DO THE EXPECTED IN SPITE OF ODDS!
THAT AFTERNOON, A CORDON OF APPREHENSIVE POLICE SURROUND THE MIDTOWN BANK--
HE WOULDN'T DARE SHOW UP!
I DON'T KNOW---THE JOKER HAS PULLED MANY A CLEVER STUNT!
MIDTOWN BANK
A TYPICAL SIDEWALK PITCHMAN AMBLES ONTO THE SCENE---
ONLY A QUARTER, FOLKS! TAKE ONE HOME TO THE CHILDREN! A LITTLE CLOWN TO MAKE YOU LAUGH!
A MECHANICAL NOVELTY, FOLKS--ONLY A QUARTER!
HAW! CUTE LITTLE JIGGERS, AREN'T THEY?
YEAH--HA! HA!
THE PITCHMAN WINDS A NEW DOLL-----
MOVE ASIDE, FOLKS! LET THE LITTLE DOLL GIVE YOU A BANG-UP DEMONSTRATION!
6
ON WADDLES THE DROLL, LITTLE CLOWN, HIS FLOPPY FEET CARRYING HIM STRAIGHT TOWARD THE BANK WALL---
--ON WADDLES. THE BULBOUS NOSE FINALLY BUMPS AGAINST THE BANK WALL---AND THEN---
BOOM

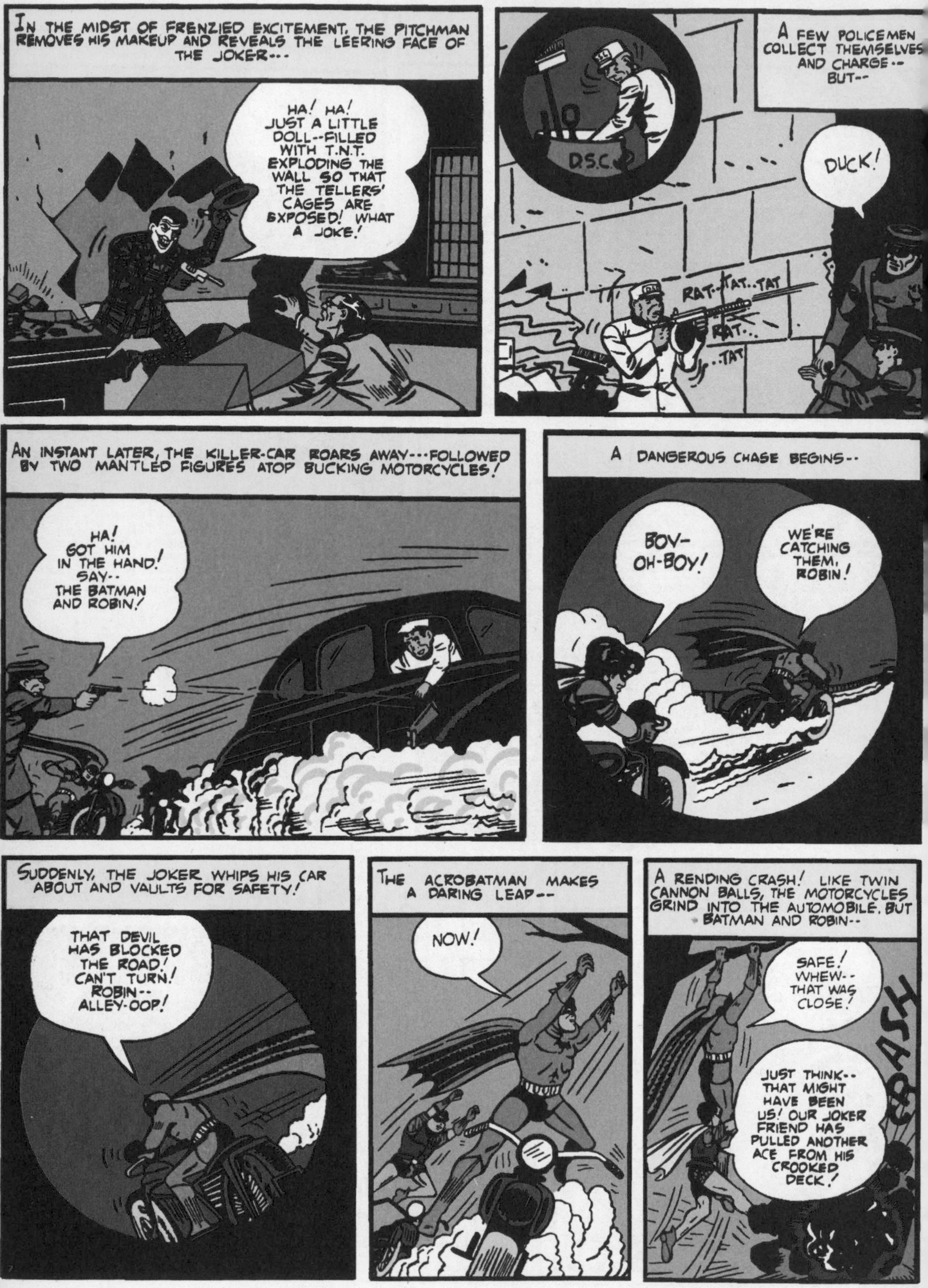

IN THE MIDST OF FRENZIED EXCITEMENT, THE PITCHMAN REMOVES HIS MAKEUP AND REVEALS THE LEERING FACE OF THE JOKER---
HA! HA! JUST A LITTLE DOLL--FILLED WITH T.N.T. EXPLODING THE WALL SO THAT THE TELLERS' CAGES ARE EXPOSED! WHAT A JOKE!
D.S.C.
A FEW POLICEMEN COLLECT THEMSELVES AND CHARGE-- BUT--
DUCK!
RAT--TAT..TAT
RAT..
..TAT
AN INSTANT LATER, THE KILLER-CAR ROARS AWAY---FOLLOWED BY TWO MANTLED FIGURES ATOP BUCKING MOTORCYCLES!
HA! GOT HIM IN THE HAND! SAY-- THE BATMAN AND ROBIN!
A DANGEROUS CHASE BEGINS--
BOY-OH-BOY!
WE'RE CATCHING THEM, ROBIN!
SUDDENLY, THE JOKER WHIPS HIS CAR ABOUT AND VAULTS FOR SAFETY!
THAT DEVIL HAS BLOCKED THE ROAD! CAN'T TURN! ROBIN-- ALLEY-OOP!
THE ACROBATMAN MAKES A DARING LEAP--
NOW!
A RENDING CRASH! LIKE TWIN CANNON BALLS, THE MOTORCYCLES GRIND INTO THE AUTOMOBILE, BUT BATMAN AND ROBIN--
SAFE! WHEW-- THAT WAS CLOSE!
JUST THINK-- THAT MIGHT HAVE BEEN US! OUR JOKER FRIEND HAS PULLED ANOTHER ACE FROM HIS CROOKED DECK!
CRASH

Panel 1: THE NEXT NIGHT...

LISTEN TO THE HEADLINE, ROBIN! JOKER NABS $20,000 AND ELUDES BATMAN! $20,000...

--AND TONIGHT THE BOWL O' BILLS PROGRAM GIVES AWAY $20,000 TO THE LUCKY PERSON WHO RECEIVES OUR TELEPHONE CALL!

DAILY FLASH
JOKER NABS $20,000 AND ELUDES BATMAN

Panel 2: AH, HERE WE ARE! THE LUCKY TELEPHONE NUMBER.. CENTRAL 8549.. HELLO, MR. MONT WILY?

MONT WILY? HE WAS JUST RELEASED FROM JAIL TWO DAYS AGO!

Panel 3: MR. WILY..YOU ARE THE WINNER OF THE BOWL O' BILLS PROGRAM!

BOWL O' BILLS

SWELL! I JUST GOT OUTTA STIR, SO THE DOUGH WILL COME IN MIGHTY HANDY TO MAKE PAYMENTS ON A NEW CAR I JUST BOUGHT!

Panel 4: COME TO THINK OF IT, WILY LOOKS LIKE THE MAN WHO HELPED THE JOKER ON HIS LAST JOB!

$20,000 -- THE SAME SUM! AND THOSE TWO WIN-O WINNERS WON $10,000.. THE SAME AMOUNT STOLEN FROM THAT OTHER BANK! HMM!

Panel 5: THE FOLLOWING DAYS SEE MORE ROBBERIES BY THE JOKER AND HIS CRIME COHORTS!

DAILY FLASH
BANK MESSENGER HELD UP BY JOKER $30,000 TAKEN!

$5000 PAYROLL ROBBED BY JOKER

Panel 6: POLICE QUESTION SUSPECTS..

WHERE DID YOU GET THE MONEY FOR THIS EXPENSIVE CAR? YOU JUST GOT OUT OF JAIL YESTERDAY!

YOU GOT NOTHIN' ON ME, COPPER! DIDN'T YOU HEAR HOW I WON $30,000 IN A BIG RAFFLE LAST NIGHT?

Panel 7: YOU JUST GET OUT OF JAIL AND ARE ABLE TO AFFORD A PLACE LIKE THIS? HOW COME?

GET THIS, COPPERS-- I WON $5,000 PLAYING WIN-O, SO JUST RELAX!

ROB A BANK, JOE?

Panel 8: ONE MAN OFFERS POLICE COMMISSIONER GORDON A LOGICAL EXPLANATION FOR THE LUCKY LAW-BREAKERS --

YES--POLICE ALWAYS CHECK UP ON NEWLY RELEASED PRISONERS WHO SUSPICIOUSLY ACQUIRE SUDDEN WEALTH. WHAT'S THAT TO DO WITH THE JOKER?

LISTEN--THE JOKER HAS A NEW RACKET, HE MAKES AN ACCOMPLICE OF A RECENTLY RELEASED CRIMINAL--THEY PULL A ROBBERY--

8

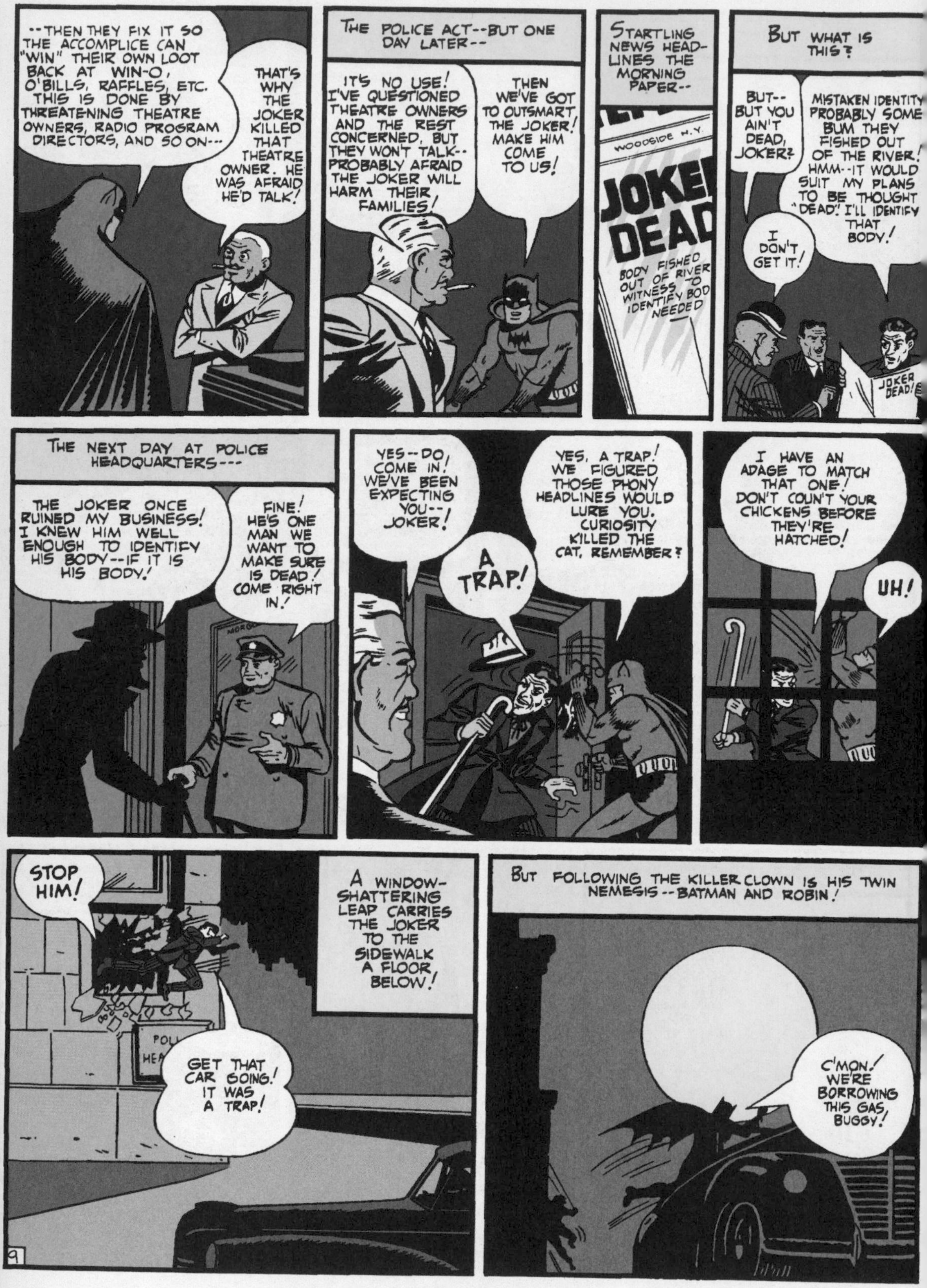
--THEN THEY FIX IT SO THE ACCOMPLICE CAN "WIN" THEIR OWN LOOT BACK AT WIN-O, O'BILLS, RAFFLES, ETC. THIS IS DONE BY THREATENING THEATRE OWNERS, RADIO PROGRAM DIRECTORS, AND SO ON---
THAT'S WHY THE JOKER KILLED THAT THEATRE OWNER. HE WAS AFRAID HE'D TALK!
THE POLICE ACT--BUT ONE DAY LATER--
IT'S NO USE! I'VE QUESTIONED THEATRE OWNERS AND THE REST CONCERNED, BUT THEY WON'T TALK--PROBABLY AFRAID THE JOKER WILL HARM THEIR FAMILIES!
THEN WE'VE GOT TO OUTSMART THE JOKER! MAKE HIM COME TO US!
STARTLING NEWS HEAD-LINES THE MORNING PAPER--
WOODSIDE N.Y.
JOKER DEAD
BODY FISHED OUT OF RIVER WITNESS TO IDENTIFY BOD NEEDED
BUT WHAT IS THIS?
BUT--BUT YOU AIN'T DEAD, JOKER?
MISTAKEN IDENTITY PROBABLY SOME BUM THEY FISHED OUT OF THE RIVER! HMM--IT WOULD SUIT MY PLANS TO BE THOUGHT "DEAD." I'LL IDENTIFY THAT BODY!
I DON'T GET IT!
JOKER DEAD!
THE NEXT DAY AT POLICE HEADQUARTERS---
THE JOKER ONCE RUINED MY BUSINESS! I KNEW HIM WELL ENOUGH TO IDENTIFY HIS BODY--IF IT IS HIS BODY!
FINE! HE'S ONE MAN WE WANT TO MAKE SURE IS DEAD! COME RIGHT IN!
YES--DO COME IN! WE'VE BEEN EXPECTING YOU--JOKER!
A TRAP!
YES, A TRAP! WE FIGURED THOSE PHONY HEADLINES WOULD LURE YOU. CURIOSITY KILLED THE CAT, REMEMBER?
I HAVE AN ADAGE TO MATCH THAT ONE! DON'T COUNT YOUR CHICKENS BEFORE THEY'RE HATCHED!
UH!
STOP HIM!
A WINDOW-SHATTERING LEAP CARRIES THE JOKER TO THE SIDEWALK A FLOOR BELOW!
GET THAT CAR GOING! IT WAS A TRAP!
BUT FOLLOWING THE KILLER CLOWN IS HIS TWIN NEMESIS--BATMAN AND ROBIN!
C'MON! WE'RE BORROWING THIS GAS BUGGY!
9

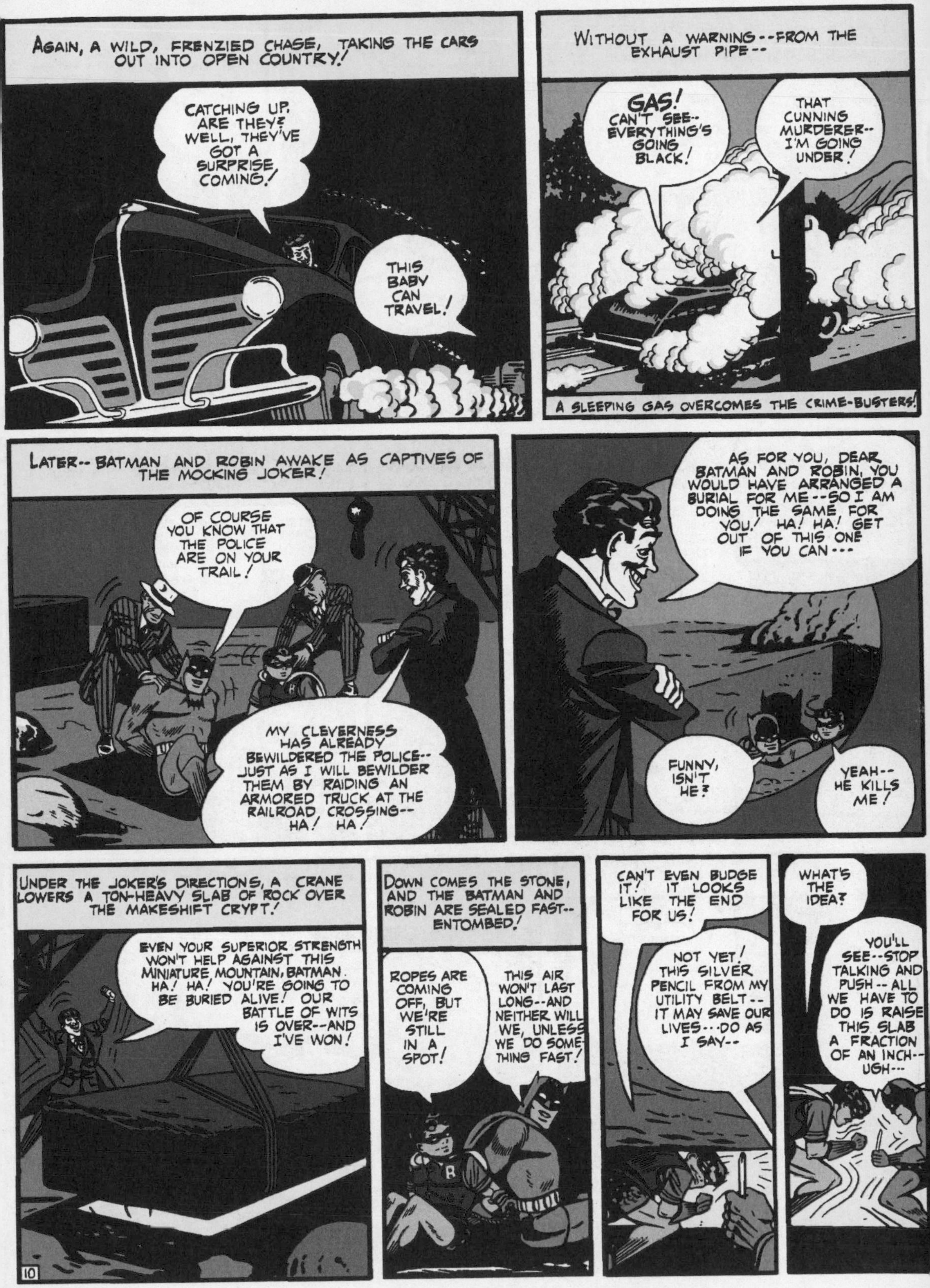
AGAIN, A WILD, FRENZIED CHASE, TAKING THE CARS OUT INTO OPEN COUNTRY!
CATCHING UP, ARE THEY? WELL, THEY'VE GOT A SURPRISE COMING!
THIS BABY CAN TRAVEL!
WITHOUT A WARNING--FROM THE EXHAUST PIPE--
GAS! CAN'T SEE-- EVERYTHING'S GOING BLACK!
THAT CUNNING MURDERER-- I'M GOING UNDER!
A SLEEPING GAS OVERCOMES THE CRIME-BUSTERS!
LATER-- BATMAN AND ROBIN AWAKE AS CAPTIVES OF THE MOCKING JOKER!
OF COURSE YOU KNOW THAT THE POLICE ARE ON YOUR TRAIL!
MY CLEVERNESS HAS ALREADY BEWILDERED THE POLICE-- JUST AS I WILL BEWILDER THEM BY RAIDING AN ARMORED TRUCK AT THE RAILROAD CROSSING-- HA! HA!
AS FOR YOU, DEAR BATMAN AND ROBIN, YOU WOULD HAVE ARRANGED A BURIAL FOR ME--SO I AM DOING THE SAME FOR YOU! HA! HA! GET OUT OF THIS ONE IF YOU CAN---
FUNNY, ISN'T HE?
YEAH-- HE KILLS ME!
UNDER THE JOKER'S DIRECTIONS, A CRANE LOWERS A TON-HEAVY SLAB OF ROCK OVER THE MAKESHIFT CRYPT!
EVEN YOUR SUPERIOR STRENGTH WON'T HELP AGAINST THIS MINIATURE MOUNTAIN, BATMAN. HA! HA! YOU'RE GOING TO BE BURIED ALIVE! OUR BATTLE OF WITS IS OVER--AND I'VE WON!
10
DOWN COMES THE STONE, AND THE BATMAN AND ROBIN ARE SEALED FAST-- ENTOMBED!
ROPES ARE COMING OFF, BUT WE'RE STILL IN A SPOT!
THIS AIR WON'T LAST LONG--AND NEITHER WILL WE, UNLESS WE DO SOMETHING FAST!
CAN'T EVEN BUDGE IT! IT LOOKS LIKE THE END FOR US!
NOT YET! THIS SILVER PENCIL FROM MY UTILITY BELT-- IT MAY SAVE OUR LIVES---DO AS I SAY--
WHAT'S THE IDEA?
YOU'LL SEE--STOP TALKING AND PUSH--ALL WE HAVE TO DO IS RAISE THIS SLAB A FRACTION OF AN INCH-- UGH---

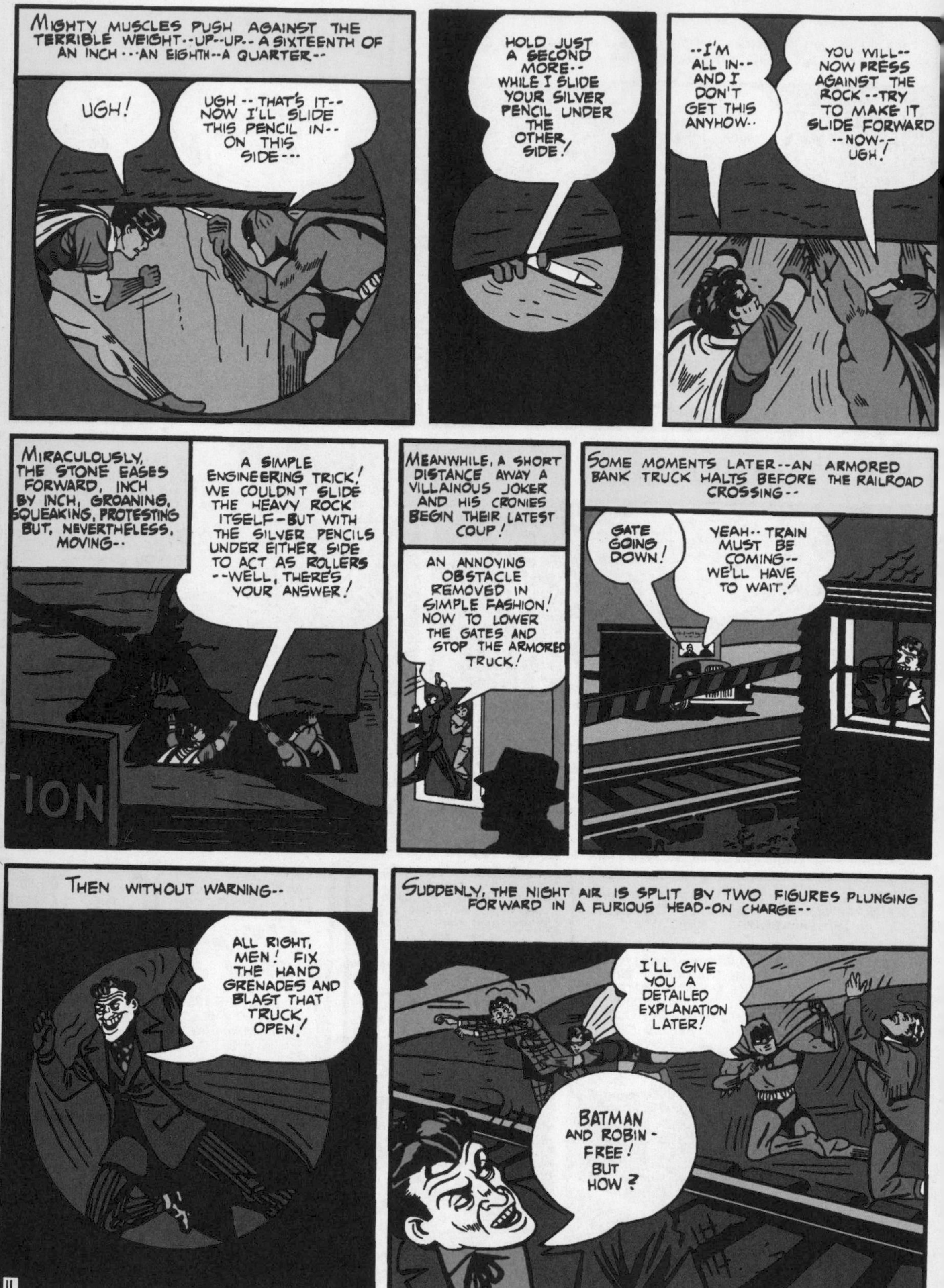
MIGHTY MUSCLES PUSH AGAINST THE TERRIBLE WEIGHT--UP--UP-- A SIXTEENTH OF AN INCH---AN EIGHTH--A QUARTER--
UGH!
UGH -- THAT'S IT-- NOW I'LL SLIDE THIS PENCIL IN-- ON THIS SIDE---
HOLD JUST A SECOND MORE-- WHILE I SLIDE YOUR SILVER PENCIL UNDER THE OTHER SIDE!
--I'M ALL IN-- AND I DON'T GET THIS ANYHOW--
YOU WILL-- NOW PRESS AGAINST THE ROCK--TRY TO MAKE IT SLIDE FORWARD --NOW-- UGH!
MIRACULOUSLY, THE STONE EASES FORWARD, INCH BY INCH, GROANING, SQUEAKING, PROTESTING BUT, NEVERTHELESS, MOVING--
A SIMPLE ENGINEERING TRICK! WE COULDN'T SLIDE THE HEAVY ROCK ITSELF-BUT WITH THE SILVER PENCILS UNDER EITHER SIDE TO ACT AS ROLLERS --WELL, THERE'S YOUR ANSWER!
TION
MEANWHILE, A SHORT DISTANCE AWAY A VILLAINOUS JOKER AND HIS CRONIES BEGIN THEIR LATEST COUP!
AN ANNOYING OBSTACLE REMOVED IN SIMPLE FASHION! NOW TO LOWER THE GATES AND STOP THE ARMORED TRUCK!
SOME MOMENTS LATER--AN ARMORED BANK TRUCK HALTS BEFORE THE RAILROAD CROSSING--
GATE GOING DOWN!
YEAH-- TRAIN MUST BE COMING-- WE'LL HAVE TO WAIT!
THEN WITHOUT WARNING--
ALL RIGHT, MEN! FIX THE HAND GRENADES AND BLAST THAT TRUCK OPEN!
11
SUDDENLY, THE NIGHT AIR IS SPLIT BY TWO FIGURES PLUNGING FORWARD IN A FURIOUS HEAD-ON CHARGE--
I'LL GIVE YOU A DETAILED EXPLANATION LATER!
BATMAN AND ROBIN- FREE! BUT HOW?

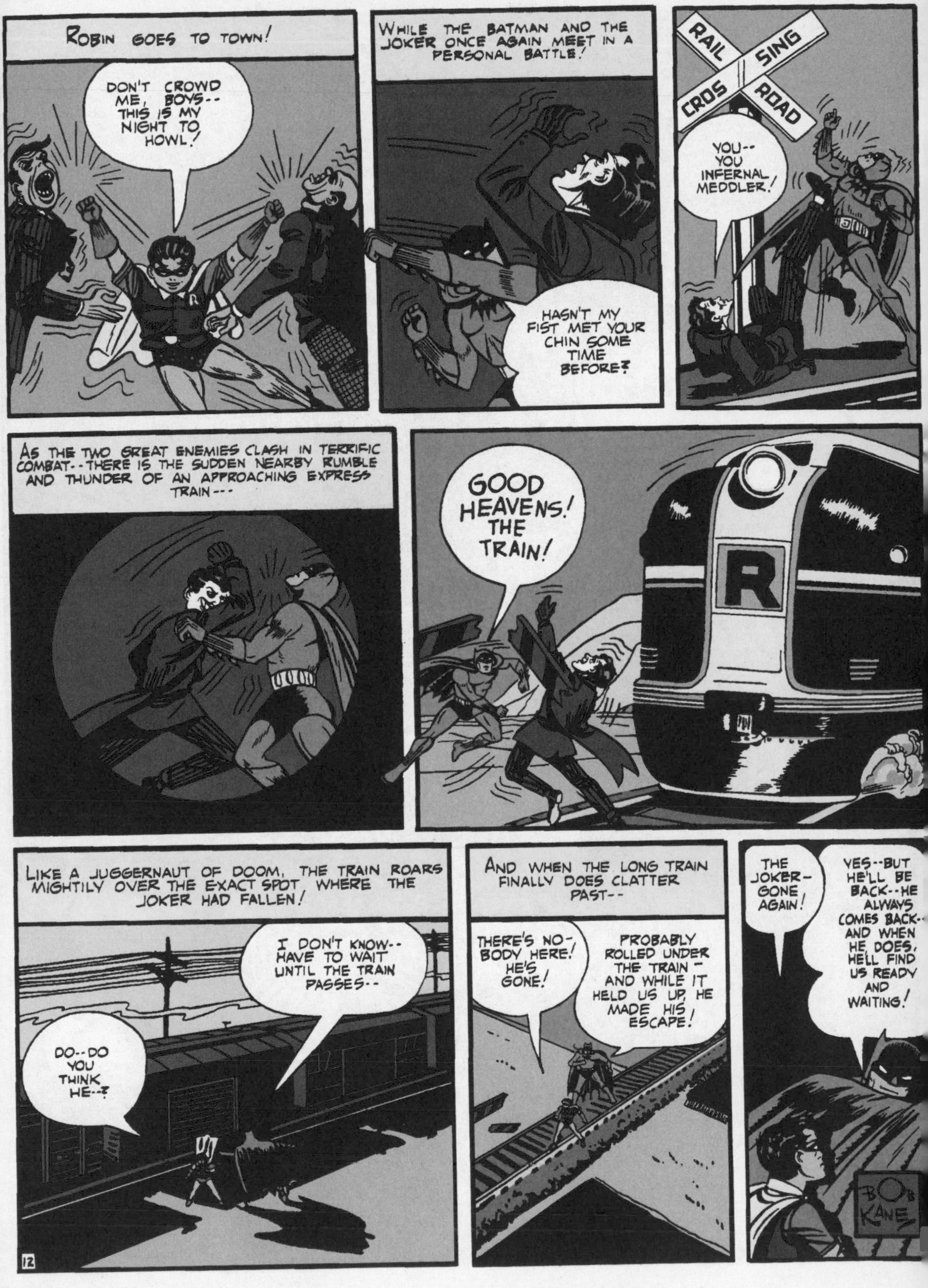

ROBIN GOES TO TOWN!
DON'T CROWD ME, BOYS-- THIS IS MY NIGHT TO HOWL!
WHILE THE BATMAN AND THE JOKER ONCE AGAIN MEET IN A PERSONAL BATTLE!
HASN'T MY FIST MET YOUR CHIN SOME TIME BEFORE?
RAIL ROAD
CROS SING
YOU-- YOU INFERNAL MEDDLER!
AS THE TWO GREAT ENEMIES CLASH IN TERRIFIC COMBAT--THERE IS THE SUDDEN NEARBY RUMBLE AND THUNDER OF AN APPROACHING EXPRESS TRAIN---
GOOD HEAVENS! THE TRAIN!
R
LIKE A JUGGERNAUT OF DOOM, THE TRAIN ROARS MIGHTILY OVER THE EXACT SPOT WHERE THE JOKER HAD FALLEN!
DO--DO YOU THINK HE--?
I DON'T KNOW-- HAVE TO WAIT UNTIL THE TRAIN PASSES--
12
AND WHEN THE LONG TRAIN FINALLY DOES CLATTER PAST--
THERE'S NOBODY HERE! HE'S GONE!
PROBABLY ROLLED UNDER THE TRAIN-- AND WHILE IT HELD US UP, HE MADE HIS ESCAPE!
THE JOKER-- GONE AGAIN!
YES--BUT HE'LL BE BACK--HE ALWAYS COMES BACK-- AND WHEN HE DOES, HE'LL FIND US READY AND WAITING!
BOB KANE

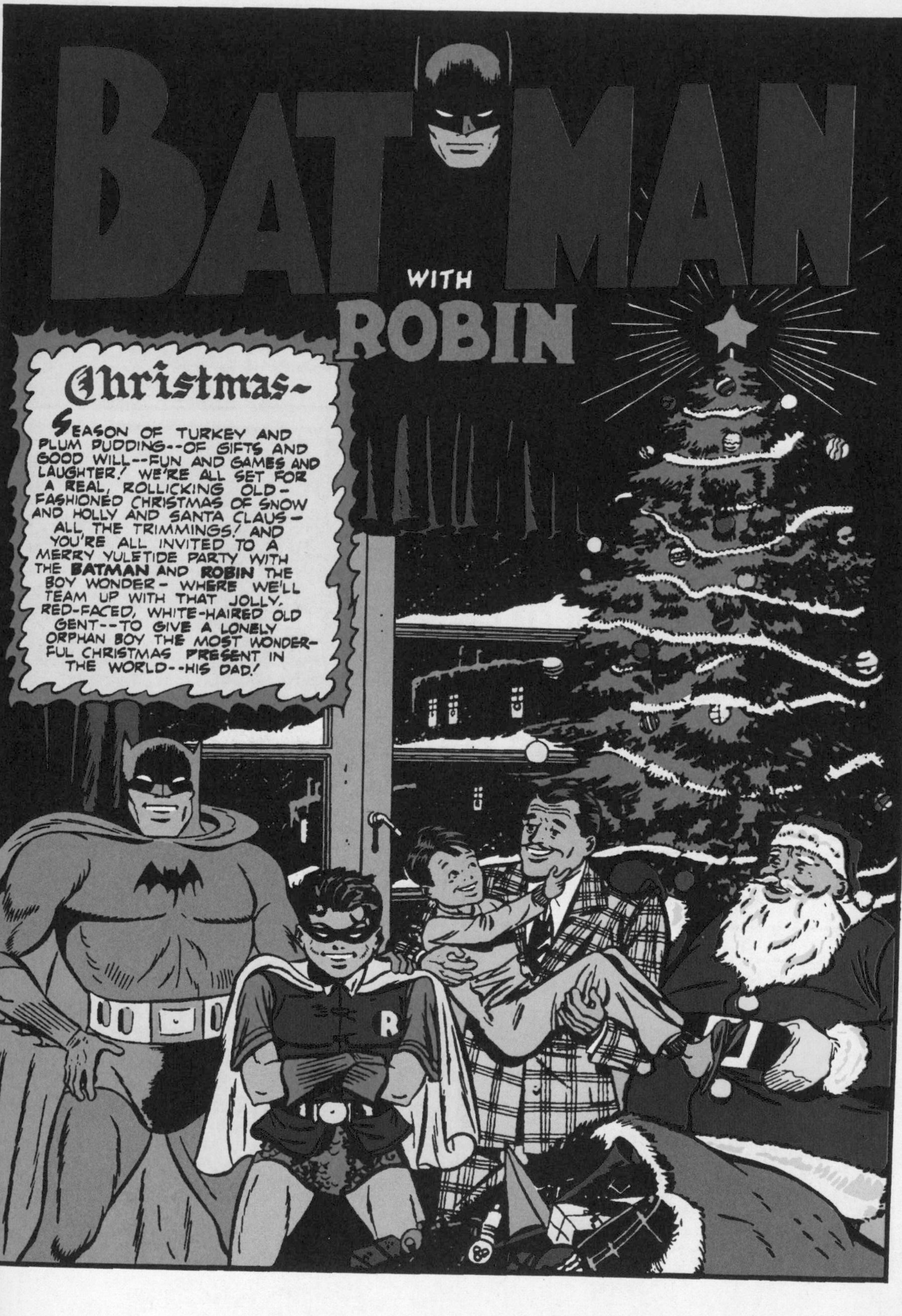
BATMAN
WITH
ROBIN
Christmas-
SEASON OF TURKEY AND PLUM PUDDING--OF GIFTS AND GOOD WILL--FUN AND GAMES AND LAUGHTER! WE'RE ALL SET FOR A REAL, ROLLICKING OLD-FASHIONED CHRISTMAS OF SNOW AND HOLLY AND SANTA CLAUS--ALL THE TRIMMINGS! AND YOU'RE ALL INVITED TO A MERRY YULETIDE PARTY WITH THE BATMAN AND ROBIN THE BOY WONDER- WHERE WE'LL TEAM UP WITH THAT JOLLY, RED-FACED, WHITE-HAIRED OLD GENT--TO GIVE A LONELY ORPHAN BOY THE MOST WONDERFUL CHRISTMAS PRESENT IN THE WORLD--HIS DAD!
R

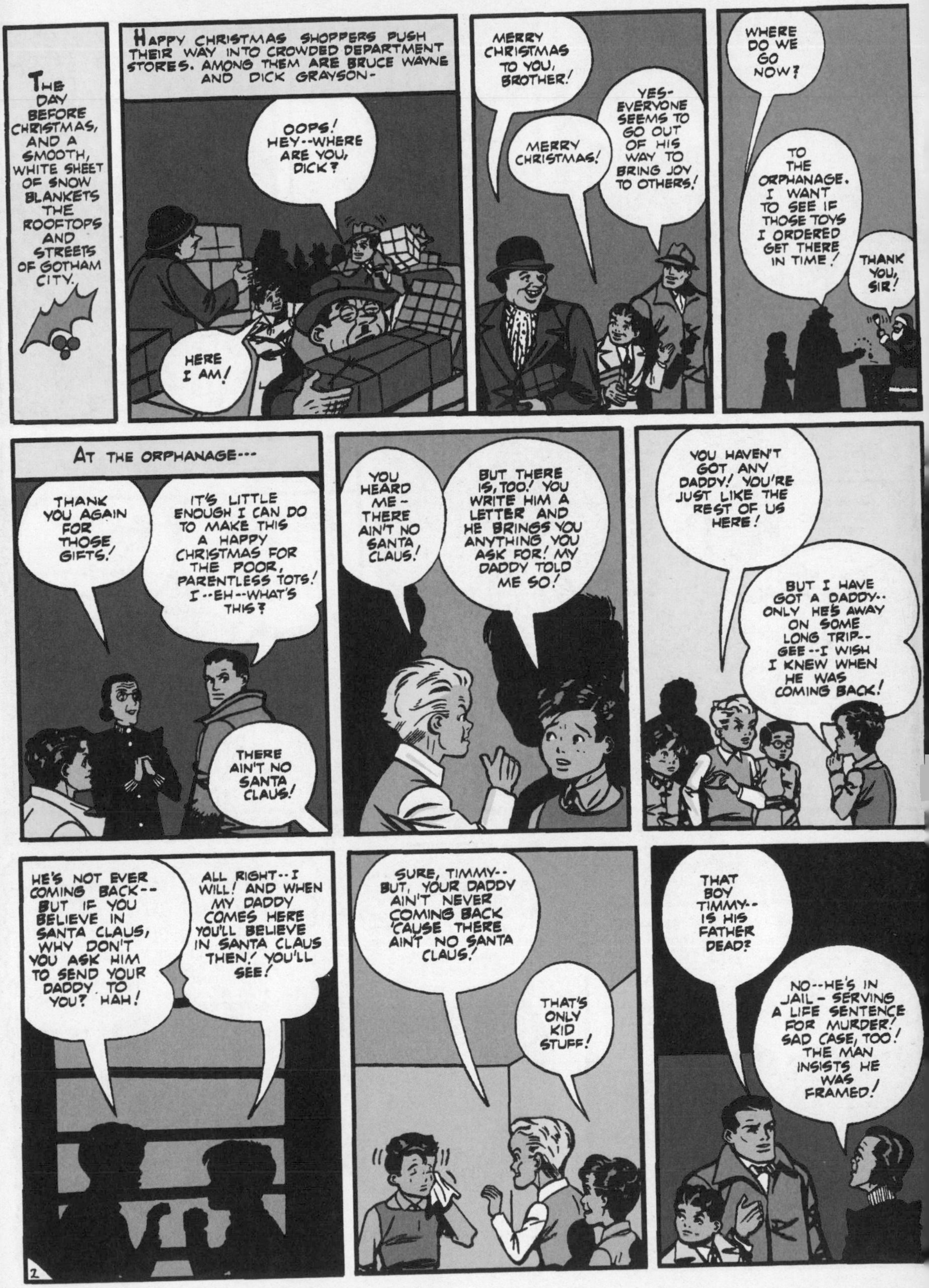
THE DAY BEFORE CHRISTMAS, AND A SMOOTH, WHITE SHEET OF SNOW BLANKETS THE ROOFTOPS AND STREETS OF GOTHAM CITY.
HAPPY CHRISTMAS SHOPPERS PUSH THEIR WAY INTO CROWDED DEPARTMENT STORES. AMONG THEM ARE BRUCE WAYNE AND DICK GRAYSON-
OOPS! HEY--WHERE ARE YOU, DICK?
HERE I AM!
MERRY CHRISTMAS TO YOU, BROTHER!
MERRY CHRISTMAS!
YES- EVERYONE SEEMS TO GO OUT OF HIS WAY TO BRING JOY TO OTHERS!
WHERE DO WE GO NOW?
TO THE ORPHANAGE. I WANT TO SEE IF THOSE TOYS I ORDERED GET THERE IN TIME!
THANK YOU, SIR!
AT THE ORPHANAGE---
THANK YOU AGAIN FOR THOSE GIFTS!
IT'S LITTLE ENOUGH I CAN DO TO MAKE THIS A HAPPY CHRISTMAS FOR THE POOR, PARENTLESS TOTS! I--EH--WHAT'S THIS?
THERE AIN'T NO SANTA CLAUS!
YOU HEARD ME- THERE AIN'T NO SANTA CLAUS!
BUT THERE IS, TOO! YOU WRITE HIM A LETTER AND HE BRINGS YOU ANYTHING YOU ASK FOR! MY DADDY TOLD ME SO!
YOU HAVEN'T GOT ANY DADDY! YOU'RE JUST LIKE THE REST OF US HERE!
BUT I HAVE GOT A DADDY.. ONLY HE'S AWAY ON SOME LONG TRIP-- GEE--I WISH I KNEW WHEN HE WAS COMING BACK!
HE'S NOT EVER COMING BACK-- BUT IF YOU BELIEVE IN SANTA CLAUS, WHY DON'T YOU ASK HIM TO SEND YOUR DADDY TO YOU? HAH!
ALL RIGHT--I WILL! AND WHEN MY DADDY COMES HERE YOU'LL BELIEVE IN SANTA CLAUS THEN! YOU'LL SEE!
2
SURE, TIMMY-- BUT, YOUR DADDY AIN'T NEVER COMING BACK 'CAUSE THERE AIN'T NO SANTA CLAUS!
THAT'S ONLY KID STUFF!
THAT BOY TIMMY-- IS HIS FATHER DEAD?
NO--HE'S IN JAIL - SERVING A LIFE SENTENCE FOR MURDER! SAD CASE, TOO! THE MAN INSISTS HE WAS FRAMED!

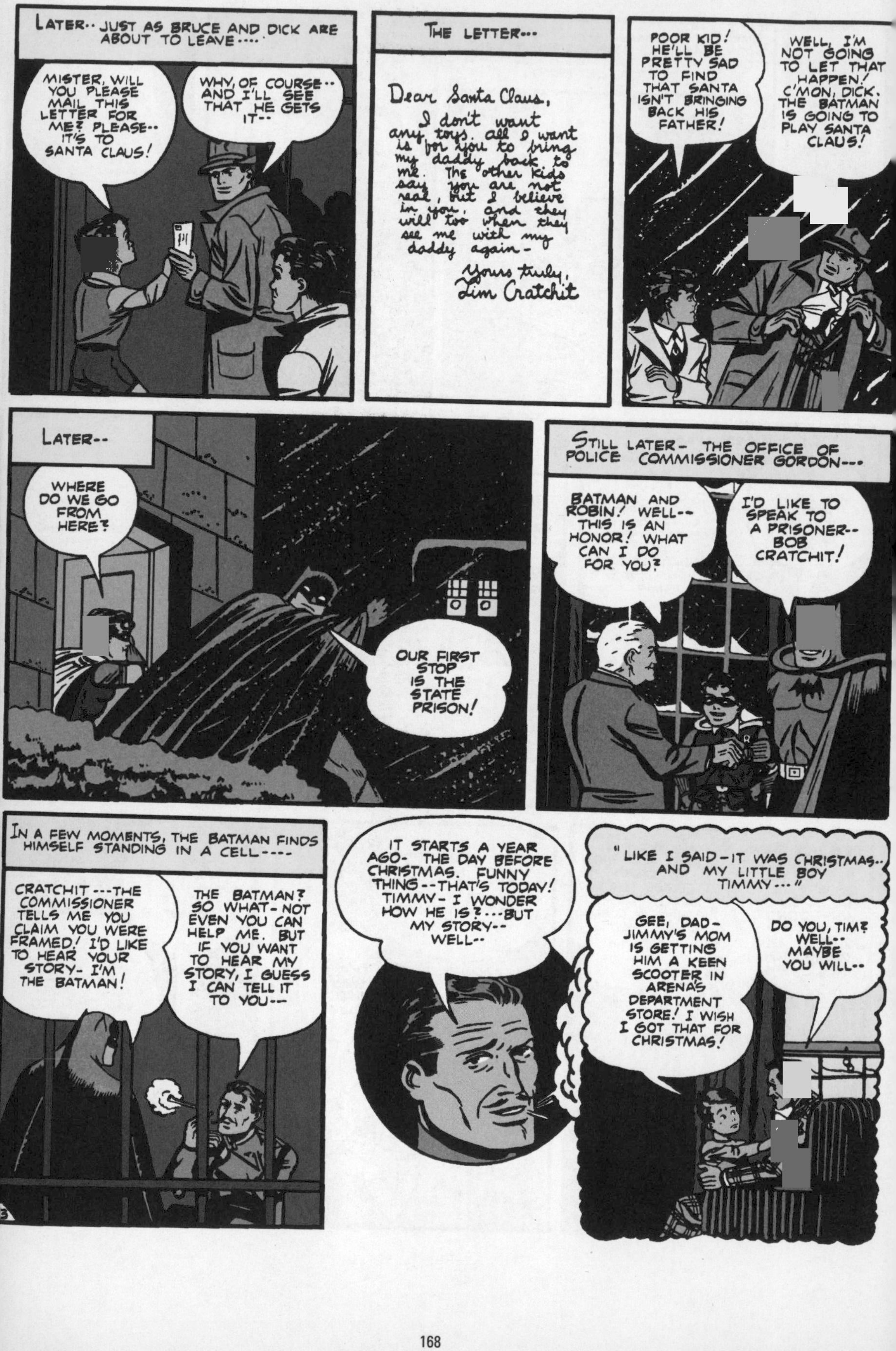
LATER.. JUST AS BRUCE AND DICK ARE ABOUT TO LEAVE....
MISTER, WILL YOU PLEASE MAIL THIS LETTER FOR ME? PLEASE.. IT'S TO SANTA CLAUS!
WHY, OF COURSE.. AND I'LL SEE THAT HE GETS IT--
THE LETTER...
Dear Santa Claus,
I don't want any toys. all I want is for you to bring my daddy back to me. The other kids say you are not real, but I believe in you, and they will too when they see me with my daddy again -
Yours truly,
Tim Cratchit
POOR KID! HE'LL BE PRETTY SAD TO FIND THAT SANTA ISN'T BRINGING BACK HIS FATHER!
WELL, I'M NOT GOING TO LET THAT HAPPEN! C'MON, DICK. THE BATMAN IS GOING TO PLAY SANTA CLAUS!
LATER--
WHERE DO WE GO FROM HERE?
OUR FIRST STOP IS THE STATE PRISON!
STILL LATER - THE OFFICE OF POLICE COMMISSIONER GORDON---
BATMAN AND ROBIN! WELL-- THIS IS AN HONOR! WHAT CAN I DO FOR YOU?
I'D LIKE TO SPEAK TO A PRISONER-- BOB CRATCHIT!
IN A FEW MOMENTS, THE BATMAN FINDS HIMSELF STANDING IN A CELL----
CRATCHIT---THE COMMISSIONER TELLS ME YOU CLAIM YOU WERE FRAMED! I'D LIKE TO HEAR YOUR STORY - I'M THE BATMAN!
THE BATMAN? SO WHAT- NOT EVEN YOU CAN HELP ME. BUT IF YOU WANT TO HEAR MY STORY, I GUESS I CAN TELL IT TO YOU---
IT STARTS A YEAR AGO- THE DAY BEFORE CHRISTMAS. FUNNY THING--THAT'S TODAY! TIMMY- I WONDER HOW HE IS?...BUT MY STORY-- WELL--
"LIKE I SAID - IT WAS CHRISTMAS.. AND MY LITTLE BOY TIMMY..."
GEE, DAD- JIMMY'S MOM IS GETTING HIM A KEEN SCOOTER IN ARENA'S DEPARTMENT STORE! I WISH I GOT THAT FOR CHRISTMAS!
DO YOU, TIM? WELL-- MAYBE YOU WILL--

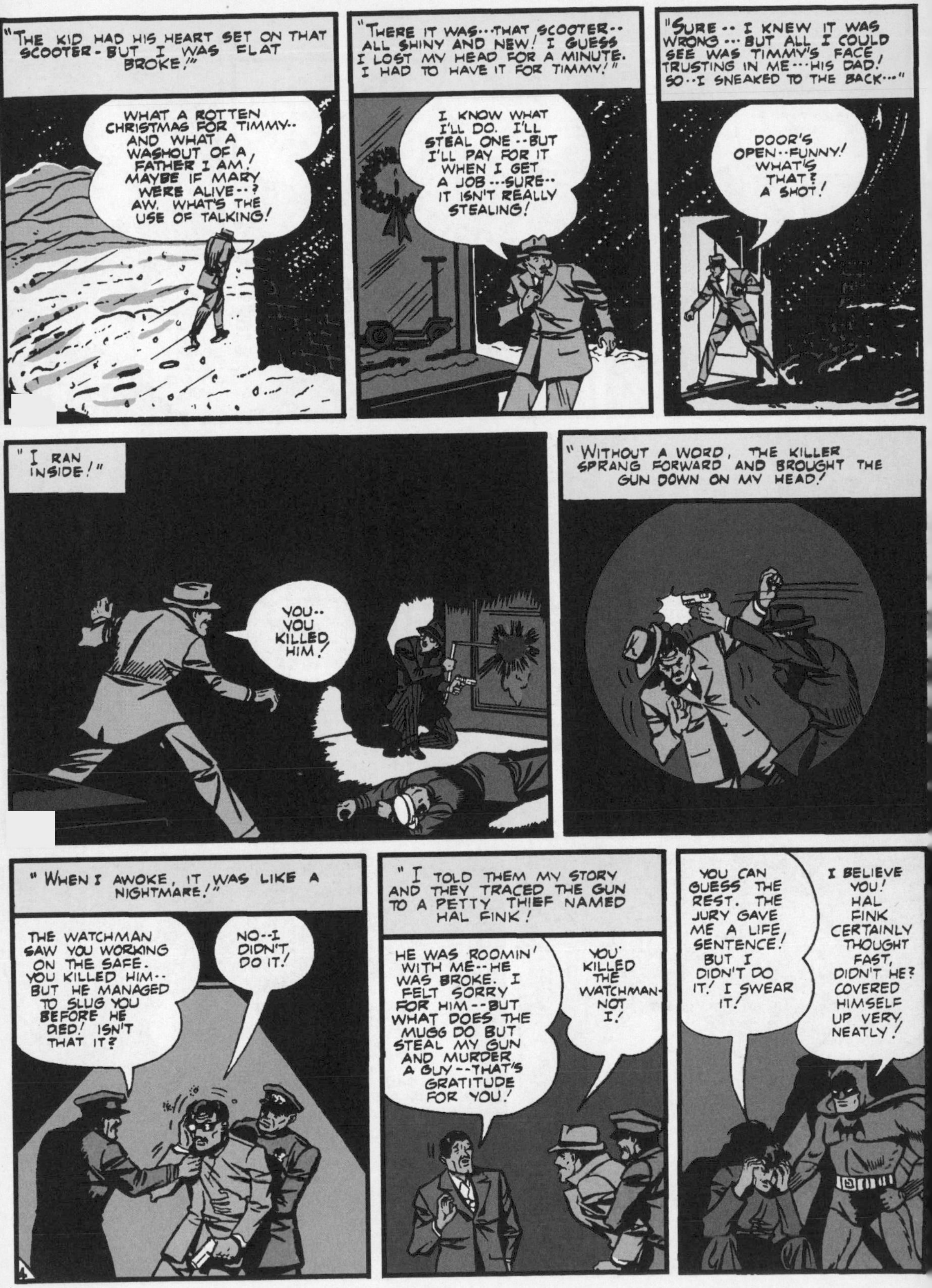
"THE KID HAD HIS HEART SET ON THAT SCOOTER - BUT I WAS FLAT BROKE!"
WHAT A ROTTEN CHRISTMAS FOR TIMMY.. AND WHAT A WASHOUT OF A FATHER I AM! MAYBE IF MARY WERE ALIVE--? AW, WHAT'S THE USE OF TALKING!
"THERE IT WAS...THAT SCOOTER.. ALL SHINY AND NEW! I GUESS I LOST MY HEAD FOR A MINUTE. I HAD TO HAVE IT FOR TIMMY!"
I KNOW WHAT I'LL DO. I'LL STEAL ONE --BUT I'LL PAY FOR IT WHEN I GET A JOB ---SURE.. IT ISN'T REALLY STEALING!
"SURE .. I KNEW IT WAS WRONG ... BUT ALL I COULD SEE WAS TIMMY'S FACE TRUSTING IN ME...HIS DAD! SO..I SNEAKED TO THE BACK..."
DOOR'S OPEN..FUNNY! WHAT'S THAT? A SHOT!
"I RAN INSIDE!"
YOU.. YOU KILLED HIM!
"WITHOUT A WORD, THE KILLER SPRANG FORWARD AND BROUGHT THE GUN DOWN ON MY HEAD!"
"WHEN I AWOKE, IT WAS LIKE A NIGHTMARE!"
THE WATCHMAN SAW YOU WORKING ON THE SAFE. YOU KILLED HIM.. BUT HE MANAGED TO SLUG YOU BEFORE HE DIED! ISN'T THAT IT?
NO--I DIDN'T DO IT!
"I TOLD THEM MY STORY AND THEY TRACED THE GUN TO A PETTY THIEF NAMED HAL FINK!
HE WAS ROOMIN' WITH ME--HE WAS BROKE. I FELT SORRY FOR HIM--BUT WHAT DOES THE MUGG DO BUT STEAL MY GUN AND MURDER A GUY--THAT'S GRATITUDE FOR YOU!
YOU KILLED THE WATCHMAN-NOT I!
YOU CAN GUESS THE REST. THE JURY GAVE ME A LIFE SENTENCE! BUT I DIDN'T DO IT! I SWEAR IT!
I BELIEVE YOU! HAL FINK CERTAINLY THOUGHT FAST, DIDN'T HE? COVERED HIMSELF UP VERY NEATLY!

CRATCHIT, I THINK I MAY BE ABLE TO DO SOMETHING! WHO KNOWS, PERHAPS YOU MAY DISCOVER THERE IS A SANTA CLAUS!

BATMAN, IF YOU GET ME OUT OF HERE, I'LL BE INDEBTED TO YOU ALL MY LIFE!

MINUTES LATER---

SAY---ISN'T HAL FINK A SORT OF A BIG SHOT NOW?

YES, HAL HAS GONE FAR FROM THAT LITTLE THIEVING RAT OF A YEAR AGO-- NOW HE'S A BIG RAT!

BACK AT THE PRISON A GUARD IN THE PAY OF CROOKDOM MAKES A PHONE CALL--

YEAH, HAL-- THE BATMAN WAS PUMPING BOB CRATCHIT-- ABOUT THAT WATCHMAN MURDER--

WELL-- THAT MEANS HE'LL BE OVER TO SEE ME NEXT. I'LL BE READY FOR HIM-- READY AND WAITING--

WHAT A DUMP! IF FINK IS SUCH A BIG SHOT, WHY DOESN'T HE LIVE IN A BETTER HOUSE?

FINK OWNS THIS PLACE, BUT HE HAS THE INSIDE FIXED UP LIKE A PALACE--GUESS HE LIKES THE ATMOSPHERE HERE!

CLANG! CLANG! CLANG! ...THE...BATMAN...IS...HERE! ...THE...BATMAN...IS...HERE!

AS THE TWO ENTER, THE ROTUND SANTA CLAUS CLANGS HIS BELL LOUDLY, PEALING A SINISTER WARNING...

SHH! WE'LL TAKE HIM BY SURPRISE!

HELLO, HAL-- BET YOU THOUGHT IT WAS SANTA CLAUS!

BATMAN!

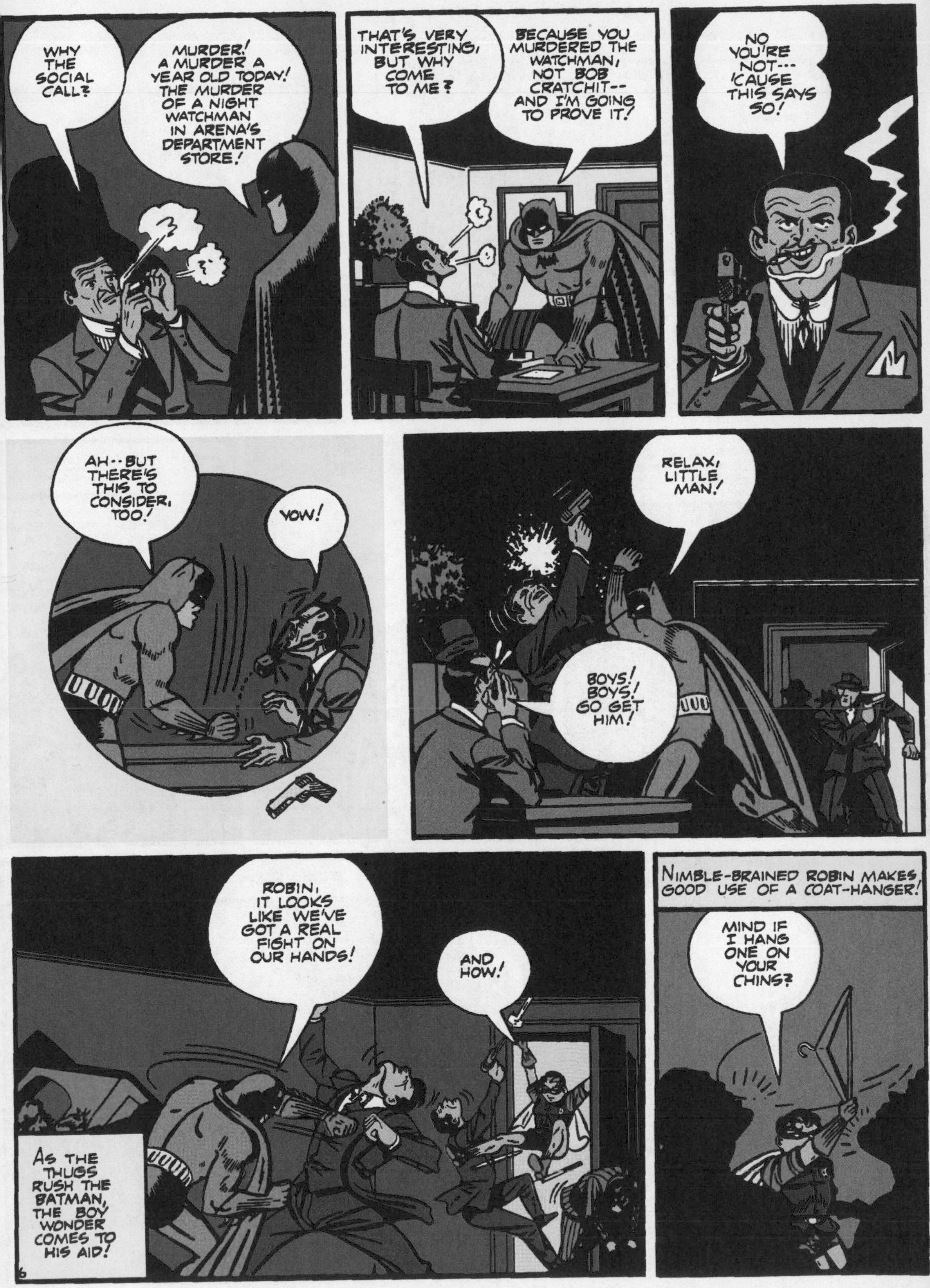
WHY THE SOCIAL CALL?
MURDER! A MURDER A YEAR OLD TODAY! THE MURDER OF A NIGHT WATCHMAN IN ARENA'S DEPARTMENT STORE!
THAT'S VERY INTERESTING, BUT WHY COME TO ME?
BECAUSE YOU MURDERED THE WATCHMAN, NOT BOB CRATCHIT-- AND I'M GOING TO PROVE IT!
NO YOU'RE NOT--- 'CAUSE THIS SAYS SO!
AH--BUT THERE'S THIS TO CONSIDER, TOO!
YOW!
RELAX, LITTLE MAN!
BOYS! BOYS! GO GET HIM!
ROBIN, IT LOOKS LIKE WE'VE GOT A REAL FIGHT ON OUR HANDS!
AND HOW!
AS THE THUGS RUSH THE BATMAN, THE BOY WONDER COMES TO HIS AID!
6
NIMBLE-BRAINED ROBIN MAKES GOOD USE OF A COAT-HANGER!
MIND IF I HANG ONE ON YOUR CHINS?

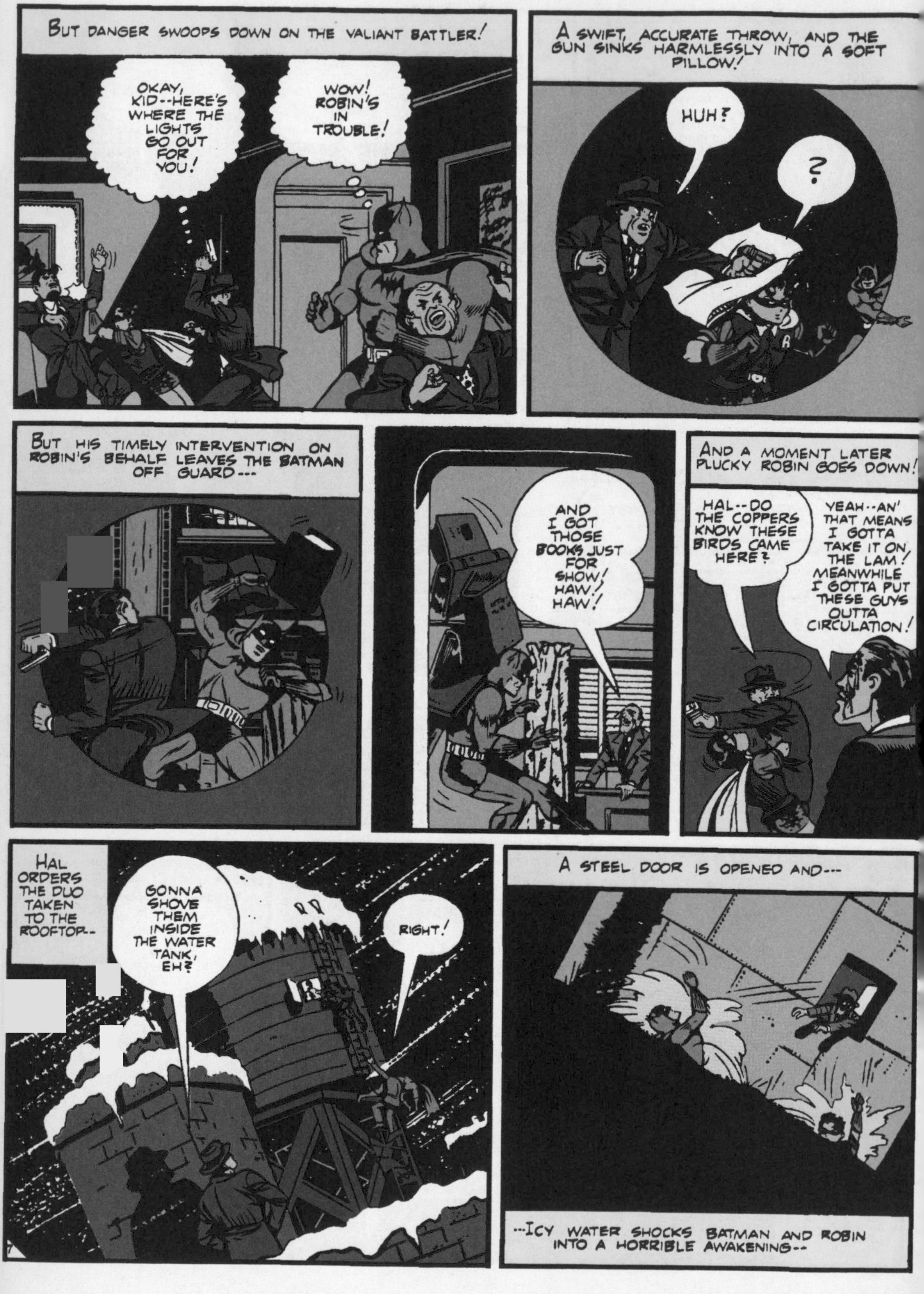
BUT DANGER SWOOPS DOWN ON THE VALIANT BATTLER!
OKAY, KID--HERE'S WHERE THE LIGHTS GO OUT FOR YOU!
WOW! ROBIN'S IN TROUBLE!
A SWIFT, ACCURATE THROW, AND THE GUN SINKS HARMLESSLY INTO A SOFT PILLOW!
HUH?
?
BUT HIS TIMELY INTERVENTION ON ROBIN'S BEHALF LEAVES THE BATMAN OFF GUARD---
AND I GOT THOSE BOOKS JUST FOR SHOW! HAW! HAW!
AND A MOMENT LATER PLUCKY ROBIN GOES DOWN!
HAL--DO THE COPPERS KNOW THESE BIRDS CAME HERE?
YEAH--AN' THAT MEANS I GOTTA TAKE IT ON THE LAM! MEANWHILE I GOTTA PUT THESE GUYS OUTTA CIRCULATION!
HAL ORDERS THE DUO TAKEN TO THE ROOFTOP--
GONNA SHOVE THEM INSIDE THE WATER TANK, EH?
RIGHT!
A STEEL DOOR IS OPENED AND---
---ICY WATER SHOCKS BATMAN AND ROBIN INTO A HORRIBLE AWAKENING--

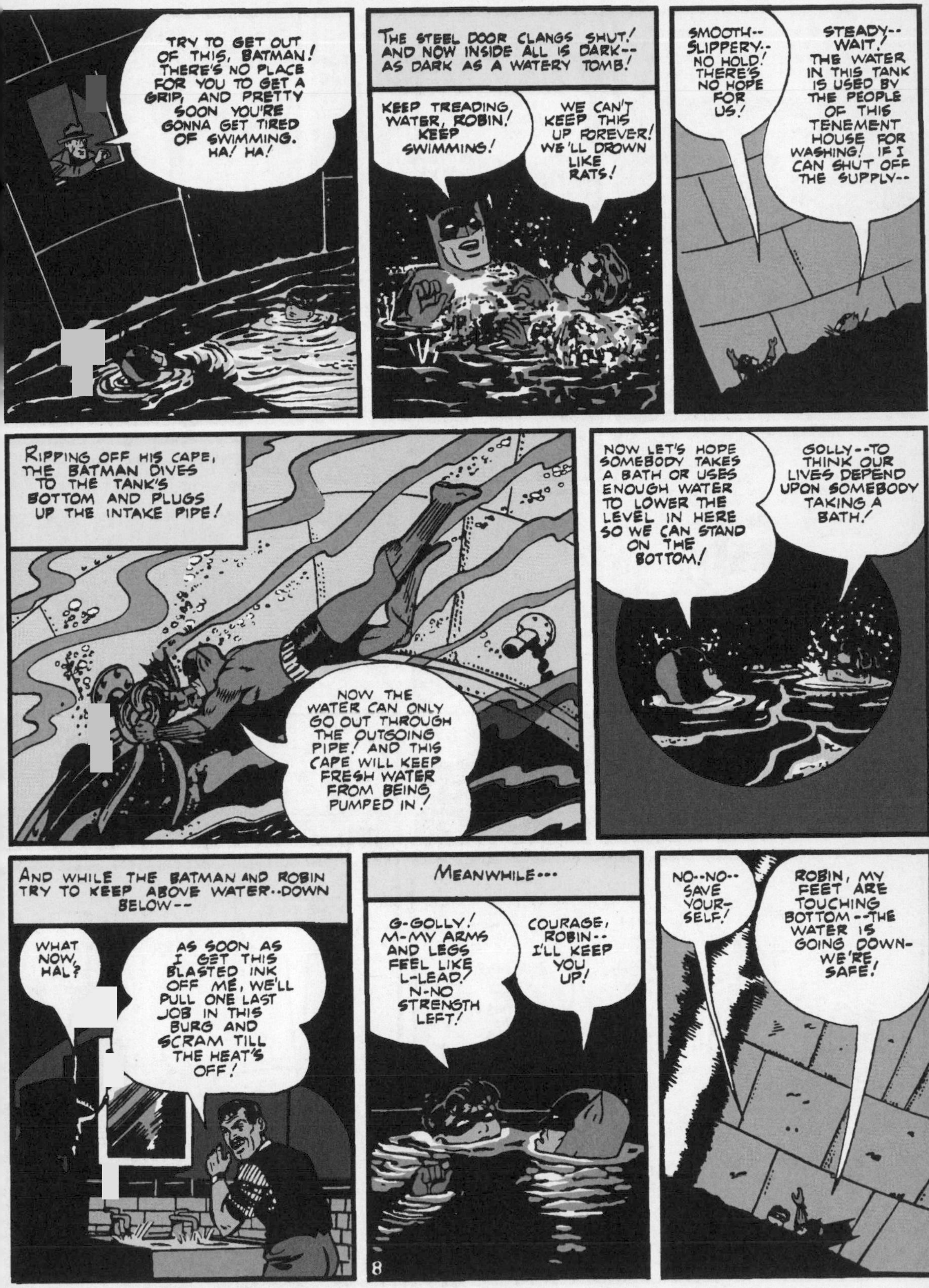
TRY TO GET OUT OF THIS, BATMAN! THERE'S NO PLACE FOR YOU TO GET A GRIP, AND PRETTY SOON YOU'RE GONNA GET TIRED OF SWIMMING. HA! HA!
THE STEEL DOOR CLANGS SHUT! AND NOW INSIDE ALL IS DARK-- AS DARK AS A WATERY TOMB!
KEEP TREADING WATER, ROBIN! KEEP SWIMMING!
WE CAN'T KEEP THIS UP FOREVER! WE'LL DROWN LIKE RATS!
SMOOTH-- SLIPPERY-- NO HOLD! THERE'S NO HOPE FOR US!
STEADY-- WAIT! THE WATER IN THIS TANK IS USED BY THE PEOPLE OF THIS TENEMENT HOUSE FOR WASHING! IF I CAN SHUT OFF THE SUPPLY--
RIPPING OFF HIS CAPE, THE BATMAN DIVES TO THE TANK'S BOTTOM AND PLUGS UP THE INTAKE PIPE!
NOW THE WATER CAN ONLY GO OUT THROUGH THE OUTGOING PIPE! AND THIS CAPE WILL KEEP FRESH WATER FROM BEING PUMPED IN!
NOW LET'S HOPE SOMEBODY TAKES A BATH OR USES ENOUGH WATER TO LOWER THE LEVEL IN HERE SO WE CAN STAND ON THE BOTTOM!
GOLLY--TO THINK OUR LIVES DEPEND UPON SOMEBODY TAKING A BATH!
AND WHILE THE BATMAN AND ROBIN TRY TO KEEP ABOVE WATER--DOWN BELOW--
WHAT NOW, HAL?
AS SOON AS I GET THIS BLASTED INK OFF ME, WE'LL PULL ONE LAST JOB IN THIS BURG AND SCRAM TILL THE HEAT'S OFF!
MEANWHILE---
G-GOLLY! M-MY ARMS AND LEGS FEEL LIKE L-LEAD! N-NO STRENGTH LEFT!
COURAGE, ROBIN-- I'LL KEEP YOU UP!
8
NO--NO-- SAVE YOURSELF!
ROBIN, MY FEET ARE TOUCHING BOTTOM--THE WATER IS GOING DOWN-- WE'RE SAFE!

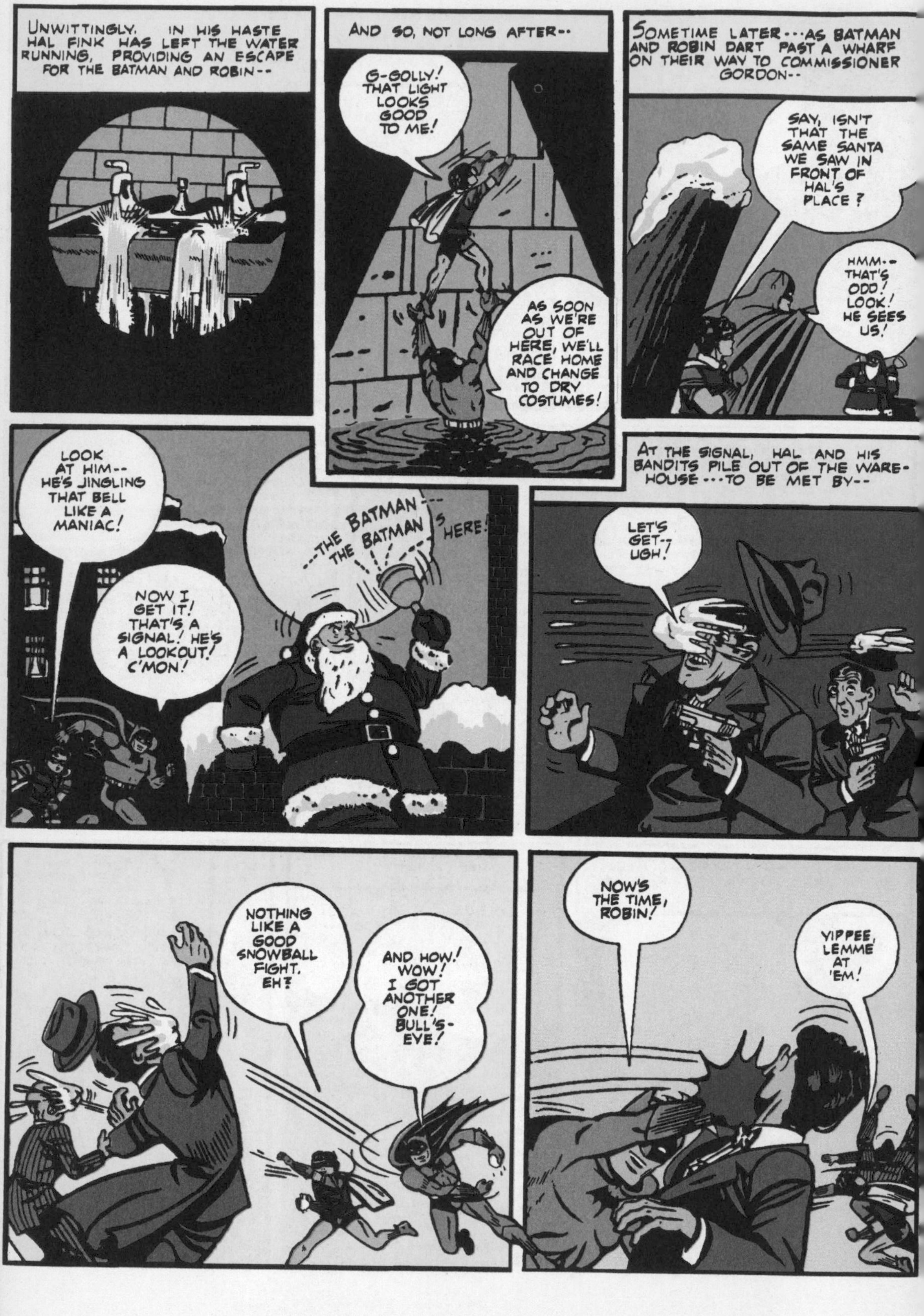
UNWITTINGLY, IN HIS HASTE HAL FINK HAS LEFT THE WATER RUNNING, PROVIDING AN ESCAPE FOR THE BATMAN AND ROBIN--
AND SO, NOT LONG AFTER--
G-GOLLY! THAT LIGHT LOOKS GOOD TO ME!
AS SOON AS WE'RE OUT OF HERE, WE'LL RACE HOME AND CHANGE TO DRY COSTUMES!
SOMETIME LATER---AS BATMAN AND ROBIN DART PAST A WHARF ON THEIR WAY TO COMMISSIONER GORDON--
SAY, ISN'T THAT THE SAME SANTA WE SAW IN FRONT OF HAL'S PLACE?
HMM-- THAT'S ODD! LOOK! HE SEES US!
LOOK AT HIM-- HE'S JINGLING THAT BELL LIKE A MANIAC!
--THE BATMAN--- THE BATMAN'S HERE!
NOW I GET IT! THAT'S A SIGNAL! HE'S A LOOKOUT! C'MON!
AT THE SIGNAL, HAL AND HIS BANDITS PILE OUT OF THE WARE-HOUSE---TO BE MET BY--
LET'S GET-- UGH!
NOTHING LIKE A GOOD SNOWBALL FIGHT, EH?
AND HOW! WOW! I GOT ANOTHER ONE! BULL'S-EYE!
NOW'S THE TIME, ROBIN!
YIPPEE, LEMME AT 'EM!

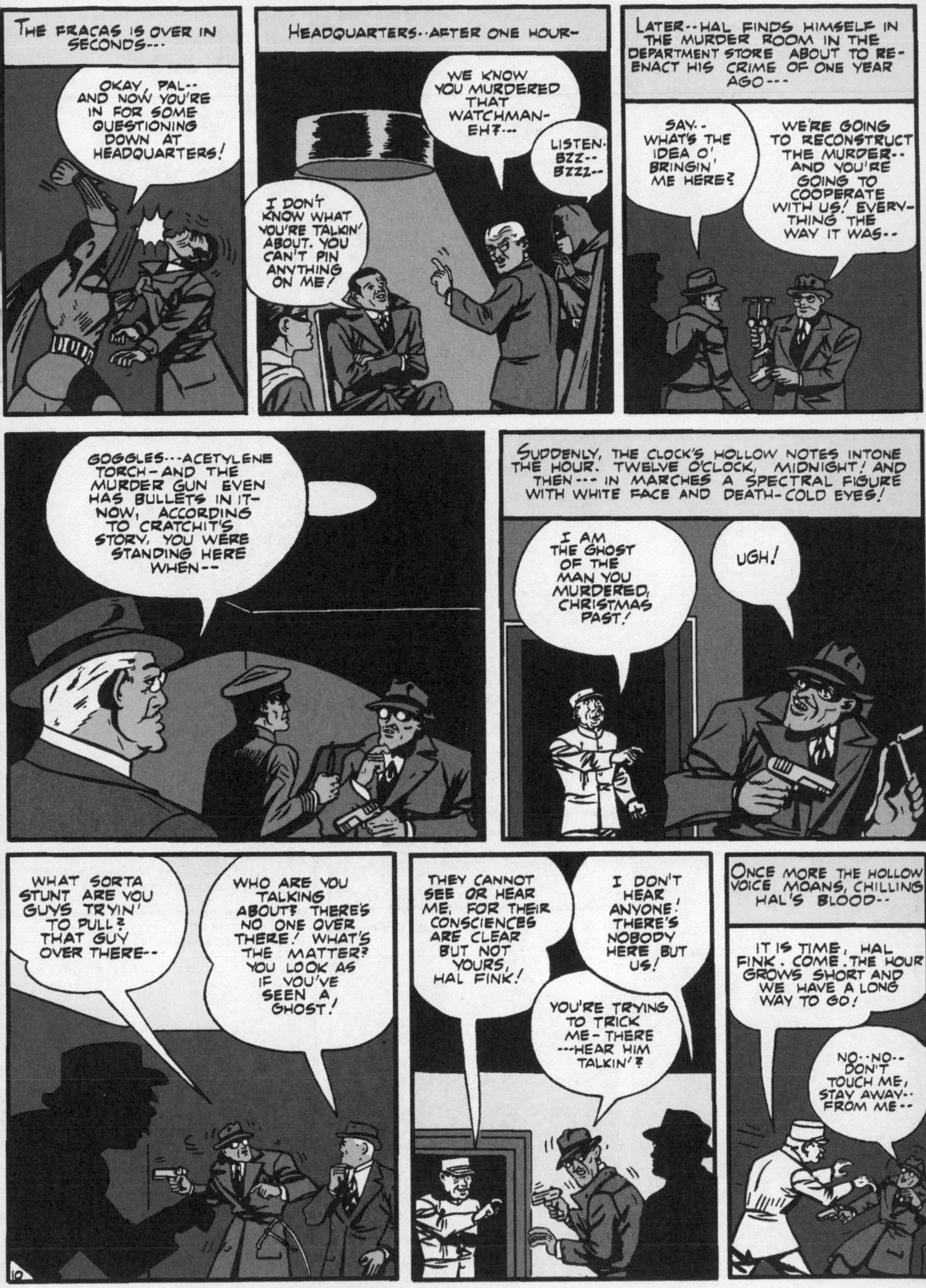

THE FRACAS IS OVER IN SECONDS---
OKAY, PAL-- AND NOW YOU'RE IN FOR SOME QUESTIONING DOWN AT HEADQUARTERS!
HEADQUARTERS..AFTER ONE HOUR-
WE KNOW YOU MURDERED THAT WATCHMAN- EH?---
LISTEN. BZZ-- BZZZ--
I DON'T KNOW WHAT YOU'RE TALKIN' ABOUT. YOU CAN'T PIN ANYTHING ON ME!
LATER--HAL FINDS HIMSELF IN THE MURDER ROOM IN THE DEPARTMENT STORE ABOUT TO RE-ENACT HIS CRIME OF ONE YEAR AGO---
SAY.- WHAT'S THE IDEA O' BRINGIN' ME HERE?
WE'RE GOING TO RECONSTRUCT THE MURDER-- AND YOU'RE GOING TO COOPERATE WITH US! EVERYTHING THE WAY IT WAS--
GOGGLES---ACETYLENE TORCH-AND THE MURDER GUN EVEN HAS BULLETS IN IT-NOW, ACCORDING TO CRATCHIT'S STORY, YOU WERE STANDING HERE WHEN--
SUDDENLY, THE CLOCK'S HOLLOW NOTES INTONE THE HOUR. TWELVE O'CLOCK, MIDNIGHT! AND THEN--- IN MARCHES A SPECTRAL FIGURE WITH WHITE FACE AND DEATH-COLD EYES!
I AM THE GHOST OF THE MAN YOU MURDERED, CHRISTMAS PAST!
UGH!
WHAT SORTA STUNT ARE YOU GUYS TRYIN' TO PULL? THAT GUY OVER THERE--
WHO ARE YOU TALKING ABOUT? THERE'S NO ONE OVER THERE! WHAT'S THE MATTER? YOU LOOK AS IF YOU'VE SEEN A GHOST!
10
THEY CANNOT SEE OR HEAR ME, FOR THEIR CONSCIENCES ARE CLEAR BUT NOT YOURS, HAL FINK!
I DON'T HEAR ANYONE! THERE'S NOBODY HERE BUT US!
YOU'RE TRYING TO TRICK ME- THERE ---HEAR HIM TALKIN'?
ONCE MORE THE HOLLOW VOICE MOANS, CHILLING HAL'S BLOOD--
IT IS TIME, HAL FINK. COME. THE HOUR GROWS SHORT AND WE HAVE A LONG WAY TO GO!
NO--NO-- DON'T TOUCH ME, STAY AWAY-- FROM ME--

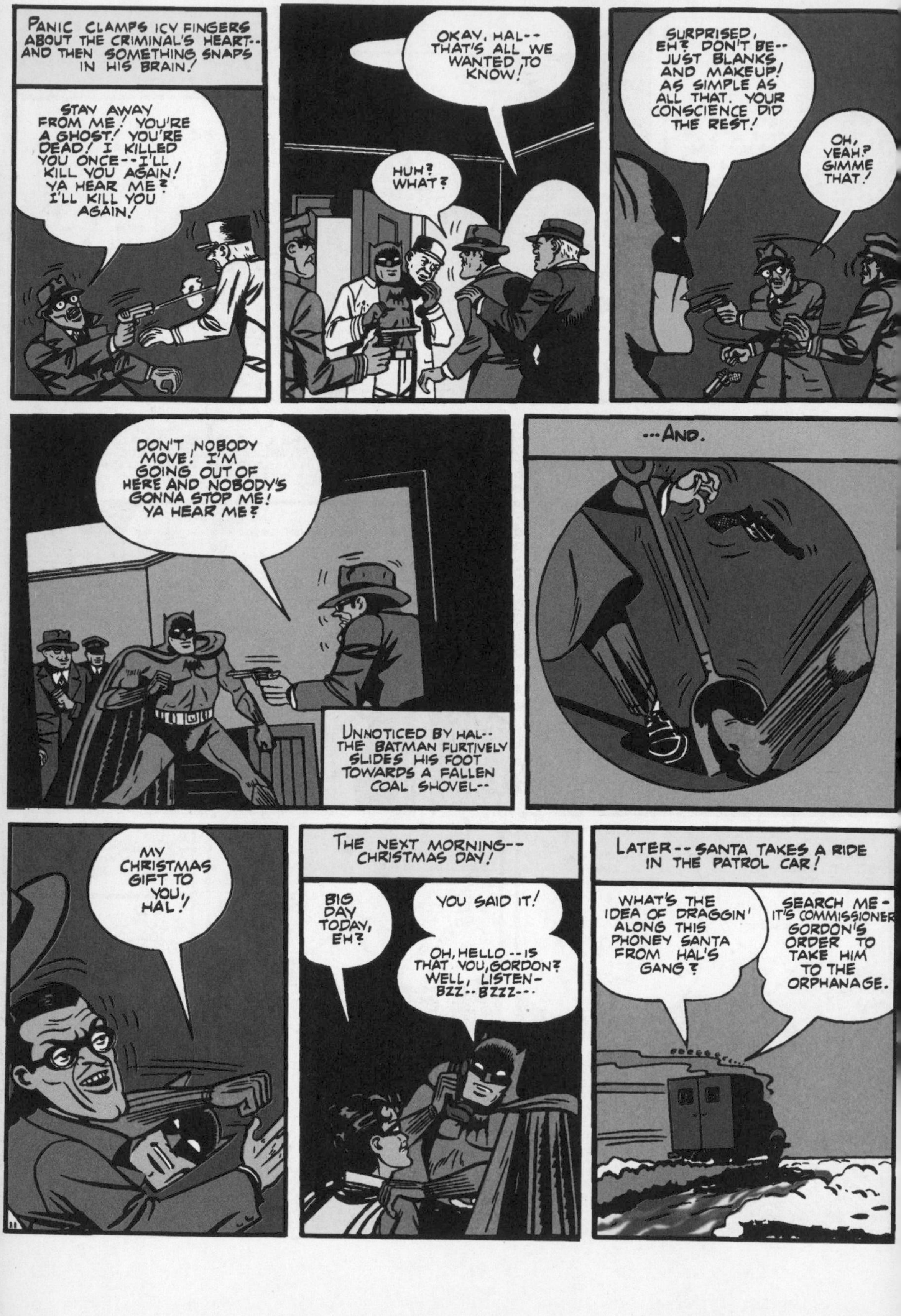
PANIC CLAMPS ICY FINGERS ABOUT THE CRIMINAL'S HEART-- AND THEN SOMETHING SNAPS IN HIS BRAIN!
STAY AWAY FROM ME! YOU'RE A GHOST! YOU'RE DEAD! I KILLED YOU ONCE--I'LL KILL YOU AGAIN! YA HEAR ME? I'LL KILL YOU AGAIN!
OKAY, HAL-- THAT'S ALL WE WANTED TO KNOW!
HUH? WHAT?
SURPRISED, EH? DON'T BE-- JUST BLANKS AND MAKEUP! AS SIMPLE AS ALL THAT. YOUR CONSCIENCE DID THE REST!
OH, YEAH? GIMME THAT!
DON'T NOBODY MOVE! I'M GOING OUT OF HERE AND NOBODY'S GONNA STOP ME! YA HEAR ME?
UNNOTICED BY HAL-- THE BATMAN FURTIVELY SLIDES HIS FOOT TOWARDS A FALLEN COAL SHOVEL--
---AND.
MY CHRISTMAS GIFT TO YOU, HAL!
THE NEXT MORNING-- CHRISTMAS DAY!
BIG DAY TODAY, EH?
YOU SAID IT!
OH, HELLO--IS THAT YOU, GORDON? WELL, LISTEN- BZZ--BZZZ---
LATER--SANTA TAKES A RIDE IN THE PATROL CAR!
WHAT'S THE IDEA OF DRAGGIN' ALONG THIS PHONEY SANTA FROM HAL'S GANG?
SEARCH ME- IT'S COMMISSIONER GORDON'S ORDER TO TAKE HIM TO THE ORPHANAGE.

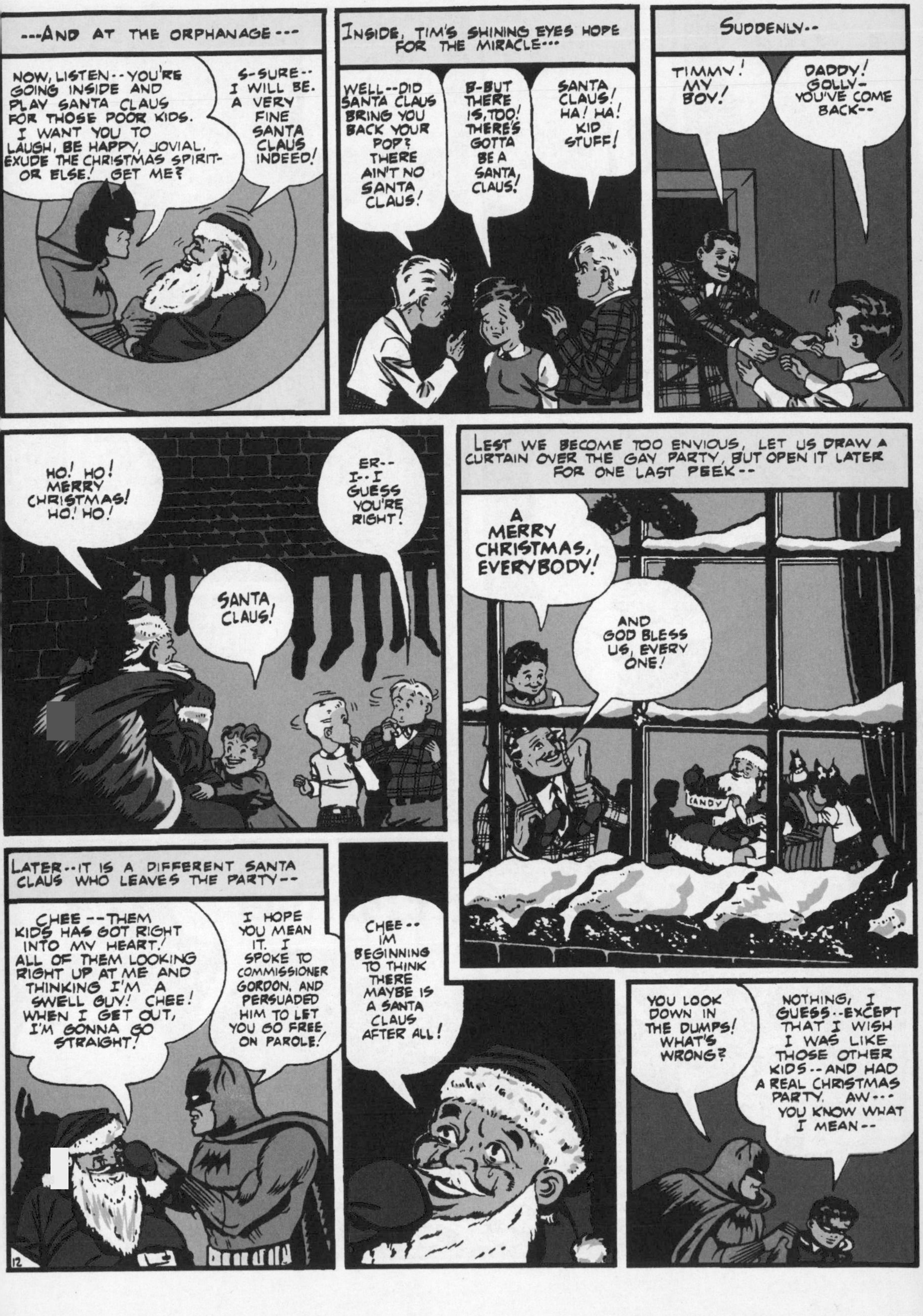
---AND AT THE ORPHANAGE---
NOW, LISTEN--YOU'RE GOING INSIDE AND PLAY SANTA CLAUS FOR THOSE POOR KIDS. I WANT YOU TO LAUGH, BE HAPPY, JOVIAL. EXUDE THE CHRISTMAS SPIRIT- OR ELSE! GET ME?
S-SURE-- I WILL BE. A VERY FINE SANTA CLAUS INDEED!
INSIDE, TIM'S SHINING EYES HOPE FOR THE MIRACLE...
WELL--DID SANTA CLAUS BRING YOU BACK YOUR POP? THERE AIN'T NO SANTA CLAUS!
B-BUT THERE IS, TOO! THERE'S GOTTA BE A SANTA CLAUS!
SANTA CLAUS! HA! HA! KID STUFF!
SUDDENLY--
TIMMY! MY BOY!
DADDY! GOLLY- YOU'VE COME BACK--
HO! HO! MERRY CHRISTMAS! HO! HO!
SANTA CLAUS!
ER-- I--I GUESS YOU'RE RIGHT!
LEST WE BECOME TOO ENVIOUS, LET US DRAW A CURTAIN OVER THE GAY PARTY, BUT OPEN IT LATER FOR ONE LAST PEEK--
A MERRY CHRISTMAS, EVERYBODY!
AND GOD BLESS US, EVERY ONE!
CANDY
LATER--IT IS A DIFFERENT SANTA CLAUS WHO LEAVES THE PARTY--
CHEE--THEM KIDS HAS GOT RIGHT INTO MY HEART! ALL OF THEM LOOKING RIGHT UP AT ME AND THINKING I'M A SWELL GUY! CHEE! WHEN I GET OUT, I'M GONNA GO STRAIGHT!
I HOPE YOU MEAN IT. I SPOKE TO COMMISSIONER GORDON, AND PERSUADED HIM TO LET YOU GO FREE ON PAROLE!
12
CHEE-- IM BEGINNING TO THINK THERE MAYBE IS A SANTA CLAUS AFTER ALL!
YOU LOOK DOWN IN THE DUMPS! WHAT'S WRONG?
NOTHING, I GUESS--EXCEPT THAT I WISH I WAS LIKE THOSE OTHER KIDS--AND HAD A REAL CHRISTMAS PARTY. AW--- YOU KNOW WHAT I MEAN--

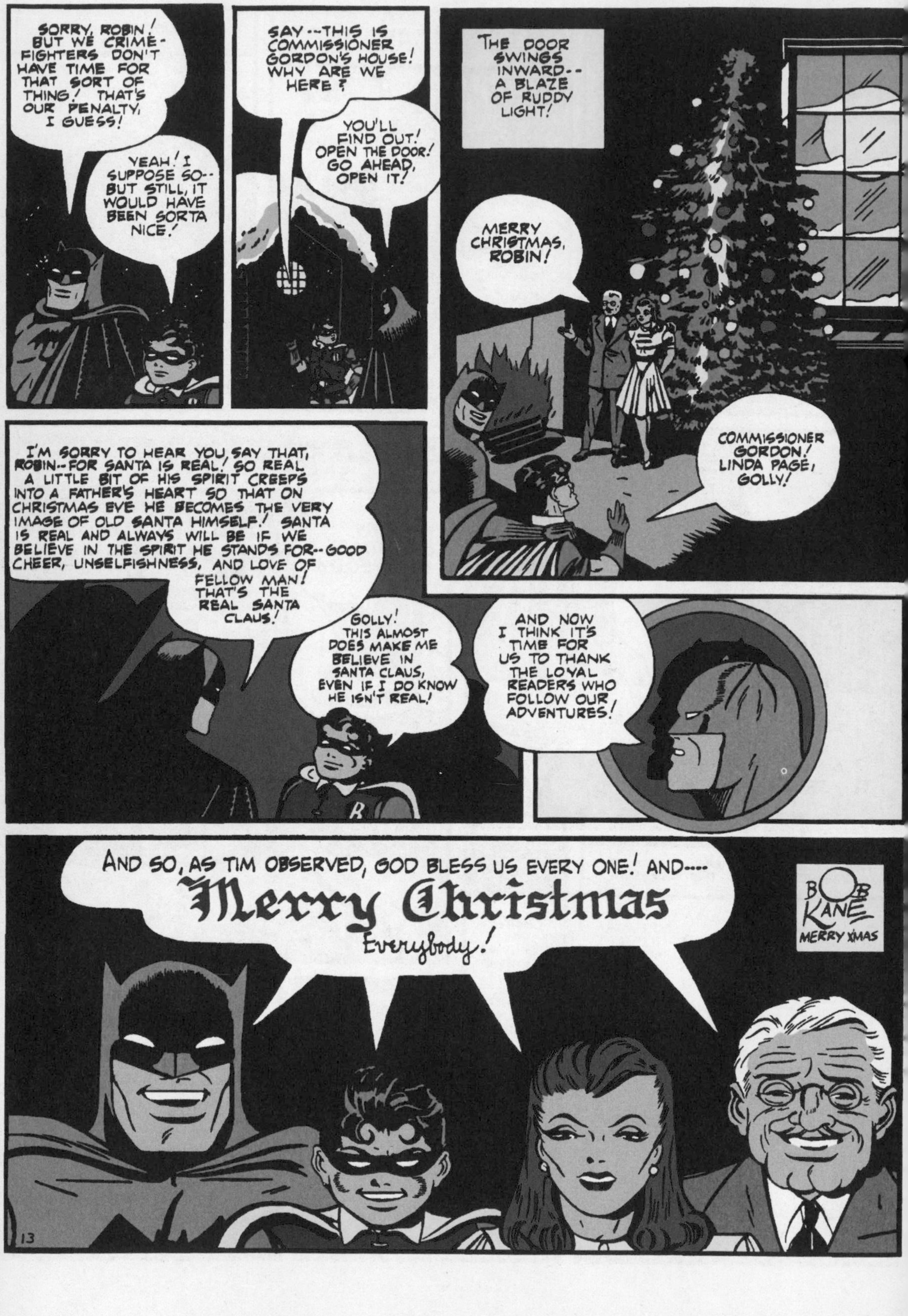

SORRY, ROBIN! BUT WE CRIME-FIGHTERS DON'T HAVE TIME FOR THAT SORT OF THING! THAT'S OUR PENALTY, I GUESS!
YEAH! I SUPPOSE SO--BUT STILL, IT WOULD HAVE BEEN SORTA NICE!
SAY--THIS IS COMMISSIONER GORDON'S HOUSE! WHY ARE WE HERE?
YOU'LL FIND OUT! OPEN THE DOOR! GO AHEAD, OPEN IT!
THE DOOR SWINGS INWARD--A BLAZE OF RUDDY LIGHT!
MERRY CHRISTMAS, ROBIN!
COMMISSIONER GORDON! LINDA PAGE, GOLLY!
I'M SORRY TO HEAR YOU SAY THAT, ROBIN--FOR SANTA IS REAL! SO REAL A LITTLE BIT OF HIS SPIRIT CREEPS INTO A FATHER'S HEART SO THAT ON CHRISTMAS EVE HE BECOMES THE VERY IMAGE OF OLD SANTA HIMSELF! SANTA IS REAL AND ALWAYS WILL BE IF WE BELIEVE IN THE SPIRIT HE STANDS FOR--GOOD CHEER, UNSELFISHNESS, AND LOVE OF FELLOW MAN! THAT'S THE REAL SANTA CLAUS!
GOLLY! THIS ALMOST DOES MAKE ME BELIEVE IN SANTA CLAUS, EVEN IF I DO KNOW HE ISN'T REAL!
AND NOW I THINK IT'S TIME FOR US TO THANK THE LOYAL READERS WHO FOLLOW OUR ADVENTURES!
AND SO, AS TIM OBSERVED, GOD BLESS US EVERY ONE! AND----
Merry Christmas
Everybody!
BOB KANE
MERRY XMAS
13

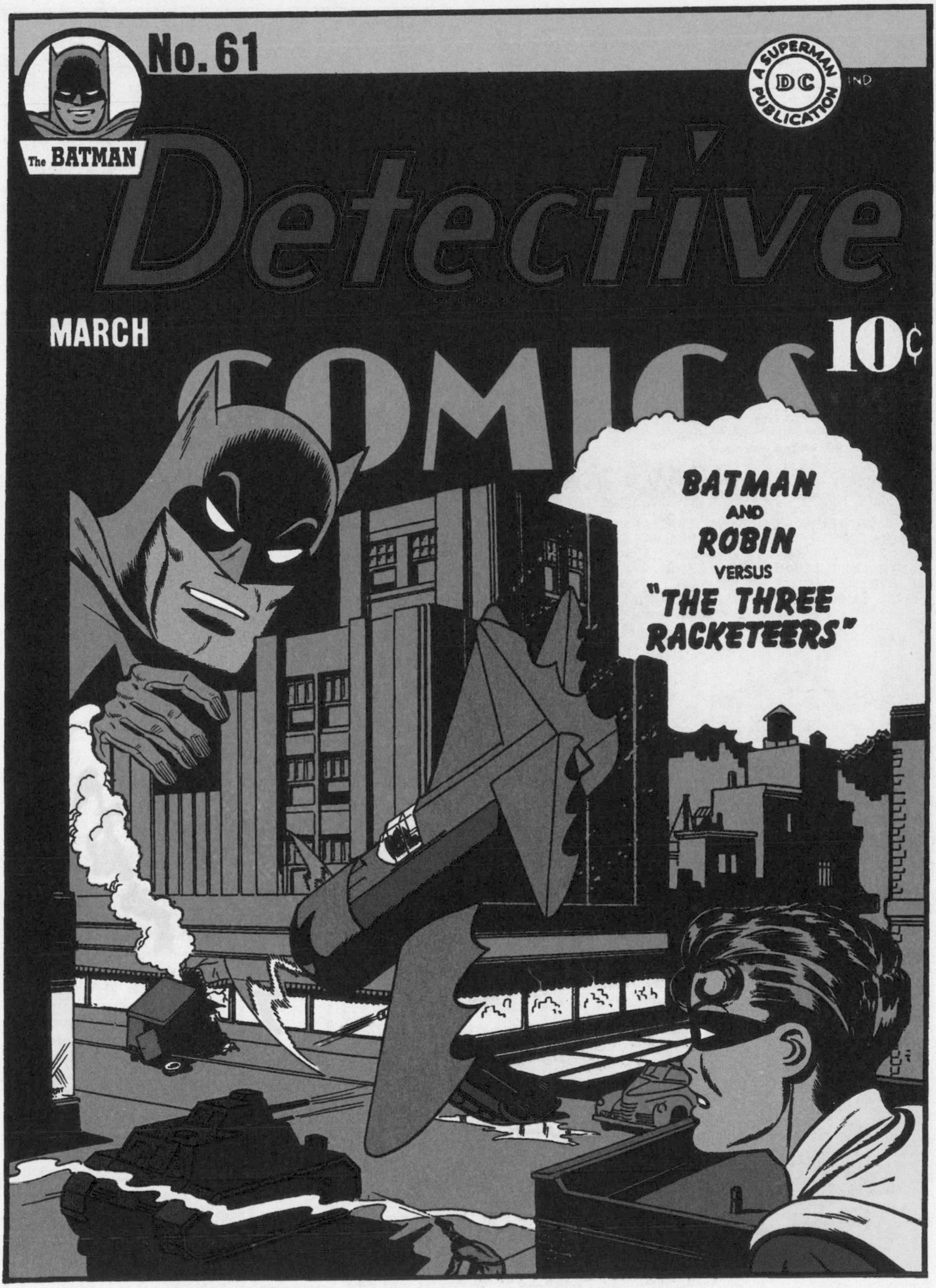
No. 61
The BATMAN
A SUPERMAN DC PUBLICATION
Detective
MARCH
10¢
COMICS
BATMAN AND ROBIN VERSUS "THE THREE RACKETEERS"

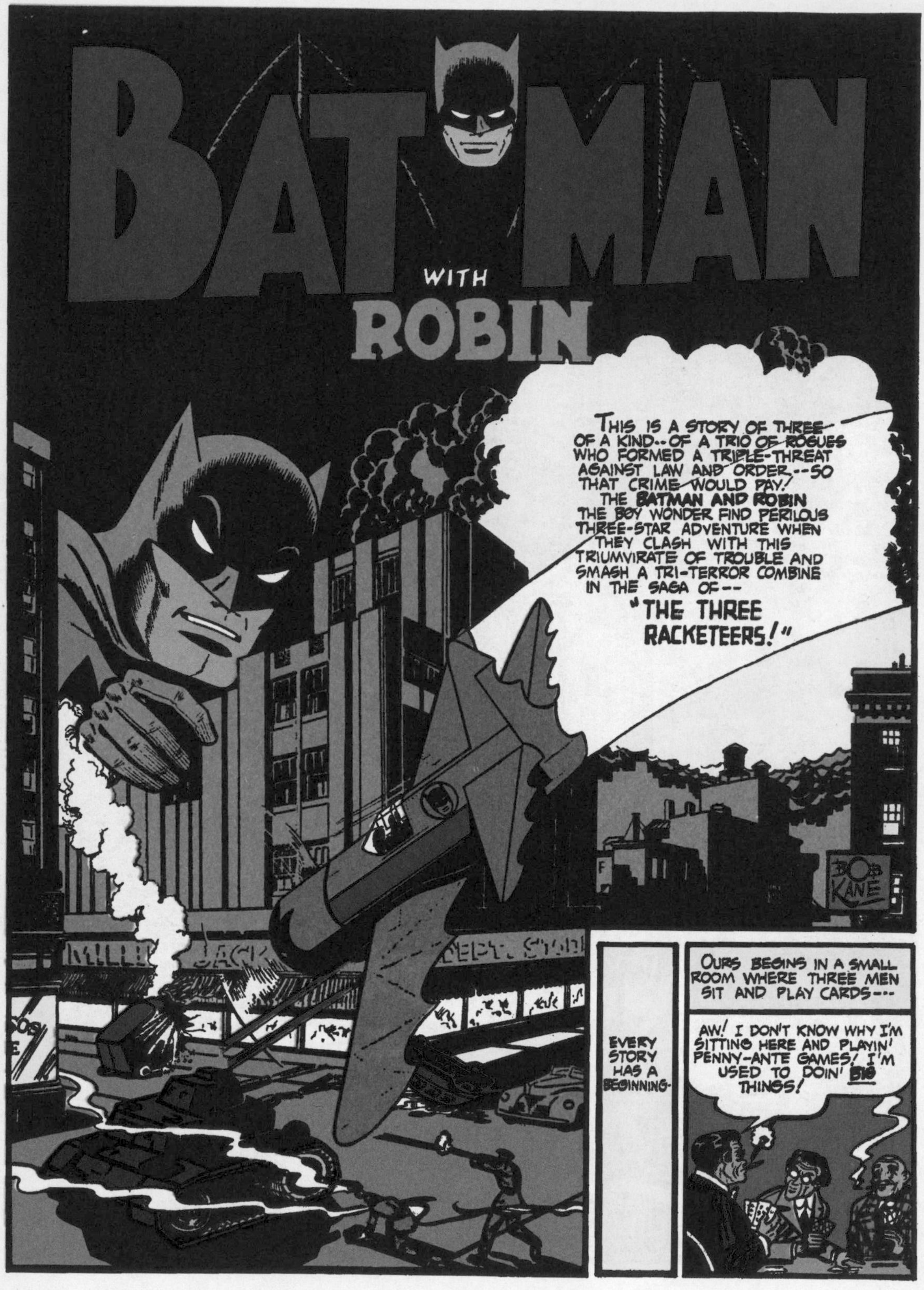
BATMAN
WITH
ROBIN
THIS IS A STORY OF THREE OF A KIND--OF A TRIO OF ROGUES WHO FORMED A TRIPLE-THREAT AGAINST LAW AND ORDER--SO THAT CRIME WOULD PAY! THE BATMAN AND ROBIN THE BOY WONDER FIND PERILOUS THREE-STAR ADVENTURE WHEN THEY CLASH WITH THIS TRIUMVIRATE OF TROUBLE AND SMASH A TRI-TERROR COMBINE IN THE SAGA OF--
"THE THREE RACKETEERS!"
BOB KANE
EVERY STORY HAS A BEGINNING-
OURS BEGINS IN A SMALL ROOM WHERE THREE MEN SIT AND PLAY CARDS---
AW! I DON'T KNOW WHY I'M SITTING HERE AND PLAYIN' PENNY-ANTE GAMES! I'M USED TO DOIN' BIG THINGS!

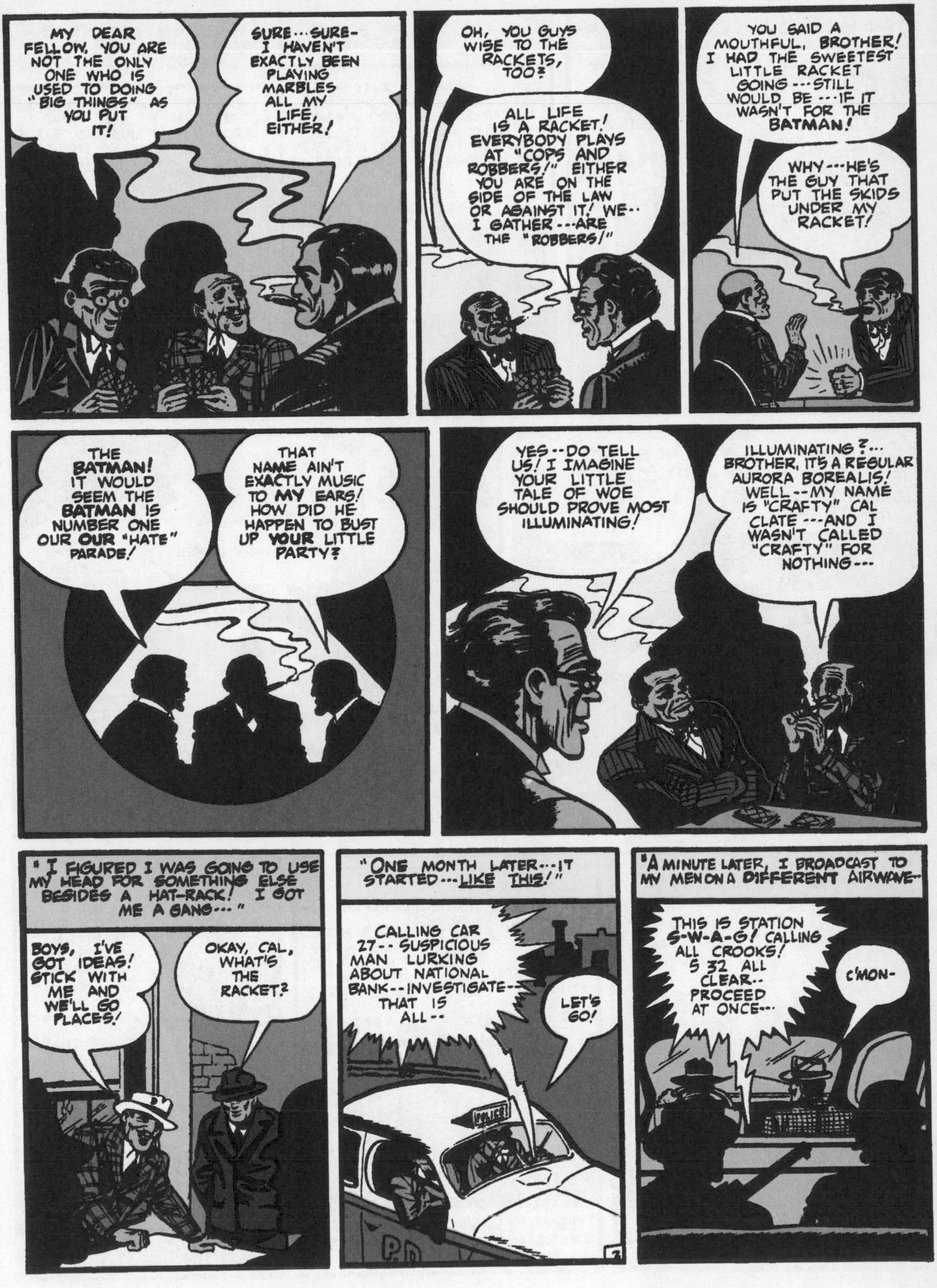
MY DEAR FELLOW, YOU ARE NOT THE ONLY ONE WHO IS USED TO DOING "BIG THINGS" AS YOU PUT IT!
SURE...SURE-- I HAVEN'T EXACTLY BEEN PLAYING MARBLES ALL MY LIFE, EITHER!
OH, YOU GUYS WISE TO THE RACKETS, TOO?
ALL LIFE IS A RACKET! EVERYBODY PLAYS AT "COPS AND ROBBERS!" EITHER YOU ARE ON THE SIDE OF THE LAW OR AGAINST IT! WE.. I GATHER---ARE THE "ROBBERS!"
YOU SAID A MOUTHFUL, BROTHER! I HAD THE SWEETEST LITTLE RACKET GOING---STILL WOULD BE---IF IT WASN'T FOR THE BATMAN!
WHY---HE'S THE GUY THAT PUT THE SKIDS UNDER MY RACKET!
THE BATMAN! IT WOULD SEEM THE BATMAN IS NUMBER ONE OUR OUR "HATE" PARADE!
THAT NAME AIN'T EXACTLY MUSIC TO MY EARS! HOW DID HE HAPPEN TO BUST UP YOUR LITTLE PARTY?
YES--DO TELL US! I IMAGINE YOUR LITTLE TALE OF WOE SHOULD PROVE MOST ILLUMINATING!
ILLUMINATING?... BROTHER, IT'S A REGULAR AURORA BOREALIS! WELL--MY NAME IS "CRAFTY" CAL CLATE---AND I WASN'T CALLED "CRAFTY" FOR NOTHING---
"I FIGURED I WAS GOING TO USE MY HEAD FOR SOMETHING ELSE BESIDES A HAT-RACK! I GOT ME A GANG..."
BOYS, I'VE GOT IDEAS! STICK WITH ME AND WE'LL GO PLACES!
OKAY, CAL, WHAT'S THE RACKET?
"ONE MONTH LATER...IT STARTED---LIKE THIS!"
CALLING CAR 27-- SUSPICIOUS MAN LURKING ABOUT NATIONAL BANK--INVESTIGATE-- THAT IS ALL--
LET'S GO!
POLICE
P.D.
"A MINUTE LATER, I BROADCAST TO MY MEN ON A DIFFERENT AIRWAVE--
THIS IS STATION S-W-A-G! CALLING ALL CROOKS! S 32 ALL CLEAR-- PROCEED AT ONCE---
C'MON-

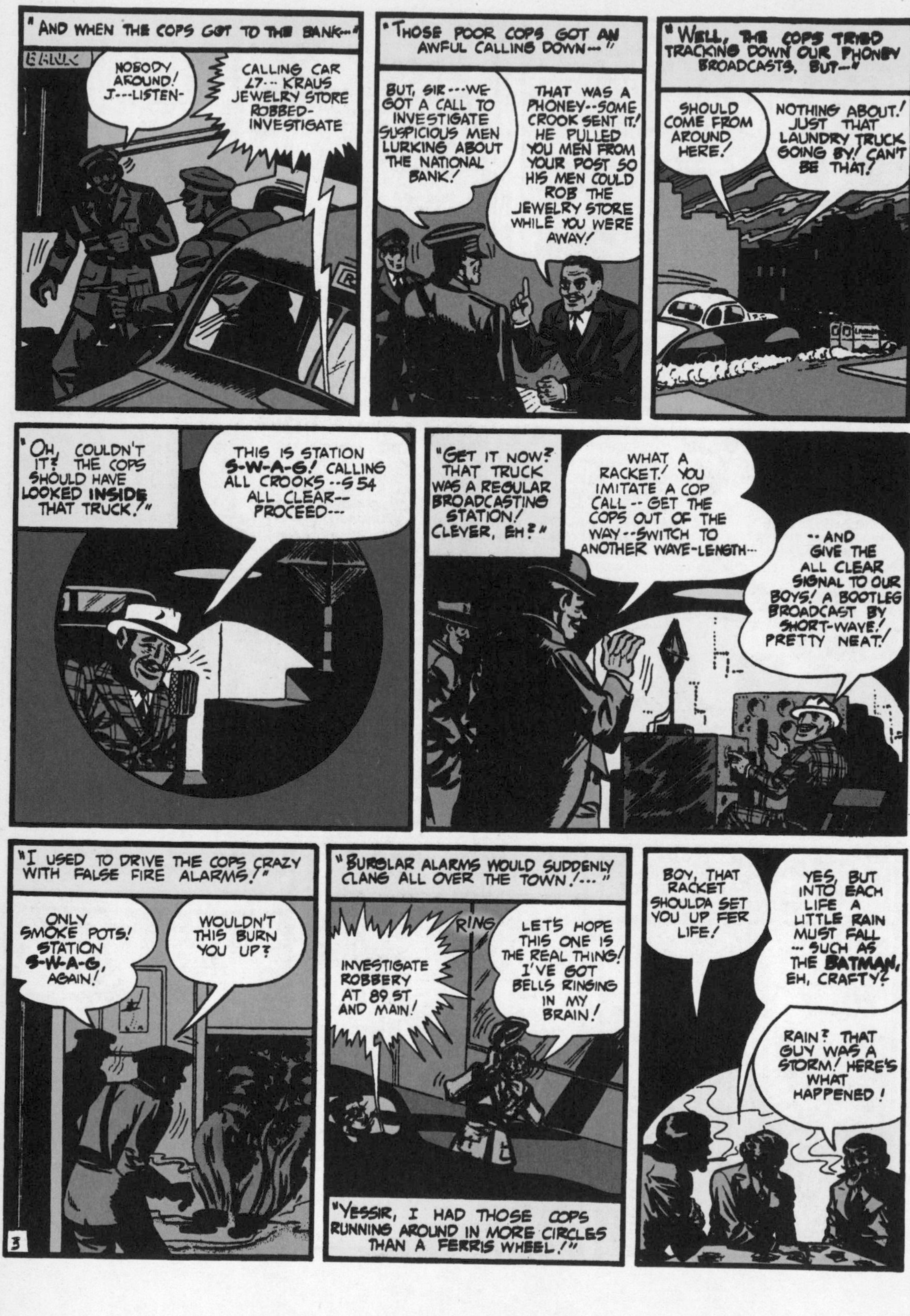
"AND WHEN THE COPS GOT TO THE BANK---"
BANK
NOBODY AROUND! J---LISTEN-
CALLING CAR L7--- KRAUS JEWELRY STORE ROBBED- INVESTIGATE
"THOSE POOR COPS GOT AN AWFUL CALLING DOWN---"
BUT, SIR---WE GOT A CALL TO INVESTIGATE SUSPICIOUS MEN LURKING ABOUT THE NATIONAL BANK!
THAT WAS A PHONEY--SOME CROOK SENT IT! HE PULLED YOU MEN FROM YOUR POST SO HIS MEN COULD ROB THE JEWELRY STORE WHILE YOU WERE AWAY!
"WELL, THE COPS TRIED TRACKING DOWN OUR PHONEY BROADCASTS, BUT---"
SHOULD COME FROM AROUND HERE!
NOTHING ABOUT! JUST THAT LAUNDRY TRUCK GOING BY! CAN'T BE THAT!
"OH, COULDN'T IT? THE COPS SHOULD HAVE LOOKED INSIDE THAT TRUCK!"
THIS IS STATION S-W-A-G! CALLING ALL CROOKS--S 54 ALL CLEAR-- PROCEED---
"GET IT NOW? THAT TRUCK WAS A REGULAR BROADCASTING STATION! CLEVER, EH?"
WHAT A RACKET! YOU IMITATE A COP CALL--GET THE COPS OUT OF THE WAY--SWITCH TO ANOTHER WAVE-LENGTH---
--AND GIVE THE ALL CLEAR SIGNAL TO OUR BOYS! A BOOTLEG BROADCAST BY SHORT-WAVE! PRETTY NEAT!
"I USED TO DRIVE THE COPS CRAZY WITH FALSE FIRE ALARMS!"
ONLY SMOKE POTS! STATION S-W-A-G, AGAIN!
WOULDN'T THIS BURN YOU UP?
3
"BURGLAR ALARMS WOULD SUDDENLY CLANG ALL OVER THE TOWN!---"
RING
INVESTIGATE ROBBERY AT 89 ST AND MAIN!
LET'S HOPE THIS ONE IS THE REAL THING! I'VE GOT BELLS RINGING IN MY BRAIN!
"YESSIR, I HAD THOSE COPS RUNNING AROUND IN MORE CIRCLES THAN A FERRIS WHEEL!"
BOY, THAT RACKET SHOULDA SET YOU UP FER LIFE!
YES, BUT INTO EACH LIFE A LITTLE RAIN MUST FALL --- SUCH AS THE BATMAN, EH, CRAFTY?
RAIN? THAT GUY WAS A STORM! HERE'S WHAT HAPPENED!

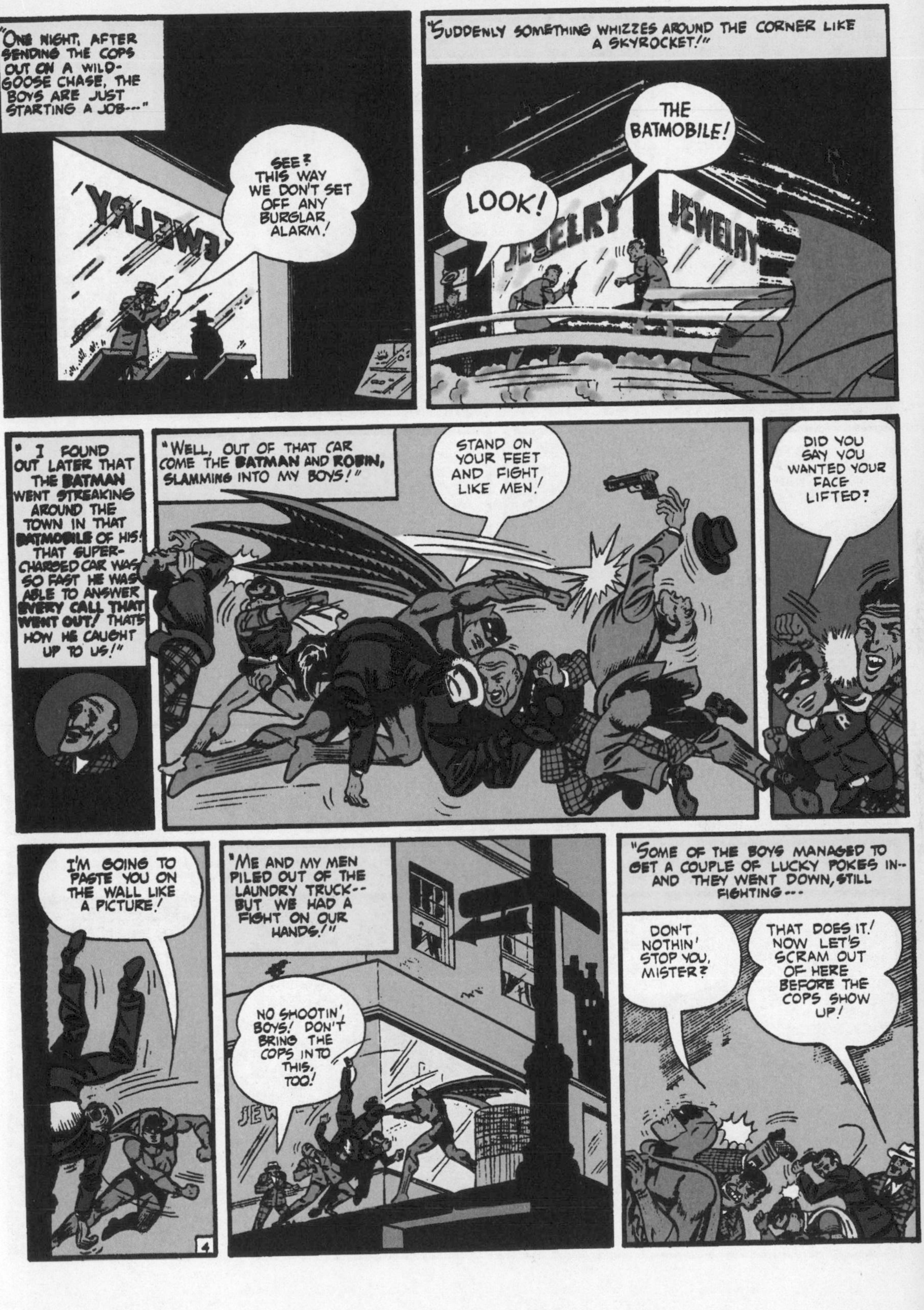
"ONE NIGHT, AFTER SENDING THE COPS OUT ON A WILD-GOOSE CHASE, THE BOYS ARE JUST STARTING A JOB---"
SEE? THIS WAY WE DON'T SET OFF ANY BURGLAR ALARM!
"SUDDENLY SOMETHING WHIZZES AROUND THE CORNER LIKE A SKYROCKET!"
LOOK!
THE BATMOBILE!
JEWELRY
" I FOUND OUT LATER THAT THE BATMAN WENT STREAKING AROUND THE TOWN IN THAT BATMOBILE OF HIS! THAT SUPER-CHARGED CAR WAS SO FAST HE WAS ABLE TO ANSWER EVERY CALL THAT WENT OUT! THAT'S HOW HE CAUGHT UP TO US!"
"WELL, OUT OF THAT CAR COME THE BATMAN AND ROBIN, SLAMMING INTO MY BOYS!"
STAND ON YOUR FEET AND FIGHT LIKE MEN!
DID YOU SAY YOU WANTED YOUR FACE LIFTED?
I'M GOING TO PASTE YOU ON THE WALL LIKE A PICTURE!
"ME AND MY MEN PILED OUT OF THE LAUNDRY TRUCK-- BUT WE HAD A FIGHT ON OUR HANDS!"
NO SHOOTIN', BOYS! DON'T BRING THE COPS INTO THIS, TOO!
"SOME OF THE BOYS MANAGED TO GET A COUPLE OF LUCKY POKES IN-- AND THEY WENT DOWN, STILL FIGHTING---"
DON'T NOTHIN' STOP YOU, MISTER?
THAT DOES IT! NOW LET'S SCRAM OUT OF HERE BEFORE THE COPS SHOW UP!

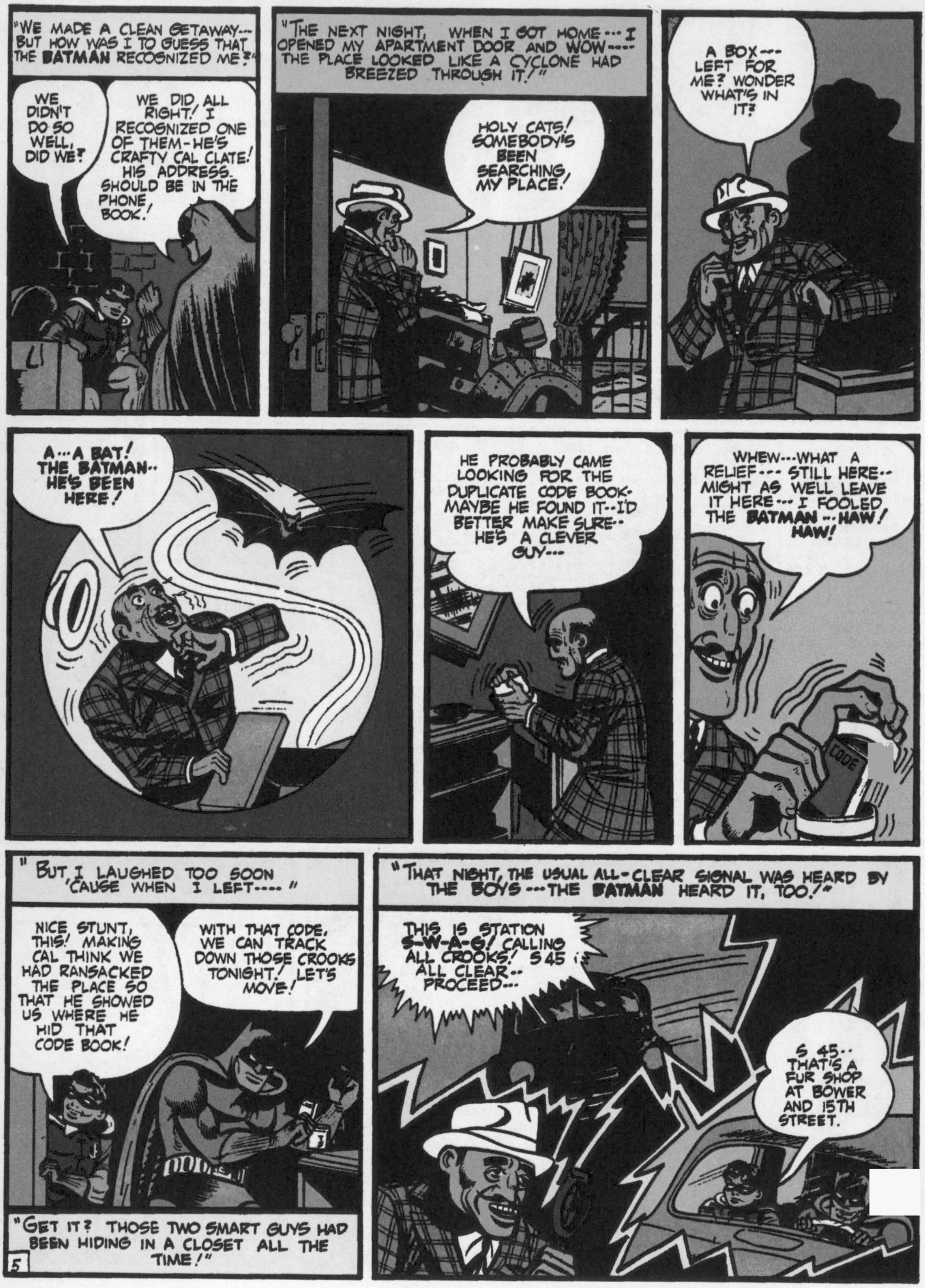
"WE MADE A CLEAN GETAWAY--- BUT HOW WAS I TO GUESS THAT THE BATMAN RECOGNIZED ME?"
WE DIDN'T DO SO WELL, DID WE?
WE DID ALL RIGHT! I RECOGNIZED ONE OF THEM-HE'S CRAFTY CAL CLATE! HIS ADDRESS SHOULD BE IN THE PHONE BOOK!
"THE NEXT NIGHT, WHEN I GOT HOME --- I OPENED MY APARTMENT DOOR AND WOW---- THE PLACE LOOKED LIKE A CYCLONE HAD BREEZED THROUGH IT!"
HOLY CATS! SOMEBODY'S BEEN SEARCHING MY PLACE!
A BOX--- LEFT FOR ME? WONDER WHAT'S IN IT?
A...A BAT! THE BATMAN.. HE'S BEEN HERE!
HE PROBABLY CAME LOOKING FOR THE DUPLICATE CODE BOOK. MAYBE HE FOUND IT--I'D BETTER MAKE SURE-- HE'S A CLEVER GUY---
WHEW---WHAT A RELIEF--- STILL HERE-- MIGHT AS WELL LEAVE IT HERE--- I FOOLED THE BATMAN ---HAW! HAW!
CODE
" BUT I LAUGHED TOO SOON 'CAUSE WHEN I LEFT---- "
NICE STUNT, THIS! MAKING CAL THINK WE HAD RANSACKED THE PLACE SO THAT HE SHOWED US WHERE HE HID THAT CODE BOOK!
WITH THAT CODE, WE CAN TRACK DOWN THOSE CROOKS TONIGHT! LET'S MOVE!
"GET IT? THOSE TWO SMART GUYS HAD BEEN HIDING IN A CLOSET ALL THE TIME!"
5
"THAT NIGHT, THE USUAL ALL-CLEAR SIGNAL WAS HEARD BY THE BOYS---THE BATMAN HEARD IT, TOO!"
THIS IS STATION S-W-A-G! CALLING ALL CROOKS! S 45 ; ALL CLEAR-- PROCEED---
S 45.. THAT'S A FUR SHOP AT BOWER AND 15TH STREET.

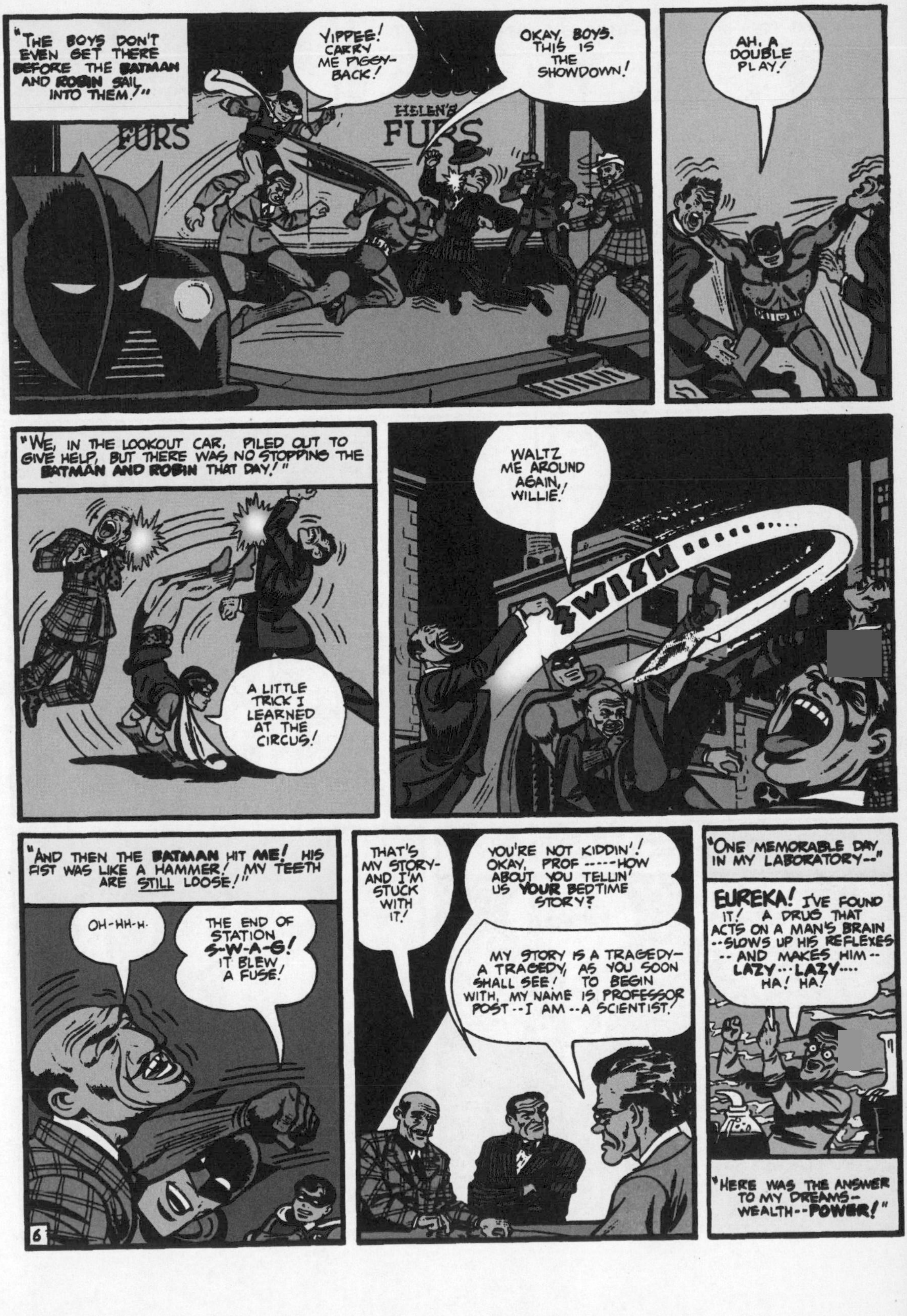
"THE BOYS DON'T EVEN GET THERE BEFORE THE BATMAN AND ROBIN SAIL INTO THEM!"
YIPPEE! CARRY ME PIGGY-BACK!
OKAY, BOYS. THIS IS THE SHOWDOWN!
FURS
HELEN'S FURS
AH, A DOUBLE PLAY!
"WE, IN THE LOOKOUT CAR, PILED OUT TO GIVE HELP, BUT THERE WAS NO STOPPING THE BATMAN AND ROBIN THAT DAY!"
A LITTLE TRICK I LEARNED AT THE CIRCUS!
WALTZ ME AROUND AGAIN, WILLIE!
SWISH
"AND THEN THE BATMAN HIT ME! HIS FIST WAS LIKE A HAMMER! MY TEETH ARE STILL LOOSE!"
OH-HH-H.
THE END OF STATION S-W-A-G! IT BLEW A FUSE!
6
THAT'S MY STORY-AND I'M STUCK WITH IT!
YOU'RE NOT KIDDIN'! OKAY, PROF -----HOW ABOUT YOU TELLIN' US YOUR BEDTIME STORY?
MY STORY IS A TRAGEDY-A TRAGEDY, AS YOU SOON SHALL SEE! TO BEGIN WITH, MY NAME IS PROFESSOR POST--I AM--A SCIENTIST!
"ONE MEMORABLE DAY IN MY LABORATORY--"
EUREKA! I'VE FOUND IT! A DRUG THAT ACTS ON A MAN'S BRAIN --SLOWS UP HIS REFLEXES --AND MAKES HIM--LAZY---LAZY---- HA! HA!
"HERE WAS THE ANSWER TO MY DREAMS-WEALTH--POWER!"

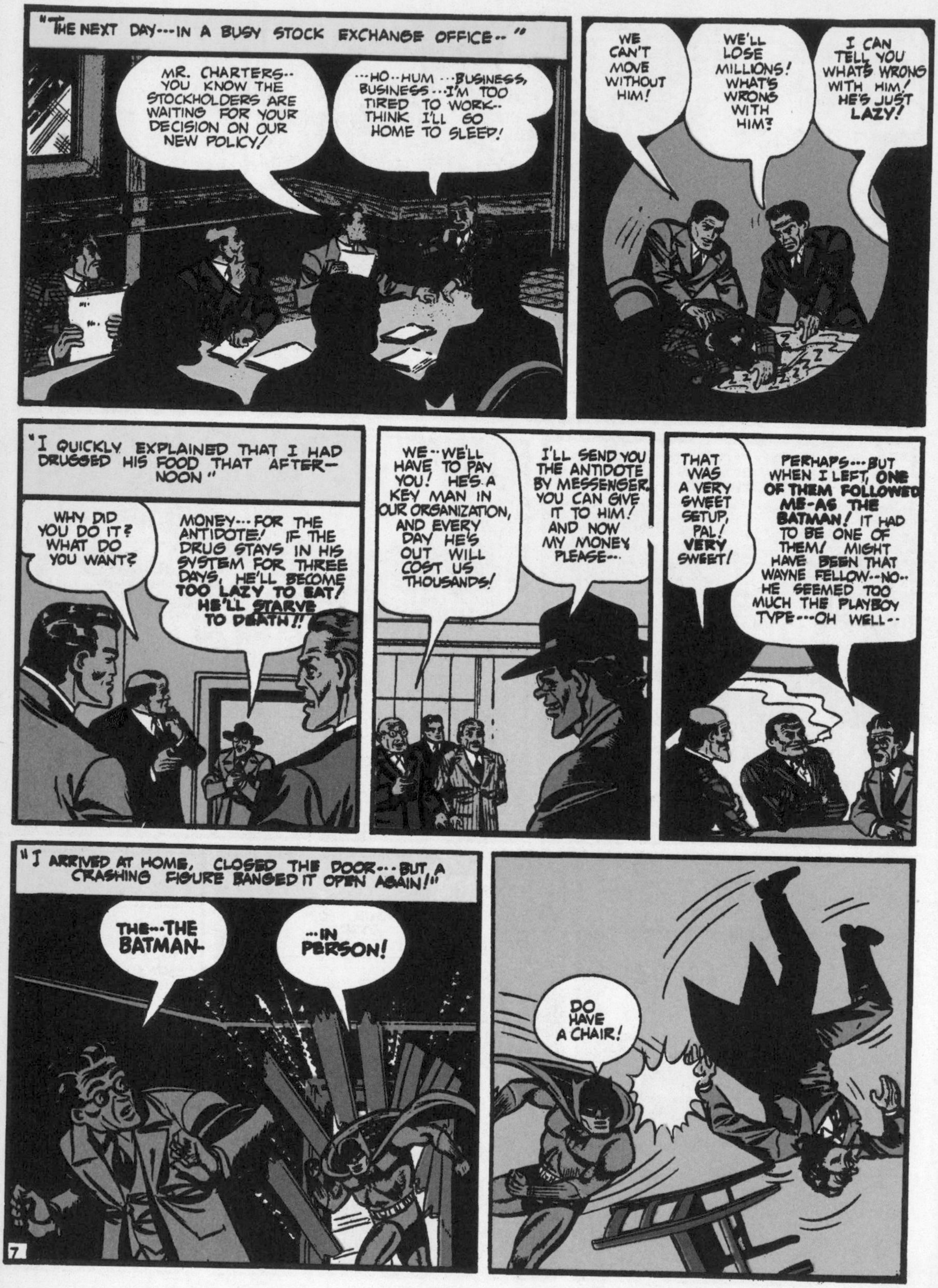
"THE NEXT DAY---IN A BUSY STOCK EXCHANGE OFFICE--"
MR. CHARTERS-- YOU KNOW THE STOCKHOLDERS ARE WAITING FOR YOUR DECISION ON OUR NEW POLICY!
--HO--HUM---BUSINESS, BUSINESS---I'M TOO TIRED TO WORK-- THINK I'LL GO HOME TO SLEEP!
WE CAN'T MOVE WITHOUT HIM!
WE'LL LOSE MILLIONS! WHAT'S WRONG WITH HIM?
I CAN TELL YOU WHAT'S WRONG WITH HIM! HE'S JUST LAZY!
"I QUICKLY EXPLAINED THAT I HAD DRUGGED HIS FOOD THAT AFTER-NOON"
WHY DID YOU DO IT? WHAT DO YOU WANT?
MONEY---FOR THE ANTIDOTE! IF THE DRUG STAYS IN HIS SYSTEM FOR THREE DAYS, HE'LL BECOME TOO LAZY TO EAT! HE'LL STARVE TO DEATH!!
WE--WE'LL HAVE TO PAY YOU! HE'S A KEY MAN IN OUR ORGANIZATION, AND EVERY DAY HE'S OUT WILL COST US THOUSANDS!
I'LL SEND YOU THE ANTIDOTE BY MESSENGER. YOU CAN GIVE IT TO HIM! AND NOW MY MONEY, PLEASE--.
THAT WAS A VERY SWEET SETUP, PAL! VERY SWEET!
PERHAPS---BUT WHEN I LEFT, ONE OF THEM FOLLOWED ME-AS THE BATMAN! IT HAD TO BE ONE OF THEM! MIGHT HAVE BEEN THAT WAYNE FELLOW--NO-- HE SEEMED TOO MUCH THE PLAYBOY TYPE---OH WELL--
"I ARRIVED AT HOME, CLOSED THE DOOR---BUT A CRASHING FIGURE BANGED IT OPEN AGAIN!"
THE---THE BATMAN-
---IN PERSON!
7
DO HAVE A CHAIR!

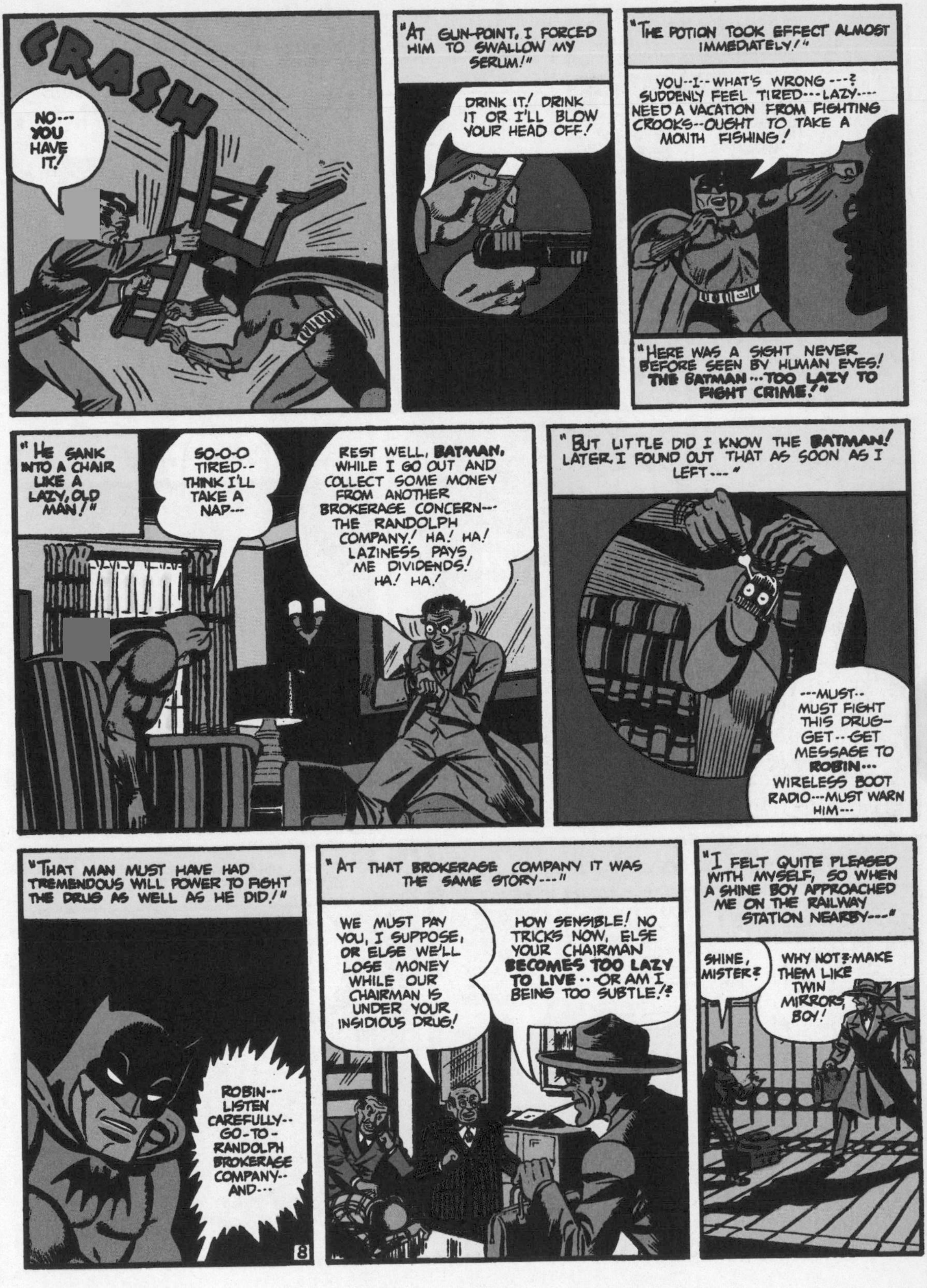
CRASH
NO--- YOU HAVE IT!
"AT GUN-POINT, I FORCED HIM TO SWALLOW MY SERUM!"
DRINK IT! DRINK IT OR I'LL BLOW YOUR HEAD OFF!
"THE POTION TOOK EFFECT ALMOST IMMEDIATELY!"
YOU--I--WHAT'S WRONG ---? SUDDENLY FEEL TIRED---LAZY---- NEED A VACATION FROM FIGHTING CROOKS--OUGHT TO TAKE A MONTH FISHING!
"HERE WAS A SIGHT NEVER BEFORE SEEN BY HUMAN EYES! THE BATMAN...TOO LAZY TO FIGHT CRIME!"
"HE SANK INTO A CHAIR LIKE A LAZY, OLD MAN!"
SO-O-O TIRED-- THINK I'LL TAKE A NAP---
REST WELL, BATMAN, WHILE I GO OUT AND COLLECT SOME MONEY FROM ANOTHER BROKERAGE CONCERN--- THE RANDOLPH COMPANY! HA! HA! LAZINESS PAYS ME DIVIDENDS! HA! HA!
"BUT LITTLE DID I KNOW THE BATMAN! LATER, I FOUND OUT THAT AS SOON AS I LEFT---"
---MUST-- MUST FIGHT THIS DRUG-- GET---GET MESSAGE TO ROBIN--- WIRELESS BOOT RADIO---MUST WARN HIM---
"THAT MAN MUST HAVE HAD TREMENDOUS WILL POWER TO FIGHT THE DRUG AS WELL AS HE DID!"
ROBIN--- LISTEN CAREFULLY-- GO-TO- RANDOLPH BROKERAGE COMPANY-- AND---
8
"AT THAT BROKERAGE COMPANY IT WAS THE SAME STORY---"
WE MUST PAY YOU, I SUPPOSE, OR ELSE WE'LL LOSE MONEY WHILE OUR CHAIRMAN IS UNDER YOUR INSIDIOUS DRUG!
HOW SENSIBLE! NO TRICKS NOW, ELSE YOUR CHAIRMAN BECOMES TOO LAZY TO LIVE---OR AM I BEING TOO SUBTLE!?
"I FELT QUITE PLEASED WITH MYSELF, SO WHEN A SHINE BOY APPROACHED ME ON THE RAILWAY STATION NEARBY---"
SHINE, MISTER?
WHY NOT?-MAKE THEM LIKE TWIN MIRRORS, BOY!

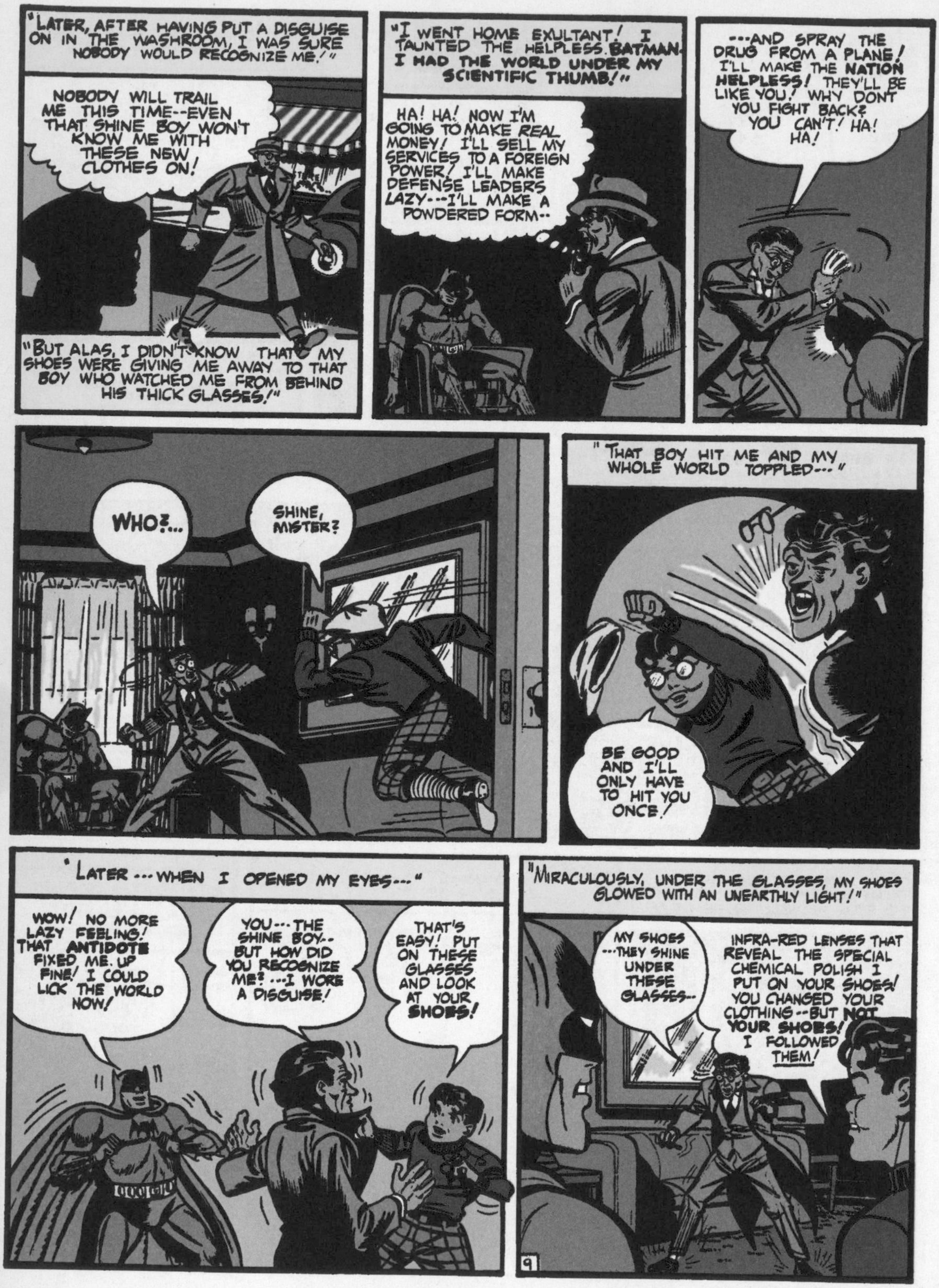
"LATER, AFTER HAVING PUT A DISGUISE ON IN THE WASHROOM, I WAS SURE NOBODY WOULD RECOGNIZE ME!"
NOBODY WILL TRAIL ME THIS TIME--EVEN THAT SHINE BOY WON'T KNOW ME WITH THESE NEW CLOTHES ON!
"BUT ALAS, I DIDN'T KNOW THAT MY SHOES WERE GIVING ME AWAY TO THAT BOY WHO WATCHED ME FROM BEHIND HIS THICK GLASSES!"
"I WENT HOME EXULTANT! I TAUNTED THE HELPLESS BATMAN. I HAD THE WORLD UNDER MY SCIENTIFIC THUMB!"
HA! HA! NOW I'M GOING TO MAKE REAL MONEY! I'LL SELL MY SERVICES TO A FOREIGN POWER! I'LL MAKE DEFENSE LEADERS LAZY---I'LL MAKE A POWDERED FORM--
---AND SPRAY THE DRUG FROM A PLANE! I'LL MAKE THE NATION HELPLESS! THEY'LL BE LIKE YOU! WHY DON'T YOU FIGHT BACK? YOU CAN'T! HA! HA!
WHO?...
SHINE, MISTER?
"THAT BOY HIT ME AND MY WHOLE WORLD TOPPLED---"
BE GOOD AND I'LL ONLY HAVE TO HIT YOU ONCE!
"LATER --- WHEN I OPENED MY EYES---"
WOW! NO MORE LAZY FEELING! THAT ANTIDOTE FIXED ME UP FINE! I COULD LICK THE WORLD NOW!
YOU---THE SHINE BOY--BUT HOW DID YOU RECOGNIZE ME? ---I WORE A DISGUISE!
THAT'S EASY! PUT ON THESE GLASSES AND LOOK AT YOUR SHOES!
"MIRACULOUSLY, UNDER THE GLASSES, MY SHOES GLOWED WITH AN UNEARTHLY LIGHT!"
MY SHOES ---THEY SHINE UNDER THESE GLASSES--
INFRA-RED LENSES THAT REVEAL THE SPECIAL CHEMICAL POLISH I PUT ON YOUR SHOES! YOU CHANGED YOUR CLOTHING--BUT NOT YOUR SHOES! I FOLLOWED THEM!
9

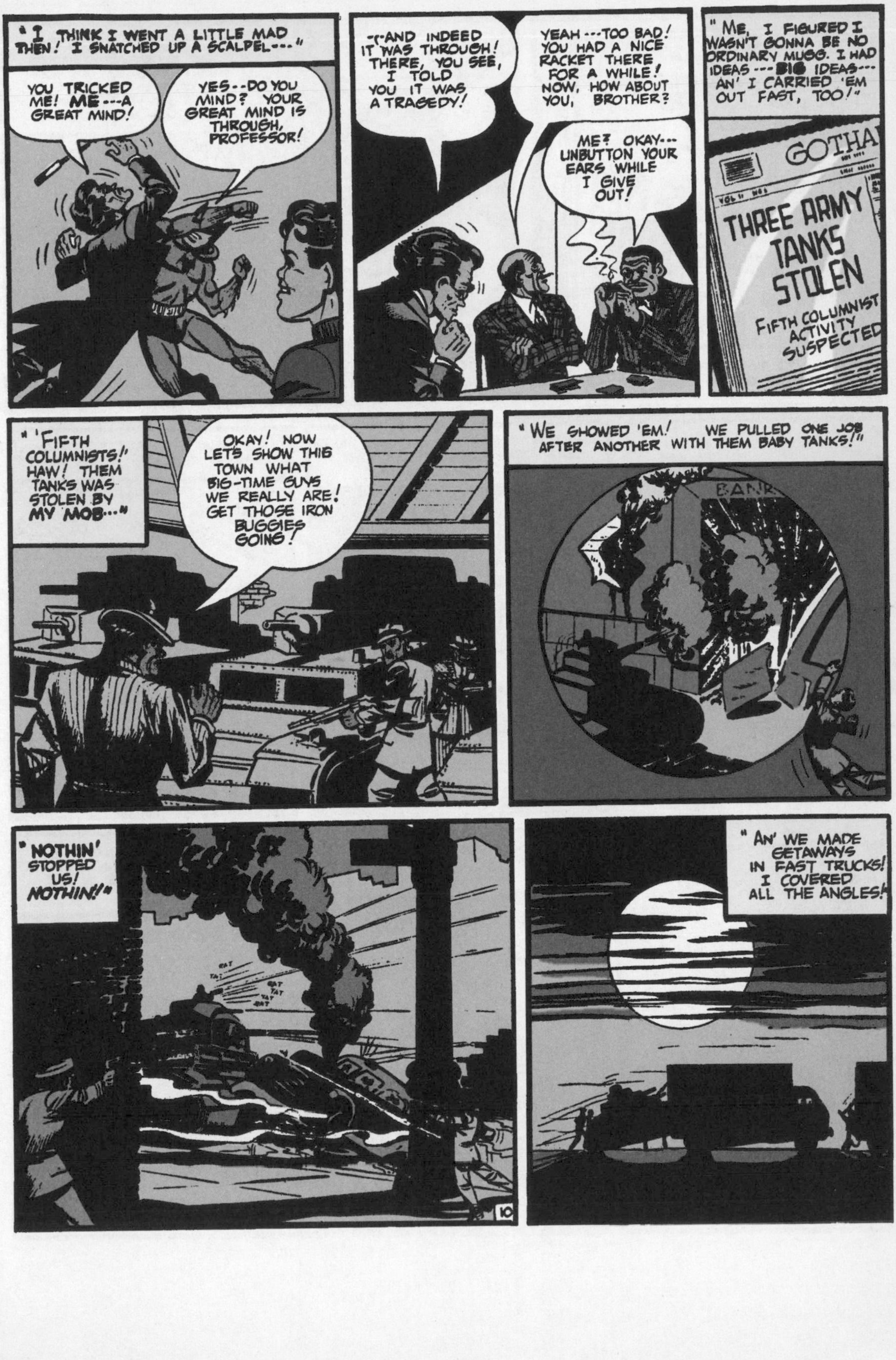
"I THINK I WENT A LITTLE MAD THEN! I SNATCHED UP A SCALPEL---"
YOU TRICKED ME! ME---A GREAT MIND!
YES--DO YOU MIND? YOUR GREAT MIND IS THROUGH, PROFESSOR!
--AND INDEED IT WAS THROUGH! THERE, YOU SEE, I TOLD YOU IT WAS A TRAGEDY!
YEAH---TOO BAD! YOU HAD A NICE RACKET THERE FOR A WHILE! NOW, HOW ABOUT YOU, BROTHER?
ME? OKAY--- UNBUTTON YOUR EARS WHILE I GIVE OUT!
"ME, I FIGURED I WASN'T GONNA BE NO ORDINARY MUGG. I HAD IDEAS---BIG IDEAS--- AN' I CARRIED 'EM OUT FAST, TOO!"
GOTHA
THREE ARMY TANKS STOLEN
FIFTH COLUMNIST ACTIVITY SUSPECTED
"'FIFTH COLUMNISTS!' HAW! THEM TANKS WAS STOLEN BY MY MOB..."
OKAY! NOW LET'S SHOW THIS TOWN WHAT BIG-TIME GUYS WE REALLY ARE! GET THOSE IRON BUGGIES GOING!
"WE SHOWED 'EM! WE PULLED ONE JOB AFTER ANOTHER WITH THEM BABY TANKS!"
BANK
"NOTHIN' STOPPED US! NOTHIN'!"
10
"AN' WE MADE GETAWAYS IN FAST TRUCKS! I COVERED ALL THE ANGLES!"

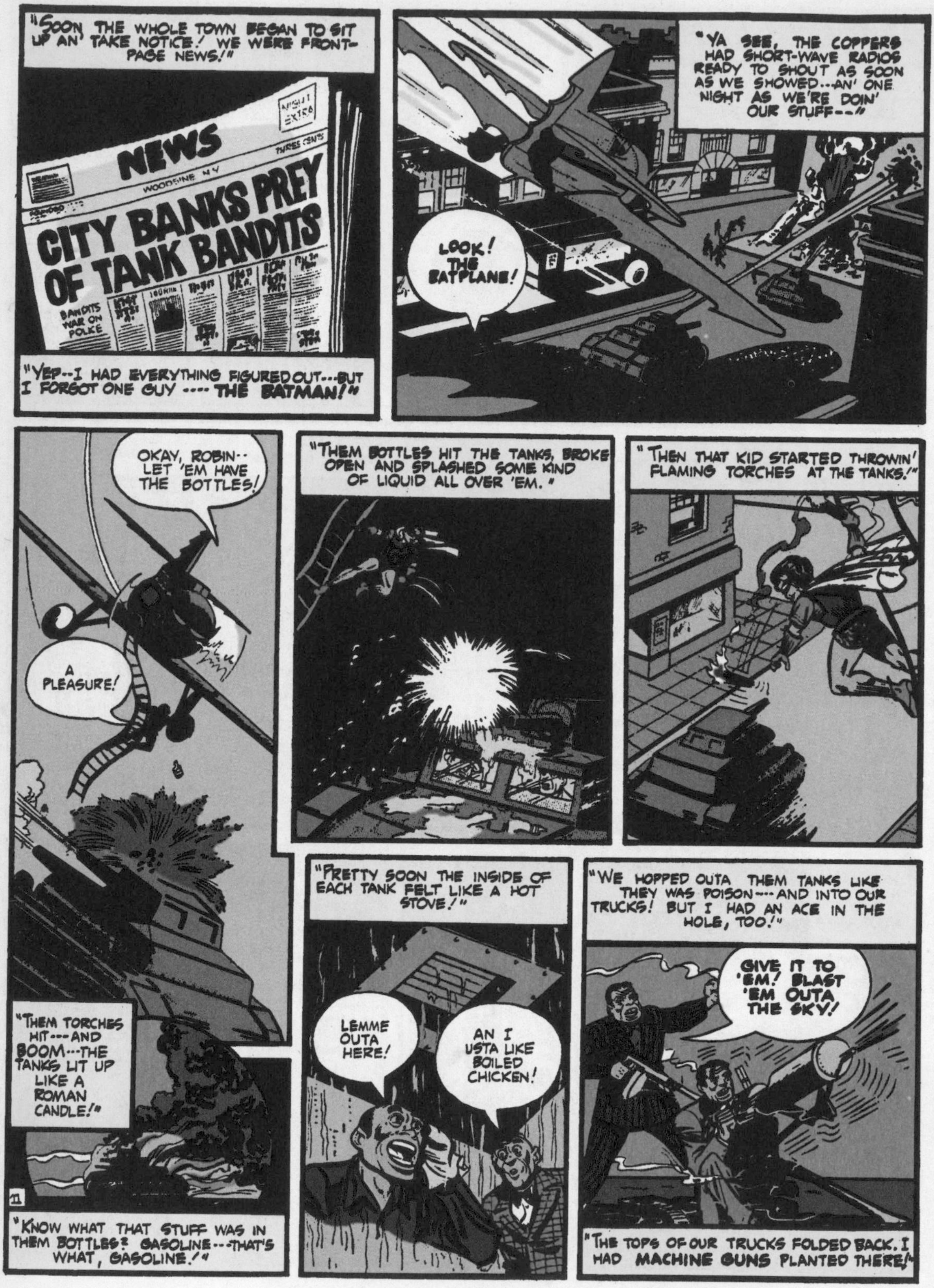
"SOON THE WHOLE TOWN BEGAN TO SIT UP AN' TAKE NOTICE! WE WERE FRONT-PAGE NEWS!"
NEWS
NIGHT EXTRA
THREE CENTS
CITY BANKS PREY OF TANK BANDITS
BANDITS WAR ON POLICE
"YEP--I HAD EVERYTHING FIGURED OUT---BUT I FORGOT ONE GUY ---- THE BATMAN!"
"YA SEE, THE COPPERS HAD SHORT-WAVE RADIOS READY TO SHOUT AS SOON AS WE SHOWED---AN' ONE NIGHT AS WE'RE DOIN' OUR STUFF--"
LOOK! THE BATPLANE!
OKAY, ROBIN-- LET 'EM HAVE THE BOTTLES!
A PLEASURE!
"THEM TORCHES HIT---AND BOOM---THE TANKS LIT UP LIKE A ROMAN CANDLE!"
11
"KNOW WHAT THAT STUFF WAS IN THEM BOTTLES? GASOLINE---THAT'S WHAT, GASOLINE!"
"THEM BOTTLES HIT THE TANKS, BROKE OPEN AND SPLASHED SOME KIND OF LIQUID ALL OVER 'EM."
"THEN THAT KID STARTED THROWIN' FLAMING TORCHES AT THE TANKS."
"PRETTY SOON THE INSIDE OF EACH TANK FELT LIKE A HOT STOVE!"
LEMME OUTA HERE!
AN' I USTA LIKE BOILED CHICKEN!
"WE HOPPED OUTA THEM TANKS LIKE THEY WAS POISON----AND INTO OUR TRUCKS! BUT I HAD AN ACE IN THE HOLE, TOO!"
GIVE IT TO 'EM! BLAST 'EM OUTA THE SKY!
"THE TOPS OF OUR TRUCKS FOLDED BACK. I HAD MACHINE GUNS PLANTED THERE!"

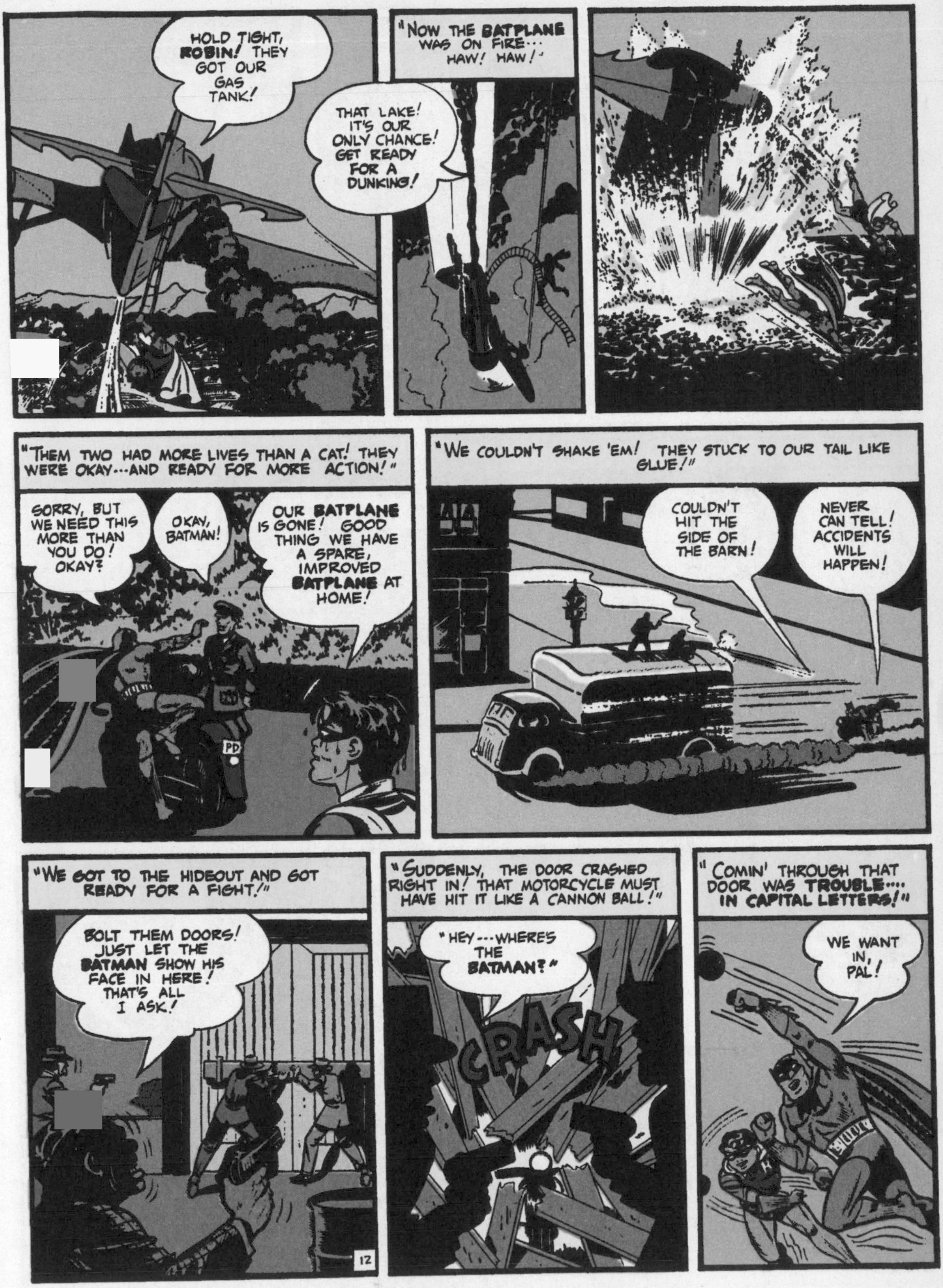
HOLD TIGHT, ROBIN! THEY GOT OUR GAS TANK!
"NOW THE BATPLANE WAS ON FIRE... HAW! HAW!"
THAT LAKE! IT'S OUR ONLY CHANCE! GET READY FOR A DUNKING!
"THEM TWO HAD MORE LIVES THAN A CAT! THEY WERE OKAY---AND READY FOR MORE ACTION!"
SORRY, BUT WE NEED THIS MORE THAN YOU DO! OKAY?
OKAY, BATMAN!
OUR BATPLANE IS GONE! GOOD THING WE HAVE A SPARE, IMPROVED BATPLANE AT HOME!
PD
"WE COULDN'T SHAKE 'EM! THEY STUCK TO OUR TAIL LIKE GLUE!"
COULDN'T HIT THE SIDE OF THE BARN!
NEVER CAN TELL! ACCIDENTS WILL HAPPEN!
"WE GOT TO THE HIDEOUT AND GOT READY FOR A FIGHT!"
BOLT THEM DOORS! JUST LET THE BATMAN SHOW HIS FACE IN HERE! THAT'S ALL I ASK!
12
"SUDDENLY, THE DOOR CRASHED RIGHT IN! THAT MOTORCYCLE MUST HAVE HIT IT LIKE A CANNON BALL!"
"HEY---WHERE'S THE BATMAN?"
CRASH
"COMIN' THROUGH THAT DOOR WAS TROUBLE.... IN CAPITAL LETTERS!"
WE WANT IN, PAL!

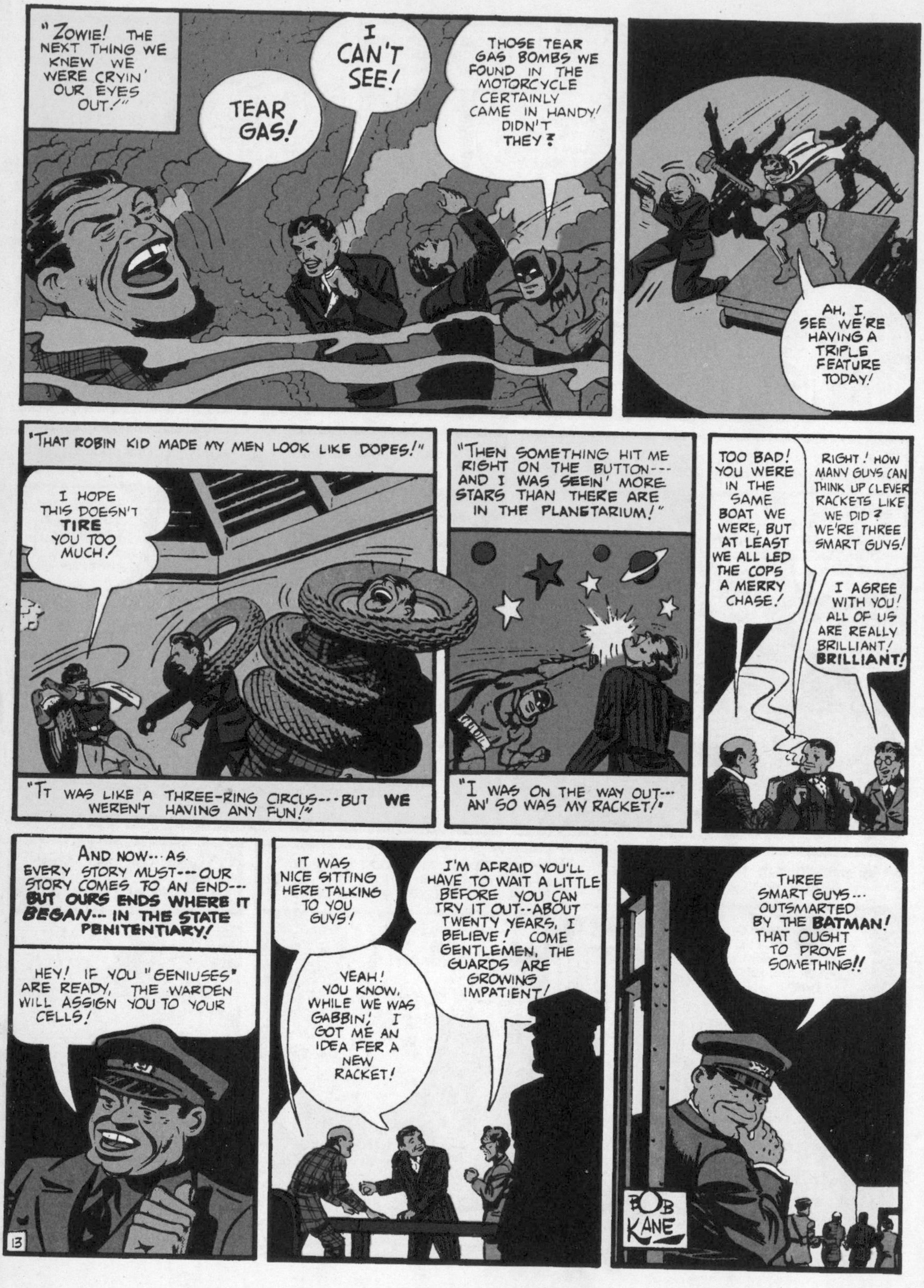
"ZOWIE! THE NEXT THING WE KNEW WE WERE CRYIN' OUR EYES OUT!"
TEAR GAS!
I CAN'T SEE!
THOSE TEAR GAS BOMBS WE FOUND IN THE MOTORCYCLE CERTAINLY CAME IN HANDY! DIDN'T THEY?
AH, I SEE WE'RE HAVING A TRIPLE FEATURE TODAY!
"THAT ROBIN KID MADE MY MEN LOOK LIKE DOPES!"
I HOPE THIS DOESN'T TIRE YOU TOO MUCH!
"IT WAS LIKE A THREE-RING CIRCUS---BUT WE WEREN'T HAVING ANY FUN!"
"THEN SOMETHING HIT ME RIGHT ON THE BUTTON---AND I WAS SEEIN' MORE STARS THAN THERE ARE IN THE PLANETARIUM!"
"I WAS ON THE WAY OUT---AN' SO WAS MY RACKET!"
TOO BAD! YOU WERE IN THE SAME BOAT WE WERE, BUT AT LEAST WE ALL LED THE COPS A MERRY CHASE!
RIGHT! HOW MANY GUYS CAN THINK UP CLEVER RACKETS LIKE WE DID? WE'RE THREE SMART GUYS!
I AGREE WITH YOU! ALL OF US ARE REALLY BRILLIANT! BRILLIANT!
AND NOW...AS EVERY STORY MUST---OUR STORY COMES TO AN END---BUT OURS ENDS WHERE IT BEGAN...IN THE STATE PENITENTIARY!
HEY! IF YOU "GENIUSES" ARE READY, THE WARDEN WILL ASSIGN YOU TO YOUR CELLS!
13
IT WAS NICE SITTING HERE TALKING TO YOU GUYS!
YEAH! YOU KNOW, WHILE WE WAS GABBIN', I GOT ME AN IDEA FER A NEW RACKET!
I'M AFRAID YOU'LL HAVE TO WAIT A LITTLE BEFORE YOU CAN TRY IT OUT--ABOUT TWENTY YEARS, I BELIEVE! COME GENTLEMEN, THE GUARDS ARE GROWING IMPATIENT!
THREE SMART GUYS...OUTSMARTED BY THE BATMAN! THAT OUGHT TO PROVE SOMETHING!!
BOB KANE